Principles and Practice of Information Theory

Principles and Practice of Information Theory

Richard E. Blahut

ADDISON-WESLEY PUBLISHING COMPANY

Reading, Massachusetts • Menlo Park, California
Don Mills, Ontario • Wokingham, England • Amsterdam
Bonn • Sydney • Singapore • Tokyo • Madrid • Bogotá
Santiago • San Juan

This book is in the **Addison-Wesley Series in Electrical and Computer Engineering.**

Richard E. Blahut
IBM Corporation
Owego, New York

Library of Congress Cataloging-in-Publication Data

Blahut, Richard E.
    Principles and practice of information theory.

    Bibliography: p.
    Includes index.
        1. Information theory.   2. Telecommunication systems.
I. Title.
Q360.B57   1987   001.53′9   86-20554
ISBN 0-201-10709-0

That which thy fathers have bequeathed to thee;
earn it anew if thou wouldst possess it.

Goethe: Faust

Preface

The development of communication systems and recording systems is ever becoming more sophisticated. A vast increase in computational power for signal processing is now available and is used within communication terminals to enhance performance. The design methods have become mathematical and algorithmic in contrast to the more intuitive and heuristic methods of bygone days. When technology was simpler, the defects and noise of the transmission media were simply overpowered by using a strong enough signal or a slow enough transmission rate. Now, however, electronics is cheap, but power and bandwidth are resources to be conserved. Channels remain impaired by noise, interference, and other defects, and one wishes to transmit ever more data through them. In a competition between different modulation schemes, the winner will more usually be the design that transmits with lower power at higher rates and with fewer errors; greater hardware complexity is a penalty that can be accepted. The search for the ultimate limits on communication systems, and for methods that come close to these limits, is the subject of information theory and the topic of this book.

It is my view that information theory is a subject of major importance to today's engineer, who too often ignores its advice because of not really hearing it. The principles and techniques of information theory must be more widely disseminated. Accordingly, this book has been written with one goal, the goal of making the subject accessible to a broader audience—this without diluting the level of the subject. To meet this goal, we must tie information theory more tightly to design problems of communication systems and other information-handling systems. The book will be a success if its readers begin to feel the laws of probability, and of mathematics in general, pulling the development of communication systems along certain inevitable paths. Having seen the general framework, they will deal more confidently with their own design tasks.

I expect that the majority of readers of this book will be engineers with no plans to become specialists in information theory. Their goal will be to develop only a working familiarity with the ideas so as to sharpen their engineering judgment. I have tried to keep this reader in mind while writing the book. At the same time, I have tried to remain true to the mathematical rigor required by the subject.

Information theory is a subject with many long and highly mathematical proofs. It is essential to understand these proofs to have a complete mastery of the subject, but it is not necessary to understand them to have a general grasp of the subject. Each reader must decide for himself how far to pursue his studies. The proofs are clearly marked in the text so that they can be skipped when desired. I recommend that on the first time through a chapter the reader skip the proofs entirely, or perhaps just skim them. They can be studied more carefully on the second reading.

Throughout the book, the presentation of the mathematics is kept to as low a level as the problem at hand allows. This means that the mathematical level is uneven and readers will find sections differing in difficulty. It is also true that some sections develop a topic in more detail than is needed to understand later sections. Therefore, it is a good idea to drop a section when reading it becomes tedious and return to it if ever the interest is reawakened. Occasionally a section uses some ideas that are not formally developed until a later section. In these cases, enough is said so that the material is understandable even though the formal proofs come later. It seemed better to do this than to defer topics just to impose a more formal order.

We begin with the study of discrete sources, discrete channels, and discrete random variables, although when the random variables have continuous probability distributions, information theory takes on a richness and beauty that are not always as striking in the discrete case. This will be seen in the later chapters where gaussian distributions and waveform channels and sources are studied in detail. In the early chapters we develop the theory for situations that are described by discrete real-valued random variables at each time instant; discrete-time continuous-amplitude random processes appear only in supplementary examples.

In most regards, the treatment is conventional, though there are a few exceptions. I have placed special emphasis on the discrimination function, hypotheses testing, and estimation theory and on their basic roles in information theory. This is the more modern view—information theory, decision theory, and estimation theory are now more closely tied together than they were a few years ago. The engineering student benefits from learning, in a unified setting, principles that underlie the designs, for example, of both radar waveforms and communication waveforms.

Two other major lines of development culminate in the continuous-time gaussian problems of Chapter 7 and in the treatment of multiterminal communication networks in Chapter 9. There are important engineering lessons in the water-pouring arguments of Chapter 7 as well as in problems dealing with the capacity of channels with restricted inputs.

Because the channel-coding theorem is so fundamental, it is proved twice, once by an "elementary" argument and then by Gallager's random-coding argument. I could not bring myself to omit either of these proofs; each yields different insights.

The book was designed so that it can be used for a one-semester introductory course on information theory by reading only the basic sections. Advanced and more difficult material is placed near the end of each chapter where it provides material for further study. For an introductory course at the graduate level, I recommend Chapters 1, 2, and 3 up to Section 3.4; Chapter 4 up to Section 4.4; Chapter 5 up to Section 5.6; Sections 6.1, 6.2, 6.3; and the first nine sections of Chapter 7. This selection bypasses the more difficult sections. Because of the importance of the additive gaussian noise channel, I believe it is important to include Chapter 7 in any introductory course.

Acknowledgments

The final shape of this book was greatly influenced by the comments of the many friends who took the time to read through the preliminary manuscript or to discuss my plans. The advice of such people is priceless. I thank Professor Toby Berger, Professor R. M. Gray, Professor L. D. Davisson, Professor B. W. Dickinson, Professor Kingo Kobayashi, and Professor M. I. Miller for their help. I am especially grateful to Professor Andrew R. Barron who recommended substantial restructuring of the book.

The writing of the book was made possible by the three institutions that dominate my life. IBM provided support over many years, Cornell University provided the stimulation of faculty and classroom. And not least, the Blahut family, especially Barbara, gave me the peace of mind and the endless amounts of time needed to finish the project.

Owego, N.Y.   R.E.B.

Contents

CHAPTER 1

Introduction

*I*nformation theory is a discipline centered around a common mathematical approach to the study of the collection and manipulation of information. It provides a theoretical basis for such activities as observation, measurement, data compression, data storage, communication, estimation, decision making, and pattern recognition. Many complex and expensive systems are built for automating or expanding these operations. As the systems become more sophisticated and performance requirements are increased, one must rely more and more on mathematical models to design systems that meet the performance requirements.

Information theory provides a guide to the development of information-transmission systems based on a study of the possibilities and limitations inherent in natural law. There are many perspectives, rooted in mathematics and physics, from which one can seek this understanding; information theory is one such perspective. Information theory is the study of how the laws of probability, and of mathematics in general, describe limits on the design of

1

information-transmission systems, but also offer opportunities. It tells how one may design strategies into a communication system by using the laws of large numbers to circumvent the noise imposed by nature and the concomitant errors that may occur in the communication channel.

1.1 THE COMMUNICATION CHANNEL

As the demand for communication capacity continues to grow in such areas as person-to-person communications, broadcast communications, inter-computer and intracomputer communications, the designer is pressed to improve performance. Under this pressure he attempts to maximize the transmitted information rate through an available communication channel subject to some requirements of message reliability and so he turns to more complex techniques. Eventually he finds his design needs to operate with signal levels close to the background thermal noise and other sources of interference. He then wishes for some sort of optimality theory that will tell him how to design waveforms or messages to ensure reliable transmission at signal levels as close as possible to the noise; for this purpose he turns to information theory. This optimality theory is one of the major goals of information theory, which gives an extensive but incomplete answer to the question.

Information theory attempts to answer a number of very basic questions:

1. What is information? That is, how do we measure it?
2. What are the fundamental limits on the transmission of information?
3. What are the fundamental limits on the extraction of information from the environment?
4. What are the fundamental limits on the compression and refinement of information?
5. How should devices be designed to approach these limits?
6. How closely do existing devices approach these limits?

In a theoretical sense, the success of information theory has been spectacular in that precise interpretations and answers to questions such as these have been obtained even though our initial reaction to such questions is that they are vague and unscientific. In a practical sense, information theory has affected the design and development of many systems. It provides guidance to those who are searching for new, more advanced communication systems.

The communication problem represented in Fig. 1.1 is the archetypal problem of information theory; much of the underlying structure and semantics of information theory is suggested by the communication channel. A source of information is to be connected to a user of information by a channel. A communication system is provided to prepare the source output for the channel and to prepare the channel output for the user. It consists of a device between the source and the channel called the *encoder/modulator* and

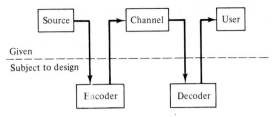

Figure 1.1   A communication system.

another device between the channel and the user called the *demodulator/decoder*.

In his study of the communication problem, Shannon in 1948 laid the foundation for the subject of information theory. By means of a nonconstructive existence proof, he showed that nearly error-free communication is possible over a noisy channel, provided an appropriate preprocessor called the *encoder* and an appropriate postprocessor called the *decoder* are allowed at each end of the communication link. However, he did not tell us how to design the best encoders and decoders, nor did he tell us how complex they must be. Considerable work has gone into an attempt to solve these problems, and although the final solutions are still unknown, many partial answers have been obtained, and work continues to yield improved communication system designs.

Information theory includes the quest for a theory of optimum communication waveforms. When restricted to this quest, the subject matter of information theory can be viewed as the existing answers to a sequence of successively weaker queries:

1. What is the best waveform family for transmitting k bits in T seconds through a specified channel? (For example, how should we send bits through an additive gaussian-noise channel with an average power constraint and a bandwidth constraint on the transmitter?)
2. What is the performance of the best such waveform family for a continuous-time channel (even though the waveform itself may be unknown)?
3. What is the approximate performance of the best waveform family (or code) for transmitting information through a discrete memoryless channel such as a binary channel?

Because we have included the word "best," none of these questions has yet been answered, not even in an approximate sense. However, the continuing search for answers has uncovered many good waveforms and codes, and also a large body of theory that is valuable for the insights it affords. A major task of this book is to develop this theory and give partial answers to the above questions.

The conventional way to partition the major functions of a modern communication system is described by the block diagram of Fig. 1.2. Data from

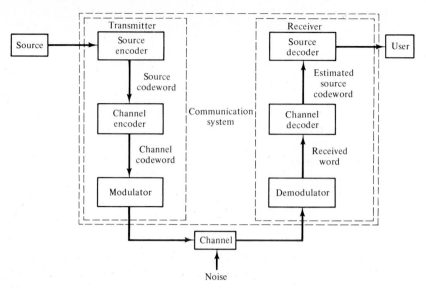

Figure 1.2   Block diagram of a communication system.

the data source is first processed by a source encoder, whose purpose is to represent the source data more compactly. A block of source data called the *sourceword* is represented by a sequence of symbols called the *source codeword*. The data then is processed by the channel encoder, which transforms a sequence of source codeword symbols into another sequence called the *channel codeword*. The channel codeword is a new, longer sequence that has more redundancy than the source codeword. Each symbol in the channel codeword might be represented by a bit or a group of bits. Next, the modulator represents each symbol of the channel codeword by its corresponding analog symbol from a finite set of possible analog symbols. The sequence of analog symbols, called a *waveform*, is transmitted through the channel. Because the channel is subject to various types of noise, distortion, and interference, the channel output differs from the channel input. The demodulator converts each analog symbol received into a discrete channel symbol based on a best estimate of the transmitted symbol, but because of channel noise sometimes makes errors. The demodulated sequence of symbols is called the *received word*. Because of error, the symbols of the received word might not always match those of the channel codeword.

   The function of the channel decoder is to use the redundancy in a channel codeword to correct the errors in the received word, and then to produce an estimate of the source codeword from it. If all errors are corrected, the estimated source codeword matches the original source codeword. The source decoder performs an operation inverse to the source encoder and delivers its output, which may be the sourceword or an approximation of the sourceword, to the user.

The source encoder and decoder are commonly split into two functions: that of expressing the output of a source compactly and that of abridging the output of a source. These are studied under the terms "data compaction codes" and "data compression codes." The channel encoder and decoder are commonly split into two functions: that of implementing error control to negate the effects of channel noise and that of preparing the sequence of transmitted symbols to be compatible with channel constraints. These are studied under the terms "data transmission codes" and "data translation codes" (or under the terms "error-control codes" and "constrained-channel codes"). The modulator and the demodulator are studied under the term "modulation theory."

A digital communication system also includes, implicitly, a function of synchronization. A continuing sequence of symbols at the output of the channel must be broken up into pieces in the right way so that each symbol can be interpreted in its proper role within the message.

Although we use the terminology of communication theory, the model is general and applies to a great variety of situations. One can interpret many other information-handling systems such as mass-storage systems in terms of this model. It only is necessary to translate the terminology and to identify the boundaries between the boxes. This is arbitrary and depends on the goals of a particular analysis. Usually the source, channel, and user are identified with those parts of the system that are fixed, and the encoder/decoder and modulator/demodulator are identified with those parts of the system that are subject to design. Therefore, in different circumstances, the identification of these functions may be different.

1.2 A BRIEF HISTORY OF INFORMATION THEORY

Information theory, like any active field of knowledge, is constantly growing, and a textbook should try to give some impression of the vitality of the subject. The brief history outlined in this section is meant to give a glimpse of this vitality, although many of the concepts mentioned will be unfamiliar at this point.

Information theory in the strictest sense of the term was largely originated by Claude Shannon. As it grew and developed, the subject gathered in other threads, and we shall consider information theory here in a somewhat broader sense. Earlier attempts to define a measure of information were made by the communication theorists Nyquist (1924) and Hartley (1928), and by the statistician Fisher (1925). However, the subject did not take its present shape until the work of Shannon (1948), and of Wiener (1948) and Kotel'nikov (1947). Of these three, Shannon laid the broadest and most central foundation in his 1948 paper, "A Mathematical Theory of Communication."[†] This paper searched for the basic theory underlying the task of communication through

---

[†]Republished in monograph form in 1949 with a slight but significant change in the title.

noisy channels and showed remarkable perceptiveness based largely on heuristic insights. Before Shannon's paper, it was generally believed that noise limited the flow of information through a channel in the sense that, with average power fixed, as one decreased the required probability of error in the received message, the necessary redundancy in the transmitted message increased—and hence the true rate of data transmission decreased. In this way, it was thought that arbitrarily low probability of error should require vanishing data rates. Shannon showed that this plausible supposition was, in fact, wrong; rather, each reasonable channel is characterized by a nonzero number called the *channel capacity* such that an arbitrarily small probability of error is achievable at any transmission rate below the channel capacity. According to Shannon, the probability of error and the rate of data transmission can be specified independently.

Shannon's ideas were influenced by work he did on cryptography during World War II. That is when he came to the realization that communication at its most fundamental level is a probabilistic process. His work in information theory followed from this realization.

The usual method considered for achieving a small error probability in digital communication is the method of coding the transmitted information in blocks; in general, large blocks are needed to achieve good performance. Shannon's original arguments took this approach. The arguments were strengthened by Feinstein (1954), who further showed that at any fixed data transmission rate, the best code for a memoryless channel has a probability of error that decays exponentially with blocklength of the code. Fano (1961) determined explicitly a representation of an exponential decay coefficient for block codes that describes the relationship between code rate, blocklength, and probability of error. This decay coefficient is nonzero only for rates below the channel capacity. By means of the latter observation, Fano provided a satisfying proof of Shannon's channel coding theorem. Gallager (1965) provided a greatly simplified proof of Fano's results and also provided the best available lower bound on the decay coefficient for low-rate codes. (The true exponential decay coefficient for optimal low-rate codes is at present still an open problem.)

These developments were based on studies of how well data can be transmitted at rates below channel capacity. In his original paper, Shannon also made a converse statement to the effect that good error performance could not be achieved at rates above channel capacity. Fano (1952) provided a simple proof that the probability of symbol error is bounded away from zero at rates above capacity. Wolfowitz (1957) proved that the probability of block error in this situation must approach 1 with increasing blocklength. The Wolfowitz and Fano bounds are not directly comparable, however, because the Wolfowitz bound is a bound on the probability of block error. One is usually more interested in the probability of symbol error. The latter question raises the issue of whether there are more complicated codes that might have occasional errors, but for which most symbols would be received correctly.

This leads into the topic of data compression codes for sources, which can be thought of as the study of the reduction of information by the judicious insertion of intentional distortion or intentional errors so that the information rate is reduced to below the capacity of the given channel. When errors must be made, it is better to make them in a controlled way prior to the channel rather than subject to the whims of the channel.

In the same paper mentioned above, Shannon (1948) raised this question of the information content of a data source and outlined an approach to treat the problem. He later (1959) published a detailed treatment that gave a precise operational significance to the information content of a source relative to a distortion measure. Later workers continued to strengthen the source coding theorems and to simplify their proofs.

During the decade of the 1970s, activity in information theory turned away from the study of point-to-point communication to the study of multiterminal problems. Shannon (1958, 1961) had earlier introduced the study of multiterminal systems, but not until the study of broadcast channels by Cover (1972) and the study of multiterminal data compaction by Slepian and Wolf (1973) did such problems begin to yield to analysis. Multiterminal problems are usually quite difficult, and there are still many open problems.

Meanwhile, related topics in decision and estimation theory were under development, sometimes motivated by problems in radar design. Kullback (1959) took the position that these topics were a part of information theory. He introduced a function that he called the *discrimination* and developed its relationship to the study of statistics. This function is of central importance in the theory of hypothesis testing and parameter estimation. The discrimination also plays a role in channel and source coding and is closely related to the entropy and mutual information functions that are so important in Shannon's work. There are many links between information theory and the field of mathematical statistics; these links are frequently expressed in terms of the discrimination.

Decision and estimation theory share with information theory the common outlook of optimally using a set of random data, so it is not surprising that the fields have been coming closer together in recent years. The links between estimation theory and information theory can be traced to Cramer (1946) and Rao (1945), who found a fundamental limit on the variance of any estimator based on the amount of information in the measurement. Neyman and Pearson (1933) had earlier described the optimum tester of simple hypotheses. The important special case of the optimum detector of a signal corrupted by white gaussian noise was developed by North (1943). This led to the development of the matched filter and threshold detector as a simple implementation of the Neyman-Pearson decision regions. The matched filter was also used in connection with the optimum estimate of the arrival time of a known waveform in gaussian noise, where it was shown to asymptotically achieve the Cramer-Rao inequality.

Sequential decision theory was developed by Wald (1947) and led to important applications in information theory. In particular, the convolutional codes of Elias (1954) were found to be well suited to a kind of sequential decoder. Sequential encoding and decoding techniques for both source codes and channel codes are currently a subject of active research. There are important connections between this part of information theory and the field of ergodic theory.

1.3 APPLICATIONS OF INFORMATION THEORY

For the scientist, information theory can be justified on the basis of its contribution to an improved understanding of natural law. For the engineer, however, information theory must be justified on the basis of its uses. The benefits that information theory gives to the engineer range from specific design procedures to advice on general evolutionary directions.

A most important reason for the study of information theory is the insight that it affords into the design of information-transmission systems. By developing a clear concept of information and its transmission, a much deeper understanding of the purposes and limitations of a technique is obtained. This insight can guide research and system design into more productive directions and has been one of the major successes of information theory.

By far the most important area of application of information theory at the present time is to the problems of communication, and we shall now discuss applications in this area. Currently, the optimum method (or family of methods) for transmitting data over a noisy channel is, in general, unknown. This is especially true when the information content of the data is greater than the information capacity of the channel, which is often the case since many information sources have a continuously distributed output, and hence infinite information content. As we shall see, it is not possible to transmit the output sequence of such a source over any real channel without distortion. By introducing the concept of the information capacity of a channel or of the information content of a source under a given distortion measure, information theory describes exactly the optimum performance of communication systems. In addition, it develops a theoretical framework which provides a means for rationally designing such communication systems.

Digital point-to-point communication systems—including satellite communications, telephone-line modems, and magnetic recording systems—now use sophisticated waveforms in which the data streams are interlocked in complex ways. We no longer transmit and receive one bit at a time serially; rather we transmit and receive at the higher level of bit packages or bit streams. Information theory provided the guidance for the development of these modern methods and also tells us how much room for improvement remains.

Digital multiterminal communication systems are more complex than digital point-to-point communication systems, and their theory is less well understood. At the present time, designers are developing many digital multiterminal systems in an ad hoc way, while theoreticians are grappling to provide a rich enough theory that can aid the designer with new methods and new insights. We shall give two examples here.

In a *binary two-way channel*, two users exchange messages through a single wire but can listen only when not transmitting. A simple model is that a user can receive a channel bit when transmitting a 0 bit but cannot receive a channel bit when transmitting a 1 bit. Intuition tells us that the two users should take turns using the channel, each using it half the time as a transmitter and half the time as a receiver. Surprisingly, the theory tells us something different; actually both users can be transmitting information successfully more than half the time, if only they cooperate.

In a *broadcast channel* there are many receivers and one transmitter. The quality of the signal or strength of the noise may vary from receiver to receiver. The transmitter wishes to send partially different or wholly different messages to each receiver. How should the transmitted waveform be designed? If the receivers are to be sent wholly different messages, then the usual technique is to use time-division or frequency-division multiplexing to divide the channel into subchannels. Information theory shows that this is not optimal and suggests practical alternatives. If the receivers are to be sent partially different messages, then existing techniques fall short. For example, suppose the transmitted message consists of high-fidelity stereo audio entertainment. Theory tells us that the communication system can be designed so that those receivers that get a weaker signal will selectively lose portions of the audio signal but will otherwise reproduce the signal perfectly. Perhaps the stereo aspect of the signal will be lost when the signal is weak; then when the signal is weaker still, the high-frequency part of the audio spectrum will be lost as well, but otherwise the surviving signal is reproduced without noise or distortion. Eventually we will learn to build digital communication systems this way. The principles of this book suggest the framework for such a system, but the details remain to be worked out.

1.4 CODES FOR SOURCES AND CHANNELS

A code is a special representation of a string of data that satisfies a given need. We shall classify codes according to their functions as data compaction codes, data compression codes, data translation codes, and data transmission codes. These terms will be defined shortly.

For any of these codes, a stream of data symbols is entered into the encoder and a stream of codeword symbols comes out of the encoder. Usually the data streams are so long as to appear infinite to the encoder and the decoder. In a practical system, the input data streams must be broken into pieces that are small enough for the encoder to work on. Long codes must be constructed from small pieces according to some plan. Hence, we shall classify codes according to their structure—for instance, as block codes, prefix codes, and tree codes.

The function of the encoders and decoders is to map strings of symbols from one alphabet into strings of symbols from a second, possibly the same, alphabet. A *block code* breaks the input data stream into blocks of fixed length N and encodes each block into a codeword of fixed length n. The blocks are concatenated to form the output data stream. A *variable-to-fixed-length block code* breaks the input data stream into blocks of variable length and encodes each block into a codeword of fixed length n; the codewords are concatenated to form the output data stream. A *fixed-to-variable-length block code* breaks the input data stream into blocks of fixed length N and encodes each block into a codeword of variable length; the codewords are concatenated to form the output data stream. It must be possible for the decoder to break the output data stream back into the individual codewords that were concatenated in the encoder. Therefore most fixed-to-variable-length block codes satisfy a condition known as the *prefix condition*, which allows self-punctuation of the code. This special kind of code is called a *prefix code* and is the kind of fixed-to-variable-length block code with which we usually deal.

There are also codes whose codewords cannot be broken into noninteracting segments. These are a little harder to understand. The encoding operation has a structure whereby, as a few data symbols enter the encoder, a few codeword symbols leave the encoder, and the specific codeword symbols depend not only on the most recent data symbols but also on the past history of sourceword or codeword symbols. A *tree code* breaks the input data stream into frames of length N_0, which are encoded into codeword frames of length n_0, with the encoding map depending on the previous m input data frames; possibly m is infinite, though it usually is finite. After encoding, the codeword frames are concatenated to form the output data stream. A tree code is called a *variable-to-fixed-length tree code* or a *fixed-to-variable-length tree code* when the input or output frames are of variable length. A tree code is called a *sliding block code* if the encoding operation is time-invariant. A sliding block code is called a *convolutional code* if the code has a linearity property in the sense that linear combinations of codewords are also codewords.

Synchronization is generally simpler for a sliding block code than for a block code because the framelength of a typical sliding block code is usually quite small in comparison with the blocklength of a typical block code.

Whenever there is a meaningful fixed ratio between the number of symbols into an encoder and the number of symbols out of the encoder, we call the ratio the *rate* of the code. The rate is expressed in units of data symbols per code symbol. For a fixed-length block code, the rate is the ratio N/n. This usage of the word rate must be carefully distinguished from other uses of the word. For example, we also speak of the *data rate* measured in units of bits per second or of the *symbol rate* through the channel measured in units of symbols per second or bits per second. Whenever it is necessary to avoid confusion, the rate of a code will be called the *code rate*.

We shall also classify codes according to their function. Codes for source

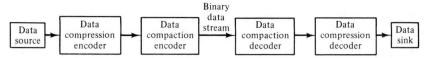

Figure 1.3   Dissection of source coding.

encoding are subdivided into *data compaction codes* and *data compression codes*. A data compaction code represents the source data more efficiently but in a way that the source data can be recovered essentially error-free. A data compression code represents the source data even more concisely than a data compaction code but does so at the cost of clean recovery of the source data. Some intentional distortion is introduced into the source data so that it can be compressed. Usually we will think of the data compression and the data compaction as two consecutive functions, as is shown in Fig. 1.3. The data compression code reduces the intrinsic information content of the source by introducing distortion or gaps into the data stream. The data compaction code then represents this compressed data efficiently, making the number of bits per second in the compacted data stream as low as possible.

Similarly, codes for channel encoding are subdivided into *data transmission codes* and *data translation codes*. A data transmission code enables data to be sent reliably through a noisy or probabilistic channel. If a data transmission code is used, the noisy channel is made to act nearly like a deterministic and reliable channel. A noisy channel may also have constraints on the allowable input sequences. For example, runs of too many successive zeros may be forbidden. Such constraints are satisfied by using a data translation code, which translates a stream of symbols into a new stream that can be accepted by the constrained channel. The use of the two codes is shown in Fig. 1.4. The inner encoder/decoder for data translation matches its input symbols to the channel constraints. When the channel makes an error, the inner decoder makes an error and can create a burst of errors in its output. The outer encoder/decoder need not obey any constraints on its output sequence, but it must deal with the errors. The data transmission code is designed to correct the errors and to provide for reliable transmission of data through the noisy channel.

Breaking a digital communication system into the four functions of data compression, data compaction, data transmission, and data translation is

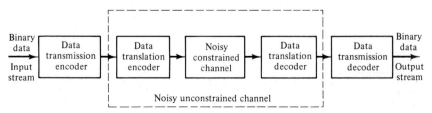

Figure 1.4   Channel coding for noisy constrained channels.

somewhat arbitrary but is important in order to develop a manageable theory of the subject. Each function can lead to a sophisticated analysis and the design of a complex code, so it is best to deal with one function at a time. In applications these four functions are usually satisfied by distinct layers in the communication system. Because of the compounded complexity, single codes that neatly combine two or more of these functions have not yet been discovered for most applications. Yet the theorems of information theory assure us that, except for a decoding delay, there is no loss in performance because of partitioning the functions in this way.

Most of this book will be devoted not to finding good codes, but rather to finding the circumstances under which good codes exist. The theorems that describe this are elegant, often reducing a bewildering complexity of possibilities into beautiful simplicity. Coming to an understanding of these results is an excellent way to build engineering insight. At the same time, however, one should be well aware of the limitations of the kind of results that we shall develop. It is one thing to say that for a given channel a code of rate R exists with probability of bit error less than 10^{-20}. But what if the decoder for this code is billions of times larger than the largest existing computer? Indeed, what if the decoder is billions of times larger than the earth or even the entire universe? Then that code is worthless in practice. This is a weakness of the theory. The codes we prove to exist may very well have decoders of such outrageous complexity. Practical codes need some sort of algorithmic structure that can be used by the encoder and decoder, but information theory has not found a way to impose this practical constraint in its basic theorems. We tolerate this weakness in the theory because by learning the circumstances under which good codes exist, we then know where to search in hopes of finding codes that have practical encoders and decoders.

1.5 PROBABILITY DISTRIBUTIONS FOR DISCRETE SOURCES AND CHANNELS

We distinguish between a *discrete* source or channel, which has a discrete symbol alphabet defined on discrete time instants; a *continuous* source or channel, which has a continuous symbol alphabet defined on discrete time instants; and a *waveform* source or channel defined on a continuum of time points. A waveform source or channel is also called an *analog* source or channel.

A *discrete information source* is a source that has only a finite (or countably infinite) set of symbols as possible outputs. Similarly, a *discrete channel* is a channel that can transmit only symbols from a finite set. The set of source symbols or channel symbols is called the *source alphabet* or the *channel alphabet* and the elements of the set are called *symbols* or *letters*. For example, a source whose output consists of strings of decimal digits has an alphabet of size 10, and the 10 decimal digits are the "letters" of the alphabet. We think of a discrete source as putting out some fixed number of source symbols per second at evenly spaced time instants called *clock times*. Likewise, a discrete channel can transmit one symbol from its input alphabet at each of its clock times. The duration in seconds of the clock's time interval determines the number of symbols transmitted per second.

Many of the situations to be discussed require two alphabets. The input to a channel will be a letter from an alphabet $\{a_0, \ldots, a_{J-1}\}$, with J letters indexed by j for $j = 0, \ldots, J - 1$. The output of the channel is a letter from an alphabet $\{b_0, \ldots, b_{K-1}\}$, with K letters indexed by k for $k = 0, \ldots, K - 1$. Often these two alphabets are the same alphabet but this need not be so, and it helps to keep them straight if different symbols are used.

A probability distribution on the source alphabet or on the channel input alphabet is denoted $p(a_j)$, abbreviated p_j, for $j = 0, \ldots, J - 1$. A probability distribution on the channel output alphabet is denoted $q(b_k)$, abbreviated q_k, for $k = 0, \ldots, K - 1$. Figure 1.5 illustrates some of the notation used for sources and channels.

The output of a channel is a random variable Y taking values in the set $\{b_0, b_1, \ldots, b_{K-1}\}$. The random variable Y is symbol b_k with a probability that is conditional on the channel input symbol a_j. The conditional probability distribution is called the *channel transition matrix* and is denoted by $\mathbf{Q}$ with elements $Q(b_k|a_j)$, abbreviated $Q_{k|j}$. For each j, $Q_{k|j}$ is the probability that the output is b_k, given that a_j is the input. The joint distribution $P(a_j, b_k)$, abbreviated P_{jk}, is the joint probability that a_j is transmitted and b_k is received. Then

$$P_{jk} = p_j Q_{k|j}$$

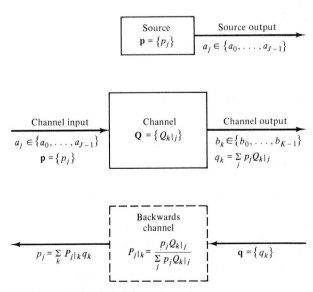

Figure 1.5   Source and channel models.

The probability distribution on the channel output alphabet is determined from the distribution on the channel input alphabet and the channel transition matrix by

$$q_k = \sum_j p_j Q_{k|j}$$

We shall also have occasion to use a fictitious channel known as the *backwards channel*, or the *a posteriori channel*, from the output to the input. Its channel transition matrix is denoted $\mathbf{P}$, with elements $P(a_j|b_k)$, abbreviated $P_{j|k}$. By the Bayes theorem, $P_{j|k}$ is given by

$$P_{j|k} = \frac{p_j Q_{k|j}}{\sum_j p_j Q_{k|j}}$$

which follows immediately from

$$p_j Q_{k|j} = q_k P_{j|k}$$

The backwards probability $P_{j|k}$ is the probability that symbol a_j was transmitted, given that symbol b_k was received.

Any function $f(Y)$ of the random variable Y is also a random variable and has a mean

$$\bar{f} = \sum_k q_k f(b_k)$$

and a variance

$$\sigma_f^2 = \sum_k q_k [f(b_k) - \bar{f}]^2$$

For a somewhat bizarre example, notice that the variable $Z = q_Y$ is a function of random variable Y taking value q_k when Y takes value k, and so Z itself can be considered as a random variable. As such, it has a mean

$$\bar{q} = \sum_k q_k q_k = \sum_k q_k^2$$

and a variance

$$\sigma_q^2 = \sum_k q_k (q_k - \bar{q})^2$$

We will often take means and variances of functions that so involve the probability distribution $\{q_k\}$.

We are frequently interested in transmitting a block of letters through a channel. Then the input to the channel is an *n*-tuple of symbols from the input alphabet, and the output from the channel is an *n*-tuple of symbols from the output alphabet. When discussing blocks of letters, we use X^n to denote a random block of input letters and Y^n to denote a random block of output letters. Thus

$$X^n = (X_1, X_2, \ldots, X_n)$$

$$Y^n = (Y_1, Y_2, \ldots, Y_n)$$

Specific realizations of these block random variables are denoted by lowercase letters **x** and **y**. Thus

$$\mathbf{x} = (a_{j_1}, a_{j_2}, \ldots, a_{j_n})$$

$$\mathbf{y} = (b_{k_1}, b_{k_2}, \ldots, b_{k_n})$$

The probability distributions on the blocks can be denoted by $p^n(\mathbf{x})$, $q^n(\mathbf{y})$, $P^n(\mathbf{x}|\mathbf{y})$, and $Q^n(\mathbf{y}|\mathbf{x})$. However, it is usually clear from the context that the random variables are blocks, so the abbreviated notation $p(\mathbf{x})$, $q(\mathbf{y})$, $P(\mathbf{x}|\mathbf{y})$, and $Q(\mathbf{y}|\mathbf{x})$ will usually be adequate.

An independent, identically distributed source probability distribution is one that satisfies

$$p^n(\mathbf{x}) = \prod_{l=1}^{n} p(a_{j_l})$$

abbreviated as

$$p(\mathbf{x}) = \prod_{l=1}^{n} p_{j_l}$$

The probability of a block is equal to the product of the probabilities of the individual letters. A source with an independent, identically distributed probability distribution is called a *memoryless source*.

We are interested also in channels that process letters independently. The probabilistic description of the channel for blocks of length n is given by

$$Q^n(\mathbf{y}|\mathbf{x}) = \prod_{l=1}^{n} Q(b_{k_l}|a_{j_l})$$

abbreviated as

$$Q(\mathbf{y}|\mathbf{x}) = \prod_{l=1}^{n} Q_{k_l|j_l}$$

This product form says that the response of the channel to the lth input symbol is independent of its response to other input symbols. Channels that satisfy this expression are called *memoryless channels*. Much of our study of channels will be concerned with memoryless channels.

The set of all probability distributions on a set of J letters is the set $\mathbf{P}^J$ and defined by

$$\mathbf{P}^J = \left\{ \langle p_0, \ldots, p_{J-1} \rangle : p_j \geq 0, \sum_j p_j = 1 \right\}$$

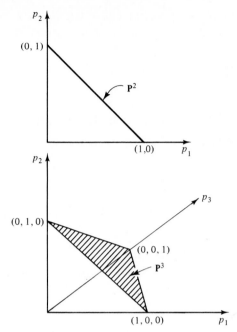

Figure 1.6   Spaces of probability vectors.

Probability distributions can be visualized geometrically as points in a space of probability distributions. This space is a convex subset of a real vector space. In Fig. 1.6 the space of two-point probability distributions and the space of three-point probability distributions are shown. Each possible probability distribution on three points corresponds to one of the points of the equilateral triangle labeled $\mathbf{P}^3$ in Fig. 1.6. We can depict $\mathbf{P}^J$ pictorially by drawing $\mathbf{P}^3$ as in Fig. 1.7. In this picture, the triangle represents the set of all probability distributions on three points, the point $\mathbf{p}$ represents one such probability distribution, and the set $\mathscr{P}$ represents a set of such probability distributions.

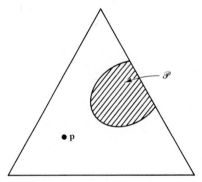

Figure 1.7   Pictorial depiction of $\mathbf{P}^3$.

1.6 MEASURES OF INFORMATION

There are three mathematical functions that are used to measure information. They are known as the *entropy*, the *mutual information*, and the *discrimination*. We shall study each of these functions in great detail when the time is right. In this chapter we shall introduce them only briefly.

Entropy is the simplest of the three functions. It is a function of a single probability distribution **p** and is given by

$$H(\mathbf{p}) = -\sum_{j=0}^{J-1} p_j \log p_j$$

We shall see that the entropy can be used to measure the prior uncertainty in the outcome of a random experiment, or equivalently, to measure the information obtained when the outcome is observed.

Mutual information is the second information measure. It is a function of a probability distribution **p** and a channel transition matrix **Q** and is given by

$$I(\mathbf{p}; \mathbf{Q}) = \sum_{j=0}^{J-1} \sum_{k=0}^{K-1} p_j Q_{k|j} \log \frac{Q_{k|j}}{\sum_i p_i Q_{k|i}}$$

We shall see that mutual information describes the amount of information that one random variable, the output of the channel, gives about a second random variable, the input to the channel.

Discrimination is the third information measure. It is a function of two probability distributions on the same alphabet and is given by

$$L(\mathbf{p}; \mathbf{p}') = \sum_{j=0}^{J-1} p_j \log \frac{p_j}{p_j'}$$

We shall see that the discrimination describes the amount of information that a measurement gives about the truth of a given hypothesis as compared with a second alternative hypothesis.

PROBLEMS

1.1 Analytically prove the "fundamental inequality of information theory"

$$\log_e x \le x - 1$$

with equality if and only if $x = 1$. Verify the inequality by a sketch. From this also show that

$$\log_e x \ge 1 - \frac{1}{x}$$

with equality if and only if $x = 1$. Sketch this also.

1.2. The binomial distribution is given by

$$q_k = \binom{n}{k} p^k (1-p)^{n-k} \qquad 0 \le k \le n$$

where p is a parameter between 0 and 1. Evaluate $L(\mathbf{q}';\mathbf{q})$ where $\mathbf{q}'$ and $\mathbf{q}$ are binomial distributions characterized by the parameters p' and p, respectively.

1.3. A block of n independent, identically distributed random variables, denoted X^n, has block probability distribution $\mathbf{p}^n$ given by

$$p^n(a_{j_1}, a_{j_2}, \ldots, a_{j_n}) = \prod_{l=1}^{n} p(a_{j_l})$$

Prove that

$$H(\mathbf{p}^n) = nH(\mathbf{p})$$

1.4. The *(weak) law of large numbers* says that for any sequence $X_1, \ldots, X_n$ of independent, identically distributed, real-valued random variables of mean $\bar{x}$, and for any $\varepsilon > 0$ and $\delta > 0$,

$$Pr\left[\left|\frac{1}{n}\sum_{i=1}^{n} X_i - \bar{x}\right| \ge \varepsilon\right] < \delta$$

for sufficiently large n. Prove the (weak) law of large numbers starting from Chebychev's inequality. (Chebychev's inequality is reviewed in Section 4.8.)

1.5. Prove the asymptotic expression for the multinomial coefficient

$$\frac{n!}{\pi_k(n_k!)} \approx e^{nH(\mathbf{p})}$$

where $\mathbf{p}$ is given by

$$p_k = \frac{n_k}{n}$$

Specifically, using Stirling's approximation to $n!$, which is

$$\sqrt{2n\pi}\left(\frac{n}{e}\right)^n < n! < \sqrt{2n\pi}\left(\frac{n}{e}\right)^n \left(1 + \frac{1}{12n-1}\right)$$

prove that

$$e^{n[H(\mathbf{p}) - \varepsilon_1(n)]} < \frac{n!}{\pi_k(n_k!)} < e^{n[H(\mathbf{p}) - \varepsilon_2(n)]}$$

where $\varepsilon_1(n)$ and $\varepsilon_2(n)$ are small terms that go to zero as n goes to infinity.

CHAPTER 2
Data Translation Codes

The simplest communication channel is an unconstrained, noiseless, memoryless channel. A *memoryless channel* is one that has no intersymbol interference and successive noise samples are independent; there is no interaction between successive symbols transmitted through the channel nor are errors interdependent from symbol to symbol. A *noiseless channel* is one that never makes errors. Whatever goes into one end of the channel comes out of the other. An *unconstrained channel* is one that allows input symbols to be transmitted in any arbitrary sequence.

The unconstrained, noiseless, memoryless channel is so simple that we shall find little to say about it. Most of this short chapter will study codes for channels that are constrained but that have neither memory nor noise. Of course, no channel is truly noiseless, but the simple case is the right one to start with. Moreover, in practice one often designs communication systems for noisy channels with constraints by dealing with the noise and the constraints separately, using two layers of coding. A data translation code, studied in this chapter, translates the data sequence into a new sequence that is consistent with the input constraints of the channel. The data translation code can be cascaded with a data transmission code, studied in Chapter 5, that is designed to prevent errors from entering the data because of channel noise.

2.1 DISCRETE NOISELESS CHANNELS

A *discrete channel* is a system in which a sequence of letters chosen from a finite alphabet of symbols $\{a_0, a_1, \ldots, a_{J-1}\}$ can be transmitted from one point to another. Historically, the most important examples of discrete channels for transmitting information are the teletype channel and the telegraphy channel. We shall illustrate many characteristics of discrete channels in terms of these two examples.

Each symbol a_j in a discrete channel has a fixed duration in time, t_j seconds. The duration need not be the same for different a_j, but often it is. In general, the system may forbid the transmission of some specified sequences of symbols from the set of a_j. On the telegraphy channel, for example, convention has fixed the symbols as a dot, a dash, a letter space, and a word space. We define these symbols as follows:

1. A dot consists of line closure for one unit of time and then line open for one unit of time.
2. A dash consists of three time units of line closure and one time unit of line open.
3. A letter space consists of three time units of line open.
4. A word space consists of six time units of line open.

We also impose the restriction on allowable sequences that no space follows another space. This definition of symbols and constraints we take as the formal definition of the telegraphy channel. The Morse code shown in Table 2.1 is one system of encoding information for this channel. Naturally, one may question the efficiency of the Morse code. Is there a limit on the amount of information that can be conveyed through the telegraphy channel and does the Morse code achieve this limit? We shall see eventually that the entropy and the average codeword length given in Table 2.1 are the basic parameters governing the answer to this question.

In the teletype channel there are 32 symbols. Each symbol can be used to represent 5 bits of information. If the system transmits r symbols per second, it is natural to say that the channel has a capacity of $5r$ bits per second. This does not mean that the teletype channel will always be transmitting information at this rate; this is simply the maximum possible rate. Whether the actual rate reaches this maximum depends on how the source of information is connected to the channel.

A more modern example is the binary channel with a so-called runlength constraint. A binary channel has two symbols in its input alphabet, a 0 and a

Table 2.1   The Morse Code

Symbol	Probability p_j	International Morse	Duration l_j
A	0.0642	· —	9
B	0.0127	— · · ·	13
C	0.0218	— · — ·	15
D	0.0317	— · ·	11
E	0.1031	·	5
F	0.0208	· · — ·	13
G	0.0152	— — ·	13
H	0.0467	· · · ·	11
I	0.0575	· ·	7
J	0.0008	· — — —	17
K	0.0049	— · —	13
L	0.0321	· — · ·	13
M	0.0198	— —	11
N	0.0574	— ·	9
O	0.0632	— — —	15
P	0.0152	· — — ·	15
Q	0.0008	— — · —	17
R	0.0484	· — ·	11
S	0.0514	· · ·	9
T	0.0796	—	7
U	0.0228	· · —	11
V	0.0083	· · · —	13
W	0.0175	· — —	13
X	0.0013	— · · —	15
Y	0.0164	— · — —	17
Z	0.0005	— — · ·	15
Space	0.1859		6

$$-\sum_j p_j \log_2 p_j = 4.03 \text{ bits} \qquad \sum_j p_j l_j = 9.296 \text{ time units}$$

1. The two symbols have the same duration. A *runlength constraint* is a constraint on the number of times that the same symbol can be sequentially repeated. A typical constraint may require that there be no strings of all 0s or of all 1s of length larger than t. This constraint ensures that transitions between 0s and 1s are not too infrequent, which would be important in a system that resynchronizes its time reference using such transitions. Another typical constrained channel requires that at least r 0s follow every 1 and that not more than s 0s occur in sequence.

2.2 STATE DIAGRAMS AND TRELLISES

A constrained channel is one that does not permit input sequences containing any of a certain collection of forbidden subsequences. In the telegraphy channel, the forbidden subsequences are those that have consecutive spaces. The user of the channel must keep a running history of recent input sequences. Such a past history can be described by a *state diagram*. This is a diagram in which each of the meaningful past histories of the channel inputs is distinguished by a node in a graph called a *state*. We imagine a number of possible states labeled $S_0, S_1, \ldots, S_{N-1}$. Each state corresponds to one or more of the possible patterns that the recent input sequence has passed through. Loosely we say that the channel is in one of these states, but to be precise we must say that the channel input history is in that state. Paths in the graph show how the state may change with time. For each state only certain symbols from the set $\{a_0, \ldots, a_{J-1}\}$ may be transmitted next. At the next channel input time, one of the allowed input symbols is transmitted and the state changes to a new state, depending both on the old state and on the particular symbol transmitted.

The telegraphy channel gives a simple illustration of a state diagram. There are two states, as shown in Fig. 2.1. State S_0 specifies that a space was the most recent symbol transmitted, and state S_1 specifies that a space was not the most recent symbol transmitted. In state S_0, only a dot or a dash can be sent next and the state always changes. In state S_1, any symbol can be transmitted next and the channel changes state only if a space is sent; otherwise it remains in the same state.

Another example of a state diagram is shown in Fig. 2.2. This state diagram is for a binary channel that forbids any sequence containing a run of more than three repetitions of the same symbol. There are six states given by

$$S_0 = 1\ 1\ 1$$
$$S_1 = 1\ 1$$
$$S_2 = 1$$
$$S_3 = 0$$
$$S_4 = 0\ 0$$
$$S_5 = 0\ 0\ 0$$

Each state denotes the most recent run of symbols of the same kind. A run is preceded by the opposite symbol. Because there can be no string of 1s longer than three, when the system is in state S_0, a 0 must be transmitted; the channel then enters state S_3. When the system is in state S_1 either a 0 or a 1 may be transmitted; the channel enters either state S_3 or S_0. The transitions from the other states are easily deduced in the same way.

In our example it is possible to eventually get from any state to any other state, although it may take several transitions. Such a channel is called an

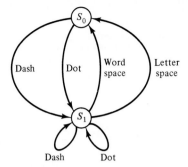

Figure 2.1   State diagram for the telegraphy channel.

irreducible channel, and its state diagram is called an *irreducible state diagram*. We will exclude from our studies those channels, which are of little practical interest, that are not irreducible.

Sometimes the state diagram is replaced by a *trellis diagram*. This is a state diagram augmented by a time axis so that one can see how the state changes with time. The trellis diagram for the telegraphy channel is shown in Fig. 2.3. The Morse code is a collection of some of the paths through this trellis; each path corresponds to one possible sequence of source symbols. An optimum code would use all of the paths, but then the mapping from the set of source output sequences to the set of trellis paths might be a complicated one. Practical codes use only a subset of the set of possible paths.

The trellis shown in Fig. 2.4 is the trellis for the binary channel whose state diagram is shown in Fig. 2.2. Notice that only one path leaves states S_0 and S_5, but two paths leave each of the other states.

Constrained channels can be described also by a matrix **B** called the *state-transition matrix* of the channel. Element b_{ij} of matrix **B** gives the number of

S_0

S_1

S_2

S_3

S_4

S_5

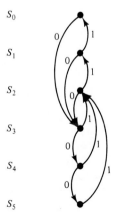

Figure 2.2   State diagram for a binary channel with runlength constraint.

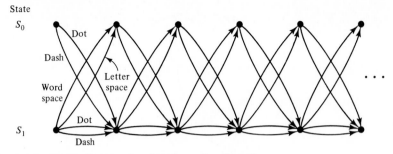

Figure 2.3   Trellis diagram for the telegraphy channel.

paths that go from state S_i to state S_j. For the telegraphy channel, the state-transition matrix is

$$\mathbf{B} = \begin{bmatrix} 0 & 2 \\ 2 & 2 \end{bmatrix}$$

This is an example of a channel that has more than one path connecting some states. For many channels there is at most one path connecting two states.

For the runlength-constrained channel with maximum runlengths of 3, the state-transition matrix is

$$\mathbf{B} = \begin{bmatrix} 0 & 0 & 0 & 1 & 0 & 0 \\ 1 & 0 & 0 & 1 & 0 & 0 \\ 0 & 1 & 0 & 1 & 0 & 0 \\ 0 & 0 & 1 & 0 & 1 & 0 \\ 0 & 0 & 1 & 0 & 0 & 1 \\ 0 & 0 & 1 & 0 & 0 & 0 \end{bmatrix}$$

This matrix is another way of presenting the same information portrayed in the trellis of Fig. 2.4.

We can also write down the two-step state-transition matrix whose ij entry gives the number of distinct paths from state S_i to state S_j that are two

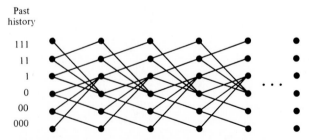

Figure 2.4   Trellis for a binary channel with runlength constraint.

"frames" long. If we count paths of length 2 in Fig. 2.4, we obtain the matrix

$$\begin{bmatrix} 0 & 0 & 1 & 0 & 1 & 0 \\ 0 & 0 & 1 & 1 & 1 & 0 \\ 1 & 0 & 1 & 1 & 1 & 0 \\ 0 & 1 & 1 & 1 & 0 & 1 \\ 0 & 1 & 1 & 1 & 0 & 0 \\ 0 & 1 & 0 & 1 & 0 & 0 \end{bmatrix}$$

which we can verify is equal to $\mathbf{B}^2$. This is a special case of the following theorem.

▢ **Theorem 2.2.1**   The trellis with state-transition matrix $\mathbf{B}$ has an m-step state-transition matrix equal to $\mathbf{B}^m$.

Proof   Let $\mathbf{B}_s$ and $\mathbf{B}_r$, with elements $b_{ij}^{(s)}$ and $b_{ij}^{(r)}$, be the s-step and the r-step state-transition matrices for the channel. Every path of length $s + r$ that starts in state S_i and ends in state S_j must pass through some state S_k after s steps. There are $b_{ik}^{(s)}$ paths into state S_k that start at state S_i and $b_{kj}^{(r)}$ paths out of state S_k that end at state S_j. Hence there are $b_{ik}^{(s)} b_{kj}^{(r)}$ paths of length $r + s$ from state S_i to state S_j that pass through state S_k after s steps. Consequently, the ij element of the m-step state-transition matrix is equal to $\sum_k b_{ik}^{(s)} b_{kj}^{(r)}$. This is nothing other than the matrix product

$$\mathbf{B}_{s+r} = \mathbf{B}_s \mathbf{B}_r$$

Because s and r are arbitrary, this implies that $\mathbf{B}_m = \mathbf{B}^m$.   ▢

The state-transition matrix corresponding to an irreducible state diagram is called an *irreducible state-transition matrix*. Specifically, $\mathbf{B}$ is called an irreducible state-transition matrix if for every i and j there is a positive integer r, possibly depending on i and j, such that $B_{ij}^{(r)}$ is larger than zero.

The state-transition matrix only specifies the number of paths between states; it does not include a description of the duration of the symbols transmitted on each path. The state-transition matrix can be replaced by another matrix that carries a more complete description of the channel. Let $t_{ij,l}$ be the duration of the lth channel input symbol that is allowable in state i and that causes a transition to state j. The structure of the set of transitions is summarized by a matrix $\mathbf{B}(x)$ whose elements are defined by

$$b_{ij}(x) = \sum_l x^{-t_{ij,l}}$$

The matrix $\mathbf{B}(x)$ is called the *augmented state-transition matrix* of the constrained channel. Now the elements are a function of a dummy variable x.

The state-transition matrix $\mathbf{B}$ can be recovered from $\mathbf{B}(x)$ by noting that $\mathbf{B} = \mathbf{B}(1)$.

For the telegraphy channel, the augmented state-transition matrix is

$$\mathbf{B}(x) = \begin{bmatrix} 0 & x^{-2} + x^{-4} \\ x^{-3} + x^{-6} & x^{-2} + x^{-4} \end{bmatrix}$$

The augmented state-transition matrix for a string of symbols is again a power of the augmented state-transition matrix for a single symbol, as is stated in the following theorem.

☐ **Theorem 2.2.2**   The trellis with augmented state-transition matrix $\mathbf{B}(x)$ has an m-step augmented state-transition matrix equal to $\mathbf{B}(x)^m$.

Proof   The proof is virtually the same as the proof of Theorem 2.2.1.   ☐

As an application of the theorem to the telegraphy channel, we can write

$$\mathbf{B}(x)^2 = \begin{bmatrix} x^{-5} + x^{-7} + x^{-8} + x^{-10} & x^{-4} + 2x^{-6} + x^{-8} \\ x^{-5} + x^{-7} + x^{-8} + x^{-10} & x^{-4} + x^{-5} + 2x^{-6} + x^{-7} + 2x^{-8} + x^{-10} \end{bmatrix}$$

from which we find that there are eight paths two symbols in length leading from state S_1 to state S_1. Of these, one has duration 4, one has duration 5, two have duration 6, one has duration 7, two have duration 8, and one has duration 10.

2.3 CAPACITY OF DISCRETE NOISELESS CHANNELS

The question we now consider is how one can measure the capacity of a constrained channel to transmit information. The following definition gives the right measure.

☐ **Definition 2.3.1**   The capacity C (in units of bits per second) of a discrete noiseless channel is given by[†]

$$C = \lim_{T \to \infty} \frac{\log_2 M(T)}{T}$$

where $M(T)$ is the number of allowed sequences of duration T.   ☐

The definition leaves open the question of whether sequences may start in an arbitrary state, or may start only in one or more specified states. For an irreducible channel, this question has no effect on the capacity because within

---

[†]Because $M(T)$ can contain fluctuations, the elementary form of the limit need not exist. The mathematically precise definition would use a limit supremum instead of a simple limit. This form of the limit disregards "bad" values of T for which $M(T)$ is small.

a few frames the channel can get from one state to any other, and these few frames are negligible in the limit as T goes to infinity.

The capacity is also expressed in units of bits per input symbol when the input symbols have the same duration. Then T must be expressed as a multiple of the input symbol duration. In units of information bits per symbol, the capacity of a discrete noiseless channel with symbols of equal duration is given by

$$C = \lim_{n \to \infty} \frac{\log_2 M(n)}{n}$$

where $M(n)$ is the number of allowed sequences of length n.

In the simple case of a noiseless unconstrained channel with J letters, $M(n) = J^n$, so the capacity is $\log_2 J$. If $J = 2$, the capacity is one information bit per bit.

The limit in the definition of capacity will be finite in cases of practical interest. From the definition, it is clear that for large T, about 2^{CT} different messages can be transmitted through the channel in time T. More simply, we say that C bits per second can be transmitted through the channel. In other words, an arbitrary binary dataword of length CT bits can be transmitted in about time T by assigning each of the 2^{CT} datawords to one of the 2^{CT} allowed sequences to form a list of datawords and associated codewords. In practice, if CT is large, such a list cannot be written down because it is exponentially large; one tries to replace the look-up table with a computational procedure or by fitting together a long message out of small pieces.

It is easily seen that the capacity of the teletype channel is $5r$ bits per second, which agrees with the intuitive result. The situation becomes more difficult if the symbols are of different duration, as for the telegraphy channel, or if certain input sequences are forbidden, as for the telegraphy channel or for the binary channel with a runlength constraint.

If all symbols have the same duration, then the matrix $\mathbf{B}^n$ can be used to find the capacity. If we choose the number of frames n to be quite large, we can count the number of paths of length n through the trellis to bound the capacity. The number of paths is the sum of the elements of $\mathbf{B}^n$. It will not be possible to use all these paths as codewords when the channel is constrained in the starting state. However, the total number of codewords cannot be larger than the total number of paths, so we have the upper bound

$$M(n) \leq \sum_{ij} b_{ij}^{(n)}$$

where $b_{ij}^{(n)}$ is the ij entry of $\mathbf{B}^n$. On the other hand, codewords that end in state S_i can always be concatenated with codewords that begin in state S_i. When n is quite large, we should do almost as well if for any i we only count paths starting in state S_i and ending in state S_i. At worst, this "wastes" a few frames at the beginning and end of the trellis because we can get to any state S_k starting in state S_i, and from any state S_k we can get back to state S_i at the end so long as $\mathbf{B}$ is irreducible. When n is very large, the waste is negligible.

Thus we have bracketed the number of paths

$$b_{ii}^{(n)} \leq M(n) \leq \sum_{ij} b_{ij}^{(n)}$$

With $C(n) = (1/n) \log_2 M(n)$, this becomes

$$\frac{1}{n}\log_2 b_{ii}^{(n)} \leq C(n) \leq \frac{1}{n}\log_2 \sum_{ij} b_{ij}^{(n)}$$

and for large n, we expect the two sides to be rather close. We are now ready to take the limit as n goes to infinity in the following theorem. In reading the theorem, recall that an eigenvalue of the N-by-N matrix $\mathbf{B}$ is a root of the polynomial equation $D(\lambda) = 0$ where $D(\lambda)$ equals the determinant of $\mathbf{B} - \lambda\mathbf{I}$ and $\mathbf{I}$ is the N-by-N identity matrix.

If all the eigenvalues of $\mathbf{B}$ are distinct, then the elementary theory of matrices tells us that $\mathbf{B}$ is similar to a diagonal matrix; there will exist the *similarity transformation*

$$\mathbf{B} = \mathbf{U}^{-1}\begin{bmatrix} \lambda_1 & & & & \\ & \lambda_2 & & & \\ & & \cdot & & \\ & & & \cdot & \\ & & & & \lambda_N \end{bmatrix}\mathbf{U}$$

for some orthogonal matrix $\mathbf{U}$. If the eigenvalues are not distinct, then the situation can be more complicated. Then the matrix $\mathbf{B}$ is similar to a block-diagonal matrix as described in the equation

$$\mathbf{B} = \mathbf{U}^{-1}\begin{bmatrix} \Lambda_1 & & & & \\ & \Lambda_2 & & & \\ & & \cdot & & \\ & & & \cdot & \\ & & & & \Lambda_N \end{bmatrix}\mathbf{U}$$

where each block is an L_k-by-L_k matrix of the form

$$\Lambda_k = \begin{bmatrix} \lambda_i & 1 & 0 & 0 \\ 0 & \lambda_i & 1 & 0 \\ 0 & 0 & \lambda_i & 1 \\ 0 & 0 & 0 & \lambda_i \end{bmatrix}$$

with the same eigenvalue λ_i in the diagonal locations, a 1 in the principal off-diagonal locations and everywhere else a 0. The block-diagonal matrix to which **B** is similar is known as the *Jordan canonical form*.

☐ **Theorem 2.3.2** The capacity of an irreducible discrete noiseless channel whose symbols have equal duration is given by

$$C = \log_2 \lambda$$

bits per channel symbol, where λ is the largest (positive) eigenvalue of the matrix **B**.

Proof Let $M_k(n)$ be the number of sequences of length n that end in state k. Then for each k, $M_k(n)$ can be related to $M_j(n-1)$ for $j = 0, \ldots, N-1$ by the matrix equation

$$
\begin{bmatrix} M_0(n) \\ \vdots \\ M_{N-1}(n) \end{bmatrix}^{\mathrm{T}} = \begin{bmatrix} M_0(n-1) \\ \vdots \\ M_{N-1}(n-1) \end{bmatrix}^{\mathrm{T}} \mathbf{B}
$$

Therefore

$$
\begin{bmatrix} M_0(n) \\ \vdots \\ M_{N-1}(n) \end{bmatrix}^{\mathrm{T}} = \begin{bmatrix} M_0(0) \\ \vdots \\ M_{N-1}(0) \end{bmatrix}^{\mathrm{T}} \mathbf{B}^n
$$

with initial conditions $M_k(0) = 1$ if the channel can start in state k, and otherwise $M_k(0) = 0$.

The matrix equation is a linear difference equation. As is well known, a solution satisfying the initial conditions is unique because if two solutions satisfy the same initial conditions, then their difference also satisfies the equation and has initial conditions equal to zero; therefore the difference is zero for all n.

We will carry through the proof for the case where the eigenvalues are distinct; then we will augment the argument to cover the more general case.

As is well known, if λ_i is an eigenvalue of **B**, then λ_i^n is an eigenvalue of $\mathbf{B}^n$. That is,

$$
\mathbf{B}^n = \mathbf{U}^{-1} \begin{bmatrix} \lambda_1^n & & & & \\ & \lambda_2^n & & & \\ & & \ddots & & \\ & & & \ddots & \\ & & & & \lambda_N^n \end{bmatrix} \mathbf{U}
$$

where **U** does not depend on n. This is seen by multiplying together n copies of the similarity representation for **B**, noting that $\mathbf{U}^{-1}\mathbf{U} = \mathbf{I}$. From this we see immediately that the elements of $\mathbf{B}^n$ have the form

$$b_{ij}^{(n)} = \sum_{k=1}^{N} a_{ijk}\lambda_k^n$$

where the a_{ijk} are constants independent of n. For each k, at least one of the a_{ijk} must be nonzero; otherwise the matrix **B** would not depend on its kth eigenvalue.

We can conclude that, because **B** is irreducible, for large enough n, any linear combination of the elements of $\mathbf{B}^n$ is dominated by a term proportional to λ^n, where λ is the eigenvalue of largest magnitude. Further, because the sum is real and positive, the eigenvalue λ must be real and positive. This completes the proof for the case where the eigenvalues are distinct.

If the eigenvalues are not distinct, then we must deal with the block-diagonal representation

$$\mathbf{B}^n = \mathbf{U}^{-1} \begin{bmatrix} \mathbf{\Lambda}_1^n & & & & \\ & \mathbf{\Lambda}_2^n & & & \\ & & \cdot & & \\ & & & \cdot & \\ & & & & \mathbf{\Lambda}_N^n \end{bmatrix} \mathbf{U}$$

By examining the successive powers of $\mathbf{\Lambda}_l$ we can see that

$$\mathbf{\Lambda}_i^n = \begin{bmatrix} \lambda_i^n & \binom{n}{1}\lambda_i^{n-1} & \binom{n}{2}\lambda_i^{n-2} & \cdots & \binom{n}{L_k}\lambda_i^{n-L_k} \\ 0 & \lambda_i^n & \binom{n}{1}\lambda_i^{n-1} & \cdots & \binom{n}{L_k-1}\lambda_i^{n-L_k-1} \\ \vdots & & & & \vdots \\ 0 & 0 & 0 & \cdots & \lambda_i^n \end{bmatrix}$$

Because L_k is fixed for each k, the elements of $b_{ij}^{(n)}$ will be dominated by terms like $\binom{n}{L_k}\lambda_i^{n-L_k}$. Ignoring all but the largest term in the expression for capacity would give

$$C = \frac{1}{n}\log\left[\binom{n}{L_k}\lambda^{n-L_k}\right]$$

$$= \frac{n-L_k}{n}\log\lambda + \frac{1}{n}\log\binom{n}{L_k}$$

which goes to $\log\lambda$ as n goes to infinity. $\square$

For an application of this theorem, consider the binary channel with no runs of length 3 whose trellis was shown in Fig. 2.4. To find the largest eigenvalue, set the determinant of $\mathbf{B} - \lambda\mathbf{I}$ equal to zero:

$$\det \begin{bmatrix} -\lambda & 0 & 0 & 1 & 0 & 0 \\ 1 & -\lambda & 0 & 1 & 0 & 0 \\ 0 & 1 & -\lambda & 1 & 0 & 0 \\ 0 & 0 & 1 & -\lambda & 1 & 0 \\ 0 & 0 & 1 & 0 & -\lambda & 1 \\ 0 & 0 & 1 & 0 & 0 & -\lambda \end{bmatrix} = 0$$

We obtain the equation

$$\lambda^6 - \lambda^4 - 2\lambda^3 - 3\lambda^2 - 2\lambda - 1 = 0$$

which must be solved for the largest real root. The largest real root is 1.8218, and so the capacity is 0.8654 information bits per channel bit.

For another application of the theorem, consider the binary channel with the constraints that at least two 0s follow every 1 and that no more than seven 0s occur in sequence. The characteristic equation can be readily evaluated as

$$\lambda^8 - \lambda^5 - \lambda^4 - \lambda^3 - \lambda^2 - \lambda - 1 = 0$$

The base-2 logarithm of the largest root of this equation is 0.518 bits per bit, which is the capacity of the channel. Codes exist that transmit up to 0.518 bits of information for each channel bit transmitted, but no code can do better.

Next we study channels whose symbols do not all have the same duration. Suppose that symbols $a_0, \ldots, a_{J-1}$ have durations $t_0, \ldots, t_{J-1}$ that are integer multiples of the unit of time. We will first try to find the capacity without recourse to matrix methods. Let $M(t)$ represent the number of sequences of duration t. There are $M(t - t_j)$ sequences that end in a_j for each j. If there are no constraints on sequences of symbols, then for each j we can take any sequence of duration $t - t_j$ and append symbol a_j to it to get a sequence of duration t. Consequently,

$$M(t) = M(t - t_0) + M(t - t_1) + \cdots + M(t - t_{J-1})$$

This is a recursive equation that can be solved by the well-known methods of finite-difference equations. Try $M(t) = x^t$. Then

$$x^t = x^{t-t_0} + x^{t-t_1} + \cdots + x^{t-t_{J-1}}$$

from which follows the characteristic equation,

$$x^{-t_0} + x^{-t_1} + \cdots + x^{-t_{J-1}} = 1$$

Any x that satisfies the characteristic equation will solve the difference equation. In general, the characteristic equation will have many solutions denoted x_i. Because the original equation is linear, the linear combination

$$M(t) = \sum_i A_i x_i^t$$

is also a solution, where the coefficients A_i are constants that can be chosen to meet known conditions on $M(t)$ for small t. So long as there are no repeated roots of the characteristic equations, this is the general solution.

Even when there are restrictions on allowed sequences we often may still obtain a difference equation of this type and find the capacity C from the characteristic equation. The telegraphy channel described above leads to the equation

$$M(t) = M(t-2) + M(t-4) + M(t-5) + M(t-7)$$
$$+ M(t-8) + M(t-10)$$

as we see by counting sequences of symbols according to the last or next-to-last symbol occurring. Hence C is equal to $\log_2 \lambda$, where λ is the largest positive root of

$$x^{-2} + x^{-4} + x^{-5} + x^{-7} + x^{-8} + x^{-10} - 1 = 0$$

Solving this, we find that $C = 0.539$ bits per unit of time. This is the maximum rate at which data can be transmitted through the telegraphy channel. We emphasize that 0.539 is the capacity of the telegraphy channel as we have defined it. If the channel is changed, as by changing the constraints, then the capacity may change also.

One may evaluate the rate at which the Morse code, shown in Table 2.1, conveys information. If it is close to 0.539 bits per unit time, then the Morse code is a good code from the point of view of bit efficiency. However, the Morse code is not designed for a binary memoryless source. It combines the functions of data compaction and data translation, matching the frequency of occurrence of English letters to the characteristics of the telegraphy channel. The information content of English text is given by its entropy, as we shall study in Chapter 3. The memoryless model of English text portrayed in Table 2.1 has an entropy of 4.03 bits per letter, and the telegraphy channel has a capacity of 0.539 bits per unit time. Hence, an optimum code uses an average of 7.48 units of signaling time per source output letter. The Morse code uses an average of 9.296 units of signaling time per source output letter, which is 124% of the time needed by the optimum code. This establishes the amount by which the Morse code could be improved for use with the memoryless model of English text. Of course, an optimum code may be too complex for an operator to learn. The Morse code is an excellent compromise between performance and simplicity.

The capacity of a channel whose letters have different durations can be computed directly from the augmented state-transition matrix. The following theorem gives a more general form of Theorem 2.3.2.

☐ **Theorem 2.3.3** A channel with an N-by-N augmented state-transition matrix $\mathbf{B}(x)$ has a channel capacity equal to the base-2 logarithm of the largest real root of the equation

$$\det\left[\mathbf{B}(x) - \mathbf{I}\right] = 0$$

where $\mathbf{I}$ is the N-by-N identity matrix.

Proof We give only an outline of a proof. Let $M_k(t)$ be the number of sequences of duration t that end in state k. Then for each k,

$$M_k(t) = \sum_j \sum_l M_j(t - t_{jk,l})$$

where $t_{jk,l}$ is the duration of the lth channel input symbol that is allowable in state j and that causes a transition to state k. This is a system of linear difference equations. Assume the form

$$M_k = A_k x^t$$

Substituting into the difference equation gives

$$A_k x^t = \sum_j \sum_l A_j x^{t - t_{jk,l}}$$

or

$$\sum_j \left(\sum_l x^{-t_{jk,l}} - \delta_{jk} \right) A_j = 0$$

where δ_{jk} equals 1 if j equals k and otherwise equals 0. This can be written as the matrix equation

$$\left[\mathbf{B}(x) - \mathbf{I}\right]\mathbf{A} = \mathbf{0}$$

But the components of $\mathbf{A}$ are not all zero. The equation can hold only if

$$D(x) = 0$$

where $D(x)$ is the determinant of $\mathbf{B}(x) - \mathbf{I}$. Let λ_i for $i = 1, \ldots,$ denote the roots of $D(x) = 0$ and let λ equal the largest of these. Supposing the roots are distinct, the total number of sequences is

$$M(t) = \sum_k M_k(t)$$

$$= \sum_i A_i \lambda_i^t$$

where the A_i are chosen to satisfy initial conditions. The capacity is

$$C = \lim_{t \to \infty} \frac{\log_2 \sum_i A_i \lambda_i^t}{t}$$

$$= \log_2 \lambda$$

because the exponentially increasing terms in the sum will be dominated by the largest. This finishes the argument if the roots of $D(x)$ are distinct. We will not enlarge the argument to cover the more general case in which $D(x)$ has repeated roots. □

If we apply Theorem 2.3.3 to the example of the telegraphy channel, the determinant equation is

$$\det \begin{bmatrix} -1 & x^{-2}+x^{-4} \\ x^{-3}+x^{-6} & x^{-2}+x^{-4}-1 \end{bmatrix} = 0$$

On expansion this leads to the equation given previously for this set of constraints.

Theorem 2.3.3 reduces to Theorem 2.3.2 if all symbols are of the same duration. This is because the matrix $\mathbf{B}(x)$ has elements equal to x^{-1} when $B_{jk} = 1$, and equal to 0 when $B_{jk} = 0$. Therefore the formula

$$\det \left[\mathbf{B}(x) - \mathbf{I} \right] = 0$$

is equivalent to

$$\det \left(\mathbf{B} - x\mathbf{I} \right) = 0$$

The roots of this equation are the eigenvalues of $\mathbf{B}$.

2.4 BLOCK CODES FOR DATA TRANSLATION

An (n,k) block code for data translation having rate k/n bits per channel symbol consists of 2^k sequences of channel symbols, each sequence of blocklength n. The sequences, called *codewords*, must satisfy the channel constraints, as must concatenated pairs of sequences.

One way to construct an (n, k) binary block code for data translation is to first write down all the binary sequences of length n that satisfy the constraints. Because the codewords will be concatenated and the concatenated pairs must still satisfy the constraints, one must discard from the list of blocks some of the entries so that the constraints will still be satisfied under concatenation. If n is large compared with the length of any forbidden subsequence, this latter detail will reduce the number of words on the list by only a small fraction. Now choose k so that there are at least 2^k words on the list and choose 2^k words as codewords. The encoder is a fixed mapping from the set of k-bit information words into the set of n-bit (or n-symbol) codewords, and the decoder is the inverse of this map.

A simple example is a $(3, 2)$ binary code in which no runs of more than two 0s occur. With little effort, we write down the five words

0 1 0

0 1 1

1 0 1

1 1 0

1 1 1

It is clear that these five words can be concatenated in any order, including repetitions, without ever forming a run of more than two 0s. To form a $(3, 2)$ code, choose any four, say the first four, as codewords and fix any map from 2-bit information words into codewords. The following map will do:

0 0 ↔ 0 1 0

0 1 ↔ 0 1 1

1 0 ↔ 1 1 0

1 1 ↔ 1 0 1

This gives a rate 2/3 binary code with no runs of more than two 0s in any concatenated sequence of codewords. The code rate of 0.667 should be compared with the channel capacity of 0.879. The rate can be increased considerably by changing the code, but to do so a longer blocklength must be chosen.

In the absence of an algorithmic rule defining the relationship between a k-bit information word and an n-bit codeword, the encoding and decoding operations will be simple look-up tables. The encoder consists of a table of 2^k n-bit words, and the decoder consists of a table of 2^n k-bit words. To encode a k-bit word, use those k bits as a memory address to look up the codeword. To decode an n-bit word, use those n bits as an address to look up the information word. The decoding table will have many unused entries; only 2^k will be meaningful. Of course, if k is as large as 20 or 30, the look-up procedure is impractical because the tables are too large. One would prefer an algorithmic procedure in the encoder that computes the codeword from the information word and an algorithmic procedure in the decoder that computes the information word from the codeword. In this book, however, we study primarily the existence of codes and not the existence of algorithmic encoders and decoders.

The set of states in which the channel can be at the start of a block and to which it must be returned at the end of the block is called the set of *terminal states*; possibly the set of terminal states is equal to the set of all states of the channel. Every codeword must be constructed so that at its end it returns the channel to a terminal state. The reason for introducing a set of terminal states is as an aid to construct codes. States that have fewer than 2^k paths of length n leaving them will not have enough codewords and so can be excluded from the set of terminal states. Consequently, no codewords can end on these states.

The following theorem describes a necessary but insufficient condition for the blocklength that a block code must have to achieve any given rate.

□   **Theorem 2.4.1**   An (n, k) block code for a constrained channel with state-transition matrix **B** does not exist unless the matrix $\mathbf{B}^n$ has all row sums not smaller than 2^k or has a submatrix, obtained by deleting any rows of $\mathbf{B}^n$ and the corresponding columns of $\mathbf{B}^n$, that has all row sums not smaller than 2^k.

Proof   Suppose that all states are terminal states so that the channel can be in any state at the start of a block. The total number of paths of length n leading out of state S_i is equal to the ith row sum of $\mathbf{B}^n$, so this row sum must be at least 2^k for each i.

Suppose that the channel is restricted at the start of a block to be only in states from a set of specified terminal states. Delete from $\mathbf{B}^n$ those rows and columns corresponding to excluded states. The total number of paths of length n leading out of state S_i that terminate in a terminal node is equal to the ith row sum of the submatrix. The row sum of the submatrix must be at least 2^k for all i that index terminal states.   □

A simple example is the channel with the runlength constraint that at least two 0s must follow every 1. The state-transition matrix is

$$\mathbf{B} = \begin{bmatrix} 0 & 1 & 0 \\ 0 & 0 & 1 \\ 1 & 0 & 1 \end{bmatrix}$$

An (n, k) rate 1/2 code must satisfy Theorem 2.4.1 with n even. If we compute $\mathbf{B}^n$ in turn for each even n until we reach

$$\mathbf{B}^{14} = \begin{bmatrix} 41 & 28 & 60 \\ 60 & 41 & 88 \\ 88 & 60 & 129 \end{bmatrix}$$

we would see that the code must have blocklength equal to at least 14 because $\mathbf{B}^{14}$ has all row sums larger than 2^7, but the condition of Theorem 2.4.1 fails for all n smaller than 14. In fact, because the lower-right element is greater than 128, we can use state S_2 as the single terminal state. By choosing 128 paths of length 14 that begin and end in state S_2, we have a $(14, 7)$ code for this channel.

The reason that the condition of Theorem 2.4.1 is not also a sufficient condition is that the codewords of a block code are fixed. They do not depend on which terminal state the channel is in at the start of a block. Therefore we also have the stronger condition that leaving each terminal state there must be an identical set of 2^k paths.

If there are 2^k paths leaving each terminal state but they are not identical sets of paths at each terminal state, then one cannot form an (n, k) block code. However, it is possible to form a code known as an (n, k) *state-dependent block code*. This is composed of a distinct (n, k) block code for each terminal state. Both the encoder and decoder are required to remember in which state the previous block left the channel. If the channel was left in state S_i, then the encoder and decoder use the ith block code. In this way, the codeword is a function both of the sourceword and the state. A state-dependent block code is an example of a tree code.

One systematic method of constructing block codes consists of forming codewords out of two parts, a prefix and a suffix. The prefix is designed to move through the trellis to a node that depends only on the prefix and not on the terminal state of the channel at the beginning. A suffix then returns the channel to any terminal state. If n is even, the prefix and suffix are each of length $n/2$. If n is odd, the prefix is of length $(n - 1)/2$ and the suffix is of length $(n + 1)/2$. A codeword consists of a prefix followed by any suffix allowed with that prefix.

As an example of this construction, we will find codewords for a $(5, 3)$ code for the channel constrained to have no runs of length greater than 3. A trellis of length 5 was shown in Fig. 2.4. To get a $(5, 3)$ code, we must choose as codewords 2^3 paths through the trellis that begin and end on a chosen set of terminal states. This property allows the codewords to be concatenated. We will choose prefixes of length 2 that will drive the channel into a state that is independent of the initial state of the channel. Figure 2.5 gives a table of the state that the channel will reach starting from each initial state for each 2-bit channel input sequence. Forbidden input sequences have no state listed. In the table, a subarray in the center is highlighted because its rows consist of identical entries. What this subarray tells us is that if the initial states are restricted as shown by the subarray and the channel input bits are also so restricted, then a prefix will take the channel to a state that is independent of the initial state. We only need to know the prefix to know which state the channel is in at the end of the prefix. For each such prefix, 01 and 10, we can tabulate the suffixes that will leave the channel in one of the allowed terminal states. These are as follows:

01	10
1 1 0	0 0 1
1 0 1	0 1 0
1 0 0	0 1 1
0 1 0	1 0 1
0 1 1	1 0 0
0 0 1	1 1 0

Channel sequence	Initial state					
	000	00	0	1	11	111
00	—	—	000	00	00	00
01	—	1	1	1	1	1
10	0	0	0	0	0	—
11	00	00	00	111	—	—

Figure 2.5   Two-step state transitions.

This gives twelve possible codewords, so we can encode at most 3 bits using any eight of these. To obtain the (5, 3) code, we arbitrarily choose any eight, say the first four from each column, and fix any map from the 3-bit information words to codewords. The following map will do:

$$0\,0\,0 \leftrightarrow 0\,1\,1\,1\,0$$
$$0\,0\,1 \leftrightarrow 0\,1\,1\,0\,1$$
$$0\,1\,0 \leftrightarrow 0\,1\,1\,0\,0$$
$$0\,1\,1 \leftrightarrow 0\,1\,0\,1\,0$$
$$1\,0\,0 \leftrightarrow 1\,0\,0\,0\,1$$
$$1\,0\,1 \leftrightarrow 1\,0\,0\,1\,0$$
$$1\,1\,0 \leftrightarrow 1\,0\,0\,1\,1$$
$$1\,1\,1 \leftrightarrow 1\,0\,1\,0\,1$$

Other encoding rules might be chosen instead. Another map may simplify the implementation, perhaps because some simple relationship can be found between information bits and code bits.

2.5 PREFIX CODES FOR DATA TRANSLATION

The capacity of a constrained channel is the largest rate of any code whose codewords will be accepted by the channel. Roughly speaking, an optimum code for an infinite stream of data uses the set of all the infinite-length sequences defining paths through the trellis. However, an optimum code may be too complex to be practical. A good code is one that has a simple description and yet uses most paths through the trellis. To find a good code whose rate is close to the channel capacity can be a difficult task. The rate of a block code often falls short of the capacity. One reason is that the number of codewords in a block usually needs to be a power of 2 (or of J), while the number of sequences that are potential codewords is not a power of 2; a large number of potential codewords are unused. To attain a larger fraction of the channel capacity, one can try to use variable-length blocks, as discussed in this section.

For some constraints one can obtain far simpler encoders and decoders by using prefix codes instead of block codes. A simple example that we have already seen in the previous section is the channel with the runlength constraint that at least two 0s must follow every 1. The state-transition matrix is

$$\mathbf{B} = \begin{bmatrix} 0 & 1 & 0 \\ 0 & 0 & 1 \\ 1 & 0 & 1 \end{bmatrix}$$

We saw in the previous section that $\mathbf{B}^{14}$ is the first even power of $\mathbf{B}$ satisfying Theorem 2.4.1. Hence a rate 1/2 block code for this channel cannot be smaller than a (14, 7) code. A blocklength of 14 is the smallest blocklength for which we could hope to construct a block code of rate 1/2 for this channel.

There is a very simple variable-length block code given by the encoding/decoding table

$$0 \quad \leftrightarrow 0\ 0$$

$$1\ 0 \leftrightarrow 0\ 1\ 0\ 0$$

$$1\ 1 \leftrightarrow 1\ 0\ 0\ 0$$

The ratio of the number of information bits to the number of codeword bits is a constant, so this is a *fixed-rate* variable-length block code. By inspection, it is clear that the codewords can be concatenated without violating channel constraints. The code has another important property; it is self-punctuating. Consider the concatenated sequence of codewords

$$0\ 1\ 0\ 0\ 1\ 0\ 0\ 0\ 0\ 0\ 0\ 1\ 0\ 0\ 0 \ldots$$

Even though the codewords are concatenated without any explicit punctuation, the structure of the code itself provides implicit punctuation so that we can uniquely punctuate this code stream as

$$0\ 1\ 0\ 0,\ 1\ 0\ 0\ 0,\ 0\ 0,\ 0\ 0,\ 1\ 0\ 0\ 0, \ldots$$

There is no other way to do it.

The prefix condition is an important property for any variable-length block code to have. The decoder must be able to break into codewords a concatenated string that is not explicitly punctuated. This implies that the punctuation is somehow built into the structure of the code, and imposing a prefix condition on the codewords is one way to do this.

☐ **Definition 2.5.1** A variable-length block code with code alphabet $\{a_0, \ldots, a_{J-1}\}$ is a set $\{\mathbf{c}_0, \ldots, \mathbf{c}_{M-1}\}$ of M strings of letters from the code alphabet. If the codeword c_m is not the beginning of $c_{m'}$ for any $m' \neq m$ and for all m, then the code is called a *prefix code*.   □

An example of a binary prefix code is as follows

$$\mathscr{C} = \begin{cases} 0\ 0 \\ 0\ 1 \\ 1\ 0 \\ 1\ 1\ 0 \\ 1\ 1\ 1\ 0\ 0 \\ 1\ 1\ 1\ 0\ 1 \\ 1\ 1\ 1\ 1\ 0 \\ 1\ 1\ 1\ 1\ 1 \end{cases}$$

Notice that no codeword is the beginning of any other codeword. Hence any indefinitely long string of concatenated codewords is self-punctuating. The string

$$0\ 1\ 1\ 1\ 0\ 1\ 1\ 1\ 0\ 0\ 0\ 1\ldots$$

can only be punctuated as

$$0\ 1,\ 1\ 1\ 0,\ 1\ 1\ 1\ 0\ 0,\ 0\ 1\ldots$$

Each comma can be inserted by working from left to right without looking at symbols to the right of it.

A prefix code can be represented graphically as an initial segment of a tree. A graphical portrayal of our above example is shown in Fig. 2.6. The prefix condition can be described graphically by the condition that every codeword corresponds to an end node. No codeword can correspond to a node that has active branches leaving it.

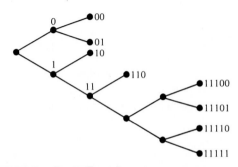

Figure 2.6   Tree structure of a prefix code.

Our example is more than just a prefix code. It has the property that whenever any branch leaving a node is used by the code, then all branches leaving it are used by the code. A formal definition is as follows:

☐ **Definition 2.5.2**   A *complete* prefix code is a prefix code with the property that *any* semi-infinite string of symbols from the code alphabet can be punctuated uniquely into a string of codewords.   ☐

A prefix code used to break apart a random data stream must be a complete prefix code. The example above could be used for this purpose.

A degenerate example of a complete prefix code is the set of n-bit binary words. The codewords are distinct, and a random binary data stream can be uniquely broken into n-bit blocks. The number of codewords M is 2^n, which can be written $M2^{-n} = 1$. This is a special case of the following theorem.

☐ **Theorem 2.5.3**   In an alphabet of size K, there exists a complete prefix code with M codewords having lengths l_m for $m = 0, \ldots, M - 1$ if and only if

$$\sum_{m=0}^{M-1} K^{-l_m} = 1$$

Proof   The proof is not given here. It can be obtained by extending the proof of the Kraft inequality, to follow in Theorem 2.5.4, to include only the equality condition.   ☐

☐ **Theorem 2.5.4   (Kraft inequality)**   In an alphabet of size K, there exists a prefix code with M codewords of length l_m for $m = 0, \ldots, M - 1$ if and only if

$$\sum_{m=0}^{M-1} K^{-l_m} \leq 1$$

Proof   The codewords of a prefix code can always be put on a tree. Pick a length l larger than any of the l_m. The tree has K^l nodes on level l. Each codeword of length l_m obstructs K^{l-l_m} nodes on level l. No two codewords obstruct the same nodes. Therefore, because there are only a total of K^l nodes on level l, we can write

$$\sum_{m=0}^{M-1} K^{l-l_m} \leq K^l$$

so that

$$\sum_{m=0}^{M-1} K^{-l_m} \leq 1$$

To prove the converse, suppose the inequality is satisfied and let n_i be the number of codewords whose length is i. Then

$$\sum_{i=1}^{l} n_i K^{-i} = \sum_{m=0}^{M-1} K^{-l_m} \leq 1$$

where l is the maximum codeword length. Therefore

$$n_1 K^{-1} \leq 1$$

$$n_2 K^{-2} + n_1 K^{-1} \leq 1$$

$$\cdots \cdots$$

$$n_l K^{-l} + \cdots + n_1 K^{-1} \leq 1$$

These inequalities are equivalent to the following

$$n_1 \leq K$$

$$n_2 \leq K^2 - n_1 K$$

$$\cdots \cdots$$

$$n_l \leq K^l - n_1 K^{l-1} - \cdots - n_{l-1} K$$

which can be interpreted in terms of a tree model. The number of nodes available on the first level of a tree is K, on the second level is K^2, and so on. The first inequality says that the number of codewords of length 1 is less than the available number of nodes on the first level. The second inequality says that the number of codewords of length 2 is less than the total number of nodes on the second level minus the number $n_1 K$ blocked by the first-level nodes already occupied by codewords. The succeeding inequalities demonstrate the availability of a sufficient number of nodes at each level after the nodes blocked by shorter length codewords have been removed. Because this is true at every codeword length up to the maximum codeword length, the assertion of the theorem is proved.   □

Although the codewords of a fixed-rate prefix code need not have the same length, each codeword must have the same rate. Each codeword has blocklength $n = mn_0$ and data length $k = mk_0$, where m is an integer and (n_0, k_0) are fixed constants.,

An example of a prefix code for data translation is the Franaszek code shown in Table 2.2. This code is designed for the runlength-constrained binary channel in which at least two 0s must follow every 1 and no more than seven 0s occur in sequence. This channel has a capacity of 0.518, while the Franaszek code in Table 2.2 has a rate of 0.5. A code that comes closer to the channel capacity will be quite complex.

By inspection of the codewords, one can see that the sourcewords of the Franaszek code satisfy the prefix condition so it can be uniquely encoded, and the codewords of the Franaszek code also satisfy the prefix condition so it can

Table 2.2   An $r = 2, s = 7$ Prefix
Code for Data Translation

Sourcewords	Codewords
11	0100
10	1000
000	000100
010	001000
011	100100
0010	00001000
0011	00100100

be uniquely decoded. Inspection also shows that the channel constraints are
satisfied by any concatenated sequence of codewords.

Finding prefix codes for data translation usually employs some kind of
disciplined search procedure. The search can proceed, much as in the case of
block codes for data translation, by selection of a set of terminal states. The
codewords begin in a terminal state and must return to a terminal state. The
terminal states must be chosen in such a way that the same set of codewords
are valid sequences out of each terminal state. If a state is not usable as a
terminal state because it has insufficient sequences leaving it, then the
sequences ending at that state cannot be used as codewords. A disciplined
search procedure for finding prefix codes works by picking a maximum
codeword length, then eliminating unusable nodes from the ends of a trellis of
this length until either a satisfactory code is obtained or the trellis is reduced to
a useless remnant.

PROBLEMS

2.1.   **a.** What is the capacity of a binary noiseless channel with transition matrix

$$\mathbf{B} = \begin{bmatrix} 1 & 1 \\ 0 & 1 \end{bmatrix}$$

Explain the result intuitively.

b. What is the capacity of a binary noiseless channel with transition matrix

$$\mathbf{B} = \begin{bmatrix} 1 & 1 \\ 1 & 0 \end{bmatrix}$$

c. What is the capacity of a ternary noiseless channel with transition matrix

$$\mathbf{B} = \begin{bmatrix} 1 & 1 & 1 \\ 1 & 1 & 1 \\ 1 & 1 & 1 \end{bmatrix}$$

2.2. A runlength-limited channel allows strings of zeros of minimum length r and of maximum length s. (Two consecutive 1s are separated by a string of 0s of length 0.) Prove that the channel capacity is given by $\log_2 \lambda$ where λ is the largest positive root of

$$x^{s+1} - \frac{x^{s+1-r} - 1}{x - 1} = 0$$

if s is finite, and of

$$x - \frac{x^{1-r}}{x - 1} = 0$$

if s is infinite.

2.3. A submarine cable channel can send a positive pulse, a negative pulse, or a zero level during each symbol time, but at least one zero must follow each positive or negative pulse.
   a. What is the capacity of this channel?
   b. What is the largest set of codewords of length 4 that you can find?
   c. Draw a trellis for the channel.

2.4. **a.** Construct a binary block code for data translation that has six codewords, a blocklength equal to 5, and a maximum runlength equal to 2.
   b. Show how to expand this block code to a fixed-rate prefix code with rate 0.6 for the same constraint by adjoining to the code 16 new codewords of length 10.

2.5. A certain transmitter tube can either be in the off state transmitting no power or in the on state transmitting a fixed amount of power. It can remain in the off state for any length of time equal to an integer multiple of the basic unit of time. It can remain in the on state either for two units of time or for three units of time. There must be at least one unit of time in the off state after leaving the on state.

   There are two ways to view this as a channel. It can be viewed as a channel with three symbols denoted 0, 1, 2 of durations one, two, and three time units, respectively, and with the constraint that symbols 1 and 2 must be followed by symbol 0. Alternatively, it can be viewed as a channel with two symbols, 0 and 1, both of one time unit, but with more complex constraints on the allowed sequences.

   Calculate the capacity of each of these perceived channels. Are the capacities the same?

2.6. By examining the eigenvalues of the state-transition matrix, verify that a noiseless unconstrained channel with J symbols of equal duration has capacity equal to $\log_2 J$.

2.7 Construct a (4, 3) binary block code for data translation for the channel that can have at most two 1s in sequence.

2.8. The binary channel with a so-called charge constraint is one in which the running difference between the total number of transmitted 1s and the total number of transmitted 0s must be in a given range. Specifically, a counter is incremented each time a 1 is transmitted and decremented each time a 0 is transmitted. The count is not allowed to become larger than q nor smaller than $-q$. If it equals q, the next bit transmitted must be a 0 and if it equals $-q$, the next bit transmitted must be a 1.

   What is the capacity of a charge-constrained channel with $q = 2$?

2.9. Prove that the trellis with augmented state-transition matrix $\mathbf{B}(x)$ has an m-step augmented state-transition matrix equal to $\mathbf{B}(x)^m$.

2.10. a. A channel can transmit in each time unit a positive pulse $p(t)$ denoting a $+1$ symbol, a negative pulse $-p(t)$ denoting a -1 symbol, or no pulse denoting a 0 symbol. A constraint on the use of the channel requires that a $+1$ or -1 be followed by at least one 0.

Compute the channel capacity and find a prefix code with rate equal to the capacity.

b. A different channel has the same symbol alphabet denoted $\{+1, 0, -1\}$. This channel has the constraint that there be no run of more than two 0s and that $+1$ and -1 cannot follow themselves (but $+1$ can follow -1 and -1 can follow $+1$). What is the capacity of this channel?

Construct a prefix code with rate 1.

2.11. The binary channel that allows no runs of 0s or 1s of length greater than 3 has capacity 0.8543. Construct a rate 3/4 prefix code for this channel having six codewords of length 4 and 16 codewords of length 8.

2.12. a. Give an example of a reducible channel with a "start-up" state that can never reoccur once it is left. Explain why such a state can play no role in computing the capacity.

b. Give an example of a reducible channel for which the states can be partitioned into two subsets such that there are no transitions from states in either subset to states in the other. Explain why the capacity can be computed using only one of these subsets. Which one?

2.13. A given noiseless channel on continuous time has two input levels, 1 and -1. Transitions between levels must not be closer than T seconds.

a. Describe a trivial communication scheme that transmits T^{-1} bits per second.

b. Now choose a channel time interval of $T/3$ and impose the channel constraint that no runs of 0s or of 1s have length greater than or equal to 3. Does this signaling scheme satisfy the original channel constraint? What is the capacity of this channel?

c. Show that this channel is equivalent to a binary channel with the constraint that every 1 be followed by at least two 0s.

d. Give a code that transmits $3/2T$ bits per second.

2.14. By inserting a comma after every 1, any binary sequence can be parsed uniquely into a concatenation of phrases, each phrase ending with a 1 and beginning with a string of none or more 0s. These phrases can themselves be regarded as variable-length symbols and the binary sequence can be regarded instead as a sequence of these new symbols. If a channel has an (r,s) runlength constraint, then only symbols with at least r and at most s zeros are allowed.

a. Show that the rate of the code satisfies

$$R = \lim_{n \to \infty} \frac{H(X_1, X_2, \ldots, X_n)}{E[l(X_1) + l(X_2) + \cdots + l(X_n)]}$$

where $l(X)$ denotes the length of the random symbol X, and E denotes the expectation.

b. Prove that, for any positive numbers,

$$\frac{A + B}{C + D} \leq \max\left(\frac{A}{C}, \frac{B}{D}\right)$$

which implies that

$$R \leq \max_{\mathbf{p}} \frac{H(X)}{E[l(X)]}$$

where $\mathbf{p}$ is the probability distribution associated with random variable X. When is equality obtained?

c. Use a Lagrange multiplier to show that

$$Pr[l(X) = l] = 2^{-lC} \qquad l = r + 1, r + 2, \ldots, s + 1$$

for some constant C satisfying

$$\sum_{l=r+1}^{s+1} 2^{-lC} = 1$$

what is the interpretation of the constant C?

NOTES

Translation codes for constrained channels were first introduced by Shannon (1948). Our treatment of the telegraphy channel and the teletype channel follows his. Further work in this area has been surprisingly sparse, being represented by the papers by Freiman and Wyner (1964), Franaszek (1969), Tang and Bahl (1970), and Blake (1982). Early work was motivated by digital telephony. More recently, motivated by the needs of the magnetic recording channel, interest in constrained channels has been primarily directed toward binary channels with runlength constraints. Zehavi and Wolf (in press) show how to develop the capacity of a runlength-constrained channel directly from the entropy of the constrained sequence.

The Kraft inequality (1949) was first used to study data compaction codes. In this chapter we have used it to study data translation codes. The trellis diagram was introduced and named by Forney (1967) as a graphical device useful for studying any tree code generated by a finite-state machine.

CHAPTER 3

Data Compaction Codes

A discrete-time information source produces messages by emitting a sequence of symbols from a fixed alphabet of symbols called the *source alphabet*. When the source alphabet is finite, the source is called a *discrete source*. The data from a discrete source can be highly redundant and hence wasteful of the resources of a communication system. A data compaction code is used to represent the output of a data source efficiently. Usually the sequence of source output symbols is represented compactly by the code as a stream of bits that can be transmitted through a communication channel. Possibly a data translation code, as discussed in Chapter 2, will then reintroduce redundancy into the data stream but in the special way that meets the needs of the channel. Practical data compaction codes are available that can reduce considerably the number of bits needed to represent the output history of a data source as compared with a naive binary representation of the source output sequence. This chapter is concerned with data compaction codes for discrete sources.

For other sources the source alphabet may be continuous, perhaps consisting of the set of real numbers, in which case the source is called a *continuous source*. Quantization techniques, which are a form of data compression code, are used to make a continuous source into a discrete source. For a continuous source, as for a discrete source, symbols are generated at discrete time instants. There are also sources, known as *waveform sources*, that produce continuous functions on the time axis. Sampling techniques are available to make a waveform source into a continuous source.

3.1 INFORMATION CONTENT OF DISCRETE SOURCES

A *discrete stationary source* is a discrete random process $\{\ldots, X_{-2}, X_{-1}, X_0, X_1, X_2, \ldots\}$, the joint probability distributions being invariant under a translation of the time origin. A special case is a *discrete memoryless source*. This is a discrete random process $\{\ldots, X_{-2}, X_{-1}, X_0, X_1, X_2, \ldots\}$ where the X_l are independent, identically distributed discrete random variables taking values in the source alphabet $\{a_0, a_1, \ldots, a_{J-1}\}$ with probability distribution $\mathbf{p} = \{p(a_0), p(a_1), \ldots, p(a_{J-1})\}$, abbreviated $\{p_0, p_1, \ldots, p_{J-1}\}$. We may assume that for all j, p_j is strictly positive; otherwise the jth symbol could be deleted from the source alphabet. Any two sources with the same probability distribution on their outputs will present the same data compaction problem because we can always rename symbols within the encoder and decoder. Thus for data compaction, the source alphabet is unimportant; only the size of this alphabet and its probability distribution matter. We can also use the symbol $\mathbf{p}$ as a handy name for the source it describes.

A long sequence of output symbols from the source is to be encoded into a string of symbols from the code alphabet $\{b_0, b_1, \ldots, b_{K-1}\}$. The code alphabet is usually binary, and this is the case we generally refer to. A data compaction code then is a way of representing a long sequence of source output symbols by a sequence of binary symbols. The encoder consists of a rule for representing each unique sequence of source output symbols by a unique sequence of binary codewords. The decoder consists of a rule for mapping from the sequence of binary codewords back to the sequence of source output symbols.

After encoding, the entire codeword may then be embedded into some longer text. Punctuation of the codeword—such as to mark its beginning or end or to delineate internal subblocks—is normally considered an implicit part of the codeword. Sometimes punctuation symbols or blanks are available at some higher level of system protocol and are not counted as part of the encoded blocklength. Then the codeword may be a little simpler. However, the more enlightened view usually is to incorporate the punctuation symbols into the code alphabet so as to devise even more compact codes.

Loosely speaking, the information content of a source is the number of bits per source symbol needed on the average by the best data compaction code for that source. We shall see that the information content of a memoryless source **p** is measured by the entropy $H(\mathbf{p})$. The entropy of a probabilistic source is equal to the average amount of information per symbol generated by that source. Another way to say this is that the entropy of a source is the average number of bits necessary to specify which symbol has been selected by the source.

When a symbol is selected by an information source, an average amount of information equal to the entropy $H(\mathbf{p})$ is produced. A binary encoding of a source whose entropy is H bits per output symbol must use on average at least H binary digits to represent the source output symbol. Further, for any positive δ, it is possible to construct a source encoder in such a way as to represent the source output symbol using, on average, fewer than $H(\mathbf{p}) + \delta$ binary digits. In general, the limit can be approached only by encoding long blocks of source symbols.

The sequence of source symbols may be too long for the encoder to deal with all at once; we may then think of the source output sequence as infinitely long. An unending stream of source output symbols enters the encoder, and an unending stream of code bits leaves the encoder. Some strategy is needed to break the sequence of source outputs into segments for encoding. The successive outputs of the encoder are strung together, which is the process of concatenation. If the encoding of successive segments in the encoder is independent of previous segments, the code is called a *block code*. If the encoder retains and uses some knowledge of earlier segments, the code is called a *tree code*. A tree code for source compaction has no definite word boundaries; it usually is more difficult to understand than is a block code. We shall have a great deal to say about both block codes and tree codes. For either kind of code, the encoder maps a source symbol into $H(\mathbf{p}) + \delta$ code bits on the average.

We shall study both fixed-length block codes and variable-length block codes. A fixed-length (n, r) block code for data compaction encodes n source output symbols into r code bits where n and r are fixed. Source output strings longer than n symbols are broken into blocks of n symbols; each block is encoded separately, and the codewords are concatenated. There are J^n possible source output blocks of length n, so it will take $\lceil \log_2 J^n \rceil$ bits to provide one binary codeword for every possible output block of length n. This is about $\log_2 J$ codeword bits per source output symbol.

We shall see that there are more efficient codes than this, codes that use about $H(\mathbf{p})$ bits per source output symbol. However, to encode at a rate close to the entropy, a fixed-length block code must introduce the possibility of an error, albeit an error of arbitrarily small probability. An efficient block code for source compaction provides only about $nH(\mathbf{p})$ bits per sourceword of blocklength n, and so there are only about $2^{nH(\mathbf{p})}$ codewords. These are assigned to the sourcewords of greatest probability. There are many sourcewords that have no codeword assigned to them, and so these blocks cannot be encoded. We shall see in Section 3.5 that by picking n large, the probability of a nonencodable sourceword can be made many orders of magnitude smaller than the probability of failure of the hardware. A fixed-length block code for source compaction must rely on this probability argument in order to encode at a rate near the entropy.

A variable-length block code also can achieve compaction rates near to the source entropy and without the need for nonencodable blocks. It breaks a long string of output symbols into blocks of n source output symbols and encodes each block into r code bits, where now either n or r, or both, are variable, depending on the specific source symbols. A variable-length code maps source output blocks of high probability into short codewords and source output blocks of low probability into long codewords. In this way, on average, compaction is obtained. Most variable-length block codes of practical interest are in that special class known as *prefix codes*, studied in Chapter 2.

It is apparent that the codewords of a good code should represent source output sequences unambiguously, at least for the vast majority of source output sequences. If all source output sequences are encoded unambiguously, the code is called a *uniquely decodable code*. Specifically, a code is uniquely decodable if, for each source output sequence of finite length, the corresponding string of concatenated codewords is different from the string of concatenated codewords for any other source output sequence of that length. Two strings of codewords that are each i symbols in length must be different if they correspond to different source output sequences.

The following theorem provides a strong condition that a uniquely decodable code must satisfy.

□ **Theorem 3.1.1**   A uniquely decodable code with K symbols in the code alphabet and with M codewords having lengths $l_0, l_1, \ldots, l_{M-1}$ must satisfy the Kraft inequality

$$\sum_{m=0}^{M-1} K^{-l_m} \leq 1$$

Proof   Let N be an arbitrary positive integer, and consider a string of N concatenated codewords, $c_1, c_2, \ldots, c_N$, having codeword lengths $l_{m_1}, l_{m_2}, \ldots, l_{m_N}$. From all such strings of codewords, we want to verify that any two strings, each i symbols in length, are distinct. To do so, we will work with the following identity:

$$\left(\sum_{m=0}^{M-1} K^{-l_m} \right)^N = \sum_{m_1=0}^{M-1} \sum_{m_2=0}^{M-1} \cdots \sum_{m_N=0}^{M-1} K^{-(l_{m_2} + l_{m_1} + \cdots + l_{m_N})}$$

There is a distinct term on the right side of this equation corresponding to each possible string of N concatenated codewords. Furthermore, the sum $l_{m_1} + l_{m_2} + \cdots + l_{m_N}$ gives the total length in code symbols of that string of concatenated codewords. Let A_i denote the number of strings of N concatenated codewords that have a total length of i code symbols.

Then we can rewrite the equation as

$$\left(\sum_{m=0}^{M-1} K^{-l_m} \right)^N = \sum_{i=1}^{LN} A_i K^{-i}$$

where L equals the largest of the l_m.

Because the code is uniquely decodable, all codeword sequences with a total length of i code symbols are distinct. Therefore $A_i \leq K^i$, and the equation becomes the inequality

$$\left(\sum_{m=0}^{M-1} K^{-l_m} \right)^N \leq LN$$

Therefore

$$\sum_{m=0}^{M-1} K^{-l_m} \leq (LN)^{1/N}$$

for each N. The proof is completed by writing

$$(LN)^{1/N} = e^{(1/N)\log LN}$$

and then noting that the limit as N goes to infinity equals 1.   □

We have already seen in Theorem 2.5.4 that, for each K and set of lengths $l_0, \ldots, l_{M-1}$ that satisfy the Kraft inequality, there is a prefix code over a code alphabet with K symbols and codeword lengths $l_0, \ldots, l_{M-1}$. Hence one can restrict the choice of a uniquely decodable code to the class of prefix codes without loss of performance.

Next we study the relationship between the average codeword length and the entropy. In the next theorem, as well as in similar statements that occur frequently, any base for the logarithm can be used, provided the same base is used in computing the entropy.

□ **Theorem 3.1.2**   For every uniquely decodable code, the average codeword length $\bar{l}$ per source symbol encoded satisfies

$$\bar{l} \log K \geq H(\mathbf{p})$$

Proof   For the proof we require that the logarithm base b is the Euler number e. (If it is not, simply multiply through the inequality by $\log_b e$.) We will show that

$$H(\mathbf{p}) - \bar{l} \log K \leq 0$$

Expand the left side as follows

$$H(\mathbf{p}) - \bar{l} \log K = -\sum_{j=0}^{J-1} p_j \log p_j - \sum_{j=0}^{J-1} l_j p_j \log K$$

$$= \sum_{j=0}^{J-1} p_j \log \frac{K^{-l_j}}{p_j}$$

Now use the inequality $\log x \leq x - 1$ to write

$$H(\mathbf{p}) - \bar{l}\log K \leq \sum_{j=0}^{J-1} p_j \left(\frac{K^{-l_j}}{p_j} - 1\right)$$

$$= \sum_{j=0}^{J-1} K^{-l_j} - \sum_{j=0}^{J-1} p_j$$

A uniquely decodable code satisfies the Kraft inequality, so the inequality becomes

$$H(\mathbf{p}) - \bar{l}\log K \leq 1 - 1 = 0$$

which completes the proof of the theorem. □

Theorem 3.1.2 applies to any uniquely decodable code—even a block code or tree code—and so it establishes the significance of the entropy function. We shall see in later sections that codes exist with rates that exceed the lower bound by not more than any arbitrarily small amount. Further, even if we allow a negligible fraction of the source output sequences to fail to be uniquely decodable, the average codeword length still is lower-bounded by the source entropy. The entropy function is clearly the right measure of the information content of a source.

Most of what we have said for memoryless sources can be extended to many sources with memory. Recall that an information source is said to be memoryless if successive symbols generated by the source are statistically independent. A source is memoryless if each symbol is selected without influence from all previous symbols. If previously selected symbols influence the selection of a symbol, then the source is said to possess memory. The simplest example of a source with memory is one in which the selection of an output symbol is influenced only by the immediately preceding symbol. This source is an example of a Markov chain.

A *discrete Markov chain* can be defined formally as a discrete random process $\{\ldots, Z_{-2}, Z_{-1}, Z_0, Z_1, Z_2, \ldots\}$, where the Z_i are dependent discrete random variables taking values in the state alphabet $\{S_0, S_1, \ldots, S_{I-1}\}$, and the dependence satisfies the *Markov condition*,

$$Pr[Z_0 = S_j | Z_{-1}, Z_{-2}, Z_{-3}, \ldots] = Pr[Z_0 = S_j | Z_{-1}]$$

where Pr denotes the probability of the event in brackets conditioned by the random variables to the right of the vertical bar. What this says is that the probability distribution on Z_0 conditional on the infinite past is equal to the probability distribution on Z_0 conditional on the single most recent source output. Given a Markov chain, one can predict an output symbol from knowledge of the previous symbol just as well as one can predict an output symbol from knowledge of all past symbols.

A Markov chain can be described by a probability transition matrix $\mathbf{P}$ with elements

$$P_{j|i} = Pr[Z_0 = S_j | Z_{-1} = S_i]$$

Products of this matrix can be computed to give the probability of subsequent source outcomes. Thus we have

$$P_{j|i}^{(2)} = Pr[Z_1 = S_j | Z_{-1} = S_i]$$

$$= \sum_{j'=0}^{J-1} Pr[Z_1 = S_j | Z_0 = S_{j'}] Pr[Z_0 = S_{j'} | Z_{-1} = S_i]$$

$$= \sum_{j'=0}^{J-1} P_{j|j'} P_{j'|i}$$

These probabilities are simply the elements of the matrix $\mathbf{P}^2$. By similar reasoning, we find that the n-step transition probabilities $Pr[Z_n = S_j | Z_0 = S_i]$ can be read from the matrix $\mathbf{P}^n$.

One may be given a probability distribution $\mathbf{p}^{(n)} = \{p^{(n)}(a_0), p^{(n)}(a_1), \ldots, p^{(n)}(a_{J-1})\}$, abbreviated $\mathbf{p}^{(n)} = \{p_0^{(n)}, p_1^{(n)}, \ldots, p_{J-1}^{(n)}\}$ on the state at the nth time. Then one can compute a probability distribution on the state at the $(n + 1)$th time. It has components

$$p_j^{(n+1)} = \sum_{i=0}^{J-1} P_{j|i} p_i^{(n)}$$

In matrix notation, this is

$$\mathbf{p}^{(n+1)} = \mathbf{P}\mathbf{p}^{(n)}$$

Consequently we also have

$$\mathbf{p}^{(n+m)} = \mathbf{P}^m \mathbf{p}^{(n)}$$

Now we are ready to describe a Markov source. In general, a *Markov source* consists of an internal Markov chain together with a function from the set of states onto the source output alphabet $\{a_0, \ldots, a_{J-1}\}$. Every time the internal Markov chain enters a new state, the source puts out the symbol from its alphabet specified by that function. In general, the number of states can be larger than the number of source output symbols, which means that one output symbol may correspond to more than one state. In many Markov sources, the number of internal states is the same as the number of output symbols. There may be no reason to distinguish the internal states from the source output symbols if the internal state can be taken to be the previous output symbol.

The simplest Markov source is the two-state source with binary output alphabet and transition matrix

$$\mathbf{P} = \begin{bmatrix} p & 1-p \\ 1-p & p \end{bmatrix}$$

This Markov source is known as the *binary symmetric Markov source*.

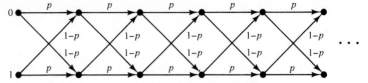

Figure 3.1   Trellis for a binary symmetric Markov source.

A Markov source can be visualized as following a path through a trellis. Figure 3.1 shows a trellis for the binary symmetric Markov source. The source can be in either of two states, which represent the source output bit. These states are depicted in a column of nodes that is periodically replicated in the diagram. As time progresses, the source moves through the trellis according to the transition probabilities, generating source output symbols as it goes.

Figure 3.2 shows a trellis for another Markov source on the binary alphabet that is known as a second-order Markov source. States correspond to the most recent pair of output bits, so there are four states. In this example, the transition probabilities are such that the same symbol never occurs three times in a row, but frequently occurs twice in a row.

Notice that in Fig. 3.2 no matter which state the source finds itself in, it can eventually reach any other state. This is an example of a kind of source known as an *ergodic Markov source*. A Markov source is not an ergodic source if there are some states that can never be reached when starting in certain other states.

An ergodic Markov source has the property that $\mathbf{p}^{(n)}$ for $n = 1, \ldots,$ the sequence of probability distributions on the set of states, will approach a limiting probability distribution $\mathbf{p}$ that is independent of the initial probability distribution. The equilibrium distribution $\mathbf{p}$ is a solution of the matrix-vector equation

$$p_j = \sum_{i=0}^{J-1} P_{j|i} p_i$$

That is, $\mathbf{p}$ is that eigenvector of $\mathbf{P}$ that is also a probability distribution. Such an eigenvector always exists because $\mathbf{P}$ is a probability transition matrix. For

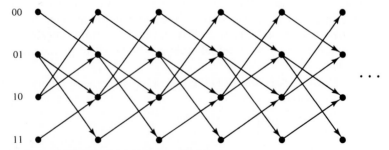

Figure 3.2   Trellis for a second-order Markov source.

an ergodic source, the equilibrium distribution is unique, and the sequence of probability distributions $\mathbf{p}^{(n)}$ will converge to the equilibrium distribution $\mathbf{p}$. If the Markov source is initialized at the first output symbol with probability distribution $\mathbf{p}$, then it has probability distribution $\mathbf{p}$ on every source output symbol, and so it is a stationary Markov source.

3.2. THE ENTROPY FUNCTION

The output of a discrete information source is a random sequence of symbols from a finite alphabet containing J symbols given by $\{a_0, a_1, \ldots, a_{J-1}\}$. The sequence is produced according to some probability rule. A source whose output is not random is completely predictable from the (infinite) past history. There is no information in the source output, and we do not study such sources further.

If a source output a_j occurs with probability $p(a_j)$, then the amount of information associated with the known occurrence of output a_j is defined to be

$$I(a_j) = -\log p(a_j)$$

The logarithm may be to the base 2 or to the base e. When the logarithm is to the base 2, the information is measured in units of *bits*. When the logarithm is taken to the base e, the information is measured in units of *nats* (a shortened form of "natural units"). Usually, the nat is more convenient for theoretical developments, but the bit is more convenient for the numerical results. The conversion factor is one nat equals 1.443 bits, because $\log_2 e = 1.443\ldots$.

If for a discrete memoryless source, the probability of selecting the source symbol a_j is $p(a_j)$, then the information generated each time a symbol a_j is selected is $-\log_2 p(a_j)$ bits. The law of large numbers tells us that the symbol a_j will, on average, be selected $np(a_j)$ times in a total of n selections, so the average amount of information obtained from n source outputs is

$$np(a_0) \log_2 p(a_0)^{-1} + \cdots + np(a_{J-1}) \log_2 p(a_{J-1})^{-1}$$

bits. Divide by n to obtain the average amount of information per source output symbol. This is known as the *average information*, the *uncertainty*, or the *entropy* $H(\mathbf{p})$:[†]

$$H(\mathbf{p}) = -\sum_{j=0}^{J-1} p(a_j) \log_2 p(a_j) \qquad \text{bits/symbol}$$

or

$$H(\mathbf{p}) = -\sum_{j=0}^{J-1} p_j \log_2 p_j$$

using p_j as an abbreviation of $p(a_j)$.

[†]The term "entropy" is used because the function is the same as that used in statistical mechanics for the thermodynamic quantity entropy.

The source output is a random variable, and we denote it by X; X takes the value a_j with probability p_j. Whenever we are thinking of the random variable X, we will write $H(X)$ for the entropy instead of $H(\mathbf{p})$. This is a convenient abuse of notation, but it incorrectly suggests that the entropy is a function of X. To be precise, the entropy is a function of a probability distribution and not of a random variable.

The entropy function can be justified by its role in source-compaction coding theorems, as in Theorem 3.1.2; by its role in combinatorics, as in Problem 1.5; by its role in laws of large numbers, as in Theorem 3.4.2; and by its intuitive properties as a measure of uncertainty. Some basic properties are as follows:

1. The entropy function is continuous in $\mathbf{p}$. This is a reasonable property because it says that small changes in the probability distribution only make small changes in the uncertainty.
2. $H(\mathbf{p}) \geq 0$ and $H(\mathbf{p}) = 0$ if and only if all of the p_j except one are equal to zero. This is a reasonable property of a measure of uncertainty because if the outcome of a selection is sure, there is no uncertainty.
3. For a given J, $H(\mathbf{p}) \leq \log J$ and is equal to $\log J$ if and only if the p_j are equal to $1/J$. This is a reasonable property, which says that the more symbols available for selection without preference, the larger the uncertainty; and the uncertainty is largest if all J symbols are equally likely.
4. Entropy is a concave[†] function of $\mathbf{p}$.
5. The entropy of a pair of independent random events is equal to the sum of the entropies of the individual events. The entropy associated with n independent selections from the same source alphabet is equal to n times the entropy per single selection.

Properties 1 and 2 are trivial. Property 3 is proved by using the inequality $\log x \leq x - 1$ to write

$$H(\mathbf{p}) - \log J = \sum_j p_j \log \frac{1}{Jp_j}$$

$$\leq \sum_j p_j \left(\frac{1}{Jp_j} - 1 \right) = 0$$

[†]A function $f(x)$ is called *convex* if for all x', x'' and all λ between 0 and 1,

$$f(\lambda x' + (1 - \lambda)x'') \leq \lambda f(x') + (1 - \lambda)f(x'')$$

That is, a straight line joining any two points of the graph of $f(x)$ never lies below the graph of $f(x)$. A function $f(x)$ is called *concave* if $-f(x)$ is convex. Convex and concave functions are studied in Appendix A.

Property 4 is proved by using the inequality $\log x \geq 1 - (1/x)$. Let $\bar{\lambda} = 1 - \lambda$ where $0 \leq \lambda \leq 1$. Then

$$H(\lambda \mathbf{p}' + \bar{\lambda} \mathbf{p}'') - \lambda H(\mathbf{p}') - \bar{\lambda} H(\mathbf{p}'')$$

$$= \lambda \sum_j p_j' \log \frac{p_j'}{\lambda p_j' + \bar{\lambda} p_j''} + \bar{\lambda} \sum_j p_j'' \log \frac{p_j''}{\lambda p_j' + \bar{\lambda} p_j''}$$

$$\geq \lambda \sum_j p_j' \left(1 - \frac{\lambda p_j' + \bar{\lambda} p_j''}{p_j'} \right) + \bar{\lambda} \sum_j p_j'' \left(1 - \frac{\lambda p_j' + \bar{\lambda} p_j''}{p_j''} \right)$$

$$= \lambda (1 - 1) + \bar{\lambda} (1 - 1) = 0$$

Property 5 will be proved as Theorem 3.2.2.

A binary source is one that contains only two symbols, a_0 and a_1; their probabilities are given by p and $1 - p$, respectively. The entropy of a binary source is described by the binary entropy function

$$H_b(p) = -p \log_2 p - (1 - p) \log_2 (1 - p)$$

which is a function of the single parameter p. The binary entropy function is shown in Fig. 3.3.

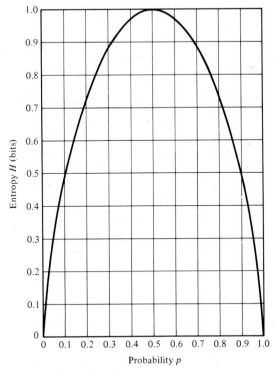

Figure 3.3   The binary entropy function.

The output of a binary source is a binary digit. The distinction between the bit used as a measure of information and the bit used as a binary output symbol should be carefully noted. Figure 3.3 shows that, on average, the amount of information provided by a binary source is always equal to or less than 1 bit per bit (one bit of information per data bit). The binary source provides 1 bit of information for each selected symbol only when the two symbols are equiprobable.

A random variable may be conditional on some side information. We then write its probability distribution as $\mathbf{Q} = \{Q_{k|j}\}$ or as $\mathbf{P} = \{P_{j|k}\}$. For each fixed value of j or of k, we have a probability distribution and hence an entropy. These are written

$$H(Y|j) = -\sum_k Q_{k|j} \log Q_{k|j}$$

$$H(X|k) = -\sum_j P_{j|k} \log P_{j|k}$$

These are read as the uncertainty (or the entropy) in Y conditional on j, or the uncertainty in X conditional on k. We define the conditional entropies by averaging over j and k:

$$H(Y|X) = -\sum_j p_j \sum_k Q_{k|j} \log Q_{k|j}$$

$$H(X|Y) = -\sum_k q_k \sum_j P_{j|k} \log P_{j|k}$$

The conditional entropies can be thought of in terms of a channel whose input is the random variable X and whose output is the random variable Y. $H(X|Y)$ is then called the *equivocation* and corresponds to the uncertainty in the channel input from the receiver's point of view. Similarly, $H(Y|X)$ is called the *prevarication* and corresponds to the uncertainty in the channel output from the transmitter's point of view. In general, the transmitter's uncertainty as to what the receiver heard is not numerically the same as the receiver's uncertainty as to what the transmitter sent; the information lost by the channel depends on which end is observed.

☐   **Theorem 3.2.1**   Side information never increases average uncertainty. That is,

$$H(X|Y) \leq H(X)$$

Proof   The proof uses the inequality $\log x \geq 1 - (1/x)$:

$$H(X) - H(X|Y) = \sum_j \sum_k q_k P_{j|k} \log \frac{P_{j|k}}{\sum_k q_k P_{j|k}}$$

$$\geq \sum_j \sum_k q_k P_{j|k} \left(1 - \frac{\sum_k q_k P_{j|k}}{P_{j|k}} \right)$$

$$= \sum_j \sum_k q_k P_{j|k} - \left(\sum_k q_k \right) \left(\sum_j \sum_k q_k P_{j|k} \right)$$

$$= 1 - 1 = 0 \qquad\qquad\qquad \square$$

The entropy for a block of random variables, denoted $H(X_1, \ldots, X_n)$, is defined by

$$H(X_1, \ldots, X_n) = -\sum_{j_1} \sum_{j_2} \cdots \sum_{j_n} p^n(a_{j_1}, a_{j_2}, \ldots, a_{j_n}) \log p^n(a_{j_1}, a_{j_2}, \ldots, a_{j_n})$$

If the random variables are independent, then

$$p^n(a_{j_1}, a_{j_2}, \ldots, a_{j_n}) = \prod_{l=1}^{n} p_l(a_{j_l})$$

where $p_l(a_j)$ is the probability of outcome a_j in the lth random variable.

□ **Theorem 3.2.2**   Entropy is additive for independent random events.

Proof   Because the logarithm of a product is a sum of logarithms, we have

$$H(X_1, \ldots, X_n) = -\sum_{j_1} \sum_{j_2} \cdots \sum_{j_n} p^n(a_{j_1}, a_{j_2}, \ldots, a_{j_n}) \left[\sum_{l=1}^{n} \log p_l(a_{j_l}) \right]$$

$$= \sum_{l=1}^{n} \left[-\sum_{j_l} p_l(a_{j_l}) \log p_l(a_{j_l}) \right]$$

$$= \sum_{l=1}^{n} H(X_l)$$

as was to be proved.   □

When the block consists of measurements that are not independent, the equality of the theorem is replaced by an inequality.

□ **Theorem 3.2.3**   For any sourceword of blocklength n,

$$H(X_1, \ldots, X_n) \leq \sum_{l=1}^{n} H(X_l)$$

with equality if and only if the source is memoryless.

Proof Let $p^n(a_{j_1}, a_{j_2}, \ldots, a_{j_n})$ be the probability distribution on the block $(X_1, X_2, \ldots, X_n)$, and let $p_l(a_{j_l})$ be the marginal on the single random variable X_l. Then

$$\sum_{l=1}^{n} H(X_l) = \sum_{l=1}^{n} \left[-\sum_{j_l} p_l(a_{j_l}) \log p_l(a_{j_l}) \right]$$

$$= -\sum_{j_1} \sum_{j_2} \cdots \sum_{j_n} p^n(a_{j_1}, a_{j_2}, \ldots, a_{j_n}) \log \prod_{l=1}^{n} p_l(a_{j_l})$$

Therefore

$$\sum_{l=1}^{n} H(X_l) - H(X_1, \ldots, X_n)$$

$$= \sum_{j_1} \sum_{j_2} \cdots \sum_{j_n} p^n(a_{j_1}, \ldots, a_{j_n}) \log \frac{p^n(a_{j_1}, \ldots, a_{j_n})}{\prod\limits_{l=1}^{n} p_l(a_{j_l})}$$

$$\geq 0$$

where the inequality follows by using the inequality $\log x \geq 1 - (1/x)$. The inequality is satisfied with equality only if the argument of the logarithm on the previous line equals 1. $\square$

$\square$ **Theorem 3.2.4** Let **Q** be the probability transition matrix for a discrete memoryless channel. Then the equivocation and prevarication satisfy

$$H(X_1, \ldots, X_n | Y_1, \ldots, Y_n) \leq \sum_{l=1}^{n} H(X_l | Y_l)$$

and

$$H(Y_1, \ldots, Y_n | X_1, \ldots, X_n) = \sum_{l=1}^{n} H(Y_l | X_l)$$

Proof The first statement follows by taking the expected value of:

$$H(X_1, \ldots, X_n | b_{k_1}, \ldots, b_{k_n}) \leq \sum_{l=1}^{n} H(X_l | b_{k_1}, \ldots, b_{k_n})$$

$$= \sum_{l=1}^{n} H(X_l | b_{k_l})$$

where the inequality is a consequence of Theorem 3.2.3.

The second statement follows by taking the expected value of

$$H(Y_1, \ldots, Y_n | a_{j_1}, \ldots, a_{j_n}) = \sum_{l=1}^{n} H(Y_l | a_{j_l})$$

which is a consequence of Theorem 3.2.2 because the channel is memoryless. $\square$

□ **Theorem 3.2.5**   Let X and Y be random variables. Then

$$H(X,Y) = H(X) + H(Y|X)$$
$$= H(Y) + H(X|Y)$$

Proof

$$H(X,Y) = -\sum_{jk} P_{jk} \log P_{jk}$$

$$= -\sum_{jk} P_{jk} \log p_j Q_{k|j}$$

$$= -\sum_j p_j \log p_j - \sum_{jk} P_{jk} \log Q_{k|j}$$

$$= H(X) + H(Y|X)$$

The second relation is proved the same way.   □

This theorem can be given a simple verbal interpretation. It says that uncertainty in the pair (X,Y) is equal to the uncertainty in X plus the uncertainty in Y when X is known.

□ **Corollary 3.2.6**   Let $(X_1,\ldots,X_n)$ be a vector random variable. Then

$$H(X_1,\ldots,X_n) = H(X_1) + H(X_2|X_1) + \cdots + H(X_n|X_1,\ldots,X_{n-1})$$

Proof The proof is by induction. The corollary is true for $n = 2$. Suppose it is true for $n - 1$. A pair of discrete random variables can be considered as a single random variable. Hence let $X'_{n-1} = (X_{n-1}, X_n)$. Then

$$H(X_1,\ldots,X_{n-1},X_n) = H(X_1,\ldots,X'_{n-1})$$
$$= H(X_1) + \cdots + H(X'_{n-1}|X_1,\ldots,X_{n-2})$$
$$= H(X_1) + \cdots + H(X_{n-1},X_n|X_1,\ldots,X_{n-2})$$

Applying Theorem 3.2.5 to the last term completes the induction argument and proves the corollary.   □

Theorem 3.2.1 says that conditioning can never increase the entropy. This leads to a number of interesting facts that are summarized in the following theorem.

□ **Theorem 3.2.7**   The entropy of a stationary source has the following properties:

(i) $H(X_n|X_1,\ldots,X_{n-1}) \le H(X_{n-1}|X_1,\ldots,X_{n-2})$

(ii) $\dfrac{1}{n} H(X_1, \ldots, X_n) \geq H(X_n | X_1, \ldots, X_{n-1})$

(iii) $\dfrac{1}{n} H(X_1, \ldots, X_n) \leq \dfrac{1}{n-1} H(X_1, \ldots, X_{n-1})$

(iv) $\lim\limits_{n \to \infty} \dfrac{1}{n} H(X_1, \ldots, X_n) = \lim\limits_{n \to \infty} H(X_n | X_1, \ldots, X_{n-1})$

Proof (i) Conditioning can never increase information. Consequently,

$$H(X_n | X_1, \ldots, X_{n-1}) \leq H(X_n | X_2, \ldots, X_{n-1})$$
$$= H(X_{n-1} | X_1, \ldots, X_{n-2})$$

where the equality holds because the source is stationary.

(ii) $H(X_1, \ldots, X_n) = \sum\limits_{l=1}^{n} H(X_l | X_1, \ldots, X_{l-1})$

$$\geq n H(X_n | X_1, \ldots, X_{n-1})$$

where part (i) has been used to bound each term in the sum.

(iii) $\dfrac{1}{n} H(X_1, \ldots, X_n) = \dfrac{1}{n} H(X_1, \ldots, X_{n-1}) + \dfrac{1}{n} H(X_n | X_1, \ldots, X_{n-1})$

$$\leq \dfrac{1}{n} H(X_1, \ldots, X_{n-1}) + \dfrac{1}{n^2} H(X_1, \ldots, X_n)$$

where the inequality uses part (ii). Now rearrange terms to obtain

$$\dfrac{n-1}{n} \dfrac{1}{n} H(X_1, \ldots, X_n) \leq \dfrac{n-1}{n} \dfrac{1}{n-1} H(X_1, \ldots, X_{n-1})$$

(iv) $H(X_n | X_1, \ldots, X_{n-1})$ is positive and nonincreasing in n by part (i); hence it has a limit. Similarly, $(1/n)H(X_1, \ldots, X_n)$ is positive and nonincreasing in n by part (iii). Therefore, both converge to a limit. Taking limits of both sides of part (ii) gives

$$\lim\limits_{n \to \infty} \dfrac{1}{n} H(X_1, \ldots, X_n) \geq \lim\limits_{n \to \infty} H(X_n | X_1, \ldots, X_{n-1})$$

To prove inequality in the opposite direction, consider the first $n + N$ terms. Then

$$\dfrac{1}{n+N} H(X_1, \ldots, X_{n+N}) = \dfrac{1}{n+N} H(X_1, \ldots, X_{n-1})$$

$$+ \dfrac{1}{n+N} \sum\limits_{l=n}^{n+N} H(X_l | X_1, \ldots, X_{l-1})$$

$$\leq \frac{1}{n+N} H(X_1, \ldots, X_{n-1})$$

$$+ \frac{N+1}{n+N} H(X_n | X_1, \ldots, X_{n-1})$$

where the inequality follows by upper-bounding each term in the sum by the largest term in the sum. Now let N go to infinity. We then have

$$\lim_{N \to \infty} \frac{1}{n+N} H(X_1, \ldots, X_{n+N}) \leq H(X_n | X_1, \ldots, X_{n-1})$$

The left side is independent of n and the inequality holds for all n. Hence we can take the limit of the right side as $n \to \infty$, obtaining

$$\lim_{n \to \infty} \frac{1}{n} H(X_1, \ldots, X_n) \leq \lim_{n \to \infty} H(X_n | X_1, \ldots, X_{n-1})$$

This combined with the opposite inequality above proves part (iv) of the theorem. □

The conditional entropy is used to study the output uncertainty of a Markov source. For a source with memory, the average information content per source output symbol is called the *entropy rate*. The entropy rate is given by

$$B = \lim_{n \to \infty} \frac{1}{n} H(X_1, \ldots, X_n)$$

provided the limit exists. For a stationary source, the limit exists and, by Theorem 3.2.7, can be written

$$B = \lim_{n \to \infty} H(X_n | X_1, \ldots, X_{n-1})$$

If the source is a Markov source, this simplifies to

$$B = H(X_n | X_{n-1})$$

□ **Theorem 3.2.8**   An ergodic Markov source has information content

$$B = H(X|Y)$$

$$= -\sum_i p_i \sum_j P_{j|i} \log P_{j|i}$$

where **p** is the equilibrium distribution.

Proof Applying part (iv) of Theorem 3.2.7 to the definition of the information content of a Markov source gives

$$B = \lim_{n \to \infty} \frac{1}{n} H(X_1, \ldots, X_n)$$

$$= \lim_{n \to \infty} H(X_n | X_1, \ldots, X_{n-1})$$

Because the source is a Markov source, the conditional entropy must satisfy

$$H(X_n | X_1, \ldots, X_{n-1}) = H(X_n | X_{n-1})$$

and

$$H(X_n | X_{n-1}) = -\sum_i p_i^{(n-1)} \sum_j P_{j|i} \log P_{j|i}$$

where $\mathbf{p}^{(n-1)}$ is the marginal distribution on the $(n-1)$th source output symbol. But the right side is continuous in $p_i^{(n-1)}$ and $\mathbf{p}^{(n-1)}$ converges to the equilibrium distribution $\mathbf{p}$. Therefore

$$\lim_{n \to \infty} H(X_1, \ldots, X_{n-1}) = -\sum_i p_i \sum_j P_{j|i} \log P_{j|i}$$

which is the claim of the theorem. □

3.3 PREFIX CODES FOR DATA COMPACTION

A discrete source puts out a sequence of symbols from an alphabet of J possible output symbols. In this section, we shall construct a class of prefix codes known as *Huffman codes*.

Suppose that a source has eight possible output symbols, with probability distribution given by

$$p_0 = p_1 = p_2 = p_3 = 1/32$$
$$p_4 = p_5 \qquad\qquad = 1/16$$
$$p_6 \qquad\qquad\quad = 1/4$$
$$p_7 \qquad\qquad\quad = 1/2$$

The entropy is $H = 2\ 1/8$ bits per octal symbol, while the common method of representing an octal symbol in binary notation requires three binary symbols. A variable-length code whose average blocklength is equal to the entropy is as follows:

Octal Symbol	Probability	Codeword	Codeword Length
0	2^{-5}	00000	5
1	2^{-5}	00001	5
2	2^{-5}	00010	5
3	2^{-5}	00011	5
4	2^{-4}	0010	4
5	2^{-4}	0011	4
6	2^{-2}	01	2
7	2^{-1}	1	1

The rate of the prefix code is the average blocklength of the codewords. For this example,

$$\bar{l} = \sum_j p_j l_j = 2\ 1/8 \qquad \text{bits/source symbol}$$

which is equal to the entropy.

The property of the code that makes it useful is that the code is a prefix code. There is no need to append extra symbols for punctuation. The codewords can be run together without possibility of ambiguity. Thus

$$00011000000000 1000101\ldots$$

can be decoded only as 30127.

The above example is a little misleading because the code rate turns out to be exactly equal to the entropy. Usually we must be satisfied with a code rate that is only approximately equal to the entropy, and a little larger. We shall see that, within this approximate sense, codes of this kind can be found for any source.

The following theorem interprets entropy in terms of the average blocklength of a prefix code over a K-ary alphabet. We shall show that $\bar{l} \log K$ is approximately equal to $H(\mathbf{p})$ by giving two inequalities, one in each direction. The lower bound is for an arbitrary code. However, in proving the upper bound, the optimum code must be considered.

□ **Theorem 3.3.1**   The average blocklength

$$\bar{l} = \sum_{j=0}^{J-1} p_j l_j$$

of a prefix code for compaction of source $\mathbf{p}$ always satisfies

$$\bar{l} \geq \frac{H(\mathbf{p})}{\log K}$$

Moreover, there exists a prefix code for which

$$\bar{l} \leq \frac{H(\mathbf{p})}{\log K} + 1$$

Proof A prefix code is uniquely decodable, so Theorem 3.1.2 gives the first part of the theorem.

To prove the second part, choose

$$l_j = \left\lceil \frac{-\log p_j}{\log K} \right\rceil$$

Then

$$p_j \geq K^{-l_j}$$

Summing both sides over j gives

$$1 \geq \sum_j K^{-l_j}$$

The Kraft inequality is satisfied so there does exist a prefix code with this set of blocklengths. The definition of l_j implies that

$$l_j \leq -\frac{\log p_j}{\log K} + 1$$

Therefore

$$\bar{l} = \sum_j p_j l_j \leq \sum_j p_j \left(\frac{-\log p_j}{\log K} \right) + 1 = \frac{H(\mathbf{p})}{\log K} + 1$$

which completes the proof of the theorem.   □

This theorem has a corollary that says that a prefix code can be found with average blocklength arbitrarily close to the entropy.

□ **Corollary 3.3.2**   Let $\varepsilon > 0$ and a memoryless source with distribution $\mathbf{p}$ be given. A prefix code can always be found to encode this source such that

$$\bar{l} \leq \frac{H(\mathbf{p})}{\log K} + \varepsilon$$

Proof Pick n with $(1/n) < \varepsilon$. Consider source output blocks of blocklength n. The block outputs have entropy $nH(\mathbf{p})$. By Theorem 3.3.1, a prefix code can be found such that the average blocklength

$$\bar{l}_n = \sum_{\mathbf{x}} p(\mathbf{x}) l(\mathbf{x})$$

satisfies

$$\bar{l}_n \leq \frac{nH(\mathbf{p})}{\log K} + 1$$

But the average blocklength per source symbol is then

$$\bar{l} = \frac{1}{n}\bar{l}_n$$

from which the corollary follows. □

One class of prefix codes, known as *Shannon codes*, is constructed by labeling the source symbols $a_0, a_1, \ldots, a_{J-1}$ in order of decreasing probability $p_0 \geq p_1 \geq \cdots \geq p_{J-1} > 0$. Let $Q_0 = 0$ and

$$Q_j = \sum_{i=0}^{j-1} p_i \qquad j = 1, \ldots, J-1$$

and

$$l_j = \lceil -\log p_j \rceil$$

The code is defined as the first l_j digits of the binary expansion of Q_j. We will not verify that a Shannon code is a prefix code; it is not difficult. Instead we will construct in detail another class of variable-length prefix codes, known as *Huffman codes*, whose average blocklength is as small as possible. Such codes have certain characterizing features which will be developed. We consider only binary code alphabets, though the source alphabet is arbitrary. Generalization to larger code alphabets is not difficult.

□ **Theorem 3.3.3** For a given J-ary source, a binary prefix code over a K-ary alphabet whose average blocklength is minimum has the following properties:

(i) If $p_j > p_{j'}$, then $l_j \leq l_{j'}$.
(ii) The two least-probable source outputs have codewords of the same blocklength.
(iii) If there are two or more codewords of the same blocklength, then two of these codewords agree in all digits except the last.

Proof
(i) If $p_j > p_{j'}$ and $l_j > l_{j'}$, then by interchanging the j and j' codewords, a better code can be obtained.
(ii) By the prefix condition, no codeword is a prefix of either of the two least-probable codewords. Suppose those two codewords have different lengths. Then the last symbol of the longer codeword can be deleted. The deletion cannot form a codeword that already exists, so the deletion forms a new prefix code with shorter average blocklength than the original code.

(iii) Suppose that all codewords of a given blocklength are different when the last symbol is discarded. No shorter codeword is the prefix of any of these, so by discarding the last symbol of all codewords of this blocklength, a new prefix code is obtained with smaller average blocklength.   □

We are now ready to find the optimum binary prefix code for a given source. Theorem 3.3.3 forms the basis for our approach. We can assume, without loss of generality, that the two codewords of part (iii) of Theorem 3.3.3 are the least-probable codewords of that particular blocklength because codewords of the same blocklength can be interchanged without changing the average blocklength of the code. Therefore, if we can construct the codewords for all but the two least-probable symbols, and can construct all but the last letter in one of the two remaining codewords, then we know immediately how to complete the code.

This suggests the following procedure. Combine the two least-probable source output symbols into a new artificial symbol whose probability is equal to the sum of the probabilities of the original two symbols. This is a new source with $J - 1$ output symbols. Find an optimum code for the new source. To obtain codewords for the two least-probable outputs of the original source, take the codeword corresponding to the artificial symbol and append a 0 and a 1 respectively. The following theorem justifies this procedure.

□   **Theorem 3.3.4**   Suppose that the two least-probable source symbols are combined into a single artificial symbol and $\mathscr{C}'$ is an optimum code for this artificial source. Obtain the code $\mathscr{C}$ from $\mathscr{C}'$ by appending a 0 and a 1 to the codeword of $\mathscr{C}'$ corresponding to the artificial symbol, thereby obtaining codewords for the two least-probable source symbols of the original source. All other symbols have the same codeword in $\mathscr{C}$ as in $\mathscr{C}'$. Then $\mathscr{C}$ is optimum for the original source.

Proof   Let p_{j_1} and p_{j_2} be the two smallest probabilities. By Theorem 3.3.3, we know that the search for the optimum code can be confined to codes such that the codewords with indices j_1 and j_2 are among the longest and differ only in the last place.

We delete index j_2 in indexing the new code $\mathscr{C}'$. The codeword lengths L_j for $j \neq j_2$ of the code for $\mathscr{C}'$ are related to the codeword lengths l_j of the code for $\mathscr{C}$ by

$$l_j = \begin{cases} L_{j_1} + 1 & j = j_1 \text{ or } j_2 \\ L_j & \text{otherwise} \end{cases}$$

Then the average blocklengths $\bar{L}$ and $\bar{l}$ are related by

$$\bar{l} = \sum_j p_j l_j$$

$$= \sum_{j \neq j_1, j_2} p_j l_j + p_{j_1} l_{j_1} + p_{j_2} l_{j_2}$$

$$= \sum_{j \neq j_1, j_2} p_j l_j + p_{j_1}(L_{j_1} + 1) + p_{j_2}(L_{j_2} + 1)$$

$$= \sum_{j \neq j_1, j_2} p_j L_j + (p_{j_1} + p_{j_2})L_{j_1} + p_{j_1} + p_{j_2}$$

$$= \bar{L} + p_{j_1} + p_{j_2}$$

But $p_{j_1} + p_{j_2}$ is a constant independent of the new code $\mathscr{C}'$. Hence, to minimize $\bar{l}$, we should minimize $\bar{L}$ by picking $\mathscr{C}'$ itself to be optimum. This completes the proof of the theorem.   □

To find the optimum code $\mathscr{C}'$ for the artificial problem, we repeat the procedure of the theorem. Combine the two symbols that now have smallest probability and search for an optimum code $\mathscr{C}''$ for this source. We continue in this way until only two symbols are left. These have the codewords 0 and 1.

Figure 3.4 gives an illustration of how the construction proceeds for the source with seven output symbols—A, B, C, D, E, F, and G—having probabilities of 3/8, 3/16, 3/16, 1/8, 1/16, 1/32, and 1/32, respectively. The original source is at the left. At each step, as the tree is constructed to the right, the two symbols of smallest probability are combined, and the final tree is labeled with 0 and 1 arbitrarily at each branch. The code is given as follows:

Source Symbol	Probability	Codeword	Blocklength
A	3/8	1	1
B	3/16	011	3
C	3/16	010	3
D	1/8	001	3
E	1/16	0001	4
F	1/32	00001	5
G	1/32	00000	5

The average blocklength is 2.44 bits per source symbol. This should be compared with the entropy, which is 2.37 bits per source symbol, which tells us that our Huffman code is very close to the best we can do for this problem. If we wish to obtain the small improvement that is still possible, we must encode larger blocks of source outputs.

Figure 3.5 gives another example where the encoding of blocks is more fruitful. The source has three symbols—A, B, and C—with probabilities 3/4,

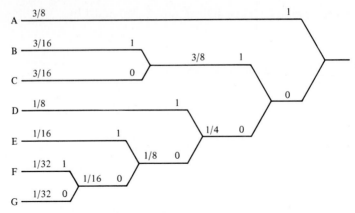

Figure 3.4   Example of a Huffman code.

3/16, and 1/16. The Huffman code for single letters has codewords 1, 01, and 00 and an average blocklength of 1.25 bits per source output symbol. Comparing this with the source entropy of 1.012 shows that a meaningful improvement of about 20% is possible. One can reduce the data rate on a communication link transmitting this source output by as much as 20% by using a Huffman code on blocks of source outputs. Figure 3.5 shows the

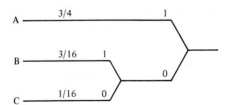

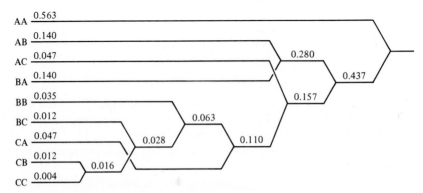

Figure 3.5   Another example of a Huffman code.

construction of the Huffman code for blocks of length 2. The code is given as follows:

Sourceword	Probability	Codeword	Blocklength
AA	0.5625	1	1
AB	0.1406	011	3
AC	0.0469	001	3
BA	0.1406	010	3
BB	0.0352	00011	5
BC	0.0117	000101	6
CA	0.0469	0000	4
CB	0.0117	0001001	7
CC	0.0039	0001000	7

The average length of the codewords is 2.09 bits, which encodes two source symbols. Hence the rate of the code is 1.045 bits per source symbol. This should be compared with 1.25 bits per source symbol, which is the rate of the simpler Huffman code, and with 1.012 bits per source symbol, which is the entropy of the source.

3.4 BLOCK CODES FOR DATA COMPACTION

Block codes differ from prefix codes in that every codeword has the same blocklength. A sourceword is to be encoded into a block of symbols from the given code alphabet, using the minimum number of code symbols per source symbol. For example, the source may put out decimal digits and these are to be encoded into binary codewords. A good code minimizes the number of binary letters required. We shall see that for block codes, as for prefix codes, the required number of binary letters per source output is essentially equal to the entropy of the source.

In the practice of data compaction, block codes are in the shadow of prefix codes and tree codes because of unavoidable defaults that can occur in the encoding, and because the encoders and decoders tend to have very little structure and so are difficult to implement. Yet there are several good reasons for studying them. The source-coding theorems are important in their own right and can help to illuminate the nature of data compaction. In addition, the study of source coding provides a vehicle for developing the close relationship between entropy and laws of large numbers.

The simplest memoryless source is the binary symmetric source. This source has two symbols in its output alphabet $\{0, 1\}$, and these symbols occur with equal probability. The binary symmetric source has entropy of 1 bit per output symbol. It is trivial to encode sourcewords of blocklength n into binary codewords of blocklength n. Simply let the n-bit codeword equal the n-bit sourceword. Such a block code requires 1 bit per output symbol, which is equal to the source entropy rate. The binary symmetric source cannot be compacted.

A block code differs from a prefix code for data compaction in that it allows some source data to be lost. The only way to avoid this with a block code is to pick r so that

$$K^r \geq J^n$$

because the source has J^n possible output blocks of length n, which are to be represented by the K^r possible K-ary sequences of length r. Such a code, however, really does no data compaction. The code rate cannot be made to approach the entropy because the code makes provision for output blocks that almost never occur. We shall see below how to ignore these improbable output blocks.

□   **Definition 3.4.1**   A block code for data compaction of blocklength n and size M is a set $\mathscr{C} = \{\mathbf{c}_m\}$ consisting of M codewords of length n; each codeword is a sequence of n source output symbols.   □

Usually $M = 2^r$ (or K^r), so the codewords can be indexed by r binary (or K-ary) symbols.[†] The ratio r/n is called the *rate R* of the code, measured in bits per source symbol (or in code symbols per source symbol).

The first $M - 1$ codewords of $\mathscr{C}$ are called *normal codewords*. The Mth codeword is called the *default codeword*. To use the block code, the source output sequence is broken into sourcewords, each a block of length n. Each sourceword is either in $\mathscr{C}$ or it is not. If it is in $\mathscr{C}$, it is left unchanged. If it is not in $\mathscr{C}$, it is replaced by the default codeword, which informs the decoder that the encoding has failed. The stream of encoded sourcewords is compactly represented by replacing each codeword with its binary index. Each block then is represented by an r-bit binary number.

Table 3.1 gives an example of a very small code for data compaction, one for a binary source with $p_0 = 0.1$ and $p_1 = 0.9$. The code has blocklength equal to 4 and rate equal to 0.75, which should be compared with the source entropy $H(\mathbf{p}) = 0.469$. The probability of encoding failure is 0.036 for this code. By increasing n and r at the same ratio, the probability of encoding failure can be made as small as is desired. With $n = 8$ and $r = 6$, the probability of encoding failure is 0.023. Similarly, if the ratio r/n is fixed at any rate R greater than 0.469, one can construct a sequence of codes whose probability of encoding failure approaches zero for arbitrarily large blocklength n.

The decoder inverts the encoding process, replacing each r-bit binary number with the appropriate codeword unless it is the default codeword. If it is the default codeword, that sourceword has been lost.

---

†The r-bit codeword index m of codeword $\mathbf{c}_m$ may also be called the codeword. The context should make it clear whether the word "codeword" refers to $\mathbf{c}_m$ or to its index m.

Table 3.1   A Trivial $(4, 3)$ Block Code for Data Compaction

Sourceword	Probability	Reproducing Codeword	Codeword Index
0000	10^{-4}	0000	000
0001	9×10^{-4}	0000	000
0010	9×10^{-4}	0000	000
0011	81×10^{-4}	0000	000
0100	9×10^{-4}	0000	000
0101	81×10^{-4}	0000	000
0110	81×10^{-4}	0000	000
0111	729×10^{-4}	0111	001
1000	9×10^{-4}	0000	000
1001	81×10^{-4}	0000	000
1010	81×10^{-4}	1010	010
1011	729×10^{-4}	1011	011
1100	81×10^{-4}	1100	100
1101	729×10^{-4}	1101	101
1110	729×10^{-4}	1110	110
1111	6561×10^{-4}	1111	111

Default Codeword $= 0000$, $p_e = 0.0361$

Suppose we have a block of n outputs of a memoryless source

$$\mathbf{x} = (a_{j_1}, \ldots, a_{j_n})$$

in which symbol a_j appears n_j times in $\mathbf{x}$. The vector $(n_0, \ldots, n_{J-1})$ is called the *composition* of the sourceword $\mathbf{x}$. The probability of $\mathbf{x}$ is given by

$$p(\mathbf{x}) = \prod_{l=1}^{n} p_{j_l}$$

$$= \prod_{j=0}^{J-1} p_j^{n_j}$$

and

$$\frac{1}{n} \log p(\mathbf{x}) = \frac{1}{n} \sum_{j=0}^{J-1} n_j \log p_j \ .$$

In the following theorem, we develop the idea that because n_j/n goes to p_j by the weak law of large numbers, then

$$-\frac{1}{n} \log p(\mathbf{x}) \to -\sum_{j=0}^{J-1} p_j \log p_j = H(\mathbf{p})$$

The essence of the theorem is often referred to as the *asymptotic equipartition property.* Loosely, it says that almost all of the output sequences are nearly equiprobable.

☐ **Theorem 3.4.2 (Shannon-McMillan theorem)** Given a discrete memoryless source **p** of entropy $H(\mathbf{p})$ and any δ greater than zero, we can choose n big enough so that the set of all possible sourcewords of blocklength n produced by the source can be partitioned into two sets $\mathcal{T}$ and $\mathcal{T}^c$ for which the following statements hold:

(i) The probability of a sourceword belonging to $\mathcal{T}^c$ is less than δ.
(ii) If a sourceword $\mathbf{x}$ is in $\mathcal{T}$, then its probability of occurrence is approximately $e^{-nH(\mathbf{p})}$ in the sense that

$$\left| -n^{-1} \log p(\mathbf{x}) - H(\mathbf{p}) \right| < \delta$$

(iii) The number of elements in $\mathcal{T}$, denoted $|\mathcal{T}|$, is at least $(1 - \delta)2^{n(H(\mathbf{p}) - \delta)}$ and at most $2^{n(H(\mathbf{p}) + \delta)}$.

Proof Let $\mathcal{T} = \{\mathbf{x}: |-\log p(\mathbf{x}) - nH(\mathbf{p})| < n\delta\}$. Then $\mathcal{T}$ satisfies the requirements of statement (ii). By Chebychev's inequality,

$$Pr[\,|-\log p(\mathbf{x}) - nH(\mathbf{p})| \geq n\delta] \leq \frac{\text{var}[-\log p(\mathbf{x})]}{n^2\delta^2}$$

$$\leq \frac{n\sigma^2}{n^2\delta^2} = \frac{\sigma^2}{n\delta^2}$$

where

$$\sigma^2 = \sum_j p_j(\log p_j)^2 - \left(\sum_j p_j \log p_j \right)^2$$

is a constant, independent of n. Consequently,

$$\sum_{\mathbf{x} \in \mathcal{T}^c} p(\mathbf{x}) \leq \delta$$

for sufficiently large n, which proves statement (i). To prove statement (iii), let $H = H(\mathbf{p})$ and write

$$1 \geq \sum_{\mathbf{x} \in \mathcal{T}} p(\mathbf{x}) \geq \sum_{\mathbf{x} \in \mathcal{T}} 2^{-n(H + \delta)} = |\mathcal{T}|2^{-n(H + \delta)}$$

and, using statement (i),

$$1 - \delta \leq \sum_{\mathbf{x} \in \mathcal{T}} p(\mathbf{x}) \leq \sum_{\mathbf{x} \in \mathcal{T}} 2^{-n(H - \delta)} = |\mathcal{T}|2^{-n(H - \delta)} \qquad\qquad ☐$$

The proof of Theorem 3.4.2 contains a slightly stronger result than the statement of the theorem. We state this separately as a corollary.

☐ **Corollary 3.4.3** The probability $Pr[\mathcal{T}^c]$ that a sourceword of blocklength n belongs to the set $\mathcal{T}^c$ is bounded by

$$Pr[\mathcal{T}^c] \leq \frac{1}{n\delta^2}\left[\sum_j p_j(\log p_j)^2 - \left(\sum_j p_j \log p_j\right)^2\right]$$ ☐

The sequences that are the elements composing the set $\mathcal{T}$ are the typical sequences generated by the source. The theorem says that there is a negligible probability that a nontypical sourceword will occur. All typical sequences are nearly equally likely, and there are about 2^{nH} of them. A formal definition is as follows.

☐ **Definition 3.4.4**   Given a memoryless source $\mathbf{p}$ with entropy $H(\mathbf{p})$, let $\delta > 0$ be given. The set of *weakly typical sequences* (or weakly δ-typical sequences) of blocklength n are the elements of the set

$$\mathcal{T}(\delta) = \left\{\mathbf{x}: \left|-\frac{1}{n}\log p(\mathbf{x}) - H(\mathbf{p})\right| < \delta\right\}$$

where the logarithm base agrees with that used in computing the entropy. The set of *strongly typical sequences* (or strongly δ-typical sequences) of blocklength n are the elements of the set

$$\mathcal{S}(\delta) = \left\{\mathbf{x}: \left|\frac{1}{n}n_j(\mathbf{x}) - p_j\right| < \frac{\delta}{J} \text{ for } j = 0, \ldots, J-1\right\}$$

where $n_j(\mathbf{x})$ is the number of occurrences of letter j in the sequence $\mathbf{x}$.   ☐

Whereas weakly typical sequences display approximately the right apparent entropy, strongly typical sequences display approximately the right relative frequency of symbols. Loosely, both weakly typical sequences and strongly typical sequences are called *typical sequences*.

We now apply the Shannon-McMillan theorem to the problem of block codes for data compaction, encoding blocks $\mathbf{x} = (a_{j_1}, \ldots, a_{j_n})$ from the discrete memoryless source into codewords of blocklength r from a code alphabet of size K. We assume that the number of codewords K^r is less than the number of sourcewords. Otherwise there is no data compaction.

During decompaction of the data, if the default codeword is observed by the decoder, it is not possible to reconstruct the sourceword. The decoder can either make a guess or raise a default flag for that block. Either case will be referred to as a decoding failure. We will show that the probability of decoding failure can be made negligibly small.

☐ **Theorem 3.4.5   (Shannon's first coding theorem)** Sourcewords of blocklength n produced by a discrete memoryless source $\mathbf{p}$ with entropy $H(\mathbf{p})$ are to be encoded into codewords of blocklength r from a coding alphabet of size K. For any $\varepsilon > 0$, the probability of block decoding failure p_e can be made less than ε, provided

$$r \log K > nH(\mathbf{p})$$

and n is sufficiently large.

Proof   Recall that the Shannon-McMillan theorem partitions the set of all sourcewords of blocklength n into two sets $\mathscr{T}$ and $\mathscr{T}^c$ such that $\mathscr{T}$, the set of typical sequences, satisfies

$$\mathscr{T} = \left\{ \mathbf{x} : e^{-n(H-\delta)} > p(\mathbf{x}) > e^{-n(H+\delta)} \right\}$$

with H expressed in units of nats. Therefore the number of sourcewords in $\mathscr{T}$ is less than $e^{n(H+\delta)}$. The theorem assumes that

$$r \log K > nH(\mathbf{p})$$

so we can choose a δ satisfying

$$r \log K \geq n(H(\mathbf{p}) + \delta)$$

Therefore, because the number of codewords of blocklength r is K^r, we see that the number of codewords is at least as large as $e^{n(H+\delta)}$. Hence we can provide a codeword for each typical sourceword. Therefore the set of nonencodable sourcewords is contained in $\mathscr{T}^c$ and, for large enough n, $p_e < \varepsilon$, as was to be proved. $\square$

This theorem and the converse theorem that follows give a precise operational interpretation of the entropy as the information content of the source. Figure 3.6 shows the various large-sample concepts, and the theorems that relate them. (Stirling's approximation was treated in Problem 1.5.)

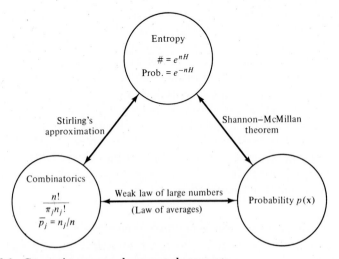

Figure 3.6   Connections among large-sample concepts.

We now show the converse, that the probability of decoding failure approaches 1 for large blocklength if the code rate is less than the source entropy. This theorem is an asymptotic bound. It does not provide an explicit formula that provides a bound for any finite n.

□ **Theorem 3.4.6** (**Converse theorem**) Let $\varepsilon > 0$ be given. Given a discrete memoryless source $\mathbf{p}$ of entropy $H(\mathbf{p})$ and a code alphabet of size K, let R satisfy

$$R \log K < H(\mathbf{p})$$

Then for all codes of rate R and sufficiently large blocklength, the probability of block decoding failure p_e satisfies

$$p_e > 1 - \varepsilon$$

Proof Let $\mathscr{C}'$ be the set of sourcewords that are encoded into distinct codewords. This is the code $\mathscr{C}$ excluding the default codeword. The number $|\mathscr{C}'|$ of codewords in $\mathscr{C}'$ satisfies

$$|\mathscr{C}'| = K^r - 1 = K^{nR} - 1 < e^{nR \log K}.$$

By assumption, we can find a positive δ such that

$$|\mathscr{C}'| < e^{n(H - 2\delta)}$$

Use the Shannon-McMillan theorem with δ equal to $\varepsilon/2$, and let $\mathscr{T}(\delta)$ be the set of weakly δ-typical sequences. Then the probability that a block can be encoded is

$$1 - p_e = \sum_{\mathbf{x} \in \mathscr{C}'} p(\mathbf{x})$$

$$= \sum_{\mathbf{x} \in \mathscr{C}' \cap \mathscr{T}'(\delta)} p(\mathbf{x}) + \sum_{\mathbf{x} \in \mathscr{C}' \cap \mathscr{T}(\delta)} p(\mathbf{x})$$

$$\leq \frac{\varepsilon}{2} + |\mathscr{C}' \cap \mathscr{T}(\delta)| \left\{ \max_{\mathbf{x} \in \mathscr{T}(\delta)} p(\mathbf{x}) \right\}$$

$$\leq \frac{\varepsilon}{2} + |\mathscr{C}'| \left\{ \max_{\mathbf{x} \in \mathscr{T}(\delta)} p(\mathbf{x}) \right\}$$

where $|\mathscr{C}' \cap \mathscr{T}(\delta)|$ denotes the number of points in $\mathscr{C}' \cap \mathscr{T}(\delta)$. Because $|\mathscr{C}'| < e^{n(H - 2\delta)}$ and $p(\mathbf{x}) < e^{-n(H - \delta)}$ for $\mathbf{x}$ in $\mathscr{T}(\delta)$, the total probability of the encoded set satisfies

$$1 - p_e < \frac{\varepsilon}{2} + e^{n(H - 2\delta)} e^{-n(H - \delta)} = \frac{\varepsilon}{2} + e^{-n\delta}$$

Consequently,

$$p_e > 1 - \varepsilon$$

for sufficiently large n.   □

3.5 ASYMPTOTIC ERROR BOUNDS

Shannon's source coding theorem tells us that for a sufficiently large n, a sourceword of blocklength n can be encoded by a block code unambiguously with probability arbitrarily close to 1, provided the code rate exceeds the source entropy. However, we have not yet given any estimate of just how large the blocklength n must be in order to make the probability of decoding failure less than some given value p_e. Here we shall study how this probability decreases with n. We shall find that for fixed rate R, the probability decreases exponentially with blocklength, the rate of decrease being given by a function of rate $F(R)$. The exponent $F(R)$ will be developed first; later its significance will be established by means of an appropriate coding theorem.

The line of development that we follow here will be used many times for other coding problems to study the relationship between blocklength and probability of coding error.

□ **Definition 3.5.1** Suppose a discrete memoryless source has probability distribution **p**. The reliability function for data compaction $F(R)$ is given by

$$F(R) = \min_{\hat{\mathbf{p}} \in \mathscr{P}_R} \sum_j \hat{p}_j \log \frac{\hat{p}_j}{p_j}$$

where the minimum is over the set of probability distributions given by

$$\mathscr{P}_R = \left\{ \hat{\mathbf{p}} : -\sum_j \hat{p}_j \log \hat{p}_j \geq R \right\}$$

□

This function $F(R)$ is defined as the minimum of a function of **p** over a set of dummy probability distributions denoted by $\hat{\mathbf{p}}$. This kind of definition will recur many times. In this case, we recognize the object function as the discrimination, whose detailed properties will be given in Section 4.3.

The simplest nontrivial example of $F(R)$ is that of a binary asymmetric source with probability distribution

$$\mathbf{p} = \{\gamma, 1 - \gamma\}$$

Because $\hat{\mathbf{p}}$ is defined on a binary alphabet, it must be of the form

$$\hat{\mathbf{p}} = \{\gamma', 1 - \gamma'\}$$

for some γ'. It turns out that only γ' between γ and $1/2$ achieve $F(R)$, as we shall see in the next theorem. Then $F(R)$ can be expressed in terms of a parameter γ':

$$F(R) = \gamma' \log \frac{\gamma'}{\gamma} + (1 - \gamma') \log \frac{1 - \gamma'}{1 - \gamma}$$

and

$$R = -\gamma' \log \gamma' - (1 - \gamma') \log (1 - \gamma')$$

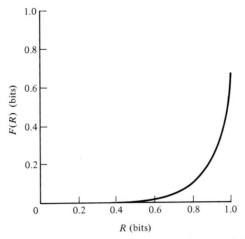

Figure 3.7   Data compaction exponent for a binary source ($p = 0.11$).

where γ' satisfies $\gamma \leq \gamma' \leq 1/2$. Each such choice of the parameter γ' gives a point $(F(R), R)$. The function $F(R)$ for the binary asymmetric source with $\gamma = 0.11$ is shown in Fig. 3.7. We shall see in Theorem 3.5.3 that the general shape of this function is the same for any source.

The symbol stream out of a discrete source can be broken into sourcewords of blocklength n. The set of such sourcewords can be considered to be the symbols of a new source with J^n letters in its output alphabet. Let $F_n(R)$ denote the reliability function for the n-tuple source. For a memoryless source, $F_n(R)$ is related simply to $F(R)$ by the following theorem.

$\square$ **Theorem 3.5.2**   Let $p^n(\mathbf{x})$ be the probability distribution on blocks of length n of independent, identically distributed letters. Then

$$F_n(nR) = nF(R)$$

Proof

$$F_n(nR) = \min_{\hat{\mathbf{p}} \in \mathscr{P}_{nR}} L(\hat{\mathbf{p}}^n; \mathbf{p}^n)$$

where

$$\mathscr{P}_{nR} = \{\hat{\mathbf{p}}^n : H(\hat{\mathbf{p}}^n) \geq nR\}$$

Whatever the single-letter projections of $\hat{\mathbf{p}}^n$ may be, $H(\hat{\mathbf{p}}^n)$ is increased and $L(\hat{\mathbf{p}}^n; \mathbf{p}^n)$ is decreased if $\hat{\mathbf{p}}^n$ is a product distribution. Hence the minimum occurs with a product distribution. It then follows that all projections of $\mathbf{p}^n$ should be the same and the theorem is proved. $\square$

$\square$ **Theorem 3.5.3** $F(R)$ is a convex and increasing function. It is zero for $R \leq H(\mathbf{p})$. It is strictly increasing in the interval $H(\mathbf{p}) \leq R \leq \log J$, and in this region the constraint is satisfied with equality.

Proof   To prove convexity, we must prove, for all λ between 0 and 1, that

$$F(\lambda R' + (1 - \lambda)R'') \le \lambda F(R') + (1 - \lambda)F(R'')$$

Let $\mathbf{p}'$ and $\mathbf{p}''$ be those values of $\mathbf{p}$ that achieve the minima defining $F(R')$ and $F(R'')$, respectively. Then

$$H(\lambda \mathbf{p}' + (1 - \lambda)\mathbf{p}'') \ge \lambda H(\mathbf{p}') + (1 - \lambda)H(\mathbf{p}'')$$

$$\ge \lambda R' + (1 - \lambda)R''$$

where the first inequality follows from the concavity of $H(\mathbf{p})$ and the second follows from the definitions of $\mathbf{p}'$ and $\mathbf{p}''$. But this inequality implies that $\lambda \mathbf{p}' + (1 - \lambda)\mathbf{p}'' \in \mathscr{P}_{\lambda R' + (1 - \lambda)R''}$. Because $F(\lambda R' + (1 - \lambda)R'')$ is a minimum over all $\hat{\mathbf{p}}$ in this set, it is not larger than $L(\hat{\mathbf{p}}; \mathbf{p})$ with $\hat{\mathbf{p}} = \lambda \mathbf{p}' + (1 - \lambda)\mathbf{p}''$. Thus

$$F(\lambda R' + (1 - \lambda)R'') \le L(\lambda \mathbf{p}' + (1 - \lambda)\mathbf{p}''; \mathbf{p})$$

$$\le \lambda L(\mathbf{p}'; \mathbf{p}) + (1 - \lambda)L(\mathbf{p}''; \mathbf{p})$$

$$= \lambda F(R') + (1 - \lambda)F(R'')$$

where the second inequality follows from the convexity of the discrimination in its first variable, which will be proved in Theorem 4.3.2. This completes the proof that $F(R)$ is a convex function.

If $H(\mathbf{p}) \ge R$, then $\mathbf{p} \in \mathscr{P}_R$ and the minimum will be where $\hat{\mathbf{p}} = \mathbf{p}$, so that $F(R)$ equals zero. If $H(\mathbf{p}) < R \le \log J$, $F(R)$ is nonzero.

If $R > R'$, then $\mathscr{P}_{R'} \supset \mathscr{P}_R$. Therefore $F(R') < F(R)$ and so $F(R)$ is increasing. It must be strictly increasing in the region $H(\mathbf{p}) < R \le \log J$ because it is convex. $\square$

$\square$ **Theorem 3.5.4**   Suppose that $R \ge H(\mathbf{p})$. Then $F(R)$ is obtained for $\hat{\mathbf{p}} = \mathbf{p}^*(s)$, where

$$p_j^*(s) = \frac{p_j^{1/(1 + s)}}{\sum\limits_{j} p_j^{1/(1 + s)}}$$

and s is nonnegative and chosen so that $H(\mathbf{p}^*(s)) = R$.

Proof   First of all there will be a nonnegative value of s for which $H(\mathbf{p}^*(s)) = R$ if R lies between $H(\mathbf{p})$ and $\log J$. This is because $H(\mathbf{p}^*(s))$ is continuous in s, and goes to $H(\mathbf{p})$ as s goes to zero and to $\log J$ as s goes to infinity. We must show that this value for $\hat{\mathbf{p}}$ does indeed achieve the minimum in Definition 3.5.1. But for any $\hat{\mathbf{p}}$ such that $H(\hat{\mathbf{p}}) = R$,

$$L(\hat{\mathbf{p}}; \mathbf{p}) = L(\hat{\mathbf{p}}; \mathbf{p}^*(s)) + \sum\limits_{j} \hat{p}_j \log \frac{p_j^*(s)}{p_j}$$

which can be seen by expanding the right side. Therefore

$$L(\hat{\mathbf{p}}; \mathbf{p}) = L((\hat{\mathbf{p}}; \mathbf{p}^*(s)) - \frac{s}{1+s} \sum_j \hat{p}_j \log p_j - \log \sum_j p_j^{1/(1+s)}$$

$$= L(\hat{\mathbf{p}}; \mathbf{p}^*(s)) + \frac{s}{1+s} [H(\hat{\mathbf{p}}) + L(\hat{\mathbf{p}}; \mathbf{p})] - \log \sum_j p_j^{1/(1+s)}$$

$$= L(\hat{\mathbf{p}}; \mathbf{p}^*(s)) + \frac{s}{1+s} [R + L(\hat{\mathbf{p}}; \mathbf{p})] - \log \sum_j p_j^{1/(1+s)}$$

Rearranging yields

$$\frac{1}{1+s} L(\hat{\mathbf{p}}; \mathbf{p}) = L(\hat{\mathbf{p}}; \mathbf{p}^*(s)) + \frac{s}{1+s} R - \log \sum_j p_j^{1/(1+s)}$$

Because $\hat{\mathbf{p}}$ appears on the right side only in the term $L(\hat{\mathbf{p}}; \mathbf{p}^*(s))$, it is clear that the right side is minimized by choosing $\hat{\mathbf{p}} = \mathbf{p}^*(s)$, and the minimum is

$$F(R) = sR - (1+s) \log \sum_j p_j^{1/(1+s)}$$

This completes the proof of the theorem. $\square$

$\square$ **Theorem 3.5.5** $F(R)$ can be represented as follows:

$$F(R) = \max_{s \geq 0} \left[sR - \log \left(\sum_j p_j^{1/(1+s)} \right)^{1+s} \right]$$

Proof For any nonnegative s,

$$F(R) \geq \min_{\hat{\mathbf{p}} \in \mathscr{P}_R} \{L(\hat{\mathbf{p}}; \mathbf{p}) + s[R - H(\hat{\mathbf{p}})]\}$$

because the term multiplying s is nonpositive. The inequality is not violated if the domain of the minimum is now enlarged to all $\hat{\mathbf{p}}$. Hence

$$F(R) \geq \min_{\hat{\mathbf{p}}} \{L(\hat{\mathbf{p}}; \mathbf{p}) + s[R - H(\hat{\mathbf{p}})]\}$$

This is true for all nonnegative s, so

$$F(R) \geq \max_{s \geq 0} \min_{\hat{\mathbf{p}}} \{L(\hat{\mathbf{p}}; \mathbf{p}) + s[R - H(\hat{\mathbf{p}})]\}$$

The minimum is found to occur at

$$\hat{p}_j = \frac{p_j^{1/(1+s)}}{\sum_j p_j^{1/(1+s)}}$$

which leads to

$$F(R) \geq \max_{s \geq 0} \left[sR - \log \left(\sum_j p_j^{1/(1+s)} \right)^{1+s} \right]$$

From the proof of Theorem 3.5.4, we see that there is one value of s for which $F(R)$ equals the right side. Hence the inequality is satisfied by equality. ☐

We shall now develop a coding theorem in terms of $F(R)$; now the asymptotic behavior with blocklength n of the probability of block decoding failure will be explicit. A block code for data compaction of size M and blocklength n will encode unambiguously a list of $M - 1$ source output blocks of length n. Any sourceword not on this list is replaced by the default codeword. If the default codeword enters the decoder, the decoder cannot determine the original sourceword and a decoding failure results. We already know that the probability of decoding failure can be made arbitrarily small, yet the data is compacted by some nontrivial amount. We shall determine bounds on the probability of such block decoding failure as a function of n.

☐ **Theorem 3.5.6** It is possible to select $M - 1$ sourcewords of blocklength n to be encoded such that M and the probability of a nonencodable sourceword satisfy

$$p_e \leq e^{-nF(R)}$$

$$M \leq e^{nR}$$

Proof Choose a *threshold* T given by

$$T = (1 + s)\left(R - \log \sum_j p_j^{1/(1+s)} \right)$$

where s parameterizes $F(R)$ at the point R. Define the following set of sourcewords:

$$\mathcal{U} = \{\mathbf{x} : p(\mathbf{x}) > e^{-nT}\}$$

The function $\phi_{\mathcal{U}^c}(\mathbf{x})$ given by

$$\phi_{\mathcal{U}^c}(\mathbf{x}) = \begin{cases} 1 & \mathbf{x} \in \mathcal{U}^c \\ 0 & \mathbf{x} \notin \mathcal{U}^c \end{cases}$$

is the indicator function of the set $\mathcal{U}^c$, the complement of $\mathcal{U}$. Then by the definition of $\mathcal{U}$,

$$\phi_{\mathcal{U}^c}(\mathbf{x}) \leq \left(\frac{e^{-nT}}{p(\mathbf{x})} \right)^\rho$$

for any positive ρ. This can be verified by checking first the case where

$\phi_{\mathcal{U}^c}(\mathbf{x})$ is equal to 1, then the case where it is equal to 0. Therefore

$$p_e = \sum_{\mathbf{x}} p(\mathbf{x}) \phi_{\mathcal{U}^c}(\mathbf{x}) \leq \sum_{\mathbf{x}} p(\mathbf{x}) \left(\frac{e^{-nT}}{p(\mathbf{x})} \right)^{s/(1+s)} = e^{-nF(R)}$$

Similarly, let $\phi_{\mathcal{U}}(\mathbf{x})$ be the indicator function of the set $\mathcal{U}$. Then

$$M = \sum_{\mathbf{x}} \phi_{\mathcal{U}}(\mathbf{x}) \leq \sum_{\mathbf{x}} \left(\frac{p(\mathbf{x})}{e^{-nT}} \right)^{1/(1+s)} = e^{nR} \qquad \square$$

□ **Corollary 3.5.7** A set of sourcewords that achieves the coding performance of the theorem is the set of $\mathbf{x}$ satisfying

$$p(\mathbf{x}) > e^{-nT}$$

where

$$T = (1+s)\left(R - \log \sum_j p_j^{1/(1+s)} \right) \qquad \square$$

The function $F(R)$ provides the asymptotically correct dependence of p_e on n, as is shown by deriving a lower bound on p_e in the next theorem, which shows that the exponents in Theorem 3.5.6 cannot be improved. Therefore

$$p_e = e^{-nF(R) + o(n)}$$

where $o(n)$ is a term that goes to zero as n goes to infinity. Notice that the equiprobable distribution, which cannot be compacted, is excluded by the theorem because there is no R satisfying the condition.

□ **Theorem 3.5.8** Let $\varepsilon > 0$ be given. Given a discrete memoryless source $\mathbf{p}$, suppose that $H(\mathbf{p}) < R < \log J$. Then for sufficiently large blocklength n, all codes with e^{nR} codewords have a probability of block decoding failure that satisfies

$$p_e \geq e^{-n[F(R) + \varepsilon]}$$

Proof The theorem does not apply to the equiprobable distribution because then $H(\mathbf{p}) = \log J$. Choose any R' larger than R. For any $\mathbf{p}$ except the equiprobable distribution, we can find a dummy probability distribution $\hat{\mathbf{p}}$ with $H(\mathbf{p}) < R < R' = H(\hat{\mathbf{p}}) < \log J$. By Theorem 3.4.6, the converse to Shannon's source coding theorem, we have for every positive constant ε',

$$\sum_{\mathbf{x} \in \mathcal{U}^c} \hat{p}(\mathbf{x}) > 1 - \varepsilon'$$

for every set $\mathcal{U}$ with no more than e^{nR} elements, provided n is large enough. Let

$$\mathcal{B} = \left\{ \mathbf{x} : \left| \log \frac{\hat{p}(\mathbf{x})}{p(\mathbf{x})} - nL(\hat{\mathbf{p}}; \mathbf{p}) \right| \leq n\delta \right\}$$

where

$$L(\hat{\mathbf{p}}; \mathbf{p}) = \sum_{\mathbf{x}} \hat{p}(\mathbf{x}) \log \frac{\hat{p}(\mathbf{x})}{p(\mathbf{x})}$$

By the law of large numbers, for sufficiently large blocklength n,

$$\sum_{\mathbf{x} \in \mathscr{B}^c} \hat{p}(\mathbf{x}) < \varepsilon'$$

Now let $\mathscr{U}$ be the set of sourcewords that are encoded. Then

$$p_e = \sum_{\mathbf{x} \notin \mathscr{U}} p(\mathbf{x}) \geq \sum_{\mathbf{x} \in \mathscr{U}^c \cap \mathscr{B}} p(\mathbf{x})$$

$$\geq \sum_{\mathbf{x} \in \mathscr{U}^c \cap \mathscr{B}} \hat{p}(\mathbf{x}) e^{-n[L(\hat{\mathbf{p}}; \mathbf{p}) + \delta]}$$

But

$$\sum_{\mathbf{x} \in \mathscr{U}^c \cap \mathscr{B}} \hat{p}(\mathbf{x}) \geq 1 - \sum_{\mathbf{x} \in \mathscr{U}} \hat{p}(\mathbf{x}) - \sum_{\mathbf{x} \in \mathscr{B}^c} \hat{p}(\mathbf{x})$$

$$= \sum_{\mathbf{x} \in \mathscr{U}^c} \hat{p}(\mathbf{x}) - \sum_{\mathbf{x} \in \mathscr{B}^c} \hat{p}(\mathbf{x})$$

$$\geq 1 - \varepsilon' - \varepsilon'$$

Therefore

$$p_e \geq (1 - 2\varepsilon') e^{-n[L(\hat{\mathbf{p}}; \mathbf{p}) + \delta]}$$

This is true for every $\hat{\mathbf{p}} \in \mathscr{R}_R$, including that achieving $F(R')$. Then

$$p_e \geq e^{-n[F(R') + \delta - (1/n) \log (1 - 2\varepsilon')]}$$

Because R' can be chosen so that $F(R')$ is arbitrarily close to R, and δ and ε' are arbitrarily small, for all sufficiently large n,

$$p_e \geq e^{-n[F(R) + \varepsilon]}$$

and the theorem is proved.   □

3.6 TREE CODES FOR DATA COMPACTION

The entropy of a source is $-\sum_j p_j \log p_j$, and the average blocklength of a Huffman code is $\sum_j p_j l_j$. To encode at a rate equal to the entropy, we should choose codeword lengths satisfying

$$l_j = -\log p_j$$

But a codeword length must be an integer, so this will not be possible except for very special cases. We have seen that one way to make the quantization from $-\log p_j$ into integer values more efficient is to Huffman-encode at the level of source blocks. Another way is to use a tree code, which differs from a block code in that it is not possible, in general, to break a codeword into a concatenated sequence of noninteracting blocks. We shall study tree codes for data compaction by studying one particular example, the Elias code.

The *Elias code* is a variable-length tree code for source compaction that encodes indefinitely long strings of source output symbols into indefinitely long strings of code symbols. The encoding operation has a sliding structure whereby, as a few source symbols enter the encoder, a few codeword bits leave the encoder. The number of codeword bits leaving the decoder per input symbol is variable, depending on the particular pattern of symbols produced by the source.

We shall first describe an impractical form of the Elias code that ignores considerations of computational precision. Suppose we wish to compact a binary source with source alphabet $\{a_0, a_1\}$ and probability distribution $\mathbf{p} = (0.7, 0.3)$. The entropy of this source is 0.88 bits. Starting at time zero, the source puts out an indefinitely long sequence of output symbols. This semi-infinite sequence of source output symbols can be represented as a string of bits. For example,

$$.011010111010\ldots$$

where here the symbols a_0 and a_1 are represented by 0 and 1, respectively. By placing a dot at the beginning of the string, we have made it look like an infinite binary expansion of a real number. We can choose to so regard the string of source symbols as the binary expansion of the real number ρ in the interval $[0, 1)$. However, we will regard the binary representation as biased in an unconventional way. Refer to Fig. 3.8. Subdivide the half-open interval $[0, 1)$ into two subintervals $[0, 0.7)$ and $[0.7, 1)$. Use the first symbol from the source, if it is a 0, to specify that ρ is in the first subinterval and, if it is a 1, to

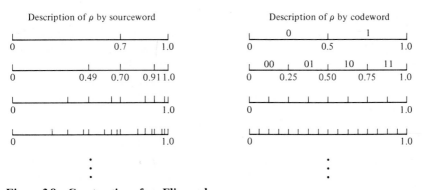

Figure 3.8   Construction of an Elias code.

specify that ρ is in the second subinterval. Next subdivide the specified subinterval further in the same proportion, either into $[0, 0.49)$ and $[0.49, 0.7)$ or into $[0.7, 0.91)$ and $[0.91, 1)$. Use the second symbol from the source to specify one of these smaller subintervals. Each source output bit is used to further subdivide the interval in the same way.

The general iterative rule is as follows: Let $p = p_0 = 1 - p_1$ be the probability of source symbol a_0. After $n - 1$ source bits, an interval $[A_{n-1}, B_{n-1})$ has been specified. If the nth source symbol is a 0, the next bit specifies a new interval with endpoints

$$A_n = A_{n-1}$$

$$B_n = A_{n-1} + p(B_{n-1} - A_{n-1})$$

If the nth source symbol is a 1, the new interval is specified by the endpoints

$$A_n = A_{n-1} + p(B_{n-1} - A_{n-1})$$

$$B_n = B_{n-1}$$

In this way, the interval specified by any sequence of source symbols has a width equal to the probability of that sequence. The interval grows ever smaller as the data sequence grows longer. Exactly one point is specified by the infinite data sequence; a data sequence of finite length specifies a small subinterval of $[0, 1)$.

The codeword, on the other hand, is a conventional binary representation of the point ρ. As soon as enough source symbols are given to the encoder to determine whether ρ is in the interval $[0, 0.5)$ or the interval $[0.5, 1)$, the first codeword bit can be transmitted. Similarly, the second codeword bit can be transmitted as soon as the encoder knows that ρ is in the interval $[0, 0.25)$ or $[0.25, 0.5)$, or in the interval $[0.5, 0.75)$ or $[0.75, 1)$. If the endpoints at the nth iteration, A_n and B_n, are expressed in a binary notation, then the codeword consists merely of the high-order bits of A_n and B_n up to the point at which they no longer agree. On average, fewer bits will appear in the codeword than appear in the sourceword. The code is a variable-length code because the number of source symbols needed to produce one codeword bit depends on the particular source sequence.

The decoder can begin to recover source symbols after receiving only a few codeword bits. For example, if the binary codeword sequence starts with 011 . . . , then the real number ρ must lie between 0.375 and 0.50; hence the first symbol from the source must be a_0. If the binary sequence starts with 0110, the real number ρ must lie between 0.375 and 0.4375; hence because $p = 0.7$, the first three symbols from the source must be $a_0 a_0 a_1$.

As the source output sequence grows longer, the original interval $[0, 1)$ becomes ever more finely divided. The number of significant places needed in the real numbers A_n and B_n grows larger. Consequently, the Elias code is not practical because of precision problems. Any wordlength chosen for the representation of A_n and B_n will soon be exceeded. Errors in the calculations, no matter how small, will eventually cause encoding and decoding errors and complete destruction of subsequent data.

The defects in the Elias code can be repaired by introducing a scaling strategy and a rounding strategy. The scaling strategy magnifies the nth interval by the factor 2^{m+L_n}, where m is a fixed integer and L_n depends on the data. The rounding strategy places the endpoints of the magnified interval only on a fixed set of finely quantized points. The role of the normalized left endpoint $2^{m+L_n}A_n$ is replaced by the integer C_n, and the normalized width $2^{m+L_n}(B_n - A_n)$ is replaced by the integer W_n. The fixed integer m determines the number of bits of precision used to measure the interval.

The parameters C_n and W_n are initialized as $C_0 = 0$ and $W_0 = 2^m - 1$. If the nth source symbol is a 0, they are updated by the equations

$$C_n = 2^s C_{n-1}$$

$$W_n = 2^s \lfloor W_{n-1} p_0 + \tfrac{1}{2} \rfloor$$

and if the nth source symbol is a 1 by the equations

$$C_n = 2^s (C_{n-1} + W_{n-1} - \lfloor W_{n-1} p_1 + \tfrac{1}{2} \rfloor)$$

$$W_n = 2^s \lfloor W_{n-1} p_1 + \tfrac{1}{2} \rfloor$$

where s is the unique integer such that

$$2^{m-1} \le W_n < 2^m$$

By choice of s, the parameter W_n stays bounded, but the parameter C_n grows without limit as n increases. The codeword bits are the high-order bits of C_n. The integer s is equal to the number of high-order bits of C_n to be shifted out of the encoder in the nth iteration. These bits are sent to the channel and then dropped from C_n in the encoder.

The magnification factor L_n is not actually computed nor is it used explicitly by the encoder or decoder. It grows without limit and is given by the recursion

$$L_n = L_{n-1} + s$$

with the initialization $L_0 = 0$.

To ensure that the parameter s is well defined, we must ensure that W_n is nonzero. This will be so if we choose m so that $p_i > 2^{-m}$ for each i. Then because $W_n \ge 2^{m-1}$, we are assured that $\lfloor W_{n-1} p_0 + \tfrac{1}{2} \rfloor$ is nonzero and also that $\lfloor W_{n-1} p_1 + \tfrac{1}{2} \rfloor$ is nonzero. Therefore W_n always remains strictly positive, and the parameter s is well defined. This is the only necessary condition on the choice of m. However, choice of a larger value of m corresponds to a finer granularity in the computation and to a tree code that will compact the data to more nearly its entropy.

3.7 UNIVERSAL CODES FOR DATA COMPACTION

One may wish to compact sourcewords generated by a source that has an unknown or incompletely known probability distribution. Surprisingly there is a certain sense in which it does not matter that the probability distribution is unknown. In this section, we shall study universal codes for data compaction. Our problem is to prove the existence of a variable-length (and variable-rate) code for data compaction that is nearly optimal for every source in a class of sources. The sources are required only to be stationary on an alphabet with J letters.

Let θ be an index designating a particular source in a class of sources. For each θ in the set of possible θ, there is a source characterized by the probability distribution on blocks $p^n(\mathbf{x}|\theta)$, abbreviated $p^n(\mathbf{x})$ when θ is fixed. A binary, variable-length code for data compaction is a binary prefix code $\mathscr{C}$ and a mapping from the set of sourcewords of blocklength n into $\mathscr{C}$, with sourceword $\mathbf{x}$ having a codeword of length $l_n(\mathbf{x})$. Loosely, the code is called a *universal code* if, for every source in the class, the average per-letter codeword length defined as

$$\bar{l}(\theta) = \frac{1}{n}\bar{l}_n(\theta) = \frac{1}{n}\sum_{\mathbf{x}} p^n(\mathbf{x}|\theta)l_n(\mathbf{x})$$

is close to the source entropy, if it exists, or to the nth-order per-letter source entropy

$$H_n(\theta) = \frac{1}{n}\left[-\sum_{\mathbf{x}} p^n(\mathbf{x}|\theta) \log p^n(\mathbf{x}|\theta)\right]$$

A formal definition is as follows.

□ **Definition 3.7.1**   Let $\varepsilon > 0$ be given and let Θ denote a collection of stationary sources indexed by θ. A code $\mathscr{C}$ of blocklength n is universal for ε if

$$\left|\frac{1}{n}\bar{l}_n(\theta) - H_n(\theta)\right| < \varepsilon$$

for every source in the collection Θ.   □

The development will proceed as follows. In the space $\mathbf{P}^{J^n}$ of probability distributions on J^n points, we will construct a finite grid $\mathscr{G}$ of 2^r probability distributions, as shown in Fig. 3.9, assigning an r-bit index to each point. We then construct a separate variable-length code for compacting each source described by one of the probability distributions in the grid $\mathscr{G}$. Given any source with block probability distribution $p^n(\mathbf{x})$, we can approximate it by $q^n(\mathbf{x})$, a nearby element of $\mathscr{G}$, and then use the code associated with $q^n(\mathbf{x})$ to encode source $p^n(\mathbf{x})$. An r-bit preamble is attached to the codeword to identify the code that the codeword comes from. By choosing the sourceword to be

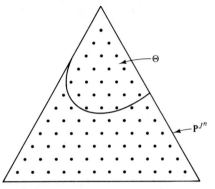

Figure 3.9   Illustrating a grid of probability distributions.

very long, the number of bits in the preamble is small compared with the average codeword length. We shall see that, asymptotically as the blocklength grows, r can grow at a negligibly slow rate. Consequently, the preamble length does not matter in an asymptotic sense, although it may be of critical importance in a practical code.

☐   **Theorem 3.7.2**   For fixed blocklength n, there exists a partition of Θ into subsets $\Theta_i, i = 1, \ldots, I$, each of which is associated with a binary code for data compaction such that when encoding source $\theta \in \Theta_i$ with the ith code, the average codeword length of the ith code

$$\bar{l}_n(\theta) = \sum_{\mathbf{x}} p^n(\mathbf{x}|\theta) l_n^{(i)}(\mathbf{x})$$

satisfies

$$\frac{1}{n} \bar{l}_n(\theta) \le H_n(\theta) + \frac{2}{n}$$

Proof   Step 1: We construct a grid $\mathscr{G}$ of points in $\mathbf{P}^{J^n}$ as follows. The grid is defined as the set of all probability distributions $\mathbf{q}^n$ that can be written

$$q^n(\mathbf{x}) = \frac{\alpha(\mathbf{x})}{2J^{2n}}$$

where $\alpha(\mathbf{x})$ is a positive, integer-valued function of $\mathbf{x}$ such that

$$\sum_{\mathbf{x}} \alpha(\mathbf{x}) = 2J^{2n}$$

For every $\mathbf{p}^n$ there is an approximating $\hat{\mathbf{q}}^n$ in the grid satisfying

$$\max_{\mathbf{x}} |p^n(\mathbf{x}) - \hat{q}^n(\mathbf{x})| \le \frac{J^n - 1}{2J^{2n}}$$

If $p''(x)$ equals 1 at one value of x, say x', then the approximating $\hat{q}''$ is unique; for x not equal to x', $\hat{q}''(x)$ equals $\frac{1}{2}J^{-2n}$ and for x equal to x', $\hat{q}''(x)$ equals $1 - \frac{1}{2}J^{-2n}(J^n - 1)$.

In general, given p'', let x' be one of the sourcewords for which $p''(x')$ is largest. Then for every x not equal to x', let

$$\hat{q}''(x) = \frac{\lfloor 1 + 2J^{2n}p''(x) \rfloor}{2J^{2n}}$$

and let

$$\hat{q}''(x') = 1 - \sum_{x \neq x'} \hat{q}''(x)$$

Then $\hat{q}'' \in \mathcal{G}$.

Step 2: We now define the distance from any p'' to the grid $\mathcal{G}$ as

$$d(p'', \mathcal{G}) = \min_{q'' \in \mathcal{G}} L(p''; q'')$$

where $L(p''; q'')$ is the discrimination between the distributions p'' and q''. The minimum is not larger than $L(p''; \hat{q}'')$.

$$d(p'', \mathcal{G}) \leq \sum_x p''(x) \log \frac{p''(x)}{\hat{q}''(x)}$$

$$< p''(x') \log \frac{p''(x')}{\hat{q}''(x')}$$

where the second inequality follows because $\log[p''(x)/\hat{q}''(x)] < 0$ for x not equal to x'. But, by the definition of $\hat{q}''$, we can easily verify that

$$\hat{q}''(x') > p''(x') - \frac{J^n - 1}{2J^{2n}}$$

Therefore, because $p''(x') \geq J^{-n}$,

$$\frac{\hat{q}''(x')}{p''(x')} \geq 1 - \frac{1}{2}\frac{J^n - 1}{J^n} > \frac{1}{2}$$

Consequently, we can complete the development of the bound on $d(p'', \mathcal{G})$:

$$d(p'', \mathcal{G}) < p''(x') \log 2$$

$$\leq 1$$

Step 3: We have seen in step 2 that

$$d(p'', \mathcal{G}) < 1$$

for every p'', so it is clear that a partition as asserted in the statement of the theorem exists for which the ith subset of the partition can be approximated by a $\mathbf{q}^n$ at a distance at most 1 from every $\mathbf{p}^n$ in the subset.

Let i index the block probability distributions in the grid $\mathscr{G}$, and let $\mathscr{C}^{(i)}$ be a Shannon code for the ith probability distribution. Then

$$l_n(\mathbf{x}) \leq -\log q^n(\mathbf{x}) + 1$$

for the Shannon code corresponding to $\mathbf{q}^n$. Therefore

$$\frac{1}{n}\sum_{\mathbf{x}} p^n(\mathbf{x}|\theta)l_n(\mathbf{x}) \leq \frac{1}{n}\sum_{\mathbf{x}} p^n(\mathbf{x}|\theta)[1 - \log q^n(\mathbf{x})]$$

$$= \frac{1}{n} + \frac{1}{n}L(\mathbf{p}^n;\mathbf{q}^n) + H_n(\theta)$$

$$= \frac{1}{n} + \frac{1}{n}d(\mathbf{p}^n,\mathscr{G}) + H_n(\theta)$$

$$\leq \frac{2}{n} + H_n(\theta)$$

which completes the proof of the theorem. $\square$

$\square$ **Theorem 3.7.3**   For every $\varepsilon > 0$, universal variable-rate codes exist for any arbitrary collection of discrete memoryless sources on a common alphabet.

Proof   We begin the proof with the partition and subcodes defined in Theorem 3.7.2 for each blocklength n. Let I_n be the number of points in the grid used for blocklength n. Let

$$L(n) = \max \{n, \lceil \log I_n \rceil\}$$

and $N = nL(n)$. The encoder works with super sourcewords of blocklength N. It uses all N source symbols to choose the source subcode $\mathscr{C}^{(i)}$, and then encodes sourcewords of blocklength n using that subcode. It requires $L(n)$ codewords to encode all N source symbols, and these are concatenated and adjoined to a preamble to form the codeword for the N source symbols. The preamble is a unique block of length $\lceil \log I_n \rceil$ bits that identifies the subcode $\mathscr{C}^{(i)}$.

To choose the subcode, the encoder tests every subcode by encoding all $L(n)$ sourcewords of blocklength n, and then chooses the subcode with the smallest total codeword length.

Let $\mathbf{y} = (\mathbf{x}_1,\mathbf{x}_2,\mathbf{x}_3,\ldots,\mathbf{x}_{L(n)})$ be the super sourceword of blocklength N composed of $L(n)$ blocks, each of blocklength n. The codeword length is

$$l_N(\mathbf{y}|\theta) = \lceil \log I_n \rceil + \min_{\mathscr{C}^{(i)}} \left[\sum_{j=1}^{L(n)} l_n^{(i)}(\mathbf{x}_j) \right]$$

and the expected codeword length is

$$\bar{l}_N(\mathbf{y}|\theta) = \sum_y l_N(\mathbf{y}|\theta)p^N(\mathbf{y}|\theta)$$

$$\leq \lceil \log I_n \rceil + \sum_{j=1}^{L(n)} p^n(\mathbf{x}_j|\theta)l_n^{(i)}(\mathbf{x}_j)$$

$$\leq L(n) + L(n)[nH_n(\theta) + 2]$$

where the last inequality follows from Theorem 3.7.2 and from the definition of $L(n)$. Consequently,

$$\bar{l}_N(\mathbf{y}|\theta) \leq L(n)[nH_n(\theta) + 3]$$

$$= N\left[H_n(\theta) + \frac{3}{n}\right]$$

Because the average codeword length cannot be smaller than the entropy, we now have

$$H_n(\theta) \leq \frac{1}{N}\bar{l}_N(\mathbf{y}|\theta) \leq H_n(\theta) + \frac{3}{n}$$

from which the theorem follows.   □

PROBLEMS

3.1. A random experiment has seven outcomes with probabilities 1/3, 1/3, 1/9, 1/9, 1/27, 1/27, and 1/27. The experiment is to be performed once and the outcome transmitted across the country. The telegraph company provides two services. Service 1 transmits binary digits at $2.00 per digit. Service 2 transmits ternary digits at $3.25 per digit. You are to select a service and design a code to minimize expected cost.
  a. Which service should be selected?
  b. What code should be used?
  c. What is the expected cost?
  d. If the ternary cost is changed, at what value of new cost would you change your mind?
  e. Suppose the experiment is to be repeated a large number of times. How do the above answers change?

3.2. A simple computer executes four instructions called ADD, SUB, MPY, and STO, which are designated by the codewords 00, 01, 10, and 11.
  a. Based on an examination of a number of computer programs, it is decided that the instruction types are used independently with probabilities 3/4, 1/16, 1/16, and 1/8. By what percentage could the average number of bits used for the instruction code be reduced by the use of a more elaborate code?
  b. Construct a Huffman code to encode a sequence of instruction codes.
  c. Now suppose a better model is constructed wherein the instruction sequence is a first-order Markov source with transition matrix and equilibrium

probability distribution

$$
P = \begin{bmatrix} \frac{13}{16} & 0 & \frac{1}{4} & 1 \\ \frac{1}{16} & 0 & \frac{1}{4} & 0 \\ \frac{1}{16} & 0 & \frac{1}{4} & 0 \\ \frac{1}{16} & 1 & \frac{1}{4} & 0 \end{bmatrix} \qquad p = \begin{bmatrix} \frac{3}{4} \\ \frac{1}{16} \\ \frac{1}{16} \\ \frac{1}{8} \end{bmatrix}
$$

(Note that $p_j = \sum_i P_{j|i} p_i$, as is required for the equilibrium distribution.) Using the model, repeat part **a**.

d. Construct a Huffman code for blocks of length 2.

3.3. An (n,k) block code can be turned into a prefix code by compacting some sourcewords of length n into $k + 1$ bits and the remaining sourcewords of length n into $n + 1$ bits as follows. If the sourceword is a typical sequence, compact it as a block code and append a single 1 as a preamble to flag it as a compacted sequence. If the sourceword is not a typical sequence, append to it a single 0 as a preamble to flag it as a noncompacted sequence. Prove that this code can compact to rates arbitrarily close to the source entropy, that every source output is recovered exactly, and that a concatenated stream of such codewords is uniquely decodable.

3.4. (A source converse theorem) Use Fano's inequality (to be proved in Chapter 5) to prove that any block code for source compaction with M codewords that encodes memoryless sourcewords of blocklength n has a probability of decoding failure p_e that satisfies

$$
p_e \geq \frac{H(\mathbf{p}) - R}{R} - \frac{1}{nR}
$$

where $R = (1/n) \log M$. An analogous converse statement for data transmission codes is known as the Wolfowitz converse.

3.5. Either prove that the following code is uniquely decodable or give an ambiguous concatenated sequence of codewords.

c_0: 101

c_1: 0011

c_2: 1001

c_3: 1110

c_4: 00001

c_5: 11001

c_6: 11100

c_7: 010100

3.6. A bridge deck is a set of 52 distinguishable objects called cards. A bridge hand is any subset containing 13 elements. A bridge deal is any partition of the bridge deck into four bridge hands. A simple but inefficient representation for a bridge hand assigns a unique 6-bit binary number to represent each card. Then a 78-bit message represents each hand. (A communication engineer would call this pulse code modulation—PCM.)

    a. Show that no binary representation of an arbitrary bridge hand can use less than approximately $52H_b(\frac{1}{4})$ bits (≈ 42 bits). Give a representation using 52 bits.

    b. Show that no representation of an arbitrary bridge deal can use less than approximately 104 bits. Give a representation using 104 bits.

    c. Show that a pair of bridge hands requires approximately 78 bits to describe. Give a representation using 78 bits.

3.7. Prove that entropy is not increased by processing. ("The uncertainty in the answer is not greater than the uncertainty in the data.")

3.8. Consider the following well-known problem: Given a pan balance and 12 pool balls of which one may be either too light or too heavy, find a method of determining with three uses of the balance which ball, if any, is faulty and whether it is too light or too heavy.

    a. Give an information-theoretic argument that suggests the problem may be solvable, that is, that the number of possible outcomes of the measurement is sufficient.

    b. What is the solution to the problem?

    c. Suppose now that there are 13 balls plus an additional ball that is known to be good. Repeat parts **a** and **b** for this problem.

    d. Give an information-theoretic argument to the effect that the task is impossible with three uses of the balance if there are 14 balls.

    e. Suppose there are 13 balls but no extra good ball. Either solve the problem or else prove there is no solution.

3.9. Let $p_0 = 1/2$, $p_1 = 1/4$, $p_2 = p_3 = 1/8$. Show that a sequence with blocklength $12m$ and composition $(5m, 5m, m, m)$ is weakly δ-typical for all δ, but is not strongly δ-typical for any sufficiently small δ.

3.10. A binary symmetric Markov source has two output symbols, a_0 and a_1; the probability of repeating a symbol is ρ and the probability of changing the symbol is $1 - \rho$.

    a. What is the information content of this source?

    b. Let $\rho = 0.25$. Construct a Huffman code that encodes sourcewords of blocklength 3 using a binary code alphabet. The source is taken as equiprobable on the first letter of each block.

    c. What is the average blocklength per symbol? How does this compare with the best possible average blocklength per symbol?

3.11. Prove that a Shannon code is a prefix code. What is the maximum codeword length? Give an example of a source for which the Shannon code and the Huffman code are different.

3.12. **a.** A binary memoryless source has probability 0.9 of producing a 0 and probability 0.1 of producing a 1. Construct a $(5, 4)$ block code for data compaction by forming a look-up table for the encoder.

    b. What is the probability of the source producing a nonencodable block?

    c. What would be the probability of a nonencodable block if a $(7, 5)$ code were used instead?

    d. Repeat part **c** for a $(14, 9)$ code. How does the code rate compare?

3.13. A source has four output letters with probabilities $p(a_0) = 1/2$, $p(a_1) = 1/4$, $p(a_2) = 1/8$, and $p(a_3) = 1/8$. Does the Elias code for this source coincide with a Huffman code for this source? State a general principle of correspondence.

3.14. Is every strongly δ-typical sequence also a weakly δ-typical sequence? If not, can one define δ' such that every strongly δ-typical sequence is also a weakly δ'-typical sequence?

3.15. Reprove Theorem 3.5.4 by using a Lagrange multiplier s (described in Appendix A) to handle the constraint $H(\hat{p}) = R$ and a Lagrange multiplier λ to handle the constraint $\sum_j p_j = 1$.

NOTES

The formal treatment of sources using the methods of this chapter was introduced by Shannon (1948). He realized that the entropy is the basic measure of the information content of a source, and explained this notion for both memoryless sources and Markov sources. The source coding theorem for block codes was proved by Shannon. The general proof that the Kraft inequality applies to any uniquely decodable code was given by McMillan (1956), and improved by Karush (1961). The relationship of entropy to the number of typical sequences as expressed by the asymptotic equipartition property was developed by Shannon (1948) and McMillan (1953), with later refinements by Breiman (1957).

Entropy was recognized to play a central role in ergodic theory by Kolmogorov (1958). A central theorem of ergodic theory tells us that if two stationary sources have the same entropy, then they have very deep similarities. This is the celebrated isomorphism theorem of Ornstein (1970). Conversely, the Kolmogorov (1958)-Sinai (1959) theorem says that two stationary sources with different entropy are very different.

The development of practical codes for data compaction has a rich history, and work has accelerated recently because of the needs of modern telecommunication and data-storage systems. Huffman (1952) gave a construction for practical codes. Because his class of codes could asymptotically achieve the entropy, many thought the problem was closed. However, more recent work has given a large variety of codes from which users can choose according to their special needs. The tree codes based on real arithmetic were introduced by unpublished work of Elias, which was further developed by Jelinek (1968). We have presented a practical version of the Elias code developed by Pasco (1976) and improved by Jones (1981). Tree codes were pushed to the forefront by Rissanen (1976), who realized their great potential and that the practical defects of the Elias code could be overcome.

Asymptotic error bounds on the performance of block codes for memoryless sources were studied by Jelinek (1968) and by Csiszár and Longo (1971), and for Markov sources by Davisson, Longo, and Sgarro (1981). Universal codes for data compaction were studied by Fitingoff (1966) and Davisson (1973).

CHAPTER 4

Testing Hypotheses

ypothesis testing is the task of deciding which of two hypotheses is true. The decision is based on a measurement (or a set of measurements) that is characterized by a probability distribution on the space of possible measurement outcomes. A *decision rule* is a prescription for deciding which of the two hypotheses is true, based on the outcome of the measurement. The optimum decision rule is given by the Neyman-Pearson theorem, which is a central theorem of hypothesis testing.

This chapter discusses hypothesis testing using the discrimination function as the basic measure of the information contained in the measurement. We study hypothesis testing because it is important and interesting in its own right, and also because the methods used to study hypothesis testing will be used later in the study of data transmission codes.

4.1 THE NEYMAN-PEARSON THEOREM

The simplest problem of decision theory is the problem of testing a simple hypothesis by means of a simple measurement. Two hypotheses H_0 and H_1 (usually called the *null hypothesis* and the *alternative hypothesis*) are given, one of which is true. The problem is to decide which hypothesis is true by collecting and processing data. We suppose that the data is random and described by a probability distribution that depends on which hypothesis is true. Even though the set of data may actually be quite extensive, it is enough for us to start out thinking of it as a measurement whose outcome can only be an element of a set of K elements called the *measurement space* and indexed by k. Of course, K could be a very large number, perhaps corresponding to many disk memories full of data. The number of possible measurement outcomes K can be exponential in the size of the data record. A set of measurements described by m bits can take on any of 2^m values, which is inconceivably large if m runs into the millions. Thus to say that K is finite is not to say that the hypothesis-testing problem is simple. Of course, a large set of measurements usually has considerable structure, often consisting of many repetitions of a simple noisy measurement. This case is included in our analysis of the simple hypothesis-testing problem because it amounts to replacing the scalar measurement by a vector measurement, as we shall see later.

Associated with each of the two simple hypotheses is a probability distribution on the measurement space with K elements. If H_0 is true, then q_{0k} gives the probability that k will be the measurement outcome; if H_1 is true, then q_{1k} gives this probability. In order to avoid the possibility of division by zero, we will always assume, unless explicitly stated otherwise, that q_{0k} and q_{1k} are strictly positive for all k, though possibly quite small. What this amounts to is that we do not consider problems in which a decision can be made with absolute certainty.

A simple measurement consists of an observation of one realization of the random variable. A measurement value k is observed, and the problem is to decide whether hypothesis H_0 or hypothesis H_1 is true. For some values of k, the decision will be that H_0 is true; for other values of k, the decision will be that H_1 is true. We can imagine a decision rule as two lists of the values of k for which each decision is made. More formally, a hypothesis-testing rule is a partition of the measurement space into two disjoint sets $\mathcal{U}_0$ and $\mathcal{U}_1 = \mathcal{U}_0^c$. If the measurement k is an element of $\mathcal{U}_0$, we decide that H_0 is true; if k is an element of $\mathcal{U}_1$, we decide that H_1 is true. Each partition is a different hypothesis-testing rule, and, except for randomized rules which we do not consider, there are no other rules. We should use the best hypothesis-testing rule, but first we must agree on what is meant by the "best" rule. Even then, when k is very large, as it often is in practice, there will be some difficulty in applying a given rule. One cannot enumerate in a table all possible values of k; a computational procedure must be used.

Accepting hypothesis H_1 when H_0 actually is true is called a *type I error*, and the probability of this event is denoted by α. Accepting hypothesis H_0 when H_1 actually is true is called a *type II error*, and the probability of this event is denoted by β.[†] Obviously

$$\alpha = \sum_{k \in \mathcal{U}_1} q_{0k} \qquad \beta = \sum_{k \in \mathcal{U}_0} q_{1k}$$

The problem is to specify $(\mathcal{U}_0, \mathcal{U}_1)$ so that α and β are as small as possible. This is not yet a well-defined problem because α generally can be made smaller by reducing $\mathcal{U}_1$, although β thereby increases. The Neyman-Pearson point of view assumes that a maximum value of β given by $\bar{\beta}$ is specified and $(\mathcal{U}_0, \mathcal{U}_1)$ must be determined so as to minimize α subject to the constraint that β is not larger than $\bar{\beta}$. Usually the constraint on β cannot be satisfied with equality, since β is obtained by adding a finite set of numbers.

A method for finding the optimum decision regions is given by the following theorem. The decision regions are specified in terms of a parameter T called a *threshold*; α and β are then functions of T.

□   **Theorem 4.1.1   (Neyman-Pearson theorem)** For any real number T, let

$$\mathcal{U}_0(T) = \{k : q_{1k} \leq q_{0k} e^{-T}\}$$

$$\mathcal{U}_1(T) = \{k : q_{1k} > q_{0k} e^{-T}\}$$

and let α^* and β^* be the probabilities of type I and type II error corresponding to this choice of decision regions. Suppose α and β are the probabilities of type I and type II errors corresponding to some other choice of decision regions and suppose $\alpha < \alpha^*$. Then $\beta > \beta^*$.

Proof   Let $(\mathcal{U}'_0, \mathcal{U}'_1)$ be any other decision procedure such that $\alpha < \alpha^*$. Define the indicator functions on k: $\phi_k = 1$ if $k \in \mathcal{U}_1(T)$ and otherwise $\phi_k = 0$; $\phi'_k = 1$ if $k \in \mathcal{U}'_1$ and otherwise $\phi'_k = 0$. Then

$$(\phi_k - \phi'_k)(q_{1k} - q_{0k} e^{-T}) \geq 0$$

for all k, which can be verified by separately examining the cases $k \in \mathcal{U}_0(T)$ and $k \in \mathcal{U}_1(T)$. Therefore

$$\sum_k (\phi_k - \phi'_k)(q_{1k} - q_{0k} e^{-T}) \geq 0$$

$$\sum_k q_{1k}\phi_k - \sum_k q_{1k}\phi'_k \geq e^{-T} \sum_k q_{0k}\phi_k - e^{-T} \sum_k q_{0k}\phi'_k$$

Hence

$$(1 - \beta^*) - (1 - \beta) \geq e^{-T}(\alpha^* - \alpha) > 0$$

Therefore $(\beta - \beta^*) > 0$, as was to be proved.   □

[†]It is unfortunately confusing that the errors are denoted type I and type II, while the hypotheses are subscripted 0 and 1. The word "type" is also used in another sense to refer to the type of a measurement or the type of a vector.

Notice that because the theorem does not explicitly define β^* as a function of α^*, but rather expresses the optimum pair $\alpha^*(T)$, $\beta^*(T)$ parametrically, many values of the threshold T must be examined in order to find the smallest α^* satisfying the constraint $\beta^* \leq \bar{\beta}$. This can best be done by constructing a graph of $\alpha^*(T)$ versus $\beta^*(T)$ parametrically in T. Parametric solutions such as this occur throughout information theory.

The Neyman-Pearson decision regions can be rewritten in the form

$$\mathcal{U}_0(T) = \mathcal{U}_1(T)^c = \left\{ k : \log \frac{q_{0k}}{q_{1k}} \geq T \right\}$$

This form is convenient in so many problems that the logarithmic term is given a special name.

☐ **Definition 4.1.2**   The *log-likelihood ratio* is given by

$$\Lambda(k) = \log \frac{q_{0k}}{q_{1k}} \qquad\qquad ☐$$

We then say simply that H_0 is true if the log-likelihood ratio is at least as large as the threshold T. It is clear that $\Lambda(k)$—or any monotonic function of $\Lambda(k)$—is the significant function in the Neyman-Pearson theorem rather than the probability distributions individually.

Suppose now that the measurement k is, in fact, a block of independent measurements of blocklength n called a *dataword*. In that case we think of the dataword as a vector of measurements. We write the vector measurement as an n-tuple of simple measurements:

$$\mathbf{y} = (k_1, \ldots, k_n)$$

where k_l indexes the value of the lth measurement. The vector $\mathbf{y}$ itself can take on only a finite number of values because each component can take on only a finite number of values. All of the theory holds just as before. However, the vector structure enables us to break the problem into pieces. The log-likelihood ratio for $\mathbf{y}$ is

$$\Lambda(\mathbf{y}) = \log \frac{q_0(\mathbf{y})}{q_1(\mathbf{y})}$$

But, because the measurements are independent, the probability distributions of the vectors are products. If the components are also identically distributed, then

$$q_0(\mathbf{y}) = \prod_{l=1}^{n} q_{0k_l}$$

$$q_1(\mathbf{y}) = \prod_{l=1}^{n} q_{1k_l}$$

so the log-likelihood ratio for the vector measurement can be written as a sum of per-letter log-likelihood ratios of the component measurements. Thus we can write

$$\Lambda(\mathbf{y}) = \sum_{l=1}^{n} \log \frac{q_{0k_l}}{q_{1k_l}}$$

$$= \sum_{l=1}^{n} \Lambda(k_l)$$

Because the logarithm of a product is the sum of the logarithms, the log-likelihood ratio for the vector measurement is the sum of the log-likelihood ratios of the component measurements.

The Neyman-Pearson decision regions for the block measurement is then expressed in terms of $\Lambda(\mathbf{y})$, as compared with a threshold. For blocks of length n, it is convenient to express the threshold in a normalized form as nT. Thus

$$\mathcal{U}_0(T) = \{\mathbf{y} : \Lambda(\mathbf{y}) \geq nT\}$$

The same description of $\mathcal{U}_0(T)$ applies even when the measurements are not independent or identically distributed. In those cases, however, the log-likelihood ratio $\Lambda(\mathbf{y})$ cannot be simply written as the sum of per-letter log-likelihood ratios.

4.2. THE NORTH FILTER

Detection of a known, finite energy signal in additive gaussian noise is a simple but important problem in hypothesis testing. It occurs in most radar systems. This detector will be found to consist of a simple linear filter followed by a threshold, as shown in Fig. 4.1. The setup is essentially the same as for the hypothesis-testing problem in the previous section, except the "measurements" consist of noisy waveforms instead of elements of a finite set. In the next section, we will return to the discussion of hypothesis testing based on measurements in a finite space. This section presents a practical example of hypothesis testing and introduces mathematical techniques that will not be used again until Chapter 7. It can be skipped by those interested in neither the example nor the techniques.

The decision problem consists of two hypotheses concerning a measured waveform $v(t)$:

$$H_0 : v(t) = n(t) \qquad \text{(noise only)}$$

$$H_1 : v(t) = s(t) + n(t) \qquad \text{(signal plus noise)}$$

where the signal $s(t)$ is a known pulse of finite energy E_p, and the noise $n(t)$ is a stationary, zero-mean gaussian-noise process of known autocorrelation function $\phi(\tau) = E[n(t)n(t+\tau)]$ and power spectral density $N(f)$, which is the Fourier transform of $\phi(\tau)$.

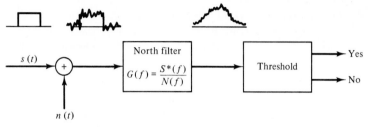

Figure 4.1   Detection of a pulse in gaussian noise.

We will need to find the likelihood function. Let $S(f)$ be the Fourier transform of the signal $s(t)$:

$$S(f) = \int_{-\infty}^{\infty} e^{-j2\pi ft} s(t)\, dt$$

The likelihood function will be expressed in terms of the filter with transfer function

$$G(f) = \frac{S^*(f)}{N(f)}$$

which is called the *North filter*, or the *matched filter*, for the pulse $s(t)$. Usually $G(f)$ is not causal. By incorporating a fixed time delay t', one can replace $G(f)$ with $G(f)e^{-j2\pi ft'}$ and then construct a suitable approximating filter that is causal. Causality is an important implementation consideration, but it does not interest us here.

To develop the maximum-likelihood detector of $s(t)$, we will expand the received signal $v(t)$ in terms of a set of orthonormal functions on an interval of time. One such expansion is a Fourier series expansion. Then the orthogonal functions are harmonically related sinusoids. The idea of the proof can be followed by visualizing a Fourier expansion. However, the Fourier expansion has the deficiency that the expansion coefficients v_k are not independent, so the log-likelihood ratio cannot be written as a simple sum. To be rigorous, we use a different expansion called a Karhunen-Loeve expansion for which the v_k are independent. The theory of a Karhunen-Loeve expansion is discussed in Appendix B. We will use Karhunen-Loeve expansions again in Chapter 7 to develop coding theorems for waveform channels and sources.

□   **Theorem 4.2.1**   The Neyman-Pearson decision rule for detecting a known pulse with spectrum $S(f)$ in stationary zero-mean gaussian noise of known power spectral density $N(f)$ is to pass $v(t)$ through the North filter with transfer function

$$G(f) = \frac{S^*(f)}{N(f)}$$

followed by a threshold test.

Proof   The received signal $v(t)$ equals $n(t)$ if it is noise only, and equals $s(t) + n(t)$ if it is signal plus noise. To find the log-likelihood ratio, restrict attention to a finite time interval $[-T/2, T/2]$ and expand the received signal $v(t)$ in terms of a set of orthonormal functions that span the interval.[†]

The Karhunen-Loeve expansion functions $\psi_i^{(T)}(t)$ are the orthonormal eigenfunctions of the integral equation

$$\int_{-T/2}^{T/2} \phi(t - s)\psi^{(T)}(s)\,ds = \lambda\psi^{(T)}(t) \qquad -T/2 \le t \le T/2$$

where $\phi(\tau)$ is the autocorrelation function of the noise. The Karhunen-Loeve expansion of the signal in noise then is

$$v(t) = \sum_{k=1}^{\infty} v_k \psi_k^{(T)}(t)$$

$$= \sum_{k=1}^{\infty} (s_k + n_k)\psi_k^{(T)}(t)$$

where $\psi_k^{(T)}(t)$ are the orthonormal expansion functions and v_k are the expansion coefficients. Now the waveform $v(t)$ is expressed in terms of a discrete set of expansion coefficients v_k for $k = 1, 2, \ldots$, that are independent gaussian random variables of variance λ_k and λ_k is the eigenvalue corresponding to the eigenfunction $\psi_k^{(T)}(t)$. Each expansion coefficient v_k consists of the sum of a noise component n_k and possibly a signal component s_k. The noise component is given by

$$n_k = \int_{-T/2}^{T/2} n(t)\psi_k^{(T)}(t)dt$$

Under hypothesis H_1, the mean of v_k is equal to s_k given by

$$s_k = \int_{-T/2}^{T/2} s(t)\psi_k^{(T)}(t)\,dt$$

and under hypothesis H_0, the mean of v_k is zero.

For each value of k, the measurement is now a gaussian random variable of variance λ_k, and with mean s_k if the signal is present. The log-likelihood ratio for component k is

$$\Lambda(k) = \frac{(v_k - s_k)^2}{2\lambda_k} - \frac{v_k^2}{2\lambda_k}$$

$$= \frac{-2v_k s_k + s_k^2}{2\lambda_k}$$

[†]The use of T to denote a time interval in this section should not be confused with the use of T to denote a threshold in the previous section.

The total log-likelihood ratio for the entire measurement $v(t)$ is

$$\sum_{k=1}^{\infty} \Lambda(k) = -\sum_{k=1}^{\infty} \frac{v_k s_k}{\lambda_k} + \frac{1}{2} \sum_{k=1}^{\infty} \frac{s_k^2}{\lambda_k}$$

The Neyman-Pearson theorem tells us that this log-likelihood ratio is to be compared with a threshold in order to decide between the two hypotheses. If

$$-\sum_{k=1}^{\infty} \frac{v_k s_k}{\lambda_k} + \frac{1}{2} \sum_{k=1}^{\infty} \frac{s_k^2}{\lambda_k} \geq T$$

then decide in favor of hypothesis H_0. The second term is a fixed constant independent of the actual received signal $v(t)$, so it can be absorbed into the threshold by redefining the threshold. Hence the decision rule for deciding in favor of H_0 is

$$\Lambda(v(t)) = \sum_{k=1}^{\infty} \frac{s_k}{\lambda_k} v_k \leq \theta$$

where θ is the redefined threshold and $\Lambda(v(t))$ is a redefined likelihood statistic, including a sign change throughout the inequality.

In order to rewrite the sum in a more useful form, we use Theorem B.2 of Appendix B. Let

$$w_k = \frac{s_k}{\lambda_k}$$

and

$$w(t) = \begin{cases} \sum_k w_k \psi_k^{(T)}(t) & -T/2 \leq t \leq T/2 \\ 0 & \text{otherwise} \end{cases}$$

By Theorem B.5, $w(t)$ satisfies

$$s(t) = \int_{-T/2}^{T/2} \phi(t - \tau) w(\tau)\, d\tau$$

and by Theorem B.2, $\Lambda(v(t))$ is given by

$$\sum_k w_k v_k = \int_{-T/2}^{T/2} w(t) v(t)\, dt$$

To complete the proof, let $T \to \infty$. Then

$$\Lambda(v(t)) = \int_{-\infty}^{\infty} w(t) v(t)\, dt$$

where $w(t)$ satisfies the convolution equation

$$s(t) = \int_{-\infty}^{\infty} \phi(t - \tau)w(\tau)\, d\tau$$

Thus

$$W(f) = \frac{S(f)}{N(f)}$$

To describe this as a filter, set $G(f) = W^*(f)$ so that

$$G(f) = \frac{S^*(f)}{N(f)}$$

and the filter output at time zero is

$$\Lambda(v(t)) = \int_{-\infty}^{\infty} g(-t)v(t)\, dt$$

as was to be proved. $\square$

To complete the analysis of the North filter detector, we must evaluate the probabilities of error α and β. For the detection problem, α is called the *probability of false alarm* and is the probability that the filter output exceeds the threshold θ when the input is noise only. Similarly, β is called the *probability of missed detection* and is the probability that the filter output does not exceed the threshold θ when the input is signal plus noise.

The matched filter collapses the received waveform $v(t)$ into a single number—the likelihood statistic $\Lambda(v(t))$. We need to determine the probability distribution of $\Lambda(v(t))$ under H_0 and under H_1. Under hypothesis H_1,

$$\Lambda(v(t)) = \int_{-\infty}^{\infty} g(-t)[s(t) + n(t)]\, dt$$

with mean

$$\bar{\Lambda} = \int_{-\infty}^{\infty} g(-t)s(t)\, dt$$

and variance

$$\sigma^2 = E\left[\int_{-\infty}^{\infty} g(-t)n(t)\, dt\right]^2$$

$$= \int_{-\infty}^{\infty} \int_{-\infty}^{\infty} g(-t')g(-t'')E[n(t')n(t'')]\, dt'\, dt''$$

$$= \int_{-\infty}^{\infty} \int_{-\infty}^{\infty} g(-t')g(-t'')\phi(t' - t'')\, dt'\, dt''$$

Under hypothesis H_0 the mean is zero and the variance is the same as the variance under hypothesis H_1.

The most common noise model is white gaussian noise, which is gaussian noise with correlation function

$$\phi(\tau) = \frac{N_o}{2} \delta(\tau)$$

where the delta function $\delta(\tau)$ is understood in the sense of a distribution as an operator defined by

$$x(\tau) = \int_{-\infty}^{\infty} x(t)\delta(t - \tau)dt$$

In the frequency domain, white gaussian noise has spectrum

$$N(f) = \frac{N_o}{2}$$

Then the North filter is

$$G(f) = \frac{2S^*(f)}{N_o}$$

so in the time domain $g(-t)$ is a multiple of $s(t)$, and

$$\bar{\Lambda} = \frac{2}{N_o} \int_{-\infty}^{\infty} s(t)^2 dt$$

$$= \frac{2E_p}{N_o}$$

The variance is

$$\sigma^2 = \left(\frac{2}{N_o}\right)^2 \int_{-\infty}^{\infty} \int_{-\infty}^{\infty} s(t')s(t'') \frac{N_o}{2} \delta(t' - t'')\, dt'\, dt''$$

$$= \frac{2}{N_o} \int_{-\infty}^{\infty} s(t)^2\, dt$$

$$= \frac{2}{N_o} E_p$$

Because the North filter is linear with gaussian noise at the input, the output must also be gaussian, and we have found its mean and variance. Therefore the probability distributions on Λ under H_0 and H_1 are

$$p_0(\Lambda) = \frac{1}{\sqrt{2\pi}\sigma} e^{-\Lambda^2/2\sigma^2}$$

$$p_1(\Lambda) = \frac{1}{\sqrt{2\pi}\sigma} e^{-(\Lambda - \bar{\Lambda})^2/2\sigma^2}$$

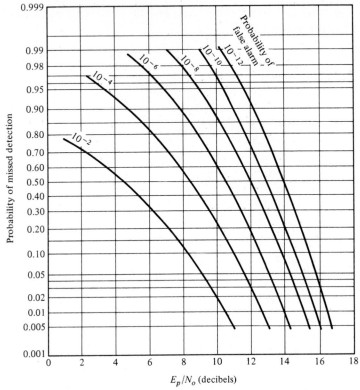

Figure 4.2   Performance of pulse detection in additive gaussian noise.

The probability of type I error and the probability of type II error are given by

$$\alpha = \int_{\theta}^{\infty} p_0(\Lambda)\,d\Lambda$$

$$\beta = \int_{-\infty}^{\theta} p_1(\Lambda)\,d\Lambda$$

These integrals depend only on the ratio E_p/N_o and the threshold θ. By crossplotting $\alpha(\theta)$ and $\beta(\theta)$, the threshold can be eliminated. The performance of the detector is shown in Fig. 4.2, with E_p/N_o expressed in decibels.[†] The performance depends only on the ratio E_p/N_o, not on the detailed structure of $s(t)$.

†The decibel is a logarithmic specification of a power ratio defined by

$$\frac{E_p}{N_o}\ (\text{decibels}) = 10\log_{10}\frac{E_p}{N_o}$$

4.3 THE DISCRIMINATION FUNCTION

The expected value of the log-likelihood ratio $l(k)$ with respect to $\mathbf{q}_0$ is a function known as the *discrimination*. For a finite measurement space, it is

$$L(\mathbf{q}_0; \mathbf{q}_1) = \sum_{k=0}^{K-1} q_{0k} \log \frac{q_{0k}}{q_{1k}}$$

$$= \sum_{k=0}^{K-1} q_{0k} l(k)$$

The discrimination is useful for forming bounds on the probability of error in the hypothesis-testing problem. It appears frequently in the subject of information theory. Occasionally, for convenience, we may write $L(Y_0; Y_1)$ when we mean $L(\mathbf{q}_0; \mathbf{q}_1)$ where Y_0 and Y_1 are random variables associated with $\mathbf{q}_0$ and $\mathbf{q}_1$.

Sometimes a symmetrical form known as the *divergence* and defined by

$$\bar{L}(\mathbf{q}_0; \mathbf{q}_1) = L(\mathbf{q}_0; \mathbf{q}_1) + L(\mathbf{q}_1; \mathbf{q}_0)$$

is used in place of the discrimination. The divergence inherits most of the properties of the discrimination. The symmetric form may appear more fundamental, but actually we will have little need for it.

The choice of logarithm base in the discrimination (and in the log-likelihood ratio) is arbitrary. Natural logs are more convenient for developing the theory, and normally will be used here, with the discrimination given in units of nats. Base-2 logarithms are usually preferred for numerical examples, with the discrimination then given in units of bits. We often will write expressions of the form $e^{L(\mathbf{q}_0; \mathbf{q}_1)}$ when L is measured in nats, with the understanding that if some other unit is used for the discrimination, then e can be replaced by the proper logarithm base.[†]

It may be that some side information is available that affects the given probability distributions. Or, to put the same thing another way, it may be that there are J different types of measurement indexed by j that can be made, and the side information tells which kind was actually made. In such cases, the probability distributions become conditional probability distributions of the form $q_{0k|j}$ and $q_{1k|j}$, and the discrimination becomes dependent on an additional parameter. The *conditional discrimination* is a family of functions indexed by a parameter j and given by

$$L(\mathbf{q}_0; \mathbf{q}_1 | j) = \sum_{k} q_{0k|j} \log \frac{q_{0k|j}}{q_{1k|j}}$$

where $\mathbf{q}_0 = \{q_{0k|j}\}$ and $\mathbf{q}_1 = \{q_{1k|j}\}$ are the probabilities of measurement outcome k, given measurement type j under hypothesis H_0 and H_1, respectively. If measurement type j occurs with probability p_j, then we define

[†]For this purpose, the identity $\log_c a = \log_c b \cdot \log_b a$ is useful. There are $\log_e 2$, or 0.6931, nats per bit.

the *expected discrimination*

$$L(\mathbf{q}_0; \mathbf{q}_1 | \mathbf{p}) = \sum_j p_j L(\mathbf{q}_0; \mathbf{q}_1 | j)$$

We shall see that discrimination has many of the properties that one might expect for a measure of the amount of information in a measurement.

☐ **Theorem 4.3.1**   Discrimination is nonnegative, and equal to zero if and only if its arguments are equal.

Proof The proof is a simple application of the inequality $\log x \geq 1 - (1/x)$:

$$L(\mathbf{q}_0; \mathbf{q}_1) = \sum_k q_{0k} \log \frac{q_{0k}}{q_{1k}} \geq \sum_k q_{0k}\left(1 - \frac{q_{1k}}{q_{0k}}\right)$$

$$= \sum_k q_{0k} - \sum_k q_{1k} = 0 \qquad\qquad ☐$$

☐ **Theorem 4.3.2**   Discrimination is convex in each of its arguments. That is, given $\lambda \in [0, 1]$ and $\bar{\lambda} = 1 - \lambda$,

$$L(\lambda \mathbf{q}_0' + \bar{\lambda} \mathbf{q}_0''; \mathbf{q}_1) \leq \lambda L(\mathbf{q}_0'; \mathbf{q}_1) + \bar{\lambda} L(\mathbf{q}_0''; \mathbf{q}_1)$$

$$L(\mathbf{q}_0; \lambda \mathbf{q}_1' + \bar{\lambda} \mathbf{q}_1'') \leq \lambda L(\mathbf{q}_0; \mathbf{q}_1') + \bar{\lambda} L(\mathbf{q}_0; \mathbf{q}_1'')$$

Proof The second inequality follows directly from the concavity of the logarithm. The first inequality is proved by an argument using the inequality $\log x \leq x - 1$ that will frequently reappear. Let $\mathbf{q}^* = \lambda \mathbf{q}_0' + \bar{\lambda} \mathbf{q}_0''$. Then

$$L(\mathbf{q}^*; \mathbf{q}_1) - \lambda L(\mathbf{q}_0'; \mathbf{q}_1) - \bar{\lambda} L(\mathbf{q}_0''; \mathbf{q}_1)$$

$$= \lambda \sum_k q_{0k}' \log \frac{q_k^*}{q_{0k}'} + \bar{\lambda} \sum_k q_{0k}'' \log \frac{q_k^*}{q_{0k}''}$$

$$\leq \lambda \sum_k (q_{0k}' - q_k^*) + \bar{\lambda} \sum_k (q_{0k}'' - q_k^*)$$

$$= 0 \qquad\qquad ☐$$

Our everyday notion of information tells us that information is increased if a measurement is made more precise, or at least the information is not decreased. Discrimination shares this behavior. Suppose that each point k in the space of measurement outcomes is replaced by several new points, with the probabilities q_{0k} and q_{1k} of the original point apportioned among the new points. This is called a *refinement* of the set of measurement outcomes. A refinement is a nontrivial refinement if, for at least one point k, the probabilities q_{0k} and q_{1k} are divided in different proportions.

☐ **Theorem 4.3.3** Discrimination is increased by a nontrivial refinement of a set of measurement outcomes.

Proof Let i index the original points and let k index the new points. Let $\mathscr{U}_i$ be the set of k into which i was subdivided; let $\mathbf{Q}_0, \mathbf{Q}_1$ be the probability distributions on the original points; and let $\mathbf{q}_0, \mathbf{q}_1$ be the probability distributions on the new points. Then

$$\sum_k q_{0k} \log \frac{q_{0k}}{q_{1k}} - \sum_i Q_{0i} \log \frac{Q_{0i}}{Q_{1i}}$$

$$= \sum_i \sum_{k \in \mathscr{U}_i} q_{0k} \log \frac{q_{0k}}{q_{1k}} - \sum_i \sum_{k \in \mathscr{U}_i} q_{0k} \log \frac{Q_{0i}}{Q_{1i}}$$

$$= \sum_i \sum_{k \in \mathscr{U}_i} q_{0k} \log \frac{q_{0k} Q_{1i}}{q_{1k} Q_{0i}}$$

$$\geq \sum_i \sum_{k \in \mathscr{U}_i} \left(q_{0k} - q_{1k} \frac{Q_{0i}}{Q_{1i}} \right)$$

$$= 0$$

The inequality is a strict inequality unless the probabilities Q_{0i}, Q_{1i} for each point i are divided among the new points in the same proportion:

$$\frac{q_{0k}}{q_{1k}} = \frac{Q_{0i}}{Q_{1i}}$$

for all k in the set $\mathscr{U}_i$.   ☐

A refinement of a space is actually the opposite of processing. From the information-theoretic point of view, processing is merely a map from the space of all possible measurements onto the space of all possible answers. Usually it is a many-to-one map. The measurement space can be viewed as a refinement of the space of possible answers.

☐ **Corollary 4.3.4** The information in a measurement as defined by the discrimination cannot be increased by subsequent processing.

Proof View the processing output as a measurement and the processing input as a refinement.   ☐

A set of data often is processed in two steps, first mapping the space of all possible measurements onto a smaller space, then mapping this interim space onto the space of all possible answers. The intermediate space is called a *statistic*. Sometimes there is no loss in discrimination in computing the statistic; the statistic summarizes the whole of the relevant information supplied by the measurement. This is then an important statistic and has a special name. A *sufficient statistic* (for discriminating H_0 from H_1) is a statistic for which the discrimination is the same as that of the raw data. The log-likelihood ratio is a sufficient statistic for hypothesis testing.

The discrimination is a function of two probability distributions. When the measurement space contains only two points, each of the two distributions is defined by a single number. To simplify discussion of this case, we define the *binary discrimination* as a function of two real numbers, with domain the unit square.

☐   **Definition 4.3.5**   The *binary discrimination* is a function of two real numbers $0 \le \alpha \le 1$ and $0 \le \beta \le 1$ given by

$$L_b(\alpha, \beta) = \alpha \log \frac{\alpha}{\beta} + (1 - \alpha) \log \frac{1 - \alpha}{1 - \beta}$$ ☐

The binary discrimination is convex in each variable and is equal to zero when α equals β.

Now consider the usefulness of side information in a measurement. We would like to say that, in some sense, additional side information never hurts. Suppose that a hypothesis-testing problem is conditional on j, which itself occurs with probability p_j. If j is known, then the probability distributions have components $q_{0k|j}$ and $q_{1k|j}$. If j is unknown, then the probability distributions describing the problem are given by the averages

$$\bar{q}_{0k} = \sum_j p_j q_{0k|j}$$

$$\bar{q}_{1k} = \sum_j p_j q_{1k|j}$$

and the appropriate discrimination is

$$L(\bar{\mathbf{q}}_0; \bar{\mathbf{q}}_1) = \sum_k \bar{q}_{0k} \log \frac{\bar{q}_{0k}}{\bar{q}_{1k}}$$

whereas, if j can be determined prior to computing the discrimination, then the expected discrimination

$$L(\mathbf{q}_0; \mathbf{q}_1 | \mathbf{p}) = \sum_j p_j \sum_k q_{0k|j} \log \frac{q_{0k|j}}{q_{1k|j}}$$

is appropriate.

☐   **Theorem 4.3.6**   Expected discrimination is nondecreasing under conditioning (side information).

Proof

$$\sum_j p_j \sum_k q_{0k|j} \log \frac{q_{0k|j}}{q_{1k|j}} - \sum_k \bar{q}_{0k} \log \frac{\bar{q}_{0k}}{\bar{q}_{1k}}$$

$$= \sum_j \sum_k p_j q_{0k|j} \log \frac{q_{0k|j}\bar{q}_{1k}}{q_{1k|j}\bar{q}_{0k}}$$

$$\geq \sum_j \sum_k p_j q_{0k|j} \left(1 - \frac{q_{1k|j}\bar{q}_{0k}}{q_{0k|j}\bar{q}_{1k}} \right)$$

$$= 1 - \sum_k \frac{\bar{q}_{0k}}{\bar{q}_{1k}} \sum_j p_j q_{1k|j}$$

$$= 0 \qquad \qquad \square$$

It is in the sense of the average given by this theorem that side information is useful. In an individual case it may be that side information is detrimental; there may be some j such that

$$\sum_k q_{0k|j} \log \frac{q_{0k|j}}{q_{1k|j}} < \sum_k \bar{q}_{0k} \log \frac{\bar{q}_{0k}}{\bar{q}_{1k}}$$

What this means is that sometimes the side information may make the false hypothesis appear more likely. Side information is only useful on the average.

We will spend a lot of time dealing with blocks of measurements. The next two theorems relate the discrimination in a block of measurements to the discrimination of the individual measurements.

□ **Theorem 4.3.7** (Additivity) Discrimination is additive for random measurements that are independent under both probability distributions.

Proof The proof is essentially the same as the proof of Theorem 3.2.2. Suppose the lth measurement has K outcomes indexed by k_l with probability distributions $\mathbf{q}_{0l}$ and $\mathbf{q}_{1l}$ under hypotheses H_0 and H_1 respectively. Then the discrimination of the block is

$$L(\mathbf{q}_0^n; \mathbf{q}_1^n) = \sum_{k_1} \sum_{k_2} \cdots \sum_{k_n} \left(\prod_{l=1}^n q_{0k_l} \right) \left[\sum_{l=1}^n \log \frac{q_{0k_l}}{q_{1k_l}} \right]$$

$$= \sum_{l=1}^n \left[\sum_{k_l} q_{0k_l} \log \frac{q_{0k_l}}{q_{1k_l}} \right]$$

$$= \sum_{l=1}^n L(\mathbf{q}_{0l}; \mathbf{q}_{1l})$$

which completes the proof.   □

An immediate consequence of the theorem is that the discrimination for n independent, identically distributed measurements is n times the discrimination for an individual measurement. Let $\mathbf{y} = (k_1, \ldots, k_n)$ denote a block of n independent, identically distributed measurements. Then the discrimination for the block measurement can be expressed as

$$L(\mathbf{q}_0^n; \mathbf{q}_1^n) = \sum_\mathbf{y} q_0(\mathbf{y}) \log \frac{q_0(\mathbf{y})}{q_1(\mathbf{y})}$$

$$= nL(\mathbf{q}_0; \mathbf{q}_1)$$

If we have n nonidentical but independent measurements drawn from a set of J measurement types then we must use a more complex statement for the same idea. As before, we have

$$L(\mathbf{q}_0^n; \mathbf{q}_1^n) = \sum_\mathbf{y} q_0(\mathbf{y}) \left[\sum_{l=1}^{n} \Lambda(k_l) \right]$$

but now the terms in the sum correspond to measurements of different types. Let n_j be the number of measurements of type j, and let $p_j = n_j/n$. The vector $\{n_j\}$ is called the *composition* of the dataword $\mathbf{y}$. The probability-like vector $\mathbf{p}$ is called the *relative frequency* or the *relative composition* of $\mathbf{y}$ or, when there is no ambiguity, simply the composition of $\mathbf{y}$. The average discrimination is defined by

$$L(\mathbf{q}_0; \mathbf{q}_1 | \mathbf{p}) = \sum_j p_j L(\mathbf{q}_0; \mathbf{q}_1 | j)$$

$$= \sum_j p_j \sum_k q_{0k|j} \log \frac{q_{0k|j}}{q_{1k|j}}$$

The total discrimination for the n measurements is then n times this average discrimination. The average discrimination under composition $\mathbf{p}$ is identical to expected discrimination under a random measurement with probability distribution $\mathbf{p}$.

When the measurements in a block are not independent, then one can make no general statement relating the discrimination in the block to the discriminations in the individual measurements. If, however, the measurements are independent under the second probability distribution, then we have an inequality relationship as expressed in the following theorem.

☐ **Theorem 4.3.8** If the measurements in a block are independent under probability distribution $\mathbf{q}_1$, then

$$L(\mathbf{q}_0^n; \mathbf{q}_1^n) \geq \sum_{l=1}^{n} L(\mathbf{q}_0^{(l)}; \mathbf{q}_1)$$

where $\mathbf{q}_0^{(l)}$ is the marginal probability distribution induced on the lth component of $\mathbf{y}$ by $\mathbf{q}_0^n$.

Proof

$$L(\mathbf{q}_0^n;\mathbf{q}_1^n) = -H(\mathbf{q}_0^n) - \sum_{\mathbf{y}} q_0(\mathbf{y}) \log q_1(\mathbf{y})$$

$$= -H(\mathbf{q}_0^n) - E\left[\log \prod_{l=1}^{n} q_1(y_l) \right]$$

$$= -H(\mathbf{q}_0^n) - \sum_{l=1}^{n} q_{0k_l}^{(l)} \log q_{1k_l}$$

By Theorem 3.2.3, we have the inequality

$$L(\mathbf{q}_0^n;\mathbf{q}_1^n) \geq - \sum_{l=1}^{n} H(\mathbf{q}_0^{(l)}) - \sum_{l=1}^{n} q_{0k_l}^{(l)} \log q_{1k_l}$$

$$= \sum_{l=1}^{n} L(\mathbf{q}_0^{(l)};\mathbf{q}_1)$$

as was to be proved. □

4.4 ELEMENTARY BOUNDS ON PERFORMANCE

Although the Neyman-Pearson theorem specifies optimum decision regions, it does not directly specify the performance in terms of type I and type II error. The probabilities of type I and type II error are given as sums possibly involving a large number of terms. These sums are such that they cannot be collapsed into more useful expressions that could be used to study behavior. Also, for large problems, it may not even be feasible to use a computer to add up all the terms in each sum. However, simple approximations can be derived. These approximations take the form of asymptotically tight upper and lower bounds on the probability of error. Aside from their use in numerical calculations, the bounds are valuable because they are expressed in terms of analytical functions. They are useful in studying how the probability of error depends on parameters such as the decision threshold or the number of measurements. This section is concerned with establishing the bounds relating α, β and the threshold T.

The measurement may be a sequence of n independent measurements. The sequence of independent measurements may be of the same type and characterized by identical probability distributions or may be of different types characterized by distributions that differ from measurement to measurement. The various theorems of this chapter can be stated and proved more concisely if the measurements are of the same type. Except for this, we are indifferent as to whether the measurements are of the same type or of different type, because the theorems and proofs are essentially the same.

◻ **Theorem 4.4.1**   For any binary partition $(\mathcal{U}_0, \mathcal{U}_1)$ of the space of measurements, the probability of type I error and the probability of type II error satisfy

$$L(\mathbf{q}_1; \mathbf{q}_0) \geq \beta \log \frac{\beta}{1 - \alpha} + (1 - \beta) \log \frac{1 - \beta}{\alpha}$$

Proof $(\mathcal{U}_0, \mathcal{U}_1)$ is a partition; hence this is just a special case of Corollary 4.3.4.   ◻

Theorem 4.4.1 is a simple information-theoretic inequality and can be interpreted by means of Fig. 4.3. The output of the hypothesis tester is binary and has distribution $(1 - \alpha, \alpha)$ and $(\beta, 1 - \beta)$ under hypotheses H_0 and H_1, respectively. The hypothesis tester in general decreases information in making a decision. Theorem 4.4.1 reflects this, by asserting that the discrimination at the input must be at least as large as the discrimination at the output.

◻ **Corollary 4.4.2**   Suppose that a block of n independent measurements is made. If the measurements are identically distributed, then

$$L(\mathbf{q}_1; \mathbf{q}_0) \geq \frac{1}{n} \left[\beta \log \frac{\beta}{1 - \alpha} + (1 - \beta) \log \frac{1 - \beta}{\alpha} \right]$$

Proof   Apply the theorem to blocks of measurements of blocklength n. The corollary is then an easy consequence of the additivity of discrimination for independent measurements.   ◻

If the frequency of measurement type j is given by p_j, then the corollary holds with the discrimination replaced by the average discrimination:

$$L(\mathbf{q}_1; \mathbf{q}_0 | \mathbf{p}) \geq \frac{1}{n} \left[\beta \log \frac{\beta}{1 - \alpha} + (1 - \beta) \log \frac{1 - \beta}{\alpha} \right]$$

◻ **Corollary 4.4.3**   Suppose that a block of n independent, identically distributed measurements is made and the probability of type II error is β. Then the probability of type I error satisfies

$$\alpha \geq 2^{-[nL(\mathbf{q}_1; \mathbf{q}_0) + 1]/(1 - \beta)}$$

with the discrimination expressed in bits.

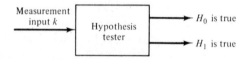

Figure 4.3   Decreasing information by a decision.

Proof Write Corollary 4.4.2 as

$$-(1 - \beta) \log_2 \alpha \leq nL(\mathbf{q}_1; \mathbf{q}_0) + H_b(\beta) + \beta \log_2 (1 - \alpha)$$

where

$$H_b(\beta) = -\beta \log_2 \beta - (1 - \beta) \log_2 (1 - \beta)$$

is not larger than 1, and $\beta \log_2 (1 - \alpha)$ is not larger than 0. Therefore

$$-(1 - \beta) \log_2 \alpha \leq nL(\mathbf{q}_1; \mathbf{q}_0) + 1$$

from which the corollary follows.   □

For a fixed value of β, the theorem and corollaries provide a lower bound to all possible α. However, they do not provide an upper bound to α. The asymptotic behavior is described in the following theorem. It is obtained from the weak law of large numbers.

□ **Theorem 4.4.4** **(Stein's lemma)** Let $\beta \in (0, 1)$ be given. Suppose that a dataword of blocklength n consists of n independent measurements. On the space of such datawords, let α_n^* be the smallest probability of type I error over all decision rules such that the probability of type II error does not exceed β. Then for all β in $(0, 1)$,

$$\lim_{n \to \infty} (\alpha_n^*)^{1/n} = e^{-L(\mathbf{q}_1; \mathbf{q}_0)}$$

Proof We give the proof only for the case where the measurements are identically distributed. Consider the set of "typical" n-tuples whose sample discrimination is about average. Specifically, choose $\varepsilon > 0$ and let $\mathscr{B}$ be the set

$$\mathscr{B} = \left\{ \mathbf{y} : L(\mathbf{q}_1; \mathbf{q}_0) - \varepsilon < \frac{1}{n} \log \frac{q_1(\mathbf{y})}{q_0(\mathbf{y})} < L(\mathbf{q}_1; \mathbf{q}_0) + \varepsilon \right\}$$

For any $\delta > 0$, the weak law of large numbers asserts that for sufficiently large n, under probability distribution $\mathbf{q}_1$,

$$Pr\left\{ \mathbf{y} : L(\mathbf{q}_1; \mathbf{q}_0) - \varepsilon < \frac{1}{n} \log \frac{q_1(\mathbf{y})}{q_0(\mathbf{y})} < L(\mathbf{q}_1; \mathbf{q}_0) + \varepsilon \right\} \geq 1 - \delta$$

Take δ equal to β. The set $\mathscr{B}^c$ then satisfies

$$\sum_{\mathbf{y} \in \mathscr{B}^c} q_1(\mathbf{y}) \leq \beta$$

and so the constraint on the probability of type II error is satisfied. Therefore the smallest probability of type I error must be at least as small as the sum of $q_0(\mathbf{y})$ over all $\mathbf{y}$ in $\mathscr{B}$. That is,

$$\alpha_n^* \leq \sum_{\mathbf{y} \in \mathscr{B}} q_0(\mathbf{y}) \leq \sum_{\mathbf{y} \in \mathscr{B}} q_1(\mathbf{y}) e^{-n[L(\mathbf{q}_1; \mathbf{q}_0) - \varepsilon]}$$

where the second inequality follows from the definition of $\mathscr{B}$. Now further weaken the inequality by replacing the sum by a sum over all $\mathbf{y}$.

$$\alpha_n^* \leq \sum_{\mathbf{y}} q_1(\mathbf{y}) e^{-n[L(\mathbf{q}_1;\mathbf{q}_0) - \varepsilon]}$$

$$= e^{-n[L(\mathbf{q}_1;\mathbf{q}_0) - \varepsilon]}$$

This completes development of the upper bound on α_n^*.

To develop a lower bound on α_n^*, let $\mathscr{U}_1$ be the set providing the smallest α_n^* for the given β. Then,

$$\alpha_n^* = \sum_{\mathbf{y} \in \mathscr{U}_1} q_0(\mathbf{y})$$

$$\geq \sum_{\mathbf{y} \in \mathscr{U}_1 \cap \mathscr{B}} q_0(\mathbf{y}) \geq \sum_{\mathbf{y} \in \mathscr{U}_1 \cap \mathscr{B}} q_1(\mathbf{y}) e^{-n[L(\mathbf{q}_1;\mathbf{q}_0) + \varepsilon]}$$

But

$$\sum_{\mathbf{y} \in \mathscr{U}_1 \cap \mathscr{B}} q_1(\mathbf{y}) = \sum_{\mathbf{y}} q_1(\mathbf{y}) - \sum_{\mathbf{y} \in \mathscr{U}_1^c \cup \mathscr{B}^c} q_1(\mathbf{y})$$

$$\geq \sum_{\mathbf{y}} q_1(\mathbf{y}) - \sum_{\mathbf{y} \in \mathscr{U}_1^c} q_1(\mathbf{y}) - \sum_{\mathbf{y} \in \mathscr{B}^c} q_1(\mathbf{y})$$

$$\geq 1 - \beta - \delta$$

Hence

$$\alpha_n^* \geq (1 - \beta - \delta) e^{-n[L(\mathbf{q}_1;\mathbf{q}_0) + \varepsilon]}$$

Therefore we have

$$e^{-n[L(\mathbf{q}_1;\mathbf{q}_0) - \varepsilon]} \geq \alpha_n^* \geq (1 - \beta - \delta) e^{-n[L(\mathbf{q}_1;\mathbf{q}_0) + \varepsilon]}$$

Taking the logarithm, dividing by n, and passing to the limit gives

$$L(\mathbf{q}_1;\mathbf{q}_0) + \varepsilon \geq \lim_{n \to \infty} \left(\frac{1}{n} \log \frac{1}{\alpha_n^*} \right) \geq L(\mathbf{q}_1;\mathbf{q}_0) - \varepsilon$$

Because $\varepsilon > 0$ is arbitrary, the theorem is proved. $\square$

4.5 ASYMPTOTIC BOUNDS ON PERFORMANCE

By finding upper and lower bounds that are asymptotically equal as the number of independent, identically distributed measurements becomes large, this section develops an explicit asymptotic relationship between α, β, and T. The Neyman-Pearson theorem states that it is only necessary to consider threshold decision regions of the form

$$\mathscr{U}_0(T) = \left\{ \mathbf{y} : \frac{1}{n} \log \frac{q_0(\mathbf{y})}{q_1(\mathbf{y})} \geq T \right\}$$

$$\mathscr{U}_1(T) = \left\{ \mathbf{y} : \frac{1}{n} \log \frac{q_0(\mathbf{y})}{q_1(\mathbf{y})} < T \right\}$$

where we have written the threshold in normalized form as nT. Clearly the log-likelihood ratio will depend only on the number of times each value k appears in the block of measurements, and not on the particular sequence in which these values appear. Therefore a dataword $\mathbf{y}$ is in the Neyman-Pearson region $\mathscr{U}_0(T)$ if and only if the composition $\hat{\mathbf{q}}$ of $\mathbf{y}$ is in the set

$$\mathscr{Q}_T = \left\{ \hat{\mathbf{q}} : \sum_k \hat{q}_k \log \frac{q_{0k}}{q_{1k}} \geq T \right\}$$

Similarly, $\mathbf{y}$ is in the Neyman-Pearson region $\mathscr{U}_1(T)$ if and only if $\hat{\mathbf{q}}$ is in the set

$$\mathscr{Q}_T^c = \left\{ \hat{\mathbf{q}} : \sum_k \hat{q}_k \log \frac{q_{0k}}{q_{1k}} < T \right\}$$

We can study decision rules by studying this partition of the space of compositions.

Figure 4.4 illustrates (in $\mathbf{P}^3$) how the set $\mathbf{P}^{K^n}$ of all probability distributions on K^n points is partitioned into the two sets $\mathscr{Q}_T$ and $\mathscr{Q}_T^c$ by the threshold T. We shall want to bound the probability under hypothesis H_0 that composition $\hat{\mathbf{q}}$ is in set $\mathscr{Q}_T^c$ and the probability under hypothesis H_1 that composition $\hat{\mathbf{q}}$ is in set $\mathscr{Q}_T$. The following theorem will show us how to find these bounds. It says that the probability of an unlikely event is determined by the discrimination distance to the closest probability distribution for which the event is likely.

The sets $\mathscr{Q}_T$ and $\mathscr{Q}_T^c$ are clearly convex sets of probability distributions. The theorem will be proved for an arbitrary convex set $\mathscr{Q}$ as shown in Fig. 4.5.

☐ **Theorem 4.5.1 (Sanov's theorem)**   Given a memoryless stationary source $\mathbf{p}$, let $\mathscr{A}$ be a subset of datawords of blocklength n such that each

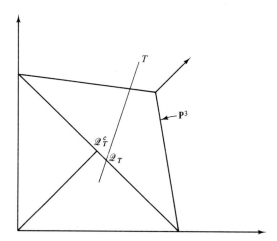

Figure 4.4   Partitioning with a threshold.

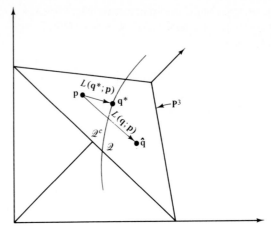

Figure 4.5   The closest probability distribution.

dataword $\mathbf{y}$ in $\mathscr{A}$ has a composition $\hat{\mathbf{q}}$ in $\mathscr{Q}$, a convex set of probability distributions. Then

$$Pr[\mathscr{A}] \leq e^{-nL(\mathbf{q}^*;\mathbf{p})}$$

where

$$L(\mathbf{q}^*;\mathbf{p}) = \min_{\hat{\mathbf{q}} \in \mathscr{Q}} L(\hat{\mathbf{q}};\mathbf{p})$$

Proof   Let $\mathbf{p}^n$ denote the product distribution having probability $p^n(\mathbf{y})$ of dataword $\mathbf{y}$. Let $p^n(\mathbf{y}|\mathbf{y} \in \mathscr{A})$ be the probability distribution on $\mathbf{y}$ when given that $\mathbf{y}$ is in the set $\mathscr{A}$. We can compute $p^n(\mathbf{y}|\mathbf{y} \in \mathscr{A})$ by using the Bayes formula,

$$p^n(\mathbf{y}|\mathbf{y} \in \mathscr{A}) = \frac{p^n(\mathbf{y})}{\sum_{\mathbf{y} \in \mathscr{A}} p^n(\mathbf{y})}$$

if $\mathbf{y}$ is in $\mathscr{A}$. Otherwise, when $\mathbf{y}$ is not in $\mathscr{A}$, $p^n(\mathbf{y}|\mathbf{y} \in \mathscr{A})$ equals zero. The discrimination $L(\mathbf{p}^n(\cdot|\mathscr{A});\mathbf{p}^n)$ is evaluated as

$$L(\mathbf{p}^n(\cdot|\mathscr{A});\mathbf{p}^n) = \sum_{\mathbf{y}} p^n(\mathbf{y}|\mathbf{y} \in \mathscr{A}) \log \frac{1}{\sum_{\mathbf{y} \in \mathscr{A}} p^n(\mathbf{y})}$$

$$= \log \frac{1}{Pr[\mathscr{A}]}$$

where $Pr[\mathscr{A}]$ denotes $\sum_{\mathbf{y} \in \mathscr{A}} p^n(\mathbf{y})$. Consequently,

$$Pr[\mathscr{A}] = e^{-L(\mathbf{p}^n(\cdot|\mathscr{A});\mathbf{p}^n)}$$

Because $p^n(\mathbf{y})$ is a product distribution, we have by Theorem 4.3.8 that the discrimination in the block is at least as large as the sum of the discriminations in each measurement. Therefore

$$Pr[\mathscr{A}] \le e^{-\sum_l L(\mathbf{p}^{(l)}(\cdot|\mathscr{A});\mathbf{p})}$$

where $\mathbf{p}^{(l)}(\cdot|\mathscr{A})$ is the single-letter probability distribution on the lth component of the random dataword $\mathbf{y}$ given that $\mathbf{y}$ is in $\mathscr{A}$:

$$p^{(l)}(y_l|\mathscr{A}) = \sum_{y_1}\cdots\sum_{y_{l-1}}\sum_{y_{l+1}}\cdots\sum_{y_n} p^n(y_1,\ldots,y_n|\mathscr{A})$$

Next use convexity as in Theorem 4.3.2 to write

$$n\sum_l \frac{1}{n}L(\mathbf{p}^{(l)}(\cdot|\mathscr{A});\mathbf{p}) \ge nL\left(\sum_l \frac{1}{n}\mathbf{p}^{(l)}(\cdot|\mathscr{A});\mathbf{p}\right)$$

so that

$$Pr[\mathscr{A}] \le e^{-nL(\mathbf{p}(\cdot|\mathscr{A});\mathbf{p})}$$

where

$$\mathbf{p}(\cdot|\mathscr{A}) = \sum_{l=1}^n \frac{1}{n}\mathbf{p}^{(l)}(\cdot|\mathscr{A})$$

All that remains is to show that $\mathbf{p}(\cdot|\mathscr{A})$ is in the set $\mathscr{Q}$, because then we could write

$$L(\mathbf{p}(\cdot|\mathscr{A});\mathbf{p}) \ge \min_{\hat{\mathbf{q}}\in\mathscr{Q}} L(\hat{\mathbf{q}};\mathbf{p})$$

to complete the proof.

Suppose that a dataword $\mathbf{y}$ is randomly chosen from set $\mathscr{A}$ using probability distribution $\mathbf{p}^n(\cdot|\mathscr{A})$. The expected composition of $\mathbf{y}$ is found by averaging across the number of times each symbol is expected in the lth component. Let $\phi_k^{(l)}$ equal one if the lth component of the randomly chosen word is the kth symbol of the data alphabet, and otherwise let $\phi_k^{(l)}$ equal zero. Then

$$\hat{q}_k = \sum_{l=1}^n \frac{1}{n}\phi_k^{(l)}$$

is the composition of the randomly selected codeword. The expected composition is

$$E[\hat{q}_k] = \sum_{l=1}^n \frac{1}{n}E[\phi_k^{(l)}]$$

$$= \sum_{l=1}^n \frac{1}{n}p^{(l)}(\cdot|\mathscr{A})$$

Therefore, $\mathbf{p}(\cdot|\mathscr{A})$ is equal to the expected composition of a dataword in $\mathscr{A}$. All datawords in $\mathscr{A}$ have composition in the convex set $\mathscr{Q}$, so $\mathbf{p}(\cdot|\mathscr{A})$ is also in $\mathscr{Q}$. The proof is now complete. $\square$

☐   **Theorem 4.5.2**   It is possible to choose decision regions for a binary hypothesis-testing problem on memoryless, stationary datawords of blocklength n such that

$$\alpha \le e^{-nL(\mathbf{q}_\lambda;\mathbf{q}_0)}$$

and

$$\beta \le e^{-nL(\mathbf{q}_\lambda;\mathbf{q}_1)}$$

where $\mathbf{q}_\lambda$ is given in terms of the parameter $0 \le \lambda \le 1$ as

$$q_{\lambda k} = \frac{q_{0k}^{1-\lambda} q_{1k}^{\lambda}}{\sum_k q_{0k}^{1-\lambda} q_{1k}^{\lambda}}$$

whenever λ can be chosen to satisfy

$$\sum_k q_{\lambda k} \log \frac{q_{0k}}{q_{1k}} = T$$

Proof   Let $\mathcal{Q}_T$ be the set of compositions $\hat{\mathbf{q}}$ given by

$$\mathcal{Q}_T = \left\{ \hat{\mathbf{q}} : \sum_k \hat{q}_k \log \frac{q_{0k}}{q_{1k}} \ge T \right\}$$

The complement of the set is

$$\mathcal{Q}_T^c = \left\{ \hat{\mathbf{q}} : \sum_k \hat{q}_k \log \frac{q_{0k}}{q_{1k}} < T \right\}$$

We only need to prove that $\mathbf{q}_\lambda$ minimizes $L(\hat{\mathbf{q}}; \mathbf{q}_0)$ over set $\mathcal{Q}_T$ and also minimizes $L(\hat{\mathbf{q}}; \mathbf{q}_1)$ over the closure of set $\mathcal{Q}_T^c$. Then Theorem 4.5.1 allows us to conclude that

$$\alpha \le e^{-nL(\mathbf{q}_\lambda;\mathbf{q}_0)}$$

$$\beta \le e^{-nL(\mathbf{q}_\lambda;\mathbf{q}_1)}$$

To verify that $\mathbf{q}_\lambda$ achieves the minimum, let $\hat{\mathbf{q}}$ be any distribution such that $\sum_k \hat{q}_k \log (q_{0k}/q_{1k}) \ge T$. Then

$$L(\hat{\mathbf{q}}; \mathbf{q}_1) = L(\hat{\mathbf{q}}; \mathbf{q}_\lambda) + \sum \hat{q}_k \log \frac{q_{\lambda k}}{q_{1k}}$$

We will show that, in the second term on the right, an inequality results if $\hat{q}_k$ is replaced by $q_{\lambda k}$. Thus

$$L(\hat{\mathbf{q}}; \mathbf{q}_1) = L(\hat{\mathbf{q}}; \mathbf{q}_\lambda) + (1 - \lambda) \sum_k \hat{q}_k \log \frac{q_{0k}}{q_{1k}} - \log \sum_k q_{0k}^{1-\lambda} q_{1k}^{\lambda}$$

$$\ge L(\hat{\mathbf{q}}; \mathbf{q}_\lambda) + (1 - \lambda)T - \log \sum_k q_{0k}^{1-\lambda} q_{1k}^{\lambda}$$

$$= L(\hat{\mathbf{q}}; \mathbf{q}_\lambda) + (1 - \lambda) \sum_k q_{\lambda k} \log \frac{q_{0k}}{q_{1k}} - \log \sum_k q_{0k}^{1-\lambda} q_{1k}^{\lambda}$$

$$= L(\hat{\mathbf{q}}; \mathbf{q}_\lambda) + L(\mathbf{q}_\lambda; \mathbf{q}_1)$$

Because $L(\hat{\mathbf{q}}; \mathbf{q}_\lambda) \geq 0$, this implies that

$$L(\hat{\mathbf{q}}; \mathbf{q}_1) \geq L(\mathbf{q}_\lambda; \mathbf{q}_1)$$

Thus $\mathbf{q}_\lambda$ does indeed achieve the minimum of $L(\hat{\mathbf{q}}; \mathbf{q}_1)$ over the set $\mathcal{Q}_T$, so by Theorem 4.5.1,

$$\beta \leq e^{-nL(\mathbf{q}_\lambda; \mathbf{q}_1)}$$

Likewise, $\mathbf{q}_\lambda$ also achieves the minimum of $L(\hat{\mathbf{q}}; \mathbf{q}_0)$ over the closure of the set $\mathcal{Q}_T^c$. This completes the proof of the theorem.   □

The probability distribution $\mathbf{q}_\lambda$ that arises in Theorem 4.5.2 is known as a *tilted probability distribution*. We can think of it as lying between $\mathbf{q}_0$ and $\mathbf{q}_1$, as illustrated in Fig. 4.6. The theorem specifies λ implicitly in terms of the threshold T.

$$T = \sum_k q_{\lambda k} \log \frac{q_{0k}}{q_{1k}}$$
$$= L(\mathbf{q}_\lambda; \mathbf{q}_1) - L(\mathbf{q}_\lambda; \mathbf{q}_0)$$

From the second line, we can see that Theorem 4.5.2 can be applied whenever the threshold T satisfies

$$L(\mathbf{q}_0; \mathbf{q}_1) \leq T \leq -L(\mathbf{q}_1; \mathbf{q}_0)$$

The gist of the next theorem is that the inequalities of Theorem 4.5.2 are asymptotically tight. While it may be that the probabilities of error are actually a little better for each finite n, as n goes to infinity the probabilities of error are accurately described by the negative exponentials in n given in Theorem 4.5.2.

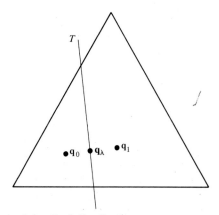

Figure 4.6   Geometry of the tilted distribution.

☐   **Theorem 4.5.3**   The Neyman-Pearson regions for a hypothesis-testing problem based on a memoryless, stationary dataword of blocklength n and normalized threshold nT have the probabilities of type I and type II error that satisfy

$$\alpha \ge e^{-nL(\mathbf{q}_\lambda;\mathbf{q}_0) - o(n)}$$

and

$$\beta \ge e^{-nL(\mathbf{q}_\lambda;\mathbf{q}_1) - o(n)}$$

where

$$q_{\lambda k} = \frac{q_{0k}^{1-\lambda}q_{1k}^{\lambda}}{\sum_k q_{0k}^{1-\lambda}q_{1k}^{\lambda}}$$

and λ is chosen such that

$$T = L(\mathbf{q}_\lambda;\mathbf{q}_1) - L(\mathbf{q}_\lambda;\mathbf{q}_0)$$

Proof   Choose $\varepsilon > 0$. The idea of the proof is to choose a distribution $\mathbf{q}$ in $\mathscr{Q}$ and within ε of the threshold T, then to apply Corollary 4.4.3, and finally to apply the law of large numbers to reduce the nuisance terms to $o(n)$. We know that the threshold satisfies

$$T = \sum_k q_{\lambda k} \log \frac{q_{0k}}{q_{1k}}$$

so we want to choose a $\hat{\mathbf{q}}$ so that $\sum_k \hat{q}_k \log (q_{0k}/q_{1k})$ is a little larger than T. Choose the tilted distribution $\mathbf{q}_\gamma$ in $\mathscr{Q}_T$ so that

$$\sum_k q_{\gamma k} \log \frac{q_{0k}}{q_{1k}} = T + \varepsilon$$

and write $\mathscr{U}_0(T)$ in the form:

$$\mathscr{U}_0(T) = \left\{ \mathbf{y} : T - \frac{1}{n}\log \frac{q_0(\mathbf{y})}{q_1(\mathbf{y})} \le 0 \right\}$$

which implies that

$$\mathscr{U}_0(T) \supset \left\{ \mathbf{y} : \left| \frac{1}{n}\log \frac{q_0(\mathbf{y})}{q_1(\mathbf{y})} - (T + \varepsilon) \right| \le \varepsilon \right\}$$

The law of large numbers implies that $\sum_{\mathbf{y} \in \mathscr{U}_0(T)} q_\gamma(\mathbf{y})$ tends to 1. Therefore, by Corollary 4.4.3 with $\mathbf{q}_\gamma$ in place of $\mathbf{q}_1$, we see that

$$\alpha \ge e^{-nL(\mathbf{q}_\gamma;\mathbf{q}_0) - o(n)}$$

for all sufficiently large n. Repeating the argument, now with $\mathbf{q}_\gamma$ in $\mathscr{Q}_T^c$, with $\sum_k q_{\gamma k} \log (q_{0k}/q_{1k})$ a little smaller than T, leads to

$$\beta \ge e^{-nL(\mathbf{q}_\gamma;\mathbf{q}_1) - o(n)}$$

Finally, use the continuity of the discrimination together with the fact that γ is arbitrary to write

$$\alpha \geq e^{-nL(\mathbf{q}_\lambda;\mathbf{q}_0) - o(n)}$$

$$\beta \geq e^{-nL(\mathbf{q}_\lambda;\mathbf{q}_1) - o(n)}$$

and the proof is complete.   □

The combination of Theorem 4.5.2 and Theorem 4.5.3 describes in terms of the parameter λ the asymptotic probabilities of error of the Neyman-Pearson hypotheses testers as

$$\alpha \sim e^{-nL(\mathbf{q}_\lambda;\mathbf{q}_0)}$$

$$\beta \sim e^{-nL(\mathbf{q}_\lambda;\mathbf{q}_1)}$$

The asymptotic behavior of α with blocklength and the asymptotic behavior of β with blocklength can be traded by varying the parameter λ.

4.6 THE ERROR-EXPONENT FUNCTION

We have seen in Section 4.5 that the probabilities of type I and type II error decrease exponentially with blocklength n. In this section we shall look more closely at how the two exponents interrelate.

□ **Definition 4.6.1**   Let the distributions $\mathbf{q}_0$ and $\mathbf{q}_1$ be fixed probability distributions on K points. Then the *error-exponent function* $e(r)$ is given by

$$e(r) = \min_{\hat{\mathbf{q}} \in \mathscr{P}_r} L(\hat{\mathbf{q}}; \mathbf{q}_0)$$

where the minimization is over the set

$$\mathscr{P}_r = \{\hat{\mathbf{q}} : L(\hat{\mathbf{q}}; \mathbf{q}_1) \leq r\}$$ □

If $L(\mathbf{q}_1; \mathbf{q}_0)$ is finite, then $e(r)$ is finite for nonnegative r, because $\mathbf{q}_1 \in \mathscr{P}_r$. Because we assume $\mathbf{q}_0$ and $\mathbf{q}_1$ have strictly positive components, $L(\mathbf{q}_1; \mathbf{q}_0)$ is always finite for finite sample spaces.

We can also define an $e(r)$ function using the average discrimination. In this case we minimize $L(\hat{\mathbf{q}}; \mathbf{q}_0 | \mathbf{p})$ over a set of transition matrices $\hat{\mathbf{q}} = \{\hat{q}_{k|j}\}$ subject to a constraint on $L(\hat{\mathbf{q}}; \mathbf{q}_1 | \mathbf{p})$. All of the theorems to be developed hold as well for the average discrimination.

The definition of $e(r)$ is given a geometric interpretation in Fig. 4.7, which supplements Fig. 4.6 with additional detail. The location of the point $\mathbf{q}^*$ in Fig. 4.7 suggests that the value of $\hat{\mathbf{q}}$ that achieves $e(r)$ is the same $\mathbf{q}_\lambda$ associated with the Neyman-Pearson threshold in the previous section. Theorem 4.6.3 will show that this is indeed the case so we can translate the conclusion of the previous section into the terminology of the error-exponent function.

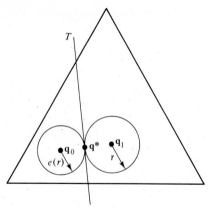

Figure 4.7   Geometry of the error-exponent function.

Therefore, for blocks of independent measurements, the probability of type I error and the probability of type II error satisfy the asymptotic expressions

$$\alpha \sim e^{-ne(r)}$$

$$\beta \sim e^{-nr}$$

for some r, but cannot simultaneously satisfy any stronger pair of asymptotic expressions. The parameter r controls the trade between the asymptotic behavior in blocklength of the probabilities of type I and type II error.

The function $e(r)$ derives a number of important properties from its definition as the minimum of a convex function subject to a convex constraint. The following theorem establishes that its general shape is as shown in Fig. 4.8.

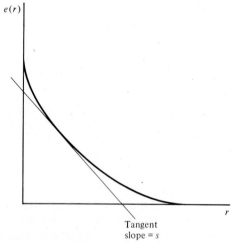

Figure 4.8   The error-exponent function.

☐ **Theorem 4.6.2** $e(r)$ is defined for $r \geq 0$. It is a convex, nonincreasing, and continuous function on the interval $0 \leq r \leq L(\mathbf{q}_0; \mathbf{q}_1)$, and equals zero for $r \geq L(\mathbf{q}_0; \mathbf{q}_1)$.

Proof If $r < 0$, then $\mathscr{P}_r$ is empty and $e(r)$ is undefined. If $r > r'$, then $\mathscr{P}_r \supset \mathscr{P}_{r'}$; hence $e(r) \leq e(r')$ and so $e(r)$ is nonincreasing. If $r \geq L(\mathbf{q}_0; \mathbf{q}_1)$, then $\mathbf{q}_0 \in \mathscr{P}_r$, so $e(r)$ equals $L(\mathbf{q}_0; \mathbf{q}_0)$, which is zero.

It remains to prove that $e(r)$ is convex; this will imply that it is continuous. Specifically, given r', r'' and $\lambda \in [0,1]$, we must show that

$$e(\lambda r' + \bar{\lambda} r'') \leq \lambda e(r') + \bar{\lambda} e(r'')$$

where $\bar{\lambda} = 1 - \lambda$. Let $\mathbf{q}'$ and $\mathbf{q}''$ achieve $e(r')$ and $e(r'')$ respectively, and let $\mathbf{q} = \lambda \mathbf{q}' + \bar{\lambda} \mathbf{q}''$. Then

$$L(\mathbf{q}; \mathbf{q}_1) \leq \lambda L(\mathbf{q}'; \mathbf{q}_1) + \bar{\lambda} L(\mathbf{q}''; \mathbf{q}_1) \leq \lambda r' + \bar{\lambda} r''$$

Therefore $\mathbf{q} \in \mathscr{P}_{\lambda r' + \bar{\lambda} r''}$ and

$$e(\lambda r' + \bar{\lambda} r'') \leq L(\mathbf{q}; \mathbf{q}_0) \leq \lambda L(\mathbf{q}'; \mathbf{q}_0) + \bar{\lambda} L(\mathbf{q}''; \mathbf{q}_0)$$
$$= \lambda e(r') + \bar{\lambda} e(r'') \qquad\qquad \Box$$

We will derive two representations for $e(r)$. Theorem 4.6.3 is derived using the classical method of Lagrange multipliers as discussed in Appendix A. Theorem 4.6.4 uses a more direct proof, with reference to the graph of the convex function $e(r)$.

☐ **Theorem 4.6.3**   In the region where it is nonzero, $e(r)$ can be expressed in terms of a parameter s as

$$e(r) = -s r_s - \log \left(\sum_k q_{0k}^{1/(1+s)} q_{1k}^{s/(1+s)} \right)^{1+s}$$

where

$$r_s = \sum_k q_k^* \log \frac{q_k^*}{q_{1k}}$$

and the tilted distribution $\mathbf{q}^*$ is given by

$$q_k^* = \frac{q_{0k}^{1/(1+s)} q_{1k}^{s/(1+s)}}{\displaystyle\sum_k q_{0k}^{1/(1+s)} q_{1k}^{s/(1+s)}}$$

Proof Temporarily ignore the inequality constraints $\hat{q}_k \geq 0$, and introduce the Lagrange multipliers s and γ so that

$$e(r) = \min_{\hat{q}} \left[\sum_k \hat{q}_k \log \frac{\hat{q}_k}{q_{0k}} + s \left(\sum_k \hat{q}_k \log \frac{\hat{q}_k}{q_{1k}} - r \right) + \gamma \left(\sum_k \hat{q}_k - 1 \right) \right]$$

Equating to zero the derivative with respect to $\hat{q}_k$ gives

$$\log \frac{\hat{q}_k}{q_{0k}} + s \log \frac{\hat{q}_k}{q_{1k}} + 1 + s + \gamma = 0$$

Solving this for $\hat{q}_k$ and choosing γ so that the solution is a probability distribution produces the tilted distribution $\mathbf{q}^*$ as the optimizing distribution. Because q_k^* is nonnegative, the inequality constraints are satisfied. Now s should be selected so that $L(\mathbf{q}^*; \mathbf{q}_1) = r$. Because we cannot solve the equation for s as a function of r, we leave the result in parametric form, expressing both r and $e(r)$ as functions of s. □

As a consequence of the theorem, we have the earlier claim that $\mathbf{q}^*$ achieving $e(r)$ is precisely that $\mathbf{q}_\lambda$ parameterizing the Neyman-Pearson threshold in Theorem 4.5.2. It is only necessary to set $\lambda = s/(1 + s)$. In particular, we see that as s goes to zero, $e(r)$ goes to zero and r goes to $L(\mathbf{q}_0; \mathbf{q}_1)$. Similarly, as s goes to ∞, $e(r)$ goes to $L(\mathbf{q}_1; \mathbf{q}_0)$ and r goes to zero.

There is an alternative representation for $e(r)$, as given in the next theorem, which will be proved independently of Theorem 4.6.3. As a consequence of the proof of this theorem, it will follow that the parameter s is nonnegative and satisfies

$$\frac{de(r)}{dr} = -s$$

whenever $e(r)$ has a derivative. Figure 4.8 shows a tangent to $e(r)$ of slope $-s$.

□   **Theorem 4.6.4**   A representation of $e(r)$ is

$$e(r) = \max_{s \geq 0} \left[-sr - \log \left(\sum_k q_{1k}^{s/(1 + s)} q_{0k}^{1/(1 + s)} \right)^{1 + s} \right]$$

Proof   For all $s \geq 0$,

$$e(r) \geq \min_{\hat{\mathbf{q}} \in \mathscr{P}_r} [L(\hat{\mathbf{q}}; \mathbf{q}_0) + s[L(\hat{\mathbf{q}}; \mathbf{q}_1) - r]]$$

because the term multiplying s is not larger than zero for all $\hat{\mathbf{q}}$ in $\mathscr{P}_r$. This inequality still holds if the domain of the minimum is now enlarged to include all probability vectors $\hat{\mathbf{q}}$, and it holds for every $s \geq 0$. Hence

$$e(r) \geq \max_{s \geq 0} \min_{\hat{\mathbf{q}}} [-sr + L(\hat{\mathbf{q}}; \mathbf{q}_0) + sL(\hat{\mathbf{q}}; \mathbf{q}_1)]$$

Carrying out the minimum over probability vectors $\hat{\mathbf{q}}$ gives

$$e(r) \geq \max_{s \geq 0} \left[-sr - \log \left(\sum_k q_{1k}^{s/(1 + s)} q_{0k}^{1/(1 + s)} \right)^{1 + s} \right]$$

All that remains to be shown is that there is equality for some value of s. Because $e(r)$ is convex and decreasing for $0 < r < L(\mathbf{q}_0; \mathbf{q}_1)$, there is a line of negative slope tangent to $e(r)$ at the value r and never larger than $e(r)$. Let $-s$ be the slope of this line as shown in Fig. 4.8. (If $e(r)$ has a derivative at r, then the derivative equals $-s$.) Therefore for any r',

$$e(r') \geq e(r) - s(r' - r)$$

The right side is the equation of a straight line of slope $-s$ through the point $(r, e(r))$. Let $\mathbf{q}^*$ achieve $e(r)$. We have by Definition 4.6.1, and for any $\hat{\mathbf{q}}$, that with $r' = L(\hat{\mathbf{q}}; \mathbf{q}_1)$,

$$e(r') + sr' \leq L(\hat{\mathbf{q}}; \mathbf{q}_0) + sL(\hat{\mathbf{q}}; \mathbf{q}_1)$$

and by choice of s,

$$e(r) + sr \leq e(r') + sr'$$

Consequently,

$$e(r) + sr \leq L(\hat{\mathbf{q}}; \mathbf{q}_0) + sL(\hat{\mathbf{q}}; \mathbf{q}_1)$$

and so

$$e(r) \leq \min_{\hat{\mathbf{q}}} \left[L(\hat{\mathbf{q}}; \mathbf{q}_0) + s[L(\hat{\mathbf{q}}; \mathbf{q}_1) - r]] \right]$$

which completes the proof of the theorem. □

The error-exponent function has been defined in terms of a single measurement, but its main role is in studying the testing of hypotheses by means of blocks of measurements. The error-exponent function for block measurements has a simple relationship to the error-exponent function for single measurements.

We will find the error-exponent function for a block of two measurements; the technique also works for blocks of n measurements. The measurements need not be of the same type. The following theorem provides a graphical construction for obtaining the error-exponent function for a pair of measurements in terms of the error-exponent functions of the two individual measurements.

□ **Theorem 4.6.5** Suppose two measurement types have error-exponent functions $e'(r)$ and $e''(r)$, respectively. Let $e(r)$ be the error-exponent function for the pair of measurements. Then

$$e(r'_s + r''_s) = e'(r'_s) + e''(r''_s)$$

where r'_s and r''_s are the values at which $e'(r)$ and $e''(r)$ have slope s, respectively. In addition, $e(r)$ has slope s at this point.

Proof Let $\mathbf{q}'_0$ and $\mathbf{q}'_1$ be the probability distributions on K' outcomes associated with the first measurement type, and let $\mathbf{q}''_0$ and $\mathbf{q}''_1$ be the probability distributions on K'' outcomes associated with the second measurement type. Then $\mathbf{q}_0'\mathbf{q}_0''$, and $\mathbf{q}_i'\mathbf{q}_i''$ are associated with the product measurement with $K'K''$ outcomes, and

$$e(r_s) = sr_s - \log\left(\sum_{k'k''}(q_{1k'}'\cdot q_{1k''}'')^{s/(1+s)}(q_{0k'}'\cdot q_{0k''}'')^{1/(1+s)}\right)^{1+s}$$

The double sum can be expanded into a product of sums. Expanding the logarithm then gives

$$e(r_s) = sr_s - \log\left(\sum_{k'}q_{1k'}'^{s/(1+s)}q_{0k'}'^{1/(1+s)}\right)^{1+s}$$

$$- \log\left(\sum_{k''}q_{1k''}''^{s/(1+s)}q_{0k''}''^{1/(1+s)}\right)^{1+s}$$

where

$$r_s = \sum_{k'k''}q_{k'k''}^* \log\frac{q_{k'k''}^*}{q_{1k'}'\cdot q_{1k''}''}$$

Again expanding the double sum into a product of sums gives

$$r_s = r_s' + r_s''$$

so that

$$e(r_s) = e'(r_s') + e''(r_s'') \qquad\qquad \square$$

This theorem expressed graphically tells us to construct the $e(r)$ function for the block measurement by adding the values of r and $e(r)$ at points having the same slope. Because the composite function again has slope s, it is immediately clear that the argument can be repeated to extend the theorem to an arbitrary number of independent measurements.

In case the n measurements are identically distributed, the error exponent for the block is given by

$$e_n(nr) = ne(r)$$

Interpreted graphically, this says that the graph of the error-exponent function for datawords of blocklength n can be obtained from the error-exponent function for a single measurement by scaling both axes by a factor of n. The graph is the same but the scale is expanded.

Theorem 4.5.3 provides lower bounds on the probabilities of error. We now provide a lower bound of another type, a lower bound based on the discrimination inequality. The bound follows from the next theorem.

$\square$ **Theorem 4.6.6**   The error-exponent function $e(r)$ is increased by a nontrivial refinement of a set of measurement outcomes. In other words,

$$e_{\text{fine}}(r) > e_{\text{coarse}}(r)$$

for all r, where $e_{\text{coarse}}(r)$ and $e_{\text{fine}}(r)$ denote the error-exponent function before and after refinement, respectively.

Proof As in the proof of Theorem 4.3.3, let i index the original points and let k index the new points. Let $\mathcal{U}_i$ be the set of k into which i was subdivided; let $\mathbf{Q}_0, \mathbf{Q}_1$ be the probability distributions on the original points; and let $\mathbf{q}_0, \mathbf{q}_1$ be the probability distributions on the new points. Next, let $\mathbf{Q}^*$ and $\mathbf{q}^*$ achieve $e_{\text{coarse}}(r)$ and $e_{\text{fine}}(r)$, respectively, at the point r. Finally let $\bar{\mathbf{q}}^*$ be the distribution on the original points induced by $\mathbf{q}^*$ according to

$$\bar{q}_i^* = \sum_{k \in \mathcal{U}_i} q_k^*$$

Then

$$\sum_k q_k^* \log \frac{q_k^*}{q_{1k}} - \sum_i \bar{q}_i^* \log \frac{\bar{q}_i^*}{Q_{1i}} = \sum_k q_k^* \log \frac{q_k^*}{q_{1k}} - \sum_i \sum_{k \in \mathcal{U}_i} q_k^* \log \frac{\bar{q}_i^*}{Q_{1i}}$$

$$= \sum_i \sum_{k \in \mathcal{U}_i} q_k^* \log \frac{q_k^* Q_{1i}}{q_{1k} \bar{q}_i^*}$$

$$\geq \sum_i \sum_{k \in \mathcal{U}_i} \left(q_k^* - \frac{q_{1k} \bar{q}_i^*}{Q_{1i}} \right)$$

$$= 0$$

Therefore,

$$L(\bar{\mathbf{q}}^*; \mathbf{Q}_1) \leq L(\mathbf{q}^*; \mathbf{q}_1)$$

and so

$$L(\bar{\mathbf{q}}^*; \mathbf{Q}_1) \leq r$$

because $L(\mathbf{q}^*; \mathbf{q}_1) \leq r$ by the definition of $e_{\text{fine}}(r)$.

Next, by the definition of $e_{\text{coarse}}(r)$ as a minimum

$$e_{\text{coarse}}(r) = L(\mathbf{Q}^*; \mathbf{Q}_0) \leq L(\bar{\mathbf{q}}^*; \mathbf{Q}_0)$$

Therefore

$$e_{\text{fine}}(r) - e_{\text{coarse}}(r) \geq L(\mathbf{q}^*; \mathbf{q}_0) - L(\bar{\mathbf{q}}^*; \mathbf{Q}_0)$$

$$= \sum_k q_k^* \log \frac{q_k^*}{q_{0k}} - \sum_i \sum_{k \in \mathcal{U}_i} q_k^* \log \frac{\bar{q}_i^*}{Q_{0i}}$$

$$= \sum_i \sum_{k \in \mathcal{U}_i} q_k^* \log \frac{q_k^* Q_{0i}}{q_{0k} \bar{q}_i^*}$$

$$\geq \sum_i \sum_{k \in \mathcal{U}_i} \left(q_k^* - \frac{q_{0k} \bar{q}_i^*}{Q_{0i}} \right)$$

$$= 0$$

At least one inequality is strict. Thus

$$e_{\text{fine}}(r) > e_{\text{coarse}}(r)$$

as was to be proved. $\quad\square$

☐ **Corollary 4.6.7**　The error-exponent function of a set of data cannot be increased by processing the data.

Proof　View the processing output as a measurement and the processing input as a refinement.　☐

An immediate application is the following theorem.

☐ **Theorem 4.6.8**　Given a hypothesis tester with probability of type I error α and probability of type II error β, let $\gamma \in [\beta, 1 - \alpha]$ be arbitrary. Suppose that α satisfies

$$e(r) < \gamma \log \frac{\gamma}{1 - \alpha} + (1 - \gamma) \log \frac{1 - \gamma}{\alpha} = L_b(\gamma, 1 - \alpha)$$

Then β satisfies

$$r \geq \gamma \log \frac{\gamma}{\beta} + (1 - \gamma) \log \frac{1 - \gamma}{1 - \beta} = L_b(\gamma, \beta)$$

Proof　View the output of the hypothesis tester as a binary measurement with probability distribution $(\alpha, 1 - \alpha)$ under H_0 and with probability distribution $(1 - \beta, \beta)$ under H_1, and denote the error-exponent function for the binary output by $e_b(r)$. Then the theorem says that for every r,

$$e(r) \geq e_b(r)$$

Because the error-exponent function is always decreasing, this implies that

$$e(r) < e_b(r')$$

only when $r > r'$. This is equivalent to the statement of the theorem because each value of γ in the specified range corresponds to one value of r'.　☐

☐ **Corollary 4.6.9**　Let $\gamma \in [\beta, 1 - \alpha]$ be arbitrary. Suppose that for a hypothesis tester using a block of n independent measurements, α satisfies

$$ne(r) < L_b(\gamma, 1 - \alpha)$$

Then β satisfies

$$nr \geq L_b(\gamma, \beta)$$

Proof　The proof follows from the theorem and the additive properties of the error-exponent function.　☐

This corollary suggests a simple graphical construction. If a given α and β are specified as the desired probabilities of type I and type II error, then plot $e(r)$ for the given problem and also plot $e_b(\alpha, \beta)(r)$. Expand the scale on both

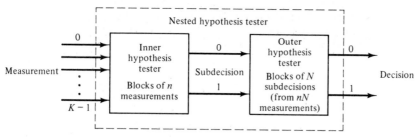

Figure 4.9   Nested hypothesis tester.

axes of the graph of $e(r)$ until $e(r)$ lies above $e_b(\alpha, \beta)(r)$ for all r. Any hypothesis-testing procedure that achieves the given α and β must use a number of measurements n that is at least as large as the scale expansion factor.

The corollary can be understood in terms of the nested hypothesis tester of Fig. 4.9. Here an inner hypothesis tester looks at a sequence of n measurements of the data and decides between H_0 and H_1, indicating its decision by 0 or 1. The outer hypothesis tester then looks at a sequence of N first-level decisions (corresponding to nN measurements) and makes a final decision. The intuitive content of the preceding theorems is that the performance of the inner hypothesis tester cannot be so good that it is possible to add an outer hypothesis tester in a way that violates lower bounds for the nested hypothesis tester. To study the achievable performance of any hypothesis tester, we can imagine it to be the inner hypothesis tester in a nested hypothesis tester.

4.7 CONVERSE THEOREMS

The previous sections have established the behavior of hypothesis testers asymptotically with blocklength. We now show that the probability of type II error cannot decay with blocklength more strongly than $e^{-nL(q_0;q_1)}$ unless the probability of type I error approaches 1 with blocklength.

□ **Theorem 4.7.1**   Given a set of independent measurements, let $c = L(\mathbf{q}_0;\mathbf{q}_1)$. Suppose that $\beta \le e^{-nr}$ where $r > c$. Then

$$\alpha > 1 - \frac{4\sigma^2}{n(r - c)^2} - e^{-n(r - c)/2}$$

where

$$\sigma^2 = \sum_k q_{0k}\left(\log \frac{q_{0k}}{q_{1k}}\right)^2 - \left(\sum_k q_{0k} \log \frac{q_{0k}}{q_{1k}}\right)^2$$

Proof Let $\mathcal{U}_0$ and $\mathcal{U}_1$ be the decision regions, and let

$$\mathcal{U}_0^* = \{y : q_1(y) \le q_0(y) e^{-n(c+\varepsilon)}\}$$
$$\mathcal{U}_1^* = \{y : q_1(y) > q_0(y) e^{-n(c+\varepsilon)}\}$$

where $\varepsilon > 0$ is arbitrary and y represents a sequence of n measurements. We now have

$$1 - \alpha = \sum_{y \in \mathcal{U}_0} q_0(y)$$

$$= \sum_{y \in \mathcal{U}_0 \cap \mathcal{U}_1^*} q_0(y) + \sum_{y \in \mathcal{U}_0 \cap \mathcal{U}_0^*} q_0(y)$$

$$< \sum_{y \in \mathcal{U}_0 \cap \mathcal{U}_1^*} q_1(y) e^{n(c+\varepsilon)} + \sum_{y \in \mathcal{U}_0 \cap \mathcal{U}_0^*} q_0(y)$$

This is further bounded by summing the first term over all of $\mathcal{U}_0$ and the second term over all of $\mathcal{U}_0^*$.

$$1 - \alpha < \sum_{y \in \mathcal{U}_0} q_1(y) e^{n(c+\varepsilon)} + \sum_{y \in \mathcal{U}_0^*} q_0(y)$$

$$< e^{-nr} e^{n(c+\varepsilon)} + \sum_{y \in \mathcal{U}_0^*} q_0(y)$$

The second term can be written

$$\sum_{y \in \mathcal{U}_0^*} q_0(y) = Pr\left[\left\{y : \log \frac{q_0(y)}{q_1(y)} \ge n(c + \varepsilon)\right\}\right]$$

where

$$nc = \sum_y q_0(y) \log \frac{q_0(y)}{q_1(y)}$$

and this can be bounded by Chebychev's inequality

$$\sum_{y \in \mathcal{U}_0^*} q_0(y) \le \frac{\text{var}\{\log [q_0(y)/q_1(y)]\}}{n^2 \varepsilon^2} = \frac{\sigma^2}{n \varepsilon^2}$$

Therefore

$$1 - \alpha < e^{n(c - r + \varepsilon)} + \frac{\sigma^2}{n \varepsilon^2}$$

This holds for any $\varepsilon > 0$. Hence pick $\varepsilon = (r - c)/2$, thereby proving the theorem. $\square$

4.8 CHERNOFF BOUNDS

Given a random variable or a collection of random variables, it is possible, in principle, to compute the probability of occurrence of a specified event. As we have already said, for many problems the calculations can be hopelessly complex, even for a computer. In addition, to make progress in theoretical studies, it is usually necessary to express the probability of an event as a simple function of the appropriate parameters. Often there is no simple formula for the exact solution, but there is a simple formula for an approximate solution, as in the bounds based on the discrimination. Because of its simplicity, an approximation may be preferable to an exact numerical solution. The Chernoff bound is another useful approximation of this kind. The Chernoff and discrimination functions are alternative characterizations of the same thing. We will develop the Chernoff bound as an extension of the more basic inequalities of Markov and Chebychev.

□ **Theorem 4.8.1 (Markov's inequality)** Suppose Y is a random variable taking values in the finite set of positive numbers $\{\xi_k, k = 0, \ldots, K - 1\}$. Then

$$Pr[Y \geq a] \leq \frac{\bar{\xi}}{a}$$

where $\bar{\xi} = \sum_k q_k \xi_k$ is the mean of Y.

Proof

$$Pr[Y \geq a] = \sum_{\xi_k \geq a} q_k \leq \sum_{\xi_k \geq a} q_k \frac{\xi_k}{a}$$

because $\xi_k/a \geq 1$ over the region of summation. The inequality is preserved if we extend the sum to all k. Hence

$$Pr[Y \geq a] \leq \sum_k q_k \frac{\xi_k}{a} = \frac{\bar{\xi}}{a} \qquad\qquad □$$

□ **Theorem 4.8.2 (Chebychev's inequality)** Suppose Y is a random variable taking values in the finite set $\{\xi_k, k = 0, \ldots, K - 1\}$. Then

$$Pr[|y - \bar{\xi}| \geq \varepsilon] \leq \frac{\sigma^2}{\varepsilon^2}$$

where $\bar{\xi} = \sum_k q_k \xi_k$ is the mean of Y and $\sigma^2 = \sum_k q_k (\xi_k - \bar{\xi})^2$ is the variance of Y.

Proof The proof consists of a change of variable in Theorem 4.8.1. Because $(Y - \bar{\xi})^2$ is a positive random variable, Theorem 4.8.1 can be applied giving

$$Pr[(Y - \bar{\xi})^2 \geq \varepsilon^2] \leq \frac{\overline{(Y - \bar{\xi})^2}}{\varepsilon^2}$$

which is equivalent to the claim of the theorem. □

We now come to the definition of the function

$$M(s) = \sum_k q_k e^{s\xi_k} = E(e^{sy})$$

which is known as the *moment generating function* in probability and statistics. In other fields, it is called the *Laplace transform*. It is well known that the moment generating function of the sum of two random variables is equal to the product of the moment generating functions of the two random variables:

$$M_{x+y}(s) = M_x(s)M_y(s)$$

A bound more delicate than Chebychev's inequality and known as the *Chernoff bound* provides a good estimate of the tail of a probability distribution of a sum. We know that when we average a large number of independent, identically distributed random variables Y_l for $l = 1, \ldots, n$, the result converges to the mean. For each value of n, the average is itself a random variable. The average has a probability distribution with tails that quickly become smaller as the number of random variables in the sum becomes large. We shall see that the Chernoff bound gives a good estimate of the tails of the form

$$Pr\left[\frac{1}{n}\sum_{l=1}^{n} Y_l \le a\right] \approx e^{-nc(a)}$$

for some function $c(a)$ that depends on the probability distribution of Y_l.

□   **Theorem 4.8.3   (Chernoff bound)** Suppose that Y is a random variable taking values in the finite set $\{\xi_k : k = 0, \ldots, K-1\}$. Then for all s greater than zero,

$$Pr[Y \ge a] \le e^{-sa}M(s)$$

and for all s less than zero,

$$Pr[Y \le a] \le e^{-sa}M(s)$$

Proof   If $s > 0$, then $Y \ge a$ is equivalent to $e^{sY} \ge e^{sa}$. Then, because e^{sY} is a positive random variable, Theorem 4.8.1 can be applied to give

$$Pr[e^{sY} \ge e^{sa}] \le e^{-sa}\sum_k q_k e^{s\xi_k}$$

Similar reasoning for $s < 0$ gives the second half of the theorem.   □

We shall see that the usefulness of the Chernoff bound is due in large measure to the fact that the random variable appears in the exponent so that a sum of random variables in the exponent yields a product of exponentials. The bound in Theorem 4.8.3 can be related to the discrimination much as the error-exponent function $e(r)$ was related to the discrimination. In the following definition, we introduce the Chernoff function $c(a)$. Then we will show that it is equal to the bound of Theorem 4.8.3.

□ **Definition 4.8.4**   The *Chernoff function* $c(a)$ for the random variable Y is defined by

$$c(a) = \min_{\hat{\mathbf{q}} \in \mathscr{P}_a} \sum_k \hat{q}_k \log \frac{\hat{q}_k}{q_k}$$

where

$$\mathscr{P}_a = \left\{ \hat{\mathbf{q}} : \sum_k \hat{q}_k \xi_k \leq a \right\}$$

where q_k is the probability that the random variable Y assumes the value ξ_k. The optimizing $\hat{\mathbf{q}}$ is called the *tilted probability distribution* corresponding to a.   □

The next theorem shows that, in the range of interest, the constraint is satisfied with equality. Therefore the minimum can be evaluated by introducing a Lagrange multiplier. This leads to a parametric representation of $c(a)$

$$c(a_s) = sa_s - \log \sum_k q_k e^{s\xi_k}$$

where

$$a_s = \sum_k q_k^* \xi_k$$

and

$$q_k^* = \frac{q_k e^{s\xi_k}}{\sum_k q_k e^{s\xi_k}}$$

A tilted probability distribution in this special form is also called an *exponential family* of probability distributions.

The simplest example of a Chernoff function is given for the binary symmetric distribution. Suppose a random variable takes the value A with probability $1/2$ and $-A$ with probability $1/2$. Because the alphabet is binary, the tilted distribution can only be of the form

$$\mathbf{q}^* = \{\lambda, 1 - \lambda\}$$

for some λ. Hence

$$c(a) = \sum_k q_k^* \log \frac{q_k^*}{q_k}$$

$$= \log 2 - H_b(\lambda)$$

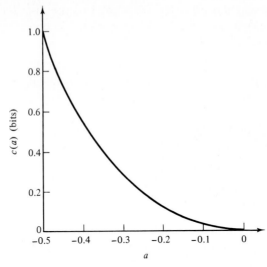

Figure 4.10   Chernoff function for a binary symmetric source.

where

$$a = \sum_k q_k^* \xi_k$$

$$= \lambda A + (1 - \lambda)(-A)$$

Eliminating λ gives

$$c(a) = \log 2 - H_b\left(\frac{a + A}{2A}\right)$$

The Chernoff function for this example is shown in Fig. 4.10. The shape of the function is typical of the general case, as is proved in the following theorem.

☐ **Theorem 4.8.5** The Chernoff function is a nonnegative, convex, strictly decreasing function of a for a less than the mean $\bar{\xi} = \sum_k q_k \xi_k$. In this range the inequality constraint is satisfied with equality.

Proof Because $\mathscr{P}_{a'} \supset \mathscr{P}_a$ if $a' > a$, it follows that $c(a)$ is nonincreasing. Convexity is proved as follows. Let $\mathbf{q}'$ and $\mathbf{q}''$ achieve $c(a')$ and $c(a'')$, and let $\lambda \in [0, 1]$ be given. Let $\mathbf{q}^* = \lambda \mathbf{q}' + \bar{\lambda} \mathbf{q}''$ where $\bar{\lambda} = 1 - \lambda$. Then

$$\sum_k q_k^* \xi_k = \lambda \sum_k q_k' \xi_k + \bar{\lambda} \sum_k q_k'' \xi_k$$

$$\leq \lambda a' + \bar{\lambda} a''$$

Therefore $\mathbf{q}^* \in \mathscr{P}_{\lambda a' + \bar{\lambda} a''}$ and

$$c(\lambda a' + \bar{\lambda} a'') \leq \sum_k q_k^* \log \frac{q_k^*}{q_k}$$

$$\leq \lambda \sum_k q_k' \log \frac{q_k'}{q_k} + \bar{\lambda} \sum_k q_k'' \log \frac{q_k''}{q_k}$$

$$= \lambda c(a') + \bar{\lambda} c(a'')$$

which establishes convexity. Because $c(a)$ is convex and nonincreasing, if it is constant on any interval, then it is constant for all a greater than this interval. Hence it is strictly decreasing on the interval of interest. Finally, it is zero if and only if $\mathbf{q}$ itself is an element of $\mathscr{P}_a$, and this implies that $a \geq \bar{\xi}$. $\square$

The following theorem provides a graphical interpretation of the Lagrange multiplier s.

☐ **Theorem 4.8.6**

$$\frac{dc(a)}{da} = s$$

Proof Show the dependence of s on a explicitly by writing $s(a)$. Then from the parametric representation

$$\frac{dc(a)}{da} = s(a) + a \frac{ds(a)}{da} - \frac{\sum_k \bar{\xi}_k q_k e^{s\xi_k}}{\sum_k q_k e^{s\xi_k}} \frac{ds(a)}{da}$$

$$= s \qquad\qquad\qquad\qquad\qquad\qquad \square$$

☐ **Theorem 4.8.7**   A representation of $c(a)$ is

$$c(a) = \max_{s \leq 0} \left[sa - \log M(s) \right]$$

Proof For each fixed s, the bracketed term is a linear function of a and is tangent to the convex function $c(a)$ at some value of a and hence lies entirely below $c(a)$. In addition, for fixed a, some value of s achieves $c(a)$. The theorem then follows. $\square$

The Chernoff function for sums of independent, identically distributed random variables is simply related to the Chernoff function for the individual random variables in the following theorem.

☐   **Theorem 4.8.8**   Suppose $\{Y_l : l = 1, \ldots, n\}$ is a block of independent, identically distributed random variables and

$$Z = \sum_{l=1}^{n} Y_l$$

If c_n is the Chernoff function for Z, then

$$c_n(na) = nc(a)$$

Proof   The additivity of the Chernoff function follows from the multiplicity of the moment generating function for independent random variables. Thus

$$M_z(s) = E\left[e^s \sum_l y_l \right] = \prod_{l=1}^{n} M_{y_l}(s)$$

Then

$$c_n(na_s) = \max_{s \le 0} \left[sna - \sum_{l=1}^{n} \log M_{y_l}(s) \right]$$

$$= \max_{s \le 0} n[sa - \log M_y(s)]$$

$$= nc(a) \qquad\qquad\qquad ☐$$

We can generalize the above discussion to the case where the random variables Y_l are different. Assume that there are J possible types of random variables occurring in the sequence and that the jth type occurs $n_j = np_j$ times. Then the Chernoff function for distributions of mixed type is

$$c(a) = \min_{\hat{Q} \in \mathcal{Q}_a} \sum_j \sum_k p_j \hat{Q}_{k|j} \log \frac{\hat{Q}_{k|j}}{Q_{k|j}}$$

where

$$\mathcal{Q}_a = \left\{ \hat{Q} : \sum_j \sum_k p_j \hat{Q}_{k|j} \xi_{kj} \le a \right\}$$

With this definition, all the theorems of this section hold virtually unchanged.

The Chernoff function provides both a lower bound and an upper bound to the distribution function of a sum of independent, identically distributed random variables. The upper bound, which follows from Theorem 4.8.3 and Theorem 4.8.8, is

$$Pr[z \le na] \le e^{-nc(a)}$$

where

$$Z = \sum_{l=1}^{n} Y_l$$

□   **Theorem 4.8.9**   Suppose Y_l are zero-mean, independent, identically distributed random variables, and let

$$Z = \sum_{l=1}^{n} Y_l$$

Then

$$Pr[z \leq na] \geq e^{-nc(a) + o(n)}$$

where $o(n)$ goes to zero as n goes to infinity.

Proof   This is proved in the same way as was Theorem 4.5.3. First choose a tilted probability distribution within distance ε of the constraint threshold na, then use Corollary 4.4.3 and the law of large numbers to reduce the nuisance terms to $o(n)$.

PROBLEMS

4.1.   The error exponent for detection of a signal of amplitude $\sqrt{S}$ in gaussian noise of variance N is given by

$$e(r) = \left(\sqrt{r} - \sqrt{\frac{S}{2N}} \right)^2$$

Suppose that n, a fixed number of independent, identically distributed measurements, are made. It is desired that the probabilities of type I and type II errors be balanced.
   Let $S = 1$ and $N = 1$. Bound the probability of error if $n = 160$. (This problem corresponds to detecting a weak target in a radar return by integrating 160 pulses.)

4.2.   Let a pair of measurements denoted by (X, Y) be given and let P_{0jk}, P_{1jk} be the probabilities that $(X, Y) = (j, k)$ under hypotheses H_0 and H_1, respectively. Let p_{0j}, p_{1j}, q_{0k}, and q_{1k} be the components of the appropriate marginals. Show that the conjecture

$$L(\mathbf{P}_0; \mathbf{P}_1) \leq L(\mathbf{p}_0; \mathbf{p}_1) + L(\mathbf{q}_0; \mathbf{q}_1)$$

is false by giving a suitable counterexample.

4.3.   Is the log-likelihood ratio a sufficient statistic for hypothesis testing? Why?

4.4.   Use the discrimination inequality to prove that

$$\sum_{j=0}^{J-1} \frac{p_j^2}{q_j} \geq 1$$

where $\mathbf{p}$ and $\mathbf{q}$ are probability distributions.

4.5.   Consider sequences of length n from an alphabet of size J. Each letter in a sequence can be one of J possibilities. The number of times letter j appears in a sequence is denoted by n_j. Clearly

$$\sum_{j=0}^{J-1} n_j = n$$

Let $\bar{p}_0, \ldots, \bar{p}_{J-1}$ denote the relative frequencies. That is, $\bar{p}_j = n_j/n$, and the vector $\bar{\mathbf{p}}$ denotes the relative composition of the sequence. Suppose the letters are randomly selected—independently and identically distributed with probability distribution $\mathbf{p} = (p_0, \ldots, p_{J-1})$. The probability of obtaining a sequence with composition $(n_0, \ldots, n_{J-1})$ is given by the multinomial distribution:

$$Pr[n_0, \ldots, n_{J-1}] = \frac{n!}{n_0! n_1! \cdots n_{J-1}!} \, p_0^{n_0} p_1^{n_1} \cdots p_{J-1}^{n_{J-1}}$$

Use Stirling's approximation to show that if $\bar{\mathbf{p}}$ is kept fixed as n increases, then

$$\lim_{n \to \infty} \left(\frac{\log Pr[n_0, \ldots, n_{J-1}]}{n} \right) = L(\bar{\mathbf{p}}; \mathbf{p})$$

This is sometimes written

$$Pr[n_0, \ldots, n_{J-1}] \simeq e^{-nL(\bar{\mathbf{p}}; \mathbf{p}) - o(n)}$$

where $o(n)$ is a term that grows more slowly than linearly with n. Note that the probability goes to zero if $\bar{\mathbf{p}} \neq \mathbf{p}$. This is a form of the weak law of large numbers.

4.6. Prove the following properties of convex functions on the real line:

a. A convex function on an open interval is continuous on that interval.

b. If $f_i(x)$ for $i = 1, \ldots, n$ are all convex functions, then

$$f(x) = \sum_i f_i(x)$$

is a convex function.

c. If $f_i(x)$ for $i = 1, \ldots, n$ are all convex funtions, then

$$f(x) = \max_i \left[f_i(x) \right]$$

is a convex function.

d. A convex function has a derivative everywhere except for, at most, a countable number of points.

4.7. Prove that on the interval $x > 0$, the function $f(x)$ is convex if and only if $x f(1/x)$ is convex.

4.8. Let $f(x, y, z) = x^2 + y^2 + x^2 z^2 + z^2$

a. Find (x, y, z) that minimizes f. What is f at this point?

b. Now find (x, y, z) that minimizes f subject to the constraint $x = y - 1$ by using direct substitution.

c. Finally, by using a Lagrange multiplier, find (x, y, z) that minimizes f subject to the constraint $x = y - 1$.

4.9. The discrimination for continuous random variables is defined by

$$L(q_0; q_1) = \int_{-\infty}^{\infty} q_0(y) \log \frac{q_0(y)}{q_1(y)} \, dy$$

Suppose $q_0(y)$ is normal of zero mean and variance N and $q_1(y)$ is normal of mean $S^{\frac{1}{2}}$ and variance N. (These are the distributions appropriate to the problem of detection of a signal in gaussian noise.) Prove that the discrimination (in nats) is

$$L(q_0; q_1) = \tfrac{1}{2}S/N$$

$$L(q_1; q_0) = \tfrac{1}{2}S/N$$

Because 1 bit $= \log_e 2$ nats, a change in units gives $L(q_0; q_1) = 0.72S/N$ bits. The ratio S/N is the signal-to-noise ratio familiar from the theory of signal detection in gaussian noise. The signal-to-noise ratio is significant only for gaussian-noise problems, while the discrimination is defined for any hypothesis-testing problem. In this sense, discrimination is a generalization of signal-to-noise ratio.

4.10. A coin is given which may be either a fair coin with probability of a head equal to 1/2 or may be a biased coin with probability of a head equal to 3/4. We are to decide which coin is given by flipping it N times and observing the outcome. Is the total number of heads a sufficient statistic for making this decision? Why or why not?

4.11. Suppose that we have a Rayleigh distribution either of mean $a\sqrt{\pi/2}$ or of mean $2a\sqrt{\pi/2}$ under hypotheses H_0 and H_1, respectively. That is,

$$H_0: q_0(y) = 2\frac{y}{a^2} e^{-y^2/a^2} \qquad y \ge 0$$

$$H_1: q_1(y) = 2\frac{y}{4a^2} e^{-y^2/4a^2} \qquad y \ge 0$$

are the probability density functions. A set of N observations is made. Find N so that probabilities of type I and type II error of less than 10^{-6} can be ensured. Take $a = 1$.

Note: This problem corresponds to the decision, based on observing the envelope (video) output of a radio receiver, as to whether the output is due to receiver internal thermal noise only or an additional external gaussian-noise signal entering the receiver.

4.12. A coin is given which may be either a fair coin with probability of a head equal to 1/2 or may be a biased coin with probability of a head equal to 3/4. We are to decide which coin is given by flipping it N times and observing the outcome. We are allowed a 1% probability of calling the coin biased when it is fair, and a 0.01% probability of calling the coin fair when it is biased. Plot $e(r)$ for this problem. Select N and a decision rule satisfying the above requirements.

4.13. Suppose that $\mathbf{q}$ is the Poisson distribution:

$$q_k = \frac{\lambda^k e^{-\lambda}}{k!} \qquad k = 0, \ldots$$

where λ is a constant. What distribution $\mathbf{q}'$ minimizes $L(\mathbf{q}'; \mathbf{q})$, given that

$$\sum_{k=1}^{\infty} k q_k' = m$$

Note: The discrimination for countably infinite distributions is defined simply by extending the sum to infinity.

4.14. Let q_k for $k = 0, \ldots, K - 1$ be any discrete probability distribution. Prove that, for any j,

$$H(\mathbf{q}) \le H_b(q_j) + (1 - q_j) \log_2 (K - 1)$$

Is this inequality stronger than the inequality $H(\mathbf{q}) \leq \log_2 K$? (The inequality anticipates the Fano inequality of Chapter 5.)

4.15. Prove that $de(r)/dr = -s$ directly by computing the derivative.

4.16. Prove in detail the Chernoff lower bound

$$Pr[z \leq na] \geq e^{-nc(a) + o(n)}$$

NOTES

The testing of binary hypotheses is a central problem of statistics and appears throughout the statistics literature. That problem is one of the meeting places of the subjects of statistics and information theory. The central theorem of binary hypothesis testing was devised by Neyman and Pearson (1933). The popularization of the discrimination as an information-theoretic function for studying hypothesis testing is due to Kullback (1951, 1959). Other techniques of mathematical statistics, developed by Sanov (1957) and Hoeffding (1965) have been distilled and applied to information theory by Csiszár (1984). The methods of asymptotic analysis based on the error-exponent function are from Csiszár and Longo (1971) and Blahut (1972). These methods are similar to the methods of Chernoff (1952) for bounding the tails of a probability distribution.

Hypothesis testing also appears with a somewhat different flavor in the engineering literature, particularly for the problem of detecting radar pulses. North (1943) first proposed the matched filter for this hypothesis-testing problem. Turin (1960) wrote a key tutorial paper to popularize these methods.

CHAPTER 5

Data Transmission Codes

A *noisy communication channel* is a channel for which the output is not completely determined by the input; there may be errors. A *data transmission code* is a code that makes a noisy channel into a reliable channel. Even though there may be errors at the output of the channel, the output of the decoder is virtually error-free. In this chapter, we shall study the conditions under which good data transmission codes exist. We shall see that most channels are characterized by a number called the *channel capacity*, which tells the maximum rate for which good data transmission codes exist.

A noisy channel is judged by the channel capacity. A block code for data transmission on this channel is judged by the probability of decoding error p_e. We shall find that an enormity of codes of arbitrarily small probability of error exist if data is to be transmitted through the channel at a rate below the channel capacity, although such codes constitute a small fraction of all possible codes. Conversely, no codes of good performance exist if data is to be transmitted at a rate above the channel capacity. Thus the capacity of a channel is a succinct statement separating the rates for which there exist good codes from the rates for which there do not.

5.1 DISCRETE NOISY CHANNELS

The noisy binary channel and the deep-space gaussian-noise channel are two important examples of noisy channels. The first example is a discrete channel. The second example is a continuous-time, continuous-amplitude channel that is usually made into a discrete channel by a modulator/demodulator.

A *discrete channel* is a system in which a sequence of letters chosen from a finite set of symbols $\{a_0, \ldots, a_{J-1}\}$ can be transmitted from one point to another. A *noisy channel* is one for which the channel output symbol is not completely determined by the channel input symbols; only some probability distribution on the output is determined by the input. If the probability distribution on the output is independent of previous channel inputs or outputs, the channel is called *memoryless*.[†]

Let $\{b_0, \ldots, b_{K-1}\}$ be the set of channel output symbols; possibly $K \neq J$. Let $Q(b_k|a_j)$, abbreviated $Q_{k|j}$, be the probability that symbol b_k is received, given that a_j was sent. It is called the *forward transition probability*, and the K-by-J matrix **Q** with elements $Q_{k|j}$ is called the *probability transition matrix* of the channel. For our purposes, any two channels with the same probability transition matrix **Q** can be regarded as the same channel. We will use **Q** as a handy name for the channel.

A representation of a channel is shown in Fig. 5.1. Some simple channels are represented symbolically in more detail in Fig. 5.2. If the input and output alphabets are the same, with a natural correspondence between input symbols and output symbols, then it is natural to say that the channel makes an error when the output is different from the input.[‡] However, many channels may have a more extensive output alphabet whose symbols are not so closely paired with channel input symbols. For such channels the term "error" does not immediately apply to individual channel outputs.

A block input **x** to the channel is an n-tuple of symbols from the channel input alphabet, with symbol a_{j_l} in the lth component x_l of **x**. We may think of a block input as a vector. A block output of the channel is a vector **y** with symbol b_{k_l} in the lth component y_l of **y**. The probability that the vector **y** is the

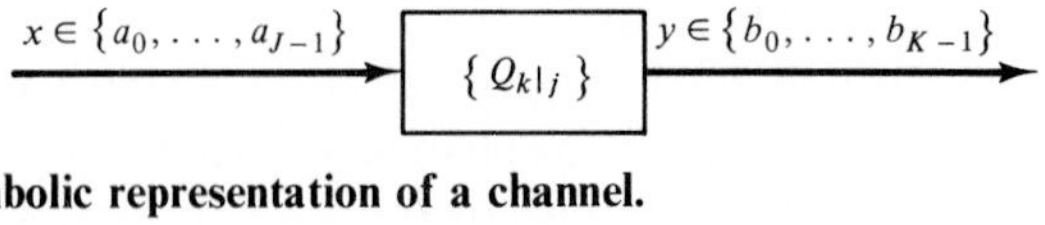

Figure 5.1   Symbolic representation of a channel.

[†]Here we are speaking of memory in the noise process. In Chapter 2 we dealt with memory in the constraints of the allowed input data stream.
[‡]In such a case, the data transmission code is also called an *error-control code* or an *error-correcting code*.

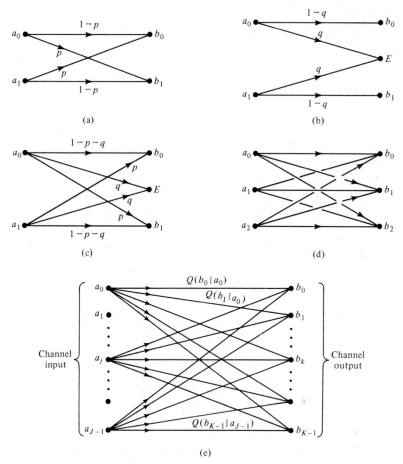

Figure 5.2   Some discrete memoryless channels: (a) binary symmetric channel; (b) binary erasure channel; (c) errors-and-erasures channel; (d) ternary symmetric channel; (e) the general case.

output of the channel after passing $\mathbf{x}$ through the memoryless channel with transition matrix $\mathbf{Q} = \{Q_{k|j}\}$ is given by the product distribution,

$$Q(\mathbf{y}|\mathbf{x}) = \prod_{l=1}^{n} Q(b_{k_l}|a_{j_l}) = \prod_{l=1}^{n} Q_{k_l|j_l}$$

A symbolic representation of the channel at the block level is shown in Fig. 5.3. From the point of view of the output, the probability that $\mathbf{x}$ was transmitted when $\mathbf{y}$ is observed is given by the Bayes formula,

$$P(\mathbf{x}|\mathbf{y}) = \frac{p(\mathbf{x})Q(\mathbf{y}|\mathbf{x})}{\sum_{\mathbf{x}} p(\mathbf{x})Q(\mathbf{y}|\mathbf{x})}$$

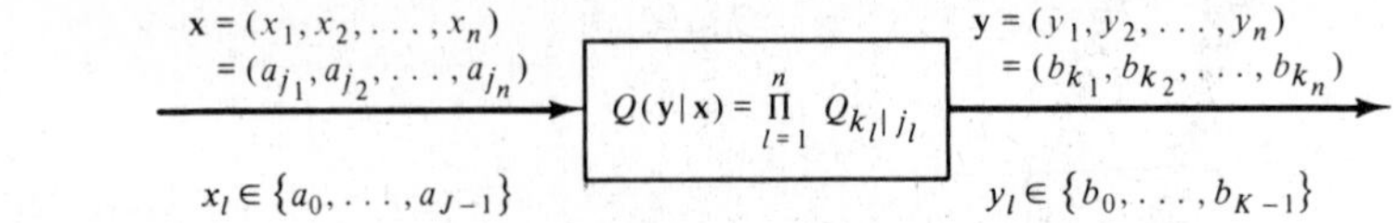

$$\mathbf{x} = (x_1, x_2, \ldots, x_n)$$
$$= (a_{j_1}, a_{j_2}, \ldots, a_{j_n})$$

$$Q(\mathbf{y}|\mathbf{x}) = \prod_{l=1}^{n} Q_{k_l|j_l}$$

$$\mathbf{y} = (y_1, y_2, \ldots, y_n)$$
$$= (b_{k_1}, b_{k_2}, \ldots, b_{k_n})$$

$$x_l \in \{a_0, \ldots, a_{J-1}\}$$

$$y_l \in \{b_0, \ldots, b_{K-1}\}$$

Figure 5.3   Symbolic representation of a channel at the block level.

A block code $\mathscr{C}$ of *blocklength n* and *size M* is a set of M n-tuples of symbols from the input alphabet. The n-tuples are called *codewords* and denoted $\mathbf{c}_m$ for $m = 0, \ldots, M - 1$. The *rate R* of the code $\mathscr{C}$ is given by $R = (1/n) \log_2 M$. The rate is expressed in units of bits per code symbol. Whenever it is necessary to avoid confusion with the rate of transmitting symbols through the channel, the rate of a code is called the *code rate*.

A simple example is the following code of blocklength 5 and size 4:

$$\mathscr{C} = \{\mathbf{c}_0, \mathbf{c}_1, \mathbf{c}_2, \mathbf{c}_3\}$$
$$= \{00000, 10101, 01010, 11111\}$$

This code has rate R equal to 0.4.

A decoder is a partition of the set of output blocks of the channel into a collection of subsets $\{\mathscr{U}_m\}_{m=0}^{M-1}$ called *decode regions*. For each m, $\mathscr{U}_m$ is the decode region for the mth codeword. Figure 5.4 gives a way to visualize the decode regions. If $\mathbf{y}$ is the block output of the channel and $\mathbf{y}$ is in decode region $\mathscr{U}_m$, then the decoder decides that $\mathbf{c}_m$ was the codeword transmitted through the channel. If some other codeword was actually transmitted, then an error occurs.

The probability of error of codeword $\mathbf{c}_m$ is

$$p_{e|m} = \sum_{\mathbf{y} \in \mathscr{U}_m^c} Q(\mathbf{y}|\mathbf{c}_m)$$

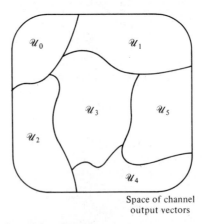

Space of channel
output vectors

Figure 5.4   Visualization of decode regions.

The average probability of error of the code $\mathscr{C}$ is

$$p_e(\mathscr{C}) = \sum_m Pr[\mathbf{c}_m]\, p_{e|m}$$

where $Pr[\mathbf{c}_m]$ is the probability of transmitting codeword $\mathbf{c}_m$.

The design of a communication system for a discrete channel consists of a choice of the code $\mathscr{C}$ and the set of decode regions $\{\mathscr{U}_m\}_{m=0}^{M-1}$. Clearly, the code can be chosen in many ways, and the set of decode regions can be defined in many ways. We shall study the error probability p_e when the decoder uses the rule that $\mathbf{y}$ is in the decode region $\mathscr{U}_m$ such that $P(\mathbf{c}_m|\mathbf{y})$ is larger than $P(\mathbf{c}_{m'}|\mathbf{y})$ for all $m' \neq m$. This rule is generally an incomplete decoding rule because there may be an m and m' for which $P(\mathbf{c}_m|\mathbf{y})$ and $P(\mathbf{c}_{m'}|\mathbf{y})$ are equal. Ties occur with such a very low probability, however, that they can be ignored in computing performance of the decoder. Any method can be used to break ties. One way to make the decoding rule into a complete decoding rule is to break ties in favor of the smallest index. The following theorem shows that this decoding rule minimizes the probability of error.

☐   **Theorem 5.1.1**   A decoder whose decode regions are given by

$$\mathscr{U}_m = \{\mathbf{y} : P(\mathbf{c}_m|\mathbf{y}) \geq P(\mathbf{c}_{m'}|\mathbf{y}) \text{ for all } m' \neq m;$$

$$P(\mathbf{c}_m|\mathbf{y}) > P(\mathbf{c}_{m'}|\mathbf{y}) \text{ for all } m' < m\}$$

is a minimum-probability-of-error decoder.

Proof   The set of decode regions can be constructed by assigning each channel output block $\mathbf{y}$ to one of the decode regions. This should be done to minimize the contribution of that $\mathbf{y}$ to the probability of decoding error. Given that word $\mathbf{y}$ is received and $\mathbf{y} \in \mathscr{U}_m$, the probability of decoding error is

$$p_{e|\mathbf{y}} = 1 - P(\mathbf{c}_m|\mathbf{y})$$

The average probability of decoding error of the code $\mathscr{C}$ is

$$p_e(\mathscr{C}) = \sum_\mathbf{y} q(\mathbf{y}) p_{e|\mathbf{y}}$$

Decode regions will have minimum probability of error if for each $\mathbf{y}$, m is chosen so that

$$P(\mathbf{c}_m|\mathbf{y}) \geq P(\mathbf{c}_{m'}|\mathbf{y})$$

for all $m' \neq m$. Then $\mathbf{y}$ is made an element of $\mathscr{U}_m$. Repeating this for each $\mathbf{y}$ forms the collection of decode regions. To make the choice unique in case of ties, we append the additional condition $P(\mathbf{c}_m|\mathbf{y}) > P(\mathbf{c}_{m'}|\mathbf{y})$ for all $m' < m$.   ☐

Using the Bayes formula, the inequality defining $\mathcal{U}_m$ may be rewritten

$$\frac{p(\mathbf{c}_m)Q(\mathbf{y}|\mathbf{c}_m)}{q(\mathbf{y})} \geq \frac{p(\mathbf{c}_{m'})Q(\mathbf{y}|\mathbf{c}_{m'})}{q(\mathbf{y})}$$

for all $m' \neq m$. If the codewords are used with equal probability, then $p(\mathbf{c}_m) = 1/M$ for all m, and the inequality becomes

$$Q(\mathbf{y}|\mathbf{c}_m) \geq Q(\mathbf{y}|\mathbf{c}_{m'})$$

The decode regions can now be written as

$$\mathcal{U}_m = \{\mathbf{y} : Q(\mathbf{y}|\mathbf{c}_m) \geq Q(\mathbf{y}|\mathbf{c}_{m'}) \text{ for all } m' \neq m;$$
$$Q(\mathbf{y}|\mathbf{c}_m) > Q(\mathbf{y}|\mathbf{c}_{m'}) \text{ for all } m' < m\}$$

It may be that the latter description of the decode regions is used to define a decoder even when the codewords are not used with equal probability. The decoder so defined is then called a *maximum-likelihood decoder*.[†] It is the same as a minimum-probability-of-error decoder when the codewords are used with equal probability.

When used on the channel $\mathbf{Q}$, a data transmission code is judged by its average probability of block decoding error p_e. If we have two codes of the same blocklength and rate, we will generally prefer the code with the smaller p_e. If we have a code $\mathscr{C} = \{\mathbf{c}_m : m = 0, \ldots, M - 1\}$, we would like to know if p_e is as small as possible for a code with this blocklength and rate. Generally we do not know how to answer this question; we can only give some coarse bounds. We may also wish to know if the rate of the code is as large as it could be on the channel $\mathbf{Q}$. To answer this question we need to define the capacity of the channel.

One way we might define the capacity of a noisy channel is as follows. For each n and p_e, let $M(n, p_e)$ denote the number of codewords in the largest block code of blocklength n having probability of block decoding error not larger than p_e. With this code we can transmit at a rate of $R = (1/n)\log_2 M(n, p_e)$ bits of information per channel symbol, but with a probability of block error of p_e and a probability of symbol error at most equal to p_e. The capacity then could be defined as

$$C = \lim_{p_e \to 0} \left[\lim_{n \to \infty} \frac{\log_2 M(n, p_e)}{n} \right]$$

Denoting the bracketed term by $C(p_e)$, we could say that for large enough n, a code of blocklength n and probability of block error p_e exists with about $2^{nC(p_e)}$ codewords. The code will transmit with a rate of about $C(p_e)$ bits of information per channel symbol. This holds for every p_e, so if we transmit at a rate of not more than about C bits of information per channel symbol, we can

---

[†]A conditional probability function $Q(\mathbf{y}|\mathbf{x})$ is called a *likelihood function* when it is viewed as a function of $\mathbf{x}$ with $\mathbf{y}$ fixed.

choose p_e as small as we like. The penalty for choosing p_e small is that the blocklength to achieve this p_e may be large.

The remarkable thing we would find by starting with such a definition is that C will be nonzero. Even though $C(p_e)$ is decreasing as p_e decreases, the limit is strictly positive. This is the significance of the capacity. However, we will not define the capacity in this way because it would be too difficult to calculate from this point of view. This is because we can see no hope of ever knowing $M(n,p_e)$. Instead, in Section 5.4, we will give a much different definition that does not involve the probability of error. Then in the remainder of the chapter we tie that definition back to the above paragraph.

5.2 THE MUTUAL-INFORMATION FUNCTION

Let $p(a_j)$, abbreviated p_j, be the probability that symbol a_j is the input of channel **Q**. The probability $q(b_k)$, abbreviated q_k, of symbol b_k being the channel output is

$$q_k = \sum_{j=0}^{J-1} p_j Q_{k|j}$$

Given the output b_k, the probability $P(a_j|b_k)$, abbreviated $P_{j|k}$, that symbol a_j was transmitted is given by the Bayes formula,

$$P_{j|k} = \frac{p_j Q_{k|j}}{\displaystyle\sum_{j=0}^{J-1} p_j Q_{k|j}}$$

The J-by-K matrix $\mathbf{P} = \{P_{j|k}\}$ is called the *backwards transition matrix* of the channel.

If the input to a channel can be regarded as a random variable X, then the uncertainty per symbol at the input to the channel is the entropy of the random variable X:

$$H(X) = -\sum_{j=0}^{J-1} p_j \log p_j \qquad \text{bits/symbol}$$

The uncertainty per symbol at the input to the channel, conditional on observing the output random variable Y, is the conditional entropy of the random variable X given by the equivocation

$$H(X|Y) = -\sum_{k=0}^{K-1} q_k \sum_{j=0}^{J-1} P_{j|k} \log P_{j|k} \qquad \text{bits/symbol}$$

The difference between the average uncertainty in the channel input before and after the channel output is received is called the *mutual information* of the channel.

$$I(X;Y) = H(X) - H(X|Y)$$

$$= -\sum_{j=0}^{J-1} p_j \log p_j + \sum_{k=0}^{K-1} \sum_{j=0}^{J-1} q_k P_{j|k} \log P_{j|k}$$

Using the Bayes formula, this becomes

$$I(X;Y) = \sum_{j=0}^{J-1} \sum_{k=0}^{K-1} p_j Q_{k|j} \log \frac{Q_{k|j}}{\sum_{i=0}^{J-1} p_i Q_{k|i}}$$

$$= I(\mathbf{p};\mathbf{Q})$$

Thus $I(X;Y)$ is another notation for the mutual information $I(\mathbf{p};\mathbf{Q})$. The notation $I(X;Y)$ is an improper notation because it incorrectly suggests that the mutual information is a function of the random variables X and Y. Mutual information is actually a function $I(\mathbf{p};\mathbf{Q})$ of probability distributions and not of random variables. However, the notation $I(X;Y)$ is convenient to use in place of $I(\mathbf{p};\mathbf{Q})$ whenever the random variables rather than their probability distributions are foremost in the discussion.

The mutual information is a measure of the average amount of information that can be received by the user by observing the symbol at the output of the channel. We say that $I(X;Y)$ is the amount of information that random variable Y has about random variable X.

The mutual information has a number of important and satisfying properties. One property is that mutual information is symmetric in X and Y. That is,

$$I(X;Y) = I(Y;X)$$

$$= H(Y) - H(Y|X)$$

where

$$I(Y;X) = \sum_{k=0}^{K-1} \sum_{j=0}^{J-1} q_k P_{j|k} \log \frac{P_{j|k}}{\sum_{k=0}^{K-1} q_k P_{j|k}}$$

Another property is that if a channel is noiseless with the same input and output alphabet and $Q_{k|j} = 1$ whenever $k = j$, then $I(X;Y) = H(X)$, so the average mutual information between the output and input of the channel is equal to the average information into the channel.

These and other properties can be proved directly, but we will get them more quickly by an indirect route. We will pose the mutual information in the form of the discrimination; then the properties are obtained easily.

Let X and Y be random variables taking discrete values in the sets $\{a_j\}$ and $\{b_k\}$, respectively. Let H_0 be the hypothesis that X and Y are dependent, with probability distribution $P_{jk} = p_j Q_{k|j}$. Let H_1 be the hypothesis that X and Y are independent, with probability distribution $\hat{P}_{jk} = (\sum_k P_{jk})(\sum_j P_{jk}) = p_j \sum_j p_j Q_{k|j}$. The mutual information between X and Y can be written as the discrimination between these two hypotheses:

$$I(X;Y) = \sum_{jk} P_{jk} \log \frac{P_{jk}}{\hat{P}_{jk}}$$

It is now obvious that $I(X;Y) = I(Y;X)$, so the mutual information is symmetric. The second property mentioned above also follows because, by symmetry,

$$I(X;Y) = H(X) - H(X|Y)$$

and $H(X|Y) = 0$ for the noiseless channel.

The definition also applies to block random variables as inputs to a memoryless channel. The formula then is written as

$$I(X_1, \ldots, X_n; Y_1, \ldots, Y_n) = H(X_1, \ldots, X_n) - H(X_1, \ldots, X_n | Y_1, \ldots, Y_n)$$
$$= H(Y_1, \ldots, Y_n) - H(Y_1, \ldots, Y_n | X_1, \ldots, X_n)$$

This mutual information for blocks can be simplified using the following theorem.

□ **Theorem 5.2.1** The mutual information between the block input and block output of a discrete memoryless channel satisfies

$$I(X_1, \ldots, X_n; Y_1, \ldots, Y_n) \le \sum_{l=1}^{n} I(X_l; Y_l)$$

with equality if and only if the input random variables $X_1, \ldots, X_n$ are independent.

Proof By Theorem 3.2.3,

$$H(Y_1, \ldots, Y_n) \le \sum_{l=1}^{n} H(Y_l)$$

with equality if and only if the Y_l are independent, which is so if and only if the X_l are independent. By Theorem 3.2.4,

$$H(Y_1, \ldots, Y_n | X_1, \ldots, X_n) = \sum_{l=1}^{n} H(Y_l | X_l)$$

The theorem is proved because mutual information is the difference between these two terms.   □

The next three theorems are immediate consequences of the corresponding properties of the discrimination.

□ **Theorem 5.2.2** Mutual information is additive for independent random events.   □

□ **Theorem 5.2.3** Mutual information is nonnegative. It equals zero if and only if the associated random variables are independent.   □

□ **Theorem 5.2.4** Refinement of the joint probability space increases mutual information.   □

The following theorem establishes convexity of the mutual information. This theorem does not follow immediately from the convexity of the discrimination and requires its own proof.

☐   **Theorem 5.2.5**   Mutual information $I(\mathbf{p};\mathbf{Q})$ is concave in $\mathbf{p}$ and is convex in $\mathbf{Q}$. That is, given $\lambda \in [0,1]$ and $\bar{\lambda} = 1 - \lambda$,

$$I(\lambda\mathbf{p}' + \bar{\lambda}\mathbf{p}'';\mathbf{Q}) \geq \lambda I(\mathbf{p}';\mathbf{Q}) + \bar{\lambda}I(\mathbf{p}'';\mathbf{Q})$$

$$I(\mathbf{p};\lambda\mathbf{Q}' + \bar{\lambda}\mathbf{Q}'') \leq \lambda I(\mathbf{p};\mathbf{Q}') + \bar{\lambda}I(\mathbf{p};\mathbf{Q}'')$$

Proof   Let $\mathbf{p}'$ and $\mathbf{p}''$ be given and let $\mathbf{p}^* = \lambda\mathbf{p}' + \bar{\lambda}\mathbf{p}''$. Then, using the inequality $\log x \geq 1 - (1/x)$, we have the following:

$$I(\mathbf{p}^*;\mathbf{Q}) - \lambda I(\mathbf{p}';\mathbf{Q}) - \bar{\lambda}I(\mathbf{p}'';\mathbf{Q})$$

$$= \lambda \sum_j \sum_k p'_j Q_{k|j} \log \frac{\sum_j p'_j Q_{k|j}}{\sum_j p^*_j Q_{k|j}} + \bar{\lambda} \sum_j \sum_k p''_j Q_{k|j} \log \frac{\sum_j p''_j Q_{k|j}}{\sum_j p^*_j Q_{k|j}}$$

$$\geq \lambda \sum_j \sum_k p'_j Q_{k|j} \left(1 - \frac{\sum_j p^*_j Q_{k|j}}{\sum_j p'_j Q_{k|j}}\right) + \bar{\lambda} \sum_j \sum_k p''_j Q_{k|j} \left(1 - \frac{\sum_j p^*_j Q_{k|j}}{\sum_j p''_j Q_{k|j}}\right)$$

$$= 0$$

The convexity in $\mathbf{Q}$ is proved by a similar argument.   ☐

It is also possible to relate mutual information to discrimination in other ways by setting up other artificial hypotheses. Suppose the null hypothesis is characterized by the distribution $\mathbf{Q} = \{Q_{k|j}\}$ conditional on some random variable on a discrete space with J symbols indexed by j, and suppose the alternative hypothesis is characterized by a dummy distribution $\hat{\mathbf{q}} = \{\hat{q}_k\}$. The average discrimination between these two hypotheses is

$$L(\mathbf{Q};\hat{\mathbf{q}}|\mathbf{p}) = \sum_j p_j \left(\sum_k Q_{k|j} \log \frac{Q_{k|j}}{\hat{q}_k}\right)$$

It is shown in the next theorem that $\hat{q}_k = \sum_j p_j Q_{k|j}$ minimizes $L(\mathbf{Q};\hat{\mathbf{q}}|\mathbf{p})$ over all choices of $\hat{\mathbf{q}}$.

☐   **Theorem 5.2.6**   Mutual information can be written in either of the following two forms:

(i) $I(\mathbf{p};\mathbf{Q}) = \min_{\hat{\mathbf{q}}} \sum_j \sum_k p_j Q_{k|j} \log \dfrac{Q_{k|j}}{\hat{q}_k}$

(ii) $I(\mathbf{p};\mathbf{Q}) = \max_{\hat{\mathbf{P}}} \sum_j \sum_k p_j Q_{k|j} \log \dfrac{\hat{P}_{j|k}}{p_j}$

Proof Both parts are proved using the inequality $\log x \geq 1 - (1/x)$. We give only the proof of part (ii). We begin with

$$P_{j|k} = \frac{p_j Q_{k|j}}{\sum_j p_j Q_{k|j}}$$

and

$$q_k = \sum_j p_j Q_{k|j}$$

so that mutual information can be rewritten

$$I(\mathbf{p}; \mathbf{Q}) = \sum_k \sum_j q_k P_{j|k} \log \frac{P_{j|k}}{p_j}$$

Therefore

$$I(\mathbf{p}; \mathbf{Q}) - \sum_j \sum_k p_j Q_{k|j} \log \frac{\hat{P}_{j|k}}{p_j} = \sum_j \sum_k q_k P_{j|k} \log \frac{P_{j|k}}{\hat{P}_{j|k}}$$

$$\geq \sum_j \sum_k q_k P_{j|k} - \sum_j \sum_k q_k \hat{P}_{j|k}$$

$$= 0$$

with equality if and only if $\hat{P}_{j|k} = P_{j|k}$. $\square$

The mutual information is defined as an expectation over the input and output alphabets. It is sometimes desirable to speak of the mutual information between specific realizations of the random variables. The *per-letter information* between symbols j and k is given by

$$I(j; k) = \log \frac{Q_{k|j}}{\sum_j p_j Q_{k|j}} = \log \frac{P_{jk}}{p_j q_k}$$

It is clear that $I(j; k) = I(k; j)$. The mutual information then can be written as the expected value of the per-letter mutual information:

$$I(X; Y) = \sum_j \sum_k p_j Q_{k|j} I(j; k)$$

The mutual information is nonnegative. However, the per-letter information $I(j; k)$ can be negative. In fact, from the definition $I(j; k)$ is nonnegative if and only if $P_{jk} \geq p_j q_k$.

If j is observed, and $Q_{k|j} < q_k$, then the probability of k is decreased by the observation and j gives negative information about k. This negative information must always be offset by positive information for other values of j and k, because the mutual information $I(X; Y)$ is never negative.

The per-letter information $I(j;k)$ can be written

$$I(j;k) = \log \frac{P_{j|k}}{p_j}$$

Suppose $P_{j|k} = 1$. Then k conveys all the information about j that j conveys about itself. That is, any information conveyed by the occurrence of symbol j is also conveyed by the occurrence of symbol k. The per-letter information in this case is also denoted by $I(j)$ so that

$$I(j;k) = -\log p_j = I(j)$$

and this is called the *self-information of j*. The self-information is a random variable and the average value of self-information is the entropy.

When three or more random variables are present in a discussion, the mutual information can be extended to a variety of forms. For example, we can express the mutual information between one set of random variables and another set of random variables. Again, however, the precise statement is that mutual information is a function of the probability distributions on the two sets of random variables.

We limit the discussion to only three random variables—X, Y, and Z indexed by j, k, and l. The joint distribution is given by P_{jkl}, and the meaning of the various conditional marginals will be apparent from the context. The marginals on X, Y, and Z are given by p_j, q_k, and s_l.

We have, first of all, the three mutual informations $I(X;Y)$, $I(Y;Z)$, and $I(Z;X)$. We also have the mutual information between X and the pair (Y,Z) given by

$$I(X;(Y,Z)) = \sum_j \sum_k \sum_l p_j Q_{kl|j} \log \frac{Q_{kl|j}}{\sum_j p_j Q_{kl|j}}$$

$$= \sum_j \sum_k \sum_l p_j Q_{kl|j} \log \frac{P_{j|kl}}{p_j}$$

These two equivalent forms can be obtained by considering the pair (Y,Z) as defining a new random variable on an alphabet with KL elements.

We can also define a *conditional mutual information* between X and Y when Z is known.

☐ **Definition 5.2.7**   The conditional mutual information is given by

$$I(X;Y|Z) = \sum_l s_l \sum_j \sum_k P_{j|l} Q_{k|jl} \log \frac{Q_{k|jl}}{\sum_j P_{j|l} Q_{k|jl}}$$

$$= \sum_l s_l \sum_j \sum_k P_{j|l} Q_{k|jl} \log \frac{P_{j|kl}}{P_{j|l}} \qquad ☐$$

These mutual informations are related by the following theorem.

☐   **Theorem 5.2.8**

$$I(X;(Y,Z)) = I(X;Z|Y) + I(X;Y)$$

$$I(X;(Y,Z)) = I(X;Y|Z) + I(X;Z)$$

Proof The proof of the first line is as follows:

$$I(X;(Y,Z)) = \sum_{jkl} P_{jkl} \log \frac{P_{j|kl}}{p_j}$$

$$= \sum_{jkl} P_{jkl} \log \frac{P_{j|kl}}{p_{j|k}} \frac{p_{j|k}}{p_j}$$

$$= \sum_{jkl} P_{jkl} \log \frac{P_{j|kl}}{p_{j|k}} + \sum_{jkl} P_{jkl} \log \frac{p_{j|k}}{p_j}$$

$$= I(X;Z|Y) + I(X;Y)$$

The second line of the theorem follows from the first by symmetry.   ☐

The expression

$$I(X;(Y,Z)) = I(X;Y) + I(X;Z|Y)$$

is read as follows: The information that the pair of random variables (Y,Z) gives about the random variable X is equal to the information that Y gives about X plus the information that Z gives about X when Y is already known.

Because any of the random variables in Theorem 5.2.8 can itself be built up from a pair of random variables, arbitrarily complicated expressions of the above type can be built up easily. For example,

$$I((X,Y);(U,V,W)) = I((X,Y);U|V,W) + I((X,Y);V|W) + I((X,Y);W)$$

It is rarely necessary to return to the original definitions to prove these more complicated expressions.

5.3 TRANSMISSION OF INFORMATION

The equivocation has been described as information lost by the channel. Consider a channel with the same input and output alphabets. The input X and the output Y then are two random variables defined on the same space. We will think of Y as an estimate of X, and say that an error occurs if X and Y have different values. This happens when X takes value j and Y takes value k that is not equal to j. The probability of error is given by

$$p_e = \sum_j \sum_{k \neq j} P_{jk}$$

We will use the equivocation to bound this probability of error in the next theorem. The theorem can be motivated by a nice intuitive argument which we give first.

The uncertainty in the estimate of the channel input symbol can be broken into two parts: the uncertainty in the binary question of whether or not an error was made and, given that an error was made, the uncertainty in the true value. But errors occur with probability p_e, so the first uncertainty is $H_b(p_e)$. The second uncertainty occurs with probability p_e and can be no larger than $\log(J - 1)$. This occurs only when all alternative errors are equally likely. Therefore, if the equivocation can be interpreted as the information lost, we should have

$$H(X|Y) \leq H_b(p_e) + p_e \log(J - 1)$$

The next theorem proves this claim rigorously.

□   **Theorem 5.3.1   (Fano's inequality)** Suppose that the channel input alphabet and output alphabet are the same. If the probability of channel symbol error is given by

$$p_e = \sum_j \sum_{k \neq j} P_{jk}$$

then

$$H(X|Y) \leq H_b(p_e) + p_e \log(J - 1)$$

Proof

$$H(X|Y) = -\sum_j \sum_k P_{jk} \log P_{j|k}$$

$$= -\sum_j \sum_{k \neq j} P_{jk} \log P_{j|k} - \sum_k P_{kk} \log P_{k|k}$$

Now consider

$$H(X|Y) - p_e \log(J - 1) - H_b(p_e)$$

$$= \sum_j \sum_{k \neq j} P_{jk} \log \frac{p_e}{(J - 1)P_{j|k}} + \sum_k P_{kk} \log \frac{1 - p_e}{P_{k|k}}$$

$$\leq \sum_j \sum_{k \neq j} P_{jk} \left[\frac{p_e}{(J - 1)P_{j|k}} - 1 \right] + \sum_k P_{kk} \left(\frac{1 - p_e}{P_{k|k}} - 1 \right)$$

$$= 0$$

□

The Fano inequality gives a lower bound on the probability of error. It may seem pointless to take an exact expression for p_e and approximate it by an inequality. However, the inequality may be far easier to evaluate because it does not require a summation over what could be a very large number of terms. We will also find Fano's inequality useful when we don't know the actual scheme for using the channel.

By simply reversing the roles of the input and output alphabets, we obtain a parallel result involving the prevarication.

☐ **Corollary 5.3.2** Suppose that X and Y assume values on the same finite space, and

$$p_e = \sum_j \sum_{k \neq j} P_{jk}$$

Then

$$H(Y|X) \leq H_b(p_e) + p_e \log (J - 1) \qquad \qquad \square$$

Fano's inequality can be used to obtain insights into the proper use of a channel. Consider a block of n symbols through a memoryless channel. Let the input and output random variables be given by X^n and Y^n. These are vector random variables, $X^n = (X_1, \ldots, X_n)$, $Y^n = (Y_1, \ldots, Y_n)$ where, in general, the components are dependent.

There are J^n output blocks, so Fano's inequality gives

$$H(Y^n|X^n) \leq H_b(p_e) + p_e \log (J^n - 1)$$
$$\leq 1 + p_e \log J^n$$

Hence

$$p_e \geq \frac{1}{n \log J}[H(Y^n|X^n) - 1]$$

where

$$H(Y^n|X^n) = -\sum_{\mathbf{x}} p(\mathbf{x}) \sum_{\mathbf{y}} Q(\mathbf{y}|\mathbf{x}) \log Q(\mathbf{y}|\mathbf{x})$$

and $Q(\mathbf{y}|\mathbf{x})$ is a product distribution. If we want p_e to go to zero as n goes to infinity, $p(\mathbf{x})$ cannot be a product distribution, since if it were, then

$$H(Y^n|X^n) = nH(Y|X)$$

and

$$p_e \geq \frac{H(Y|X)}{\log J}$$

which does not go to zero as n goes to infinity. The performance of the codes for the channel then would not improve with blocklength.

We will conclude this section with a statement that processing cannot increase mutual information. The statement places no limit on the sophistication or complexity of the encoder and decoder. They could be processors of any type or complexity. The only condition is that the encoder and decoder cannot pass information through some hidden channel. They are connected only by the specified channel. This qualification is expressed mathematically by the conditions

$$Pr[Y|X, U] = Pr[Y|X]$$
$$Pr[V|Y, X, U] = Pr[V|Y]$$

where the random variables U, X, Y, and V are as defined in Fig. 5.5. When these conditions hold, the variables form a Markov chain $U \rightarrow X \rightarrow Y \rightarrow V$ because

$$Pr[V, Y, X, U] = Pr[V|Y]Pr[Y|X]Pr[X|U]Pr[U]$$

We say that the source U is connected to the destination V by means of the channel with input X and output Y.

□   **Theorem 5.3.3   (Data-processing theorem)** If U, X, Y, and V form the Markov chain $U \rightarrow X \rightarrow Y \rightarrow V$, then

$$I(U; V) \leq I(X;Y)$$

Proof From the condition

$$Pr[Y|X, U] = Pr[Y|X]$$

it follows that

$$I(U; Y|X) = 0 = I(Y; U|X)$$

Now

$$I(Y; (X, U)) = I(Y; X) + I(Y; U|X)$$
$$= I(Y; U) + I(Y; X|U)$$

Therefore

$$I(Y; X) = I(Y; U) + I(Y; X|U) \geq I(Y; U)$$

The last inequality holds because $I(Y; X|U)$ is nonnegative. Similar reasoning using $I(U; V|Y) = 0$ leads to

$$I(U; Y) \geq I(U; V)$$

Combining the two inequalities gives

$$I(X; Y) \geq I(U; Y) \geq I(U; V)$$

which proves the theorem.   □

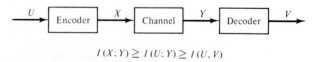

$$I(X; Y) \geq I(U; Y) \geq I(U, V)$$

Figure 5.5   The data-processing theorem.

A channel with block input X^n and block output Y^n can be used to transmit blocks of N data symbols by encoding N data symbols into a channel input block and decoding the channel output block into N data symbols. The data-processing theorem then becomes the following corollary.

□ **Corollary 5.3.4**   If encoder input blocks of length N, denoted U^N, are connected to decoder output blocks of length N, denoted V^N, by means of a channel with codewords of blocklength n, then

$$I(U^N; V^N) \leq I(X^n; Y^n)$$

Proof   Simply replace U, V, X, and Y with U^N, V^N, X^n, and Y^n, respectively, in Theorem 5.3.3.   □

The data-processing theorem is a mathematical statement. Though it has been expressed from a communication point of view, it also applies to other problems. By changing the wording, it becomes applicable to an estimation problem. Here the decoder becomes a processor, the channel becomes a sensor, and the encoder disappears so that U and X are the same. The theorem becomes the following.

□ **Corollary 5.3.5**   Suppose that $\hat{X}$ is an estimate of a random variable X based on a measurement Z. Then

$$I(X; \hat{X}) \leq I(X; Z)$$

Proof   The proof follows from Theorem 5.3.3 by setting $U = X, Y = Z$, and $V = \hat{X}$.   □

5.4. CAPACITY OF DISCRETE NOISY CHANNELS

Loosely, the channel capacity of a channel **Q** is defined to be the maximum rate at which information can be transmitted through the channel. Intuitively, in a well-designed message, we may expect that channel input symbols should occur with a probability distribution such that the average mutual information between channel input and channel output is maximized. This intuitive idea does lead to the right definition of channel capacity. However, it will be some time yet before we give a formal proof, demonstrating that information can be reliably transmitted at any rate smaller than the capacity and yet cannot be reliably transmitted at any rate larger than the capacity.

The capacity of a channel expresses the maximum rate at which information can be conveyed reliably by the channel. We shall see that any coding scheme that superficially appears to operate at a rate higher than C will cause enough data to be lost, because of uncorrectable channel errors, that the information rate at the receiver will actually be less than C. We shall also see that with proper code design, one can come as close to C as is desired.

☐ **Definition 5.4.1** The capacity of a memoryless channel with transition matrix $\mathbf{Q}$ is given by

$$C = \max_{\mathbf{p}} I(\mathbf{p}; \mathbf{Q})$$

$$= \max_{\mathbf{p}} \sum_{j} \sum_{k} p_j Q_{k|j} \log \frac{Q_{k|j}}{\sum_j p_j Q_{k|j}}$$

where the maximum is over the set of all probability distributions on the channel input alphabet. ☐

If the channel is not memoryless, then capacity cannot be defined based on a single channel input symbol. One must use a stronger definition of the capacity, such as

$$C = \lim_{n \to \infty} \frac{1}{n} \max I(X_1, \ldots, X_n; Y_1, \ldots, Y_n)$$

where the maximum is over all probability distributions on input blocks of length n. Evaluation of the capacity of a channel with memory usually is a difficult task. Accordingly, we shall only deal with memoryless channels in this chapter.

We always transmit long sequences through a channel, yet we have defined the capacity of a memoryless channel based on a single channel input symbol. The reason is that, by Theorem 5.2.1,

$$I(X_1, \ldots, X_n; Y_1, \ldots, Y_n) \leq \sum_{l=1}^{n} I(X_l; Y_l)$$

with equality if the input random variables are independent. The capacity of the block channel is obtained by maximizing the right side over all probability distributions on the input blocks. To achieve equality in the inequality, we should choose a product distribution and then maximize over each component. Therefore

$$\max I(X_1, \ldots, X_n; Y_1, \ldots, Y_n) = \sum_{l=1}^{n} \max I(X_l; Y_l)$$

$$= nC$$

By solving the capacity of a memoryless channel for a single input, we implicitly have the capacity of the memoryless channel used for blocks. This is an extraordinary statement because we have already seen, as a consequence to Fano's inequality, that the probability of using a block input cannot be a product distribution if the channel is to be used wisely. Nevertheless, simply to compute the capacity of a memoryless channel, a product distribution suffices. We must try to convey some insight into this seemingly paradoxical statement.

Channel encoding is a deterministic process. The same block of data symbols will always produce the same block of channel input symbols. Nevertheless, if attention is restricted to a single channel input symbol without knowledge of the previous or subsequent channel input symbols, the channel input symbol is not predetermined. At the level of a single letter, the input symbol a_j can be thought of as a random variable. Similarly, small subblocks of input symbols appear to have independent symbols. If one observes a segment of the stream of code symbols entering the channel that is short compared with the code's blocklength, then the symbols in that segment will appear to be independent. The constraints built into the code will become apparent only when a large fraction of a codeword is observed.

The capacity of many simple channels can be evaluated by finding the maximum analytically. We shall see that if the channel is symmetric,[†] the probability distribution **p** that achieves the capacity is the equiprobable probability distribution. This is the right intuitive answer; it says that if the channel treats all input symbols the same, then all input symbols should be used equally often. Symmetric channels are good models for many channels that occur in practice, so it is fortunate that their capacities are easy to compute.

The capacity of the binary symmetric channel with error probability ρ is achieved by the equiprobable input probability distribution $\mathbf{p} = (\frac{1}{2}, \frac{1}{2})$. The capacity is

$$C = 1 + \rho \log_2 \rho + (1 - \rho) \log_2 (1 - \rho)$$

$$= 1 - H_b(\rho) \qquad \text{bits/input symbol}$$

The binary erasure channel fails our definition of a symmetric channel, though it does have its own symmetry. The capacity of the binary erasure channel with erasure probability ρ is also achieved by the equiprobable input probability distribution $\mathbf{p} = (\frac{1}{2}, \frac{1}{2})$. The capacity is

$$C = 1 - \rho \qquad \text{bits/input symbol}$$

This is somewhat surprising because it says that the erasures cause a loss in capacity exactly equal to the fraction of symbols erased, despite the fact that the encoder does not know which symbols will be erased, only that there will be $n\rho$ erasures on average.

The capacities of these two simple channels are shown in Fig. 5.6 as a function of the channel crossover probability ρ.

[†]A *symmetric channel* **Q** is a discrete memoryless channel such that every row is a permutation of the first row and every column is a permutation of the first column.

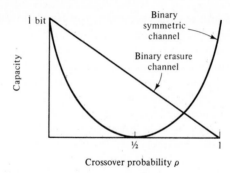

Figure 5.6   Capacity of binary symmetric and binary erasure channels.

☐   **Theorem 5.4.2**   The capacity of any symmetric channel is given by

$$C = \sum_j \frac{1}{J} \sum_k Q_{k|j} \log Q_{k|j} + \log K$$

and is achieved using the equiprobable distribution on the input alphabet.

Proof

$$C = \max_{\mathbf{p}} \left[\sum_j p_j \sum_k Q_{k|j} \log Q_{k|j} - \sum_k q_k \log q_k \right]$$

where $q_k = \sum_j p_j Q_{k|j}$. But because of symmetry, $\sum_k Q_{k|j} \log Q_{k|j}$ is the same for every j, so the first term is unaffected by choice of p_j. Hence

$$C = \sum_j \frac{1}{J} \sum_k Q_{k|j} \log Q_{k|j} + \max_{\mathbf{p}} \left[-\sum_k q_k \log q_k \right]$$

The second term can be maximized if **p** can be chosen to make **q** the equiprobable distribution. By symmetry of **Q**, this will be so if **p** itself is chosen as the equiprobable distribution.   ☐

For more general channels, it can be difficult to find the input probability distribution that achieves the capacity. The next theorem gives a test that sometimes can be used to verify that a plausible probability distribution does, in fact, achieve the capacity. Later in the section we shall give an efficient numerical algorithm that can be used to compute the capacity.

☐   **Theorem 5.4.3**   A probability distribution **p** on the channel input achieves capacity of the channel with transition matrix **Q** if and only if there exists a number C such that

$$\sum_k Q_{k|j} \log \frac{Q_{k|j}}{\sum_j p_j Q_{k|j}} = C \qquad \text{if } p_j \neq 0$$

$$\sum_k Q_{k|j} \log \frac{Q_{k|j}}{\sum_j p_j Q_{k|j}} \leq C \qquad \text{if } p_j = 0$$

Proof The proof is an application of the Kuhn-Tucker theorem, which is given as Theorem A.6 in Appendix A. The Kuhn-Tucker theorem can be applied because $I(\mathbf{p};\mathbf{Q})$ is a concave function in $\mathbf{p}$. Using a Lagrange multiplier to constrain $\sum_j p_j = 1$, the Kuhn-Tucker theorem gives

$$\frac{\partial}{\partial p_j}\left(-\sum_j \sum_k p_j Q_{k|j} \log \frac{Q_{k|j}}{\sum_j p_j Q_{k|j}} - \lambda \sum_j p_j\right) \geq 0$$

$$\sum_k Q_{k|j} \log \frac{Q_{k|j}}{\sum_j p_j Q_{k|j}} \leq -\lambda + 1$$

with equality for all j for which p_j is nonzero. Setting $-\lambda + 1 = C$ completes the proof of the theorem. $\square$

The constant C is evaluated by multiplying each equation by p_j and summing. Thus

$$\sum_j p_j \sum_k Q_{k|j} \log \frac{Q_{k|j}}{\sum_j p_j Q_{k|j}} = C$$

This shows that the constant C is the capacity of the channel.

It is relatively easy to show that there are no reliable data transmission codes with rate greater than the capacity, a fact known as the *converse theorem*, but the direct theorem is much longer and appears in the next section. The converse theorem can be obtained from Fano's inequality. The information rate into a channel is given by

$$R = \frac{1}{n} H(X^n)$$

where $H(X^n)$ is the entropy of the set of input words of blocklength n. The entropy is largest if the M input words are used equiprobably so that

$$R \leq \frac{1}{n} \log M$$

$\square$ **Theorem 5.4.4 (Channel-coding converse theorem)** Let a channel with capacity C be used to transmit codewords of blocklength n and input information rate R. Then the probability of block decoding error satisfies

$$p_e \geq \frac{1}{\log J}\left(R - C - \frac{1}{n}\right)$$

In particular, if R is greater than C, the probability of block decoding error is bounded away from zero.

Proof

$$H(Y^n|X^n) = H(X^n) - I(X^n; Y^n)$$

$$\geq H(X^n) - \max_{\mathbf{p}} \sum_{\mathbf{x}} \sum_{\mathbf{y}} p(\mathbf{x})Q(\mathbf{y}|\mathbf{x})\log \frac{Q(\mathbf{y}|\mathbf{x})}{\sum_{\mathbf{x}} p(\mathbf{x})Q(\mathbf{y}|\mathbf{x})}$$

But the maximum is just nC. Hence

$$H(Y^n|X^n) \geq n(R - C)$$

Then Fano's inequality (Theorem 5.3.1) applied to blocks gives

$$n(R - C) \leq H_b(p_e) + p_e \log (J^n - 1)$$
$$\leq 1 + p_e \log J^n$$

from which the theorem follows.   □

One can also prove a channel-coding converse theorem based on probability of decoded symbol error in place of probability of decoded block error. This is a stronger form of a converse coding theorem and will be presented in Section 6.1.

Except for simple special cases, the maximization problem defining channel capacity cannot be evaluated analytically. It is possible, however, to obtain many useful conditions on the solution as well as efficient numerical techniques. To obtain these conditions, we artificially enlarge the definition of capacity to a larger maximization problem. In this larger problem we have room to work. This enlargement is done in the following theorem by introducing as a dummy variable a backwards transition matrix $\hat{\mathbf{P}}$. Here (as elsewhere) maxima and minima are understood to be over the appropriate spaces of probability vectors or probability transition matrices.

□   **Theorem 5.4.5**   The capacity can be expressed as a double maximum as

$$C = \max_{\mathbf{p}} \max_{\hat{\mathbf{P}}} \sum_{j} \sum_{k} p_j Q_{k|j} \log \frac{\hat{P}_{j|k}}{p_j}$$

where $\hat{\mathbf{P}}$ is a dummy K-by-J transition matrix. For fixed $\mathbf{p}$, the right side is maximized by

$$\hat{P}_{j|k} = \frac{p_j Q_{k|j}}{\sum_{j} p_j Q_{k|j}}$$

For fixed $\hat{\mathbf{P}}$, the right side is maximized by

$$p_j = \frac{\exp\left(\sum_{k} Q_{k|j} \log \hat{P}_{j|k}\right)}{\sum_{j} \exp\left(\sum_{k} Q_{k|j} \log \hat{P}_{j|k}\right)}$$

Proof The double maximum follows immediately from Theorem 5.2.6, and the maximizing $\hat{\mathbf{P}}$ is an immediate consequence of the condition of equality of Theorem 5.2.6. We only need to prove the final statement.

For any value of j, if $\hat{P}_{j|k} = 0$, for some value of k, then p_j should be set equal to zero in order to obtain the maximum. Such j can be deleted from the sum and dropped from further consideration. To find the maximum over $\mathbf{p}$, temporarily ignore the constraint $p_j \geq 0$, and use a Lagrange multiplier λ to constrain $\sum_j p_j = 1$. Then

$$\frac{\partial}{\partial p_j} \left\{ \sum_j \sum_k p_j Q_{k|j} \log \frac{\hat{P}_{j|k}}{p_j} + \lambda \left(\sum_j p_j - 1 \right) \right\} = 0$$

$$-\log p_j - 1 + \sum_k Q_{k|j} \log \hat{P}_{j|k} + \lambda = 0$$

Hence

$$p_j = \frac{\exp \sum_k Q_{k|j} \log \hat{P}_{j|k}}{\sum_j \exp \sum_k Q_{k|j} \log \hat{P}_{j|k}}$$

where λ is selected so that $\sum_j p_j = 1$. The inequality constraint $p_j \geq 0$, which was ignored until now, turns out to be satisfied because the solution for p_j is always positive. $\square$

Combining the two parts of the theorem implies that the maximizing $\mathbf{p}$ satisfies

$$p_j = \frac{p_j \exp \sum_k Q_{k|j} \log \dfrac{Q_{k|j}}{\sum_j p_j Q_{k|j}}}{\sum_j p_j \exp \sum_k Q_{k|j} \log \dfrac{Q_{k|j}}{\sum_j p_j Q_{k|j}}}$$

This equation is obtained by substituting the expression for $\hat{\mathbf{P}}$ given by the theorem into the expression given for $\mathbf{p}$. If one knows the $\mathbf{p}$ that achieves capacity, it can be inserted into the right side of the equation, and it will reproduce itself.

The form of the equation suggests that any $\mathbf{p}$ can be inserted into the right side of the equation and it will generate a new $\mathbf{p}$ on the left, though not necessarily the same one. We shall prove below that under appropriate conditions, this new $\mathbf{p}$ gives a larger value of mutual information. It can be reinserted into the right side to generate yet another new $\mathbf{p}$ on the left, which gives yet a larger value of mutual information. This leads to a simple recursive algorithm for finding the capacity. We give this algorithm in the next theorem. Even when one can find an explicit closed-form solution for the capacity, as when the channel transition matrix is square and invertible, the recursive algorithm is usually preferable. This is because it involves no matrix inversions, so it is practical even for very large alphabet sizes. It also can be used when there is no closed-form solution.

☐   **Theorem 5.4.6**   For any probability distribution $\mathbf{p}$ on the channel input alphabet, let

$$c_j(\mathbf{p}) = \exp \sum_k Q_{k|j} \log \frac{Q_{k|j}}{\sum_j p_j Q_{k|j}}$$

If $\mathbf{p}^{(0)}$ is any probability distribution on the channel input alphabet with all components strictly positive, then the sequence of probability vectors $\mathbf{p}^{(0)}, \mathbf{p}^{(1)}, \mathbf{p}^{(2)}, \ldots$, defined by

$$p_j^{(r+1)} = p_j^{(r)} \frac{c_j(\mathbf{p}^{(r)})}{\sum_j p_j^{(r)} c_j(\mathbf{p}^{(r)})}$$

is such that the sequence $I(\mathbf{p}^{(r)}, \mathbf{Q})$ converges to C from below.

Proof   Theorem 5.4.5 states that

$$C = \max_{\mathbf{p}} \max_{\hat{\mathbf{P}}} \sum_j \sum_k p_j Q_{k|j} \log \frac{\hat{P}_{j|k}}{p_j}$$

Given any $\mathbf{p}^{(r)}$, we increase the value of the double summation on the right by using the second condition of Theorem 5.4.5 to choose $\mathbf{P}^{(r)}$:

$$P_{j|k}^{(r)} = \frac{p_j^{(r)} Q_{k|j}}{\sum_j p_j^{(r)} Q_{k|j}}$$

Then, with $\mathbf{P}^{(r)}$ fixed, we use the third condition of Theorem 5.4.5 to choose $\mathbf{p}^{(r+1)}$:

$$p_j^{(r+1)} = \frac{\exp \sum_k Q_{k|j} \log P_{j|k}^{(r)}}{\sum_j \exp \sum_k Q_{k|j} \log P_{j|k}^{(r)}}$$

The composition of these two operations is just the statement of the theorem to be proved. Hence the algorithm of the theorem increases mutual information at each step. To make the argument precise, let

$$I^{(r)} = \sum_j \sum_k p_j^{(r)} Q_{k|j} \log \frac{P_{j|k}^{(r)}}{p_j^{(r)}}$$

$$= I(\mathbf{p}^{(r)}; \mathbf{Q})$$

$$J^{(r)} = \sum_j \sum_k p_j^{(r+1)} Q_{k|j} \log \frac{P_{j|k}^{(r)}}{p_j^{(r+1)}}$$

$$= \sum_j \sum_k p_j^{(r+1)} Q_{k|j} \left[\log P_{j|k}^{(r)} - \log \left(\frac{\exp \sum_k Q_{k|j} \log P_{j|k}^{(r)}}{\sum_j \exp \sum_k Q_{k|j} \log P_{j|k}^{(r)}} \right) \right]$$

$$= \log \sum_j p_j^{(r)} \exp \sum_k Q_{k|j} \log \frac{Q_{k|j}}{\sum_j p_j^{(r)} Q_{k|j}}$$

Then, because the terms are obtained by successive maximizations, we have the nondecreasing sequence

$$\cdots \leq I^{(r)} \leq J^{(r)} \leq I^{(r+1)} \leq J^{(r+1)} \leq I^{(r+2)} \leq \cdots$$

This sequence is upper-bounded by C and is nondecreasing, so it must have a limit point. We only need to show that a number smaller than C cannot be a limit point. Let $\mathbf{p}^*$ achieve C and consider the following:

$$\sum_j p_j^* \log \frac{p_j^{(r+1)}}{p_j^{(r)}} = \sum_j p_j^* \log \frac{c_j(\mathbf{p}^{(r)})}{\sum_j p_j^{(r)} c_j(\mathbf{p}^{(r)})}$$

$$= \sum_j p_j^* \sum_k Q_{k|j} \log \frac{Q_{k|j}}{\sum_j p_j^{(r)} Q_{k|j}}$$

$$- \log \sum_j p_j^{(r)} \exp \sum_k Q_{k|j} \log \frac{Q_{k|j}}{\sum_j p_j^{(r)} Q_{k|j}}$$

The first term on the right is decreased if $\mathbf{p}^{(r)}$ is replaced by $\mathbf{p}^*$ because the discrimination inequality states that

$$\sum_k \sum_j p_j^* Q_{k|j} \log \frac{\sum_j p_j^* Q_{k|j}}{\sum_j p_j^{(r)} Q_{k|j}} \geq 0$$

Therefore

$$\sum_j p_j^* \log \frac{p_j^{(r+1)}}{p_j^{(r)}} \geq \sum_j p_j^* \sum_k Q_{k|j} \log \frac{Q_{k|j}}{\sum_j p_j^* Q_{k|j}}$$

$$- \log \sum_j p_j^{(r)} \exp \sum_k Q_{k|j} \log \frac{Q_{k|j}}{\sum_j p_j^{(r)} Q_{k|j}}$$

We now recognize the first term as C and the second as $J^{(r)}$:

$$\sum_j p_j^* \log \frac{p_j^{(r+1)}}{p_j^{(r)}} \geq C - J^{(r)}$$

Now sum on r:

$$\sum_{r=0}^{R} (C - J^{(r)}) \le \sum_{r=0}^{R} \left(\sum_j p_j^* \log \frac{p_j^{(r+1)}}{p_j^{(r)}} \right)$$

$$= \sum_j p_j^* \log \frac{p_j^{(R+1)}}{p_j^{(0)}}$$

$$\le \sum_j p_j^* \log \frac{p_j^*}{p_j^{(0)}}$$

where the last inequality follows from the discrimination inequality. The right side now is a constant independent of R, and the left side is smaller than this for any R. But $J^{(r)} \le C$, so $C - J^{(r)}$ is positive and nonincreasing. Because the sum is bounded, $C - J^{(r)}$ must go to zero. This implies that $J^{(r)}$ converges to C, which completes the proof of the theorem.   □

The application of Theorem 5.4.6 to the computation of channel capacity is illustrated in Fig. 5.7. The termination is based on the following theorem.

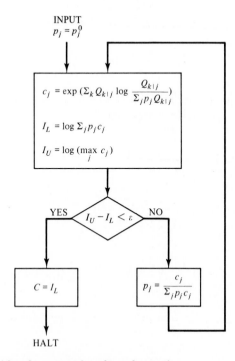

INPUT
$p_j = p_j^0$

$$c_j = \exp \left(\Sigma_k Q_{k|j} \log \frac{Q_{k|j}}{\Sigma_j p_j Q_{k|j}} \right)$$

$$I_L = \log \Sigma_j p_j c_j$$

$$I_U = \log (\max_j c_j)$$

YES $I_U - I_L < \varepsilon$ NO

$C = I_L$

$$p_j = \frac{c_j}{\Sigma_j p_j c_j}$$

HALT

Figure 5.7   Algorithm for computing channel capacity.

□ **Theorem 5.4.7** For any probability assignment **p**, the following hold:

(i) $C \leq \log \left(\max_j c_j \right)$

(ii) $C \geq \log \sum_j p_j c_j$

where

$$c_j = \exp \sum_k Q_{k|j} \log \frac{Q_{k|j}}{\sum_j p_j Q_{k|j}}$$

Proof To prove part (i), let **p*** achieve C. Then for any **p**,

$$C - \log \left(\max_j c_j \right) = \sum_j \sum_k p_j^* Q_{k|j} \log \frac{Q_{k|j}}{\sum_j p_j^* Q_{k|j}}$$

$$- \sum_j p_j^* \left(\max_j \sum_j Q_{k|j} \log \frac{Q_{k|j}}{\sum_j p_j Q_{k|j}} \right)$$

$$\leq \sum_j \sum_k p_j^* Q_{k|j} \log \frac{Q_{k|j}}{\sum_j p_j^* Q_{k|j}}$$

$$- \sum_j \sum_k p_j^* Q_{k|j} \log \frac{Q_{k|j}}{\sum_j p_j Q_{k|j}}$$

$$= \sum_j \sum_k p_j^* Q_{k|j} \log \frac{\sum_j p_j Q_{k|j}}{\sum_j p_j^* Q_{k|j}}$$

$$\leq 0$$

To prove part (ii), we use Theorem 5.4.5. In that theorem, substitute the expression for the maximizing **p** into the expression for C to obtain

$$C = \max_{\hat{P}} \log \sum_j \exp \left(\sum_k Q_{k|j} \log \hat{P}_{j|k} \right)$$

which no longer depends on **p**. Now in this expression, given any arbitrary probability distribution **p**, let

$$\hat{P}_{j|k} = \frac{p_j Q_{k|j}}{\sum_j p_j Q_{k|j}}$$

Then

$$C \geq \log \sum_j \exp \sum_k Q_{k|j} \log \frac{p_j Q_{k|j}}{\sum_j p_j Q_{k|j}}$$

which reduces to the statement being proved.   □

For some channels, some of the channel input symbols are more expensive to use than others. This will be true for those channels that use energy to transmit a symbol, for which different symbols use different amounts of energy. For example, the *binary on-off keyed channel* transmits a pulse to represent a 1 and omits a pulse to represent a 0. Each transmitted 1 uses a fixed amount of energy and each transmitted 0 uses no energy. We want to design codewords that maximize information rate for a given energy cost.

A *cost schedule* for a channel is a vector **s** whose component s_j is called the *cost* of using the jth channel input letter. The capacity at cost S is defined as

$$C(S) = \max_{\mathbf{p} \in \mathbf{P}_S} I(\mathbf{p}; \mathbf{Q})$$

where

$$\mathbf{P}_S = \left\{ \mathbf{p} : \sum_j p_j s_j \leq S \right\}$$

This definition of capacity differs from the original definition only in that the maximum is over a restricted set of probability distributions, those that satisfy the cost constraint. To deal with the cost constraint, the theorems given earlier in this section should be reformulated, with the constraint appended via a Lagrange multiplier.

The capacity-cost function for the binary on-off keyed channel is shown in Fig. 5.8 for various values of error probability. Because this channel treats 0s and 1s differently, the error probabilities are asymmetric. By inspection of Fig. 5.8, with $p_1 = 0.9$, we see for example that by transmitting 20% 1s, we can achieve an information rate of about 0.6 bits per bit. No transmission scheme exists that does better.

5.5 BLOCK CODES FOR DATA TRANSMISSION

Powerful codes for data transmission are widely used, especially for channels whose input alphabet has size equal to power of 2. Codes in use can achieve very small probability of symbol error, but the known codes are not good enough to achieve a code rate near the channel capacity.

A block code for the channel **Q** is to be used to transmit a block of symbols of length n. Altogether there are J^n possible channel input blocks, and a code is some subset of these possible block inputs. The codewords themselves

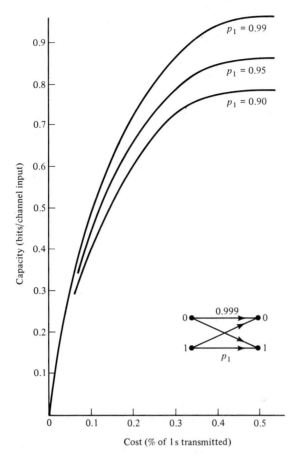

Figure 5.8   Capacity-cost function $C(S)$ for a binary asymmetric channel, $p_0 = 0.999$.

are denoted by $\mathbf{c}_m$ for $m = 0, \ldots, M - 1$. We allow any arbitrary collection of M codewords to be a code of size M. This lack of structure in the codes will simplify our proof of the coding theorem. In practice, however, structure in the code is necessary if the code is to be useful. Otherwise it is not practical to design an acceptable encoder and decoder. Thus, although we shall prove that good codes exist, we will not guarantee that these codes are practical to use.

An extremely simple example of a block code for a binary channel, known as the *Hamming (7,4) code*, is shown in Fig. 5.9. This code is so simple that we can list all of the codewords, and by inspection we can verify that every codeword differs from every other codeword in at least three places. Therefore, if one error is made by the channel, the received word will differ from the true codeword in one place and will differ from every other codeword in at least two places. The single error is corrected by choosing as the correct codeword the one that most closely agrees with the received word. The

0	0	0	0	0	0	0
0	0	0	1	0	1	1
0	0	1	0	1	1	0
0	0	1	1	1	0	1
0	1	0	0	1	1	1
0	1	0	1	1	0	0
0	1	1	0	0	0	1
0	1	1	1	0	1	0
1	0	0	0	1	0	1
1	0	0	1	1	1	0
1	0	1	0	0	1	1
1	0	1	1	0	0	0
1	1	0	0	0	1	0
1	1	0	1	0	0	1
1	1	1	0	1	0	0
1	1	1	1	1	1	1

Figure 5.9   The Hamming (7, 4) code.

Hamming $(7, 4)$ code is a single-error-correcting code for a binary channel. The probability of block error is the probability that two or more errors occur. When the code is used with a binary symmetric channel with crossover probability ρ, the probability of block error is

$$p_e = \sum_{l=2}^{7} \binom{7}{l} \rho^l (1 - \rho)^{7-l}$$

and the rate is $4/7$. The question that now arises is whether one can find another code of larger blocklength n, but of the same rate, such that the probability of block error is much smaller.

In this section, we shall show that block codes with arbitrarily small probability of block error exist at every rate smaller than channel capacity. This provides the practical significance of the channel capacity. The proof employs a "random-coding" argument. This is a method of proof that analyzes the performance of a randomly constructed code. Remarkably, by using the law of large numbers, one can give meaningful bounds on the performance of good codes without actually finding the codes. The reason we resort to a random-coding argument is that we do not know how to find the best codes of large blocklength nor, if we did know them, could we compute their probability of decoding error. Fortunately, the probability of decoding error of an average code is practical to compute.

We will consider the ensemble of all possible codes and draw a code from the ensemble. We imagine a probability distribution on this ensemble of codes and, by means of this distribution, randomly select a code. By calculating the expected value over the ensemble of the selected code's performance, we estimate the performance of the best code in the ensemble. The number of codes in an ensemble is enormous. For example, if we choose the modest values of $n = 20$ and $M = 2^{10}$ for a binary code, the number of possible codes is $2^{20480} \approx 10^{6144}$. Of course, the great majority of these codes are worthless. Shannon sidestepped the complex and seemingly hopeless problem of finding the best code by making use of the law of large numbers to estimate the performance of a good code.

Because we are deriving an upper bound on the performance of codes, we can choose any decoder, not necessarily the best decoder. We will choose a decoder that we are able to analyze easily. Specifically, we will decode based on the idea of jointly typical pairs of sequences, which will be defined in the same way as were typical sequences in Definition 3.4.4. Channel output $\mathbf{y}$ will be decoded into codeword $\mathbf{c}_m$ if the pair $(\mathbf{y}, \mathbf{c}_m)$ is a jointly typical pair in the sense of the following definition.

□ **Definition 5.5.1** Given a memoryless pair of random variables (X, Y) with joint probability distribution $\mathbf{P}$ and with joint entropy $H(\mathbf{P})$, let $\delta > 0$ be given. The set of *jointly weakly typical pairs of sequences* (or jointly weakly δ-typical pairs of sequences) of blocklength n are the pairs $(\mathbf{x}, \mathbf{y})$ in the set

$$\mathcal{T}_{xy}(\delta) = \left\{ (\mathbf{x}, \mathbf{y}) : \left| -\frac{1}{n} \log P(\mathbf{x}, \mathbf{y}) - H(\mathbf{P}) \right| < \delta \right\}$$

provided $\mathbf{x}$ and $\mathbf{y}$ are elements, respectively, of $\mathcal{T}_x(\delta)$ and $\mathcal{T}_y(\delta)$, the sets of weakly typical $\mathbf{x}$ and $\mathbf{y}$ sequences, and where the logarithm base agrees with that used in computing the entropy. The set of *jointly strongly typical pairs of sequences* (or jointly strongly δ-typical pairs of sequences) of blocklength n are the elements of the set

$$\mathcal{S}_{xy}(\delta) = \left\{ (\mathbf{x}, \mathbf{y}) : \left| \frac{1}{n} n_{jk} - P_{jk} \right| < \frac{\delta}{JK}; j = 0, \ldots, J-1, k = 0, \ldots, K-1 \right\}$$

where $n_{jk}(\mathbf{x}, \mathbf{y})$ is the number of simultaneous occurrences of letter j in the sequence $\mathbf{x}$ and letter k in the sequence $\mathbf{y}$. □

It is easy to verify that if $(\mathbf{x}, \mathbf{y})$ is in $\mathcal{S}_{xy}(\delta)$, then $\mathbf{x}$ and $\mathbf{y}$ are individually in $\mathcal{S}_x(\delta)$ and $\mathcal{S}_y(\delta)$.

The sets $\mathcal{T}_{xy}(\delta)$ and $\mathcal{S}_{xy}(\delta)$ each are loosely called the *set of jointly typical pairs of sequences*. More generally, when there are m random variables in a discussion, we can speak of the set of jointly typical m-tuples of sequences as an immediate generalization.

Jointly typical sequences behave very much as do typical sequences. This is apparent simply by observing that the pair of discrete sources (X, Y) can be reinterpreted as a single new source Z with a pair of letters from (X, Y) defined as a single letter of Z. In particular, the Shannon-McMillan theorem can be restated for the pair of sources as follows.

☐ **Theorem 5.5.2** (**Shannon-McMillan theorem for pairs**) Given a dependent pair of discrete memoryless sources of entropy $H(X, Y)$ and any δ greater than zero, we can choose n big enough so that the set $\{(\mathbf{x}, \mathbf{y})\}$ of all pairs of sourcewords of blocklength n produced by the pair of sources can be partitioned into two sets $\mathcal{T}_{xy}(\delta)$ and $\mathcal{T}_{xy}^{c}(\delta)$ for which the following statements hold:

(i) The probability of a pair of sourcewords belonging to $\mathcal{T}_{xy}^{c}(\delta)$ is less than δ.

(ii) If a pair of sourcewords $(\mathbf{x}, \mathbf{y})$ is in $\mathcal{T}_{xy}(\delta)$, then the probability $p(\mathbf{x}, \mathbf{y})$ is approximately $e^{-nH(X,Y)}$ in the sense that

$$\left| -n^{-1} \log p(\mathbf{x}, \mathbf{y}) - H(X, Y) \right| < \delta$$

(iii) If a pair of sourcewords $(\mathbf{x}, \mathbf{y})$ is in $\mathcal{T}_{xy}(\delta)$ and $\mathbf{x}$ is fixed, then the conditional probability $p(\mathbf{y}|\mathbf{x})$ is approximately $e^{-nH(Y|X)}$ in the sense that $\left| n^{-1} \log p(\mathbf{y}|\mathbf{x}) - H(Y|X) \right| < 2\delta$.

(iv) The number of elements in $\mathcal{T}_{xy}(\delta)$, denoted $\left| \mathcal{T}_{xy}(\delta) \right|$, is at most $2^{nH(X,Y)+\delta}$.

Proof Statements (i) and (ii) follow from the Shannon-McMillan theorem by interpreting the pair (X, Y) as a single source Z. Statement (iii) follows from statement (ii) here and statement (ii) of Theorem 3.4.2, together with the elementary relationship

$$p(\mathbf{y}|\mathbf{x}) = \frac{p(\mathbf{x}, \mathbf{y})}{p(\mathbf{x})}$$

and

$$H(Y|X) = H(X, Y) - H(X)$$

Statement (iv) follows from statement (ii) and the fact that the sum of the probabilities cannot be greater than 1. ☐

☐ **Theorem 5.5.3** (**Shannon's second coding theorem**) Suppose $R < C$, where C is the capacity of the memoryless channel $\mathbf{Q}$. Then for any $\varepsilon > 0$ there exist a blocklength n and a code of blocklength n and rate R whose probability of block decoding error satisfies

$$p_e \leq \varepsilon$$

when the code is used on channel $\mathbf{Q}$.

Proof We shall employ a random-coding argument with blocklength fixed at n. The proof consists of examining typical sequences of blocklength n that will be seen at the receiver when using a randomly selected code. Define the decoder as follows. If $\mathbf{y}$ is the output of the channel, the decoder output is the unique codeword $\mathbf{c}_m$ such that the pair $(\mathbf{c}_m, \mathbf{y})$ is jointly weakly typical, provided there is such a unique codeword. If there is no such codeword or more than one such codeword, then the decoder output can be defined in any way, and we will presume in our analysis that an error then occurs.

Step 1: Let $\mathscr{C} = \{\mathbf{c}_0, \mathbf{c}_1, \ldots, \mathbf{c}_{M-1}\}$ be a code of blocklength n. When codeword $\mathbf{c}_m$ is transmitted, the probability of error $p_{e|m}$ can be bounded by using the union bound.[†]

$$p_{e|m} \leq Pr[(\mathbf{c}_m, \mathbf{y}) \notin \mathscr{T}_{xy}(\delta)] + \sum_{m' \neq m} Pr[(\mathbf{c}_{m'}, \mathbf{y}) \in \mathscr{T}_{xy}(\delta)]$$

By Theorem 5.5.2, we know that the first term on the right is smaller than δ for sufficiently large blocklength. Therefore, choosing $\delta \leq \varepsilon$,

$$p_{e|m} \leq \varepsilon + \sum_{m' \neq m} Pr[(\mathbf{c}_{m'}, \mathbf{y}) \in \mathscr{T}_{xy}(\delta)]$$

Define the indicator function:

$$\phi(\mathbf{x}, \mathbf{y}) = \begin{cases} 1 & \text{if } (\mathbf{x}, \mathbf{y}) \in \mathscr{T}_{xy}(\delta) \\ 0 & \text{if } (\mathbf{x}, \mathbf{y}) \notin \mathscr{T}_{xy}(\delta) \end{cases}$$

Then we can rewrite the bound on $p_{e|m}$ as

$$p_{e|m} \leq \varepsilon + \sum_{m' \neq m} \sum_{\mathbf{y}} \phi(\mathbf{c}_{m'}, \mathbf{y}) Q(\mathbf{y}|\mathbf{c}_m)$$

The second term on the right need not be small in general. However, we will show that it is small for an average code. This argument requires us to consider a randomly constructed code, which we do in step 2.

Step 2: Construct the code $\mathscr{C} = \{\mathbf{c}_0, \mathbf{c}_1, \ldots, \mathbf{c}_{M-1}\}$ by random selection. For the probability $Pr[\{\mathbf{c}_0, \mathbf{c}_1, \ldots, \mathbf{c}_{M-1}\}]$ of picking code $\mathscr{C}$, use the product distribution

$$Pr[\{\mathbf{c}_0, \mathbf{c}_1, \ldots, \mathbf{c}_{M-1}\}] = \prod_{m=0}^{M-1} p(\mathbf{c}_m)$$

[†]The *union bound* says that

$$Pr[\textstyle\bigcup_i \mathscr{E}_i] \leq \sum_i Pr[\mathscr{E}_i]$$

for any set of events $\{\mathscr{E}_i\}$.

For the probability of picking codeword $\mathbf{c}_m = (a_{j_{m1}}, a_{j_{m2}}, \ldots, a_{j_{mn}})$, use the product distribution on the components

$$p(\mathbf{c}_m) = \prod_{l=1}^{n} p(c_{ml}) = \prod_{l=1}^{n} p(a_{j_{ml}})$$

This means that each component of each codeword is randomly chosen independently and with replacement. Finally, for the single-letter probability distribution, use the probability distribution that achieves channel capacity, $p(a_j) = p_j$.

Let E denote the expectation operator with respect to the random-code selection. Then

$$E[p_{e|m}] \leq \varepsilon + \sum_{m' \neq m} E\left[\sum_y \phi(\mathbf{c}_{m'}, \mathbf{y}) Q(\mathbf{y} | \mathbf{c}_m) \right]$$

$$\leq \varepsilon + \sum_{m' \neq m} Pr[(\mathbf{x}, \mathbf{y}) \in \mathcal{T}_{xy}(\delta)]$$

where now the probability is over the ensemble of codes and $\mathbf{c}_m$ is replaced by $\mathbf{x}$ as a reminder that it is now a realization of the random variable associated with the random-code selection. All terms in the sum are now the same, so we have

$$E[p_{e|m}] \leq \varepsilon + (M - 1) Pr[(\mathbf{x}, \mathbf{y}) \in \mathcal{T}_{xy}(\delta)]$$

Because $\mathbf{x}$ is a randomly chosen codeword other than the codeword actually transmitted and $\mathbf{y}$ is the response of the channel to the randomly selected codeword that is transmitted, $\mathbf{x}$ and $\mathbf{y}$ are realizations of independent random variables. In step 3, we shall show that the second term can be made smaller than ε.

Before giving the next step of the proof, we will drop the m on the left side of the inequality based on the following argument. The right side of the bound no longer depends on m. Let $Pr[\mathbf{c}_m]$ be the probability of using the mth codeword. The average probability of error of the code is $p_e = \sum_m Pr[\mathbf{c}_m] p_{e|m}$. Over the ensemble, the expected value of the average probability of error is now bounded as follows:

$$E[p_e] = E\left[\sum_m Pr[\mathbf{c}_m] p_{e|m} \right]$$

$$= \sum_m Pr[\mathbf{c}_m] E[p_{e|m}]$$

$$\leq \varepsilon + (M - 1) Pr[(\mathbf{x}, \mathbf{y}) \in \mathcal{T}_{xy}(\delta)]$$

where $\mathbf{x}$ and $\mathbf{y}$ are independently selected n-tuples.

Step 3: All that remains is to evaluate $Pr[(\mathbf{x}, \mathbf{y}) \in \mathcal{T}_{xy}(\delta)]$, given that $\mathbf{x}$ and $\mathbf{y}$ are independent with probability $p(\mathbf{x})$ and $q(\mathbf{y})$ respectively. This is the probability that the pair $(\mathbf{x}, \mathbf{y})$ turns out to be jointly typical even though $\mathbf{x}$ and $\mathbf{y}$ are generated independently. But

$$Pr[(\mathbf{x}, \mathbf{y}) \in \mathcal{T}_{xy}(\delta)] = \sum_{(\mathbf{x},\mathbf{y}) \in \mathcal{T}_{xy}(\delta)} p(\mathbf{x})q(\mathbf{y})$$

$$\leq |\mathcal{T}_{xy}(\delta)| e^{-n[H(X) - \delta]} e^{-n[H(Y) - \delta]}$$

The inequality follows because, if $(\mathbf{x},\mathbf{y}) \in \mathcal{T}_{xy}(\delta)$, then $\mathbf{x}$ and $\mathbf{y}$ are each typical individually. Then using Theorem 5.5.2 to bound $|\mathcal{T}_{xy}(\delta)|$ and replacing $M - 1$ with M gives

$$(M - 1)Pr[(\mathbf{x}, \mathbf{y}) \in \mathcal{T}_{xy}(\delta)] \leq M e^{n[H(X,Y) + \delta]} e^{-n[H(X) - \delta]} e^{-n[H(Y) - \delta]}$$

$$= e^{nR} e^{-n[I(X;Y) - 3\delta]}$$

$$= e^{-n[C - R - 3\delta]}$$

Because $R < C$ and δ is an arbitrary positive number, we can choose δ to satisfy the inequality $C - R - 3\delta > 0$. Hence for sufficiently large n,

$$(M - 1)Pr[(\mathbf{x},\mathbf{y}) \in \mathcal{T}_{xy}(\delta)] < \varepsilon$$

Step 4: We have shown that for large enough blocklength n, the average probability of block decoding error over all codes satisfies

$$E[p_e] < 2\varepsilon$$

There must be at least one code at least as good as the average. Consequently, there exists at least one code whose probability of block decoding error satisfies

$$p_e < 2\varepsilon$$

Because ε is arbitrary, we can replace 2ε with ε to complete the proof of the theorem.   □

5.6 THE RANDOM-CODING BOUND

The channel coding theorem of the previous section shows that codes with arbitrarily small probability of block decoding error exist at any rate smaller than the channel capacity C. However, we made no attempt to estimate how large the blocklength needed to be to attain a specified probability of decoding error. In this section we shall re-prove the channel coding theorem using an alternative and more delicate method that describes a little of the dependence between blocklength and probability of decoding error.

This time the derivation will be based on the maximum-likelihood decoder. Recall that the decoder with minimum probability of error estimates the transmitted codeword by comparing the a posteriori distributions $P(\mathbf{c}_m | \mathbf{y})$ and selecting that m for which $P(\mathbf{c}_m | \mathbf{y})$ is largest for the particular output $\mathbf{y}$ that was received. In the proof of the next theorem, we shall use instead the decoding rule that m is selected if $Q(\mathbf{y} | \mathbf{c}_m) > Q(\mathbf{y} | \mathbf{c}_{m'})$ for all $m' \neq m$. This is potentially a decoder with a larger probability of error, but when all codewords are used with equal probability, it is equivalent to the minimum probability-of-error decoder. Because the theorem we are proving is an upper bound on p_e, it is permissible to use the maximum-likelihood decoding rule, even if the codewords are not used with equal probability. The probability of error of the optimum decoding rule can only be smaller.

□   **Theorem   5.6.1**   Let $R = (1/n) \log M$.   There   exists   a   data transmission code of size M and blocklength n for the memoryless channel with block transition matrix $Q(\mathbf{y}|\mathbf{x})$ whose probability of block decoding error p_e satisfies

$$p_e \leq \min_{s \in [0,1]} \min_{p(\mathbf{x})} \left\{ e^{nsR} \sum_{\mathbf{y}} \left[\sum_{\mathbf{x}} p(\mathbf{x}) Q(\mathbf{y}|\mathbf{x})^{1/(1+s)} \right]^{1+s} \right\}$$

Proof   Let $\{\mathbf{c}_0, \ldots, \mathbf{c}_{M-1}\}$ denote the set of codewords, and let the decoding rule be that the mth codeword is decoded when $\mathbf{y}$ is received if

$$Q(\mathbf{y}|\mathbf{c}_m) > Q(\mathbf{y}|\mathbf{c}_{m'})$$

for all $m' \neq m$. In case several values of m show the same maximum, we allow any arbitrary method of breaking the tie, but for bounding the probability of error, we assume that an error is then always made. The set of $\mathbf{y}$ that decode into $\mathbf{c}_m$ is

$$\mathscr{U}_m = \{\mathbf{y} : Q(\mathbf{y}|\mathbf{c}_m) > Q(\mathbf{y}|\mathbf{c}_{m'})   \text{ for all } m' \neq m\}$$

The characteristic function of this set $\phi_m(\mathbf{y})$ is by definition equal to 0 if $\mathbf{y} \notin \mathscr{U}_m$ and equal to 1 if $\mathbf{y} \in \mathscr{U}_m$. The first step in the proof is to bound $\phi_m(\mathbf{y})$ as follows:

$$1 - \phi_m(\mathbf{y}) \leq \left\{ \sum_{m' \neq m} \left[\frac{Q(\mathbf{y}|\mathbf{c}_{m'})}{Q(\mathbf{y}|\mathbf{c}_m)} \right]^{1/(1+s)} \right\}^s   \qquad \text{for all } s > 0$$

This inequality is true if $\phi_m(\mathbf{y}) = 1$ because the right side is nonnegative. It is also true if $\phi_m(\mathbf{y}) = 0$ because then there is at least one m' with $Q(\mathbf{y}|\mathbf{c}_m) \leq Q(\mathbf{y}|\mathbf{c}_{m'})$. For this value of m'

$$1 \leq \frac{Q(\mathbf{y}|\mathbf{c}_{m'})}{Q(\mathbf{y}|\mathbf{c}_m)}$$

The right side is greater than 1, so it can be raised to any positive power and will still be greater than 1. Hence

$$1 \leq \left[\frac{Q(\mathbf{y}|\mathbf{c}_{m'})}{Q(\mathbf{y}|\mathbf{c}_m)} \right]^{1/(1+s)}$$

for all $s > 0$. The equality is preserved if any number of nonnegative terms are added to the right side, and still preserved if the resulting sum is raised to any positive power. Therefore the above bound follows.

Given that the mth codeword is transmitted, the probability of block decoding error is given by

$$P_{e|m} = \sum_{\mathbf{y} \notin \mathcal{U}_m} Q(\mathbf{y}|\mathbf{c}_m)$$

$$= \sum_{\mathbf{y}} Q(\mathbf{y}|\mathbf{c}_m)[1 - \phi_m(\mathbf{y})]$$

$$\leq \sum_{\mathbf{y}} Q(\mathbf{y}|\mathbf{c}_m) \left\{ \sum_{m' \neq m} \left[\frac{Q(\mathbf{y}|\mathbf{c}_{m'})}{Q(\mathbf{y}|\mathbf{c}_m)} \right]^{1/(1+s)} \right\}^s$$

$$= \sum_{\mathbf{y}} Q(\mathbf{y}|\mathbf{c}_m)^{1/(1+s)} \left[\sum_{m' \neq m} Q(\mathbf{y}|\mathbf{c}_{m'})^{1/(1+s)} \right]^s$$

We are now ready to randomly select a code. Define a probability distribution on the set of codes such that the codewords are selected independently, with probability of selecting $\mathbf{x}$ as a codeword equal to $p(\mathbf{x})$. Thus the probability of the code $\{\mathbf{c}_0, \ldots, \mathbf{c}_{M-1}\}$ is given by

$$Pr[\{\mathbf{c}_0, \ldots, \mathbf{c}_{M-1}\}] = \prod_{m=0}^{M-1} p(\mathbf{c}_m)$$

For the moment, the probability distribution $p(\mathbf{x})$ will be arbitrary. The expected value $p_{e|m}$ over the ensemble is the ensemble average

$$E[p_{e|m}] \leq E\left\{ \sum_{\mathbf{y}} Q(\mathbf{y}|\mathbf{c}_m)^{1/(1+s)} \left[\sum_{m' \neq m} Q(\mathbf{y}|\mathbf{c}_{m'})^{1/(1+s)} \right]^s \right\}$$

$$= \sum_{\mathbf{y}} E\left\{ Q(\mathbf{y}|\mathbf{c}_m)^{1/(1+s)} \left[\sum_{m' \neq m} Q(\mathbf{y}|\mathbf{c}_{m'})^{1/(1+s)} \right]^s \right\}$$

$$= \sum_{\mathbf{y}} E[Q(\mathbf{y}|\mathbf{c}_m)^{1/(1+s)}] E\left[\sum_{m' \neq m} Q(\mathbf{y}|\mathbf{c}_{m'})^{1/(1+s)} \right]^s$$

where the first step follows because the expectation of a sum equals the sum of the expectations. The second step follows because the codewords are selected independently and the first term depends only on $\mathbf{c}_m$, while the second term does not depend on $\mathbf{c}_m$. Now suppose $s \leq 1$. Then t^s is a concave function of t, so Jensen's inequality is applicable. That is,

$$E[t^s] \leq [E(t)]^s$$

Therefore

$$E[p_{e|m}] \leq \sum_{\mathbf{y}} E[Q(\mathbf{y}|\mathbf{c}_m)^{1/(1+s)}] \left[E \sum_{m' \neq m} Q(\mathbf{y}|\mathbf{c}_{m'})^{1/(1+s)} \right]^s$$

$$= \sum_{\mathbf{y}} E[Q(\mathbf{y}|\mathbf{c}_m)^{1/(1+s)}] \left\{ \sum_{m' \neq m} E[Q(\mathbf{y}|\mathbf{c}_{m'})^{1/(1+s)}] \right\}^s$$

The M codewords are selected with identical distributions. Therefore $E[Q(\mathbf{y}|\mathbf{c}_m)^{1/(1+s)}]$ does not depend on m, so that

$$E[p_{e|m}] \leq \sum_{\mathbf{y}} E[Q(\mathbf{y}|\mathbf{x})^{1/(1+s)}]\{(M-1)E[Q(\mathbf{y}|\mathbf{x})^{1/(1+s)}]\}^s$$

$$= (M-1)^s \sum_{\mathbf{y}} \{E[Q(\mathbf{y}|\mathbf{x})^{1/(1+s)}]\}^{1+s}$$

We can replace $M-1$ with M without violating the inequality. Write the expectation explicitly in terms of $p(\mathbf{x})$:

$$E[p_{e|m}] \leq M^s \sum_{\mathbf{y}} \left[\sum_{\mathbf{x}} p(\mathbf{x})Q(\mathbf{y}|\mathbf{x})^{1/(1+s)} \right]^{1+s}$$

The right side no longer depends on m, so we can remove the conditioning on m. Specifically, if $Pr[\mathbf{c}_m]$ is the probability of using the mth codeword, then $p_e = \sum_m Pr[\mathbf{c}_m] p_{e|m}$. Over the ensemble, the average probability of error has the expected value

$$E[p_e] = E\left[\sum_m Pr[\mathbf{c}_m] p_{e|m} \right]$$

$$= \sum_m Pr[\mathbf{c}_m] E[p_{e|m}]$$

$$\leq M^s \sum_{\mathbf{y}} \left[\sum_{\mathbf{x}} p(\mathbf{x})Q(\mathbf{y}|\mathbf{x})^{1/(1+s)} \right]^{1+s}$$

Because the expected value over the ensemble of codes satisfies this bound, there must be at least one code that itself satisfies the bound. Hence there exists a code whose probability of block decoding error satisfies

$$p_e \leq M^s \sum_{\mathbf{y}} \left[\sum_{\mathbf{x}} p(\mathbf{x})Q(\mathbf{y}|\mathbf{x})^{1/(1+s)} \right]^{1+s}$$

This is true for any $s \in [0, 1]$ and for any $\mathbf{p}$, and so holds even if we choose s and $\mathbf{p}$ to make the right side smallest.   □

Theorem 5.6.1 is expressed in terms of block probabilities on the input blocks. Our next step is to express the bound in terms of per-letter probabilities. The bound will be given in terms of the random-coding exponent, which is given in the following definition.

□ **Definition 5.6.2**   The *random-coding exponent*[†] is given by

$$E_r(R) = \max_{0 \leq s \leq 1} \max_{\mathbf{p}} \left[-sR - \log \sum_{k=0}^{K-1} \left(\sum_{j=0}^{J-1} p_j Q_{k|j}^{1/(1+s)} \right)^{1+s} \right]$$ □

[†]The use of E to denote the random-coding exponent should not be confused with the use of E to denote the expectation.

In Chapter 10, we will find that $E_r(R)$ is always positive for R smaller than C and is always equal to zero for R larger than C. A sketch of $E_r(R)$ for a binary symmetric channel with crossover probability 0.01 is shown in Fig. 5.10. The region where $E_r(R)$ is a straight line is the region where the maximum over s is achieved at $s = 1$. It turns out that for every channel, $E_r(R)$ has such a straight line whose slope is -1.

☐ **Theorem 5.6.3** Let p_e be the probability of error of the best block code of size M and blocklength n for a memoryless channel and let $R = (1/n) \log M$. Then

$$p_e \leq e^{-nE_r(R)}$$

Proof From the proof of Theorem 5.6.1, we have that

$$p_e \leq e^{nsR} \sum_{\mathbf{y}} \left[\sum_{\mathbf{x}} p(\mathbf{x}) Q(\mathbf{y}|\mathbf{x})^{1/(1+s)} \right]^{1+s}$$

for every $\mathbf{p}$ and for all $s \in [0, 1]$. For a memoryless channel, $Q(\mathbf{y}|\mathbf{x})$ is given by the product distribution

$$Q(\mathbf{y}|\mathbf{x}) = \prod_{l=1}^{n} Q(y_l|x_l)$$

so we will choose $\mathbf{p}$ to be a product distribution as well:

$$p(\mathbf{x}) = \prod_{l=1}^{n} p(x_l)$$

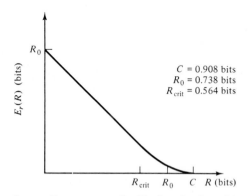

Figure 5.10   **A random-coding exponent for block codes for a binary symmetric channel, $p = 0.01$.**

We need not bother to prove that a product distribution gives the tightest bound because the inequality holds for any choice of $p(\mathbf{x})$. Therefore

$$p_e \leq e^{nsR} \sum_y \left[\sum_x \prod_{l=1}^{n} p(x_l) \, Q(y_l|x_l)^{1/(1+s)} \right]^{1+s}$$

The next step is to replace the sum of products with a product of sums. Notice that the sum over all $\mathbf{x}$ is a sum over all vectors $(x_1, x_2, \ldots, x_n)$. Similarly, the sum over all $\mathbf{y}$ is a sum over all vectors $(y_1, y_2, \ldots, y_n)$. That is,

$$p_e \leq e^{nsR} \sum_{y_1} \sum_{y_2} \cdots \sum_{y_n} \left[\sum_{x_1} \sum_{x_2} \cdots \sum_{x_n} \prod_{l=1}^{n} p(x_l) Q(y_l|x_l)^{1/(1+s)} \right]^{1+s}$$

Now apply the general rule[†]

$$\sum_{x_1} \sum_{x_2} \cdots \sum_{x_n} \left[\prod_{l=1}^{n} A(x_l) \right] = \prod_{l=1}^{n} \left[\sum_{x_l} A(x_l) \right]$$

twice to interchange the sums and the product. This gives

$$p_e \leq e^{nsR} \prod_{l=1}^{n} \left\{ \sum_{y_l} \left[\sum_{x_l} p(x_l) Q(y_l|x_l)^{1/(1+s)} \right]^{1+s} \right\}$$

For each l, the term in braces is the same. Replace $p(x_l)$ and $Q(y_l|x_l)$ with the abbreviated notation p_j and $Q_{k|j}$, now independent of l, to give the product of n identical terms. Therefore

$$p_e \leq e^{nsR} \left[\sum_k \left(\sum_j p_j Q_{k|j}^{1/(1+s)} \right)^{1+s} \right]^n$$

Picking s and $\mathbf{p}$ to make this bound the tightest gives

$$p_e \leq e^{-nE_r(R)}$$

to complete the proof of the theorem.   □

We can state as a corollary to Theorem 5.6.3 Shannon's second coding theorem, which was already given as Theorem 5.5.3. This gives us an alternative proof of the channel coding theorem, and some new insights.

□ **Corollary 5.6.4 (Shannon's second coding theorem)** Suppose $R < C$, Then for any $\varepsilon > 0$ there exist a blocklength n and a code of blocklength n and rate R whose probability of block decoding error satisfies

$$p_e \leq \varepsilon$$

[†]This is a more general form of the obvious expression

$$\left(\sum_j A_j \right) \left(\sum_k B_k \right) = \sum_j \sum_k A_j B_k$$

Proof We shall prove in Theorem 10.1.2 and Corollary 10.1.6 that $E_r(R)$ is positive for all R smaller than channel capacity. Therefore, in the theorem, pick n satisfying

$$p_e \le e^{-nE_r(R)} \le \varepsilon$$

Such an n always exists if $R < C$ because $E_r(R) > 0$. $\square$

5.7 THE CHANNEL RELIABILITY FUNCTION

The random-coding exponent gives a bound on the probability of error as a function of blocklength. It is suggestive of the error exponent for hypothesis testing that was studied in Section 4.6. That error exponent was found to be asymptotically tight with blocklength.

It is natural to ask how the behavior of the average probability of decoding error of block codes depends asymptotically on blocklength, and whether the random-coding exponent is tight. These are difficult questions, which we introduce briefly in this section and return to more fully in Chapter 10. In that chapter, we shall expend a great deal of effort in learning how, for good codes, the probability of block decoding error $p_e(\mathscr{C})$ behaves as a function of the code's rate and blocklength, and in learning something about the structure of good codes.

The probability of block decoding error when codeword $\mathbf{c}_m$ is the transmitted codeword is

$$p_{e|m} = \sum_{\mathbf{y} \in \mathscr{U}_m^c} Q(\mathbf{y}|\mathbf{c}_m)$$

If the M codewords are used with equal probability, then the average probability of decoded block error for the code $\mathscr{C}$ is

$$p_e(\mathscr{C}) = \sum_{m=0}^{M-1} \frac{1}{M} \sum_{\mathbf{y} \in \mathscr{U}_m^c} Q(\mathbf{y}|\mathbf{c}_m)$$

Even when the code $\mathscr{C}$ is known, this expression is impractical to evaluate unless the code is very small, and small codes are not very good. Further, we do not know how to find good codes of large blocklength. Nevertheless, we will not be discouraged, but will press on and try to get some idea of how $p_e(\mathscr{C})$ for an optimal code $\mathscr{C}$ depends on the blocklength and rate of the code. Remarkably, we can get a partial answer even though we do not know how to find the optimal codes.

Let $p_e(n,R)$ denote the smallest possible probability of block decoding error of any code of blocklength n and rate R. That is,

$$p_e(n, R) = \min_{\mathscr{C}} p_e(\mathscr{C})$$

where the minimum is over all codes of blocklength n and rate R. The channel reliability at rate R is defined as

$$E^*(R) = \lim_{n \to \infty} \left[-\frac{1}{n} \log p_e(n, R) \right]$$

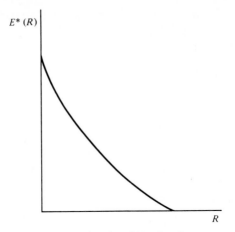

Figure 5.11 Typical reliability function for channel codes.

providing the limit exists. If the limit does exist,[†] the asymptotic behavior in n of $p_e(n, R)$ is given by

$$p_e(n, R) = e^{-nE^*(R) + o(n)}$$

where $o(n)$ is a term that goes to zero as n goes to infinity.

A channel reliability function $E^*(R)$ is defined for each channel $\mathbf{Q}$. A sketch of a typical $E^*(R)$ is shown in Fig. 5.11. The function is monotonically decreasing in R and is conjectured to be convex. The true function $E^*(R)$ is known only for rates greater than that rate at which the random-coding bound $E_r(R)$ deviates from a straight line of slope -1. This is the *critical rate* R_{crit}. The rate R_{crit} occurs at the largest R where $E^*(R)$ has a slope of -1. For lower rates, only bounds on $E^*(R)$ are known.

The *cutoff rate* R_0, another parameter used to characterize a channel, is defined as the rate at which that tangent to $E_r(R)$ (or to $E^*(R)$) of slope -1 intersects the R axis. This rate can be expressed as

$$R_0 = \max_{\mathbf{p}} \left[-\log \sum_k \left(\sum_j p_j Q_{k|j}^{1/2} \right)^2 \right]$$

Whereas the channel capacity of a channel $\mathbf{Q}$ is the rate beyond which it is impossible to communicate over the channel, the cutoff rate of $\mathbf{Q}$ is widely believed to be the rate beyond which it is very expensive to communicate over the channel. This belief stems from the fact that for some kinds of decoders for data transmission codes, known as sequential decoders, the complexity of the decoders grows very rapidly as the code rate is increased above R_0. However, a general proof of this significance for R_0 has never been discovered, and

---

[†]If the limit does not exist, then the lower and upper bounds described in this chapter become lower bounds on the limit infimum and upper bounds the limit supremum, respectively.

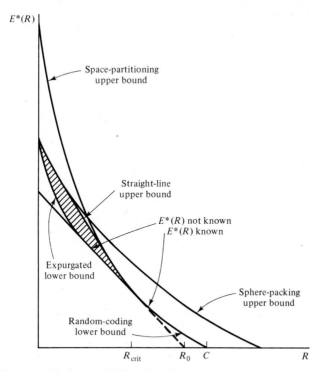

Figure 5.12   Bounds on the reliability function.

examples of channels are known for which the cutoff rate clearly has no meaning. (See Problem 5.26.)

The $E^*(R)$ function, to the extent it is known, is established by proving five bounds, three upper and two lower. These correspond respectively to three lower bounds and two upper bounds on the probability of block decoding error. These are the *random-coding* lower bound, which was derived in Section 5.6; the *expurgated* lower bound; the *space-partitioning*[†] upper bound; the *sphere-packing* upper bound; and the *straight-line* upper bound. Derivations of the latter four bounds will be found in Chapter 10; they are all rather difficult. Figure 5.12 gives a sketch of the five bounds. Figure 5.13 gives the bounds evaluated for a specific example—a binary symmetric channel with symbol error probability equal to 0.1.

The upper bounds on $E^*(R)$, corresponding to lower bounds on p_e, are derived by identifying a binary hypothesis-testing problem in the decoding problem and applying the methods of Chapter 4. A lower bound on the probability of error of the hypothesis-testing problem then is used to infer a lower bound on the probability of error of the decoding problem.

[†]This is the bound usually called the "sphere-packing bound." We apologize for the nonstandard terminology, which is selected here so that the latter bound, proved by packing spheres, can be referred to as the sphere-packing bound.

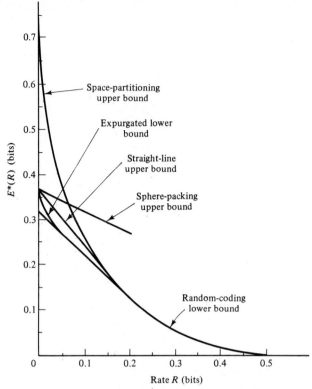

Figure 5.13   Bounds on the reliability function for a binary symmetric channel, $p = 0.1$.

For high-rate codes, the lower bound on p_e is called the *space-partitioning bound*. The nib of its derivation is the hypothesis-testing problem given by

$$H_0 : \mathbf{c}_m = \text{transmitted codeword}$$

$$H_1 : \mathbf{c}_m \neq \text{transmitted codeword}$$

where $\mathbf{c}_m$ is chosen to be one of the more difficult codewords to decode.

For low-rate codes, the lower bound on p_e is called the *sphere-packing bound*. The nib of its derivation is a different hypothesis-testing problem given by

$$H_0 : \text{of } \mathbf{c}_m \text{ and } \mathbf{c}_{m'}, \; \mathbf{c}_m = \text{transmitted codeword}$$

$$H_1 : \text{of } \mathbf{c}_m \text{ and } \mathbf{c}_{m'}, \; \mathbf{c}_{m'} = \text{transmitted codeword}$$

where $\mathbf{c}_m$ and $\mathbf{c}_{m'}$ are chosen to be two of the more difficult codewords to distinguish.

Speaking very loosely, and only from the nature of the derivations of the bounds, it appears that the performance of good codes of large blocklength has a different cause above R_{crit} than below. Below R_{crit}, the average probability of error of a code is dominated by the fact that a typical codeword has a few neighboring codewords with which it is often confused. Then it seems important to design the code so that all codewords are far apart in the sense of a distance known as *Bhattacharyya distance*. Above R_{crit}, an average codeword is surrounded by a cloud of codewords with any one of which it can be confused. Then it seems that it is not important to maximize the minimum Bhattacharyya distance. Pairwise distance between codewords seems not to be the fundamental limitation for high-rate codes. Rather, the more distant codewords are so numerous when the rate is high that their great number is more of a factor than the smaller distance to the nearer codewords. For these rates, each codeword should cause a channel output very different from the average channel output.

5.8 DISTANCE AND COMPOSITION NOTIONS

In a word of blocklength n over a finite alphabet of size J, we can count how many times each letter occurs. The *composition* of a word of blocklength n is a vector of length J whose jth component n_j specifies the number of times that letter a_j appears in the word. The number of distinct words with composition n_j is given by the multinomial distribution, and the multinomial distribution can be approximated using the entropy function. Thus, as stated in Problem 1.5,

$$N = \frac{n!}{\pi_j n_j!} = e^{nH(\mathbf{p}) + o(n)}$$

where $\mathbf{p}$ is the relative frequency vector whose components are given by

$$p_j = \frac{n_j}{n}$$

We will also be interested in the joint composition of a pair of words of blocklength n. The *joint composition* of a pair of words is an array n_{ij} whose ij entry is the number of locations in which the first word contains symbol a_i and the second contains symbol a_j. A *conditional composition* is an array $n_{j|i}$ which, for the locations where the first word contains symbol a_i, specifies the number of locations where the second contains symbol a_j. Because these are just different ways of saying the same thing, we have

$$n_{ij} = n_{j|i}$$

The *relative frequency*, or relative joint composition, of an array n_{ij} is defined by

$$P_{ij} = \frac{n_{ij}}{n}$$

Similarly, the *conditional relative frequency* is

$$P_{j|i} = \frac{n_{j|i}}{n_i}$$

Therefore

$$P_{ij} = p_i P_{j|i}$$

A code is called a *constant-composition code* if all of its codewords have the same composition. An arbitrary code $\mathscr{C}$ can be broken into a collection of constant-composition subcodes. The subcode $\mathscr{C}_n$ is the set of all codewords of $\mathscr{C}$ that have composition vector $\mathbf{n} = \{n_j\}$. Then $\mathscr{C}$ is the union of all its constant-composition subcodes. In an asymptotic sense, the largest constant-composition subcode of $\mathscr{C}$ of rate R is nearly as large as $\mathscr{C}$. This is because the composition $\{n_j\}_{j=0}^{J-1}$ can take on only $n + 1$ values in each of J components; there are less than $(n + 1)^J$ distinct constant-composition subcodes. In contrast, the number of codewords is exponential in n.

Let M be the number of codewords in $\mathscr{C}$ and let M^* be the number of codewords in the largest constant-composition subcode $\mathscr{C}^*$. Let r and R^* be the rates of the respective codes. Then

$$M \leq (n + 1)^J M^*$$

Therefore

$$\frac{1}{n} \log M^* \geq \frac{1}{n} \log M - \frac{J}{n} \log (n + 1)$$

In terms of the rates, this can be rewritten

$$R^* \geq R - \frac{J}{n} \log (n + 1)$$

The second term on the right goes to zero as n to infinity with R fixed. Hence R^* goes to R.

The minimum distance of a code is a measure of the amount of difference between the two most similar codewords. The minimum Hamming distance is given by the following two definitions.

☐ **Definition 5.8.1**   The *Hamming distance* $d(\mathbf{c}_m, \mathbf{c}_{m'})$ between two sequences $\mathbf{c}_m$ and $\mathbf{c}_{m'}$ of length n is the number of places in which they differ.   ☐

For example, if $\mathbf{x} = 10101$ and $\mathbf{y} = 01100$, then $d(10101, 01100) = 3$. If $\mathbf{x} = 30102$ and $\mathbf{y} = 21103$, then $d(30102, 21103) = 3$.

The Hamming distance is related to the joint composition as follows:

$$d(\mathbf{c}_m, \mathbf{c}_{m'}) = \sum_j \sum_{i \neq j} n_{ij} = n \sum_j \sum_{i \neq j} P_{ij}$$

$$= n - \sum_i n_{ii}$$

Intuitively, good codes spread the codewords far apart to the extent possible; no two codewords should be similar. One way to judge a code is by the distance between the closest pair of codewords.

☐ **Definition 5.8.2**   Let $\mathscr{C} = \{\mathbf{c}_0, \ldots, \mathbf{c}_{M-1}\}$ be a code. The *minimum Hamming distance* of $\mathscr{C}$ is the Hamming distance of the pair of codewords with smallest Hamming distance. That is,

$$d^* = \min_{\substack{\mathbf{c}_m, \mathbf{c}_{m'} \in \mathscr{C} \\ m \neq m'}} d(\mathbf{c}_m, \mathbf{c}_{m'}) \qquad \qquad ☐$$

The minimum Hamming distance is a useful descriptor for a code. It does not depend on the channel transition matrix $\mathbf{Q}$. It should be apparent that the Hamming distance is most appropriate for channels that are symmetric. If the channel has some degree of skewing or asymmetry in its transition matrix, then the minimum Hamming distance is less appropriate. The generalization of Hamming distance to an arbitrary channel is the Bhattacharyya distance. Before studying the Bhattacharyya distance between two codewords, we define the Bhattacharyya distance between two letters.

☐ **Definition 5.8.3**   For a specified channel $\mathbf{Q}$, the *Bhattacharyya distance* between channel input letters a_i and a_j is given by

$$d_{ij} = -\log \sum_k Q_{k|i}^{1/2} Q_{k|j}^{1/2} \qquad \qquad ☐$$

Each channel $\mathbf{Q}$ is associated with the symmetric matrix $\Delta = \{d_{ij}\}$ of Bhattacharyya distances between input letters. The properties of the distance matrix can be used to define several classes of channel. Channels such as the examples shown in Fig. 5.14 that have $d_{ij} = \infty$ for some pair of letters a_i, a_j have the property that it is possible to find two input letters and a binary partition of the set of output letters such that the first input letter always causes an output in one half of the partition while the second input letter always causes an output in the other half of the partition. For such channels a message can be sent without error. These are called channels with a nonzero zero-error capacity. Some of our general theorems in Chapter 10 will not hold for such a good channel; those channels need to be studied separately. A channel for which $d_{ij} \neq \infty$ for all i and j is called an *indivisible channel*.

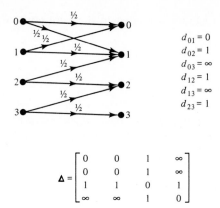

$$\Delta = \begin{bmatrix} 0 & 0 & 1 & \infty \\ 0 & 0 & 1 & \infty \\ 1 & 1 & 0 & 1 \\ \infty & \infty & 1 & 0 \end{bmatrix}$$

Figure 5.14   A Bhattacharyya distance matrix.

Another class of channels is the class for which d_{ij} equals a constant A, which must be positive, whenever $i \neq j$. This class is known as the class of *equidistant channels* because any two distinct letters are at the same distance. Every binary input channel is equidistant. For an equidistant channel, Bhattacharyya distance is the same as Hamming distance except for a constant multiplier equal to A. Therefore any result we derive for Bhattacharyya distance can be applied to Hamming distance by taking the channel to be equidistant and dividing out A.

☐ **Definition 5.8.4**   The Bhattacharyya distance between codewords $\mathbf{c}_m$ and $\mathbf{c}_{m'}$ in a code of blocklength n is given by

$$d(\mathbf{c}_m, \mathbf{c}_{m'}) = -\log \sum_k Q(\mathbf{y}|\mathbf{c}_m)^{1/2} Q(\mathbf{y}|\mathbf{c}_{m'})^{1/2}$$

$$= -n \sum_{ij} P_{ij} \log \sum_k Q_{k|i}^{1/2} Q_{k|j}^{1/2}$$

where nP_{ij} is the joint composition of $\mathbf{c}_m$ and $\mathbf{c}_{m'}$.   ☐

☐ **Definition 5.8.5**   Let $\mathscr{C} = \{\mathbf{c}_0, \ldots, \mathbf{c}_{M-1}\}$ be a code. The minimum Bhattacharyya distance of $\mathscr{C}$ is the Bhattacharyya distance of the pair of codewords with the smallest Bhattacharyya distance. That is,

$$d^* = \min_{\substack{\mathbf{c}_m, \mathbf{c}_{m'} \in \mathscr{C} \\ m \neq m'}} d(\mathbf{c}_m, \mathbf{c}_{m'})$$ ☐

If we know the minimum Bhattacharyya distance of a code for a channel $\mathbf{Q}$, then we can make some estimates of the probability of decoding error when the code is used on $\mathbf{Q}$. This we do in Chapter 10 by studying the probability of confusing two codewords that differ by the minimum distance.

5.9 TREE CODES FOR DATA TRANSMISSION

A tree code encodes a stream of data symbols into a stream of codeword symbols. It cannot be broken into a succession of noninteracting blocks. A data stream is shifted into the encoder beginning at time zero and continued indefinitely into the future, while a code stream is shifted out. The duration of the data stream and the code stream is so long that it is effectively infinite; the duration does not enter into the design of the encoder and decoder. Most tree codes for data transmission are built upon the structure of a fixed framelength, as in the tree code whose encoder is shown in Fig. 5.15. The stream of incoming data symbols is broken into pieces; each piece has k_0 data symbols and is called a *data frame*. The stream of code symbols is broken into segments of n_0 code symbols called *code frames*. The encoder can store the m most recent frames of input symbols, a total of mk_0 data symbols. During each frame time, a new frame is shifted into the encoder and the oldest data frame is shifted out and discarded. From the new incoming data frame and the m previously stored data frames, the encoder computes a single codeword frame of length n_0 symbols. This codeword frame is shifted out of the encoder as the next data frame is shifted in. Hence the channel must transmit n_0 codeword symbols for each k_0 data symbols. The rate R of the tree code is defined as $R = k_0/n_0$, provided the data alphabet and the code alphabet are the same.

The constraint length v of a tree code is defined as $v = mk_0$. In the example of Fig. 5.15, the constraint length is 21 and the rate is 0.6. For practical codes, the constraint length is always finite, though it may be infinite in theoretical studies. When the constraint length is finite, the encoder is a finite-state machine. The v most recent J-ary input symbols define the set of J^v states of the finite-state machine. Then the code can be described by a trellis with J^v states and is called a *trellis code*.

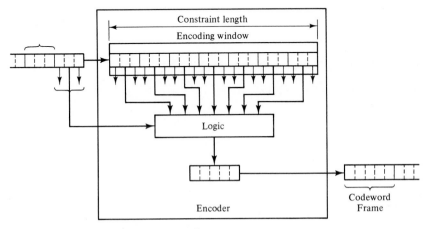

Figure 5.15   An encoder for a tree code.

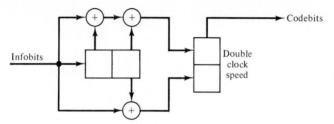

Figure 5.16   Encoder for a trellis code with constraint length 2.

An encoder for a simple binary trellis code of constraint length 2 with $k_0 = 1$ and $n_0 = 2$ is shown in Fig. 5.16. The code is the set of all semi-infinite binary words that can be generated by this encoder. The code can also be described using the trellis diagram in Fig. 5.17. The code is the set of all semi-infinite binary words that can be read off any path through the trellis.

In this section we will develop the elementary information-theoretic parameters describing the performance of trellis codes. The information-theoretic study of trellis codes is more difficult than that of block codes because it is not possible to discuss the probability of decoding error without discussing something about the decoder. For block codes, we could simply assume a convenient decoding rule and avoid any close scrutiny of it. Trellis codes, on the other hand, are infinitely long. We must somehow restrict our analysis of the performance of decoders to those decoders of finite complexity.

A trellis code can be decoded as follows. The decoder receives a noisy codeword and examines it against a beginning segment of the trellis to decide which path through the trellis the encoder took to start. It chooses the beginning segment that best agrees with the received noisy codeword along the beginning segment. That is, it chooses the path that differs from the received word in the fewest number of places in that beginning segment. In this way it makes a firm decoding decision for the first frame.

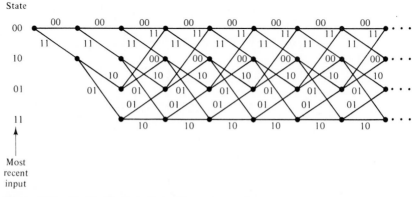

Figure 5.17   Trellis diagram for a binary tree code.

Specifically, suppose the decoder has received $N + 1$ frames, and it knows the state of the encoder at the start of these $N + 1$ frames. There are $J^{k_0(N+1)}$ paths leaving the initial node of the trellis that are $N + 1$ frames long, so the decoder compares the received word to these $J^{k_0(N+1)}$ paths and finds the closest path—in particular, the first frame of this closest path. In this way, it decodes the first information frame. Then the decoder moves forward one frame, dropping the first frame of the received word and appending a new frame to the received word and decodes another frame. It then repeats the process, continuing indefinitely to decode information frames.

In this section we will use the random-coding bound for block codes to derive a random-coding bound for trellis codes, which is given in the next theorem, to describe the probability of error as a function of encoded constraint length $v_e = v(n_0/k_0)$. There may be a temptation to compare the random-coding bound for trellis codes with the random-coding bound for block codes. However, this is a meaningless comparison. The random-coding bound for block codes expresses the probability of block decoding error asymptotically in terms of blocklength, while the random-coding bound for tree codes expresses the probability of symbol error asymptotically in terms of encoded constraint length. There is no sense in which blocklength is comparable to constraint length, so the bounds cannot be compared. Even if we were to insist on equating these two lengths, a comparison of the asymptotic behavior would not say much about a comparison of practical codes. This is because the random-coding bound for trellis codes includes a very large constant multiplying the bound, and for practical values of n, this constant can be as important as the exponentially decreasing term.

The maximum-likelihood decoder for trellis codes looks at a long segment of the trellis and finds that path that most closely agrees with the received word. Visualize two paths through the trellis, the correct path and the decoded path. There will be symbol errors in the decoded data stream if these two paths are different. This is the case we visualize, with the two paths agreeing for some time, then diverging for a number of symbols, then recombining. The interval where the paths differ is called an *error event*. There may be any number of such error events along the indefinitely long decoded data stream.

□   **Theorem 5.9.1**   Let p_e be the probability of symbol error of the best trellis code of rate R and constraint length v_e for a discrete memoryless channel. Then for any s and probability distribution $\mathbf{p}$,

$$p_e \leq A e^{-v_e E_o(s, \mathbf{p})}$$

provided s satisfies $0 \leq s \leq 1$ and

$$s < \frac{E_o(s, \mathbf{p})}{R}$$

where

$$E_o(s, \mathbf{p}) = -\log \sum_k \left(\sum_j p_j Q_{k|j}^{1/(1+s)} \right)^{1+s}$$

and A is a constant independent of v_e.

Proof A particular code symbol x_l can be decoded incorrectly only if it is contained within an error event, say an error event of length r symbols, with r a multiple of n_0. We will bound the probability of this error event by using the random-coding bound for block codes.

Let the code symbols on the trellis be assigned randomly. The segment of the trellis $v_e + r$ symbols long forms a block code. The probability of an error event is essentially the probability of block decoding error with $M_r = e^{rR}$ codewords and blocklength $N_r = v_e + r$. The rate of the fabricated block code is

$$R_r = \frac{\log M_r}{N_r} = \frac{rR}{v_e + r}$$

Let $p_e(r)$ be the probability of error for an event of length r. Then by the random-coding bound,

$$p_e(r) \le e^{-(v_e + r)[E_o(s,\mathbf{p}) - srR/(v_e + r)]}$$

$$= e^{-r[E_o(s,\mathbf{p}) - sR]} e^{-v_e E_o(s,\mathbf{p})}$$

where $0 \le s \le 1$.

To have a decoding error in symbol x_l, there must be an error event of length $v_e + r$ that started not more than r symbols earlier. This is because the paths in the trellis will not remerge unless the last v_e received symbols are correct. Let E_{ri} denote an error event of length $v_e + r$ starting i frames earlier for $i = 0, 1, \ldots, j$ and for $r = 0, 1, \ldots$. The union bound gives

$$p_e = Pr[\hat{X}_l \ne X_l]$$

$$\le \sum_{r=0}^{\infty} \sum_{i=0}^{r} Pr[E_{ri}]$$

We will bound the probability of error over a randomly constructed ensemble of codes. The ensemble average is bounded by replacing the inner sum with $(r + 1)$ times a bound on the largest summand. Thus

$$E[p_e] \le \sum_{r=0}^{\infty} (r + 1) E[p_e(r)]$$

$$\le e^{-v_e E_o(s,\mathbf{p})} \sum_{r=0}^{\infty} (r + 1) e^{-r[E_o(s,\mathbf{p}) - sR]}$$

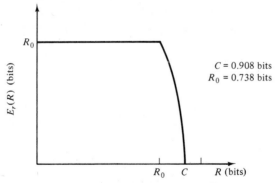

Figure 5.18   A random-coding exponent for trellis codes for a binary symmetric channel, $p = 0.01$.

The series in the second line converges, provided

$$E_o(s, \mathbf{p}) - sR > 0$$

We know from study of the random-coding exponent that there must be an s between 0 and 1 for which the inequality is satisfied as long as R is less than C. Summing the series gives

$$E[p_e] \le \frac{e^{-v_e E_o(s, \mathbf{p})}}{(1 - e^{-[E_o(s, \mathbf{p}) - sR]})^2}$$

The denominator is independent of v_e and the best code has a probability of symbol error at least as small as the ensemble average, so we have

$$p_e \le A e^{-v_e E_o(s, \mathbf{p})}$$

as was to be proved.   □

The random-coding exponent for trellis codes is obtained by maximizing the bound given in Theorem 5.9.1 over all s satisfying the conditions, and over all $\mathbf{p}$. If R is sufficiently small, the maximum will occur with $s = 1$ and for the maximizing $\mathbf{p}$ independent of R. Therefore the random-coding exponent for small R will be constant. The sketch of the random-coding exponent in Fig. 5.18 illustrates this behavior.

PROBLEMS

5.1. Prove that for discrete random variables

$$I(X; (Y; Z)) = I(X; Z|Y) + I(X; Y)$$

5.2. Prove the following for discrete random variables:

$$H(X_1,\ldots,X_n) \le H(X_1) + \cdots + H(X_n)$$

$$H(X_1,\ldots,X_n,Y_1,\ldots,Y_n) \le H(X_1,\ldots,X_n) + H(Y_1,\ldots,Y_n)$$

When are the inequalities satisfied with equality?

5.3. Suppose that the probability distribution of Y conditional on X and Z is the same as the probability distribution of Y conditional on Z. That is,

$$P_{k|jl} = P_{k|j}$$

for all k, j, l. Prove that

$$I(Z;Y|X) = 0$$

5.4. Show that the capacity of the channel

$$\mathbf{Q} = \begin{bmatrix} 2/3 & 1/3 & 0 \\ 1/3 & 1/3 & 1/3 \\ 0 & 1/3 & 2/3 \end{bmatrix}$$

is obtained by setting equal to zero the probability of using one of the input letters. What is the channel capacity? Give an intuitive reason for why this letter is not used.

5.5. Consider the channel whose input symbols are 2-bit binary words and whose transmission matrix is described by the transitions

$$00 \rightarrow 00$$
$$01 \rightarrow 10$$
$$10 \rightarrow 11$$
$$11 \rightarrow 01$$

with probability 1. Suppose the input letters are independent and equiprobable. Show that the mutual information between input symbols and output symbols is 2 bits, while the mutual information between any single bit and the corresponding output bit is zero.

Conclude that for any pair of random vectors whose marginal probability distributions are known, the mutual information is not necessarily maximized if the vector components are independent.

5.6. The channel with probability transition matrix

$$\mathbf{Q} = \begin{bmatrix} 0.5 & 0.3 & 0.2 \\ 0.2 & 0.5 & 0.3 \\ 0.3 & 0.2 & 0.5 \end{bmatrix}$$

exhibits a kind of symmetry. Does it satisfy our definition of a symmetric channel? What probability distribution achieves the capacity?

5.7. The binary errors-and-erasures channel is given by

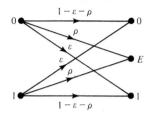

   a. Find the capacity.
   b. Specialize to erasures only ($\varepsilon = 0$).
   c. Specialize to the binary symmetric channel ($\rho = 0$).
   d. Would you prefer a binary symmetric channel with crossover probability $= 0.125$ or a simple erasure channel with probability of erasure $= 0.5$?

5.8. Consider the following channel:

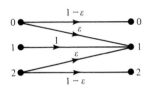

Is $(\frac{1}{2}, 0, \frac{1}{2})$ an input distribution that achieves capacity?

5.9. Each of the three channels shown below is used with probability distribution on the input letters of $\mathbf{p} = (p_0, p_1) = (\frac{1}{2}, \frac{1}{2})$. In each case find $I(X;Y)$.

Which channel, with this distribution $\mathbf{p}$ on the input letters, has the largest mutual information between input and output?

5.10. Is the following statement correct?

One way of deriving the relationship $I(X;Y) = H(X) - H(X|Y)$ is to average the expression $I(X;k) = H(X) - H(X|k)$, over all k.

If so, why? if not, why not?

5.11. Suppose that two channels are to be connected end to end to form a composite channel. Each of the original channels is a binary symmetric channel with crossover probability ε.

   a. Suppose that the output of the first channel is connected directly to the input of the second with no processing between:

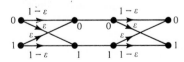

What is the capacity of the composite channel?

b. Suppose that a decoder/encoder (a recoder) is allowed between the channels:

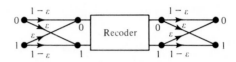

What is the capacity?

5.12. A channel $\mathbf{Q}'$ has capacity C' and a channel $\mathbf{Q}''$ has capacity C''. Let

$$Q_{k|j} = \sum_{r=0}^{R-1} Q'_{k|r} Q''_{r|j}$$

assuming that $\mathbf{Q}'$ has R inputs and $\mathbf{Q}''$ has R outputs. Let C be the capacity of $\mathbf{Q}$. Prove that

$$C \le \min\left[C', C''\right]$$

5.13. Compute the capacity-cost function for the ternary channel with probability transition matrix

$$\mathbf{Q} = \begin{bmatrix} p & q & 0 \\ q & p & 0 \\ 0 & 0 & 1 \end{bmatrix}$$

and with cost schedule $(1,0,0)$.

5.14. Verify that the equiprobable distribution on the input alphabet of a symmetric channel does indeed satisfy the Kuhn-Tucker conditions.

5.15. The capacity-cost function $C(S)$ can be studied by introducing a Lagrange multiplier.

   a. Prove that $C(S)$ is an increasing, concave, and continuous function in its region of interest.

   b. Modify the algorithm for computing capacity to get an algorithm for computing $C(S)$.

5.16. For the channel $\mathbf{Q}$, define the capacity per unit cost by

$$C_r = \max_{\mathbf{p}} \frac{I(\mathbf{p};\mathbf{Q})}{\sum_i p_i e_i} \qquad \text{bits/unit cost}$$

where $\{e_i\}$ is an expense schedule with $e_i \ge 0$ for all i. Show that C_r can be read off a graph of $C(S)$.

5.17. a. Sketch the random-coding exponent $E_r(R)$ for a binary symmetric channel with crossover probability $\rho < 1/2$.

   b. R_{crit} is defined as the largest value of R for which $dE_r(R)/dR = -1$. Find R_{crit} as a function of ρ.

   c. If $\rho = 0.01$, what is the smallest n for which the proof of the direct part of the coding theorem guarantees the existence of a code of blocklength n and rate R_{crit} for which $p_e \le 10^{-6}$?   .

   d. Repeat for $p_e \le 10^{-12}$.

5.18. A binary symmetric Markov channel has a binary input alphabet and probability transition matrix $\{P_{j|i}\}$ given by

$$\mathbf{P} = \begin{bmatrix} 1-\rho & \rho \\ \rho & 1-\rho \end{bmatrix}$$

Find the capacity.

5.19. A channel $\mathbf{Q}$ has the property that for every permutation of the input symbols, there is a permutation of the output symbols that returns $\mathbf{Q}$ to its original form. Prove that $\mathbf{Q}$ is an equidistant channel.

5.20. Prove the useful rule

$$\prod_{l=1}^{n}\left(\sum_{j_l} A_{j_l}\right) = \sum_{j_1}\sum_{j_2}\cdots\sum_{j_n}\left(\prod_{l=1}^{n} A_{j_l}\right)$$

where $(A_{j_0}, \ldots, A_{j_l}, \ldots, A_{j_{n-1}})$ is a vector whose range of values in the lth component are indexed by j_l.

5.21. Prove that

$$I((X,Y);(U,V,W)) = I((X,Y);U|V,W) + I((X,Y);V|W) + I((X,Y);W)$$

5.22. Let U, V, X, Y, and Z be random variables. Do the conditions

$$I(V;Y,Z|U,X) = 0$$

and

$$I(X;U,Z|V,Y) = 0$$

imply that

$$I(Z;X,V|U,Y) = 0?$$

5.23. Conditioning reduces the entropy. However, no such property exists for the mutual information. Show that neither $I(X;Y)$ nor $I(X;Y|Z)$ dominates the other in general by giving the following counterexamples:

a. Find P_{ijk} with $X, Y,$ and Z binary random variables such that $I(X;Y) = 0$ and $I(X;Y|Z) \neq 0$.

b. Find P_{ijk} with $X, Y,$ and Z binary random variables such that $I(X;Y|Z) = 0$ with $I(X;Y) \neq 0$.

5.24. Suppose that $I(X;Y) = 0$. Does this imply that $I(X;Z) = I(X;Z|Y)$?

5.25. Show that the rate at which a tangent to $E_r(R)$ of slope -1 intersects the R axis is equal to $E_r(0)$ and is given by

$$R_0 = \max_{\mathbf{p}}\left[-\log\sum_{k}\left(\sum_{j} p_j Q_{k|j}^{1/2}\right)^2\right]$$

5.26. A quaternary erasure channel has probability transition matrix

$$\mathbf{Q} = \begin{bmatrix} 1-\varepsilon & 0 & 0 & 0 \\ 0 & 1-\varepsilon & 0 & 0 \\ 0 & 0 & 1-\varepsilon & 0 \\ 0 & 0 & 0 & 1-\varepsilon \\ \varepsilon & \varepsilon & \varepsilon & \varepsilon \end{bmatrix}$$

Let the input symbols be denoted as $\{00, 01, 10, 11\}$. If the first and second bits are viewed separately, the quaternary erasure channel can be used as two binary erasure channels, possibly with some degradation. Consequently, the quaternary erasure channel is at least as good as two binary erasure channels, and fundamental descriptions of code rates should be at least as large.

a. Show that the capacity of the quaternary erasure channel is the same as the capacity of the two binary erasure channels.

b. Show that the cutoff rate of the quaternary erasure channel is smaller than the cutoff rate of the two binary erasure channels. This implies that the cutoff rate is not a fundamental limit on communication rate.

NOTES

The basic ideas of this chapter can be found in Shannon's epic 1948 paper. The definitions of mutual information and channel capacity for discrete or continuous channels are his, and he developed the basic properties of mutual information. The notion of mutual information was generalized to abstract alphabets by several Soviet mathematicians, culminating in work of Dobrushin (1959). Fano (1952) contributed both his basic inequality and his converse theorems. Some other kinds of converse theorems were contributed by Wolfowitz (1957) and Arimoto (1973). The latter will be studied in Chapter 6.

Shannon introduced the use of typical sequences and Wolfowitz (1961) refined the application of typical sequences in the proof of coding theorems. Csiszár and Körner (1981) reconstructed much of information theory from the point of view of typical sequences and used composition arguments to derive an error exponent directly in the form of a discrimination. The idea of a random-coding argument originated with Shannon. Its adaptation to proving the random-coding exponent was done by Gallager (1965). The recursive algorithm for computing capacity was devised by Arimoto (1972) and Blahut (1972). The Bhattacharyya distance appeared in the statistical literature as early as 1943.

The random-coding and other exponential bounds for trellis codes were developed by Yudkin (1964), Viterbi (1967), and Forney (1974). The cutoff rate has a prominent role in the theory of sequential decoding. Arikan (1985) has provided a satisfying explanation of its essential character in terms of list decoders for block codes.

CHAPTER 6

Data Compression Codes

O ne sometimes wishes to represent the output of a source using a bit rate that is less than the source entropy rate. No such data compaction code exists; every such representation must fail to describe the output of the source exactly. Such a distorting representation is called a *data compression code*. A data compression code intentionally discards the fine details of the data. The source output no longer can be recovered exactly; some distortion will ensue. One tries to minimize distortion by design of the data compression code.

It may seem that there are not many instances where it is important to reduce the data rate below the source entropy, and this is usually true for sources that originate as discrete sources. However, in most instances of the digitization of continuous signals or of multidimensional images, the source entropy is infinite. It always requires an infinite number of bits to digitize such a source exactly. A data compression code must be used to reduce the output of a continuous source to a finite number of bits. Distortion will always occur, but one tries to get the least distortion for the number of bits expended. Thus our study of data compression for discrete sources is primarily a preparation for the study of data compression for continuous sources.

6.1 TRANSMISSION AT RATES ABOVE CAPACITY

The requirement for data compression comes when one needs to communicate source data that is generated at rates above channel capacity. The Fano inequality tells us that in such cases there must be some symbol errors in a decoded block, but it does not say how many. Before entering into the study of data compression codes, in this section we shall study stronger bounds on the probability of decoding error for channel codes. First we will develop an improved block converse, which states that for rates larger than channel capacity, the probability of correct block decoding goes to zero exponentially in the blocklength. Then we will rework the Fano inequality into the alternative form of a per-symbol converse, which states that the probability of *symbol* error is bounded away from zero if the code rate is larger than the channel capacity.

The block converse is given in the following theorem in terms of the probability of correct decoding, $p_c = 1 - p_e$.

□ **Theorem 6.1.1** Suppose that a block code for a discrete memoryless channel of capacity C has $M = e^{nR}$ equiprobable codewords, and suppose that $R > C$. Then the probability of correct decoding satisfies

$$p_c \le e^{-nE^-(R)}$$

where

$$E^-(R) = \max_{-1 \le s \le 0} \min_{\mathbf{p}} \left[-sR - \log \sum_k \left(\sum_j p_j Q_{k|j}^{1/(1+s)} \right)^{1+s} \right]$$

which is always positive if $R > C$.

Proof The probability of error is least if a maximum-likelihood decoder is used, as was shown in Theorem 5.1.1. Because the codewords are used with equal probability, the output block $\mathbf{y}$ is decoded into the mth message if

$$Q(\mathbf{y}|\mathbf{c}_m) > Q(\mathbf{y}|\mathbf{c}_{m'})$$

for all $m' \ne m$. The probability of correct decoding is

$$p_c = \sum_{m=0}^{M-1} \frac{1}{M} \sum_{\mathbf{y} \in \mathcal{U}_m} Q(\mathbf{y}|\mathbf{c}_m)$$

and $Q(\mathbf{y}|\mathbf{c}_m)$ satisfies

$$Q(\mathbf{y}|\mathbf{c}_m) = \max_{m'} Q(\mathbf{y}|\mathbf{c}_{m'})$$

for all $\mathbf{y}$ in $\mathcal{U}_m$. Therefore

$$p_c = \frac{1}{M} \sum_{m=0}^{M-1} \sum_{\mathbf{y} \in \mathcal{U}_m} \max_{m'} Q(\mathbf{y}|\mathbf{c}_{m'})$$

The argument of the summand is now independent of m. The $\mathcal{U}_m$ are disjoint so we can carry out the sum over all m to give

$$p_c \le \sum_{\mathbf{y}} \frac{1}{M} \max_{m'} Q(\mathbf{y}|\mathbf{c}_{m'})$$

which is an inequality because there may be some $\mathbf{y}$ that are in no decoding set $\mathcal{U}_m$. Now drop the prime on m and rewrite this as

$$p_c \le \frac{1}{M} \sum_{\mathbf{y}} \left\{ \left[\max_m Q(\mathbf{y}|\mathbf{c}_m) \right]^{1/\rho} \right\}^{\rho}$$

for any positive ρ. The introduction of ρ allows us to use the inequality

$$\left[\max_m Q(\mathbf{y}|\mathbf{c}_m) \right]^{1/\rho} \le \sum_{m=0}^{M-1} Q(\mathbf{y}|\mathbf{c}_m)^{1/\rho}$$

which leads to an inequality on p_c:

$$p_c \le \frac{1}{M} \sum_{\mathbf{y}} \left[\sum_{m=0}^{M-1} Q(\mathbf{y}|\mathbf{c}_m)^{1/\rho} \right]^{\rho}$$

This is an intractable expression for large unknown codes, so we intend to simplify it by further weakening the inequality. First we replace the sum on codewords by a sum over all $\mathbf{x}$ by defining the probability distribution

$$p(\mathbf{x}) = \begin{cases} 1/M & \text{if } \mathbf{x} \text{ is a codeword} \\ 0 & \text{otherwise} \end{cases}$$

Then we can write

$$p_c \le \frac{1}{M} \sum_{\mathbf{y}} \left[M \sum_{\mathbf{x}} p(\mathbf{x}) Q(\mathbf{y}|\mathbf{x})^{1/\rho} \right]^{\rho}$$

We do not know the code $\mathscr{C}$, so we do not know $p(\mathbf{x})$. Therefore we replace this with the weaker expression

$$p_c \le \max_{\mathbf{p}} \frac{1}{M^{1-\rho}} \sum_{\mathbf{y}} \left[\sum_{\mathbf{x}} p(\mathbf{x}) Q(\mathbf{y}|\mathbf{x})^{1/\rho} \right]^{\rho}$$

Now let $\rho = 1 + s$, with $-1 \le s \le 0$, and rewrite the inequality as

$$p_c \le \exp\left[-\min_{\mathbf{p}} \left\{ -snR - \log \sum_{\mathbf{y}} \left[\sum_{\mathbf{x}} p(\mathbf{x}) Q(\mathbf{y}|\mathbf{x})^{1/(1+s)} \right]^{1+s} \right\} \right]$$

The right side is a concave function of $\mathbf{p}$ for $-1 \le s \le 0$, and $Q(\mathbf{y}|\mathbf{x})$ is a product distribution. Therefore the maximum over $\mathbf{p}$ must occur for a product distribution. To verify this, one can write out the Kuhn-Tucker conditions for a blocklength of 1, and from this show that the product distribution must satisfy the Kuhn-Tucker conditions for a blocklength of n. Therefore

$$p_e \leq \exp\left\{-n\min_{\mathbf{p}}\left[-sR - \log\sum_k\left(\sum_j p_j Q_{k|j}^{1/(1+s)}\right)^{1+s}\right]\right\}$$

where now $\mathbf{p}$ is a probability distribution on single letters. Because s is arbitrary in the interval from -1 to 0, we can choose it to make the bound the tightest, thereby establishing the first claim of the theorem.

It remains to show that the exponent is positive for $R > C$. Let

$$E_o(s, \mathbf{p}) = -\log\left[\sum_k\left(\sum_j p_j Q_{k|j}^{1/(1+s)}\right)\right]^{1+s}$$

We will expand $E_o(s, \mathbf{p})$ in a Taylor series in s. By Jensen's inequality (Theorem A.4), if d_j for $j = 0, \ldots, J - 1$ are nonnegative, then

$$\sum_j p_j d_j \leq \left(\sum_j p_j d_j^{1/t}\right)^t$$

for all $0 < t < 1$. Therefore, for $-1 < s < 0$,

$$E_o(s, \mathbf{p}) \leq 0$$

with equality when $s = 0$. This implies that the Taylor series is of the form

$$E_o(s, \mathbf{p}) = s\frac{\partial E_o(s, \mathbf{p})}{\partial s} + \cdots$$

The partial derivative can be calculated (see Problem 6.10) to obtain

$$\frac{\partial E_o(s, \mathbf{p})}{\partial s} = I(\mathbf{p}; \mathbf{Q})$$

Now we have

$$E^-(R) = \max_{-1 < s < 0}\min_{\mathbf{p}}\left\{-s[R - I(\mathbf{p}; \mathbf{Q})] + s^2\frac{\partial^2 E_o(s, \mathbf{p})}{\partial s^2} + \cdots\right\}$$

For sufficiently small s, the term in braces depends primarily on the linear term. Choose $s = -\varepsilon$ for ε very small, and write

$$E^-(R) \geq \min_{\mathbf{p}}\{\varepsilon[R - I(\mathbf{p}; \mathbf{Q})] + o(\varepsilon^2)\}$$

which is expressed as an inequality because $-\varepsilon$ need not be the maximizing value of s. We can evaluate the minimum over $\mathbf{p}$ to write

$$E^-(R) \geq \varepsilon(R - C) + o(\varepsilon^2)$$

which is positive if $R > C$. This completes the proof of the theorem.　□

Every block converse for data transmission codes has a subtle weakness, and the converse statement in Theorem 6.1.1 is no exception. The weakness is that we have not demonstrated that a block decoding error is necessarily a serious error. It is conceivable that codes of very long blocklength exist such that when a block decoding error occurs, the erroneous block output is only wrong in a very few symbols. A block converse theorem, in fact, only asserts that one symbol must be in error. If the blocks are millions of symbols long, this may be relatively unimportant.

For this reason, the per-letter converse that we prove next may be considered a stronger converse because it precludes the above circumstance. It says that the probability of *symbol* error must be bounded away from zero for any blocklength if the rate is larger than channel capacity. The per-letter converse is proved by combining an averaging procedure with the Fano inequality.

The symbol errors that we wish to study are those errors at the output of the decoder. An error occurs in the lth symbol out of the decoder if that symbol is not the same as the lth symbol into the encoder. If we standardize the encoder input to be a stream of binary symbols, then the probability of symbol error is called the *bit-error rate*.

The probability of symbol error is defined as

$$\langle p_e \rangle = \frac{1}{N} \sum_{l=1}^{N} p_{e,l}$$

where $p_{e,l}$ is the probability of error in the lth symbol of the decoder output.

The encoder input is a block of length N of symbols in the encoder input alphabet, and the decoder output is a block of length N in this same alphabet. Let U^N and V^N denote the encoder input block and the decoder output block respectively, as block random variables. Let $I(U^N; V^N)$ denote the average mutual information between an encoder input block and a decoder output block, and let $I(X^n; Y^n)$ denote the average mutual information between a channel input block and a channel output block.

□   **Theorem 6.1.2**   Given an encoder, whose input alphabet has J symbols, that encodes blocks of N input symbols into codewords of blocklength n, the probability of symbol error $\langle p_e \rangle$ at the output of a channel decoder satisfies

$$\langle p_e \rangle \log (J - 1) + H_b(\langle p_e \rangle) \geq \frac{1}{N} H(X^n) - \frac{1}{N} I(X^n; Y^n)$$

Proof   Let U_l and V_l denote the lth symbol into the encoder and the lth symbol out of the decoder, respectively. By Theorem 5.3.1,

$$p_{e,l} \log (J - 1) + H_b(p_{e,l}) \geq H(U_l | V_l)$$

Averaging over l gives

$$\frac{1}{N}\sum_{l=1}^{N}\left[p_{e,l}\log\left(J-1\right)+H_b(p_{e,l})\right]\geq\frac{1}{N}\sum_{l=1}^{N}H(U_l|V_l)$$

Because the binary entropy is concave, we can move the average over l inside the binary entropy without violating the inequality. We then have

$$\langle p_e\rangle\log\left(J-1\right)+H_b(\langle p_e\rangle)\geq\frac{1}{N}\sum_{l=1}^{N}H(U_l|V_l)$$

Now we work on the right side by writing

$$H(U^N|V^N)=H(U_1|V^N)+H(U_2|V^N,U_1)+\cdots+H(U_N|V^N,U_1,\ldots,U_{N-1})$$
$$\leq\sum_{l=1}^{N}H(U_l|V_l)$$

The proof is completed as follows

$$\langle p_e\rangle\log\left(J-1\right)+H_b(\langle p_e\rangle)\geq\frac{1}{N}H(U^N|V^N)$$

$$=\frac{1}{N}H(U^N)-\frac{1}{N}I(U^N;V^N)$$

$$\geq\frac{1}{N}H(X^n)-\frac{1}{N}I(X^n;Y^n)$$

where we have used the fact that the encoder is deterministic to change the first term on the right and the data-processing theorem (Theorem 5.3.3) to change the second. □

□ **Corollary 6.1.3** For an encoder with input alphabet of size J, the probability of symbol error of a block code of rate R used on a channel of capacity C satisfies

$$\langle p_e\rangle\log\left(J-1\right)+H_b(\langle p_e\rangle)\geq\frac{R-C}{R}\log J$$

Proof From the facts that $H(X^n)=nR$ and $I(X^n;Y^n)\leq nC$, the theorem gives the inequality

$$\langle p_e\rangle\log\left(J-1\right)+H_b(\langle p_e\rangle)\geq\frac{n}{N}(R-C)$$

Because

$$R=\frac{1}{n}\log J^N$$

the corollary follows. □

If the encoder input is a binary data stream, then $J = 2$, and $\langle p_e \rangle$ is the bit-error rate. We have then that the bit-error rate satisfies

$$H_b(\langle p_e \rangle) \geq \frac{R - C}{R}$$

6.2 COMPRESSION OF INFORMATION

Data compression is the practice of intentionally reducing the information content of a data record. This should be done in such a way that the reproduction has as little distortion as is possible. We think of a data compressor as a device for intentionally blurring the fine details of a source output so as to reduce the information content. We wish to determine the amount of information still needed to describe the source output to within an allowed distortion.

We will develop the theory of data compression primarily for discrete memoryless sources because then the main ideas can be developed in the simplest mathematical setting. However, this is the least interesting case in applications for two reasons. First, many sources have memory, and memory constitutes a form of redundancy that a data compression code can remove. Second, by far the most important sources for data compression are continuous sources. Practically speaking, compression of a discrete memoryless source is unusual. However, most of the theoretical ideas can be understood by studying this simple source.

The data compression problem is shown in Fig. 6.1. The output of a discrete information source is a random sequence of symbols from a finite alphabet containing J symbols given by $\{a_0, a_1, \ldots, a_{J-1}\}$. The output of a discrete memoryless source is the jth symbol with probability $p(a_j)$, abbreviated p_j. Because source letters that occur with probability zero can be deleted from the source alphabet, we can assume that p_j is strictly positive. The source output is to be reproduced in terms of a second alphabet, called the *reproducing alphabet*, containing K symbols given by $\{b_0, b_1, \ldots, b_{K-1}\}$. The reproducing alphabet often is identical to the source alphabet, but it need not be. For example, the reproducing alphabet might consist of the union of the source alphabet and a single new symbol denoting "data erased".

A *distortion matrix* is a J-by-K matrix with nonnegative elements ρ_{jk}. The jk element specifies the distortion associated with reproducing the jth source letter by the kth reproducing letter. The largest element of the matrix is denoted ρ_m.

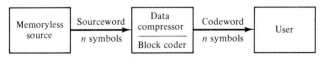

Figure 6.1   Data compression using a block code.

Usually we assume that ρ_m is finite and call the distortion matrix a *bounded distortion measure*. It can also be assumed that for each source letter, there is at least one reproducing letter such that the resulting distortion equals zero. Otherwise we can replace the distortion matrix with a new distortion matrix with elements $\rho'_{jk} = \rho_{jk} - \min_k \rho_{jk}$. The average distortion for a data compression scheme using ρ'_{jk} differs from that using ρ_{jk} by $\sum_j p_j[\min_k \rho_{jk}]$, which is a constant independent of the data compression code. There is no loss of generality in the theory in assuming this constant is zero.

A distortion matrix for a block of letters of length n is a K^n-by-J^n matrix with nonnegative elements $\rho(\mathbf{x}, \mathbf{y})$. The element $\rho(\mathbf{x}, \mathbf{y})$ specifies the block distortion that occurs when representing sourceword $\mathbf{x}$ by reproducing word $\mathbf{y}$. Usually $\rho(\mathbf{x}, \mathbf{y})$ has a simple structure, called a *single-letter distortion measure*, in which the distortion in a block is simply the sum of the distortions in each letter of the block

$$\rho(\mathbf{x}, \mathbf{y}) = \sum_{l=1}^{n} \rho_{j_l k_l}$$

The opposite case is called a *context-dependent distortion measure*. A context-dependent distortion measure is often felt to be more appropriate in applications, but it is much more difficult to handle mathematically. We shall only study single-letter distortion measures.

An important distortion matrix is the *probability-of-error distortion matrix*. For this case the alphabets are identical, $\rho_{jk} = 0$ if $j = k$, and $\rho_{jk} = 1$ otherwise. For example, if J and $K = 4$, the probability-of-error distortion matrix is

$$\rho = \begin{bmatrix} 0 & 1 & 1 & 1 \\ 1 & 0 & 1 & 1 \\ 1 & 1 & 0 & 1 \\ 1 & 1 & 1 & 0 \end{bmatrix}$$

This distortion matrix says that each error is counted as one unit of distortion. A different data compression problem with the same source and reproducing alphabets is obtained if one takes the distortion matrix

$$\rho = \begin{bmatrix} 0 & 1 & 2 & 1 \\ 1 & 0 & 1 & 2 \\ 2 & 1 & 0 & 1 \\ 1 & 2 & 1 & 0 \end{bmatrix}$$

This distortion matrix says that, modulo 4, an error of two units is counted as two units of distortion. Yet another distortion matrix with the same source alphabet is

$$\rho = \begin{bmatrix} 0 & 2 & 2 & 2 & 1 \\ 2 & 0 & 2 & 2 & 1 \\ 2 & 2 & 0 & 2 & 1 \\ 2 & 2 & 2 & 0 & 1 \end{bmatrix}$$

Now there are five letters in the reproducing alphabet. The fifth letter can be called an *erasure*. With this distortion matrix, it is half as serious to erase a symbol as to make an error.

☐ **Definition 6.2.1**   A block code for data compression of blocklength n and size M is a set $\mathscr{C}$ consisting of M codewords of length n, each codeword a sequence of n reproducing letters.   ☐

One way to use the data compression code is as follows. The set of codewords is partitioned into two disjoint subsets $\mathscr{C}_1$ and $\mathscr{C}_2$. The set $\mathscr{C}_1$ contains the first $M - 1$ codewords, and these are called *normal codewords*. The set $\mathscr{C}_2$ contains solely the Mth codeword and this is called the *default codeword*. Each sourceword of blocklength n is mapped onto that one of the first $M - 1$ codewords that results in the least block distortion, provided the distortion of the block is not larger than a maximum allowable block distortion, denoted nD. Otherwise the sourceword is mapped onto the default codeword. In this case, a coding failure is said to occur. The distortion is then less than $n\rho_m$.

The output sourceword is random, so the block distortion of the code $\mathscr{C}$ is a random variable, and the expected value of this random variable is referred to as the *average* block distortion, denoted $\rho(\mathscr{C})$, and given by

$$\rho(\mathscr{C}) = E\rho(\mathbf{x}, \mathbf{y}(\mathbf{x}))$$

where $\mathbf{y}(\mathbf{x})$ is the codeword into which $\mathbf{x}$ is encoded. We shall study bounds on the rate needed by any block code for data compression such that the average per-letter distortion satisfies $(1/n)\rho(\mathscr{C}) \le D$. It turns out that for good codes, almost all codewords have block distortions of about nD or less. Therefore, we can speak of nD interchangeably as the maximum distortion of a normal codeword or as the average block distortion of the code. The two interpretations are not completely equivalent for finite blocklength, but the differences vanish asymptotically.

The minimum achievable rate of a code with average per-letter distortion D is denoted $B(D)$ and is called the *source-distortion function.*[†] The source-

---

[†]The accepted term here is the *rate-distortion function* of the source. We prefer to reserve the word "rate," in the sense of "information rate," for the description of codes. We avoid using the word to describe the information content of a source, just as we do not use it to describe the information capacity of a channel. There is already enough confusion with the word "rate" used in the sense of "symbol rate," measured in symbols per second.

distortion function measures the abridged information content at distortion D. The function $B(D)$ divides the rate-distortion plane into the set of points for which good codes for data compression exist and the set of points for which no codes for data compression exist.

The central topic of the chapter is the source-compression coding theorem for discrete sources. Loosely stated, this theorem says that data compression codes exist that have average per-letter distortion equal to D and have rate R only a little larger than the function $B(D)$, while conversely, no codes can exist that compress the source with average per-letter distortion equal to D and with rate less than $B(D)$. This function $B(D)$ concisely expresses the conditions under which data compression codes exist.

6.3 INFORMATION CONTENT OF COMPRESSED DATA

Data compression replaces a stream of source output symbols with a stream of symbols from the reproducing alphabet. This is done in such a way that the new sequence has less entropy but at the cost of some distortion. A block code for data compression does this by encoding the source data in blocks; each sourceword, consisting of a block of n source symbols, is replaced with a codeword, consisting of a block of n reproducing symbols. The new sequence of blocks then can be compacted by assigning an index to each reproducing block. When it is convenient, we may refer to the *indices* of these reproducing blocks as the codewords rather than the blocks themselves. A reproducing block of length n is a noncompacted version of the codeword, while its index is a compacted form of the codeword.

Data compression is a deterministic process. The same block of source symbols will always produce the same block of reproducing symbols. Nevertheless, when restricting attention to a single source output symbol (or a relatively small subblock) without knowledge of the previous or subsequent source output symbols nor of that symbol's position within a block, then the reproducing symbol is not predetermined. In this way, at the level of a single letter, the symbol b_k into which source symbol a_j is encoded can be thought of as a random variable, even though at the block level the encoding is deterministic. This random variable can be described by a transition matrix $\mathbf{Q}$, whose entropy $Q(b_k|a_j)$, abbreviated $Q_{k|j}$, gives the probability that data symbol a_j will be reproduced as symbol b_k. Heuristically, we think of $\mathbf{Q}$ as describing an artificial memoryless channel that approximates the data compression. Each time the source produces symbol a_j, it is reproduced by symbol b_k with probability $Q_{k|j}$ as shown in Fig. 6.2.

We shall show that in a well-designed data compression code, the reproducing symbol b_k should occur, conditional on the source symbol a_j, with a probability $Q_{k|j}$ such that the average mutual information between source symbol and reproducing symbol is minimized subject to the constraint on average distortion. It is not easy to grasp the intuition behind this idea by thinking of single letters. In a block code of blocklength n, however, the

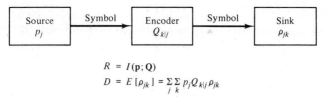

$$R = I(\mathbf{p};\mathbf{Q})$$
$$D = E[\rho_{jk}] = \sum_j \sum_k p_j Q_{k|j}\rho_{jk}$$

Figure 6.2 Idealized single-letter view of data compression.

mutual information between sourceword and codeword is

$$I(X^n; Y^n) = H(Y^n) - H(Y^n|X^n)$$

But $H(Y^n|X^n) = 0$ because the encoding is deterministic. We want to reduce the entropy $H(Y^n)$ of the codeword, and so we want to reduce the mutual information $I(X^n; Y^n)$. This implies the mutual information should be minimized subject to the constraint on average distortion. It will be some time yet before we formalize the coding theorem behind this idea. First we study the appropriate performance measure.

   ☐ **Definition 6.3.1** The *source-distortion function B(D)* is given by the function

$$B(D) = \min_{\mathbf{Q}\in\mathscr{2}_D} \sum_j \sum_k p_j Q_{k|j} \log \frac{Q_{k|j}}{\sum_j p_j Q_{k|j}}$$

where $\mathscr{2}_D$ is the set of probability transition matrices given by

$$\mathscr{2}_D = \left\{ \mathbf{Q}: \sum_j \sum_k p_j Q_{k|j}\rho_{jk} \le D \right\}$$
          ☐

The source-distortion function $B(D)$ is measured in units of bits if the base-2 logarithm is used. If the natural logarithm is used, then $B(D)$ is measured in units of nats. The definition of the source-distortion function will be justified by the data-compression coding theorems of this chapter. Intuitively, if average distortion D is specified, then any code for data compression must use an average of at least $B(D)$ bits per source letter, and conversely, compression to a rate arbitrarily close to $B(D)$—but not smaller— is possible by appropriate selection of the data compression code.

The function $B(D)$ depends on the probability distribution $\mathbf{p}$. When we need to emphasize this, we shall write $B(\mathbf{p}, D)$. For a fixed source-alphabet size J and distortion matrix $\{\rho_{jk}\}$, there will be one probability distribution on the source alphabet that makes the source the most difficult to compress. Define

$$B^*(D) = \max_{\mathbf{p}} B(\mathbf{p}, D)$$

Then for any $\mathbf{p}$, we have the bound

$$B(\mathbf{p}, D) \le B^*(D)$$

Sometimes it is convenient to use the inverse of $B(D)$ instead. It can be defined by interchanging the elements in the definition of $B(D)$:

$$D(B) = \min_{\mathbf{Q} \in \mathcal{Q}_R} d(\mathbf{Q})$$

where now

$$\mathcal{Q}_R = \{\mathbf{Q} : I(\mathbf{p}; \mathbf{Q}) \leq R\}$$

For simple sources and distortion matrices, $B(D)$ can be evaluated by finding the minimum analytically. For more difficult problems, an efficient algorithm for computing $B(D)$ is available. We shall prove that if the source symbols are equiprobable and the distortion matrix is the probability-of-error distortion matrix, then the conditional probability distribution $\mathbf{Q}$ that achieves $B(D)$ has the same value in each off-diagonal element and the same value in each diagonal element. This is the right intuitive answer. It says that if the source and the distortion matrix treat all symbols the same, then, in the compressed sequence, all errors should occur equally often.

The source-distortion function of a binary symmetric source with probability-of-error distortion matrix is easy to compute:

$$\begin{aligned}
D &= \sum_{j=0}^{1} \sum_{k=0}^{1} p_j Q_{k|j} \rho_{jk} \\
&= \tfrac{1}{2} Q_{0|1} + \tfrac{1}{2} Q_{1|0}
\end{aligned}$$

But, because of symmetry $Q_{0|1} = Q_{1|0}$, the matrix $\mathbf{Q}$ must be

$$\mathbf{Q} = \begin{bmatrix} 1 - D & D \\ D & 1 - D \end{bmatrix}$$

Finally, because $B(D) = I(\mathbf{p}; \mathbf{Q})$, we can complete the solution to write

$$\begin{aligned}
B(D) &= 1 + (1 - D) \log (1 - D) + D \log D \\
&= 1 - H_b(D)
\end{aligned}$$

The source-distortion function for a binary symmetric source under the probability-of-error distortion measure is shown in Fig. 6.3. The general appearance of this function is quite typical, as is proved in the following theorem.

□   **Theorem 6.3.2** $B(D)$ is a decreasing, convex, and hence continuous function defined in the interval $0 \leq D \leq D_{\max}$, where

$$D_{\max} = \min_k \sum_j p_j \rho_{jk}$$

In this interval, the inequality constraint on D is satisfied with equality.

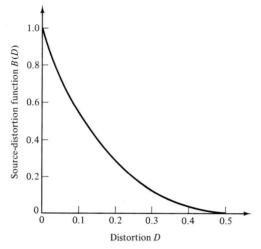

Figure 6.3   Source-distortion function for a binary symmetric source.

Proof We shall prove continuity only on the open interval $0 < D < D_{max}$. Otherwise the theorem will be proved as stated.

If D is negative, the set $\mathcal{D}_D$ is empty and $B(D)$ is not defined. If D is nonnegative, $\mathcal{D}_{D'}$ contains $\mathcal{D}_D$ if D' is larger than D, which implies that $B(D)$ is nonincreasing.

Let D_{max} represent the smallest average distortion that can be obtained with zero information. This is the maximum distortion that ever needs to be tolerated for that source. Because the information $I(\mathbf{p}; \mathbf{Q}) = 0$, we must have that

$$Q_{k|j} = Q_k$$

independent of j. Therefore the expression for average distortion becomes

$$D = \sum_k Q_k \sum_j p_j \rho_{jk}$$

subject to $Q_k \geq 0$ and $\sum_k Q_k = 1$. The smallest such value of D is D_{max}. Distortion D_{max} can be obtained with zero information simply by always choosing reproducing symbol b_k where k achieves the above minimum.

To prove that $B(D)$ is convex, choose any two points $(D', B(D'))$ and $(D'', B(D''))$ on the graph and let $\mathbf{Q}'$ and $\mathbf{Q}''$ achieve these points. Let λ be any number in the interval $[0, 1]$ and set

$$Q_{k|j} = \lambda Q'_{k|j} + (1 - \lambda)Q''_{k|j}$$

This is a conditional probability distribution. The average distortion associated with $\mathbf{Q}$ is

$$D = \sum_j \sum_k p_j Q_{k|j} \rho_{jk}$$

$$= \lambda \sum_j \sum_k p_j Q'_{k|j} \rho_{jk} + (1 - \lambda) \sum_j \sum_k p_j Q''_{k|j} \rho_{jk}$$

$$= \lambda D' + (1 - \lambda) D''$$

and $\mathbf{Q} \in \mathcal{Q}_D$. Therefore

$$B(D) \le I(\mathbf{p}; \mathbf{Q})$$

Now we use the fact that $I(\mathbf{p}; \mathbf{Q})$ is convex in $\mathbf{Q}$ as given in Theorem 5.2.5,

$$B(D) \le \lambda I(\mathbf{p}; \mathbf{Q}') + (1 - \lambda) I(\mathbf{p}; \mathbf{Q}'')$$

from which we have that

$$B(\lambda D' + (1 - \lambda) D'') \le \lambda B(D') + (1 - \lambda) B(D'')$$

and convexity is proved.

Finally, because $B(D)$ is convex on $[0, D_{max}]$, it is continuous on $(0, D_{max})$. Because $B(D)$ is nonnegative, nonincreasing, convex, and zero at D_{max}, it must be strictly decreasing for D smaller than D_{max}. Because it is strictly decreasing, the constraint on D must be satisfied with equality. $\square$

The theorem tells us that the inequality constraint in the definition of $B(D)$ can be replaced with an equality constraint. This is significant because it means that we can accommodate the constraint by introducing a Lagrange multiplier s. The function $B(D)$ then can be expressed as

$$B(D_s) = \min_{\mathbf{Q}} \left[\sum_j \sum_k p_j Q_{k|j} \log \frac{Q_{k|j}}{\sum_j p_j Q_{k|j}} - s \left(\sum_j \sum_k p_j Q_{k|j} \rho_{jk} - D \right) \right]$$

where now $\mathbf{Q}$ is unconstrained except that it must be a probability transition matrix. For each choice of the Lagrange multiplier s, the minimum will be achieved by some probability transition matrix $\mathbf{Q}^*$. In this way, the Lagrange multiplier s becomes the independent parameter. The value of D for which one has found the solution is then given by the formula:

$$D_s = \sum_j \sum_k p_j Q^*_{k|j} \rho_{jk}$$

The representation of $B(D)$ is now in a parametric form; a value of s is specified whereupon both D and $B(D)$ are generated for the point on the $B(D)$ curve that is parameterized by s.

Our remaining tasks in this section are to give the Kuhn-Tucker conditions on the solution for $B(D)$ and to give an efficient algorithm for computing $B(D)$. We will first enlarge the minimization problem into a double minimization problem. The larger problem will give us more room in which to work.

☐ **Theorem 6.3.3** The source-distortion function $B(D)$ can be expressed as a double minimum:

$$B(D) = sD + \min_{\mathbf{q}} \min_{\mathbf{Q}} \left[\sum_j \sum_k p_j Q_{k|j} \log \frac{Q_{k|j}}{q_k} - s \sum_j \sum_k p_j Q_{k|j} \rho_{jk} \right]$$

where

$$D = \sum_j \sum_k p_j Q^*_{k|j} \rho_{jk}$$

and $\mathbf{Q}^*$ achieves the minimum. For fixed $\mathbf{Q}$, the right side is minimized by

$$q_k = \sum_j p_j Q_{k|j}$$

For fixed $\mathbf{q}$, the right side is minimized by

$$Q_{k|j} = \frac{q_k e^{s\rho_{jk}}}{\sum_k q_k e^{s\rho_{jk}}}$$

Proof The double minimum follows immediately from Theorem 5.2.6, and the minimizing $\mathbf{q}$ follows from the condition of equality in that theorem. We only need to prove the final statement. Temporarily ignore the inequality constraint $Q_{k|j} \geq 0$ and introduce Lagrange multipliers λ_j to constrain $\sum_k Q_{k|j} = 1$. Then

$$\frac{\partial}{\partial Q_{k|j}} \left(\sum_j \sum_k p_j Q_{k|j} \log \frac{Q_{k|j}}{q_k} - s \sum_j \sum_k p_j Q_{k|j} \rho_{jk} + \sum_j \lambda_j \sum_k Q_{k|j} \right) = 0$$

$$p_j \log Q_{k|j} - p_j \log q_k + p_j - s p_j \rho_{jk} + \lambda_j = 0$$

Hence solving for $Q_{k|j}$ and choosing λ_j so that $\sum_k Q_{k|j} = 1$ gives

$$Q_{k|j} = \frac{q_k e^{s\rho_{jk}}}{\sum_k q_k e^{s\rho_{jk}}}$$

This is always nonnegative so that the inequality constraint $Q_{k|j} \geq 0$ is satisfied.   ☐

The simultaneous conditions of the theorem imply that if $\mathbf{Q}$ achieves a point on the $B(D)$ curve parameterized by s, then

$$q_k = \sum_j p_j Q_{k|j} = q_k \sum_j p_j \frac{e^{s\rho_{jk}}}{\sum_k q_k e^{s\rho_{jk}}}$$

The simultaneous conditions will form the basis of the algorithm to be given in Theorem 6.3.8.

☐ **Corollary 6.3.4**   In terms of the parameter s,

$$B(D_s) = sD_s + \min_{\mathbf{q}} \left[-\sum_j p_j \log \sum_k q_k e^{s\rho_{jk}} \right]$$

$$D_s = \sum_j \sum_k p_j \frac{q_k^* e^{s\rho_{jk}}}{\sum_k q_k^* e^{s\rho_{jk}}} \rho_{jk}$$

where $\mathbf{q}^*$ achieves $B(D_s)$.

Proof   This follows immediately by substituting the third part of the theorem into the first part.   ☐

☐ **Corollary 6.3.5**   The source-distortion function can be expressed in either of the two forms:

$$B(D) = \max_{s \in [-\infty, 0]} \min_{\mathbf{q}} \left[sD - \sum_j p_j \log \sum_k q_k e^{s\rho_{jk}} \right]$$

$$D(B) = \max_{s \in [-\infty, 0]} \min_{\mathbf{q}} \left[\frac{1}{s} B + \frac{1}{s} \sum_j p_j \log \sum_k q_k e^{s\rho_{jk}} \right]$$

Proof   We will prove only the first line.

For fixed s, the equation on the right is that of a straight line in D. From the definition of $B(D)$, we can write

$$B(D) \geq \min_{Q \in \mathscr{Q}_D} \left[\sum_j \sum_k p_j Q_{k|j} \log \frac{Q_{k|j}}{\sum_j p_j Q_{k|j}} - s \left(\sum_j \sum_k p_j Q_{k|j} \rho_{jk} - D \right) \right]$$

for any $s \leq 0$. The inequality holds because the term multiplying s is negative for all $\mathbf{Q}$ in $\mathscr{Q}_D$. The inequality is still valid if the domain of the minimum is enlarged. Therefore

$$B(D) \geq \min_{Q} \left[\sum_j \sum_k p_j Q_{k|j} \log \frac{Q_{k|j}}{\sum_j p_j Q_{k|j}} - s \left(\sum_j \sum_k p_j Q_{k|j} \rho_{jk} - D \right) \right]$$

Now, as in Theorem 6.3.3, replace the mutual information with a minimum over $\mathbf{q}$ and then explicitly evaluate the minimum over $\mathbf{Q}$. This gives

$$B(D) \geq \min_{\mathbf{q}} \left[sD - \sum_j p_j \log \sum_k q_k e^{s\rho_{jk}} \right]$$

for any $s \leq 0$. Therefore

$$B(D) \geq \max_{s \leq 0} \min_{\mathbf{q}} \left[sD - \sum_j p_j \log \sum_k q_k e^{s\rho_{jk}} \right]$$

But Corollary 6.3.4 says that for some value of $s \leq 0$, the inequality is achieved with equality, so the proof is complete.   ☐

The analog of Theorem 5.4.3 is the following.

☐ **Theorem 6.3.6** A probability assignment $\mathbf{q}$ on the reproducing alphabet yields a point on the $B(D)$ curve via the transition matrix

$$Q_{k|j} = \frac{q_k e^{s\rho_{jk}}}{\sum\limits_k q_k e^{s\rho_{jk}}}$$

if and only if

$$c_k = \sum_j p_j \frac{e^{s\rho_{jk}}}{\sum\limits_k q_k e^{s\rho_{jk}}} \leq 1$$

for all k, with equality for any k for which q_k is nonzero.

Proof By Corollary 6.3.4, we have

$$B(D_s) = sD_s + \min_{\mathbf{q}} \left[-\sum_j p_j \log \sum_k q_k e^{s\rho_{jk}} \right]$$

The minimization operates on a convex function of $\mathbf{q}$, so we can apply the Kuhn-Tucker theorem. Then the minimum is at a $\mathbf{q}$ satisfying

$$\frac{\partial}{\partial q_k} \left(-\sum_j p_j \log \sum_k q_k e^{s\rho_{jk}} - \lambda \sum_k q_k \right) \geq 0$$

which reduces to

$$-\sum_j p_j \frac{e^{s\rho_{jk}}}{\sum\limits_k q_k e^{s\rho_{jk}}} - \lambda \geq 0$$

with equality for any k for which q_k is nonzero. The Lagrange multiplier λ is evaluated by multiplying the equation by q_k and summing over k. This gives $\lambda = -1$. Therefore

$$\sum_j p_j \frac{e^{s\rho_{jk}}}{\sum\limits_k q_k e^{s\rho_{jk}}} \leq 1 \qquad\qquad ☐$$

Let $\mathbf{p}'$ be the probability distribution on the output of a discrete memoryless source with alphabet $\{a'_0, \ldots, a'_{J'-1}\}$, and let ρ' be a distortion matrix for that source. Let $\mathbf{p}''$ be the probability distribution for a second discrete memoryless source with alphabet $\{a''_0, \ldots, a''_{J''-1}\}$, and let ρ'' be a distortion matrix for the second source. The product source is the source whose outputs are pairs of letters—one from the first source and one from the second—and the probability distribution is the product distribution. That is, the product source alphabet consists of the pairs of letters in the set

$\{(a'_0, a''_0), \ (a'_0, a''_1), \ldots, (a'_{J'-1}, a''_{J''-1})\}$, and $p(a'_{j'}, a''_{j''}) = p(a'_{j'})p''(a''_{j''})$. The *sum distortion measure* for the product source is the sum of the two distortions in reproducing each of the two letters of the pair.

☐   **Theorem 6.3.7**   Given a product source with a sum distortion measure, the source-distortion function $B(D)$ can be obtained from the source-distortion functions for the component problems $B'(D')$ and $B''(D'')$ by adding ordinates and abscissas parameterized respectively by the same value of s. That is,

$$B(D_s) = B'(D'_s) + B''(D''_s)$$

and

$$D_s = D'_s + D''_s$$

Proof   This is a consequence of Theorem 6.3.6. Let $q'_{k'}$ and $q''_{k''}$ achieve $B(D')$ and $B(D'')$, as in Theorem 6.3.6. Let $q_{k'k''} = q'_{k'}q''_{k''}$. This achieves $B(D)$ because

$$c_{k'k''} = \sum_{j'}\sum_{j''} p'_{j'} p''_{j''} \frac{e^{s\rho'_{j'k'} + s\rho''_{j''k''}}}{\sum_{k'k''} q'_{k'}q''_{k''} e^{s\rho'_{j'k'} + s\rho''_{j''k''}}}$$

$$= \left(\sum_{j'} p'_{j'} \frac{e^{s\rho'_{j'k'}}}{\sum_{k'} q'_{k'} e^{s\rho'_{j'k'}}}\right)\left(\sum_{j''} p''_{j''} \frac{e^{s\rho''_{j''k''}}}{\sum_{k''} q''_{k''} e^{s\rho''_{j''k''}}}\right)$$

$$= c'_{k'}c''_{k''}$$

$$\leq 1$$

with equality if $q'_{k'}$ and $q''_{k''}$ are both nonzero so that Theorem 6.3.6 applies. Therefore the probability transition matrix is

$$Q_{k'k''|j'j''} = \frac{q'_{k'}q''_{k''} e^{s\rho'_{j'k'} + s\rho''_{j''k''}}}{\sum_{k'}\sum_{k''} q'_{k'}q''_{k''} e^{s\rho'_{j'k'} + s\rho''_{j''k''}}}$$

$$= Q'_{k'|j'}Q''_{k''|j''}$$

The theorem follows by substituting this into the formulas for the mutual information and the average distortion.   ☐

☐   **Theorem 6.3.8**   Let the parameter $s < 0$ be given and let $A_{jk} = e^{s\rho_{jk}}$. Let $\mathbf{q}^{(0)}$ be any probability vector such that all components are nonzero. Let $\mathbf{q}^{(r+1)}$ be given in terms of $\mathbf{q}^{(r)}$ by

$$q_k^{(r+1)} = q_k^{(r)} \sum_j \frac{p_j A_{jk}}{\sum_k q_k^{(r)} A_{jk}}$$

Then

$$D(\mathbf{Q}(\mathbf{q}^{(r)})) \to D_s \qquad \text{as } r \to \infty$$

$$I(\mathbf{p}; \mathbf{Q}(\mathbf{q}^{(r)})) \to B(D_s) \qquad \text{as } r \to \infty$$

where

$$\mathbf{Q}(\mathbf{q}^{(r)}) = \frac{q_k^{(r)} A_{jk}}{\sum_k q_k^{(r)} A_{jk}}$$

and $(D_s, B(D_s))$ is a point on the $B(D)$ curve parameterized by s.

Proof We use the shorthand notation $I(\mathbf{q}) = I(\mathbf{p}; \mathbf{Q}(\mathbf{q}))$, and $V(\mathbf{q}) = I(\mathbf{q}) - sD(\mathbf{q})$ where

$$D(\mathbf{q}) = \sum_j \sum_k p_j Q_{k|j}(\mathbf{q}) \rho_{jk}$$

To show that $V(\mathbf{q})$ is nonincreasing, we use Theorem 6.3.3, first fixing $\mathbf{q}$ and minimizing over $\mathbf{Q}$, then fixing $\mathbf{Q}$ and minimizing over $\mathbf{q}$. Minimizing over $\mathbf{Q}$ gives a value $W(\mathbf{q}^{(r)})$ between $V(\mathbf{q}^{(r+1)})$ and $V(\mathbf{q}^{(r)})$ given by

$$W(\mathbf{q}^{(r)}) = -\sum_j p_j \left(\log \sum_k q_k^{(r)} A_{jk} \right)$$

and, because of the successive minimizations, we have the nonincreasing sequence

$$\ldots \geq V(\mathbf{q}^{(r)}) \geq W(\mathbf{q}^{(r)}) \geq V(\mathbf{q}^{(r+1)}) \geq W(\mathbf{q}^{(r+1)}) \geq \ldots$$

The composition of the above two operations gives the recursive definition for $\mathbf{q}^{(r)}$ of the theorem, which by construction is such that $\mathbf{q}^{(r)}$ has only positive components and $V(\mathbf{q}^{(r)})$ is nonincreasing. Therefore, because $V(\mathbf{q}^{(r)})$ is bounded, $V(\mathbf{q}^{(r)})$ converges to some number V^∞. We must show that $V^\infty = B(D) - sD$.

Let $\mathbf{Q}^{(r+1)} = \mathbf{Q}(\mathbf{q}^{(r)})$. Let $\mathbf{q}^*$ be such that $V(\mathbf{q}^*) = B(D) - sD$ and let $\mathbf{Q}^* = \mathbf{Q}(\mathbf{q}^*)$. Now consider

$$\sum_j \sum_k p_j Q_{k|j}^* \log \frac{Q_{k|j}^{(r)}}{Q_{k|j}^{(r+1)}} = \sum_j \sum_k p_j Q_{k|j}^* \log \frac{Q_{k|j}^{(r)}}{q_k^{(r)}} - \sum_j \sum_k p_j Q_{k|j}^* \log A_{jk}$$

$$+ \sum_j \sum_k p_j Q_{k|j}^* \log \sum_k q_k^{(r)} A_{jk}$$

The following calculation shows that the first term on the right is increased if $\mathbf{Q}^{(r)}$ and $\mathbf{q}^{(r)}$ are replaced by $\mathbf{Q}^*$ and $\mathbf{q}^*$:

$$\sum_j \sum_k p_j Q^*_{k|j} \log \frac{Q^{(r)}_{k|j}}{q^{(r)}_k} - \sum_j \sum_k p_j Q^*_{k|j} \log \frac{Q^*_{k|j}}{q^*_k}$$

$$= \sum_j \sum_k p_j Q^*_{k|j} \log \frac{Q^{(r)}_{k|j} q^*_k}{q^{(r)}_k Q^*_{k|j}}$$

$$\leq \sum_j \sum_k p_j Q^{(r)}_{k|j} \frac{q^*_k}{q^{(r)}_k} - \sum_j \sum_k p_j Q^*_{k|j}$$

$$= 0$$

Therefore

$$\sum_j \sum_k p_j Q^*_{k|j} \log \frac{Q^{(r)}_{k|j}}{Q^{(r+1)}_{k|j}} \leq \sum_j \sum_k p_j Q^*_{k|j} \log \frac{Q^*_{k|j}}{\sum_j p_j Q^*_{k|j}}$$

$$- s \sum_j \sum_k p_j Q^*_{k|j} \rho_{jk} + \sum_j p_j \log \sum_k q^{(r)}_k A_{jk}$$

$$= V(\mathbf{q}^*) - W(\mathbf{q}^{(r)})$$

Now sum on r:

$$\sum_{r=1}^R [V(\mathbf{q}^*) - W(\mathbf{q}^{(r)})] \geq \sum_j \sum_k p_j Q^*_{k|j} \sum_{r=1}^R \log \frac{Q^{(r)}_{k|j}}{Q^{(r+1)}_{k|j}}$$

$$= \sum_j \sum_k p_j Q^*_{k|j} \log \frac{Q^{(1)}_{k|j}}{Q^{(R+1)}_{k|j}}$$

$$\geq \sum_j \sum_k p_j Q^*_{k|j} \log \frac{Q^{(1)}_{k|j}}{Q^*_{k|j}}$$

where the last inequality follows from the discrimination inequality. Consequently, with a change in sign, we have the inequality

$$\sum_{r=1}^R [W(\mathbf{q}^{(r)}) - V(\mathbf{q}^*)] \leq L(\mathbf{q}^*; \mathbf{q}^{(1)})$$

The right side is a constant independent of R, and the left side is smaller than this for any R. Because $W(\mathbf{q}^{(r)})$ is larger than $V(\mathbf{q}^*)$ and is nonincreasing, the term in brackets is positive and so must go to zero as r increases. This implies that $W(\mathbf{q}^{(r)})$ converges to $V(\mathbf{q}^*)$, which proves the theorem. $\square$

The application of Theorem 6.3.8 to the computation of the source-distortion function is illustrated in Fig. 6.4. The termination is based on Theorem 6.3.10 below. To develop the method of termination, we need a way of estimating the residual error after each iteration. The following theorem

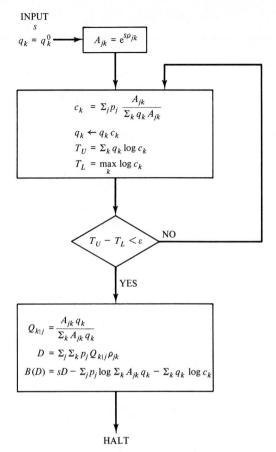

Figure 6.4   Computation of the source-distortion function.

will be useful in this regard, because it expresses $B(D)$ as a maximum rather than as a minimum.

□ **Theorem 6.3.9** The source-distortion function can be expressed as follows:

$$B(D) = \max_{s \le 0} \max_{\lambda \in \Lambda_s} \left[sD + \sum_j p_j \log \lambda_j \right]$$

where

$$\Lambda_s = \left\{ \lambda \in \mathbf{R}^J : \lambda_j \ge 0; \sum_j p_j \lambda_j e^{s\rho_{jk}} \le 1 \right\}$$

Proof Let $s \leq 0, \lambda \in \Lambda_s$, and $\mathbf{Q} \in \mathcal{Q}_D$ be given. Then, using the fact that

$$\sum_j \sum_k p_j Q_{k|j} \rho_{jk} \leq D$$

gives

$$I(\mathbf{p}; \mathbf{Q}) - sD - \sum_j p_j \log \lambda_j$$

$$\geq I(\mathbf{p}; \mathbf{Q}) - s\sum_j \sum_k p_j Q_{k|j} \rho_{jk} - \sum_j \sum_k p_j Q_{k|j} \log \lambda_j$$

$$= \sum_j \sum_k p_j Q_{k|j} \log \frac{Q_{k|j} e^{-s\rho_{jk}}}{q_k \lambda_j}$$

$$\geq \sum_j \sum_k p_j Q_{k|j} \left(1 - \frac{q_k \lambda_j e^{s\rho_{jk}}}{Q_{k|j}} \right)$$

$$= 1 - \sum_k q_k \sum_j p_j \lambda_j e^{s\rho_{jk}}$$

$$\geq 1 - \sum_k q_k = 0$$

Therefore

$$B(D) \geq sD + \sum_j p_j \log \lambda_j$$

But we know that for some values of s and λ this inequality holds with equality, in particular for

$$\lambda_j = \sum_k q_k^* e^{s\rho_{jk}}$$

where s and $\mathbf{q}^*$ achieve $B(D)$. Therefore the theorem is proved.   □

□   **Theorem 6.3.10**   Let the parameter $s \leq 0$ be given, and let $A_{jk} = e^{s\rho_{jk}}$. Suppose $\mathbf{q}$ is any output probability vector, and let

$$c_k = \sum_j p_j \frac{A_{jk}}{\sum_k q_k A_{jk}}$$

Then at the point

$$D = \sum_j \sum_k p_j \frac{q_k A_{jk}}{\sum_k q_k A_{jk}} \rho_{jk}$$

we have

(i) $B(D) \leq sD - \sum_j p_j \log \sum_k q_k A_{jk} - \sum_k q_k c_k \log c_k$

(ii) $B(D) \geq sD - \sum_j p_j \log \sum_k q_k A_{jk} - \max_k \log c_k$

Proof (i) The matrix with elements

$$Q_{k|j} = \frac{q_k A_{jk}}{\sum_k q_k A_{jk}}$$

is a transition matrix giving distortion D. Hence

$$B(D) \leq I(\mathbf{p}; \mathbf{Q}) = \sum_j \sum_k p_j Q_{k|j} \log \frac{Q_{k|j}}{\sum_j p_j Q_{k|j}}$$

$$= \sum_j \sum_k p_j Q_{k|j} \log \frac{q_k A_{jk}}{\left(\sum_k q_k A_{jk}\right)\left(\sum_j p_j Q_{k|j}\right)}$$

$$= sD - \sum_j p_j \log \sum_k q_k A_{jk} - \sum_k q_k c_k \log c_k$$

(ii) Theorem 6.3.9 states that for any $s \leq 0$,

$$B(D) \geq sD + \sum_j p_j \log \lambda_j$$

where λ is any vector such that $\sum_j p_j \lambda_j A_{jk} \leq 1$. Let

$$c_{\max} = \max_k \sum_j p_j \frac{A_{jk}}{\sum_k q_k A_{jk}}$$

and let

$$\lambda_j = \left(c_{\max} \sum_k q_k A_{jk}\right)^{-1}$$

Then

$$\sum_j p_j \lambda_j A_{jk} \leq 1$$

and

$$B(D) \geq sD - \sum_j p_j \log \sum_k q_k A_{jk} - \max_k \log c_k \qquad \square$$

To end this section, we will look at the n-fold product source obtained by taking blocks of n symbols at a time from the source. Each symbol of the product source is composed of a block of n symbols from the original source. Intuitively, the source should be neither more compressible nor less compressible just because we choose to think about the output differently. This is the gist of the following theorem.

☐ **Theorem 6.3.11**   Let $B_n(D)$ denote the source-distortion function of a memoryless source viewed at the level of blocks of length n under a per-letter distortion measure. Then

$$B_n(nD) = nB(D)$$

Proof   This is an n-fold product source, so the proof is a consequence of Theorem 6.3.7.   ☐

6.4 THE INFORMATION-TRANSMISSION THEOREM

The source-compression coding theorem, stated here, will not be proved until the next two sections. The source-compression converse theorem, however, is easy to prove.

☐ **Theorem 6.4.1**   (**Source-compression converse**) Every block code for data compression of blocklength n and average per-letter distortion D for a finite alphabet memoryless source has rate R satisfying

$$R \geq B(D)$$

Proof   Let $\mathbf{x}$ range over the set of all sourcewords of blocklength n, and let $\mathbf{y}$ range over the set of all reproducing words of blocklength n. Let

$$\hat{Q}(\mathbf{y}|\mathbf{x}) = \begin{cases} 1 & \text{if } \mathbf{x} \text{ is encoded into } \mathbf{y} \\ 0 & \text{otherwise} \end{cases}$$

This is a conditional probability matrix. Because of the assumption of the theorem, the average block distortion of the code given by

$$\rho(\mathscr{C}) = \sum_{\mathbf{x}} \sum_{\mathbf{y}} p(\mathbf{x})\hat{Q}(\mathbf{y}|\mathbf{x})\rho(\mathbf{x},\mathbf{y})$$

is at most nD. Hence, by the definition of $B(D)$ and Theorem 6.3.11, we have

$$nB(D) = \min_{Q \in \mathscr{Q}_{nD}} \sum_{\mathbf{x}} \sum_{\mathbf{y}} p(\mathbf{x})Q(\mathbf{y}|\mathbf{x}) \log \frac{Q(\mathbf{y}|\mathbf{x})}{\sum_{\mathbf{x}} p(\mathbf{x})Q(\mathbf{y}|\mathbf{x})}$$

$$\leq \sum_{\mathbf{x}} \sum_{\mathbf{y}} p(\mathbf{x})\hat{Q}(\mathbf{y}|\mathbf{x}) \log \frac{\hat{Q}(\mathbf{y}|\mathbf{x})}{\sum_{\mathbf{x}} p(\mathbf{x})\hat{Q}(\mathbf{y}|\mathbf{x})}$$

But $\hat{Q}(\mathbf{y}|\mathbf{x})$ is either 0 or 1, so this reduces to

$$nB(D) \leq -\sum_{\mathbf{y}} q(\mathbf{y}) \log q(\mathbf{y})$$

where

$$q(\mathbf{y}) = \sum_{\mathbf{x}} p(\mathbf{x})\hat{Q}(\mathbf{y}|\mathbf{x})$$

Because $q(\mathbf{y})$ is nonzero only on codewords, we have

$$nB(D) \leq -\sum_{\mathbf{y}\in\mathscr{C}} q(\mathbf{y}) \log q(\mathbf{y})$$

$$\leq \log M$$

which completes the proof of the theorem because $\log M = nR$. □

□ **Theorem 6.4.2 (Shannon's third coding theorem)** For any finite alphabet memoryless source with bounded distortion measure, it is possible to find a block code for data compression of rate R such that the average per-letter distortion is less than D, provided

$$R > B(D)$$

and the blocklength n is chosen sufficiently large.

Proof This is an immediate consequence of Theorem 6.5.1 and Theorem 6.6.3 to be proved in the next two sections. □

Shannon's second and third coding theorems—the channel-transmission coding theorem and the source-compression coding theorem—are two of the major theorems of information theory. They can be merged into a single statement. The source output alphabet and the channel input alphabet may be different alphabets, but this does not matter as long as the source content $B(D)$ and the channel capacity $C(S)$ are expressed in consistent units such as bits per source output letter or bits per channel input letter.

□ **Theorem 6.4.3 (Information-transmission theorem)** The output sequence of a discrete memoryless source with content $B(D)$ can be reproduced with distortion at most D at the output of any discrete memoryless channel of capacity $C(S)$, provided

$$C(S) > B(D)$$

Proof We shall initially prove only that the output sequence can be reproduced with distortion at most $D + \varepsilon$ for any small positive ε.

Choose a value of ε satisfying $\varepsilon \leq C(S) - B(D)$. Choose a source-compression code so that the average distortion is not more than D and the code rate satisfies

$$R < B(D) + \frac{\varepsilon}{2}$$

Theorem 6.4.2, the source-compression coding theorem, guarantees that such a code exists. The entropy of the source encoder output is no larger than $B(D) + (\varepsilon/2)$ so that the channel coding theorem implies that the source codewords can be transmitted with arbitrarily small probability of symbol error by using a code of rate at most $B(D) + (\varepsilon/2) + (\varepsilon/2)$. The probability of symbol error can be specified so small that the additional distortion due to channel errors is as small as is desired. This is because the distortion caused by a block decoding error in the channel decoder is at worst linear in the blocklength, while the probability of such a decoding error is exponentially decreasing in the blocklength. In particular, the total system can operate with total distortion smaller than $D + \varepsilon$.

We have proved that the system can have distortion smaller than $D + \varepsilon$ if $C(S) > B(D)$. Now replace D with $D - \varepsilon$. The system can have distortion D if $C(S) > B(D - \varepsilon)$. Because $B(D)$ is continuous and this is true for all ε, the system can have distortion D if $C(S) > B(D)$.   □

In practice, the number of symbols produced by the source each second need not correspond to the number of symbols accepted by the channel each second. Then it is necessary to normalize the information transmission system to the time interval. Let $1/T_s$ be the number of source symbols per second and let $1/T_c$ be the number of channel symbols per second. The theorem then becomes the following.

□ **Theorem 6.4.4 (Information-transmission theorem)** A discrete memoryless source with content $B(D)$ bits per symbol and $1/T_s$ symbols per second can be reproduced with distortion at most D at the output of any channel of capacity $C(S)$ bits per symbol and $1/T_c$ symbols per second, provided

$$\frac{C(S)}{T_c} > \frac{B(D)}{T_s}$$

□

It is worth commenting that the information-transmission theorem presumes a binary data stream between source encoder and channel encoder. There is never any need to make the interface more elaborate. The channel encoder only needs to encode bit streams; it need not care where the bit streams come from. The source encoder only needs to create bit streams; it need not care what the bit streams will go through.

We should emphasize further that the theory tells us that we *can* partition the encoder into a source encoder and a channel encoder, not that we *must* do so.

☐ **Theorem 6.4.5 (Converse information-transmission theorem)** It is not possible to reproduce a discrete memoryless source of content $B(D)$ with average distortion D or smaller at the output of a discrete memoryless channel of capacity $C(S)$ satisfying

$$\frac{C(S)}{T_c} < \frac{B(D)}{T_s}$$

Proof This is an easy consequence of the data-processing theorem. Let N be the total number of source symbols in a stream of finite duration, and let n be the total number of symbols in the channel code stream. Define the random variables U^N, X^n, Y^n, and V^N, as in Fig. 6.5. The data-processing theorem (Theorem 5.3.3) says that, for any system of encoding and decoding,

$$I(U^N; V^N) \le I(X^n; Y^n)$$

By definition of $B(D)$,

$$NB(D) \le I(U^N; V^N)$$

By the definition of $C(S)$,

$$I(X^n; Y^n) \le nC(S)$$

Therefore

$$NB(D) \le I(U^N; V^N) \le I(X^n; Y^n) \le nC(S)$$

and the theorem follows. ☐

The major information-theoretic performance measures associated with the point-to-point communication of information for discrete problems have now been developed, especially $C(S)$, the channel capacity at cost S, and $B(D)$, the source content at distortion D. We will pause here to summarize, in Table 6.1, the most important performance measures; some of them have not been studied yet. In order to strengthen the analogies, entropy is given in the summary table as the minimum of a mutual information, although that minimum can be trivially evaluated. Similarly, the function $F(R)$ is expressed in terms of a maximum, although that maximum can be trivially evaluated also. The function $F(R, D)$ is studied in Section 6.6.

$$NB(D) \le I(U^N; V^N) \le I(X^n; Y^n) \le nC(S)$$

Figure 6.5   The converse information transmission theorem.

Table 6.1   A Table of Performance Measures

Channel $(Q_{k\|j})$	Source (p_j)
Capacity	Entropy
$C = \max_{\mathbf{p}} I(\mathbf{p};\mathbf{Q})$	$H = \min_{\mathbf{Q}} I(\mathbf{p};\mathbf{Q})$
Cost schedule (e_j)	Distortion measure (ρ_{jk})
Information capacity at cost S	Information content at distortion D
$C(S) = \max_{\mathbf{p}\in\mathscr{P}_S} I(\mathbf{p};\mathbf{Q})$	$B(D) = \min_{\mathbf{Q}\in\mathscr{Q}_D} I(\mathbf{p};\mathbf{Q})$
$\mathscr{P}_S = \{\mathbf{p}\mid e(\mathbf{p}) \le S\}$	$\mathscr{Q}_D = \{\mathbf{Q}\mid d(\mathbf{Q}) \le D\}$
Channel reliability function	Source reliability function
$E(R) = \max_{\mathbf{p}} \min_{\hat{\mathbf{Q}}\in\mathscr{Q}_R} L(\hat{\mathbf{Q}};\mathbf{Q})$	$F(R) = \max_{\mathbf{Q}} \min_{\hat{\mathbf{p}}\in\mathscr{P}_R} L(\hat{\mathbf{p}};\mathbf{p})$
$\mathscr{Q}_R = \{\hat{\mathbf{Q}}\mid I(\mathbf{p};\hat{\mathbf{Q}}) \le R\}$	$\mathscr{P}_R = \{\hat{\mathbf{p}}\mid I(\hat{\mathbf{p}};\mathbf{Q}) \ge R\}$
	(*Note:* Maximum is achieved when $\mathbf{Q}$ is the identity matrix.)
Constrained reliability function	Constrained reliability function
$E(R,S) = \max_{\mathbf{p}\in\mathscr{P}_S} \min_{\hat{\mathbf{Q}}\in\mathscr{Q}_R} L(\hat{\mathbf{Q}};\mathbf{Q})$	$F(R,D) = \max_{\mathbf{Q}} \min_{\hat{\mathbf{p}}\in\mathscr{P}_{R,D}} L(\hat{\mathbf{p}};\mathbf{p})$
$\mathscr{Q}_R = \{\hat{\mathbf{Q}}\mid I(\mathbf{p};\hat{\mathbf{Q}}) \le R\}$	$\mathscr{P}_{R,D} = \{\hat{\mathbf{p}}\mid I(\hat{\mathbf{p}};\mathbf{Q}) \ge R, \hat{d}(\mathbf{Q}) \ge D\}$
$\mathscr{P}_S = \{\mathbf{p}\mid e(\mathbf{p}) \le S\}$	

6.5 THE SOURCE-COMPRESSION CODING THEOREM

We are ready now to prove the source-compression coding theorem. Given a blocklength n and distortion D, we are interested in the probability of occurrence of a sourceword that cannot be encoded with block distortion less than or equal to nD. We shall see that, for appropriate codes, an upper bound on this probability goes to zero exponentially with blocklength. The source-compression coding theorem then follows by showing that the exponential decay coefficient, denoted $F(R,D)$, is positive if $R > B(D)$.

The random-coding exponent for source-compression codes $F(R,D)$ is an analog of the random-coding exponent for channel-transmission codes $E_r(R)$. The exponent will be defined in terms of a dummy probability distribution on the reproducing alphabet. An output probability distribution $\mathbf{q}$ will enter the proof as a probability distribution on a random ensemble of codes. The distribution $\mathbf{q}$ can be given a heuristic interpretation. As the blocklength becomes large, the relative frequency with which symbol b_k occurs in the set of codewords is approximately q_k. Thus the output distribution $\mathbf{q}$ achieving $F(R, D)$ is the proper distribution with which to randomly select codewords for a code of rate R and distortion D. Such a random selection of codewords will usually give a good code.

Later, we will study the exponent $F(R, D)$ in detail. We will see that it is associated with a probability matrix $\mathbf{Q}$. The transition matrix $\mathbf{Q}$ can also be given a heuristic interpretation, $Q_{k|j}$ being the relative frequency with which source symbol a_j is reproduced by code symbol b_k for a compression code of rate R and distortion D.

☐ **Theorem 6.5.1 (Random-coding bound)** It is possible to select $M = e^{nR}$ codewords of blocklength n so that the probability of a sourceword of blocklength n occurring that cannot be encoded within block distortion at most nD satisfies

$$p_e \le e^{-nF(R,D) + o(n)}$$

where

$$F(R, D) = \max_{s \ge 0} \min_{t \le 0} \max_{\mathbf{q}} \left[sR - stD - \log \sum_j p_j \left(\sum_k q_k e^{t\rho_{jk}} \right)^{-s} \right]$$

and for large enough n, $o(n) = 0$.

Proof The proof employs a random-coding argument.

Step 1: For any sourceword $\mathbf{x}$, let $\mathscr{S}(\mathbf{x})$ denote the set of all reproducing words $\mathbf{y}$ that could represent $\mathbf{x}$ with distortion at most nD. Let $\mathscr{T}(\mathbf{y})$ denote the set of all sourcewords $\mathbf{x}$ that, with distortion at most nD, can be represented by reproducing word $\mathbf{y}$. That is, for each $\mathbf{x}$, $\mathscr{S}(\mathbf{x})$ is the "sphere" around it given by

$$\mathscr{S}(\mathbf{x}) = \{\mathbf{y} : \rho(\mathbf{x}, \mathbf{y}) \le nD\}$$

and for each $\mathbf{y}$, $\mathscr{T}(\mathbf{y})$ is given by

$$\mathscr{T}(\mathbf{y}) = \{\mathbf{x} : \rho(\mathbf{x}, \mathbf{y}) \le nD\}$$

Let $\mathscr{C} = \{\mathbf{c}_m : m = 0, \ldots, M - 1\}$ denote one of the randomly chosen codes. Let the function $\phi_{\mathscr{T}(\mathbf{c}_m)}(\mathbf{x})$ denote the indicator function of the set $\mathscr{T}(\mathbf{c}_m)$. It is equal to 1 if $\mathbf{x}$ is an element of $\mathscr{T}(\mathbf{c}_m)$ and otherwise it is equal to 0. The probability of a sourceword that cannot be encoded within distortion nD with code $\mathscr{C}$ is

$$p_e = \sum_{\mathbf{x}} p(\mathbf{x}) \prod_{m=0}^{M-1} [1 - \phi_{\mathscr{T}(\mathbf{c}_m)}(\mathbf{x})]$$

because the product term is 1 only for $\mathbf{x}$ that cannot be encoded. Now randomly select the M codewords independently with product distribution on the symbols $q(\mathbf{y})$. Because the codewords are chosen independently, the ensemble average is

$$E[p_e] = \sum_{\mathbf{x}} p(\mathbf{x}) \left[1 - \sum_{\mathbf{y}} q(\mathbf{y}) \phi_{\mathcal{T}(\mathbf{y})}(\mathbf{x}) \right]^M$$

But $\mathbf{x}$ is in $\mathcal{T}(\mathbf{y})$ if and only if $\mathbf{y}$ is in $\mathcal{S}(\mathbf{x})$. Therefore

$$E[p_e] = \sum_{\mathbf{x}} p(\mathbf{x}) \left[1 - \sum_{\mathbf{y} \in \mathcal{S}(\mathbf{x})} q(\mathbf{y}) \right]^M$$

It will be necessary in step 2 to restrict attention to a subset of sourcewords of constant composition. Therefore, let $\mathcal{N}$ be a subset of all sourcewords having a given composition and define

$$E[p_e | \mathcal{N}] = \sum_{\mathbf{x} \in \mathcal{N}} p(\mathbf{x}) \left[1 - \sum_{\mathbf{y} \in \mathcal{S}(\mathbf{x})} q(\mathbf{y}) \right]^M$$

The bulk of the proof consists of upper-bounding the right side of this equation by breaking the sum into several sums over subsets. Because the number of distinct compositions is algebraic, we will be able to upper-bound $E[p_e]$ in terms of the upper bound on $E[p_e | \mathcal{N}]$.

Step 2: In the equation at the end of step 1, break the sum on $\mathbf{x}$ into two parts:

$$E[p_e | \mathcal{N}] = \sum_{\mathbf{x} \in \mathcal{U}^c} p(\mathbf{x}) \left[1 - \sum_{\mathbf{y} \in \mathcal{S}(\mathbf{x})} q(\mathbf{y}) \right]^M + \sum_{\mathbf{x} \in \mathcal{U}} p(\mathbf{x}) \left[1 - \sum_{\mathbf{y} \in \mathcal{S}(\mathbf{x})} q(\mathbf{y}) \right]^M$$

$$\leq \sum_{\mathcal{U}^c} p(\mathbf{x}) + \sum_{\mathcal{U}} p(\mathbf{x}) \left[1 - \sum_{\mathbf{y} \in \mathcal{S}(\mathbf{x})} q(\mathbf{y}) \right]^M$$

For the set $\mathcal{U}$, we choose

$$\mathcal{U} = \left\{ \mathbf{x} : \sum_{\mathbf{y}} q(\mathbf{y}) e^{t[\rho(\mathbf{x},\mathbf{y}) - nD]} > e^{-nR} \right\} \cap \mathcal{N}$$

for some parameter t not larger than zero. In the first term of the equation for $E[p_e | \mathcal{N}]$, we can use the fact that for $\mathbf{x}$ an element of $\mathcal{U}^c$,

$$1 \leq \left[\frac{e^{-nR}}{\sum_{\mathbf{y}} q(\mathbf{y}) e^{t[\rho(\mathbf{x},\mathbf{y}) - nD]}} \right]^s$$

for any positive s. This gives

$$E[p_e | \mathcal{N}] \leq \sum_{\mathcal{U}^c} p(\mathbf{x}) \left[\frac{e^{-nR}}{\sum_{\mathbf{y}} q(\mathbf{y}) e^{t[\rho(\mathbf{x},\mathbf{y}) - nD]}} \right]^s + \sum_{\mathcal{U}} p(\mathbf{x}) \left[1 - \sum_{\mathbf{y} \in \mathcal{S}(\mathbf{x})} q(\mathbf{y}) \right]^M$$

The first term is finished by extending the sum to all $\mathbf{x}$. Then

$$E[p_e | \mathcal{N}] \leq \sum_{\mathbf{x}} p(\mathbf{x}) \left[\frac{e^{-nR}}{\sum_{\mathbf{y}} q(\mathbf{y}) e^{t[\rho(\mathbf{x},\mathbf{y}) - nD]}} \right]^s + p_{e2}$$

where

$$p_{e2} = \sum_{\mathcal{U}} p(\mathbf{x}) \left[1 - \sum_{\mathbf{y} \in \mathcal{S}(\mathbf{x})} q(\mathbf{y}) \right]^M$$

Because $M = 2^{nR}$, the term p_{e2} is doubly exponential in n, which suggests that it goes to zero very quickly. We will show that this is indeed the case under the conditions of the theorem.

Step 3: We will now use a Chernoff bound on the second term. By Theorem 4.8.9 and the definition of $\mathcal{S}(\mathbf{x})$, we have

$$\sum_{\mathbf{y} \in \mathcal{S}(\mathbf{x})} q(\mathbf{y}) \geq e^{-c_x(nD) + o'(n)}$$

where

$$c_x(nD) = \max_{t \leq 0} \left[-\log \sum_{\mathbf{y}} q(\mathbf{y}) e^{t(\rho(\mathbf{x}, \mathbf{y}) - nD)} \right]$$

is the Chernoff function depending on the composition of sourceword $\mathbf{x}$. Because all sourcewords under consideration have the same composition, and $q(\mathbf{y})$ is a product distribution, there is only one maximizing t.

We can write

$$p_{e2} \leq \sum_{\mathbf{x} \in \mathcal{U}} p(\mathbf{x}) [1 - e^{-c_x(nD) + o'(n)}]^M$$

$$= \sum_{\mathbf{x} \in \mathcal{U}} p(\mathbf{x}) \exp \{ M \log [1 - e^{-c_x(nD) + o'(n)}] \}$$

Using the inequality

$$\log (1 - z) \leq -z$$

and $M = e^{nR}$, this becomes

$$p_{e2} \leq \sum_{\mathbf{x} \in \mathcal{U}} p(\mathbf{x}) \exp \{ -e^{nR - c_x(nD) + o'(n)} \}$$

By the definition of $\mathcal{U}$, for some $t \leq 0$,

$$nR > -\log \sum_{\mathbf{y}} q(\mathbf{y}) e^{t(\rho(\mathbf{x}, \mathbf{y}) - nD)}$$

for each $\mathbf{x}$ in $\mathcal{U}$. Thus the exponent is positive for every $\mathbf{x}$ in $\mathcal{U}$. Consequently, $p_{e2} \to 0$ doubly exponentially fast. For large enough n, it is a negligible contributor to $E[p_e]$ and can be buried by attaching an $o(n)$ term to p_{e1}. Extending the outer sum to all $\mathbf{x}$, we now have

$$E[p_e | \mathcal{N}] \leq \sum_{\mathbf{x}} p(\mathbf{x}) \left[\frac{e^{-nR}}{\sum_{\mathbf{y}} q(\mathbf{y}) e^{t\rho(\mathbf{x}, \mathbf{y}) - nD}} \right]^s (1 + e^{o''(n)})$$

In this inequality, both $p(\mathbf{x})$ and $q(\mathbf{y})$ are product distributions. Then

$$E[p_e|\mathcal{N}] \le \left[\sum_j p_j \left(\frac{e^{-R}}{\sum_k q_k e^{t(\rho_{jk}-D)}}\right)^s\right]^n (1 + e^{o''(n)})$$

We can choose $\mathbf{q}$ to make the bound the tightest. Having chosen $\mathbf{q}$, we should choose t as required by the Chernoff bound. It is enough to choose t to make the bound the weakest. Finally, s is chosen to make the bound the tightest.

There is an identical such bound for each composition subset $\mathcal{N}$, and the number of such composition subsets is algebraic. Therefore, within another $o(n)$ terms the bound also applies to $E[p_e]$. There must be at least one code for which p_e is smaller than the average $E[p_e]$, so the first claim of the theorem is proved.

Step 4: Because p_{e2} is doubly exponentially decreasing, it must be exactly zero for large enough n. This is because the probability p_e is always computed as a sum of finitely many terms, the smallest of which is

$$p_{\min} = \left(\min_j p_j\right)^n$$

$$= e^{-n \log (\min_j p_j)^{-1}}$$

This term is decreasing at a singly exponential rate, so p_{e2} will eventually be smaller than $p_{\min}$. Because p_{e2} is smaller than any possible term in the sum for p_{e2}, the sum must be empty, and $p_{e2} = 0$. Thus the term $o(n)$ is eventually zero. $\square$

6.6 THE SOURCE-COMPRESSION ERROR EXPONENT

The source-compression coding theorem is stated in terms of a random-coding exponent $F(R,D)$ for sources that plays the same role for data compression codes that the random-coding exponent $E_r(R)$ plays for data transmission codes. The source-compression coding theorem states that every sourceword of blocklength n can be encoded with distortion at most nD, except for a set of sourcewords whose probability p_e is at most $e^{-nF(R,D)+o(n)}$. Thus knowledge of where $F(R,D)$ is positive provides a sufficient condition for the existence of good codes of large blocklength. Therefore we will investigate the region of the R,D plane where $F(R,D)$ is positive and find that it is positive for $R > B(D)$. This provides the last piece of the proof of the data-compression coding theorem, which was given as Theorem 6.4.2.

We begin with a definition of the function $F(R, D)$ that appears to be much different from that given in the previous section, but we will show that it is the same function.

☐ **Definition 6.6.1** Let $[\rho_{jk}]$ be a single-letter distortion matrix. The reliability function for data compression codes for a discrete memoryless source with probability distribution $\mathbf{p}$ is given by

$$F(R, D) = \max_{\mathbf{Q}} \ \min_{\hat{\mathbf{p}} \in \mathscr{P}_{R,D}(\mathbf{Q})} \sum_j \hat{p}_j \log \frac{\hat{p}_j}{p_j}$$

where

$$\mathscr{P}_{R,D}(\mathbf{Q}) = \left\{ \hat{\mathbf{p}} : I(\hat{\mathbf{p}}; \mathbf{Q}) \geq R, \sum_j \sum_k \hat{p}_j Q_{k|j} \rho_{jk} \geq D \right\}$$

and the maximum is over all $\mathbf{Q}$ for which $\mathscr{P}_{R,D}(\mathbf{Q})$ is nonempty.   ☐

Notice that the set $\mathscr{P}_{R,D}(\mathbf{Q})$ involves constraints that are related to the usual definition of the source-distortion function:

$$B(D) = \min_{\mathbf{Q} \in \mathscr{Q}_D} I(\mathbf{p}; \mathbf{Q})$$

$$\mathscr{Q}_D = \left\{ \mathbf{Q} : \sum_j \sum_k p_j Q_{k|j} \rho_{jk} \leq D \right\}$$

so we expect that $F(R, D)$ should have an intimate relationship with $B(D)$.

For fixed D, $F(R, D)$ need not exist for each R. This is because, for some R, there will be no element $\hat{\mathbf{p}}$ in the set $\mathscr{P}_{R,D}(\mathbf{Q})$ for any $\mathbf{Q}$. To find the domain of the function, we must find those R for which $\mathscr{P}_{R,D}(\mathbf{Q})$ is nonempty for some $\mathbf{Q}$. Fix the distortion matrix ρ and fix the source alphabet. It will follow from Theorem 6.6.4 that $F(R, D)$ is defined only for rates satisfying

$$R \leq B^*(D)$$

where $B^*(D)$ is the largest source-distortion function of any source with the specified alphabet and distortion matrix.

The general nature of $F(R, D)$ is shown in the example of Fig. 6.6, which shows $F(R, D)$ for a binary source with $\mathbf{p} = (\gamma, 1 - \gamma)$ and probability-of-error distortion matrix. As shown in the following theorem, the general shape will be the same for any source.

☐ **Theorem 6.6.2** $F(R, D)$ is convex and increasing in both R and in D.

Proof The mutual information $I(\mathbf{p}; \mathbf{Q})$ is concave in $\mathbf{p}$. The inequality constraints of Definition 6.6.1 can be multiplied through by -1 to make them into convex constraints. The inner minimization is now the minimum of a convex function subject to convex constraints. Therefore for each $\mathbf{Q}$ this gives a convex function. The outer maximum is then over a set of convex functions and hence yields a convex function. Similarly, the inner minimum on $\mathbf{p}$ is increasing in both R and D and hence $F(R, D)$ also behaves in this way.   ☐

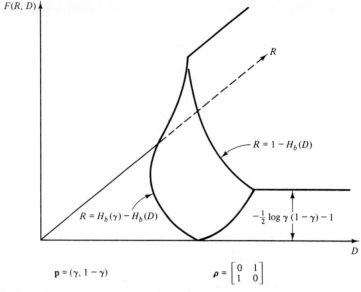

Figure 6.6   Source-compression exponent for a binary memoryless source.

☐   **Theorem 6.6.3** $F(R, D)$ is positive if $R > B(D)$ and is zero if $R \leq B(D)$.

Proof $F(R, D) = 0$ if and only if $\hat{\mathbf{p}} = \mathbf{p}$ and otherwise $F(R, D)$ is positive. Thus the minimization problem defining $F(R, D)$ achieves its minimum of zero at $\hat{\mathbf{p}} = \mathbf{p}$ if and only if $\mathbf{p} \in \mathscr{P}_{R,D}(\mathbf{Q})$ for every value of $\mathbf{Q}$. In particular, $\mathbf{p} \in \mathscr{P}_{R,D}(\mathbf{Q})$ even for the value of $\mathbf{Q}$ achieving $B(D)$, which implies that $B(D) = I(\mathbf{p}; \mathbf{Q}) \geq R$. Thus $F(R, D) = 0$ implies that $R \leq B(D)$. Conversely, if $R > B(D)$, then $\mathbf{Q}$ achieving $B(D)$ is such that $I(\mathbf{p}; \mathbf{Q}) < R$, and hence $\mathbf{p}$ is not an element of $\mathscr{P}_{R,D}(\mathbf{Q})$. Therefore $F(R, D) > 0$.   ☐

The following theorem provides an alternative representation of $F(R, D)$. This representation is less well suited to proving convexity properties of $F(R, D)$ but is better matched to proving the coding theorems.

☐   **Theorem 6.6.4**   A representation of $F(R, D)$ is

$$F(R, D) = \min_{\hat{\mathbf{p}} \in \mathscr{P}_{R,D}} \sum_j \hat{p}_j \log \frac{\hat{p}_j}{p_j}$$

where

$$\mathscr{P}_{R,D} = \{\hat{\mathbf{p}} : B(\hat{\mathbf{p}}, D) \geq R\}$$

Proof In the definition of $F(R, D)$ (Definition 6.6.1), $\mathbf{Q}$ does not appear in the object function, but only in the set $\mathscr{P}_{R,D}(\mathbf{Q})$. The maximum is achieved if for each $\hat{\mathbf{p}}$ that might achieve the minimum, $\mathbf{Q}$ is chosen to exclude $\hat{\mathbf{p}}$ from the set $\mathscr{P}_{R,D}(\mathbf{Q})$. By the definition of $B(\hat{\mathbf{p}}, D)$, this can be done if and only if

$$B(\hat{\mathbf{p}}, D) < R$$

Then $F(R, D)$ is found by minimizing $L(\hat{\mathbf{p}}; \mathbf{p})$ over the remaining $\hat{\mathbf{p}}$.   □

It is easy to compute $F(R, D)$ using this representation. For example, consider the binary asymmetric source with probability distribution

$$\mathbf{p} = (\gamma, 1 - \gamma)$$

and distortion matrix

$$\rho = \begin{bmatrix} 0 & 1 \\ 1 & 0 \end{bmatrix}$$

Now because it is a binary distribution, $\hat{\mathbf{p}}$ must be of the form

$$\hat{\mathbf{p}} = (\gamma', 1 - \gamma')$$

for some γ'. Therefore

$$F(R, D) = L_b(\gamma', \gamma)$$

where γ' satisfies

$$R = H_b(\gamma') - H_b(D)$$

This parametric solution gives the equations for Fig. 6.6.

□ **Theorem 6.6.5** The source reliability function $F(R, D)$ can be expressed as follows:

$$F(R, D) = \max_{s \geq 0} \min_{t \leq 0} \max_{\mathbf{q}} \left[sR - stD - \log \sum_j p_j \left(\sum_k q_k e^{t\rho_{jk}} \right)^{-s} \right]$$

Proof We begin with the representation given in Theorem 6.6.4. In the range of R for which $F(R, D)$ is strictly increasing, we can express $F(R, D)$ using a Lagrange multiplier as

$$F(R, D) = \min_{\hat{\mathbf{p}}} \sum_j \hat{p}_j \log \frac{\hat{p}_j}{p_j} + s[R - B(\hat{\mathbf{p}}, D)]$$

Alternatively, for each $s \geq 0$, we can write

$$F(R, D) \geq \min_{\hat{\mathbf{p}} \in \mathscr{P}_{R,D}} \sum_j \hat{p}_j \log \frac{\hat{p}_j}{p_j} + s[R - B(\hat{\mathbf{p}}, D)]$$

because the term multiplying s is nonpositive. Without violating the inequality, we can take the minimum over all $\hat{\mathbf{p}}$. Then because the inequality is true for all nonnegative s, we can choose the maximizing s to give

$$F(R, D) \geq \max_{s \geq 0} \min_{\hat{\mathbf{p}}} \sum_j \hat{p}_j \log \frac{\hat{p}_j}{p_j} + s[R - B(\hat{\mathbf{p}}, D)]$$

But we know from the Lagrange-multiplier formulation that the right side has the form of $F(R, D)$ for some value of s, so the inequality can be replaced by equality

$$F(R, D) = \max_{s \geq 0} \min_{\hat{\mathbf{p}}} \sum_j \hat{p}_j \log \frac{\hat{p}_j}{p_j} + s[R - B(\hat{\mathbf{p}}, D)]$$

Now apply Corollary 6.3.5, using t in place of s. This gives

$$F(R, D) = \max_{s \geq 0} \min_{\hat{\mathbf{p}}} \min_{t \leq 0} \max_{\mathbf{q}}$$

$$\left[\sum_j \hat{p}_j \log \frac{\hat{p}_j}{p_j} + sR - stD + s \sum_j \hat{p}_j \log \sum_k q_k e^{t \rho_{jk}} \right]$$

because $B(\hat{\mathbf{p}}, D)$ appears with a negative sign.

All that remains is to evaluate the minimum on $\hat{\mathbf{p}}$. To do so we must justify pushing the minimum to the other side of the maximum on $\mathbf{q}$. But the argument is convex in $\hat{\mathbf{p}}$ and concave in $\mathbf{q}$. We are looking for a saddle point; the minimax equals the maximin. We are justified in evaluating the minimum on $\hat{\mathbf{p}}$, and by differentiation, it occurs where

$$\hat{p}_j = \frac{p_j \left(\sum_k q_k e^{t \rho_{jk}} \right)^{-s}}{\sum_j p_j \left(\sum_k q_k e^{t \rho_{jk}} \right)^{-s}}$$

Substituting this into the previous equation for $F(R, D)$ completes the proof of the theorem. $\quad\Box$

6.7 LOWER BOUNDS FOR DATA COMPRESSION CODES

An upper bound on the performance of block codes for data compression was developed in Section 6.5. The probability of a sourceword of blocklength n that cannot be encoded within maximum block distortion nD satisfies

$$p_e \leq e^{-nF(R, D) + o(n)}$$

We shall show now that this probability is lower-bounded by

$$p_e \geq e^{-nF(R, D) + o'(n)}$$

Combining the two bounds shows that the asymptotic behavior of the probability of decoding failure is given by $F(R, D)$.

The next theorem says that if $R < B(D)$, the probability of decoding failure is bounded away from zero. The second theorem says that if $R > B(D)$, the probability of decoding failure can be lower-bounded by reference to a dummy source $\hat{\mathbf{p}}$ such that $R < B(\hat{\mathbf{p}}, D)$, whose probability of decoding failure is bounded away from zero.

☐ **Theorem 6.7.1** Suppose the rate of a source code for data compression satisfies $R < B(D)$. Then for all n, the probability that a sourceword of blocklength n cannot be encoded within maximum distortion nD satisfies

$$p_e \geq \frac{B(D) - R}{|s|\rho_m}$$

where

$$s = \frac{dB(D)}{dD}$$

Proof According to Theorem 6.4.1 and Theorem 6.3.11, for a sourceword of blocklength n, the average distortion $\bar{D}$ satisfies

$$nR \geq nB(\bar{D}) = B_n(n\bar{D})$$

The distortion is at most nD except when, with probability p_e, it is at most $n\rho_m$. Therefore the average distortion $n\bar{D}$ satisfies

$$n\bar{D} \leq nD + np_e\rho_m$$

Then, because $B(D)$ is convex and decreasing, we can write the following string of inequalities:

$$nR \geq B_n(n\bar{D})$$

$$\geq B_n(nD + np_e\rho_m)$$

$$\geq B_n(nD) + n\frac{dB(D)}{dD}p_e\rho_m$$

$$= nB(D) + nsp_e\rho_m$$

Because s is negative, this is equivalent to the statement of the theorem. ☐

☐ **Theorem 6.7.2** Suppose that $\mathbf{p}$ satisfies $B(\mathbf{p}, D) < B^*(D)$. Every data compression code of blocklength n for source $\mathbf{p}$ with rate R satisfying

$$B(\mathbf{p}, D) < R < B^*(D)$$

has a probability of block decoding failure that satisfies

$$p_e \geq e^{-nF(R,D) + o(n)}$$

where $o(n)$ is a term that goes to zero as n goes to infinity.

Proof Let $\mathscr{C}$ be any code of rate R and blocklength n, and let $\mathscr{U}$ be the set of sourcewords that are encoded within maximum distortion nD. By assumption, $\mathbf{p}$ does not achieve $B^*(D)$. Therefore we can find a probability vector $\hat{\mathbf{p}}$ with

$$B(\mathbf{p}, D) < R < B(\hat{\mathbf{p}}, D) < B^*(D)$$

Therefore, by Theorem 6.7.1, we have that

$$\sum_{\mathbf{x} \in \mathscr{U}^c} \hat{p}(\mathbf{x}) > 2\alpha$$

for some positive constant α. Let $\mathscr{B}$ be the set

$$\mathscr{B} = \left\{ \mathbf{x} : \left| \frac{1}{n} \log \frac{\hat{p}(\mathbf{x})}{p(\mathbf{x})} - L(\hat{\mathbf{p}}; \mathbf{p}) \right| \leq \varepsilon \right\}$$

By the law of large numbers, for sufficiently large blocklength n,

$$\sum_{\mathbf{x} \in \mathscr{B}^c} \hat{p}(\mathbf{x}) < \alpha$$

Now bound p_e as follows:

$$p_e = \sum_{\mathbf{x} \notin \mathscr{U}} p(\mathbf{x}) \geq \sum_{\mathbf{x} \in \mathscr{U}^c \cap \mathscr{B}} p(\mathbf{x})$$

$$\geq \sum_{\mathbf{x} \in \mathscr{U}^c \cap \mathscr{B}} \hat{p}(\mathbf{x}) e^{-nL(\hat{\mathbf{p}}; \mathbf{p}) + n\varepsilon}$$

But

$$\sum_{\mathbf{x} \in \mathscr{U}^c \cap \mathscr{B}} \hat{p}(\mathbf{x}) \geq \sum_{\mathbf{x} \in \mathscr{U}^c} \hat{p}(\mathbf{x}) - \sum_{\mathbf{x} \in \mathscr{B}^c} \hat{p}(\mathbf{x})$$

$$\geq 2\alpha - \alpha = \alpha$$

Therefore

$$p_e \geq \alpha e^{-nL(\hat{\mathbf{p}}; \mathbf{p}) + n\varepsilon}$$

This is true for every $\hat{\mathbf{p}}$ that satisfies $B(\hat{\mathbf{p}}, D) > R$. Hence, of such $\hat{\mathbf{p}}$, we choose the $\hat{\mathbf{p}}$ that makes $L(\hat{\mathbf{p}}; \mathbf{p})$ the smallest, so that

$$p_e \geq e^{-nF(R,D) + n\varepsilon - \log \alpha}$$

This completes the proof of the theorem. $\square$

PROBLEMS

6.1 A ternary channel accepts 1000 symbols per second and has a capacity of 0.5 bits per input symbol. This channel is used to transmit the output symbols of a binary equiprobable source that has 1000 output symbols per second. What is the best probability of error that can be attained?

6.2. Consider a source that puts out binary symbols. Successive letters are independent and both 0 and 1 occur with probability $\frac{1}{2}$. You are to compress this output data. The reproducing alphabet is $\{0, 1, e\}$ where the symbol e denotes an *erasure*. The distortion matrix is

$$\rho = \begin{bmatrix} 0 & 1 & 0.25 \\ 1 & 0 & 0.25 \end{bmatrix}$$

That is, an error is judged to be four times as severe as an erasure. By what factor can the data be compressed so that the average distortion is no worse than D?

6.3. Suppose a binary equiprobable source is to be compressed. The distortion matrix is

$$\rho = \begin{bmatrix} 0 & 2 \\ 1 & 0 \end{bmatrix}$$

That is, it is twice as serious to reproduce a 0 by a 1 as it is to reproduce a 1 by a 0. Find $B(D)$.

6.4. A discrete memoryless ternary source is given having probability distribution

$$\mathbf{p} = \left(\frac{1-\rho}{2}, \rho, \frac{1-\rho}{2} \right)$$

where $\rho \leq 1/3$. A discrete memoryless ternary channel is given having transition matrix

$$\mathbf{Q} = \begin{bmatrix} 1-\varepsilon & \varepsilon/2 & \varepsilon/2 \\ \varepsilon/2 & 1-\varepsilon & \varepsilon/2 \\ \varepsilon/2 & \varepsilon/2 & 1-\varepsilon \end{bmatrix}$$

The source puts out symbols at the same rate that the channel accepts symbols (for example, one per microsecond).

a. Show how to build a trivial system for transmitting the source outputs over the channel with a per-letter probability of error of ε.

b. Evaluate the capacity of the channel.

c. Suppose that the distortion measure is probability of error. Evaluate $B(D)$. What is $B(D)$ at $D = 0$? Comment on this.

d. Suppose that $\rho = 0.25$ and $\varepsilon = 0.6$. What is the smallest attainable per-letter probability of error p_e?

e. There may be some combination of values of ρ, ε, and $p_e (= D)$ such that direct connection of the source to the channel satisifes the information-theoretic bounds and hence is the best possible encoder. Are there such values of (ρ, ε, p_e) and if so, what are they?

f. Now suppose that the channel requires 1 microjoule to transmit symbol 1 or 3 and no energy to transmit symbol 2. (Think of a positive pulse representing 1, a negative pulse representing 3, and no pulse representing 2.) What is the smallest amount of average power that can be expended and still attain the results of part **d**?

6.5. There are approximately 2^{78} distinct pairs of bridge hands. (See Problem 3.6.) A partnership is a pair of people, each with a concealed bridge hand which he wishes to disclose to the other. An idealized procedure (which ignores the need to deceive opponents) is as follows: A bid collection is an ordered set of 35 objects called bids. A bid sequence consists of each partner alternatively naming a bid that is higher in the order than any previous bid until either partner declines to make a further bid. A bid strategy is an announced rule which both partners use to select their next bid based upon their hands and the previous bids.

   Prove that any bid strategy has approximatley 2^{43} pairs of bridge hands associated with an average bid sequence. A bid strategy has some of the elements of a data compression code but is more complicated because it also performs the task of two-way communication.

6.6. Suppose that a given source is binary. Is the bound expressed by Corollary 6.1.3 tighter than, looser than, or the same as the bound given by the source-compression coding theorem? Explain.

6.7. Prove that, under a per-letter distortion matrix, the average information content at distortion D of a discrete source with memory is strictly less than a memoryless source having the same per-letter probability distribution, except at maximum distortion.

6.8. Prove that if two transition matrices $\mathbf{Q}'$ and $\mathbf{Q}''$ both achieve the same point $(D, B(D))$, then so does $\mathbf{Q} = \lambda\mathbf{Q}' + (1 - \lambda)\mathbf{Q}''$ for all $\lambda \in [0, 1]$.

6.9. This problem will show that for many channels the expurgated exponent, studied in Chapter 10, has the form of a source-distortion function. For these channels the expurgated bound evaluated for block inputs must be achieved by a product distribution because the source-distortion function is always achieved by a product distribution. Define

$$E_{L2}(R) = \max_{\mathbf{p}} \min_{\hat{\mathbf{P}} \in \mathscr{P}_R} \left[-\sum_{ij} p_i \hat{P}_{j|i} \log \sum_k Q_{k|i}^{1/2} Q_{k|j}^{1/2} \right]$$

where

$$\mathscr{P}_R(\mathbf{p}) = \left\{ \hat{\mathbf{P}} : \sum_{ij} p_i \hat{P}_{j|i} \log \frac{\hat{P}_{j|i}}{\sum_i p_i \hat{P}_{j|i}} \leq R \right\}$$

(This differs from Definition 10.4.1 in that the symmetrizing constraint $\sum_i p_i P_{j|i} = p_j$ is eliminated.) With the proof of Theorem 10.4.3 as a guide, prove that $E_{L2}(R) = E_L(R)$ whenever $E_L(R)$ is achieved by a probability distribution with all components strictly positive. Prove further that all equidistant channels satisfy this condition.

6.10. Prove that $\partial E_o(s, \mathbf{p})/\partial s = I(\mathbf{p}; \mathbf{Q})$.

6.11. Suppose that both the source alphabet and the reproducing alphabet consist of binary n-tuples and the distortion between two n-tuples is their Hamming distance. Let $A_{jk} = e^{s\rho_{jk}}$. Show that if $\sum_j A_{jk}^{-1} p_j \geq 0$ for all k, then

$$B(D) = -\sum_i p_j \log p_j - H_b(D)$$

6.12. Prove that the Lagrange multiplier s for $B(D)$ satisfies

$$s = \frac{dB(D)}{dD}$$

NOTES

In his 1948 paper, Shannon briefly discussed the question of choosing messages to be sent over a communication system, but he did not yet follow the thought to any depth. He returned to this question in 1959 when he introduced the study of performance measures for data compression and provided the first source-compression coding theorems. Strengthened versions of the coding theorem were proved by Berger (1971), Omura (1973), Gray (1975), and many others. The recursive algorithm for computing the source-distortion function was found by Blahut (1972). A lower bound on the performance of data compression codes came from Marton (1974). The idea of an error exponent for source compression codes is implicit in Jelinek's textbook and was developed explicitly by Marton (1974) and Blahut (1974, 1976). The information content of a class of sources under distortion was studied by Sakrison (1969) and by Ziv (1972). Universal variable-length codes for data compression were studied by Pursley and Davisson (1976). Singh and Kambo (1977) discuss codes for which all sourcewords are encodable within a maximum distortion.

Data compression would be unmotivated were it not for the converse to the channel coding theorem. The Fano inequality (1952) and the Wolfowitz inequality (1957) were the basis of the original converse theorems. The exponential form of the block converse theorem that we have given comes from Arimoto (1973). It was shown by Dueck and Körner (1979) that the Arimoto exponent cannot be improved.

CHAPTER 7

Continuous Channels and Sources

A discrete information source generates information at a finite rate; the entropy rate must be finite if the source alphabet is finite. In contrast, a continuous information source can assume any one of an uncountably infinite number of amplitude values and so requires an infinite number of binary digits for its exact specification; the entropy is infinite. An immediate consequence of this is that, in order to transmit the output of a continuous information source and recover it exactly, a channel of infinite capacity is required. Because in practice every channel is perturbed by noise and so has a finite capacity, it is not possible to transmit the output of a continuous source over any channel and recover it exactly; there is alway some distortion.

We distinguish between a discrete source or channel; a continuous source or channel defined on discrete time instants; and a waveform source or channel defined on a continuum of time points.

A waveform channel can be made into a discrete channel by choosing a finite set of modulation waveforms for the channel. A waveform source can be made into a continuous source by sampling, provided the bandwidth is finite, and into a discrete source by sampling and quantization, provided a small amount of distortion can be introduced.

7.1 CONTINUOUS-AMPLITUDE SIGNALS

The *differential entropy* (in bits) of a continuous random variable X with probability density function $p(x)$ is defined as

$$H(X) = -\int_{-\infty}^{\infty} p(x) \log_2 p(x)\, dx$$

The differential entropy has no fundamental physical meaning, but occurs often enough to have a name. The differential entropy is not invariant under invertible coordinate transformations. It is *not* the limiting case of the entropy; the entropy of a random variable with a continuous distribution is infinite.

Consider how we might generalize the entropy to continuous random variables. A continuous probability density function can be approximated by means of probability densities that are constant on intervals of width Δx. The approximating probability density function has value p_j on the jth interval. To ensure that $\sum_j p_j = 1$, set $p_j = p(x_j)\,\Delta x$ where x_j is a point in the jth interval such that $p(x_j)\,\Delta x$ is the area under $p(x)$ in the jth interval. The entropy of the approximating probability distribution is

$$H(\mathbf{p}) = -\sum_j p_j \log p_j$$

$$= -\sum_j p(x_j)\,\Delta x \log\left[p(x_j)\,\Delta x \right]$$

$$= -\sum_j p(x_j)\,\Delta x \log p(x_j) - \log \Delta x$$

We may wish to define the entropy of the continuous probability density function $p(x)$ to be the limit of this expression as $\Delta x \to 0$. However, even if the first term converges to an integral, the second term becomes infinite. Because there is no way to avoid the divergence of the second term, the entropy of a continuous random variable is always infinite.

The mathematical behavior has a physical interpretation. If we consider entropy to be the average number of yes/no answers necessary to resolve the uncertainty in the outcome of an experiment, then we almost always need an infinite number of answers to specify a continuously distributed outcome. The binary representation of almost all real numbers requires an infinite number of nonrepeating bits. This suggests that an infinite number of bits is required to represent a single output of a continuous source.[†] Consequently, when such sources are represented with a finite number of bits, distortion must always occur.

Problems such as data compaction, which in the discrete case are treated in terms of the entropy, require infinite information in the continuous case and so do not have interesting generalizations. However, problems that in the discrete case are treated in terms of the mutual information or the discrimination do have interesting generalizations. The reason is that the mutual information and the discrimination are well behaved for continuous probability density functions, since the argument of the logarithm is a ratio.

The average mutual information between two continuous random variables X and Y is defined as in the discrete case:

$$I(X;Y) = H(X) + H(Y) - H(X,Y)$$

$$= H(X) - H(X|Y) = H(Y) - H(Y|X)$$

$$= \int_{-\infty}^{\infty} \int_{-\infty}^{\infty} P(x,y) \log_2 \frac{P(x,y)}{p(x)p(y)} \, dy \, dx$$

$$= \int_{-\infty}^{\infty} p(x) \int_{-\infty}^{\infty} Q(y|x) \log_2 \frac{Q(y|x)}{\int_{-\infty}^{\infty} p(x)Q(y|x) \, dx} \, dy \, dx \quad \text{bits}$$

where $H(X|Y)$ and $H(Y|X)$ are conditional differential entropies, which are defined analogously to the differential entropy. The mutual information is expressed as the difference between two terms that are each a differential entropy. The two terms individually are not invariant under an invertible coordinate transformation, but their difference is invariant. The mutual information does have a fundamental significance. For example, if X is replaced by $2X$, as in a change of units, then both $H(X)$ and $H(X|Y)$ change their values but $I(X;Y)$ is unchanged.

The discrimination also extends to the continuous case without difficulty. Given the probability density functions $p_0(x)$ and $p_1(x)$, the discrimination is given by

$$L(p_0; p_1) = \int p_0(x) \log \frac{p_0(x)}{p_1(x)} \, dx$$

Again, because there is a ratio under the logarithm, the discrimination is invariant under invertible coordinate transformations such as scale changes and rotation of coordinate axes.

[†]However, this need not imply that the entropy *rate* of every continuous-amplitude random *process* is infinite. For example, if a discrete-time continuous-amplitude random process does not change with time, the process can be described to any desired accuracy at any fixed rate simply by making the blocklength long enough.

7.2. INFORMATION MEASURES OF GAUSSIAN SIGNALS

The gaussian distribution is the most important continuous probability distribution. Problems that involve gaussian random variables and quadratic constraints are common. Many communication channels are additive gaussian-noise channels because every radio receiver is limited by thermal noise, which is always gaussian. The quadratic constraint comes from a constraint on the average energy or average power. It is a basic physical constraint. The study of gaussian channels under a quadratic constraint is very well motivated.

Source models are usually more subjective. Most sources are rather complex and more difficult to model; a gaussian model may be only a rough approximation. The distortion measure is also a matter of judgment. Mean-squared error is a quadratic constraint that is commonly used as a convenient distortion measure for data compression, but it is not usually mandated by the essentials of the problem. Thus the study of gaussian sources under a quadratic constraint may not be as fundamental as the study of gaussian channels under a quadratic constraint.

The gaussian distribution is important for other reasons. Its mathematical structure allows a much more thorough analysis than is possible with many other distributions. Also, in many classes of problems, gaussian noise can be shown to be a worst case. For example, of all additive noise processes with fixed variance N, independent gaussian noise results in the smallest channel capacity. Therefore one often is satisfied with codes designed for the gaussian case when the true noise distribution is unknown.

One reason the gaussian probability distribution plays the major role it does is that it maximizes the differential entropy for a fixed variance. That is, if Y is a continuous random variable, then the differential entropy

$$H(Y) = -\int_{-\infty}^{\infty} q(y) \log_2 q(y)\, dy$$

is maximized over the set of all probability density functions with variance σ^2 by choosing the gaussian density function. This fact follows from the property that the logarithm of a gaussian distribution is a quadratic function. Suppose that $q^*(y)$ is gaussian. Then

$$\log q^*(y) = \log\left(\frac{1}{\sqrt{2\pi}\,\sigma} e^{-(y-\bar{y})^2/2\sigma^2}\right)$$

$$= -\log\sqrt{2\pi}\,\sigma - \frac{(y-\bar{y})^2}{2\sigma^2}$$

For any other random variable $q(y)$ of mean $\bar{y}_q$ and variance σ_q, we have

$$-\int_{-\infty}^{\infty} q(y) \log q^*(y)\, dy = \log\sqrt{2\pi}\,\sigma + \frac{\sigma_q^2 - (\bar{y} - \bar{y}_q)^2}{2\sigma^2}$$

Only the mean and variance of $q(y)$ affect this computation. If $q(y)$ and $q'(y)$ have the same mean and the same variance, then

$$-\int_{-\infty}^{\infty} q(y) \log q^*(y)\, dy = -\int_{-\infty}^{\infty} q'(y) \log q^*(y)\, dy$$

This leaves us ready for the theorem.

☐ **Theorem 7.2.1**   The gaussian distribution has the largest differential entropy of any distribution with a specified mean and variance.

Proof   Let $q^*(y)$ be gaussian of mean $\bar{y}$ and variance σ^2, and let $q(y)$ be any other probability distribution with the same mean and variance. Then

$$H(q^*) - H(q) = -\int_{-\infty}^{\infty} q^*(y) \log q^*(y)\, dy + \int_{-\infty}^{\infty} q(y) \log q(y)\, dy$$

$$= -\int_{-\infty}^{\infty} q(y) \log q^*(y)\, dy + \int_{-\infty}^{\infty} q(y) \log q(y)\, dy$$

$$= L(q; q^*) \geq 0 \qquad\qquad\qquad ☐$$

☐ **Theorem 7.2.2**   The differential entropy of a gaussian distribution with any mean and with variance σ^2 is given by

$$H(q) = \frac{1}{2} \log (2\pi e \sigma^2)$$

Proof

$$H(q) = \int_{-\infty}^{\infty} q(y) \left[-\log \sqrt{2\pi}\, \sigma - \frac{(y - \bar{y})^2}{2\sigma^2} \right] dy$$

$$= \frac{1}{2} \log 2\pi\sigma^2 + \frac{1}{2}$$

$$= \frac{1}{2} \log (2\pi e \sigma^2) \qquad\qquad\qquad ☐$$

The differential entropy of a vector of length n whose components are independent, identically distributed, gaussian random variables of variance σ^2 is

$$H(X^n) = \frac{n}{2} \log (2\pi e \sigma^2)$$

because entropy adds for independent events.

Mutual information assumes a simple form when the two random variables differ by an additive-noise term.

☐ **Theorem 7.2.3** Suppose that $Y = X + Z$ where X and Z are independent continuous random variables. Then

$$I(X;Y) = H(Y) - H(Z)$$

Proof Let $Q(z)$ be the probability density function of Z. Then

$$H(Y|X) = -\int_{-\infty}^{\infty} \int_{-\infty}^{\infty} p(x)Q(y-x)\log Q(y-x)\,dy\,dx$$

$$= \int_{-\infty}^{\infty} p(x)H(Z)\,dx = H(Z)$$

Hence

$$I(X;Y) = H(Y) - H(Y|X) = H(Y) - H(Z)$$ ☐

☐ **Theorem 7.2.4** Suppose that $Y = X + Z$ where X and Z are gaussian random variables of variance S and N, respectively. Then

$$I(X;Y) = \frac{1}{2}\log\left(1 + \frac{S}{N}\right)$$

Proof Y is gaussian of variance $S + N$. Using Theorem 7.2.3,

$$I(X;Y) = \frac{1}{2}\log\left[2\pi e(S+N)\right] - \frac{1}{2}\log(2\pi eN)$$

$$= \frac{1}{2}\log\frac{S+N}{N}$$ ☐

The expected value of the square of additive noise is also referred to as the *average noise power*. The average noise power is equal to the variance if the mean is zero. The next theorem says that if the input to an additive-noise channel is gaussian, then the kind of additive noise of a fixed noise power that is most efficient in reducing mutual information is additive gaussian noise of zero mean.

☐ **Theorem 7.2.5** Suppose that $Y = X + Z$ where X is a gaussian random variable and Z is a random variable having average noise power N and independent of X. Then $I(X;Y)$ is smallest if Z is gaussian with zero mean.

Proof If Z is gaussian, then it must have zero mean to minimize $I(X;Y)$ because, by Theorem 7.2.4, mutual information is decreased by increasing the noise variance and, if $E[Z]^2 = N$, the variance is increased by reducing the mean to zero. Hence we only need to prove that Z is gaussian.

Let $p(x)$ be the density function for X. Suppose that Q^* is a gaussian density for Z and Q is any other density having the same mean and variance. Let

$$q^*(y) = \int_{-\infty}^{\infty} p(x)Q^*(y-x)\,dx$$

$$q(y) = \int_{-\infty}^{\infty} p(x)Q(y-x)\,dx$$

Then $q^*(y)$ is also a gaussian density function and has the same mean and variance as $q(y)$. Consequently, as we have seen,

$$H(q^*) = -\int_{-\infty}^{\infty} q(y)\log q^*(y)\,dy$$

and

$$H(Q^*) = -\int_{-\infty}^{\infty} Q(y)\log Q^*(y)\,dy$$

Therefore, by Theorem 7.2.3,

$$I(p;Q) - I(p;Q^*) = H(q) - H(Q) - H(q^*) + H(Q^*)$$

$$= -\int q(y)\log q(y)\,dy + \int Q(z)\log Q(z)\,dz$$

$$+ \int q(y)\log q^*(y)\,dy - \int Q(z)\log Q^*(z)\,dz$$

$$= \int\int p(x)Q(y-x)\log\frac{q^*(y)}{q(y)}\frac{Q(y-x)}{Q^*(y-x)}\,dy\,dx$$

$$\geq \int\int p(x)Q(y-x)\left[1 - \frac{q(y)Q^*(y-x)}{q^*(y)Q(y-x)}\right]dy\,dx$$

The final term is equal to zero, so the theorem is proved. □

□ **Theorem 7.2.6**   Suppose that $q_1^*(y)$ is gaussian and $q_0(y)$ is an arbitrary density function having mean $\bar{y}_0$ and variance σ_0^2. Then $L(q_0;q_1^*)$ is smallest if $q_0(y)$ is also gaussian.

Proof   Let q_0^* be gaussian of mean $\bar{y}_0$ and variance σ_0^2. Then

$$L(q_0^*;q_1^*) = \int q_0^*(y)\left[\frac{(y-\bar{y}_1)^2}{2\sigma_1^2} - \frac{(y-\bar{y}_0)^2}{2\sigma_0^2} + \log\frac{\sigma_1}{\sigma_0}\right]dy$$

$$= \int q_0(y)\left[\frac{(y-\bar{y}_1)^2}{2\sigma_1^2} - \frac{(y-\bar{y}_0)^2}{2\sigma_0^2} + \log\frac{\sigma_1}{\sigma_0}\right]dy$$

$$= \int q_0(y)\log\frac{q_0^*(y)}{q_1^*(y)}\,dy$$

Therefore

$$L(q_0;q_1^*) - L(q_0^*;q_1^*) = \int_{-\infty}^{\infty} q_0(y)\log\frac{q_0(y)}{q_1^*(y)}dy - \int_{-\infty}^{\infty} q_0(y)\log\frac{q_0^*(y)}{q_1^*(y)}dy$$

$$= \int_{-\infty}^{\infty} q_0(y)\log\frac{q_0(y)}{q_0^*(y)} \geq 0 \qquad \square$$

The parallel statement, that q_1 should be gaussian to minimize $L(q_0; q_1)$ when q_0 is gaussian, is not true.

Next we expand the discussion to consider multivariate gaussian distributions. We will use the following fact from matrix theory, which we prove by an indirect argument that serves to review matrix technique.

□ **Theorem 7.2.7** Let **A** be a symmetric n-by-n matrix and let **x** be a column vector of length n. Then[†]

$$\mathbf{x}^T\mathbf{A}\mathbf{x} = \text{tr}\left[\mathbf{A}\mathbf{x}\mathbf{x}^T\right]$$

Proof Let **M** be an orthogonal matrix chosen to diagonalize **A**. Then $\mathbf{M}^T\mathbf{M} = \mathbf{I}$, $\mathbf{M}^T = \mathbf{M}^{-1}$, and

$$\mathbf{B} = \mathbf{M}^{-1}\mathbf{A}\mathbf{M}$$

where **B** is a diagonal matrix, a similarity transformation of **A**. The trace of a matrix is invariant under a similarity transformation. Under the orthogonal coordinate transformation defined by $\mathbf{M}^T$, let

$$\mathbf{y} = \mathbf{M}^T\mathbf{x}$$

Then

$$\text{tr}\left[\mathbf{A}\mathbf{x}\mathbf{x}^T\right] = \text{tr}\left[\mathbf{M}^T\mathbf{A}\mathbf{x}\mathbf{x}^T\mathbf{M}\right]$$

$$= \text{tr}\left[\mathbf{M}^T\mathbf{A}\mathbf{M}\mathbf{M}^T\mathbf{x}\mathbf{x}^T\mathbf{M}\right]$$

$$= \text{tr}\left[\mathbf{B}\mathbf{y}\mathbf{y}^T\right]$$

But **B** is diagonal, so the last term is easily seen to be

$$\text{tr}\left[\mathbf{B}\mathbf{y}\mathbf{y}^T\right] = \mathbf{y}^T\mathbf{B}\mathbf{y}$$

Finally, because

$$\mathbf{y}^T\mathbf{B}\mathbf{y} = \mathbf{x}^T\mathbf{A}\mathbf{x}$$

the theorem is proved. □

[†]The notation tr[**A**] denotes the *trace* of the matrix **A** defined to be the sum of the diagonal elements of **A**.

☐ **Theorem 7.2.8** Let $q_0(\mathbf{y})$ and $q_i(\mathbf{y})$ be multivariate gaussian distributions of dimension n, with means $\mathbf{y}_0$ and $\mathbf{y}_1$ and covariance matrices $\boldsymbol{\Sigma}_0$ and $\boldsymbol{\Sigma}_1$. Then

$$L(\mathbf{q}_0;\mathbf{q}_1) = \frac{1}{2}\,\mathrm{tr}\,\boldsymbol{\Sigma}_1^{-1}[\boldsymbol{\Sigma}_0 - \boldsymbol{\Sigma}_1 + (\mathbf{y}_0 - \mathbf{y}_1)(\mathbf{y}_0 - \mathbf{y}_1)^T] + \frac{1}{2}\log\frac{|\boldsymbol{\Sigma}_1|}{|\boldsymbol{\Sigma}_0|}$$

Proof

$$L(\mathbf{q}_0;\mathbf{q}_1) = \int q_0(\mathbf{y})\log\frac{q_0(\mathbf{y})}{q_1(\mathbf{y})}\,d\mathbf{y}$$

$$= \int q_0(\mathbf{y})\left[\frac{1}{2}\log\frac{|\boldsymbol{\Sigma}_1|}{|\boldsymbol{\Sigma}_0|} + \frac{1}{2}(\mathbf{y} - \mathbf{y}_1)^T\boldsymbol{\Sigma}_1^{-1}(\mathbf{y} - \mathbf{y}_1)\right.$$

$$\left. - \frac{1}{2}(\mathbf{y} - \mathbf{y}_0)^T\boldsymbol{\Sigma}_0^{-1}(\mathbf{y} - \mathbf{y}_0)\right]d\mathbf{y}$$

Now make use of Theorem 7.2.7 so that

$$L(\mathbf{q}_0;\mathbf{q}_1) = \frac{1}{2}\log\frac{|\boldsymbol{\Sigma}_1|}{|\boldsymbol{\Sigma}_0|} + \frac{1}{2}\,\mathrm{tr}\int q_0(\mathbf{y})$$

$$\times\,[\boldsymbol{\Sigma}_1^{-1}(\mathbf{y} - \mathbf{y}_1)(\mathbf{y} - \mathbf{y}_1)^T - \boldsymbol{\Sigma}_0^{-1}(\mathbf{y} - \mathbf{y}_0)(\mathbf{y} - \mathbf{y}_0)^T]\,d\mathbf{y}$$

Because $E[(\mathbf{y} - \mathbf{y}_0)(\mathbf{y} - \mathbf{y}_0)^T] = \boldsymbol{\Sigma}_0$ and $E[(\mathbf{y} - \mathbf{y}_0)] = \mathbf{0}$, the equation

$$(\mathbf{y} - \mathbf{y}_1)(\mathbf{y} - \mathbf{y}_1)^T = (\mathbf{y} - \mathbf{y}_0)(\mathbf{y} - \mathbf{y}_0)^T + (\mathbf{y}_0 - \mathbf{y}_1)(\mathbf{y} - \mathbf{y}_0)^T$$

$$+ (\mathbf{y} - \mathbf{y}_0)(\mathbf{y}_0 - \mathbf{y}_1)^T + (\mathbf{y}_0 - \mathbf{y}_1)(\mathbf{y}_0 - \mathbf{y}_1)^T$$

then completes the proof of the theorem. ☐

For univariate gaussian distributions, the theorem reduces to

$$L(q_0;q_1) = \frac{1}{2\sigma_1^2}[\sigma_0^2 - \sigma_1^2 + (y_0 - y_1)^2] + \log\frac{\sigma_1}{\sigma_0}$$

☐ **Theorem 7.2.9** Let $\mathbf{q}$ be a multivariate gaussian distribution of dimension n, with arbitrary mean and with covariance matrix $\boldsymbol{\Sigma}$. Then

$$H(\mathbf{q}) = \frac{1}{2}\log\left[(2\pi e)^n|\boldsymbol{\Sigma}|\right]$$

Proof It suffices to prove the theorem for the case in which the mean is equal to zero:

$$H(\mathbf{q}) = -\int q(\mathbf{y})\log q(\mathbf{y})\,d\mathbf{y}$$

$$= \int q(\mathbf{y})\left[\frac{1}{2}\log(2\pi)^n|\boldsymbol{\Sigma}| + \frac{1}{2}\mathbf{y}^T\boldsymbol{\Sigma}^{-1}\mathbf{y}\right]d\mathbf{y}$$

By Theorem 7.2.7,

$$H(\mathbf{q}) = \frac{1}{2}\log (2\pi)^n |\mathbf{\Sigma}| + \frac{1}{2}\mathrm{tr}\left[\int q(\mathbf{y})\mathbf{\Sigma}^{-1}\mathbf{y}\mathbf{y}^T\,d\mathbf{y}\right]$$

Then, because $E[\mathbf{y}\mathbf{y}^T] = \mathbf{\Sigma}$,

$$H(\mathbf{q}) = \frac{1}{2}\log (2\pi)^n |\mathbf{\Sigma}| + \frac{n}{2}$$

which completes the proof of the theorem.   □

7.3 GAUSSIAN CHANNELS AND SOURCES WITHOUT MEMORY

To calculate the capacity of a channel can be a difficult task requiring numerical methods, but the important case of an additive gaussian-noise channel subject to an average power constraint can be solved analytically. Likewise, the content at distortion D of a memoryless gaussian source under a quadratic distortion measure can be obtained in closed form. We start out computing these, then repeat the analysis for gaussian channels and sources with memory. Later in the chapter we shall study gaussian waveform channels and gaussian waveform sources.

A continuous channel always has some constraint on the input probability distribution; otherwise the channel input could be any number on the infinite real line. This would be a physically (and mathematically) unreasonable situation. Therefore $p(x)$ must satisfy at least one constraint equation of the form

$$\int_{-\infty}^{\infty} e(x)p(x)\,dx \le S$$

where $e(x)$ is a nonnegative cost schedule. The most common constraint is the average power constraint, which uses a quadratic cost schedule $e(x) = x^2$ so that

$$\int_{-\infty}^{\infty} x^2 p(x)\,dx \le S$$

The average value of the input x^2 is called the *average input power*.

The capacity of the continuous channel is the maximum value of the average mutual information over all probability distributions on the input alphabet consistent with the constraints

$$C = \max_{p(x)} I(X; Y)$$

$$= \max_{p(x)} \int_{-\infty}^{\infty} p(x) \int_{-\infty}^{\infty} Q(y|x) \log \frac{Q(y|x)}{\int_{-\infty}^{\infty} p(x)Q(y|x)\,dx}\,dy\,dx$$

where the maximum[†] is taken over the set of probability distributions that satisfy the specified constraints.

□ **Theorem 7.3.1**   A discrete-time memoryless channel with additive gaussian noise and quadratic constraint has capacity

$$C(S) = \frac{1}{2} \log \left(1 + \frac{S}{N} \right)$$

where S is the input power constraint and N is the channel noise variance.

Proof   The additive gaussian-noise channel is described by $Y = X + Z$ where Z is gaussian.

By Theorem 7.2.3, for any input distribution the gaussian channel with input X and output Y has mutual information given by

$$I(X; Y) = H(Y) - H(Z)$$

The differential entropy $H(Y)$ is to be maximized by choice of probability distribution on X subject to the constraint $\operatorname{var}(Y) = \operatorname{var}(X) + \operatorname{var}(Z) \leq S + N$. But $H(Y)$ is maximized if Y is gaussian with variance $S + N$, and this occurs if and only if X is gaussian with variance S. Hence

$$H(Y) = \frac{1}{2} \log \left[2\pi e(S + N) \right]$$

$$H(Z) = \frac{1}{2} \log (2\pi e N)$$

and

$$C = \frac{1}{2} \log \frac{S + N}{N} \qquad\qquad\qquad\qquad □$$

Of all channels with additive noise of average noise power N, the channel with the smallest capacity is the one whose additive noise is zero mean and gaussian. That is shown by the following theorem.

[†]The maximum need not exist, so to be precise we should use the supremum in place of the maximum.

☐ **Theorem 7.3.2** Let $Y = X + Z$ denote a discrete-time additive-noise channel where Z has average noise power N, and let $C(S)$ be the capacity-cost function of the channel under a quadratic power constraint. Then

$$C(S) \geq \frac{1}{2} \log\left(1 + \frac{S}{N}\right)$$

with strict inequality unless Z is zero mean and gaussian.

Proof Let $Y = X + Z'$ describe a second additive-noise channel, where Z' is now gaussian of zero mean and variance N, and let $C'(S)$ be the capacity-cost function of the gaussian channel under the same power constraint. Let p' be the gaussian density achieving $C'(S)$. Then, because p' must satisfy the constraint on average power,

$$C(S) = \max I(p; Q)$$

$$\geq I(p'; Q)$$

By Theorem 7.2.5, because p' is gaussian,

$$I(p'; Q) \geq I(p'; Q')$$

where Q and Q' are the probability density functions of Z and Z'. Consequently,

$$C(S) \geq I(p'; Q') = C'(S)$$

and the theorem is proved. ☐

If a channel has additive but nongaussian noise and a power constraint, then the capacity may be difficult to calculate exactly. However, upper and lower bounds on the capacity are easy to obtain as a corollary to the previous theorem.

☐ **Corollary 7.3.3** For a discrete-time, additive-noise channel, the capacity-cost function is bounded by the inequalities

$$\frac{1}{2} \log \frac{S + N}{N_e} \geq C(S) \geq \frac{1}{2} \log \frac{S + N}{N}$$

where S is the average transmitted power, N is the average noise power, and

$$N_e = \frac{1}{2\pi e} e^{2H(Z)}$$

Proof The upper bound on the right side is given by Theorem 7.3.2. The lower bound on the left side can be obtained using $1/2 \log [2\pi e(S + N)]$

as an upper bound on $H(Y)$. Then for any X having variance S,

$$I(X;Y) = H(Y) - H(Z)$$

$$\leq \frac{1}{2}\log\left[2\pi e(S + N)\right] - \frac{1}{2}\log\left[2\pi e N_e\right]$$

The maximum of $I(X;Y)$ over all X of variance S must also satisfy this bound. □

The term N_e appearing in Corollary 7.3.3 is known as the *entropy power*. Section 7.10 studies the entropy power in detail. An inequality known as the *entropy-power inequality* is developed in that section, from which the inequalities

$$\frac{1}{2}\log_2\frac{S + N}{N_e} \geq C(S) \geq \frac{1}{2}\log_2\frac{S + N_e}{N_e}$$

can be derived as an improvement to Corollary 7.3.3

Suppose we have two parallel channels, both of them additive gaussian-noise channels with independent noise but not necessarily with the same noise power. How should the total available signal power S be apportioned between the two channels? It is obvious that half the signal power should be used with each channel if the noise powers are equal. The following theorem says that for the general case the power should be distributed over L channels in such a way that $S_l + N_l = \theta$ for $l = 1, \ldots, L$, where θ is a constant and $S = \Sigma_l S_l$, but with the exception that S_l cannot be negative. Figure 7.1 illustrates the idea of the

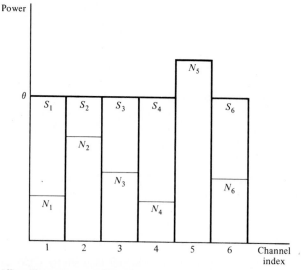

Figure 7.1   Allocating power to channels.

theorem. The fifth subchannel in that figure is so noisy that it is given no power and it carries no information. If the total power S is increased, then the level θ is raised. Eventually, if S is made large enough, there will be nonzero power in the fifth subchannel.

The wording of the following theorem gives the capacity implicitly in terms of the parameter θ. To apply the theorem at fixed S, one must try various values of the parameter θ until one gets the desired value of S.

□ **Theorem 7.3.4** Given a set of parallel, discrete-time, memoryless, additive gaussian-noise channels with independent noises having variance N_l for $l = 1, \ldots, L$, let the channel inputs be constrained to have a total average power of S:

$$\sum_{l=1}^{L} E[X_l^2] \leq S$$

The capacity of the set of parallel channels is

$$C(S) = \sum_{l=1}^{L} \frac{1}{2} \log\left(1 + \frac{S_l}{N_l}\right)$$

and is achieved with inputs being independent, zero mean, gaussian random variables having variances S_l for $l = 1, \ldots, L$, where the S_l satisfy

$$S_l = \max\left[0, \theta - N_l\right]$$

for θ such that $\Sigma_l S_l = S$.

Proof The capacity is the maximum of $I(X^L; Y^L)$ where $X^L = (X_1, \ldots, X_L)$ and $Y^L = (Y_1, \ldots, Y_L)$. But by Theorem 5.2.1,

$$I(X^L; Y^L) \leq \sum_{l=1}^{L} I(X_l; Y_l)$$

with equality if and only if the inputs are independent. To maximize $I(X^L; Y^L)$, we must choose the inputs to be independent because this choice can be made without constraining the individual terms $I(X_l; Y_l)$.

Next, by using Corollary 7.3.3 we see that

$$I(X_l; Y_l) \leq \frac{1}{2} \log\left(1 + \frac{S_l}{N_l}\right)$$

with equality if and only if X_l is of zero mean and is gaussian. So whatever the value of S_l, we should choose X_l to be gaussian of zero mean and variance S_l. Hence

$$C = \sum_{l=1}^{L} \frac{1}{2} \log\left(1 + \frac{S_l}{N_l}\right)$$

All that remains is to choose the nonnegative numbers S_l for $l = 1, \ldots, L$ such that $\Sigma_l S_l = S$ and C is maximized. This is a problem of maximizing a concave function subject to a constraint, and the Kuhn-Tucker theorem applies. Taking partial derivatives gives

$$\frac{1}{2(S_l + N_l)} \leq \lambda$$

with equality if S_l is nonzero, where λ is a Lagrange multiplier. Choose $\lambda = 1/(2\theta)$, and the proof is complete. □

The theorem can be interpreted in terms of the graph $C^{(l)}(S_l)$ of the lth subchannel. Graphically the point on the $C(S)$ curve having slope s is computed by finding the point on each $C^{(l)}(S_l)$ having slope s. This is the point satisfying

$$\frac{dC^{(l)}(S_l)}{dS_l} = \frac{1}{2} \frac{1}{N_l + S_l}$$

$$= \frac{1}{2\theta}$$

so $s = (2\theta)^{-1}$. If it has no point of slope s, the lth subchannel is not used. Then add all abscissas of points with slope s and add all ordinates of points with slope s to obtain $C(S)$.

Now we turn attention to gaussian sources. The information content of a gaussian source is described by the source-distortion function $B(D)$. This function is a little harder to derive than the capacity-cost function for a gaussian channel. In both cases we have a mutual information $I(p;Q)$ relating X and Y. In the problem of finding the capacity, we are given that $Y = X + Z$ for some Z independent of X. In the source problem, we are not restricted to this form. There might be a more complicated relationship between Y and X. However, among the candidate channels are those of the additive form $Y = aX + Z$ where Z is independent of X. They can be used to give an upper bound. It is an upper bound for any source.

□   **Theorem 7.3.5**   Under the quadratic distortion measure

$$E[X - Y]^2 \leq D$$

a continuous memoryless source with variance σ^2 has information content at distortion D satisfying the inequality

$$B(D) \leq \frac{1}{2} \log \frac{\sigma^2}{D} \qquad 0 \leq D \leq \sigma^2$$

Proof   By definition

$$B(D) = \min_{Q \in \mathcal{Q}_D} I(p;Q)$$

where the test channel Q is in the set

$$\mathcal{Q}_D = \left\{ Q(y|x) \colon \iint p(x)Q(y|x)(x-y)^2 \, dx \, dy \le D \right\}$$

We can obtain an upper bound on $B(D)$ by choosing any test channel from $\mathcal{Q}_D$. We choose an additive noise channel of the form

$$Y = aX + Z$$

where Z is an independent, zero-mean, gaussian-noise process with $E[Z]^2 = aD$. We choose the constant a so that $E[X - Y]^2 = D$. The distortion is

$$D = E[X - Y]^2$$

$$= E[(1 - a)X]^2 + E[Z]^2$$

$$= (1 - a)^2 \sigma^2 + aD$$

which is satisfied by choosing

$$a = 1 - \frac{D}{\sigma^2}$$

Therefore

$$B(D) \le I(p;Q)$$

$$= H(Y) - H(Y|X)$$

$$= H(Y) - H(Z)$$

$$= H(Y) - \frac{1}{2} \log (2\pi e a D)$$

The variance of Y is

$$E[Y^2] = E[a^2 X^2] + E[Z^2]$$

$$= a^2 \sigma^2 + aD$$

$$= \sigma^2 - D$$

so we can bound $H(Y)$ as

$$H(Y) \le \frac{1}{2} \log \left[2\pi e (\sigma^2 - D) \right]$$

Accordingly,

$$B(D) \le \frac{1}{2} \log \left[2\pi e (\sigma^2 - D) \right] - \frac{1}{2} \log (2\pi e a D)$$

$$= \frac{1}{2} \log \frac{\sigma^2 - D}{aD}$$

$$= \frac{1}{2} \log \frac{\sigma^2}{D}$$

which completes the proof of the theorem. $\square$

Before giving the lower bound for a gaussian source, we give an alternative representation of $B(D)$ valid for any continuous source. This is the continuous alphabet version of Theorem 6.3.9, which was proved previously for discrete sources.

☐ **Theorem 7.3.6** For any continuous source, $B(D)$ can be expressed as follows:

$$B(D) = \max_{s \le 0} \max_{\lambda \in \Lambda_s} \left[sD + \int_{-\infty}^{\infty} p(x) \log \lambda(x) \, dx \right]$$

where

$$\Lambda_s = \left\{ \lambda(x) : \lambda(x) \ge 0, \int_{-\infty}^{\infty} p(x)\lambda(x)e^{s\rho(x,y)} \, dx \le 1 \right\}$$

Proof The proof is the same as the proof of Theorem 6.3.9.   ☐

☐ **Theorem 7.3.7** Under the quadratic distortion measure, a continuous memoryless gaussian source with variance σ^2 has information content at distortion D given by

$$B(D) = \frac{1}{2} \log \frac{\sigma^2}{D} \qquad 0 \le D \le \sigma^2$$

Proof By Theorem 7.3.5,

$$B(D) \le \frac{1}{2} \log \frac{\sigma^2}{D}$$

so we need only prove the inequality in the other direction.

We will apply Theorem 7.3.6 to get an inequality. Choose

$$\lambda(x) = \frac{K}{p(x)}$$

for some K not depending on x. The requirement that $\lambda(x)$ be an element of Λ_s simplifies to

$$K \int_{-\infty}^{\infty} e^{s(x-y)^2} \, dx \le 1$$

or, with a change in the variable of integration,

$$K \int_{-\infty}^{\infty} e^{sz^2} \, dz \le 1$$

Evaluating the definite integral gives

$$K = \sqrt{\frac{-s}{\pi}}$$

With this value for K, the inequality is satisfied with equality. Then, by Theorem 7.3.6,

$$B(D) \geq sD + \int_{-\infty}^{\infty} p(x) \log \lambda(x) \, dx$$

$$= sD + \int_{-\infty}^{\infty} p(x) \log \frac{\sqrt{-s/\pi}}{p(x)} \, dx$$

$$= sD + \frac{1}{2} \log \left(\frac{-s}{\pi} \right) + \frac{1}{2} \log (2\pi e \sigma^2)$$

Finally, choose $s = -(2D)^{-1}$ to get

$$B(D) \geq \frac{1}{2} \log \frac{\sigma^2}{D}$$

which completes the proof of the theorem. □

Suppose we have two independent sources, each gaussian and memoryless, and a distortion measure defined as the sum of the quadratic distortion in reproducing each of the two source outputs. If the two gaussian sources have the same variance, it is apparent that half of the total distortion should be due to reproducing each source. The following theorem treats the general case of L independent gaussian sources with variance S_l for $l = 1, \ldots, L$.

□ **Theorem 7.3.8** Given a set of L discrete-time, memoryless gaussian sources with variance S_l for $l = 1, \ldots, L$, and the sum quadratic distortion measure

$$\sum_l E[X_l - Y_l]^2 \leq D$$

the source-distortion function is given by

$$B(D) = \sum_{l=1}^{L} \frac{1}{2} \log \frac{S_l}{D_l}$$

where

$$D_l = \min [\theta, S_l]$$

and the parameter θ is such that

$$\sum_{l=1}^{L} D_l = D$$

Proof The proof is analogous to the proof of Theorem 7.3.4. □

7.4 GAUSSIAN CHANNELS AND SOURCES WITH MEMORY

Now we will introduce channels and sources with memory. These can be defined quite generally, but we will only pursue the study of those channels and sources that can be described in terms of a gaussian process with a Markov memory structure.

We begin with the channel capacity. Consider the channel used with input blocks of length n. We think of the channel at the block level as a new channel whose inputs are blocks of length n of the original channel input, and we ignore the memory from block to block. The block channel has an average power constraint of nS and has a capacity of $C_n(nS)$ bits per block. The (per-letter) capacity of the original channel is defined as follows.

☐ **Definition 7.4.1**   Let $Q(\mathbf{y}|\mathbf{x}) = Q(y_1, \ldots, y_n | x_1, \ldots, x_n)$ be the probability of block output $(y_1, \ldots, y_n)$, given block input $(x_1, \ldots, x_n)$, of a discrete-time stationary channel and let $e(x)$ be a cost schedule on the channel inputs. Then the capacity-cost function of the channel is

$$C(S) = \lim_{n \to \infty} \frac{1}{n} C_n(nS)$$

where $C_n(S)$ is the capacity-cost function defined on blocks of length n.   ☐

We will determine the capacity-cost function for a discrete-time gaussian-additive-noise channel with memory.

☐ **Theorem 7.4.2**   Let a discrete-time channel with quadratic cost schedule be corrupted by additive gaussian noise of power spectral density

$$N(f) = \sum_{k=-\infty}^{\infty} \Phi_k e^{-j2\pi k f}$$

Then the capacity-cost function has the parametric representation

$$C(S_\theta) = \frac{1}{2} \int_{-1/2}^{1/2} \max\left[0, \log \frac{\theta}{N(f)}\right] df$$

$$S_\theta = \int_{-1/2}^{1/2} \max\left[0, \theta - N(f)\right] df$$

Proof   The proof will make use of the discrete-time Toeplitz distribution theorem, which is given in Appendix C. Take any finite blocklength n and consider the noise correlation matrix $\mathbf{\Sigma}$:

$$\mathbf{\Sigma} = E[z_i z_j]$$

$$= \phi_{i-j}$$

Because it is symmetric, $\boldsymbol{\Sigma}$ can be diagonalized by an orthonormal coordinate transformation. The maximization problem defining the capacity is unaffected by the transformation for two reasons. The transformation is invertible so it preserves mutual information, and the quadratic constraint is unaffected under an orthonormal transformation.

In the new coordinate system, the new correlation matrix is $\mathbf{M}^T\boldsymbol{\Sigma}\mathbf{M}$ for some orthogonal matrix $\mathbf{M}$. The new correlation matrix is diagonal, so that the n new coordinates form n independent, but not identical, channels. The kth channel has noise power equal to λ_k, the kth eigenvalue of $\boldsymbol{\Sigma}$. We can compute the capacity-cost function for each of these channels. The capacity-cost function for the total collection of n channels then can be found in terms of a parameter θ using Theorem 7.3.4. Then the input power normalized to a single input symbol is

$$S(\theta) = n^{-1} \sum_l \max \left[0, \theta - N_l\right]$$

and the normalized per-letter capacity is

$$C_n(S(\theta)) = n^{-1} \sum_l \max \left[0, \frac{1}{2}\log\left(1 + \frac{S_l}{N_l}\right)\right]$$

$$= n^{-1} \sum_l \max \left[0, \frac{1}{2}\log \frac{\theta}{N_l}\right]$$

where $S_l = \theta - N_l$.

Finally, to complete the proof of the theorem, let $n \to \infty$ and apply the Toeplitz distribution theorem (given as Theorem C.2 of Appendix C). The Toeplitz distribution theorem says that in the limit as $n \to \infty$, the sums can be replaced by integrals, as in the statement of the theorem.   □

Now we turn to discrete-time gaussian sources with memory. The development of $B(D)$ for this problem closely follows the development of $C(S)$.

□ **Definition 7.4.3**   Let $p(\mathbf{x}) = p(x_1, \ldots, x_n)$ be the probability of a discrete-time stationary source producing block $\mathbf{x}$ and let ρ_{jk} be a single-letter distortion measure. Then the per-letter information content of the source with distortion D is

$$B(D) = \lim_{n \to \infty} \frac{1}{n} B_n(nD)$$

where $B_n(D)$ is the information content of a sourceword of blocklength n under distortion D. This limit always exists so that $B(D)$ is well defined.   □

☐   **Theorem 7.4.4**   Suppose a discrete-time gaussian source has a power spectral density given by

$$S(f) = \sum_{k=-\infty}^{\infty} \phi_k e^{-j2\pi kf}$$

Then the information content of the source with respect to a quadratic distortion measure has the following parametric representation:

$$B(D(\theta)) = \frac{1}{2} \int_{-1/2}^{1/2} \max\left[0, \log \frac{S(f)}{\theta}\right] df$$

$$D(\theta) = \int_{-1/2}^{1/2} \min\left[\theta, S(f)\right] df$$

Proof   As in the proof of Theorem 7.4.2, we will make use of the discrete-time Toeplitz distribution theorem. Take any finite blocklength n and consider the correlation matrix of the source output $\Sigma = E[x_i x_j]$. Because it is symmetric, Σ can be diagonalized by an orthonormal coordinate transformation. The quadratic distortion measure is unaffected by an orthonormal coordinate transformation, and the coordinate transformation is invertible so it preserves mutual information. Therefore the minimization problem defining the source-distortion function is unaffected under the coordinate transformation. In the new coordinate system, we have a set of n independent sources for which Theorem 7.3.8 can be applied. The remainder of the proof follows the ideas of the proof of Theorem 7.4.2.   ☐

7.5 THE SAMPLING THEOREM

Next we will want to study waveform channels and sources, which are defined on continuous time. Before studying these, we need to develop the sampling theorem. The sampling theorem provides a link between continuous-time signals and discrete-time signals. It provides the connection portrayed in Fig. 7.2 between waveform sources and channels, which use continuous-time

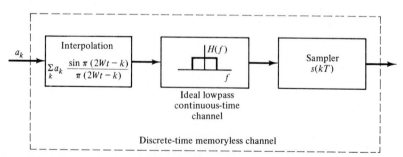

Figure 7.2   Discretizing a continuous-time channel.

functions of finite bandwidth, and continuous sources and channels, which use discrete-time sequences of real or complex numbers. The sampling theorem states that if a function of time $s(t)$ has Fourier transform $S(f) = 0$ for $|f|$ larger than W hertz, then it is completely determined by giving the value of the function at a series of points spaced $1/2W$ seconds apart. The values $s_k = s(k/2W)$ are called the *samples* of $s(t)$. The sampling rate of $2W$ samples per second is called the *Nyquist rate*.

☐ **Theorem 7.5.1   (Sampling theorem)** If $S(f) = 0$ for $|f|$ greater than W hertz, then $s(t)$ can be recovered from its samples by the *Nyquist-Shannon interpolation formula*:

$$s(t) = \sum_{k=-\infty}^{\infty} s\left(\frac{k}{2W}\right) \frac{\sin \pi(2Wt - k)}{\pi(2Wt - k)}$$

Further, if s_k is any sequence of real numbers, and

$$s(t) = \sum_{k=-\infty}^{\infty} s_k \frac{\sin \pi(2Wt - k)}{\pi(2Wt - k)}$$

then $S(f) = 0$ for $|f| > W$ hertz.

Proof The second statement of the theorem follows from the properties of the Fourier transform and from the fact that the Fourier transform of $\sin(2Wt)/(2Wt)$ equals zero for $|f|$ larger than W.

The first step in proving the first statement is to verify that $s(t)$ given by the Nyquist-Shannon formula does indeed have the correct samples. The second step is to show that there is only one function $s(t)$ satisfying the constraint on the spectrum that has the given set of samples. Let $T = 1/(2W)$. Then

$$s(k'T) = \sum_{k=-\infty}^{\infty} s(kT) \frac{\sin 2\pi W(k' - k)T}{2\pi W(k' - k)T}$$

$$= \sum_{k=-\infty}^{\infty} s(kT)\delta_{k'k}$$

where $\delta_{k'k} = 1$ when $k' = k$ and $\delta_{k'k} = 0$ otherwise. Hence

$$s(k'T) = s(k'T)$$

so the formula is consistent.

Now suppose that $s(t)$ and $s'(t)$ both satisfy the constraint on their Fourier transforms and have the same samples $s(kT) = s'(kT)$. We need to verify that $s(t) = s'(t)$. This we do by using the uniqueness of the Fourier series. Let $R(f) = S(f) - S'(f)$. Then

$$s(t) - s'(t) = \int_{-W}^{W} R(f)e^{j2\pi ft}\, df$$

But $R(f)$ is nonzero only in the interval $-W \leq f \leq W$. Therefore $R(f)$ can be expanded in a Fourier series with coefficients

$$r_{-k} = \int_{-W}^{W} R(f) e^{j2\pi fk/2W} \, df$$

$$= s(kT) - s'(kT)$$

$$= 0$$

Because the Fourier coefficients uniquely determine $R(f)$, this implies that $R(f) = 0$, and so $s(t) = s'(t)$. □

Next we show that if a gaussian-noise process with rectangular power spectrum

$$N(f) = \begin{cases} N_0/2 & |f| \leq W \\ 0 & \text{otherwise} \end{cases}$$

is sampled at the Nyquist rate, the samples are independent. This fact and the sampling theorem will be used in the next section to analyze a continuous-time channel by treating it as a discrete-time channel.

□ **Theorem 7.5.2**   The Nyquist samples of a gaussian-noise process with rectangular spectrum are independent gaussian random variables.

Proof   Let the gaussian process X have a rectangular power spectral density. This means that the autocorrelation function is the inverse Fourier transform of the power spectral density. Therefore

$$\phi(\tau) = \sigma^2 \frac{\sin 2\pi W}{2\pi W}$$

where $\sigma^2 = \text{var}(X)$. The correlation between Nyquist samples is

$$E[n_k n_{k'}] = \phi[(k - k')T]$$

$$= A \frac{\sin 2\pi W(k - k')T}{2\pi W(k - k')T}$$

which equals zero if $k \neq k'$. □

7.6 GAUSSIAN WAVEFORM CHANNELS AND SOURCES

A waveform channel is a channel whose inputs are functions on continuous time. A waveform channel with additive gaussian noise is shown in Fig. 7.3. This kind of channel arises repeatedly in the physical world, so the calculation of its capacity is of fundamental importance. Our interest in this section is in the calculation of the capacity and extends in later sections to an investigation of the implications for reliable communication. Gaussian waveform sources can be treated in an analogous way.

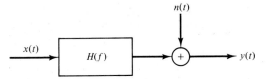

Figure 7.3   Filtered gaussian channel.

☐ **Definition 7.6.1**   The capacity-cost function in bits per second of a waveform channel corrupted by additive stationary noise is

$$C(S) = \lim_{T \to \infty} \frac{1}{T} C_T(TS)$$

where C_T is the capacity-cost function defined on an interval of length T.   ☐

The simplest example of a waveform channel is the channel with an ideal rectangular filter and white gaussian noise, as shown in Fig. 7.4. We can assume that the noise lies only within the band of the filter; noise outside this band can be filtered out. The output of this channel is completely described by sampling at the Nyquist rate, and any input can be formed from a discrete-time input by the Nyquist-Shannon interpolation formula. Consequently, because the Nyquist noise samples are independent, the channel is equivalent to a discrete-time channel with $2W$ samples per second. Hence, by Theorem 7.3.1 the capacity, in bits per second, is

$$C = W \log \left(1 + \frac{S}{N} \right)$$

for the ideal rectangular channel. To find the capacity of other additive-gaussian-noise channels will be more difficult.

The continuous-time channel needs to be constrained both in bandwidth and in transmitted power so that the model is physically meaningful. The bandwidth constraint is part of the channel and takes the form of a linear filter through which the signal passes. The power constraint is part of the transmitter. Except for its average power, the channel input signal is arbitrary, but only those frequency components that are in the passband of the filter will be seen at the output. To achieve channel capacity, the spectrum of the input signal must be somehow matched to the channel.

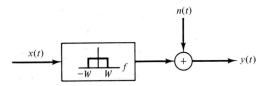

Figure 7.4   Ideal rectangular gaussian channel.

In analyzing the channel we are free to change it into any equivalent form that suits our purpose. Let $N(f)$ be the power spectral density of the additive gaussian noise. Let

$$N'(f) = \frac{N(f)}{|H(f)|^2}$$

Figure 7.4 shows a form of the channel with noise $n'(t)$ appearing before the filter. This form of the channel will be more convenient to analyze. It is equivalent, except at those frequencies where $H(f) = 0$. Because we will find that $S(f) = 0$ at such frequencies, this will not matter.

We want to express the waveform channel as an infinite sum of independent channels, and this requires us to decompose the channel using a Karhunen-Loeve expansion, as described in Appendix B. Consider a time interval of duration T running from $-T/2$ to $T/2$. Let $\psi_k^{(T)}(t)$ for $k = 1, \ldots,$ be the infinite collection of Karhunen-Loeve orthonormal expansion functions based on the noise autocorrelation function $\phi(\tau)$, which is the inverse Fourier transform of the power spectral density $N'(f)$. The functions $\psi_k^{(T)}(t)$ are the orthonormal eigenfunctions of the integral equation

$$\int_{-T/2}^{T/2} \phi'(t - s)\psi(s)\, ds = \lambda\psi(t) \qquad -T/2 \le t \le T/2$$

and $\phi'(\tau)$ is the autocorrelation function associated with the power spectral density $N'(f)$. Fortunately, there is never any need to actually compute the Karhunen-Loeve eigenfunctions. They will not appear in the final formulas that we will derive. Let λ_k for $k = 1, \ldots,$ be the eigenvalues associated with these eigenfunctions. Because the eigenfunctions are an orthonormal set, the noise can be written as the expansion

$$n'(t) = \sum_{k=1}^{\infty} n_k' \psi_k^{(T)}(t)$$

where the noise components n_k' are independent and gaussian. The input signal can be also represented in terms of the orthonormal expansion

$$s(t) = \sum_{k=1}^{\infty} s_k \psi_k^{(T)}(t)$$

In this way, over time interval T, the channel decomposes into an infinite set of discrete additive gaussian-noise channels. We know the capacity of each of these subchannels. It is given by applying to each subchannel the general formula

$$C(S) = \frac{1}{2}\log\left(1 + \frac{S}{N}\right)$$

replacing S and N with the signal power and noise power in the kth subchannel, respectively. By summing the subchannels, we can compute the capacity of the waveform channel on an interval of length T with average power constraint. Letting $T \to \infty$ then gives the capacity of the channel, as expressed in the following theorem.

□ **Theorem 7.6.2**   The capacity at cost S of a channel with additive gaussian noise of noise spectrum $N(f)$ and input filter $H(f)$ is given in terms of a parameter θ by the formulas

$$C(S) = \frac{1}{2} \int_{-\infty}^{\infty} \max\left[0, \log \frac{\theta}{N(f)/|H(f)|^2}\right] df$$

$$S = \int_{-\infty}^{\infty} \max\left[0, \theta - \frac{N(f)}{|H(f)|^2}\right] df$$

Proof Figure 7.5 shows the equivalent gaussian waveform channel with the noise at the input to the channel filter. The equivalent gaussian-noise process $n'(t)$ has power spectral density

$$N'(f) = \frac{N(f)}{|H(f)|^2}$$

and has autocorrelation function $\phi'(\tau)$ given by the inverse Fourier transform of $N'(f)$. Consider a finite time interval $[-T/2, T/2]$ and, by means of a Karhunen-Loeve expansion, represent the gaussian process $n'(t)$ and the input signal $s(t)$ in this interval as follows:

$$n'(t) = \sum_{k=1}^{\infty} n'_k \psi_k^{(T)}(t)$$

$$s(t) = \sum_{k=1}^{\infty} s_k \psi_k^{(T)}(t)$$

The expansion coefficients n'_k are independent gaussian random variables of variance λ_k. The waveform channel now has been decomposed into a countably infinite set of independent discrete gaussian channels. By Theorem 7.3.4, the capacity is

$$C_T(TS_\theta) = \sum_{k=1}^{\infty} \max\left[0, \frac{1}{2}\log \frac{\theta}{\lambda_k}\right]$$

$$TS_\theta = \sum_{k=1}^{\infty} \max[0, \theta - \lambda_k]$$

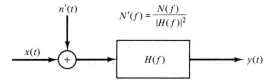

Figure 7.5   Equivalent channel.

Then by Definition 7.6.1,

$$C(S) = \lim_{T \to \infty} \frac{1}{T} \sum_{k=1}^{\infty} \max \left[0, \frac{1}{2} \log \frac{\theta}{\lambda_k} \right]$$

$$S = \lim_{T \to \infty} \frac{1}{T} \sum_{k=1}^{\infty} \max \left[0, \theta - \lambda_k \right]$$

Finally, let $T \to \infty$ and apply the second Toeplitz distribution theorem of Appendix C to complete the proof. □

This theorem can be interpreted in terms of a "water-pouring" picture. The equivalent noise spectrum at the input $N(f)/|H(f)|^2$ is plotted as in Fig. 7.6. For realistic channels, this will always take the shape of a bowl because as f goes to infinity, $|H(f)|^2$ goes to zero faster than $N(f)$ does. Water is imagined as poured into the "bowl" to level θ. The water then assumes the shape of the optimum transmission power spectrum. The integral of the "water" is the waveform power, and the integral of the logarithm of the "water" is the amount of information $C(S)$ that can be transmitted at this power.

For example, consider the class of channel filters of the form

$$|H(f)|^2 = \frac{1}{1 + (f/f_0)^{2n}}$$

Suppose the channel noise is additive gaussian noise with noise power spectral density equal to a constant. Specifically, let $N(f) = N_o/2$. Noise of this form with power spectral density equal to a constant is called *white noise*, with single-sided noise power spectral density equal to N_o (and often measured in

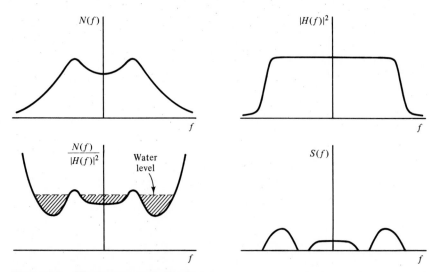

Figure 7.6   The "water-pouring" schema.

units of watts per hertz). For this example, the channel capacity is

$$C(S_\theta) = \frac{1}{2} \int_{-W}^{W} \log \frac{\theta}{(N_o/2)[1 + (f/f_o)^{2n}]} \, df$$

$$S_\theta = \int_{-W}^{W} \left\{ \theta - \frac{N_o}{2} \left[1 + \left(\frac{f}{f_o} \right)^{2n} \right] \right\} df$$

where W is the positive solution of

$$\frac{N_o}{2} \left[1 + \left(\frac{f}{f_o} \right)^{2n} \right] = \theta$$

These equations can be integrated numerically to obtain the graph of $C(S)$.

The case of the idealized baseband filter given by

$$H(f) = \begin{cases} 1 & |f| \leq W \\ 0 & |f| > W \end{cases}$$

with additive gaussian noise has a simple closed-form solution. This is Shannon's celebrated capacity formula, which we wrote down at the start of the section as a consequence of the sampling theorem. The next theorem derives it as a consequence of the water-pouring theorem.

□ **Theorem 7.6.3** The capacity of an ideal bandlimited channel of bandwidth W hertz that contains additive white gaussian noise of variance $N(= WN_o)$ in the band is given by

$$C(S) = W \log \left(1 + \frac{S}{N} \right)$$

Proof The formulas of Theorem 7.6.2 are easily evaluated to give

$$C(S_\theta) = W \log \frac{\theta}{N_o/2}$$

$$S_\theta = 2W \left(\theta - \frac{N_o}{2} \right)$$

Eliminating the parameter θ gives

$$C(S) = W \log \left(1 + \frac{S}{N} \right)$$

□

The same closed-form expression can be obtained for the idealized passband filter given by

$$H(f) = \begin{cases} 1 & f_o - \dfrac{W}{2} \leq |f| \leq f_o + \dfrac{W}{2} \\ 0 & \text{otherwise} \end{cases}$$

where f_o is a "center frequency" larger than $W/2$.

7.7 BIT ENERGY AND BIT-ERROR RATE

Whenever the decoder output is presented in the form of a bit stream, the probability of bit error is called the *bit-error rate*. We know that the bit-error rate can be made arbitrarily small at any data rate smaller than the channel capacity. In this section, we shall look more closely at the channel capacity, especially at how it depends on the transmitted energy per bit. The channel we study is the continuous-time additive-noise channel with gaussian white noise and an ideal rectangular filter.

The bit energy E_b is calculated from the message energy and the number of information bits in the message. Given a waveform $s(t)$ of finite length T representing K information bits, the energy in the message E_m is given by $E_m = \int_0^T s(t)^2 \, dt$ and the energy per bit E_b is given by

$$E_b = \frac{E_m}{K}$$

For an infinite-length message of rate R information bits per second, as would be used by a tree code, E_b is defined as

$$E_b = \frac{S}{R}$$

where S is the average power of the message.

The noise signal has a one-sided spectral density of N_o watts per hertz (joules). We wish to reformulate the capacity in terms of the ratio E_b/N_o. Our starting point for developing bounds on E_b/N_o is Theorem 7.6.3. The signal power is $S = E_b R$ and the noise power $N = N_o W$. Then Theorem 7.6.3 becomes

$$\frac{C}{W} = \log_2 \left(1 + \frac{RE_b}{N_o W} \right)$$

and

$$\frac{R}{W} < \frac{C}{W}$$

Define the spectral bit rate r (measured in bits per second per hertz) by

$$r = \frac{R}{W}$$

The spectral bit rate r and E_b/N_o are two important figures of merit of a digital communication system.

We now have

$$r < \log_2 \left(1 + r\frac{E_b}{N_o} \right)$$

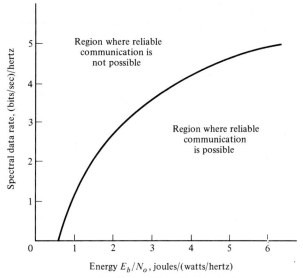

Figure 7.7 Capacity of a baseband gaussian-noise channel.

or

$$\frac{E_b}{N_o} > \frac{2^r - 1}{r}$$

The inequality is shown graphically in Fig. 7.7. Every digital communication system can be described by a point lying below the curve of Fig. 7.7, and for any point below the curve one can design a digital communication system that has as small a bit-error rate as one desires. The graph tells us that increasing the bit rate per unit bandwidth increases the required energy per bit. This is the basis of the energy/bandwidth trade of digital communication theory, where increasing bandwidth at a fixed information rate can reduce power requirements.

If bandwidth W is a plentiful resource, then E_b/N_o can be reduced by letting W go to infinity. This reduces the spectral bit rate r to zero, and we have the bound

$$\frac{E_b}{N_o} \geq \log_e 2 = 0.69$$

This is a fundamental limit.[†] The ratio E_b/N_o is not less than 0.69 for any "reliable" digital communication system in gaussian noise, and by using a sufficiently complex system one can communicate reliably with any E_b/N_o larger than 0.69.

[†]In units of decibels, this becomes the bound $E_b/N_o \geq -1.6$ db.

In many applications the spectral noise N_o arises through thermal effects. Thermodynamics may be used to deduce that, because of thermal noise, any receiver at absolute temperature T (in degrees kelvin) develops a noise density of kT watts per hertz, where k is Boltzmann's constant ($k = 1.38 \times 10^{-23}$ joules/degree). Therefore the energy needed to transmit a bit to a receiver at temperature T satisfies the bound

$$E_b \geq 0.69kT$$

This is a rather unusual result because it relates things that we don't expect to be related. It suggests a physical connection between the "soft" concept of information and the "hard" concepts of energy and temperature.

7.8 SIGNALING WITH A BANDWIDTH CONSTRAINT

When channel bandwidth is constrained, it becomes important to transmit with large spectral bit rate (measured in bits per second per hertz). We can conclude from Fig. 7.7 that this will require larger values of E_b/N_o.

A practical way to signal with a bandwidth constraint is to use the waveform channel as a discrete channel. A discrete-time continuous-amplitude channel can be created from the waveform channel by means of the sampling theorem. As was shown in Fig. 7.2, a discrete-time waveform is made into a continuous-time waveform at the channel input by using the Nyquist-Shannon interpolation formula. At the channel output, the continuous-time waveform is made into a discrete-time waveform by sampling.

The discrete-time channel can be converted in turn into a discrete-input channel by choosing a finite set of real numbers as the input alphabet of the channel. This set is called the *signaling alphabet* or the *signaling constellation*. Figure 7.8 shows some typical choices for the signaling alphabet. Each signaling alphabet is a set of 2^m real numbers. When a 2^m-ary signaling alphabet is used, each channel input symbol is assigned a unique m-bit binary label. Thus each channel input symbol is the equivalent of m code bits.

Even though the channel input is restricted to a finite set, the channel output need not be so restricted. If the channel is an additive gaussian-noise channel, the channel output is a real-valued random variable on the entire real line, conditional on the symbol transmitted. When c_j is the transmitted symbol, an output sample is the real number y with probability density function

$$Q(y|c_j) = \frac{1}{\sqrt{2\pi}\,\sigma} e^{-(y-c_j)^2/2\sigma^2}$$

It has a gaussian distribution conditioned on input symbol c_j.

A common option in using the channel is to incorporate at the channel output a demodulator that forms an estimate $\hat{c}_j$ of the transmitted symbol c_j, using only the single channel output sample y. The estimate $\hat{c}_j$ is then passed

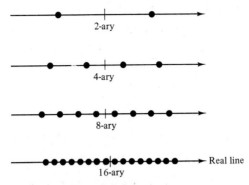

Figure 7.8   Some real-valued signaling alphabets.

to the decoder. This is called a *hard-decision* demodulator output. A second
option is to pass *y* as a real number directly to the decoder. This is called a *soft-decision* demodulator output.

To choose between ways of restricting the input and output of a channel
one can examine the channel capacity under the restriction. If the reduction in
channel capacity is negligible, then we may conclude that we have lost nothing
in restricting the channel input and output. In using this argument, however,
one must be wary of coding complexity. Codes needed to achieve a large
fraction of the capacity of the restricted channel may be more complex than
codes needed to achieve the same fraction of the capacity of the original
channel. By going to the restricted channel one may end up with a more
complex code.

The capacity of the additive gaussian-noise channel with restriction of the
channel input to points in a signaling constellation $\{c_j : j = 0, \ldots, J-1\}$, but
with no restrictions on the channel output, is given by the formula

$$C = \max_{\mathbf{p}} \sum_{j=0}^{J-1} p_j \int_{-\infty}^{\infty} Q(y|c_j) \log \frac{Q(y|c_j)}{\sum_i p_i Q(y|c_i)} \, dy$$

and the average transmitted power is

$$S = \sum_{j=0}^{J-1} p_j c_j^2$$

Before we think about evaluating the formula for capacity, let us think about
what it is we want to learn. The most straightforward calculation is to first
choose the c_j and then carry through the maximization on $\mathbf{p}$. But in many
applications we might wish to design the code in such a way that all symbols
are used equally often. In such a case, we would insist that $\mathbf{p}$ be the
equiprobable distribution. Then the capacity will depend only on the c_j. We
may wish to maximize the capacity over possible choices of the signaling

alphabet subject to the power constraint. Then the capacity becomes

$$C = \max_{\mathbf{c}} \sum_{j=0}^{J-1} \frac{1}{J} \int_{-\infty}^{\infty} Q(y|c_j) \log \frac{Q(y|c_j)}{J^{-1} \sum_i Q(y|c_i)} \, dy$$

given that

$$\sum_{j=0}^{J-1} \frac{1}{J} c_j^2 \le S$$

We will evaluate yet a simpler case, which corresponds to how one often wishes to use the channel. We take the signaling alphabet as given, and consisting of equally spaced real numbers. We also retain the constraint that the probability distribution is an equiprobable probability distribution. With these constraints, the capacity calculation becomes trivial because there is only one probability distribution in the set over which we are maximizing. There are no variables remaining. Thus

$$C = \sum_{j=0}^{J-1} \frac{1}{J} \int_{-\infty}^{\infty} Q(y|c_j) \log \frac{Q(y|c_j)}{\sum_i J^{-1} Q(y|c_i)} \, dy$$

$$= \sum_{j=0}^{J-1} \frac{1}{J} \int_{-\infty}^{\infty} \frac{1}{\sqrt{2\pi}\,\sigma} e^{-(y-c_j)^2/2\sigma^2} \log \frac{e^{-(y-c_j)^2/2\sigma^2}}{J^{-1} \sum_i e^{-(y-c_i)^2/2\sigma^2}}$$

In each term of the outer sum, replace y with $z\sigma + c_j$ and replace c_i with $c_i'\sigma$. Then, dropping the prime on c_j', the final formula becomes

$$C = \log J - \sum_j \frac{1}{J} \int_{-\infty}^{\infty} \frac{1}{\sqrt{2\pi}} e^{-z^2/2} \log \sum_i e^{-(c_j-c_i)^2/2} e^{-z(c_j-c_i)} \, dz$$

and, because $N = \sigma^2$,

$$\frac{S}{N} = \sum_j \frac{1}{J} c_j^2$$

where now c_j is normalized by the noise variance. To proceed further, we must employ numerical integration to evaluate C as a function of S/N for each choice of signaling constellation. The result of the computation is given in Fig. 7.9 for selected examples of signaling constellation. By inspection of this figure, we see, for example, that below 18 dB an 8-ary signaling constellation attains most of the capacity of the gaussian-noise channel.

When the channel is a complex gaussian-noise channel,[†] similar methods can be used. Now one chooses the signaling alphabet as a set of points in the

---

[†] A complex channel is a waveform channel whose inputs are complex functions of time. It arises as a convenient way of representing a passband channel—that is, a channel for which $H(f)$ is nonzero for an interval of frequencies not including the zero frequency.

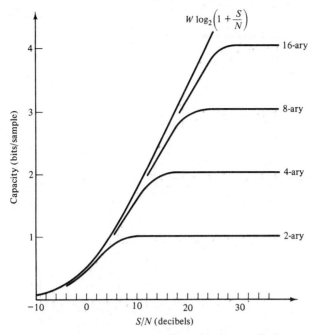

Figure 7.9   Channel capacity for some one-dimensional constellations.

complex plane. Figure 7.10 shows some possible choices for the signaling constellation. The signaling constellations with all points equidistant from the origin are called *PSK* (*phase-shift keyed*) *signaling constellations*. Now the channel input is a complex number c_j, and the channel output is a complex number that is a random variable conditional on the transmitted complex number. The output sample is the complex number y with probability density function:

$$p(y|c_j) = \frac{1}{2\pi\sigma^2} e^{-|y-c_j|^2/2\sigma^2}$$

under the usual model that the additive complex gaussian noise has independent and identically distributed real and imaginary components. Using this probability density function, the channel capacity can be expressed just as when the signaling constellation is real. Replace y with $z\sigma + c_j$, where z is complex with components u and v, and replace c_i with $c_i\sigma$. With the constraint that all points of the signaling constellation are used with equal probability, the capacity is

$$C = \log J - \sum_j \frac{1}{J} \int_{-\infty}^{\infty} \int_{-\infty}^{\infty} \frac{1}{2\pi} e^{-|z|^2/2} \log \sum_i e^{-|c_j-c_i|^2/2} e^{-\text{Re}[z^*(c_j-c_i)]} \, du \, dv$$

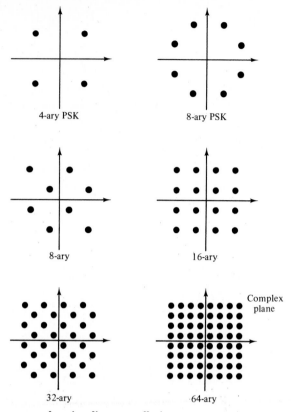

4-ary PSK

8-ary PSK

8-ary

16-ary

32-ary

64-ary

Complex plane

Figure 7.10   Some complex signaling constellations.

and, for the passband waveform,

$$\frac{S}{N} = \frac{1}{2} \sum_j \frac{1}{J} |c_j|^2$$

where c_j is the jth point of the signal constellation now normalized so that the noise variance is 1. Numerical integration of this equation provides the capacity curves shown in Fig. 7.11 for a variety of signaling constellations as portrayed in Fig. 7.10.

One may notice in Fig. 7.11 that the lower parts of the capacity curves for the PSK signaling constellations seem to be conspiring to define a single increasing curve; it might be called the "PSK limit". It is instructive to derive this asymptote. To do so, we must return to the original passband gaussian-noise channel. We will convert our description of the complex number x representing the input to the channel from rectangular coordinates to polar coordinates in proving the following theorem.

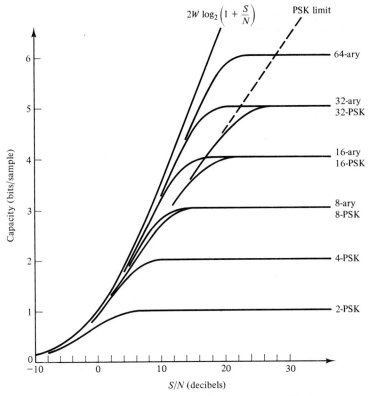

Figure 7.11 **Channel capacity for some two-dimensional constellations.**

□ **Theorem 7.8.1** As signal-to-noise ratio becomes large, the capacity (in bits per sample) of the discrete-time, complex gaussian channel with phase-only modulation approaches the asymptote

$$C = \log_2 \sqrt{\frac{4\pi}{e}\frac{S}{N}}$$

Proof The probability density of the complex output $z = u + iv$ when $\bar{z} = \bar{u} + i\bar{v}$ is transmitted is the two-dimensional gaussian distribution

$$Q(u,v|\bar{u},\bar{v}) = \frac{1}{2\pi\sigma^2}e^{-[(u-\bar{u})^2+(v-\bar{v})^2]/2\sigma^2}$$

To transform this equation into polar coordinates, make the change of variable:

$$\bar{u} = A\cos\theta \qquad \bar{v} = A\sin\theta$$

$$u = r\cos\phi \qquad v = r\sin\phi$$

With these substitutions, we obtain the probability density function in polar coordinates as

$$Q(r,\phi\,|\,A,\theta) = \frac{r}{2\pi\sigma^2}\,e^{-[(r-A)^2 - 2rA\cos(\theta-\phi) + 2rA]/2\sigma^2}$$

Next we temporarily introduce the difference coordinates

$$\rho = r - A$$

$$\alpha = \theta - \phi$$

and we make the assumption that the signal-to-noise ratio A^2/σ^2 is large so that α is small. Then we will make the approximation that $\cos\alpha = 1 - \alpha^2/2$. Now the probability density function in difference coordinates is

$$Q(\rho,\alpha\,|\,A,\theta) = \frac{A+\rho}{2\pi\sigma^2}\,e^{-[\rho^2 + (A^2 + A\rho)\alpha^2]/2\sigma^2}$$

The term ρ can be neglected in comparison with A when the signal-to-noise ratio is large. Then the right side can be factored so that

$$Q(\rho,\alpha\,|\,A,\theta) = \left(\frac{1}{\sqrt{2\pi}\,\sigma}\,e^{-\rho^2/2\sigma^2}\right)\left(\frac{A}{\sqrt{2\pi}\,\sigma}\,e^{-(A\alpha)^2/2\sigma^2}\right)$$

$$= p(\rho\,|\,A,\theta)p(\alpha\,|\,A,\theta)$$

The first term does not depend on θ, so when phase-only modulation is used and the signal-to-noise ratio is large, there is no information in the amplitude of the received signal. The capacity depends only on the second term. We conclude that we have a channel with probability density function

$$Q(\phi\,|\,\theta) = \frac{A}{\sqrt{2\pi}\,\sigma}\,e^{-A^2(\phi-\theta)^2/2\sigma^2}$$

The capacity is

$$C = \max_{p(\theta)}\int_0^{2\pi}\int_0^{2\pi} p(\theta)Q(\phi\,|\,\theta)\log\frac{Q(\phi\,|\,\theta)}{\displaystyle\int_0^{2\pi} p(\theta)Q(\phi\,|\,\theta)\,d\theta}\,d\phi\,d\theta$$

The variance is much less than 1 radian, so to compute one integral we can make the approximation

$$\int_0^{2\pi} p(\theta)Q(\phi\,|\,\theta)\,d\theta \approx \int_{-\infty}^{\infty} p(\theta)Q(\phi\,|\,\theta)\,d\theta$$

Even though θ is an angle, the integral on θ now has limits from $-\infty$ to ∞, which are convenient because we have approximated the probability density function using a gaussian density. We then have

$$\int_{-\infty}^{\infty} Q(\phi|\theta) \log Q(\phi|\theta) \, d\phi = -\frac{1}{2} \log\left(2\pi e \frac{\sigma^2}{A^2}\right)$$

which is independent of θ. Therefore $p(\theta)$ only affects the computation through the term

$$H = -\int\int p(\theta)Q(\phi|\theta) \log\left[\int p(\theta)Q(\phi|\theta) \, d\theta\right] d\theta \, d\phi$$

This is maximized if the argument of the logarithm is uniform on the interval $[0, 2\pi]$. We conclude that the maximizing $p(\theta)$ is uniform on $[0, 2\pi]$. Consequently,

$$C = -\log\frac{1}{2\pi} + \log\frac{A}{\sqrt{2\pi e}\,\sigma}$$

$$= \log\sqrt{\frac{2\pi}{e}}\frac{A}{\sigma}$$

Finally, the substitution

$$\frac{A}{\sigma} = \sqrt{2\frac{S}{N}}$$

completes the proof.   □

7.9 SIGNALING WITHOUT A BANDWIDTH CONSTRAINT

For an additive gaussian-noise channel with no bandwidth constraint, one can signal at any value of E_b/N_o satisfying the bound $E_b/N_o > 0.69$. In this section we shall introduce M-ary orthogonal signaling, which is known to be one way to signal with arbitrarily small probability of error at any value of E_b/N_o satisfying this bound.

An *M-ary orthogonal waveform alphabet* is a set of M functions $s_m(t)$ for $m = 0, \ldots, M - 1$ on the interval $[0, T]$ that are pairwise orthogonal

$$\int_0^T s_m(t)s_n(t) \, dt = 0$$

for $n \neq m$ and that have equal energy

$$\int_0^T s_m^2(t) \, dt = E_p$$

The energy per bit of an M-ary alphabet is

$$E_b = \frac{E_p}{\log_2 M}$$

An example of an M-ary orthogonal waveform alphabet is a set of M harmonically related sinusoids.

For convenience, we usually choose $M = 2^k$ for some k. The modulator maps each k-bit word at its input into one of the 2^k waveforms in the signaling alphabet. The demodulator compares the received signal in each signaling time interval with each of the 2^k possible transmitted waveforms and chooses the most likely. An M-ary demodulator is a device that forms an estimate $\hat{m}$ of the input to the modulator based on the noisy output of the waveform channel. It is an M-ary hypothesis tester.

There are a great many sets of M-ary orthogonal signaling alphabets that can be used when bandwidth is unconstrained. Because the modulator puts k bits into one waveform symbol, it can make E_p k times as large as E_b. Because the demodulator must make a 2^k-way decision rather than a binary decision, it needs more energy in the waveform to ensure a small error probability. It turns out that the additional energy needed grows more slowly with k than the additional energy available. The net effect is that the waveform can operate at a very low E_b/N_o but occupies a bandwidth much greater than the bit rate.

The probability of symbol error of M-ary signaling as a function of E_b/N_o is shown in Fig. 7.12. These curves were obtained by numerical integration. For large M, the probability of bit error is equal to approximately one-half of the probability of symbol error. The curves could be replotted for probability of bit error—the appearance would not change much.

Notice that the curves in Fig. 7.12 are moving left as M increases. One can show that the curves converge on the vertical line at -1.6 db as $M \to \infty$. We already know that they cannot go to the left of this vertical line. Because the curves converge to this vertical line, we can conclude that M-ary orthogonal signaling alphabets are asymptotically optimal in the absence of a bandwidth constraint.

7.10 THE ENTROPY-POWER INEQUALITY

We have seen in Corollary 7.3.3 that the capacity of a discrete-time, continuous-amplitude, additive-noise channel can be bounded using as a measure of the effective noise power a functional known as the *entropy power*, which will be studied in this section.

□ **Definition 7.10.1**   Given a continuous random variable X with differential entropy $H(X)$, the *entropy power* of X is

$$N_e = \frac{1}{2\pi e} e^{2H(X)} \qquad\qquad \square$$

The entropy power of a random variable X is the average noise power of a gaussian random variable having the same differential entropy as the random variable X. The entropy power of any noise is less than or equal to its actual

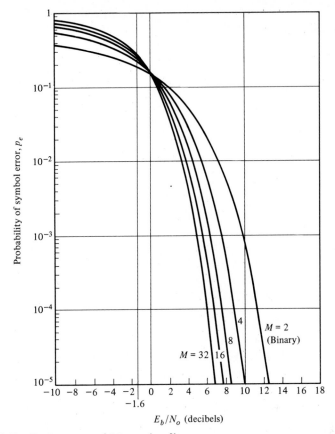

Figure 7.12   **Performance of M-ary signaling.**

noise power because gaussian noise has the maximum differential entropy of any noise of a given fixed average power.

The ratio of the entropy power of a random variable X to the variance of X is a measure of the efficiency of the random variable in producing uncertainty under a power constraint. This ratio is always less than 1, and equals 1 if and only if the noise is gaussian. Thus the "noisiest" form a noise waveform can take is the form of gaussian noise.

Whenever two independent random variables are added, the power in the sum is equal to the sum of the power in the two random variables. The differential entropy of the sum of the two, however, is generally not so simply stated. We know that the sum of two independent gaussian random variables is another gaussian random variable with variance equal to var (X) + var (Y). Consequently, for the gaussian case, because

$$\text{var}\,(X) = \frac{1}{2\pi e}\,e^{2H(X)}$$

and

$$\operatorname{var}(X + Y) = \operatorname{var}(X) + \operatorname{var}(Y)$$

we can write

$$e^{2H(X + Y)} = e^{2H(X)} + e^{2H(Y)}$$

as the desired relationship. When the noise is nongaussian, this becomes the inequality

$$e^{2H(X + Y)} \geq e^{2H(X)} + e^{2H(Y)}$$

which is known as the *entropy-power inequality*. It will be proved later as Theorem 7.10.4. This inequality says that the entropy power of the sum is always at least as large as the sum of the entropy powers of the two component noise signals, and is strictly larger than the sum unless both signals are gaussian. The entropy-power inequality has the flavor of a fundamental result but, with a few exceptions, its role in information theory so far has been as more of a curiosity than a useful tool.

The proof of the entropy-power inequality is surprisingly difficult and without general interest. Many readers will prefer to pass over the formal proof which, except for justifying several interchanges of integration and differentiation, is given in the remainder of this section.

The proof will be broken down into several steps which will be presented in the form of a sequence of lemmas. For the development of these lemmas, we use the notation[†]

$$K(X) = \int_{-\infty}^{\infty} \frac{1}{p(x)} \left[\frac{\partial p(x)}{\partial x} \right]^2 dx$$

$$= \int_{-\infty}^{\infty} p(x) \left[\frac{\partial}{\partial x} \log p(x) \right]^2 dx$$

for any random variable X with probability density function $p(x)$. This is well defined as long as $p(x)$ is everywhere nonzero and differentiable. In proving the entropy-power inequality, it is enough to consider only differentiable $p(x)$, because any probability density function can be approximated arbitrarily closely by a differentiable $p(x)$.

We will work with the mixture random variable $X_\tau = X + \sqrt{\tau}\, Z$, where X is any continuous random variable and Z is an independent gaussian random variable with variance 1. By adding $\sqrt{\tau}\, Z$ to X, we are mixing X with an independent gaussian random variable of variance τ. As we let τ increase, X becomes dominated by the gaussian random variable.

We can presume that, as a function of τ, the entropy power of X_τ can be sketched as in Fig. 7.13. The motivation for the sketch is that as τ becomes

---

[†]The function $K(X)$ is a form of the Fisher information to be defined in Section 8.2.

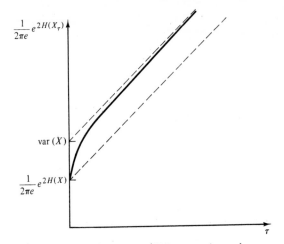

Figure 7.13   Entropy-power growth with additive gaussian noise.

large, X_τ will come to look like a gaussian random variable with variance

$$\text{var}(X_\tau) = \text{var}(X) + \tau$$

In the proof of Theorem 7.10.4, we will use the fact that the reciprocal $e^{-H(X_\tau)}$ is an integrable function of τ, but no other property of Fig. 7.13 is used.

☐   **Lemma 7.10.2   (de Bruijn's identity)** Let X be a continuous random variable with finite variance and probability density $p(x)$, and let Z be an independent gaussian random variable with unit variance. Then the differential entropy of the mixture $X + \sqrt{\tau}\, Z$ satisfies

$$\frac{dH(X + \sqrt{\tau}\, Z)}{d\tau} = \frac{1}{2} K(X + \sqrt{\tau}\, Z)$$

Proof   Let $Y = X + \sqrt{\tau}\, Z$. Suppose for the moment that $p(x)$ is strictly positive and differentiable with finite Fisher information. The probability density function for Y is

$$p_\tau(y) = \frac{1}{\sqrt{2\pi\tau}} \int_{-\infty}^{\infty} p(x) e^{-(y-x)^2/2\tau}\, dx$$

Differentiate $p_\tau(y)$ with respect to τ by differentiating under the integral sign with respect to τ:

$$\frac{\partial p_\tau(y)}{\partial \tau} = \frac{1}{\sqrt{2\pi\tau}} \int_{-\infty}^{\infty} \frac{(y-x)^2 - 1}{2\tau^2}\, p(x)\, e^{-(y-x)^2/2\tau}\, dx$$

which, except for a factor of $1/2$, is the same as would be obtained by twice differentiating $p_\tau(y)$ with respect to y. Therefore

$$\frac{\partial p_\tau(y)}{\partial \tau} = \frac{1}{2} \frac{\partial^2 p_\tau(y)}{\partial y^2}$$

This equation is called the *diffusion equation* in the theory of partial differential equations. It will be used in the manipulations that follow.

Now suppose that the differential entropy

$$H(Y) = -\int_{-\infty}^{\infty} p_\tau(y) \log p_\tau(y) \, dy$$

is finite and differentiate under the integral sign

$$\frac{dH(Y)}{d\tau} = -\int_{-\infty}^{\infty} \frac{\partial p_\tau(y)}{\partial \tau} \, dy - \int_{-\infty}^{\infty} \frac{\partial p_\tau(y)}{\partial \tau} \log p_\tau(y) \, dy$$

$$= -\frac{\partial}{\partial \tau} \int_{-\infty}^{\infty} p_\tau(y) \, dy - \frac{1}{2} \int_{-\infty}^{\infty} \frac{\partial^2 p_\tau(y)}{\partial y^2} \log p_\tau(y) \, dy$$

The first term on the right is zero and the second can be integrated by parts:

$$\frac{dH(Y)}{d\tau} = \frac{1}{2} \frac{\partial p_\tau(y)}{\partial y} \log p_\tau(y) \Big|_{-\infty}^{\infty} + \frac{1}{2} \int_{-\infty}^{\infty} \left(\frac{\partial p_\tau(y)}{\partial y} \right)^2 \frac{dy}{p_\tau(y)}$$

All that remains is to show that the first term on the right is zero. Consider the equality

$$\left| \frac{\partial p_\tau(y)}{\partial \tau} \log p_\tau(y) \right| = \left| \frac{\frac{\partial}{\partial y} p_\tau(y)}{\sqrt{p_\tau(y)}} \right| \left| 2\sqrt{p_\tau(y)} \log \sqrt{p_\tau(y)} \right|$$

The second term on the right tends to zero as $|y|$ goes to infinity because $u \log u$ goes to zero as u goes to zero. Consequently, the right side goes to zero if only the first term on the right is bounded as y goes to infinity. But the integral of the square of the first term on the right is the Fisher information $K(X + \sqrt{\tau} Z)$, which is finite, so the term itself must be bounded for large y. We can conclude that the above product is zero when evaluated in the limit of infinite y. Then

$$\frac{dH(Y)}{d\tau} = \frac{1}{2} \int_{-\infty}^{\infty} \left[\frac{\partial p_\tau(y)}{\partial y} \right]^2 \frac{dy}{p_\tau(y)}$$

as was to be proved.

We can now remove the restriction that $p(x)$ is strictly positive and differentiable. If X does not satisfy these conditions, simply pick the constant a satisfying $0 < a < \tau$ and define $X_a = X + \sqrt{a} Z$, which does have a probability density function that is strictly positive and differentiable, so the theorem applies to X_a. Therefore, replacing τ with $\tau - a$, we have

$$\frac{d}{d\tau} H(X_a + \sqrt{\tau - a}\, Z) = \frac{1}{2} K(X_a + \sqrt{\tau - a}\, Z)$$

from which we conclude that the theorem is true for X. $\square$

$\square$ **Lemma 7.10.3** Suppose that X and Y are independent random variables with probability density functions everywhere nonzero and differentiable. Then

$$\frac{1}{K(X + Y)} \geq \frac{1}{K(X)} + \frac{1}{K(Y)}$$

with equality if and only if X and Y are both gaussian. In addition, for all real constants a and b,

$$(a + b)^2 K(X + Y) \leq a^2 K(X) + b^2 K(Y)$$

Proof Denote the probability densities of X, Y, and $X + Y$ by $p(x), q(y)$, and

$$r(z) = \int_{-\infty}^{\infty} p(x)q(z - x)\, dx$$

respectively. Then dr/dz is given by

$$r'(z) = \int_{-\infty}^{\infty} p'(x)q(z - x)\, dx$$

which leads to

$$\frac{r'(z)}{r(z)} = \int_{-\infty}^{\infty} \frac{p(x)q(z - x)}{r(z)} \frac{p'(x)}{p(x)}\, dx$$

This is the conditional expectation of $p'(x)/p(x)$ for a given value of z:

$$\frac{r'(z)}{r(z)} = E\left[\frac{p'(x)}{p(x)}\bigg| z\right]$$

Likewise, because the convolution is symmetric,

$$\frac{r'(z)}{r(z)} = E\left[\frac{q'(y)}{q(y)}\bigg| z\right]$$

Therefore, for any constants a and b,

$$(a + b)\frac{r'(z)}{r(z)} = E\left[a\frac{p'(x)}{p(x)} + b\frac{q'(y)}{q(y)}\bigg| z\right]$$

The square of the mean of any random variable is never greater than its second moment. This allows us to write

$$(a + b)^2 \left[\frac{r'(z)}{r(z)} \right]^2 = \left\{ E \left[a \frac{p'(x)}{p(x)} + b \frac{q'(y)}{q(y)} \Big| z \right] \right\}^2$$

$$\leq E \left[\left(a \frac{p'(x)}{p(x)} + b \frac{q'(y)}{q(y)} \right)^2 \Big| z \right]$$

Equality holds only if

$$a \frac{p'(x)}{p(x)} + b \frac{q'(y)}{q(y)} = (a + b) \frac{r'(z)}{r(z)}$$

with probability 1 whenever $z = x + y$.

Averaging both sides of the inequality over the distribution of z, and recalling that X and Y are independent, gives us

$$(a + b)^2 E \left[\left(\frac{r'(z)}{r(z)} \right)^2 \right] \leq E \left[\left(a \frac{p'(x)}{p(x)} + b \frac{q'(y)}{q(y)} \right)^2 \right]$$

$$= a^2 E \left[\left(\frac{p'(x)}{p(x)} \right)^2 \right] + b^2 E \left[\left(\frac{q'(y)}{q(y)} \right)^2 \right]$$

or

$$(a + b)^2 K(X + Y) \leq a^2 K(X) + b^2 K(Y)$$

which is the second inequality of the lemma. Setting $a = 1/K(X)$ and $b = 1/K(Y)$, we obtain the first inequality of the lemma.

It remains to prove the equality condition. We have already found that equality occurs only if

$$a \frac{p'(x)}{p(x)} + b \frac{q'(y)}{q(y)} = (a + b) \frac{r'(z)}{r(z)}$$

Substituting $x = z - y$ and integrating with respect to y, we get

$$-a \log p(z - y) + b \log q(y) = (a + b) \frac{r'(z)}{r(z)} y + c(z)$$

for some function $c(z)$. Setting $y = 0$ shows that $c(z)$ is differentiable, and it follows that $r'(z)/r(z)$ is also differentiable. Thus differentiating with respect to z and setting $z = 0$, we have

$$-a \frac{p'(-y)}{p(-y)} = (a + b) \frac{r(0)r''(0) - r'^2(0)}{r^2(0)} y + c(0)$$

from which we see that $p(x)$ must be a gaussian density function. Further, because X and Y play symmetric roles, we can conclude that $q(y)$ is gaussian also. □

We are now ready to prove the main theorem of this section.

☐   **Theorem 7.10.4   (Entropy-power inequality)** Let X and Y be independent continuous random variables of finite variance. Then the differential entropy satisfies

$$e^{2H(X+Y)} \geq e^{2H(X)} + e^{2H(Y)}$$

with equality if and only if X and Y are gaussian.

Proof   Let $f(t)$ and $g(t)$ be any nonnegative functions of a parameter t such that $f(0) = g(0) = 0$. Let Z be a zero-mean gaussian random variable of unit variance. Define

$$X_f = X + \sqrt{f(t)}\, Z$$

$$Y_g = Y + \sqrt{g(t)}\, Z$$

Because of the smoothing effect of adding a gaussian random variable, the probability density functions of X_f and Y_g are everywhere differentiable and positive. Define

$$s(t) = e^{-2H(X_f + Y_g)}\big(e^{2H(X_f)} + e^{2H(Y_g)}\big)$$

Because X and Y have finite variance, we can write

$$\lim_{t \to 0} s(t) = s(0)$$

$$= e^{-2H(X+Y)}\big(e^{2H(X)} + e^{2H(Y)}\big)$$

To prove the theorem, we will prove that $s(0)$ is not larger than 1. This we prove by showing that $s(t)$ has a nonnegative derivative for all positive t, and that $s(t) \to 1$ as $t \to \infty$. Indeed, the latter claim holds because if X has finite variance, then the differential entropy $H(X + \sqrt{\tau}\, Z)$ is trapped between $(1/2)\log 2\pi e \tau$ and $(1/2)\log[2\pi e(\tau + \mathrm{var}(X))]$.
    Consequently,

$$\frac{f(t) + g(t)}{\mathrm{var}(X) + \mathrm{var}(Y) + f(t) + g(t)} \leq s(t) \leq \frac{\mathrm{var}(X) + \mathrm{var}(Y) + f(t) + g(t)}{f(t) + g(t)}$$

which means that $s(t) \to 1$ as $t \to \infty$, provided either $f(t)$ or $g(t)$ goes to infinity as t does.
    The last step is to compute the derivative of $s(t)$ and then define the still-unspecified functions $f(t)$ and $g(t)$ to obtain the desired properties.
    Differentiate $s(t)$ with respect to t. With the help of Lemma 7.10.2 and denoting derivatives of $f(t)$ and $g(t)$ by $f'(t)$ and $g'(t)$, we have

$$e^{2H(X_f + Y_g)}s'(t) = e^{2H(X_f)}f'(t)K(X_f) + e^{2H(Y_g)}g'(t)K(Y_g)$$

$$- (e^{2H(X_f)} + e^{2H(Y_g)})[f'(t) + g'(t)]K(X_f + Y_g)$$

We now use Lemma 7.10.3 in the form

$$K(X_f + Y_g) \leq \frac{K(X_f)K(Y_g)}{K(X_f) + K(Y_g)}$$

With this substitution, we can rearrange terms to obtain the inequality

$$e^{2H(X_f + Y_g)}s'(t) \geq \frac{[e^{2H(X_f)}K(X_f) - e^{2H(Y_g)}K(Y_g)][f'(t)K(X_f) - g'(t)K(Y_g)]}{K(X_f) + K(Y_g)}$$

provided $f'(t)$ and $g'(t)$ exist and are positive. Our goal is to define $f(t)$ and $g(t)$ so that the right side is defined and nonnegative for all t. If we could define

$$\frac{df}{dt} = e^{2H(X_f)}$$

$$\frac{dg}{dt} = e^{2H(Y_g)}$$

we would obtain the inequality

$$e^{2H(X_f + Y_g)}s'(t) \geq \frac{[e^{2H(X_f)}K(X_f) - e^{2H(Y_g)}K(Y_g)]^2}{K(X_f) + K(Y_g)}$$

which implies that $s'(t)$ is nonnegative. Because $s(\infty) = 1$ and $s'(t)$ is nonnegative, we could conclude that $s(0)$ is at most equal to 1. Therefore

$$1 \geq e^{-2H(X+Y)}(e^{2H(X)} + e^{2H(Y)})$$

as was to be proved. Thus it only remains to argue that df/dt and dg/dt are well defined. For simplicity of notation, let

$$A(f) = e^{-2H(X_f)}$$

The function $A(f)$ is continuous (and differentiable). The definition now written

$$\frac{df}{dt} = A(f)^{-1}$$

has the solution

$$t(f) = \int_0^f A(\xi)\, d\xi$$

The right side goes to infinity monotonically with f, so for every positive f the solution $f(t)$ exists. (In fact, because $A(f)$ behaves as f^{-1} asymptotically, we can expect that for large t, $f(t)$ behaves as e^t.) Hence $f(t)$ and $g(t)$ exist with the required properties and derivatives, and the theorem is proved. $\square$

The next theorem extends the entropy-power inequality to vector random variables. While we will not prove the equality conditions explicitly, if one examines every step of the proof for equality, it can be seen that equality holds only for gaussian random vectors with proportional covariance matrices.

☐ **Theorem 7.10.5**   Let $X^n = (X_1, \ldots, X_n)$ and $Y^n = (Y_1, \ldots, Y_n)$ be independent, continuous, vector-valued random variables with finite variances. Then

$$e^{2H(X^n + Y^n)/n} \geq e^{2H(X^n)/n} + e^{2H(Y^n)/n}$$

Proof   Step 1: In the first step, we will prove the following inequality for any random variables U and V:

$$E[\log (e^U + e^V)] \geq \log (e^{E[U]} + e^{E[V]})$$

This inequality will be used in step 2 and again in step 3. To prove the inequality, first notice that the function

$$y = \log (1 + e^x)$$

has second derivative

$$\frac{d^2 y}{dx^2} = \frac{e^x}{(1 + e^x)^2} \geq 0$$

so that y is a convex function of x. Consequently, we can write

$$E[\log (1 + e^{V - U})] \geq \log (1 + e^{E[V - U]})$$

Add $E[U]$ to both sides, and rewrite as

$$E[\log e^U (1 + e^{V - U})] \geq \log e^{E[U]} (1 + e^{E[V - U]})$$

which reduces to the inequality being proved.

Step 2: The remainder of the proof is by mathematical induction. By Theorem 7.10.4, the theorem is true for vectors of length 1. We assume it is true for vectors of length n and show that this implies it is true for vectors of length $n + 1$. Let

$$X^n = (X_1, \ldots, X_n)$$
$$Y^n = (Y_1, \ldots, Y_n)$$
$$Z^n = (X_1 + Y_1, \ldots, X_n + Y_n)$$
$$X^{n+1} = (X_1, \ldots, X_n, X_{n+1})$$
$$Y^{n+1} = (Y_1, \ldots, Y_n, Y_{n+1})$$
$$Z^{n+1} = (X_1 + Y_1, \ldots, X_n + Y_n, X_{n+1} + Y_{n+1})$$

and let **x** and **y** be realizations of the vector random variables X^n and Y^n. Then, by Theorem 7.10.4,

$$e^{2H(X_{n+1} + Y_{n+1} | \mathbf{x}, \mathbf{y})} \geq e^{2H(X_{n+1} | \mathbf{x})} + e^{2H(Y_{n+1} | \mathbf{y})}$$

where we have set $H(X_{n+1}|\mathbf{x},\mathbf{y}) = H(X_{n+1}|\mathbf{x})$ and $H(Y_{n+1}|\mathbf{x},\mathbf{y}) = H(Y_{n+1}|\mathbf{y})$ because X^{n+1} and Y^{n+1} are independent random variables. We can now write

$$
\begin{aligned}
2H(X_{n+1} + Y_{n+1}|Z^n) &\geq 2H(X_{n+1} + Y_{n+1}|X^n, Y^n) \\
&= E[2H(X_{n+1} + Y_{n+1}|\mathbf{x},\mathbf{y})] \\
&\geq E[\log(e^{2H(X_{n+1}|\mathbf{x})} + e^{2H(Y_{n+1}|\mathbf{y})})] \\
&\geq \log(e^{2H(X_{n+1}|X^n)} + e^{2H(Y_{n+1}|Y^n)})
\end{aligned}
$$

where the second inequality is a consequence of Theorem 7.10.4 and the third inequality is the inequality proved in step 1.

Step 3: We have now proved a conditional form of the entropy-power inequality. Next write

$$
\begin{aligned}
H(Z^{n+1}) &= H(X_{n+1} + Y_{n+1}|Z^n) + H(Z^n) \\
&\geq H(X_{n+1} + Y_{n+1}|X^n, Y^n) + H(Z^n)
\end{aligned}
$$

Use the inequality proved in step 2 on the first term on the right and the induction hypothesis on the second. In this way, we can write

$$
\frac{2}{n+1}H(Z^{n+1}) \geq \frac{1}{n+1}2H(X_{n+1} + Y_{n+1}|X^n, Y^n) + \frac{n}{n+1}\frac{2}{n}H(Z^n)
$$

$$
\geq \frac{1}{n+1}\log(e^{2H(X_{n+1}|X^n)} + e^{2H(Y_{n+1}|Y^n)})
$$

$$
+ \frac{n}{n+1}\log(e^{2H(X^n)/n} + e^{2H(Y^n)/n})
$$

Now examine the right side of the inequality in the light of the inequality proved in step 1. Define the two-valued random variables U and V as follows. With probabiltiy $1/(n+1)$, let

$$
U = 2H(X_{n+1}|X^n)
$$

$$
V = 2H(Y_{n+1}|Y^n)
$$

and with probability $n/(n+1)$, let

$$
U = e^{2H(X^n)/n}
$$

$$
V = e^{2H(Y^n)/n}
$$

We can now apply the indicated inequality to write

$$
\frac{2}{n+1}H(Z^{n+1}) \geq \log(e^{2H(X_{n+1}|X^n)/(n+1) + 2H(X^n)/(n+1)}
$$

$$
+ e^{2H(Y_{n+1}|Y^n)/(n+1) + 2H(Y^n)/(n+1)})
$$

Finally, combine the terms in each of the two exponents to write

$$\frac{2H(Z^{n+1})}{n+1} \geq \log\left(e^{2H(X^{n+1})/(n+1)} + e^{2H(Y^{n+1})/(n+1)}\right)$$

which completes the proof of the theorem. $\square$

7.11 THE CENTRAL LIMIT THEOREM

Information theory depends for its development on the theorems of probability theory. To conclude this chapter, we shall study a contribution of information theory back to probability theory. Specifically, we shall outline a proof of the central limit theorem that is based on properties of the discrimination.

Given a sequence of independent, identically distributed, real random variables $X_1, X_2, \ldots$, with mean m and variance σ^2, the nth standardized sum is defined as

$$Y_n = \frac{1}{\sqrt{n}} \sum_{l=1}^{n} X_l$$

Each of the random variables Y_n has the same mean and variance as the X_l. However, the Y_n are not identically distributed. Rather, they approach gaussian densities in appearance. Specifically, if Z is a gaussian density, with mean m and variance σ^2, then as $n \rightarrow \infty$,

$$L(Y_n; Z) \rightarrow 0$$

As measured by the discrimination, the "distance" between Y_n and Z goes to zero. This is a stronger form of the central limit theorem. The usual statement of the central limit theorem, that Y_n converges to Z in distribution, follows as a corollary by using the inequality given by the following theorem.

$\square$ **Theorem 7.11.1**

$$\int p(x) \log \frac{p(x)}{q(x)} \, dx \geq \frac{1}{2 \log e} \left[\int |p(x) - q(x)| \, dx\right]^2$$

Proof Step 1: We prove in step 1 a discrete binary version of the theorem, that for $p \in [0, 1]$ and $q \leq p$,

$$p \log \frac{p}{q} + (1 - p) \log \frac{1-p}{1-q} \geq \frac{4}{2 \log e} (p - q)^2$$

To prove this simplified inequality, consider

$$f(p, q) = p \log \frac{p}{q} + (1 - p) \log \frac{1-p}{1-q} - \frac{4}{2 \log e} (p - q)^2$$

We will show that the function $f(p, q) \geq 0$ for $0 \leq q \leq p \leq 1$ by noting that $f(p, q) = 0$ if $q = p$ and that the derivative df/dq is negative for $q < p$. Indeed,

$$\frac{df(p,q)}{dq} = \left[4(p - q) - \frac{p - q}{q(1 - q)} \right] \frac{1}{\log e}$$

$$\leq 0$$

for $q \leq p$. Therefore $f(p, q) \geq 0$ for $0 \leq q \leq p \leq 1$, and step 1 is complete.

Step 2: Let $\mathscr{S}$ denote the set of x for which $p(x) \geq q(x)$. By the refinement property of the discrimination, and the earlier inequality,

$$L(p; q) \geq p(\mathscr{S}) \log \frac{p(\mathscr{S})}{q(\mathscr{S})} + p(\mathscr{S}^c) \log \frac{p(\mathscr{S}^c)}{q(\mathscr{S}^c)}$$

$$\geq \frac{4}{2 \log e} [p(\mathscr{S}) - q(\mathscr{S})]^2$$

where $p(\mathscr{S})$ denotes $\int_{\mathscr{S}} p(x) \, dx$, and so forth. We now have

$$p(\mathscr{S}) - q(\mathscr{S}) = \int_S [p(x) - q(x)] \, dx$$

$$= - \int_{S^c} [p(x) - q(x)] \, dx$$

and so

$$p(\mathscr{S}) - q(\mathscr{S}) = \frac{1}{2} \int |p(x) - q(x)| \, dx$$

We can conclude that

$$L(p; q) \geq \frac{1}{2 \log e} \left(\int |p(x) - q(x)| \, dx \right)^2$$

which completes the proof of the theorem. ☐

Our approach to the central limit theorem is to use the entropy-power inequality to show that the sequence of positive numbers $L(Y_n; Z)$ is monotonically decreasing and so has a limit. Let L_∞ denote the limit of the powers-of-2 subsequence. Consider the "sphere" consisting of all probability densities $\hat{p}$ of variance σ^2 such that $L(\hat{p}; \phi) = L_\infty$ as illustrated in Fig. 7.14. Intuitively, the probabilities associated with the sequence of standardized sums are converging to this sphere. However, if L_∞ if nonzero, then no point on the sphere is itself stable under the operation of forming standardized sums. Therefore it appears that the original sequence cannot be converging to the sphere unless $L_\infty = 0$. To prove this, however, requires a difficult argument involving functional analysis, which is not given.

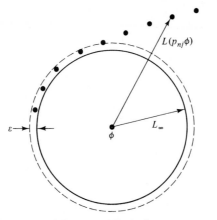

Figure 7.14   Heuristic view of the central limit theorem.

☐   **Theorem 7.11.2**   The standardized sums Y_n satisfy

$$L(Y_n; Z) \to 0$$

as $n \to \infty$.

Proof   We prove only that $L(Y_n; Z)$ decreases to a limit. All random variables in the proof will have variance σ^2. The entropy-power inequality is

$$e^{2H(X+Y)} \geq e^{2H(X)} + e^{2H(Y)}$$

where X and Y are independent, and equality holds if and only if X and Y are gaussian. Replace X and Y with $\sqrt{\alpha}\, X$ and $\sqrt{1-\alpha}\, Y$ and recall that $H(aX) = H(X) + \log_e a$. Therefore the inequality becomes

$$e^{2H(\sqrt{\alpha}X + \sqrt{1-\alpha}Y)} \geq \alpha e^{2H(X)} + (1-\alpha)e^{2H(Y)}$$

Multiply through by $\exp\left[2 \int \phi(x) \log \phi(x) \, dx\right]$, where $\phi(x)$ is a gaussian density of variance σ^2, and recall that

$$-\int \phi(x) \log \phi(x) \, dx = -\int p(x) \log \phi(x) \, dx$$

wherever $p(x)$ has the same variance as $\phi(x)$. The inequality now becomes

$$e^{-2L(\sqrt{\alpha}X + \sqrt{1-\alpha}Y;Z)} \geq \alpha e^{-2L(X,Z)} + (1-\alpha)e^{-2L(Y;Z)}$$

A more convenient, though weaker, form is obtained by using Jensen's inequality to write

$$e^{-2L(\sqrt{\alpha}X + \sqrt{1-\alpha}Y;Z)} \geq e^{-2[\alpha L(X;Z) + (1-\alpha)L(Y;Z)]}$$

or

$$L(\sqrt{\alpha}\, X + \sqrt{1-\alpha}\, Y; Z) \le \alpha L(X; Z) + (1-\alpha) L(Y; Z)$$

with equality if and only if X and Y are gaussian.

Let Y_n be the standardized sum of the first n of the X_l and let Y'_m be the standardized sum of the next m of the X_l. The random variables are independent and both have variance σ^2. Replace X and Y in the inequality with Y_n and Y'_m, and let $\alpha = n/(n+m)$. Then

$$L\left(\sqrt{\frac{n}{n+m}}\, Y_n + \sqrt{\frac{m}{n+m}}\, Y'_m; Z\right) \le \frac{n}{n+m} L(Y_n; Z)$$

$$+ \frac{m}{n+m} L(Y'_m; Z)$$

or

$$L(Y_{n+m}; Z) \le \frac{n}{n+m} L(Y_n; Z) + \frac{m}{n+m} L(Y'_m; Z)$$

A sequence obeying this kind of relationship is called a *subadditive sequence*.

Consider the powers-of-2 indices $n = m = 2^r$. Then

$$L(Y_{2^{r+1}}; Z) \le \frac{1}{2} L(Y_{2^r}; Z) + \frac{1}{2} L(Y'_{2^r}; Z)$$

The two terms on the right are equal, so

$$L(Y_{2^{r+1}}; Z) \le L(Y_{2^r}; Z)$$

with equality if and only if Y_{2^r} is gaussian.

We now have a decreasing sequence of nonnegative numbers. Hence the powers-of-2 subsequence converges (which implies that the full sequence converges). The difficult part of the proof, to show that it cannot be stalled at some value away from zero, is not given.   ☐

☐   **Theorem 7.11.3   (Central limit theorem)**

$$\int |p_n(x) - \phi(x)|\, dx \to 0$$

as $n \to \infty$.

Proof Combining the general inequality of Theorem 7.11.1,

$$\int p(x) \log \frac{p(x)}{\phi(x)}\, dx \ge \frac{1}{2\log e} \left(\int |p(x) - \phi(x)|\, dx\right)^2$$

with the conclusion of Theorem 7.11.2,

$$L(Y_n; Z) \to 0$$

proves the theorem.   □

PROBLEMS

7.1. The exponential probability density function is given by

$$p(x) = \frac{1}{\bar{x}} e^{-x/\bar{x}}$$

where $\bar{x}$ is the mean. Evaluate $L(p_0; p_1)$ where p_0 and p_1 are exponential density functions with means $\bar{x}_0, \bar{x}_1$. Evaluate the log-likelihood ratio for a sequence of independent measurements described by exponential probability density functions with means $\bar{x}_{0i}, \bar{x}_{1i}$ under hypotheses H_0 and H_1.

7.2. Suppose that the random variable X has gaussian probability density function with zero mean and variance σ^2; then X^2 has the probability density function

$$p(x) = \frac{1}{\sqrt{2\pi\sigma}} x^{-1/2} e^{-x/2\sigma^2}$$

and is known as a chi-squared random variable of order 1.

Given two chi-squared random variables of order 1 with parameters σ_0 and σ_1, compute the discrimination $L(q_0; q_1)$. Compare the result with the discrimination of two gaussian random variables of zero mean. What does this say about the information lost in squaring these gaussian random variables? Explain.

7.3. A vector random variable X^n has entropy $H(X^n)$. Let

$$\mathbf{y} = (y_1, \ldots, y_n) = [f_1(\mathbf{x}), f_2(\mathbf{x}), \ldots, f_n(\mathbf{x})] = \mathbf{f}(\mathbf{x})$$

be a one-to-one vector function of the vector $\mathbf{x}$ with each f_i having continuous first partial derivatives. The probability density function associated with new random variable $Y^n = f(X^n)$ is

$$q(\mathbf{y}) = \frac{[\mathbf{f}^{-1}(\mathbf{y})]}{|\mathbf{J}|}$$

where $\mathbf{J}$ is the jacobian of the transformation

$$\mathbf{J} = \frac{\partial(f_1, \ldots, f_n)}{\partial(x_1, \ldots, x_n)}$$

Prove that the entropy is not invariant under the transformation by proving that

$$H(Y^n) = H(X^n) - \log|\mathbf{J}|$$

7.4. Prove that, of all probability density functions defined on the interval $[0, 1]$, the uniform density function has the largest differential entropy.

7.5. Prove that

$$\mathbf{x}^T \mathbf{A} \mathbf{x} = \text{tr}[\mathbf{A}\mathbf{x}\mathbf{x}^T]$$

by a direct argument, expressing both sides as summations.

7.6. Suppose that X and Y are real-valued, independent, random variables. Use Jensen's inequality to prove that

$$H(X + Y) \geq H(X)$$

7.7. **a.** Prove that if a real-valued random variable has finite variance, then it also has finite entropy.
b. If a real-valued random variable has finite entropy, does this imply that it has finite variance?

7.8. Suppose we wish to detect a rectangular-shaped pulse of amplitude A and duration T in noise of power spectral density ·

$$N(f) = \frac{1}{1 + (f/f_o)^2}$$

Calculate the error-exponent function $e(r)$, and bound the probability of type II error for a threshold that achieves a probability of type I error of α_o.

7.9. Suppose a gaussian-noise channel with average power constraint has a noise spectrum

$$N(f) = \frac{N_o}{2}$$

and an input filter

$$H(f) = \frac{1}{1 + (f/f_o)^2}$$

Find $C(S)$.

7.10. Using the entropy-power inequality, prove that

$$\frac{1}{2} \log_2 \frac{S + N}{N_e} \geq C(S) \geq \frac{1}{2} \log_2 \frac{S + N_e}{N_e}$$

for a discrete-time, additive-noise channel and show that the inequality implies Corollary 7.3.3.

7.11. An adversary called a *jammer* intends to disrupt communication on a discrete-time channel by adding noise of power N. Using the entropy-power inequality, prove that his best strategy for reducing capacity is to use additive gaussian noise.

7.12. It may be that by removing the constraint that symbols must be used with equal probability, the capacity curves presented in Fig. 7.9 could be increased. On a sketch of Fig. 7.9 shade in the obvious region where the increased capacity for a 16-ary alphabet must lie.

7.13. Discuss the multivariate generalization of Theorem 7.2.1. Specifically argue that, of all vector random variables of blocklength n and covariance matrix Σ, the gaussian has the largest differential entropy.

7.14. Let X and X' be independent, continuous, real-valued random variables with the same probability density function and let $Y = X + X'$. Prove that

$$I(X; Y) \geq \frac{1}{2} \log 2$$

with equality if and only if X and X' are gaussian.

7.15. Prove the following statement. It is a discrete-alphabet version of a theorem known as the *Boltzmann H theorem*.

Let $\{Q_{k|j}\}$ be a doubly stochastic K-by-K matrix. That is,

$$\sum_{j=0}^{K-1} Q_{k|j} = \sum_{k=0}^{K-1} Q_{k|j} = 1$$

Then the probability distribution with components

$$q_k = \sum_{j=0}^{K-1} Q_{k|j}\, p_j$$

has entropy greater than or equal to the "input" probability distribution with components p_j, with equality only for the equiprobable distribution. Further, if $Q_{k|j}$ is nonzero for all j and k, the sequence of probability distributions defined by

$$p_k^{(r)} = \sum_{j=0}^{K-1} Q_{k|j} p_j^{(r-1)}$$

has entropy that converges to $\log K$.

7.16. Let $s_m(t)$ for $m = 0, \ldots, M-1$ be an M-ary orthogonal waveform alphabet with "pulse energy" E_p. A *simplex waveform alphabet* is given by

$$s_m'(t) = s_m(t) - \frac{1}{M}\sum_{m=0}^{M-1} s_m(t)$$

Prove that, when used on an additive gaussian-noise channel, the simplex alphabet has the same probability of decoding error as the orthogonal alphabet, and yet has smaller pulse energy.

It is widely believed that with pulse energy fixed, of all M-ary alphabets, an M-ary simplex waveform alphabet has the smallest probability of decoding error for an additive gaussian-noise channel, but this "simplex conjecture" has never been proved.

7.17. **a.** Set up an expression for the probability of symbol error for M-ary orthogonal signaling.

b. Use l'Hôpital's rule to show that as $M \to \infty$, $p_e \to 0$ if $E_b/N_o > -1.6$ db.

7.18. A PSK signaling constellation consists of four points in the complex plane of equal magnitude. Prove that, if the four points are to be used equiprobably and if each point has a mate $180°$ away, then the capacity is maximum if the points are separated by multiples of $90°$.

7.19. The capacity of an additive-noise waveform channel is given by the water-pouring formulas

$$C(S) = \frac{1}{2}\int_{-\infty}^{\infty} \max\left[0, \log\frac{\theta}{N(f)/|H(f)|^2}\right] df$$

$$S = \int_{-\infty}^{\infty} \max\left[0, \theta - \frac{N(f)}{|H(f)|^2}\right] df$$

An adversary, called a "jammer," intends to interfere with the communication system by creating gaussian noise having spectrum $N(f)$. How should the jammer choose $N(f)$ subject to his power constraint

$$J \le \int_{-\infty}^{\infty} N(f)\, df$$

so as to minimize the capacity? Could the jammer reduce the capacity further by using other than gaussian noise?

7.20. Motivate the multivariate generalization of the central limit theorem in the form

$$L(\mathbf{Y}_n; \boldsymbol{\phi}) \to 0$$

where $\mathbf{Y}_n$ is the standardized sum

$$\mathbf{Y}_n = \frac{1}{n} \sum_{r=1}^{n} \mathbf{X}_r$$

the $\mathbf{X}_r$ are independent, identically distributed, vector random variables, and $\boldsymbol{\phi}$ is a vector gaussian random variable with the same covariance matrix as the $\mathbf{X}_r$.

7.21. Write out a proof for Theorem 7.3.8.

7.22. The channel reliability exponent $E(R)$ is defined in Section 10.1 for discrete channels. Give a definition of $E(R,S)$ for a discrete-time, continuous-amplitude, memoryless gaussian channel with additive noise of variance N and power constraint S. Express $E(R,S)$ in terms of water-pouring formulas for the case where the noise has memory with power spectral density $N(f)$.

NOTES

Shannon (1948) included continuous random variables in his original treatment of information theory. The introductory sections of this chapter are based on his work. The optimum power allocation on parallel discrete-time gaussian-noise channels was studied by Ebert (1966). The water-pouring solution to the continuous-time gaussian-noise channel was developed by Holsinger (1964). The capacity of a passband channel that uses only phase modulation was studied by Blachman (1953).

The entropy-power inequality was first stated by Shannon (1948). A proof was given by Stam (1959) and refined by Blachman (1965). We have incorporated further refinements by Barron (1984). The information-theoretic approach to the central limit theorem was developed by Brown (1982) and by Barron (1986). The inequality relating discrimination and L_1 distance was expressed in the form given by Csiszár (1967).

CHAPTER 8

Estimation Theory

Estimation theory is concerned with the problem of finding a best value for an unknown parameter from a continuum of possible values when given a collection of imperfect measurements. The quality of the estimate is limited by the quality of the measurements. These limitations are information-theoretic and can be expressed by means of information-theoretic functions. The most important information inequality that pertains to the estimation problem is known as the *Cramer-Rao inequality*. It is a bound on the performance of an estimator that is related to the fact that the discrimination cannot be increased by processing.

The simplest problem of estimation theory involves an unknown real parameter θ and a random measurement X from which θ is to be determined. An understanding of this problem leads to an understanding of the more general problems: the estimation of one or several parameters based upon observing a collection of random measurements; the estimation of one or several parameters based upon observing a sample waveform of a stochastic process; and the estimation of a function on an interval based upon observing a sample waveform of a stochastic process.

8.1 ESTIMATION OF PARAMETERS

The simplest problem of estimation theory involves an unknown real parameter θ and a random measurement X from which θ is to be determined. The measurement X is a random variable that has a continuous probability density function $q(x|\theta)$ depending on the parameter θ. The unknown parameter θ must be estimated based upon an observation of X. The estimate of θ, given the measurement X, is a function $\hat{\theta}(x)$. This estimate $\hat{\theta}$ is itself a random variable because it is a function of the random variable X. Estimation theory studies various criteria for making good estimates—that is, for selecting the function $\hat{\theta}(x)$.

The quality of an estimator is judged by its mean value conditional on θ:

$$E[\hat{\theta}] = E[\hat{\theta}(x)]$$

and by its conditional variance:

$$\sigma_\theta^2 = E[(\hat{\theta}(x) - E[\hat{\theta}(x)])]^2$$

where E denotes the expectation taken using $q(x|\theta)$.

Intuitively, one hopes to choose the estimator $\hat{\theta}(x)$ so that its conditional mean satisfies $E[\hat{\theta}(x)] = \theta$, a so-called unbiased estimator, and so that, simultaneously, the conditional variance is as small as possible. Such an estimator is called a *minimum-variance unbiased estimator*. Sometimes, however, another estimator is used because the minimum-variance unbiased estimator does not exist or the other estimator has some advantage; the variance is not the only measure of quality of an estimator. Nevertheless, the variance is the most important figure of merit, and the one we shall study.

The Cramer-Rao bound is a lower bound on the conditional variance of any estimator. For an unbiased estimator of a single parameter θ, the most common form of the bound is

$$\sigma_\theta^2 \geq \frac{1}{E[(\partial/\partial\theta)\log q(x|\theta)]^2}$$

provided the derivative exists. The Cramer-Rao bound holds even if the measurement X is replaced by a vector of measurements. Simply replace $q(x|\theta)$ with $q(x_1, \ldots, x_n|\theta)$.

The Cramer-Rao bound can be expressed in other, equivalent forms. Expressed in terms of a second derivative, it is

$$\sigma_\theta^2 \geq \frac{-1}{E[(\partial^2/\partial\theta^2)\log q(x|\theta)]}$$

provided the derivatives exist. We shall see that it can also be expressed in terms of the discrimination:

$$\sigma_\theta^2 \geq \left[\lim_{\gamma \to \theta} \frac{2L(q_\gamma; q_\theta)}{(\theta - \gamma)^2}\right]^{-1}$$

where

$$L(q_\gamma; q_\theta) = \int_{-\infty}^{\infty} q(x|\gamma) \log \frac{q(x|\gamma)}{q(x|\theta)} dx$$

Two elements of the family $q(x|\cdot)$ are used in this formula, those with parameters θ and γ. We think of γ as a value in the neighborhood of θ; taking the limit then is suggestive of the differentiation in the first form of the bound.

Rather than prove the Cramer-Rao bound directly, we will prove a stronger bound that implies the Cramer-Rao bound.

□ **Theorem 8.1.1**   For any unbiased estimate $\hat{\theta}$,

$$\sigma_\theta^2 \left\{ \int_{-\infty}^{\infty} q(x|\gamma) \left[\frac{q(x|\gamma)}{q(x|\theta)} - 1\right] dx \right\} \geq (\theta - \gamma)^2$$

for all θ and γ for which $q(x|\theta)$ and $q(x|\gamma)$ are defined.

Proof Let E denote expectation with respect to $q(x|\theta)$. By Schwarz's inequality,[†]

$$E[\hat{\theta}(x) - E[\hat{\theta}]]^2 E\left[1 - \frac{q(x|\gamma)}{q(x|\theta)}\right]^2$$

$$\geq \left\{E\left[(\hat{\theta}(x) - E[\hat{\theta}])\left(1 - \frac{q(x|\gamma)}{q(x|\theta)}\right)\right]\right\}^2$$

$$= \left\{\int q(x|\theta)(\hat{\theta}(x) - \theta)\left(1 - \frac{q(x|\gamma)}{q(x|\theta)}\right) dx\right\}^2$$

$$= \left\{\int (q(x|\theta) - q(x|\gamma))(\hat{\theta}(x) - \theta) dx\right\}^2$$

$$= (\theta - \gamma)^2$$

Finally, because

$$\sigma_\theta^2 = E[\hat{\theta}(x) - E[\hat{\theta}]]^2$$

and

$$\int q(x|\theta)\left[1 - \frac{q(x|\gamma)}{q(x|\theta)}\right]^2 dx = \int q(x|\gamma)\left[\frac{q(x|\gamma)}{q(x|\theta)} - 1\right] dx$$

the theorem is proved. □

[†]Schwarz's inequality for expectations is $E[X^2]E[Y^2] \geq (E[XY])^2$.

Although the bound in Theorem 8.1.1 is stronger than the Cramer-Rao bound, it is not as useful, because if X is replaced by a vector of independent measurements, the bound does not reduce to a simple form. The Cramer-Rao bound is weaker but is more useful because the probability density function appears inside a logarithm. This means that, for independent measurements, the Cramer-Rao bound contains the form of a sum of simple terms.

☐ **Theorem 8.1.2 (Cramer-Rao bound)** Suppose that $q(x|\theta)$ is differentiable in θ. The variance of an unbiased estimate of θ is bounded by

$$\sigma_\theta^2 \geq \frac{1}{E[(\partial/\partial\theta)\log q(x|\theta)]^2}$$

Proof With $\gamma = \theta + \Delta\theta$, rewrite Theorem 8.1.1 in the form

$$\sigma_\theta^2 \geq \frac{1}{\int q(x|\theta)\left[\frac{1}{\Delta\theta}\left(1 - \frac{q(x|\theta+\Delta\theta)}{q(x|\theta)}\right)\right]^2 dx}$$

and take the limit as $\Delta\theta \to 0$. ☐

An estimator that satisfies the Cramer-Rao bound with equality is called an *efficient estimator*. An efficient estimator need not exist for a given problem. The Cramer-Rao bound can be expressed as an information inequality by expressing the variance of the estimate in terms of the discrimination as in the next theorem.

☐ **Theorem 8.1.3** Suppose that

$$\lim_{\gamma\to\theta}\max_x \left|\frac{q(x|\theta) - q(x|\gamma)}{q(x|\theta)}\right| = 0$$

Then

$$\sigma_\theta^2\left[\lim_{\gamma\to\theta}\frac{2L(q_\gamma; q_\theta)}{(\theta-\gamma)^2}\right] \geq 1$$

Proof By the Taylor series formula with remainder of elementary calculus,

$$y\log_e y = (y-1) + \frac{1}{2}(y-1)^2 + \frac{1}{6}\frac{(y-1)^3}{\tilde{y}^2}$$

for some $\tilde{y} = c(y)$ lying between y and 1. Therefore, for any $p(x)$ and $q(x)$,

$$\frac{p(x)}{q(x)}\log\frac{p(x)}{q(x)} = \left(\frac{p(x)}{q(x)} - 1\right) + \frac{1}{2}\left(\frac{p(x)}{q(x)} - 1\right)^2$$
$$+ \frac{1}{6}\left(\frac{p(x)}{q(x)} - 1\right)^3\frac{1}{c^2(p(x)/q(x))}$$

Consequently,

$$L(p;q) = \frac{1}{2}\int q(x)\left(\frac{p(x)}{q(x)} - 1\right)^2 dx + O\left(\left|\frac{p(x)}{q(x)} - 1\right|\right)^3$$

Now replace $p(x)$ and $q(x)$ with $q(x|\gamma)$ and $q(x|\theta)$, respectively. By the assumption of the theorem, the argument of the second term on the right of the equation goes to zero as $\gamma \to \theta$. Rewriting the first term then gives

$$2L(q_\gamma;q_\theta) = \int_{-\infty}^{\infty} q(x|\gamma)\left[\frac{q(x|\gamma)}{q(x|\theta)} - 1\right]dx$$

up to terms of second order. A reference to Theorem 8.1.1 then completes the proof of the theorem. □

In Chapter 4, we defined the notion of a sufficient statistic for problems of hypothesis testing. We can apply the same idea to the problem of estimation. A function of the data, $t(x)$, is called a *sufficient statistic* if for all γ and θ in the space of parameters

$$L(p_\gamma; p_\theta) = L(q_\gamma; q_\theta)$$

where q_θ abbreviates $q(x|\theta)$, the distribution on the measurement conditional on θ, and p_θ abbreviates $p(t|\theta)$, the induced distribution on the statistic t conditional on θ.

The Cramer-Rao inequality is easily generalized in a number of ways. We know that discrimination adds for independent measurements. Hence, if several independent measurements are made in order to estimate a parameter, we can use the following.

□ **Theorem 8.1.4**   The variance of an unbiased estimate of θ based on a set of n independent measurements is bounded by

$$\sigma_\theta^2 \lim_{\gamma \to \theta}\left[\frac{2\sum_{l=1}^{n} L_l(q_\gamma; q_\theta)}{(\theta - \gamma)^2}\right] \geq 1$$

where L_l denotes the discrimination of the lth measurement.

Proof The discrimination is additive for independent measurements. □

As a simple example, suppose that the variance N of a zero-mean gaussian-noise process is to be estimated based on n samples. Then the discrimination is

$$L(q_N;q_{N'}) = \frac{N - N'}{2N'} + \frac{1}{2}\log\frac{N'}{N}$$

and

$$\lim_{N' \to N} \frac{2nL(q_N; q_{N'})}{(N - N')^2} = \frac{n}{2N^2}$$

Therefore

$$\sigma_N^2 > \frac{2N^2}{n}$$

Thus the variance in any estimate of noise power approaches zero no faster than the reciprocal of the number of measurements.

It is clear how to generalize Theorem 8.1.4 if the successive measurements are dependent. Simply replace the numerator with the block discrimination $L(q_\gamma^n; q_\theta^n)$. Another way of generalization is to remove the requirement that the estimate be unbiased. One then has that the variance of any estimate of θ is bounded by

$$\sigma_\theta^2 \lim_{\gamma \to \theta} \left[\frac{2L(q_\gamma; q_\theta)}{(\theta - \gamma)^2} \right] \geq \left[\frac{dE(\hat{\theta})}{d\theta} \right]^2$$

where $E(\hat{\theta})$ is the expectation of $\hat{\theta}$, given θ.

8.2 THE FISHER INFORMATION MATRIX

It may be that several parameters are to be estimated simultaneously. In this case, $\boldsymbol{\theta} = \{\theta_1, \ldots, \theta_m\}$ is a vector parameter to be estimated, and the measurement X is a random variable that has probability distribution dependent on the unknown vector $\boldsymbol{\theta}$;

$$q(x|\boldsymbol{\theta}) = q(x|\theta_1, \ldots, \theta_m)$$

A multiple-parameter estimator is a vector function $\hat{\boldsymbol{\theta}}(x)$ that provides an estimate of the vector parameter $\boldsymbol{\theta}$ based on a measurement X. The vector estimator is judged by its vector mean

$$E[\hat{\boldsymbol{\theta}}] = E[\hat{\boldsymbol{\theta}}(x)]$$

and by its covariance matrix

$$\boldsymbol{\Sigma}(\hat{\boldsymbol{\theta}}) = E[[\hat{\boldsymbol{\theta}}(x) - E[\hat{\boldsymbol{\theta}}]][\hat{\boldsymbol{\theta}}(x) - E[\hat{\boldsymbol{\theta}}]]^T]$$

The Cramer-Rao bound for multiple-parameter estimation will be proved in Section 8.3. It states that the covariance matrix $\boldsymbol{\Sigma}(\boldsymbol{\theta})$, or more simply $\boldsymbol{\Sigma}$, of any unbiased estimator satisfies the matrix inequality

$$\boldsymbol{\Sigma}(\boldsymbol{\theta}) \geq \mathbf{K}^{-1}(\boldsymbol{\theta})$$

where $\mathbf{K}(\boldsymbol{\theta})$ is a matrix to be defined. The meaning of the matrix inequality is that $\mathbf{\Sigma} - \mathbf{K}^{-1}$ is a nonnegative-definite matrix. That is,

$$\delta^T(\mathbf{\Sigma} - \mathbf{K}^{-1})\delta \geq 0$$

for all vectors δ of length m.

□ **Definition 8.2.1** Let $q(x|\theta)$ be a probability distribution that is differentiable in the components of the vector parameter θ. The *Fisher information matrix* $\mathbf{K}(\theta)$ at the point θ is an *m*-by-*m* matrix whose elements are given by

$$K_{ij}(\theta) = \int_{-\infty}^{\infty} q(x|\theta)\left[\frac{\partial}{\partial\theta_i}\log q(x|\theta)\right]\left[\frac{\partial}{\partial\theta_j}\log q(x|\theta)\right]dx \qquad \square$$

When there is only a single parameter, the Fisher information matrix becomes a real function of θ. The *Fisher information* at the point θ is given by

$$K(\theta) = \int_{-\infty}^{\infty} q(x|\theta)\left[\frac{\partial}{\partial\theta}\log q(x|\theta)\right]^2 dx$$

The Fisher information matrix is closely related to the discrimination. The following theorem says that it is a matrix of second partial derivatives of the discrimination.

□ **Theorem 8.2.2** Suppose that

$$\lim_{\gamma \to \theta} \max_x \left|\frac{q(x|\theta) - q(x|\gamma)}{q(x|\theta)}\right| = 0$$

for every sequence of γ converging to θ. Let $\Delta\theta = \theta - \gamma$. Then

$$L(q_\gamma; q_\theta) = \frac{1}{2}\Delta\theta^T \mathbf{K}(\theta)\Delta\theta$$

up to terms of second order in $\Delta\theta$. Therefore

$$K_{ij}(\theta) = 2\frac{\partial}{\partial\theta_i}\frac{\partial}{\partial\theta_j}L(q_\gamma; q_\theta)\big|_{\gamma=\theta}$$

Proof As in the proof of Theorem 8.1.3, we have, up to terms of second order,

$$L(q_\gamma; q_\theta) = \frac{1}{2}\int q(x|\theta)\left(\frac{q(x|\gamma)}{q(x|\theta)} - 1\right)^2 dx$$

$$= \frac{1}{2}\int q(x|\theta)\left(\frac{\Delta q(x|\theta)}{q(x|\theta)}\right)\left(\frac{\Delta q(x|\theta)}{q(x|\theta)}\right)dx$$

where

$$\Delta q(x|\theta) = q(x|\theta) - q(x|\gamma)$$

But, up to terms of second order,

$$\frac{\Delta q(x|\boldsymbol{\theta})}{q(x|\boldsymbol{\theta})} = \sum_i \Delta\theta_i \frac{\partial}{\partial\theta_i} \log q(x|\boldsymbol{\theta})$$

from which the theorem follows. □

We also consider cases wherein the measurement is a vector. The probability density q then becomes a function of the vector measurement $\mathbf{x} = (x_1,\ldots,x_n)$ conditional on the vector parameter $\boldsymbol{\theta} = (\theta_1,\ldots,\theta_m)$. The Fisher information matrix elements are now expressed as multiple integrals:

$$K_{ij}(\boldsymbol{\theta}) = \int_{-\infty}^{\infty} \cdots \int_{-\infty}^{\infty} q(\mathbf{x}|\boldsymbol{\theta})\left[\frac{\partial}{\partial\theta_i}\log q(\mathbf{x}|\boldsymbol{\theta})\right]\left[\frac{\partial}{\partial\theta_j}\log q(\mathbf{x}|\boldsymbol{\theta})\right]dx_1,\ldots,dx_n$$

If the density q is a product density, then $K_{ij}(\boldsymbol{\theta})$ becomes a sum of n terms, one corresponding to each component of the measurement.

8.3 MULTIPLE SIMULTANEOUS ESTIMATES

Let $\hat{\boldsymbol{\theta}}$ be an estimate of the vector parameter $\boldsymbol{\theta}$ and let $\boldsymbol{\Sigma}(\boldsymbol{\theta})$ be the covariance matrix of the vector random variable $\hat{\boldsymbol{\theta}}$, which will depend on $\boldsymbol{\theta}$. We will find a Cramer-Rao bound on $\boldsymbol{\Sigma}(\boldsymbol{\theta})$ by considering the estimation of the single parameter

$$\psi = a_1\theta_1 + \cdots + a_m\theta_m$$

for an arbitrary weighting vector $\mathbf{a}$. This is now a single-parameter estimation problem, so the results of Section 8.1 apply. We can then consider many particular values of the weight vector $\mathbf{a}$ in order to obtain the desired bound on the covariance matrix $\boldsymbol{\Sigma}(\boldsymbol{\theta})$.

We first develop two general inequalities dealing with quadratic forms. The first is a generalization of Schwarz's inequality. It reduces to the Schwarz inequality when the matrix $\mathbf{A}$ is the identity matrix.

□   **Theorem 8.3.1**   Let $\mathbf{A}$ be a positive-definite symmetric matrix. Then for any vectors $\mathbf{x}$ and $\mathbf{y}$,

$$(\mathbf{x}^T\mathbf{y})^2 \leq (\mathbf{x}^T\mathbf{A}\mathbf{x})(\mathbf{y}^T\mathbf{A}^{-1}\mathbf{y})$$

with equality when

$$\mathbf{y} = \mathbf{A}\mathbf{x}$$

where the vectors $\mathbf{x}^T$ and $\mathbf{y}^T$ are the transposes of $\mathbf{x}$ and $\mathbf{y}$.

Proof   The condition for equality is obvious. The inequality is proved by an argument often used to prove Schwarz's inequality. Because $\mathbf{A}$ is a positive-definite matrix,

$$\mathbf{z}^T\mathbf{A}\mathbf{z} \geq 0$$

In particular, this holds with $\mathbf{z} = r\mathbf{x} + \mathbf{A}^{-1}\mathbf{y}$, where r is any real number and $\mathbf{x}$ and $\mathbf{y}$ are any vectors:

$$(r\mathbf{x} + \mathbf{A}^{-1}\mathbf{y})^T\mathbf{A}(r\mathbf{x} + \mathbf{A}^{-1}\mathbf{y}) \geq 0$$

Hence

$$r^2\mathbf{x}^T\mathbf{A}\mathbf{x} + 2r\mathbf{x}^T\mathbf{y} + \mathbf{y}^T\mathbf{A}^{-1}\mathbf{y} \geq 0$$

where we have used the fact that the inverse of a symmetric matrix is symmetric and that $\mathbf{x}^T\mathbf{y} = \mathbf{y}^T\mathbf{x}$. We now have a quadratic equation in r that is nonnegative for all r. The zeros of the quadratic equation must be either equal or complex. Therefore the discriminant is not positive:

$$4(\mathbf{x}^T\mathbf{y})^2 - 4(\mathbf{x}^T\mathbf{A}\mathbf{x})(\mathbf{y}^T\mathbf{A}^{-1}\mathbf{y}) \leq 0$$

and the theorem follows. $\square$

□ **Theorem 8.3.2** Suppose that $\mathbf{A}$ and $\mathbf{B}$ are positive-definite symmetric real matrices, and for all $\mathbf{x}$,

$$\mathbf{x}^T\mathbf{A}\mathbf{x} \geq \mathbf{x}^T\mathbf{B}\mathbf{x}$$

Then for all $\mathbf{y}$,

$$\mathbf{y}^T\mathbf{A}^{-1}\mathbf{y} \leq \mathbf{y}^T\mathbf{B}^{-1}\mathbf{y}$$

Proof Because $\mathbf{A}$ is a positive-definite symmetric matrix, the matrix $\mathbf{A}^{-1/2}$ exists and is symmetric. Because the matrix $\mathbf{A}^{-1/2}\mathbf{B}\mathbf{A}^{-1/2}$ is a real symmetric matrix, there is a matrix $\mathbf{M}$ such that $\mathbf{M}^T = \mathbf{M}^{-1}$ and

$$\mathbf{T} = \mathbf{M}(\mathbf{A}^{-1/2}\mathbf{B}\mathbf{A}^{-1/2})\mathbf{M}^{-1}$$

is a diagonal matrix. The diagonal elements of the diagonal matrix $\mathbf{T}$ are nonzero because $\mathbf{A}$ and $\mathbf{B}$ are positive-definite. For any $\mathbf{x}$, define

$$\mathbf{z} = \mathbf{M}\mathbf{A}^{1/2}\mathbf{x}$$

Because

$$\mathbf{x}^T\mathbf{A}\mathbf{x} \geq \mathbf{x}^T\mathbf{B}\mathbf{x}$$

for all $\mathbf{x}$, it follows that

$$\mathbf{z}^T\mathbf{z} \geq \mathbf{z}^T\mathbf{T}\mathbf{z}$$

Therefore every diagonal element of $\mathbf{T}$ must be less than or equal to 1, and the reciprocal of every diagonal element is greater than or equal to 1. Therefore, for all $\mathbf{z}$,

$$\mathbf{z}^T\mathbf{z} \leq \mathbf{z}^T\mathbf{T}^{-1}\mathbf{z}$$

Finally, given any $\mathbf{y}$, let $\mathbf{z} = \mathbf{M}^{-1}\mathbf{A}^{-1/2}\mathbf{y}$. Then

$$\mathbf{y}^T\mathbf{A}^{-1}\mathbf{y} = \mathbf{z}^T\mathbf{z}$$

$$\leq \mathbf{z}^T\mathbf{M}^{-1}\mathbf{A}^{1/2}\mathbf{B}^{-1}\mathbf{A}^{1/2}\mathbf{M}\mathbf{z}$$

$$= \mathbf{y}^T\mathbf{B}^{-1}\mathbf{y}$$

as was to be proved.   □

□   **Theorem 8.3.3**   Up to second-order terms in $\Delta\theta$,

$$2L(q_{\theta+\Delta\theta}; q_\theta) \geq \Delta\theta^T \Sigma^{-1}(\theta)\,\Delta\theta$$

where $\theta = (\theta_1, \ldots, \theta_m)$, provided q_θ satisfies the condition of uniform continuity

$$\lim_{\gamma \to \theta} \max_x \left| \frac{q(x\,|\,\theta) - q(x\,|\,\gamma)}{q(x\,|\,\theta)} \right| = 0$$

Proof   Let

$$\psi = a_1\theta_1 + \cdots + a_m\theta_m$$

where $\mathbf{a} = (a_1, \ldots, a_m)^T$ is a weight vector to be chosen later, and consider the estimate

$$\hat{\psi}(x) = a_1\hat{\theta}_1(x) + \cdots + a_m\hat{\theta}_m(x)$$

where $\hat{\theta}_1(x), \ldots, \hat{\theta}_m(x)$ are estimates of $\theta_1, \ldots, \theta_m$. Then

$$\sigma_\psi^2 = \mathbf{a}^T\Sigma(\theta)\mathbf{a}$$

where $\Sigma(\theta)$ is the covariance matrix of the vector random variable $(\hat{\theta}_1(x), \ldots, \hat{\theta}_m(x))$. Because $\hat{\psi}(x)$ is an estimate, it must satisfy Theorem 8.1.3. That is, up to second-order terms in $\Delta\theta$,

$$\sigma_\psi^2 \frac{2L(q_\gamma; q_\theta)}{\Delta\psi^2} \geq 1$$

or

$$\frac{2L(q_\gamma; q_\theta)}{\Delta\psi^2} \geq \frac{1}{\mathbf{a}^T\Sigma(\theta)\mathbf{a}}$$

Now apply Theorem 8.3.1 in the form

$$(\Delta\psi)^2 = (\mathbf{a}^T\,\Delta\theta)^2 = (\mathbf{a}^T\Sigma(\theta)\mathbf{a})(\Delta\theta^T\Sigma^{-1}(\theta)\,\Delta\theta)$$

where $\mathbf{a}$ has been chosen so that equality holds in the theorem. Then

$$\frac{2L(q_{\theta+\Delta\theta}; q_\theta)}{\Delta\psi^2} \geq \frac{\Delta\theta^T\Sigma^{-1}(\theta)\,\Delta\theta}{\Delta\psi^2}$$

□

☐ **Corollary 8.3.4**

$$\Delta\theta^T \mathbf{K}(\theta) \, \Delta\theta \geq \Delta\theta^T \mathbf{\Sigma}^{-1}(\theta) \, \Delta\theta$$

Proof We will base the proof on Theorem 8.3.3, so the corollary is proved only under the condition of that theorem. The inequality holds for sufficiently small $|\Delta\theta|$ by the theorem because

$$L(q_{\theta + \Delta\theta}; q_\theta) = \Delta\theta^T \mathbf{K}(\theta) \, \Delta\theta$$

up to terms of second order in $\Delta\theta$. Therefore, because both sides are quadratic, the inequality holds for all $\Delta\theta$.   ☐

☐ **Theorem 8.3.5 (Multiple-parameter Cramer-Rao bound)** For any vector $\Delta\theta$ the covariance matrix $\mathbf{\Sigma}(\theta)$ of an unbiased estimator satisfies

$$\Delta\theta^T \mathbf{\Sigma}(\theta) \, \Delta\theta \geq \Delta\theta^T \mathbf{K}^{-1}(\theta) \, \Delta\theta$$

Proof Apply Theorem 8.3.2 to Corollary 8.3.4.   ☐

The statement of Theorem 8.3.5 can be expressed more concisely as

$$\mathbf{\Sigma} \geq \mathbf{K}^{-1}$$

where the matrix inequality is interpreted to mean that $\mathbf{\Sigma} - \mathbf{K}^{-1}$ is a nonnegative-definite matrix.

One way to use Theorem 8.3.5 is as a collection of bounds on the variances of the individual parameters. Simply take $\Delta\theta$ equal to 1 in the jth component and equal to 0 otherwise. The theorem then gives the bound for the jth parameter:

$$\sigma_j^2 \geq \left[\mathbf{K}^{-1}(\theta) \right]_{jj}$$

Theorem 8.3.5 also can be given a geometrical meaning by interpreting it as a relationship between ellipsoids in m-dimensional space. The expression

$$\Delta\theta^T \mathbf{\Sigma}^{-1} \, \Delta\theta = 1$$

defines an ellipsoid in the m-dimensional space of estimator errors $(\Delta\theta_1, \ldots, \Delta\theta_m)$. Corollary 8.3.4 tells us that for any estimator whatsoever, this ellipsoid must always lie outside (or touching) the ellipsoid defined by $\Delta\theta^T \mathbf{K} \, \Delta\theta = 1$. Equivalently, the ellipsoid defined by $\Delta\theta^T \mathbf{\Sigma} \, \Delta\theta = 1$ always lies inside (or touching) the ellipsoid defined by $\Delta\theta^T \mathbf{K}^{-1} \, \Delta\theta = 1$. The geometrical relationship is illustrated in Fig. 8.1.

The Cramer-Rao bound says that the outer ellipse can never pass inside the inner ellipse. If we can design an estimator such that the outer ellipse coincides with the inner ellipse, then we have managed to squeeze the data dry; there is no better estimation algorithm. If we want a better estimation accuracy, then we must collect more data.

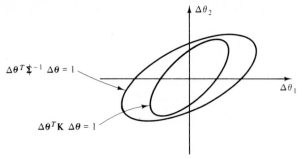

Figure 8.1   Illustration of the Cramer-Rao bound.

8.4 ESTIMATION OF PULSE ARRIVAL TIME

The estimation of pulse arrival time is based on a received signal of the form

$$v(t) = s(t - \alpha) + n(t)$$

where $s(t)$ is a known waveform with finite energy E_p and $n(t)$ is a stationary gaussian-noise process whose correlation function $\phi(\tau)$ and power spectral density $N(f)$ are known. The estimation problem is to determine the unknown delay α from $v(t)$; we will find the minimum-variance unbiased estimate.

The error in any estimate of pulse arrival time must have a variance at least as great as the Cramer-Rao bound. We will evaluate the Cramer-Rao bound for this problem and then give an estimator, called the *matched-filter estimator*, that achieves the Cramer-Rao bound—at least when the signal-to-noise ratio is high. Hence, asymptotically for high signal-to-noise ratio, no unbiased estimator can then have a smaller variance than the matched-filter estimator.

The estimation of arrival time might also be based on a received waveform of the form

$$v(t) = s(t - \alpha)\cos 2\pi(f_0 t + \theta) + n_R(t)\cos 2\pi f_0 t - n_I(t)\sin 2\pi f_0 t$$

or possibly

$$v(t) = s_R(t - \alpha)\cos 2\pi(f_0 t + \theta) - s_I(t - \alpha)\sin 2\pi(f_0 t + \theta)$$
$$+ n_R(t)\cos 2\pi f_0 t - n_I(t)\sin 2\pi f_0 t$$

where f_0 is a known carrier frequency and $n_R(t)$ and $n_I(t)$ are independent, stationary gaussian-noise processes with identical power spectral density $N(f)$. These are called *passband waveforms* whenever the carrier frequency f_0 is much larger than the bandwidth.

It might be the case that $\theta = -f_0\alpha$, so that the argument of the sinusoids is $f_0(t - \alpha)$. However, if f_0 is very large, as is often the case, this dependence on α is not usable for estimation purposes, since $f_0\alpha$ would also be extremely large, and tiny errors in α can cause large changes in the sinusoid. Suppressing the α dependence forces the bound to correspond to the practical aspects of the problem. For such reasons, the passband waveform usually is modeled with an unknown phase angle θ as a further complication. This is called a *noncoherent passband waveform*. Any lower bound on the arrival-time variance for the baseband waveform must also be a lower bound for the noncoherent passband waveform, since including an unknown phase angle cannot possibly be beneficial.

☐ **Theorem 8.4.1** Suppose that a known waveform $s(t)$ is received with an unknown delay α and in the presence of additive gaussian noise of spectral density $N(f)$. Then the variance of any estimate of α satisfies

$$\sigma_\alpha^2 \geq \left[(2\pi)^2 \int_{-\infty}^{\infty} f^2 \frac{|S(f)|^2}{N(f)} \, df \right]^{-1}$$

Proof For a gaussian random variable, of variance λ and mean $m(\alpha)$, a simple calculation gives

$$E\left[\frac{\partial}{\partial \alpha} \log p(x|\alpha) \right]^2 = \frac{1}{\lambda} \left(\frac{\partial m}{\partial \alpha} \right)^2$$

We will express the received signal as a sum of independent gaussian random variables and apply this formula to each term. Restrict attention to a finite interval $[-T/2, T/2]$ and find a Karhunen-Loeve expansion:

$$v(t) = s(t - \alpha) + n(t)$$

$$= \sum_{k=1}^{\infty} v_k \psi_k^{(T)}(t)$$

where the Karhunen-Loeve expansion functions $\psi_k^{(T)}(t)$ are the orthonormal eigenfunctions of the integral equation

$$\int_{-T/2}^{T/2} \phi(t - s)\psi^{(T)}(s) \, ds = \lambda \psi^{(T)}(t) \qquad -T/2 \leq t \leq T/2$$

where $\phi(\tau) = E[n(t)n(t + \tau)]$. The expansion coefficients v_k for $k = 1, 2, \ldots$ are independent gaussian random variables of variance λ_k, where λ_k is the eigenvalue of the above integral equation corresponding to the eigenfunction $\psi_k^{(T)}(t)$. The mean of v_k is

$$s_k(\alpha) = \int_{-T/2}^{T/2} s(t - \alpha)\psi_k^{(T)}(t) \, dt$$

Because $s(t - \alpha)$ is unrelated to $n(t)$, the expansion functions $\psi_k^{(T)}(t)$ are independent of α. The Cramer-Rao bound is obtained by summing the single component Cramer-Rao bounds. That is,

$$\sigma_\alpha^2 \geq \left\{ \sum_{k=1}^{\infty} E\left[\frac{\partial}{\partial\alpha} \log p_k(y_k|\alpha)\right]^2 \right\}^{-1} = \left\{ \sum_{k=1}^{\infty} \frac{1}{\lambda_k}\left[\frac{ds_k(\alpha)}{d\alpha}\right]^2 \right\}^{-1}$$

This is the bound if $v(t)$ is observed from $-T/2$ to $T/2$. We now let $T \to \infty$ to obtain the Cramer-Rao bound:

$$\sigma_\alpha^2 \geq \left\{ \lim_{T\to\infty} \sum_{k=1}^{\infty} \frac{1}{\lambda_k}\left[\frac{ds_k(\alpha)}{d\alpha}\right]^2 \right\}^{-1}$$

We can evaluate the limit using the same methods of functional analysis as were used in the proof of Theorem 4.2.1. There it was found that in a similar problem,

$$\lim_{T\to\infty} \sum_{k=1}^{\infty} \frac{s_k}{\lambda_k} v_k = \int_{-\infty}^{\infty} \frac{S^*(f)}{N(f)} V(f)\,df$$

We can borrow this formula, replacing both s_k and v_k by the derivative of s_k so that it fits the problem at hand. Alternatively, the steps of the derivation can be written out for the new problem. In either case, the proof is completed by recalling that the Fourier transform of $ds(t)/dt$ is $j2\pi f S(f)$. □

The Cramer-Rao bound for the case where the noise is white gaussian noise is of primary practical interest. In this case,

$$N(f) = \frac{N_o}{2} \quad \text{watts/hertz}$$

and the bound becomes

$$\sigma_\alpha^2 \geq \frac{1}{(2\pi)^2 \overline{f^2}(2E_p/N_0)}$$

where $(\overline{f^2})^{1/2}$ in hertz is known as the *Gabor bandwidth* (or the *rms bandwidth*) and is given by

$$\overline{f^2} = \frac{\displaystyle\int_{-\infty}^{\infty} f^2 |S(f)|^2\,df}{\displaystyle\int_{-\infty}^{\infty} |S(f)|^2\,df}$$

and

$$E_p = \int_{-\infty}^{\infty} s(t)^2\,dt = \int_{-\infty}^{\infty} |S(f)|^2\,df$$

is the energy of the pulse.

To the extent that the Cramer-Rao bound is tight, the waveform design can affect the timing accuracy only through the Gabor bandwidth and the pulse energy E_p. Any other aspect of the waveform shape is irrelevant to the timing accuracy.

There is an important estimator whose performance agrees with the Cramer-Rao bound, at least in an asymptotic sense. As before, the signal $s(t - \alpha)$ is received in additive noise, but we drop the assumption that $n(t)$ is gaussian noise. Only the covariance properties of the noise will be needed. The estimator that we choose to analyze passes $v(t)$ through a linear filter $g(t)$ and sets the estimate $\hat{\alpha}$ equal to the time at which the filter output is maximum. This structure is referred to as a *linear estimator*. If the filter transform satisfies

$$G(f) = \frac{S^*(f)}{N(f)}$$

it is called a *matched-filter estimator*.

Normally, a fixed time delay must be included in $g(t)$ to make the filter causal. However, this fixed delay plays no other role in the discussion. When $N(f)$ is not a constant, the matched filter is called a *whitened* matched filter, this because the denominator $N(f)$ can be thought of as a term to "whiten" the noise.

□ **Theorem 8.4.2** Asymptotically, as the filter output signal is made sufficiently strong, the matched-filter estimator has the smallest variance of any linear estimator. The variance is given asymptotically by

$$\sigma_\alpha^2 = \left[(2\pi)^2 \int_{-\infty}^{\infty} f^2 \frac{|S(f)|^2}{N(f)} \, df \right]^{-1}$$

Proof The argument is a bit clumsy in that it is based on the linearization of Fig. 8.2. This is why the requirement of a sufficiently

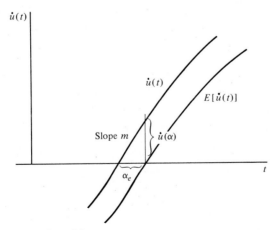

Figure 8.2   A linearized model.

strong signal is included. Denote the filter output by the random variable $u(t)$. The time derivative of $u(t)$ can be written

$$\dot{u}(t) = \int_{-\infty}^{\infty} \dot{g}(\xi)v(t - \xi)\, d\xi$$

where $\dot{g}$ is the time derivative of g. The estimator $\hat{\alpha}$ is taken as the peak of $u(t)$. This is the value $\hat{\alpha}$ such that $\dot{u}(\hat{\alpha}) = 0$. The mean of $\dot{u}(t)$ at the point $t = \alpha$ is given by

$$E[\dot{u}(\alpha)] = E \int \dot{g}(\xi)v(\alpha - \xi)\, d\xi$$

$$= \int \dot{g}(\xi)s(\alpha - \xi)\, d\xi$$

$$= \int_{-\infty}^{\infty} jf G(f)S(f)\, df$$

where $G(f)$ is the Fourier transform of $g(t)$. The output variance is due to the noise only:

$$\text{var}\,[\dot{u}(t)] = \int\int \dot{g}(\xi)\dot{g}(\xi')E[n(t - \xi)n(t - \xi')]\, d\xi\, d\xi'$$

$$= \int\int \dot{g}(\xi)\dot{g}(\xi')\phi(\xi - \xi')\, d\xi\, d\xi'$$

This result is independent of t. Now make the change in variables

$$\eta = \xi - \xi'$$

so that

$$\text{var}\,[\dot{u}(t)] = \int \phi(\eta) \int \dot{g}(\xi)\dot{g}(\xi - \eta)\, d\xi\, d\eta$$

Transform this formula into the frequency domain using Parseval's theorem and noting that the convolution $\int \dot{g}(\xi)\dot{g}(\xi - \eta)\, d\xi$ has transform $(2\pi f)^2|G(f)|^2$. Then

$$\text{var}\,[\dot{u}(t)] = (2\pi)^2 \int_{-\infty}^{\infty} f^2 N(f)|G(f)|^2\, df$$

We now are ready to find the variance in the estimate $\hat{\alpha}$. The analysis is only valid when the signal out of the matched filter is large compared with the noise, because otherwise second-order terms become important and the linearized approximation breaks down. Based on the linearized model defined by the triangle of Fig. 8.2, we have for the error in α

$$\alpha_e = \frac{\dot{u}(\alpha)}{m}$$

and the variance is

$$\sigma_\alpha^2 = \frac{\text{var}\,[\dot{u}(\hat{\alpha})]}{m^2}$$

where the slope m is given by

$$m = \frac{d}{dt}\,E[\dot{u}(t)]_{t=\hat{\alpha}} = (2\pi)^2 \int_{-\infty}^{\infty} f^2 S(f) G(f)\,df$$

Therefore

$$\sigma_\alpha^2 = \left(\frac{1}{2\pi}\right)^2 \frac{\displaystyle\int_{-\infty}^{\infty} f^2 N(f) |G(f)|^2\,df}{\left[\displaystyle\int_{-\infty}^{\infty} f^2 S(f) G(f)\,df\right]^2}$$

To minimize the error variance by choice of $G(f)$, we manipulate the denominator into an appropriate form and use the Schwarz inequality:

$$\left[\int_{-\infty}^{\infty} f^2 S(f) G(f)\,df\right]^2 = \left\{\int_{-\infty}^{\infty} [fG(f)N^{1/2}(f)]\left[\frac{fS(f)}{N^{1/2}(f)}\right]df\right\}^2$$

$$\leq \int_{-\infty}^{\infty} f^2 |G(f)|^2 N(f)\,df \int_{-\infty}^{\infty} \frac{f^2 |S(f)|^2}{N(f)}\,df$$

with equality if and only if

$$G(f) = \frac{S^*(f)}{N(f)}$$

So for this choice of filter, we have the conclusion of the theorem.   □

We can draw a number of important conclusions from the above theorem. Because it agrees with the Cramer-Rao bound derived for gaussian processes, the matched-filter estimator is the minimum-variance unbiased estimator for gaussian processes, at least to the extent that the linearized model is valid. For any covariance stationary process, the matched-filter estimator is the best linear estimator, but for nongaussian processes there may be better nonlinear estimators. Consequently, if a designer knows only the power spectral density of covariance stationary noise but not higher-order moments, it can be assumed that the noise is gaussian. If the noise is actually nongaussian, the performance—in the sense of error variance—will be no worse than that predicted for gaussian noise. This property justifies the common assumption of gaussian noise when the true noise is not known.

We can also conclude that of all noise processes having a fixed power spectral density, none is more damaging to a linear estimator than the gaussian process. The optimum strategy for an adversary who intends to degrade the estimation process by inserting stationary noise of a fixed power spectral density is to use gaussian noise.

8.5 ESTIMATION OF PULSE ARRIVAL FREQUENCY

A received passband pulse with unknown frequency offset is a signal of the form

$$v(t) = s(t)\cos 2\pi(f_o t + \beta t + \theta) + n_R(t)\cos 2\pi f_o t - n_I(t)\sin 2\pi f_o t$$

where $s(t)$ is a known waveform with finite energy whose bandwidth is much less than the known carrier frequency f_o, and $n_R(t)$ and $n_I(t)$ are independent, stationary, gaussian-noise processes with identical and known power spectral density $N(f)$. More generally, $v(t)$ may consist of $s_R(t)$ multiplying a cosine carrier and $s_I(t)$ multiplying a sine carrier, as well as the noise terms. The passband waveform can be represented in the equivalent form of a complex baseband waveform:

$$v(t) = \left[s_R(t)\cos 2\pi(\beta t + \theta) + s_I(t)\sin 2\pi(\beta t + \theta) + n_R(t) \right]$$
$$+ j\left[-s_R(t)\sin 2\pi(\beta t + \theta) + s_I(t)\cos 2\pi(\beta t + \theta) + n_I(t) \right]$$

The estimation problem is to determine the unknown frequency offset β from $v(t)$ by means of a minimum-variance unbiased estimator.

We will consider the artificial problem in which the phase angle θ is known. Usually both β and θ are unknown and the problem is more complicated to analyze completely. Any lower bound on the arrival frequency of a waveform of known phase is also a lower bound on the arrival frequency of a waveform of unknown phase, because to know the value of the phase cannot possibly be detrimental.

The error in any estimate of pulse arrival frequency must have a variance at least as great as the Cramer-Rao bound. We will evaluate the Cramer-Rao bound for this problem.

☐   **Theorem 8.5.1**   Suppose that a known complex waveform $s(t)$ is received with an unknown frequency offset β and in the presence of additive gaussian noise of power spectral density $N(f)$. Then any estimate of β satisfies

$$\sigma_\beta^2 \geq \left[(2\pi)^2 \int_{-\infty}^{\infty} \frac{|S'(f)|^2}{N(f)}\, df \right]^{-1}$$

where $S'(f)$ is the derivative of $S(f)$.

Proof   We will restrict attention to a finite time interval $[-T/2, T/2]$, and express the received signal $v(t)$ using a Karhunen-Loeve expansion. The real and imaginary components of the complex signal have the same Karhunen-Loeve expansion functions because the noise components have equal correlation functions. The expansion of the complex baseband waveform is

$$v(t) = \sum_{k=1}^{\infty} v_{Rk}\psi_k^{(T)}(t) + j\sum_{k=1}^{\infty} v_{Ik}\psi_k^{(T)}(t) = \sum_{k=1}^{\infty} v_k\psi_k^{(T)}(t)$$

where the Karhunen-Loeve expansion functions $\psi_k^{(T)}(t)$ are the orthonormal eigenfunctions of the integral equation

$$\int_{-T/2}^{T/2} \phi(t - s)\psi^{(T)}(s)\, ds = \lambda\psi^{(T)}(t) \qquad -T/2 \le t \le T/2$$

in which

$$\phi(t - s) = E[n_R(t)n_R(s)] = E[n_I(t)n_I(s)]$$

The expansion coefficients

$$v_k = v_{Rk} + jv_{Ik}$$

for $k = 1, \ldots$ are independent, complex gaussian random variables whose real and imaginary components are independent and have variance λ_k, where λ_k is the eigenvalue of the above integral equation corresponding to the eigenfunction $\psi_k^{(T)}(t)$. The mean of v_k is

$$s_k(\beta) = \int_{-T/2}^{T/2} [s_R(t) + js_I(t)][\cos 2\pi\beta t - j\sin 2\pi\beta t]\psi_k^{(T)}(t)\, dt$$

Because the noise terms do not depend on β, the expansion functions $\psi_k^{(T)}(t)$ are independent of β. For each k, we have an independent contribution to the Cramer-Rao bound. The Cramer-Rao bound is obtained by summing the single component contributions:

$$\sigma_\beta^2 \ge \sum_{k=1}^{\infty} E\left[\frac{\partial}{\partial\beta}\log p_k(v_k|\beta)\right]^2 = \sum_{k=1}^{\infty} \frac{1}{\lambda_k}\left|\frac{ds_k(\beta)}{d\beta}\right|^2$$

This is the Cramer-Rao bound if $v(t)$ is only observed from $-T/2$ to $T/2$. We now let $T \to \infty$ to obtain the following bound:

$$\sigma_\beta^2 \ge \left[\lim_{T\to\infty} \sum_{k=1}^{\infty} \frac{1}{\lambda_k}\left(\frac{ds_k(\beta)}{d\beta}\right)^2\right]^{-1}$$

This limit can be evaluated in the same way as in the proofs of Theorem 4.2.1 and Theorem 8.4.1. We need only recall that the Fourier transform of $ts(t)$ is $dS(f)/df$ to complete the proof. □

The Cramer-Rao bound for the case where the noise is white is of considerable practical interest. In this case,

$$N(f) = \frac{N_o}{2} \qquad \text{watts/hertz}$$

and the bound becomes

$$\sigma_\beta^2 \ge \frac{1}{(2\pi)^2 \overline{t^2} 2E_p/N_o}$$

where

$$\overline{t^2} = \frac{\displaystyle\int_{-\infty}^{\infty} |S'(f)|^2\, df}{\displaystyle\int_{-\infty}^{\infty} |S(f)|^2\, df}$$

The maximum-likelihood estimator achieves the Cramer-Rao bound whenever the signal-to-noise ratio is sufficiently large. The variance of this estimator could be derived directly, as was done for estimation of time of arrival in the previous section. The analysis would be valid for any stationary noise process with power spectral density $N(f)$; that analysis would not require an assumption of gaussian noise. Consequently, because the variance must asymptotically agree with the Cramer-Rao bound, we expect that

$$\sigma_\beta^2 = \left[(2\pi)^2 \int \frac{|S'(f)|^2}{N(f)} \, df \right]^{-1}$$

for the maximum-likelihood estimator, provided the signal-to-noise ratio is sufficiently large.

8.6 PRINCIPLES OF INFERENCE

A limited set of data can be extrapolated or interpolated only if one has a model underlying the data. For example, time sampling represents a continuous-time function $s(t)$ by its value at a discrete set of time instants. However, samples $s(k\Delta t)$ for $k = 0, \pm 1, \pm 2, \ldots$ are useless for specifying $s(t)$ at other values of t unless one accepts a model that imposes conditions on $s(t)$. One possible condition is that the transform $S(f) = 0$ for $|f| > 2/\Delta t$. Then, using the Nyquist-Shannon interpolation formula, $s(t)$ can be computed for any t. By requiring $S(f)$ to satisfy such a condition, we are imposing a model onto the data that the data by itself cannot justify. Sometimes a model of this kind may not be available; it then must be construed using the data and some general principle of inference.

The *Jaynes maximum-entropy principle* is a principle of data reduction that says that when reducing a set of data into the form of an underlying model, one should be maximally noncommittal with respect to missing data. If one must estimate a probability distribution $\mathbf{q}$ on the data source satisfying certain known constraints on $\mathbf{q}$, such as

$$\sum_k q_k f_k = t$$

then, of those distributions that are consistent with the constraints, one should choose as the estimate of $\mathbf{q}$ the probability distribution $\hat{\mathbf{q}}$ that has maximum entropy. A nice example can be given for a probabilistic source with a real output. Suppose the source produces a real-valued random variable X whose mean and variance are known, and otherwise the probability distribution governing the source is unknown. Then the maximum-entropy principle says that one should estimate that the probability density $q(x)$ is a gaussian probability density with the given mean and variance. This is a consequence of Theorem 7.2.1, which says that a gaussian random variable has the largest differential entropy of a given mean and variance.

The *Kullback minimum-discrimination principle* is a more general principle that applies when, in addition to a set of constraints on the source probability distribution $\mathbf{q}$, one is also given a probability distribution $\mathbf{p}$ that is a prior estimate of $\mathbf{q}$. The principle of minimum discrimination states that, of the probability distributions that satisfy the constraints, one should choose as the new estimate that distribution $\hat{\mathbf{q}}$ that minimizes the discrimination $L(\hat{\mathbf{q}};\mathbf{p})$. Then

$$L(\hat{\mathbf{q}};\mathbf{p}) = \min_{\mathbf{q}} L(\mathbf{q};\mathbf{p})$$

where the minimum is over the set of $\mathbf{q}$ that satisfy the constraint

$$\sum_k q_k f_k = t$$

Because $L(\mathbf{p};\mathbf{p}) = 0$, if the prior distribution $\mathbf{p}$ satisfies the constraints, then $\mathbf{p}$ itself will be chosen as the new estimate of the source probability distribution satisfying the constraints.

If the source is a discrete source and $\mathbf{p}$ is the equiprobable distribution, then the minimum-discrimination principle reduces to the maximum-entropy principle because

$$\min_{\mathbf{q}} L(\mathbf{q};\mathbf{p}) = \min_{\mathbf{q}} \left[\sum_j q_j \log \frac{q_j}{1/J} \right]$$

$$= \log J - \max_{\mathbf{q}} \left[H(\mathbf{q}) \right]$$

The maximum-entropy principle is the minimum-discrimination principle with an equiprobable distribution as the prior distribution. In this sense, the principle of minimum discrimination is the more general principle.

When the source is continuous, the maximum-entropy principle refers to the differential entropy. One can relate the maximum-entropy principle for continuous sources to the minimum-discrimination principle by using a gaussian density as the prior density $\mathbf{p}$.

Neither the minimum-discrimination principle nor the maximum-entropy principle is universally accepted as a fundamental principle. However, both are consequences of the properties of conditional probability. We shall derive the principle of minimum discrimination from the properties of conditional probability for the case where the constraints are simple moments of the form $E[f(X)] = t$. The derivation for the case of correlation-like constraints of the form $E[f(X_i, X_j)] = t$ is more difficult.

We shall begin by replacing the equality constraints with more general constraints in the form of inequalities:

$$\sum_k q_k f_k \leq t$$

An equality constraint can be accommodated by writing it as two inequality constraints,

$$\sum_k q_k f_k \le t$$

and

$$\sum_k q_k(-f_k) \le -t$$

so we have not reduced the generality by treating only inequality constraints.

A list of constraints is written in vector form as

$$\sum_k q_k \mathbf{f}_k \le \mathbf{t}$$

A dataword $\mathbf{x}$ will satisfy the constraints if and only if its composition $\mathbf{q}$ is in the convex set $\mathcal{Q}$ given by

$$\mathcal{Q} = \left\{ \mathbf{q} : \sum_k q_k \mathbf{f}_k \le \mathbf{t} \right\}$$

This set is illustrated in Fig. 8.3 for the case of two constraints.

The gist of the following theorem is that if one has a memoryless source $\mathbf{p}$ to which is imposed a side constraint that certain source output sequences of composition in a particular class are prohibited, then that source essentially becomes a memoryless source with probability distribution $\hat{\mathbf{q}}$ satisfying the minimum-discrimination principle. Let $\mathcal{A}$ be the set of sequences $\mathbf{x}$ that satisfy the constraints, and let $\mathbf{p}^n(\cdot \mid \mathcal{A})$ denote the probability distribution on sequences when restricted to set $\mathcal{A}$. Specifically, $p^n(\mathbf{x} \mid \mathbf{x} \in \mathcal{A})$ is the probability of $\mathbf{x}$, given that $\mathbf{x}$ is in the set $\mathcal{A}$. The theorem implies that for large enough n, $\mathbf{p}^n(\cdot \mid \mathcal{A})$ approaches the product distribution $\hat{\mathbf{q}}^n$.

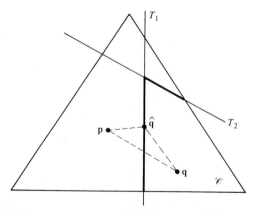

Figure 8.3   Illustrating the principle of minimum discrimination.

That is,

$$\lim_{n \to \infty} \frac{1}{n} L(\mathbf{p}^n(\cdot|\mathscr{A}); \hat{\mathbf{q}}^n) = 0$$

where $\hat{\mathbf{q}}$ achieves the minimum discrimination of the theorem.

☐ **Theorem 8.6.1** Given a discrete memoryless source $\mathbf{p}$ and a subset $\mathscr{A}$ of source output blocks $\mathbf{x} = (x_1, \ldots, x_n)$ of blocklength n satisfying the constraints on sample averages,

$$\frac{1}{n} \sum_{l=1}^{n} \mathbf{f}(x_l) \le \mathbf{t}$$

Then

$$\lim_{n \to \infty} \frac{1}{n} L(\mathbf{p}^n(\cdot|\mathscr{A}); \mathbf{p}^n) = \min_{\mathbf{q} \in \mathscr{Q}} L(\mathbf{q}; \mathbf{p})$$

where

$$\mathscr{Q} = \left\{ \mathbf{q} : \sum_k q_k \mathbf{f}_k \le \mathbf{t} \right\}$$

Proof The theorem and its proof use the same ideas as were used in the proof of Theorem 4.5.1. As in the proof of Theorem 4.5.1, we can write

$$Pr[\mathscr{A}] = e^{-L(\mathbf{p}^n(\cdot|\mathscr{A}); \mathbf{p}^n)}$$

which is easy to show by using the Bayes formula to express $\mathbf{p}^n(\cdot|\mathscr{A})$. Then, using Theorem 4.3.8,

$$Pr[\mathscr{A}] \le e^{-\Sigma_l L(\mathbf{p}^{(l)}(\cdot|\mathscr{A}); \mathbf{p}^n)}$$

$$\le e^{-nL(\mathbf{p}(\cdot|\mathscr{A}); \mathbf{p})}$$

where $\mathbf{p}(\cdot|\mathscr{A})$ is the average single-letter probability distribution defined as in the proof of Theorem 4.5.1. The upper bound is completed by writing

$$Pr[\mathscr{A}] \le \exp\left\{ -n\left[\min_{\mathbf{q} \in \mathscr{Q}} L(\mathbf{q}; \mathbf{p}) \right] \right\}$$

The last inequality is valid because $\mathbf{p}(\cdot|\mathscr{A})$ satisfies the constraints defining the convex set $\mathscr{Q}$ as can be verified in the same way as in the proof of Theorem 4.5.1.

Now we need to derive the corresponding lower bound. Choose $\varepsilon > 0$, and choose any $\mathbf{q}$ in $\mathscr{Q}$ with discrimination $L(\mathbf{q}; \mathbf{p})$ within ε of the minimum $L(\hat{\mathbf{q}}; \mathbf{p})$. The law of large numbers implies that

$$Pr\left[\frac{1}{n} \sum_{l=1}^{n} f(x_l) \ge t \right]$$

tends to 1 as n goes to infinity. Therefore, as in Theorem 4.5.1,

$$Pr[\mathscr{A}] \geq e^{-n[L(\hat{q};p) + 2\varepsilon]}$$

for sufficiently large n. Consequently, combining this lower bound with the earlier upper bound gives

$$Pr[\mathscr{A}] = e^{-nL(\hat{q};p) - o(n)} \qquad \square$$

To understand the sense in which $\mathbf{p}^n(\cdot|\mathscr{A})$ behaves like the product distribution $\hat{\mathbf{q}}^n$, consider the projection inequality:

$$L(\mathbf{q};\mathbf{p}) \geq L(\mathbf{q};\mathbf{q}^*) + L(\mathbf{q}^*;\mathbf{p})$$

for all $\mathbf{q} \in \mathscr{Q}$ where $\mathscr{Q}$ is a convex set of probability vectors and

$$L(\mathbf{q}^*;\mathbf{p}) = \min_{\mathbf{q} \in \mathscr{Q}} L(\mathbf{q};\mathbf{p})$$

As applied to the situation of Theorem 8.6.1, the projection inequality gives

$$L(\mathbf{p}^n(\cdot|\mathscr{A});\mathbf{p}^n) \geq L(\mathbf{p}^n(\cdot|\mathscr{A});\hat{\mathbf{q}}^n) + L(\hat{\mathbf{q}}^n;\mathbf{p}^n)$$

But the theorem says that

$$L(\mathbf{p}^n(\cdot|\mathscr{A});\mathbf{p}^n) = L(\hat{\mathbf{q}}^n;\mathbf{p}^n) + o(n)$$

which leads to

$$L(\mathbf{p}^n(\cdot|\mathscr{A});\hat{\mathbf{q}}^n) \leq o(n)$$

so we have the heuristic notion that $\mathbf{p}^n(\cdot|\mathscr{A})$ approaches the product distribution $\hat{\mathbf{q}}^n$.

8.7 SPECTRAL ESTIMATION

Spectral estimation involves the problem of estimating the power spectrum of a stochastic process, given the value of its autocorrelation function $\phi(\tau)$ at a finite number of values of τ. We consider only discrete-time stochastic processes for which $m + 1$ consecutive values of the autocorrelation function are known. Spectral-estimation methods in common use ignore the possibility of noise on the autocorrelation samples. Only the problem of computing the spectrum from the exactly known autocorrelation samples is treated.

Every method of spectral estimation can be interpreted as a method of filling in the missing autocorrelation samples and must assume an underlying model. Sometimes the assumption is partially hidden and not immediately seen to be an assumption. For example, the simplest spectral-estimation procedure takes as the estimated spectrum a discrete Fourier transform of the known values of the autocorrelation function, possibly padding the known values of the autocorrelation function with zero components to make the number of components equal to the blocklength of the Fourier transform. Because a discrete Fourier transform is used, the implicit assumption is that the autocorrelation function is periodic, with a period equal to the blocklength of the Fourier transform.

The Jaynes maximum-entropy principle, when applied to spectral estimation, yields an alternative procedure known as *maximum-entropy spectral estimation*. Suppose that a discrete-time covariance-stationary stochastic process $\{X_i\}_{i=1}^{\infty}$ is known to have $m + 1$ specified consecutive autocorrelation values:

$$E[X_iX_{i+k}] = \phi_k \qquad k = 0, 1, 2, \dots, m$$
$$i = 1, 2, \dots$$

We wish to find ϕ_k for all values of k. This is equivalent to finding the power spectral density of the stochastic process.

□ **Theorem 8.7.1   (Burg's theorem)** The stochastic process $\{X_i\}_{i=1}^{\infty}$ that maximizes the differential entropy rate subject to the auto-correlation constraints

$$E[X_iX_{i+k}] = \phi_k \qquad k = 0, 1, 2, \dots, m$$
$$i = 1, 2, \dots$$

is the mth-order Markov zero-mean gaussian process satisfying these constraints.

Proof   Choose any blocklength n larger than m. Let $X_1, X_2, \dots, X_n$ be any collection of random variables satisfying the conditions of the theorem. Let $Z_1, Z_2, \dots, Z_n$ be any zero-mean multivariate gaussian random variables with a covariance matrix satisfying the conditions of the theorem, and let $Z_1', Z_2', \dots, Z_n'$ be the mth-order Markov zero-mean gaussian process satisfying the conditions of the theorem.

The proof involves two inequalities, one relating to the gaussian assumption and one relating to the Markov assumption. Both inequalities will be tight under the conditions of the theorem. The first inequality, a consequence of the gaussian assumption, is

$$H(X_1, X_2, \dots, X_n) \le H(Z_1, Z_2, \dots, Z_n)$$

This is the multivariate generalization of Theorem 7.2.1 and is proved the same way.

The second inequality is developed starting with the chain rule for entropy:

$$H(Z_1, Z_2, \dots, Z_n)$$
$$= H(Z_1, Z_2, \dots, Z_m) + \sum_{k=m+1}^{n} H(Z_k | Z_{k-1}, \dots, Z_1)$$
$$\le H(Z_1, Z_2, \dots, Z_m) + \sum_{k=m+1}^{n} H(Z_k | Z_{k-1}, Z_{k-2}, \dots, Z_{k-m})$$

The inequality is the conditional entropy inequality $H(A|B,C) \le H(A|B)$. Each term on the right side depends only on the covariance matrix because of the gaussian assumption. Therefore we have

$$H(Z_1, Z_2, \ldots, Z_n)$$

$$\le H(Z'_1, Z'_2, \ldots, Z'_m) + \sum_{k=m+1}^{n} H(Z'_k | Z'_{k-1}, Z'_{k-2}, \ldots, Z'_{k-m})$$

$$= H(Z'_1, Z'_2, \ldots, Z'_m) + \sum_{k=m+1}^{n} H(Z'_k | Z'_{k-1}, Z'_{k-2}, \ldots, Z'_1)$$

$$= H(Z'_1, Z'_2, \ldots, Z'_n)$$

Therefore

$$H(X_1, X_2, \ldots, X_n) \le H(Z'_1, Z'_2, \ldots, Z'_n)$$

and

$$\lim_{n \to \infty} \frac{1}{n} H(X_1, \ldots, X_n) \le \lim_{n \to \infty} \frac{1}{n} H(Z'_1, \ldots, Z'_n)$$

for all stochastic processes $\{X_i\}$ satisfying the autocorrelation constraints, thus proving the theorem. $\square$

The maximum-entropy stochastic process can be thought of as the output of an autoregressive filter excited by discrete-time white noise. The maximum-entropy estimate of the stochastic process is

$$X_i = -\sum_{j=1}^{m} g_j X_{i-j} + n_i$$

where the filter coefficients g_j are chosen so that the correlation coefficients of this process agree with the specified correlation coefficients. Multiply by X_0 and take the expectation to see that the filter coefficients can be computed as the solution of the matrix equation:

$$\phi_i = -\sum_{j=1}^{m} g_j \phi_{i-j}$$

where the correlation coefficients ϕ_i for $i = 0, \ldots, m$ are known.

PROBLEMS

8.1. The variance of a zero-mean gaussian process is estimated, based on n samples x_l for $l = 1, \ldots, n$, by using the estimate

$$\hat{N} = \frac{1}{n} \sum_{l=1}^{n} x_l^2$$

Show that this is a minimum-variance unbiased estimate by showing it is unbiased and has variance that equals the Cramer-Rao bound.

8.2. Derive the Cramer-Rao bound for a biased estimator.

8.3. Derive the alternative form of the Cramer-Rao bound:

$$\sigma_\theta^2 \geq \frac{-1}{E[(\partial^2/\partial\theta^2) \log q(x|\theta)]}$$

8.4. Suppose a two-dimensional vector random variable is observed having a bivariate gaussian distribution with covariance matrix

$$\Sigma(\rho) = \begin{bmatrix} S+N & S\rho \\ S\rho & S+N \end{bmatrix}$$

depending on a parameter ρ. Show that an unbiased estimate of ρ has variance satisfying

$$\sigma_\rho^2 \geq \frac{(2SN + N^2)^2}{S^2(2S^2 + 2SN + N^2)}$$

How does the bound behave when S is much larger than N, and when S is much smaller than N?

8.5. (Estimation under a prior distribution) Suppose that $p(\theta)$ is a prior distribution on the parameter θ and define the expected value of the variance as

$$\sigma^2 = \int p(\theta)\sigma_\theta^2 \, d\theta$$

Give a bound on σ^2 in the spirit of the Cramer-Rao bound. In particular, show that the expected variance of any estimate of a zero-mean gaussian random variable θ with variance S in the presence of additive gaussian noise of variance N must satisfy

$$\sigma^2 \geq N\left(1 + \frac{N}{S}\right)^2$$

8.6. Show that the variance of a matched-filter estimator is insensitive to small perturbations in the filter transfer function.

8.7. **a.** Prove that, as long as enough energy exists in each segment so that the linearized analysis holds, with no loss in arrival-time estimation accuracy a waveform can be chopped up into segments and the arrival time of the waveform estimated by averaging estimates of the arrival time of each segment. This justifies the common practice of estimating the arrival time of a pulse train by estimating the arrival time of each pulse individually and then averaging (after suitable correction for pulse offset time). For time-of-arrival estimation it is not necessary to maintain coherence in long-duration waveforms.

b. Prove that the arrival frequency of a pulse train can be estimated much more accurately than one can estimate the arrival frequency of a single pulse. Estimating the arrival frequency of a pulse train by averaging estimates made on individual pulses can result in excessive degradation in accuracy.

8.8. A coin is given whose probability p of landing heads up is unknown. The probability p is to be estimated by flipping the coin N times and observing the result. Intuitively, there is no need to record the full sequence of heads and tails. Prove that the number of heads observed is a sufficient statistic for estimating p.

8.9. Suppose that $\hat{\theta}(\mathbf{x})$ is an unbiased estimate of the vector parameter θ, given a vector measurement that is gaussian with a mean $\bar{\mathbf{x}}(\theta)$ that depends on θ and a covariance matrix Φ that does not depend on θ. Prove that the covariance matrix of the estimate satisfies

$$\Delta\theta^T \Sigma(\theta) \, \Delta\theta \geq \Delta\theta^T \left[\text{tr} \left[\frac{\partial \bar{\mathbf{x}}(\theta)^T}{\partial \theta_i} \Phi^{-1} \frac{\partial \bar{\mathbf{x}}(\theta)}{\partial \theta_j} \right]^{-1} \right] \Delta\theta$$

for all $\Delta\theta$.

8.10. Using the Schwarz inequality, prove that, for any additive, covariance, stationary noise of power spectral density $N(f)$ and finite-energy input waveform $s(t)$ with transform $S(f)$, the filter

$$G(f) = \frac{S^*(f)}{N(f)}$$

uniquely maximizes the output signal-to-noise ratio at time zero.

8.11. For each positive integer r, there is an *exponential family* of probability distributions, which is the parameterized family of the form

$$p(x) = \exp\left(-\sum_{i=0}^{r} a_i x^i \right)$$

where $(a_0, \ldots, a_r)$ is a parameter vector designating $p(x)$. (The set of all gaussian distributions on x is an example of an exponential family.) Find conditions so that if the prior distribution $\mathbf{p}$ is in an exponential family, the minimum-discrimination distribution $\hat{\mathbf{q}}$ will be in the same exponential family.

8.12. A received passband waveform with unknown time of arrival, offset frequency, and carrier phase is expressed as

$$v(t) = s(t - \alpha) \cos 2\pi(f_0 t + \beta t + \theta) + n(t)$$

where $s(t)$ is a known pulse of finite energy and $n(t)$ is stationary gaussian noise of power spectral density $N(f)$.
   a. Give the Cramer-Rao bound for simultaneous estimation of α, β, and θ.
   b. Give the structure of a matched filter estimator for α, β, θ.

8.13. Prove the *projection inequality*:

$$L(\mathbf{q};\mathbf{p}) \geq L(\mathbf{q};\mathbf{q}^*) + L(\mathbf{q}^*;\mathbf{p})$$

for all $\mathbf{q} \in \mathcal{Q}$ where $\mathcal{Q}$ is a convex set of probability distributions, and

$$L(\mathbf{q}^*;\mathbf{p}) = \min_{\mathbf{q} \in \mathcal{Q}} L(\mathbf{q};\mathbf{p})$$

NOTES

The Cramer-Rao bound (1946, 1945) is a central inequality of mathematical statistics. It is a more general form of the earlier inequality of Fisher (1925). Our presentation of the Cramer-Rao bound as an information inequality is not the standard approach. Slepian (1954) first evaluated the Cramer-Rao bound for the estimation of pulse arrival time in white gaussian noise. This approach leads to a matched filter as a maximum-likelihood estimator. Mallinckrodt and Sollenberger (1954) approached the problem from another point of view by using variational arguments to derive the best linear filter to be used in conjunction with a signal-peak detector in order to obtain a minimum-variance, unbiased time-of-arrival estimate of a certain type. Later treatments have followed one or the other of these approaches. Besides the Cramer-Rao bound, other bounds are of interest when the signal-to-noise ratio is low such as the bounds of Ziv and Zakai (1969) and Seidman (1970).

The two most important estimators in engineering practice are the matched filter, which has something of a block structure, and the Kalman (1960) or Kalman-Bucy (1961) filter, which has something of a sequential structure.

The Jaynes principle of maximum entropy first appeared in 1957 and the Kullback principle of minimum discrimination was given in 1959. Shore and Johnson (1980) formulated a set of axioms of consistency and showed that these principles are consequences of those axioms. Van Campenhout and Cover (1981) and Csiszár (1984) developed the principle of maximum entropy as a consequence of properties of conditional probability. The maximum-entropy spectral estimate is credited to Burg (1975); we use the more powerful information-theoretic proof of Choi and Cover (1984).

CHAPTER 9

Multiterminal Information Networks

A point-to-point information system consists of one data source, one data user, and one channel between them. A multiterminal network is more general, allowing for more than one data source, more than one data user, or more than one channel between them. Information networks can have conflicting requirements imposed by the several terminals. An efficient communication system tries to satisfy several goals at once—perhaps to interlock several independent messages into one efficient waveform; perhaps to share a multiaccess channel among several users; or perhaps to break a message into two distorted replicas, which together contain enough information to reconstruct the original message. In this chapter we shall study to what extent it is possible in such problems to satisfy several goals at once.

9.1 FEEDBACK CHANNELS

A feedback channel, shown in Fig. 9.1, is used to transmit information in one

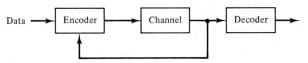

Figure 9.1   The feedback channel.

direction from a transmitter to a receiver. However, there is also a side channel in the reverse direction that informs the transmitter about the message reaching the receiver. The transmitter can then modify its subsequent message to include errata pertaining to earlier parts of the message.

A discrete memoryless feedback channel has one input alphabet $\{a_j\}$ and one output alphabet $\{b_k\}$. Given input symbol a_j, the channel output is symbol b_k with probability $Q(b_k \,|\, a_j)$, abbreviated $Q_{k|j}$. This much is the same as a simple point-to-point channel. The difference is that both the encoder and the decoder receive the channel input symbol b_k.

In this section we shall show that the capacity in the forward direction is not increased by the addition of feedback to the channel; one can communicate at the same rates without feedback as with it. This is a remarkable result because one might readily expect the opposite: that the transmitter could transmit, rather carelessly, at a higher net rate if it knew which symbols needed to be re-sent because they were received in error. What is true, however, is that to achieve any given rate smaller than capacity, the *complexity* of the codes will be much less when there is feedback, because then much simpler coding schemes can be used. Thus feedback is of practical importance because of its effect on complexity, not because of its effect on capacity.

Because we are proving a negative result, it is permissible to use strong assumptions. We will prove that feedback does not increase capacity even in the best case—that is, when the feedback is error-free and instantaneous. It is clear then that more restricted forms of feedback will not increase capacity either.

Let m index the set of possible transmitted messages. A block code for a feedback channel is a vector function whose lth component is a function of m and the first $l - 1$ components of the received block. We can think of the codewords as trees truncated at blocklength n. Figure 9.2 shows this new form of a codeword for $n = 4$. The encoder chooses the upward path if the feedback of the previous bit is a 0 and chooses the lower path if the feedback is a 1. The crosshatched path is the path that will be taken if there are no channel errors in the first three channel bits. An error in the last channel bit has no effect on the encoding of a block. It must be emphasized that we are speaking here of an *encoding* operation. The decoding operation consists of finding which of M codetrees best fits the received data. The assignment of bits to the branches of a codetree should be done so as to make the trees very different, but not necessarily to make the branches on a single tree different.

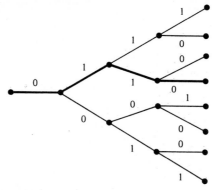

Figure 9.2   A codeword for a binary feedback channel.

We can express the *l*th input to the channel functionally as the variable $x_l = f(m, y_{l-1}, y_{l-2}, \ldots, y_1)$ taking values in $\{a_j\}$, where the variable y_l is the *l*th output of the channel taking values in $\{b_k\}$ and *m* is the message index ranging from 0 to $M - 1$.

☐ **Theorem 9.1.1**   The channel capacity of a discrete memoryless channel with feedback is equal to the capacity of that channel without feedback.

Proof   Certainly anything that can be done without feedback can be done with feedback simply by ignoring the feedback, so we only need to prove that the capacity is not larger than *C*. To prove this converse statement we need only prove that at rates above capacity the block equivocation is bounded away from zero, because then Fano's inequality tells us that the probability of error is bounded away from zero.

Let X^n denote the block random variable at the input to the channel, and let Y^n denote the block random variable at the output. To carry through the proof we need to find an upper bound on the mutual information $I(X^n; Y^n)$. Accordingly, write

$$I(X_1, \ldots, X_n; Y_1, \ldots, Y_n) = H(Y_1, \ldots, Y_n) - H(Y_1, \ldots, Y_n | X_1, \ldots, X_n)$$

$$\leq \sum_{l=1}^{n} H(Y_l) - \sum_{l=1}^{n} H(Y_l | X_1, \ldots, X_n, Y_1, \ldots, Y_{l-1})$$

where we have used Theorem 3.2.3 on the first term, and Corollary 3.2.6 on the second term. But the channel is memoryless, so the probability of y_l depends on previous channel outputs only because the channel input depends on previous channel outputs. Thus

$$Pr[y_l | x_1, \ldots, x_n, y_1, \ldots, y_{l-1}] = Pr[y_l | x_l]$$

Consequently,

$$H(Y_l | X_1, \ldots, X_n, Y_1, \ldots, Y_{l-1}) = H(Y_l | X_l)$$

Therefore

$$I(X_1, \ldots, X_n; Y_1, \ldots, Y_n) \leq \sum_{l=1}^{n} H(Y_l) - \sum_{l=1}^{n} H(Y_l | X_l)$$

$$= \sum_{l=1}^{n} I(X_l; Y_l)$$

$$\leq nC$$

where the last inequality applies because, for every l, $I(X_l; Y_l)$ is not larger than C.

Let W be a random variable denoting the message; $W = m$ with probability of p_m. Let $\hat{W}$ be a random variable denoting the output of the decoder. Therefore by the data-processing theorem,

$$I(W; \hat{W}) \leq I(X^n; Y^n)$$

$$\leq nC$$

Now we can apply Fano's inequality. The per-symbol form of Fano's inequality given in Theorem 6.1.2 says that in a dataword of blocklength N transmitted by a codeword of blocklength n, the per-symbol probability of decoding error, $\langle p_e \rangle$ satisfies

$$\langle p_e \rangle \log (J - 1) + H_b(\langle p_e \rangle) \geq \frac{1}{N} H(W) - \frac{1}{N} I(W; \hat{W})$$

where J is the size of the data alphabet. Because $H(W) = nR$ and $I(W; \hat{W}) \leq nC$, this becomes

$$\langle p_e \rangle \log (J - 1) + H_b(\langle p_e \rangle) \geq \frac{n}{R} (R - C)$$

$$= \frac{R - C}{R} \log J$$

and if $R > C$, the probability of symbol error is bounded away from zero for all blocklengths. $\square$

9.2 MULTIACCESS CHANNELS

A multiaccess channel consists of two or more transmitters and one receiver, as shown in Fig. 9.3; we shall study the case with two transmitters, the X transmitter and the Y transmitter. The channel has two input alphabets $\{a_j\}$ and $\{a'_{j'}\}$, which need not be the same alphabet nor of the same size. The channel has one output alphabet $\{b_k\}$. Given input symbols a_j and $a'_{j'}$, the

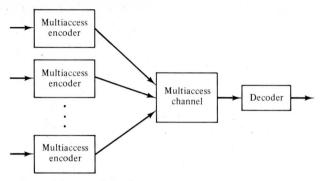

Figure 9.3   The multiaccess channel.

channel output is symbol b_k with probability $Q(b_k|a_j,a'_{j'})$, abbreviated $Q_{k|jj'}$. The multiaccess channel is memoryless if the output probability does not depend on symbols transmitted or received at earlier times.

The multiaccess channel $\{Q_{k|jj'}\}$ becomes a point-to-point channel $\{Q_{k|j}(j')\}$ if the second transmitter sends only the fixed symbol $a'_{j'}$ by prearrangement among all terminals. We think of that transmitter as turned off and the symbol $a'_{j'}$—perhaps the zero symbol—is the standard channel input symbol from that transmitter when it is turned off. The prearranged symbol should be chosen so that the first transmitter sees a channel of the largest capacity. For each $a'_{j'}$, let $C(j')$ be the capacity of the channel $Q_{k|j}(j')$. Then $a'_{j'}$ should be chosen so that $C(j')$ is largest.

The *capacity region* of the multiaccess channel is formally defined as the convex hull[†] of the set of all pairs (R_x, R_y) for which codes exist that can transmit information with arbitrarily small probability of error. Two points in the capacity region are given by $(C_x, 0)$ and $(0, C_y)$, where $C_x = \max_{j'} C(j')$ and $C_y = \max_j C(j)$.

One way to use a multiaccess channel is by timesharing. Each transmitter takes a turn using the channel for a period of time. To timeshare the channel, the first transmitter uses the channel a fraction λ of the time with the second transmitter turned off, and the second transmitter uses the channel a fraction $1 - \lambda$ of the time with the first transmitter turned off.

This is the reason that the convex hull is included in the definition of the capacity region: If any two points are in the capacity region then, by timesharing, the straight line joining them is also in the region. This is because any point on the straight line can be obtained by using one coding scheme a fraction λ of the time and the other a fraction $1 - \lambda$ of the time. In this way we see that the point $(\lambda C_x, (1 - \lambda)C_y)$ is in the capacity region for all λ between 0 and 1. Therefore the straight line between $(C_x, 0)$ and $(0, C_y)$ lies in the capacity

---

[†]The *convex hull* of a set of points is the intersection of all convex sets that contain that set of points.

region, as do all points below this line. To find other points in the capacity region requires a more direct approach.

□ **Definition 9.2.1**   Let $M_x = 2^{nR_x}$ and $M_y = 2^{nR_y}$. A block code $\mathscr{C}$ of rates R_x and R_y and blocklength n for a multiaccess channel consists of two component codes $\mathscr{C}_x$ and $\mathscr{C}_y$. Set $\mathscr{C}_x$ consists of the set of M_x codewords $\{\mathbf{c}_m\}$. Set $\mathscr{C}_y$ consists of the set of M_y codewords $\{\mathbf{c}'_{m'}\}$.   □

Given input blocks $\mathbf{x}$ and $\mathbf{y}$, the probability that the output of a memoryless multiaccess channel is the output block $\mathbf{z}$, is given by the product distribution

$$Q(\mathbf{z}|\mathbf{x}, \mathbf{y}) = \prod_{l=1}^{n} Q_{k_l|j_l j'_l}$$

When codewords $\mathbf{c}_m$ and $\mathbf{c}'_{m'}$ are transmitted, the channel output is the received word $\mathbf{z}$ with probability $Q(\mathbf{z}|\mathbf{c}_m, \mathbf{c}'_{m'})$. The maximum-likelihood decoder finds that pair of codewords $\mathbf{c}_m$ and $\mathbf{c}'_{m'}$ such that the likelihood function $Q(\mathbf{z}|\mathbf{c}_m, \mathbf{c}'_{m'})$ is maximum. This decoder has the minimum probability of error if the inputs are used equiprobably. In proving the coding theorem we shall use another decoder that is not quite as good as the maximum-likelihood decoder, but is good enough to prove the theorem. The decoder will look for codewords that are jointly weakly typical with the received word. Usually the decoder will find a unique pair of jointly typical codewords, and these will be the same as would be found by the maximum-likelihood decoder. Occasionally our decoder will fail where the maximum-likelihood decoder would decode correctly, but this is negligibly often.

We shall see that even though the coding is at the block level, because the channel is memoryless, the description of the capacity region is at the level of a single letter. The single-letter description is portrayed in Fig. 9.4. Single-letter descriptions in coding theorems occur throughout multiterminal information theory just as they do for point-to-point channels. Intuitively, the input random variables X and Y in Fig. 9.4 are independent, taking values with a product probability distribution $p_j p'_{j'}$. The mutual informations that are then naturally suggested are the right ones for describing the capacity region, as is asserted in the next theorem.

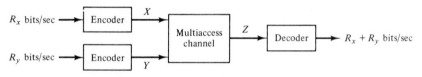

Figure 9.4   Single-letter view of a multiaccess channel.

☐ **Theorem 9.2.2** The capacity region of the memoryless multiaccess channel consists of the convex hull of the set of all rates R_x and R_y for which

$$R_x \leq I(X;Z|Y)$$
$$R_y \leq I(Y;Z|X)$$

and

$$R_x + R_y \leq I(X,Y;Z)$$

for some product probability distribution $p_j p'_{j'}$ on the input pair (X,Y).

Proof The proof follows directly from Theorem 9.2.3 and Theorem 9.2.4, which are forthcoming. ☐

☐ **Theorem 9.2.3** (**Direct theorem**) Let $\varepsilon > 0$ be given. For sufficiently large blocklength n, a code for a memoryless multiaccess channel exists having rates R_x and R_y and error probability smaller than ε, provided

$$R_x \leq I(X;Z|Y)$$
$$R_y \leq I(Y;Z|X)$$

and

$$R_x + R_y \leq I(X,Y;Z)$$

for some product probability distribution $p_j p'_{j'}$ on the input pair (X,Y).

Proof The proof involves a random-coding argument. Given $P_{jj'} = p_j p'_{j'}$, let $\mathcal{C}_x$ and $\mathcal{C}_y$ be component codes randomly and independently chosen with probability distributions **p** and **p'**, respectively. For each code, the codewords and their letters are chosen independently.

Fix $\delta > 0$. For decoding of a received word **z**, simply choose the pair $(\mathbf{c}_m, \mathbf{c}'_{m'})$ such that the triplet $(\mathbf{c}_m, \mathbf{c}'_{m'}, \mathbf{z})$ is jointly weakly δ-typical, provided such a jointly typical triplet exists and is unique. Otherwise, declare an error.

The probability of decoding error satisfies the union bound

$$p_e \leq Pr[(\mathbf{c}_m, \mathbf{c}'_{m'}, \mathbf{z}) \notin \mathcal{T}_{xyz}(\delta)] + \sum_{r,r'} Pr[(\mathbf{c}_r, \mathbf{c}'_{r'}, \mathbf{z}) \in \mathcal{T}_{xyz}(\delta) | (r,r') \neq (m,m')]$$

where $\mathcal{T}_{xyz}(\delta)$ is the set of jointly weakly δ-typical triplets. Call the two terms on the right p_{e1} and p_{e2}. The first term p_{e1} is the probability that the channel output block **z** is not jointly typical with the pair of channel codewords; the second term p_{e2} is the probability that the channel output block is jointly typical with some other pair of channel codewords. For every code, the first term goes to zero with blocklength as a consequence of the Shannon-McMillan theorem. The second term need not be small for every code; we shall show only that the ensemble average is small, and this is enough to imply that there must be some codes for which p_{e2} is small.

Because of the random nature of the code construction, the probability of error averaged over the ensemble of codes is independent of the indices (m, m') of the codeword actually transmitted. Without loss of generality, any fixed m and m' can be assumed. The ensemble average of p_{e2} is

$$E[p_{e2}] = \sum_{r, r'} Pr[(\mathbf{x}, \mathbf{y}, \mathbf{z}) \in \mathcal{T}_{xyz}(\delta) | (r, r') \neq (m, m')]$$

where we are now using $\mathbf{x}$ and $\mathbf{y}$ in place of $\mathbf{c}_r$ and $\mathbf{c}'_{r'}$ as a reminder that the codewords are realizations of random variables arising because of the random code selection.

Break the summation into three terms based on the conditions $r \neq m$ and $r' = m'$; or $r = m$ and $r' \neq m'$; or $r \neq m$ and $r' \neq m'$. We denote these by $E[p_{e2}^{(1)}]$, $E[p_{e2}^{(2)}]$, and $E[p_{e2}^{(3)}]$. As we shall see, each of these three terms corresponds to one of the three inequalities of the theorem and goes to zero if that inequality is satisfied. First consider $E[p_{e2}^{(1)}]$:

$$E[p_{e2}^{(1)}] = (M_x - 1)Pr[(\mathbf{x}, \mathbf{y}, \mathbf{z}) \in \mathcal{T}_{xyz}(\delta) | r \neq m, r' = m']$$

because there is one term in the sum over r', and $M_x - 1$ terms in the sum over r. We now rewrite the equation in the form

$$E[p_{e2}^{(1)}] = (M_x - 1) \sum_{(\mathbf{x}, \mathbf{y}, \mathbf{z}) \in \mathcal{T}_{xyz}(\delta)} p(\mathbf{x})P(\mathbf{y}, \mathbf{z})$$

where $P(\mathbf{y}, \mathbf{z})$ denotes the probability of the pair $(\mathbf{y}, \mathbf{z})$. Writing the argument of the summation as a product in this way is valid because $m \neq r$, so over the ensemble of codes X is independent of (Y, Z). We know from the properties of typical sequences that $p(\mathbf{x}) \approx 2^{-nH(X)}$ and $P(\mathbf{y}, \mathbf{z}) \approx 2^{-nH(Y, Z)}$, so we have the asymptotic equality

$$E[p_{e2}^{(1)}] \approx (M_x - 1)|\mathcal{T}_{xyz}(\delta)|2^{-nH(X)}2^{-nH(Y, Z)}$$

But we also know that the number of weakly typical triplets is given by

$$|\mathcal{T}_{xyz}(\delta)| \approx 2^{nH(X, Y, Z)}$$

Therefore

$$E[p_{e2}^{(1)}] \approx (M_x - 1)2^{n[H(X, Y, Z) - H(X) - H(Y, Z)]}$$

Now write

$$H(X, Y, Z) = H(Y) + H(X|Y) + H(Z|X, Y)$$

and

$$H(Y, Z) = H(Y) + H(Z|Y)$$

and recall that the messages are independent, so $H(X|Y) = H(X)$. Then

$$E[p_{e2}^{(1)}] \approx 2^{nR_x} 2^{-n[H(Z|Y) - H(Z|X,Y)]}$$

$$\approx 2^{nR_x} 2^{-nI(X;Z|Y)}$$

By similar analyses, we also obtain asymptotic expressions for the other terms:

$$E[p_{e2}^{(2)}] \approx 2^{nR_y} 2^{-nI(Y;Z|X)}$$

$$E[p_{e2}^{(3)}] \approx 2^{n(R_x + R_y)} 2^{-nI(X,Y;Z)}$$

It follows that, within some $o(n)$ terms in the exponents,

$$E[p_e] \le E[p_{e1}] + 2^{nR_x} 2^{-nI(X;Z|Y)} + 2^{nR_y} 2^{-nI(Y;Z|X)} + 2^{n(R_x + R_y)} 2^{-nI(X,Y;Z)}$$

The conditions of the theorem ensure that every term goes to zero as n goes to infinity. Hence

$$E[p_e] \le \varepsilon$$

for sufficiently large n. At least one code in the ensemble has a probability of error at least this small. Consequently, because ε is arbitrary, every such rate pair (R_x, R_y) is in the capacity region. The theorem is now proved because timesharing allows any point in the convex hull to be achieved. □

□   **Theorem 9.2.4   (Converse theorem)** If for every product distribution $p_j p'_{j'}$ on the inputs (X, Y) of a memoryless multiaccess channel, either

$$R_x > I(X;Z|Y)$$

$$R_y > I(Y;Z|X)$$

or

$$R_x + R_y > I(X, Y; Z)$$

then there exist no codes of rate (R_x, R_y) with arbitrarily small probability of decoded symbol error.

Proof   The proof is based on Fano's inequality. Let $\langle p_{ex} \rangle$ and $\langle p_{ey} \rangle$ be the probabilities of symbol error of symbols sent by the X encoder and sent by the Y encoder, respectively. We will need a version of Theorem 6.1.2 that deals with both $\langle p_{ex} \rangle$ and $\langle p_{ey} \rangle$. Let V_l and V'_l denote the lth symbols into the X encoder and Y encoder, respectively, and let U_l and U'_l denote the lth symbols out of the decoder corresponding to the X and Y messages, respectively.

Applying Theorem 5.3.1 to each l and then averaging over l gives

$$\langle p_{ex} \rangle \log (J - 1) + H_b(\langle p_{ex} \rangle) \geq \frac{1}{N} \sum_{l=1}^{N} H(U_l | V_l)$$

$$\langle p_{ey} \rangle \log (J' - 1) + H_b(\langle p_{ey} \rangle) \geq \frac{1}{N'} \sum_{l=1}^{N'} H(U'_l | V'_l)$$

where N and N' are the number of symbols in a data block *into* the X and Y encoders and J and J' are the sizes of the alphabets into the encoders. In forming the above expressions, the concavity of the binary entropy allows the averaging on l to be moved inside the binary entropy.

Now, as in the proof of Theorem 6.1.2, write

$$\sum_{l=1}^{N} H(U_l | V_l) \geq H(U^N | V^N)$$

$$= H(U^N) - I(U^N; V^N)$$

$$\geq H(X^n) - I(X^n; Z^n)$$

$$\geq H(X^n) - I(X^n; Z^n | Y^n)$$

The second inequality follows from the data-processing theorem and from the fact that the encoding is deterministic. The last inequality follows because Y^n is independent of X^n so that

$$I(X^n; Z^n | Y^n) = I(X^n; Y^n, Z^n) = I(X^n; Z^n) + I(X^n; Y^n | Z^n)$$

$$\geq I(X^n; Z^n)$$

Using Theorem 5.2.1 and the fact that $H(X^n) = nR_x$, we now have

$$\sum_{l=1}^{N} H(U_l | V_l) \geq nR_x - \sum_{l=1}^{n} I(X_l; Z_l | Y^n)$$

$$= nR_x - \sum_{l=1}^{n} I(X_l; Z_l | Y_l)$$

$$= \sum_{l=1}^{n} [R_x - I(X_l; Z_l | Y_l)]$$

where the second line follows because the channel is memoryless.

The same sequence of steps can be applied to give a second inequality,

$$\sum_{l=1}^{N'} H(U'_l | V'_l) \geq \sum_{l=1}^{n} [R_y - I(Y_l; Z_l | X_l)]$$

and also applied to the sum of both to give a third inequality,

$$\sum_{l=1}^{N} H(U_l | V_l) + \sum_{l=1}^{N'} H(U'_l | V'_l) \geq H(U^N, U'^{N'} | V^N, V'^{N'})$$

$$\geq \sum_{l=1}^{n} [R_x + R_y - I(X_l, Y_l; Z_l)]$$

We now have the three inequalities

$$N[\langle p_{ex} \rangle \log (J - 1) + H_b(\langle p_{ex} \rangle)] \geq \sum_{l=1}^{n} [R_x - I(X_l; Z_l | Y_l)]$$

$$N'[\langle p_{ey} \rangle \log (J' - 1) + H_b(\langle p_{ey} \rangle)] \geq \sum_{l=1}^{n} [R_y - I(Y_l; Z_l | X_l)]$$

and

$$N[\langle p_{ex} \rangle \log (J - 1) + H_b(\langle p_{ex} \rangle)] + N'[\langle p_{ey} \rangle \log (J' - 1) + H_b(\langle p_{ey} \rangle)]$$

$$\geq \sum_{l=1}^{n} [R_x + R_y - I(X_l, Y_l; Z_l)]$$

The probability of symbol error will be bounded away from zero unless the right side of each inequality is negative, and, by the assumption of the theorem, the right side of at least one of the three inequalities is positive for every l. This completes the proof of the theorem. $\square$

9.3 BROADCAST CHANNELS

A broadcast channel consists of a single transmitter and two or more receivers, as shown in Fig. 9.5; we shall study the case with two receivers. The channel has one input alphabet $\{a_j\}$ and two output alphabets $\{b_k\}$ and $\{b'_{k'}\}$, which need not be the same alphabet nor of the same size. Given input symbol a_j, the channel outputs are symbols b_k and $b'_{k'}$ with probability $Q(b_k, b'_{k'} | a_j)$, abbreviated $Q_{kk'|j}$. We can also consider the probability of an individual output by writing $Q_{k|j} = \sum_{k'} Q_{kk'|j}$ as the probability of output symbol b_k, and $Q'_{k'|j} = \sum_{k} Q_{kk'|j}$ as the probability of output symbol $b'_{k'}$. The broadcast channel is memoryless if the output probability of a block depends on the input block by a product probability distribution.

If the same message is to be sent to all receivers and the individual channels have the same transition matrix, then the task of designing the

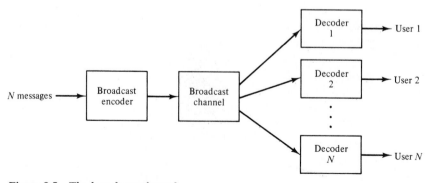

Figure 9.5   The broadcast channel.

communication waveform is no different from the situation where there is a single receiver, and we need not consider it further. If different messages are to be sent to each receiver, the problem is more complex. In the most general case, there is a part of the message that is intended for both receivers and parts of the message that are different for the two receivers.

The *capacity region* of the broadcast channel is defined as the convex hull of the set of rate triplets (R_0, R_1, R_2) for which codes exist that can simultaneously transmit, with arbitrarily small probability of decoding error, a common message at rate R_0 to both receivers, an individual message at rate R_1 to receiver 1, and an individual message at rate R_2 to receiver 2.

One way to share the channel among the different messages is to divide the channel according to the needs of the receivers. The method of time-division signaling breaks the channel into subchannels, which can then be used as point-to-point channels. Optimum techniques are more tightly interlocked and do better. Time-division signaling cannot achieve the capacity region of a broadcast channel.

□ **Definition 9.3.1** A block code $\mathscr{C}$ of blocklength n and rate (R_0, R_1, R_2) for a broadcast channel consists of M n-tuples of channel input symbols where

$$M = 2^{nR_0} 2^{nR_1} 2^{nR_2}$$ □

The codeword index m takes on M values. It can be expressed conveniently in terms of three indices as (m_0, m_1, m_2). The first index m_0 is the common part of the message, while m_1 and m_2 compose the individual part of the message. The task of decoder 1 is to determine (m_0, m_1). The task of decoder 2 is to determine (m_0, m_2). We will say that there is a decoding error if either decoder output is incorrect.

A special case of a broadcast channel, known as a *degraded* broadcast channel, is shown in Fig. 9.6. A degraded broadcast channel is a broadcast channel whose probability transition matrix $Q_{kk'|j}$ can be written in the form

$$Q_{kk'|j} = \tilde{Q}_{k'|k} Q_{k|j}$$

for some probability transition matrix $\tilde{Q}$ from alphabet $\{b_k\}$ to alphabet $\{b_{k'}'\}$. This is the form of the broadcast channel that we shall study. The structure of a degraded broadcast channel is such that the receivers can be thought of as arranged in sequence so that successive receivers see a successively degraded message. The random variables describing a degraded broadcast channel have the structure of a Markov chain,

$$X \rightarrow Y \rightarrow Z$$

where X is the channel input and Y and Z are the successively degraded channel outputs. Consequently,

$$I(Z; X) \leq I(Y; X)$$

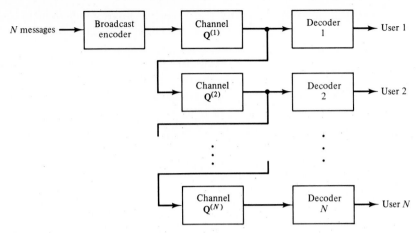

Figure 9.6   The degraded broadcast channel.

For the degraded broadcast channel, it turns out that decoder 1 will actually recover the entire message and then discard the individual part of the message intended for decoder 2. Consequently, m_0 and m_2 play nearly the same role. Therefore we will simplify notation when the channel is a degraded broadcast channel by allowing m to play the role of the pair (m_0, m_2). Then the index m_0 is dropped from the discussion and m_1 is replaced by m'.

The heuristic idea for the coding theorem that we shall prove is illustrated in Fig. 9.7. The codewords are selected so as to form "clouds" of codewords. There are 2^{nR_2} clouds and they are indexed by m. Within each cloud there are 2^{nR_1} codewords and they are indexed by m'. The decoder observing the output of the poorer channel only tries to determine the index of the transmitted cloud, not of the individual codeword within the cloud. The decoder observing the output of the better channel tries to determine both the cloud and the specific codeword. Consequently, that decoder gets both the common part of the message and its own individual message (as well as the other decoder's individual message, which it discards).

Each cloud center, a vector of blocklength n in a dummy input alphabet $\{a'_{j'}\}$, is called a *protocodeword* and denoted $\mathbf{s}$. (Possibly the symbols of the channel input alphabet are used in forming protocodewords; then the vectors

Figure 9.7   A visualization of broadcast codewords.

may be over a subset of the channel input alphabet.) Scattered about each protocodeword are the codewords associated with that protocodeword. The code consists of the set of all codewords so associated with the set of protocodewords.

□ **Theorem 9.3.2** The capacity region of the memoryless degraded broadcast channel consists of the convex hull of the set of all rates R_1 and R_2 for which

$$R_1 \leq I(X; Y \mid U)$$

$$R_2 \leq I(U; Z)$$

for any random variable U jointly distributed with X.

Proof The proof follows directly from Theorem 9.3.3 and Theorem 9.3.4, which are forthcoming. □

Once again we see that, because the channel is memoryless, the description of the capacity is at the level of single letters, even though the coding is at the block level. By now this should come as no surprise.

The statement of the capacity region of the broadcast channel requires the introduction of a random variable that was not in the problem to start with. The random variable U is called an *auxiliary* random variable. The block random variable U^n takes the role of the protocodeword and is understandable to both decoders. Figures 9.8 and 9.9 illustrate the intuitive role of the auxiliary random variable U as that part of the channel input intended for the second decoder. Figure 9.8 shows the elements connected in a natural way. Figure 9.9 is an alternative depiction from the point of view of the second decoder, in which the encoder and the two channel elements connecting U to Z combine into a single channel.

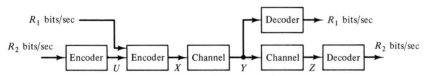

Figure 9.8 **Single-letter view of a degraded broadcast channel.**

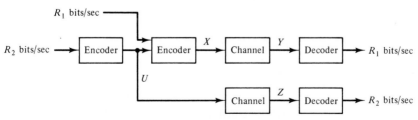

Figure 9.9 **Another view of a degraded broadcast channel.**

□   **Theorem 9.3.3**   **(Direct theorem)** Let $\varepsilon > 0$ be given. Let U be any discrete random variable. Let $p_i P_{j|i}$ be any joint probability distribution on U and X. If

$$R_1 \leq I(X; Y|U)$$

$$R_2 \leq I(U; Z)$$

then for sufficiently large blocklength n, there exists a block code for the memoryless degraded broadcast channel of rates (R_1, R_2) and with error probability smaller than ε.

Proof   The proof involves a random-coding argument. Let $M_1 = 2^{nR_1}$ and $M_2 = 2^{nR_2}$. First we randomly choose the protocodewords for $m = 0, \ldots, M_2 - 1$ using probability distribution **p**. Then we randomly choose a set of M_1 codewords associated with each protocodeword by using the conditional probability distribution **P**.

To randomly choose the protocodewords, independently choose M_2 sequences, each of blocklength n. For the probability of choosing the set of protocodewords $\{s_0, s_1, \ldots, s_{M_2-1}\}$, use the product distribution

$$p(s_0, s_1, \ldots, s_{M_2-1}) = \prod_{m=0}^{M_2-1} p(s_m)$$

and in turn for the probability of picking protocodeword s_m, use the product distribution on the components

$$p(s_m) = \prod_{l=1}^{n} p(s_{ml}) = \prod_{l=1}^{n} p(a'_{i_{ml}})$$

where $p(a'_i) = p_i$.

To randomly choose the codewords, for every protocodeword s_m conditionally independently choose M_1 sequences $c_{mm'}$ for $m' = 0, \ldots, M_1 - 1$. These are the codewords associated with that protocodeword. Given s_m, for the conditional probability of choosing the set of codewords $\{c_{m0}, c_{m1}, \ldots, c_{m(M_1-1)}\}$, use the product distribution

$$P(c_{m0}, c_{m1}, \ldots, c_{m(M_1-1)}) = \prod_{m'=0}^{M_1-1} P(c_{mm'}|s_m)$$

and in turn for the conditional probability of picking codeword $c_{mm'}$, use the product distribution on the components,

$$P(c_{mm'}|s_m) = \prod_{l=1}^{n} P(c_{mm'l}|s_{ml}) = \prod_{l=1}^{n} P(a_{j_{mm'l}}|a'_{i_{ml}})$$

where $P(a_j|a'_i) = P_{j|i}$.

To decode at the first receiver: If **y** is the received word, declare that $c_{rr'}$ is the transmitted codeword if (r, r') is the unique pair of indices for which $(s_r, c_{rr'}, y)$ are jointly weakly δ-typical. Otherwise declare an error.

To decode at the second receiver: If $\mathbf{z}$ is the received word, declare that $\mathbf{s}_r$ is the transmitted protocodeword if r is the unique index for which $\mathbf{s}_r$ and $\mathbf{z}$ are jointly weakly δ-typical. Otherwise declare an error.

The probability of decoding error satisfies the union bound

$$p_e \leq p_{ey} + p_{ez}$$

where p_{ey} is the probability of error in decoding $\mathbf{y}$ and p_{ez} is the probability of error in decoding $\mathbf{z}$. These can be bounded as in the proof of Theorem 9.2.3. We shall show that p_e can be made smaller than ε by showing that p_{ey} and p_{ez} can each be made smaller than $\varepsilon/2$.

We have the inequalities

$$p_{ez} \leq Pr\big[(\mathbf{s}_m, \mathbf{z}) \notin \mathcal{T}_{uz}(\delta)\big] + \sum_{r \neq m} Pr\big[(\mathbf{s}_r, \mathbf{z}) \in \mathcal{T}_{uz}(\delta)\big]$$

$$p_{ey} \leq Pr\big[(\mathbf{s}_m, \mathbf{c}_{mm'}, \mathbf{y}) \notin \mathcal{T}_{uxy}(\delta)\big] + \sum_{(r,r') \neq (m,m')} Pr\big[(\mathbf{s}_r, \mathbf{c}_{rr'}, \mathbf{y}) \in \mathcal{T}_{uxy}(\delta)\big]$$

The first term of each inequality goes to zero for every code as a consequence of the Shannon-McMillan theorem. The second term of each inequality corresponds to the event that some incorrect codeword belongs to the decoding set because it has the correct typicality property. These latter terms need not be small for every code. We will show that they are small for some codes by showing that the ensemble average is small. Because of the random nature of the code construction, the probability of error averaged over the ensemble of codes is independent of the codeword indices (m, m') transmitted. Without loss of generality, any fixed pair (m, m') can be assumed. Indeed, we can later average over (m, m') without changing the bounds.

For randomly constructed codes, we have the inequalities for large enough n:

$$E[p_{ez}] \leq \frac{\varepsilon}{2} + \sum_{r \neq m} Pr\big[(\mathbf{u}_r, \mathbf{z}) \in \mathcal{T}_{uz}(\delta)\big]$$

$$E[p_{ey}] \leq \frac{\varepsilon}{2} + \sum_{(r,r') \neq (m,m')} Pr\big[(\mathbf{u}_r, \mathbf{x}_{rr'}, \mathbf{y}) \in \mathcal{T}_{uxy}(\delta)\big]$$

where we now use $\mathbf{u}_r$ and $\mathbf{x}_{rr'}$ in place of $\mathbf{s}_r$ and $\mathbf{c}_{rr'}$ because they are now realizations of random variables associated with the random code selection.

Because of the definition of the random code construction, the second term of the first inequality can be bounded by observing that U_r and Z are independent random variables if $r \neq m$. Therefore, by the same argument used in the proof of Theorem 5.5.3,

$$Pr\big[(\mathbf{u}_r, \mathbf{z}) \in \mathcal{T}_{uz}(\delta)\big] \approx 2^{-nI(U;Z)}$$

and

$$\sum_{r \neq m} Pr[(\mathbf{u}_r, \mathbf{z}) \in \mathcal{T}_{uz}(\delta)] \approx 2^{-n[I(U;Z) - R_2]}$$

This term goes to zero with increasing blocklength if

$$R_2 < I(U;Z)$$

The second term of the second inequality is treated in a similar way. It is a more complicated term, so we first break it into two pieces by noting that $(r, r') \neq (m, m')$ is equivalent to $r \neq m$ or $r = m$ and $r' \neq m'$:

$$\sum_{(r,r') \neq (m,m')} Pr[(\mathbf{u}_r, \mathbf{x}_{rr'}, \mathbf{y}) \in \mathcal{T}_{uxy}(\delta)] \leq \sum_{r \neq m} Pr[(\mathbf{u}_r, \mathbf{y}) \in \mathcal{T}_{uy}(\delta)]$$

$$+ \sum_{r' \neq m'} Pr[(\mathbf{u}_m, \mathbf{x}_{mr'}, \mathbf{y}) \in \mathcal{T}_{uxy}(\delta)]$$

where we have used the inequality

$$Pr[(\mathbf{u}_r, \mathbf{x}_{rr'}, \mathbf{y}) \in \mathcal{T}_{uxy}(\delta)] \leq Pr[(\mathbf{u}_r, \mathbf{y}) \in \mathcal{T}_{uy}(\delta)]$$

The first term on the right is of the same form as was already studied in the bound on $E[p_{ez}]$. By the same argument, it goes to zero with increasing blocklength if

$$R_2 < I(U;Y)$$

The channel is a degraded broadcast channel, so $I(U;Z) \leq I(U;Y)$. Because $R_2 < I(U, Z)$, we can conclude that this requirement is satisfied.

Finally, we must bound the second term on the right of the above inequality. The summand can be written as

$$Pr[(\mathbf{u}_m, \mathbf{x}_{mr'}, \mathbf{y}) \in \mathcal{T}_{uxy}(\delta)] = \sum_{(\mathbf{u},\mathbf{x},\mathbf{y}) \in \mathcal{T}_{uxy}(\delta)} p(\mathbf{u})P(\mathbf{x}|\mathbf{u})q(\mathbf{y}|\mathbf{u})$$

where the summand on the right is written in this factored form because $r' \neq m'$ implies that the received word $\mathbf{y}$ is independent of the randomly selected codeword $\mathbf{x}$. Again, following the same argument used in Theorem 5.5.3, the probabilities of typical sequences are approximated by negative exponentials in the entropy. Thus

$$Pr[(\mathbf{u}_m, \mathbf{x}_{mr'}, \mathbf{y}) \in \mathcal{T}_{uxy}(\delta)] \approx 2^{nH(X,Y,U)}(2^{-nH(U)}2^{-nH(X|U)}2^{-nH(Y|U)})$$

$$\approx 2^{-nI(X;Y|U)}$$

So the second term on the right side of the earlier inequality above goes to zero if

$$R_1 < I(X;Y|U)$$

We now have proved that $E[p_e] < \varepsilon$ for sufficiently large blocklength. Some code must be at least as good as the average. This completes the proof of the theorem. □

□ **Theorem 9.3.4** (**Converse theorem**) Given a degraded broadcast channel, if for every auxiliary random variable U and channel input X with probability distribution $p_i P_{j|i}$ on the pair (U, X), either

$$R_1 > I(X; Y|U)$$

or

$$R_2 > I(U; Z)$$

then there exist no codes of rate (R_1, R_2) for this broadcast channel having arbitrarily small probability of decoding error.

Proof The proof is based on Fano's inequality. We will show that the inequalities of the theorem imply that at least one of the probabilities of symbol error $\langle p_{ey} \rangle$ or $\langle p_{ez} \rangle$ is bounded away from zero.

Step 1: Let W_1 and W_2 be independent random variables taking the values m' and m. These random variables denote the selected messages. The degraded channel then can be described as the Markov chain

$$(W_1, W_2) \to X^n \to Y^n \to Z^n$$

It is immediately apparent that

$$R_2 = \frac{1}{n} H(W_2) = \frac{1}{n} \left[I(W_2; Z^n) + H(W_2|Z^n) \right]$$

and

$$R_1 = \frac{1}{n} H(W_1|W_2) = \frac{1}{n} \left[I(W_1; Y^n|W_2) + H(W_1|Y^n, W_2) \right]$$

$$\leq \frac{1}{n} \left[I(X^n; Y^n|W_2) + H(W_1|Y^n) \right]$$

We shall prove in step 2 that there exists an auxiliary random variable U such that

$$\frac{1}{n} I(W_2; Z^n) \leq I(U; Z)$$

and in step 3 that for the same U,

$$\frac{1}{n} I(X^n; Y^n|W_2) = I(X; Y|U)$$

Using these equations and the per-symbol form of Fano's inequality, as given in Theorem 6.1.2, brings us to

$$N[\langle p_{ez}\rangle \log (J_2 - 1) + H_b(\langle p_{ez}\rangle)] \geq nH(W_2|Z'')$$

$$\geq n(R_2 - I(U;Z))$$

$$N[\langle p_{ey}\rangle \log (J_1 - 1) + H_b(\langle p_{ey}\rangle)] \geq nH(W_1|Y'')$$

$$\geq n(R_1 - I(X;Y|U))$$

where J_1 and J_2 are the alphabet sizes at the input to the encoders and N is the blocklength at the input to the encoders.

By assumption of the theorem, for every random variable U, the right side is positive for at least one of the two inequalities. Thus it is not possible to make $\langle p_{ey}\rangle$ and $\langle p_{ez}\rangle$ both go to zero with blocklength, which is the claim of the theorem. Therefore the theorem is proved except for the claims to be proved in steps 2 and 3.

Step 2: The development of this step consists of the manipulation of the properties of the mutual information and conditional entropy. From basic principles, we have

$$I(W_2;Z'') = H(Z'') - H(Z''|W_2)$$

$$\leq \sum_{l=1}^{n} H(Z_l) - \sum_{l=1}^{n} H(Z_l|W_2, Z_{l-1}, \ldots, Z_1)$$

$$\leq \sum_{l=1}^{n} [H(Z_l) - H(Z_l|W_2, Z_{l-1}, \ldots, Z_1, Y_{l-1}, \ldots, Y_1)]$$

where the second inequality is due to including $Y_{l-1}, \ldots, Y_1$ in the conditioning of the entropy.

For every fixed value of W_2, the output Z_l of the discrete memoryless channel is conditionally independent of the previous outputs $Z_{l-1}, \ldots, Z_1$ if W_2 and the previous inputs $Y_{l-1}, \ldots, Y_1$ are given. Therefore we drop the conditioning on $Z_{l-1}, \ldots, Z_1$ in the last term of the inequality above to yield

$$I(W_2;Z'') \leq \sum_{l=1}^{n} I(Z_l; W_2, Y_{l-1}, \ldots, Y_1)$$

We now want to find a way to summarize $(W_2, Y_{l-1}, \ldots, Y_1)$ by a random variable U. Introduce a random variable L, uniformly distributed over the set $\{1, 2, \ldots, n\}$ and independent of all other random variables. Let U be the discrete random variable defined as the collection

$$U = (W_2, Y_{L-1}, \ldots, Y_1, L)$$

and define a new random variable Z by $Z = Z_L$. Then we can write

$$I(Z_l; W_2, Y_{l-1}, \ldots, Y_1) = I(Z; U|l)$$

and the right side of our inequality takes the form of an expectation. Thus

$$\frac{1}{n}I(W_2;Z^n) \le \sum_{l=1}^{n}\frac{1}{n}I(Z;U|l)$$

$$= I(Z;U|L)$$

$$= I(Z;U)$$

where the last equality holds because L is independent of Z.

Step 3: The argument parallels that of step 2:

$$I(X^n;Y^n|W_2) = H(Y^n|W_2) - H(Y^n|W_2,X^n)$$

$$= \sum_{l=1}^{n} [H(Y_l|W_2,Y_{l-1},\ldots,Y_1)$$

$$- H(Y_l|W_2,X^n,Y_{l-1},\ldots,Y_1)]$$

Now we argue that

$$H(Y_l|W_2,X^n,Y_{l-1},\ldots,Y_1) = H(Y_l|W_2,X_l,Y_{l-1},\ldots,Y_1)$$

because Y^n is connected to X^n by a discrete memoryless channel. Therefore, as in step 2,

$$\frac{1}{n}I(X^n;Y^n|W_2) = \sum_{l=1}^{n}\frac{1}{n}I(X_l;Y_l|W_2,Y_{l-1},\ldots,Y_1)$$

$$= I(X;Y|U)$$

and the proof is complete.   □

9.4 TWO-WAY CHANNELS

A two-way channel has two terminals, as shown in Fig. 9.10. Each terminal attempts to send a message to the other terminal through the two-way channel, but the transmission in one direction interferes with the transmission in the other direction. The problem is to design the message structure so as to achieve high data rates in both directions simultaneously.

Many practical channels are intrinsically two-way channels. Often the designer elects to break such a channel into two one-way channels using a technique such as time division. This technique schedules the direction in which data can be sent, say one-half of the time in one direction and one-half of the time in the other. Time division is a simple and workable technique, but one wishes to know if there is a performance penalty. What is the two-way capacity region, and what sort of communication scheme is optimal?

The simplest example of a two-way channel is the noiseless channel known as the *binary multiplying channel*. It has a binary input and binary output alphabet at each terminal. At each clock interval, each transmitter can send either a 0 or a 1. However, a terminal can receive a bit reliably only

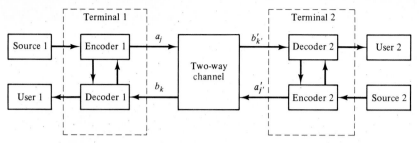

Figure 9.10   The two-way channel.

during those bit intervals when it is transmitting a 1. One way to say this is that the channel delivers to both users the logical "and" of both inputs. This two-way channel is shown in Fig. 9.11. By cooperating on the message structure, the terminals can reliably send data at rates greater than 1/2 bit per clock interval simultaneously in both directions. However, the exact capacity region of this two-way channel is not yet known.

In this section we shall derive upper and lower bounds on the capacity region for two-way channels. Figure 9.12 shows these bounds for the binary multiplying channel. From Fig. 9.12, we see that it is possible to simultaneously send data at a rate of 0.62 bit per clock interval in both directions, while it is impossible to simultaneously send data at rates greater than 0.69 bit per clock interval in both directions.

The *capacity region* is formally defined as the convex hull of the set of all rates R_1 and R_2 for which codes exist that can transmit information with arbitrarily small probability of error. An error occurs if either decoder is in error.

In general, a discrete memoryless two-way channel has two input alphabets and two output alphabets, which need not be the same. Terminal 1 selects symbols from input alphabet $\{a_j\}$ and observes an output symbol from alphabet $\{b'_{k'}\}$. Terminal 2 selects the input $a'_{j'}$ and observes the output b_k. The channel is described by a set of transition probabilities $Q(b_k, b'_{k'} | a_j, a'_{j'})$, abbreviated $Q_{kk'|jj'}$ for $j = 0, \ldots, J - 1; j' = 0, \ldots, J' - 1; k = 0, \ldots, K - 1;$ and $k' = 0, \ldots, K' - 1$. This four-dimensional array has $JJ'KK'$ entries. The binary multiplying channel has 16 elements in its transition matrix, but, because it is a noiseless channel, each element is either 0 or 1.

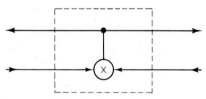

Figure 9.11   The binary multiplying channel.

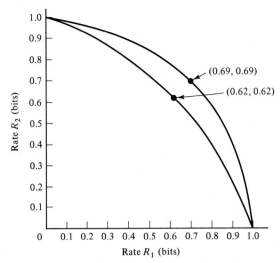

Figure 9.12   Inner and outer bounds on the capacity region of a binary multiplying two-way channel.

Each terminal transmits a sequence of symbols based upon the information bits coming from the source and the sequence of channel output symbols that it observes. Loosely, a block code $\mathscr{C}$ of rate (R_1, R_2) and blocklength n consists of a pair of component codes—$\mathscr{C}_1$ with 2^{nR_1} codewords and $\mathscr{C}_2$ with 2^{nR_2} codewords. However, the codewords are not the simple blocks of channel input symbols we are used to. Instead, a codeword becomes a more complicated structure called a *codetree* in which a channel input symbol depends on previous channel output symbols. The block code for a two-way channel consists of two sets of codetrees, as shown in Fig. 9.13. This figure shows an extremely small code for a two-way binary channel in which $\mathscr{C}_1$ and $\mathscr{C}_2$ each have only four codetrees. The code has rate $2/3$ in each direction. By reference to the bounds of Theorem 9.4.2, we see that a decoder for this code cannot recover all transmitted bits error-free if that pair of rates is outside the capacity region.

We will not try to design good codes. Just as for point-to-point data transmission, our only intention is to find conditions on the existence of two-way codes by studying the capacity region. Nor, in general, are we able to describe the capacity region exactly. This is an unsolved problem. Instead we will give an outer bound and an inner bound on the capacity region. For some channels, these bounds are equal. For those channels, the capacity region is completely determined.

Let X and X' denote random variables on the channel input alphabets, and let Y and Y' denote random variables on the channel output alphabets. We will see that, because the channel is memoryless, the bounds can be expressed at the level of single letters.

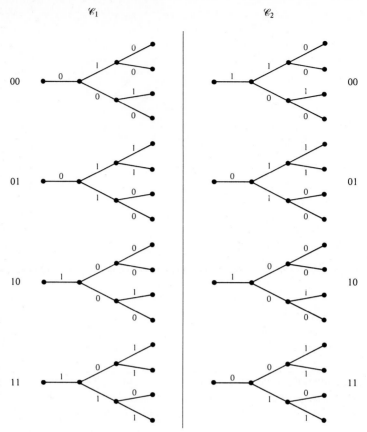

Figure 9.13   A block code for a binary two-way channel.

The outer bound and inner bound are motivated as follows: Each encoder has only partial knowledge of which codeword the other encoder is sending. An encoder has no such knowledge at the beginning of a block, but considerable knowledge by the end of the block. We do not know how to completely model this partial knowledge to develop a coding theorem. Instead we observe that partial knowledge is not as good as total knowledge but is not worse than no knowledge at all. If the two encoders could cooperate completely in choosing codewords, then any probability distribution $p_{jj'}$ on pairs of input letters could be used. We could then calculate the two mutual informations $I(X; Y'|X')$ and $I(X'; Y|X)$ and find a coding theorem that says that we can communicate up to these rates. Because in truth we cannot expect to do this well, this gives only an outer bound.

On the other hand, if the two encoders did not cooperate at all, then only independent probability distributions $p_j p'_{j'}$ on pairs of input letters could be used. We would then calculate $I(X;Y'|X')$ and $I(X';Y|X)$ and find a coding theorem. Because in truth we can expect to do better than this, this gives only an inner bound.

□ **Theorem 9.4.1   (Outer bound)** Let (X,X',Y,Y') have the joint probability distribution $p_{jj'}Q_{kk'|jj'}$ for any joint probability distribution $p_{jj'}$. For all such (X,X',Y,Y'), the set

$$\{(R_1,R_2): R_1 \le I(X;Y'|X') \text{ and } R_2 \le I(X';Y|X)\}$$

contains the capacity region of the memoryless two-way channel **Q**.

Proof We must prove that if (R_1,R_2) is any pair of rates that cannot be so written in terms of such mutual-information functions, then the probability of error of any sequence of codes is bounded away from zero. To do this, we use Fano's inequality. We begin with the two equations,

$$R_1 = \frac{1}{n}H(W|W') = \frac{1}{n}[I(W;Y'^n|W') + H(W|Y'^n,W')]$$

$$R_2 = \frac{1}{n}H(W'|W) = \frac{1}{n}[I(W';Y^n|W) + H(W'|Y^n,W)]$$

where W and W' are independent random variables denoting the messages entering the two encoders. The encoders are deterministic, so $W = X^n$ and $W' = X'^n$. Therefore

$$R_1 = \frac{1}{n}[I(X^n;Y'^n|X'^n) + H(X^n|Y'^n,X'^n)]$$

$$R_2 = \frac{1}{n}[I(X'^n;Y^n|X^n) + H(X'^n|Y^n,X^n)]$$

We will work on the first of these two equations:

$$I(X^n;Y'^n|X'^n) \le \sum_{l=1}^{n} I(X_l;Y'_l|X'^n)$$

$$= \sum_{l=1}^{n} H(Y'_l|X'^n) - \sum_{l=1}^{n} H(Y'_l|X_l,X'^n)$$

$$\le \sum_{l=1}^{n} H(Y'_l|X'_l) - \sum_{l=1}^{n} H(Y'_l|X_l,X'_l,X'_{l-1},\dots,X'_1)$$

The channel is memoryless, and Y'_l can depend on $X'_{l-1},\dots,X'_1$ only because X_l depends on them. This implies

$$H(Y'_l|X_l,X'_l,X'_{l-1},\dots,X'_1) = H(Y'_l|X_l,X'_l)$$

Therefore

$$I(X^n; Y'^n \mid X'^n) \leq \sum_{l=1}^{n} I(X_l; Y'_l \mid X'_l)$$

$$= nI(X; Y' \mid X')$$

Use this in the equation for R_1 with which we started and also use Fano's inequality as given in Theorem 6.1.2 to obtain

$$N[\langle p_{e1} \rangle \log (J_1 - 1) + H_b(\langle p_{e1} \rangle)] \geq n[R_1 - I(X; Y' \mid X')]$$

Likewise, the equation for R_2 leads to

$$N[\langle p_{e2} \rangle \log (J_2 - 1) + H_b(\langle p_{e2} \rangle)] \geq n[R_2 - I(X'; Y \mid X)]$$

If, for every quadruple (X, X', Y, Y'), either $R_1 - I(X; Y' \mid X') > 0$ or $R_2 - I(X'; Y \mid X) > 0$, then the probability of symbol error is bounded away from zero.   □

Next we prove the inner bound by restricting the problem, as shown in Fig. 9.14. In the restricted form of the problem, the encoder is not allowed to look at what is coming out at its end of the channel. Clearly, the original two-way channel has at least as much capacity as the restricted two-way channel. The restriction would be a pointless one except that it simplifies the codes. There is no longer any need to use codetrees; simple block codes will do, so the random-coding argument will be manageable. The restricted two-way channel resembles the multiaccess channel, and the proof will be similar.

□   **Theorem 9.4.2   (Inner bound)** Let (X, X', Y, Y') have the joint probability distribution $p_j p'_{j'} Q_{kk' \mid jj'}$ for any two probability distributions p_j and $p'_{j'}$ on the alphabets of X and X'. For all such (X, X', Y, Y'), the convex hull of the set

$$\{(R_1, R_2): R_1 \leq I(X; Y' \mid X') \text{ and } R_2 \leq I(X'; Y \mid X)\}$$

is contained in the capacity region of the memoryless two-way channel $\mathbf{Q}$.

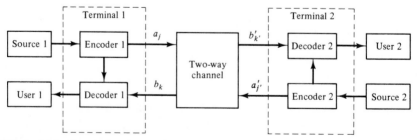

Figure 9.14   Restricting the two-way channel.

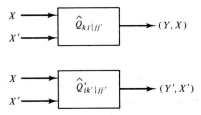

Figure 9.15   Viewing the restricted two-way channel as two multiaccess channels.

Proof The proof uses a random-coding argument. Given $p_j p'_{j'}$, let $\mathcal{C}_1$ and $\mathcal{C}_2$ be component codes randomly and independently chosen, with probabilities **p** and **p'**, respectively. For each code, the codewords and their letters are chosen independently.

At the end of a block, decoder 1 knows the word **y** that it received as well as the codeword **x** that it sent. We can think of this pair $(\mathbf{x}, \mathbf{y})$ as the output of the fictitious multiaccess channel of Fig. 9.15 in which **x** is transmitted to decoder 1 through an error-free channel. The probability transition matrix of the fictitious channel is

$$\hat{Q}(b_k, a_i | a_j, a'_{j'}) = \delta(i, j) \sum_{k'} Q(b_k, b'_{k'} | a_j, a'_{j'})$$

which we abbreviate $\hat{Q}_{ki|jj'}$. The Kronecker delta $\delta(i, j)$ equals 1 if $i = j$, and equals 0 otherwise. The factor $\delta(i, j)$ simply means that the multiaccess channel always gets symbol a_j perfectly.

Similarly, data available to decoder 2 can be thought of as the output of the fictitious multiaccess channel

$$\hat{Q}'(a'_{i'}, b'_{k'} | a_j, a'_{j'}) = \delta(i', j') \sum_k Q(b_k, b'_{k'} | a_j, a'_{j'})$$

The remainder of the proof consists of applying the methods that were used to prove the expression for the capacity region of the multiaccess channel in Theorem 9.2.3. The probability of block decoding error for the two-way channel satisfies

$$p_e \leq p_{e1} + p_{e2}$$

where p_{e1} and p_{e2} are the probabilities of block decoding error at decoders 1 and 2, respectively. Averaged over the ensemble,

$$E[p_e] \leq E[p_{e1}] + E[p_{e2}]$$

and $E[p_{e1}]$ and $E[p_{e2}]$ can be made arbitrarily small if the inequalities of Theorem 9.2.3 are satisfied. For $E[p_{e1}]$, this requires

$$R_1 \leq I(X; (X, Y) | X')$$

$$R_2 \leq I(X'; (X, Y) | X)$$

$$R_1 + R_2 \leq I(X, X'; (X, Y))$$

The third inequality is found to be superfluous by the following argument:

$$I(X, X'; (X, Y)) = I(X; (X, Y)) + I(X'; (X, Y)|X)$$
$$\geq I(X; (X, Y)|X') + I(X'; (X, Y)|X)$$

Hence the third inequality is satisfied if the other two inequalities are satisfied.

The first inequality can be written

$$R_1 \leq I(X; X|X') + I(X; Y|X, X')$$

The second term equals zero, and the first term is $H(X)$ because X and X' are independent. Thus

$$R_1 \leq H(X)$$

which must be satisfied if

$$R_1 \leq I(X; Y'|X')$$

as assured in the theorem.

The second inequality can be written

$$R_2 \leq I(X'; Y|X) + I(X'; X|X, Y)$$

The second term is zero, so this reduces to the inequality of the theorem. We conclude that $E[p_{e1}]$ can be made arbitrarily small under the conditions of the theorem.

The same analysis can be repeated for $E[p_{e2}]$ to conclude that $E[p_{e2}]$ can be made arbitrarily small under the conditions of the theorem. Consequently, if the conditions of the theorem are satisfied, the ensemble average $E[p_e]$ can be made arbitrarily small. There must be at least one code in the ensemble as good as the average, so all such rate pairs are in the capacity region. Because the capacity region is convex, the theorem is proved. □

9.5 REMOTE COMPACTION OF DEPENDENT DATA

There are applications in which information is collected at several places and must be brought to a common site for processing or for other use. The simplest example is shown in Fig. 9.16. There are two data sources and one data user, all remotely located. Data sources X and Y, with entropy $H(X)$ and $H(Y)$, respectively, are dependent. The data is to be sent to a common site at rates R_x and R_y, but the encoders do not communicate with each other. Individually the encoders cannot compact their data to less than $H(X)$ or $H(Y)$ bits, but if they could cooperate, they could jointly compact their combined data to $H(X, Y)$ bits. In this section we shall show that they can cooperate even without communicating; neither needs see the other's data stream!

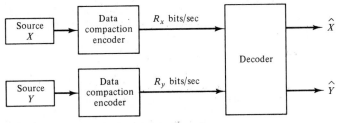

Figure 9.16   Remote compaction of dependent data.

A pair of discrete memoryless sources has two source alphabets: $\{a_j\}$ of size J and $\{a'_{j'}\}$ of size J'. The probability that the pair of sources produces output pair $(a_j, a'_{j'})$ is $P(a_j, a'_{j'})$, abbreviated $P_{jj'}$. The individual distributions are denoted $p_j = \sum_{j'} P_{jj'}$ and $p'_{j'} = \sum_j P_{jj'}$.

The *achievable-rate region* is defined as the convex hull of the set of all R_x and R_y for which codes exist that can transmit pairs (X^n, Y^n) of long blocks of source output symbols with arbitrarily small probability of error. We shall derive the achievable-rate region in this section. It is shown in Fig. 9.17. An encoder and decoder for data compaction can be built with rate pairs corresponding to any point in the upper-right region. The region can be described quite simply. Each individual rate, R_x or R_y, must be larger than the conditional entropy, $H(X|Y)$ or $H(Y|X)$, respectively, and the total rate $R_x + R_y$ must be at least as large as the joint entropy, $H(X, Y)$. It is quite remarkable that the latter bound would not be any different even if both encoders could each see the output of both sources. This is a significant conclusion, but it should not be read as saying more than it does. It does not say that there would be *no* benefit in providing either encoder with side information from the other source. Side information does not affect the data rates that can be achieved, but it can be quite useful in reducing the complexity of the encoder and decoder. The coding methods needed to achieve a specified pair of rates will be much more complex when there is no side information.

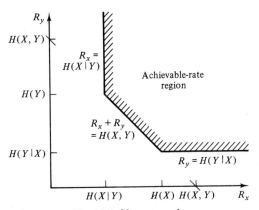

Figure 9.17   The Slepian-Wolf achievable-rate region.

We first give a converse theorem establishing that the achievable-rate region is contained within the region shown in Fig. 9.17. In a later theorem we shall see that the converse theorem is tight; the set of rate pairs that it excludes exactly gives the complement of the achievable-rate region.

☐ **Theorem 9.5.1   (Slepian-Wolf converse theorem)** Given a pair of dependent sources (X, Y), no coding scheme can give arbitrarily small probability of block decoding failure unless its rates satisfy

$$R_x \geq H(X|Y)$$
$$R_y \geq H(Y|X)$$
$$R_x + R_y \geq H(X, Y)$$

Proof   The proof is based on Theorem 3.4.6. First consider the pair of sources as a single source. Then Theorem 3.4.6 requires that

$$R_x + R_y \geq H(X, Y)$$

which is the third inequality of the present theorem.

Because we are proving a converse, we are free to assume gratuitous information. The actual performance cannot be any better. Thus, in proving the first inequality, suppose that the Y data stream is given perfectly to both the X encoder and the X decoder by an error-free side channel. Then Theorem 3.4.6 requires that

$$R_x \geq H(X|Y)$$

and so this inequality must hold even when Y is not given perfectly to the X encoder and the X decoder.

The proof is completed by noting that

$$R_y \geq H(Y|X)$$

follows by the same argument, with X and Y interchanged.   ☐

Now we are ready to give the direct theorem. First we must define the code more specifically. Recall that a data compaction code of blocklength n and size M was defined as a set $\mathscr{C}$ consisting of M codewords of blocklength n; each codeword is a sequence of n source output letters. A block code for compacting a pair of dependent sources is defined in a similar but more complicated way. The role of the codewords is replaced by that of *codebins*. Each codebin contains a list of sourcewords of blocklength n. Each of the two source encoders has its own code consisting of a set of codebins, as given in the following definition.

☐ **Definition 9.5.2**   Let $M_x = 2^{nR_x}$ and $M_y = 2^{nR_y}$. A block code $\mathscr{C}$ of blocklength n and rates R_x and R_y for a pair of dependent sources consists of two component codes $\mathscr{C}_x$ and $\mathscr{C}_y$; each component code is a set of codebins. Set $\mathscr{C}_x$ consists of M_x codebins, each codebin containing N_x sourcewords of blocklength n from source X. Set $\mathscr{C}_y$ consists of M_y codebins, each codebin containing N_y sourcewords of blocklength n from source Y. □

The codebins for source X are denoted $\mathscr{B}_m$ for $m = 0,\ldots, M_x - 1$, and codebins for source Y are denoted $\mathscr{B}'_{m'}$ for $m' = 0,\ldots, M_y - 1$. Thus each component code is a set of codebins, and each codebin contains a set of sourcewords.

The first $M_x - 1$ codebins of $\mathscr{C}_x$ and the first $M_y - 1$ codebins of $\mathscr{C}_y$ are called *normal codebins*. The M_xth codebin of $\mathscr{C}_x$ and the M_yth codebin of $\mathscr{C}_y$ are called *default codebins*. To use the block code, each source encoder breaks the stream of source output symbols into sourcewords of blocklength n. (The X and Y encoders must be synchronized so they begin new source blocks at the same time.) Each sourceword of source X is represented by any codebin containing that sourceword. In turn, that codebin is designated by the nR_x-bit binary number that indexes that codebin. If the sourceword appears in no codebin, it is assigned to the default codebin of $\mathscr{C}_x$ and represented by the largest index $M_x - 1$.

The sourcewords of source Y are encoded in the same way, using component code $\mathscr{C}_y$.

The decoder makes use of a decoding table consisting of an nR_x-by-nR_y array, which is used as follows: The decoder receives the indices of codebin $\{\mathbf{c}_x\}$ and codebin $\{\mathbf{c}_y\}$ and looks in the decoding table under that pair of indices to find the decoded output pair $(\mathbf{x}, \mathbf{y})$. The decoding table is constructed as follows: Choose $\delta > 0$. For each pair of codebins $\{\mathbf{c}_x\}$ and $\{\mathbf{c}_y\}$, choose a pair of sourcewords $\mathbf{x}$ and $\mathbf{y}$ from the pair of codebins such that the pair $(\mathbf{x}, \mathbf{y})$ is jointly weakly δ-typical. This pair $(\mathbf{x}, \mathbf{y})$ then composes the entry in the decoding table corresponding to that pair of codebin indices. If there is no such jointly typical pair, then any null symbol can compose the entry in the decoding table corresponding to that pair of codebins. Such a case will be counted as a decoding error.

The following theorem gives conditions such that codes of large blocklength can be constructed for which the decoded sourcewords are almost always correct. The proof involves a random-coding argument. The details of the random-coding proof are complex and fill the remainder of the section.

□ **Theorem 9.5.3** (**Slepian-Wolf direct theorem**) Let $\varepsilon > 0$ be given. Given a pair of dependent sources, X and Y, let the pair of rates (R_x, R_y) satisfy

$$R_x > H(X|Y)$$

$$R_y > H(Y|X)$$

$$R_x + R_y > H(X, Y)$$

Then for sufficiently large n, there exists a block code $\mathscr{C}$ composed of component code $\mathscr{C}_x$ of rate at most R_x and blocklength n for source X, and component code $\mathscr{C}_y$ of rate at most R_y and blocklength n for source Y, such that the probability of block decoding failure p_e is less than ε.

Proof Choose a small positive number δ, which eventually will be sent to zero. Given any $\varepsilon > 0$, choose any point (R_x, R_y) that satisfies the conditions of the theorem and also satisfies the secondary constraints $R_x \leq H(X) + \delta$ and $R_y \leq H(Y) + \delta$. We shall prove that there exists a sequence of codes with rates at most (R_x, R_y) of increasing blocklength such that the probability of decoding error goes to zero as the blocklength goes to infinity. The secondary constraints are included to facilitate the proof, but need not appear in the statement of the theorem because, if the theorem is true for any (R_x, R_y), it is also true for all larger rate pairs.

Let $\mathscr{T}_{xy}(\delta)$ be the set of jointly weakly δ-typical sequences:

$$\mathscr{T}_{xy}(\delta) = \left\{ (\mathbf{x}, \mathbf{y}): \left| -\frac{1}{n} \log P(\mathbf{x}, \mathbf{y}) - H(X, Y) \right| < \delta \right\}$$

Let $\mathscr{T}_x(\delta)$ and $\mathscr{T}_y(\delta)$ be the corresponding sets of weakly δ-typical sourcewords of blocklength n given by

$$\mathscr{T}_x(\delta) = \left\{ \mathbf{x}: \left| -\frac{1}{n} \log p(\mathbf{x}) - H(X) \right| < \delta \right\}$$

$$\mathscr{T}_y(\delta) = \left\{ \mathbf{y}: \left| -\frac{1}{n} \log p'(\mathbf{y}) - H(Y) \right| < \delta \right\}$$

It follows from Theorem 3.4.2 that there are most $2^{n[H(X)+\delta]}$ and $2^{n[H(Y)+\delta]}$ sourcewords in $\mathscr{T}_x(\delta)$ and $\mathscr{T}_y(\delta)$, respectively. Define

$$N_x = 2^{n[H(X) - R_x + 2\delta]}$$

$$N_y = 2^{n[H(Y) - R_y + 2\delta]}$$

to be the sizes of the X and Y codebins, respectively. Because we require that $R_x < H(X) + \delta$ and $R_y < H(Y) + \delta$, we are assured that $|N_x|$ and $|N_y|$ are at least equal to 1. Therefore the construction is meaningful.

Form the codebins by random selection with replacement from the sets of weakly typical sequences $\mathscr{T}_x(\delta)$ and $\mathscr{T}_y(\delta)$. Thus, in the X encoder, codebin $\mathscr{B}_1$ is formed by randomly choosing N_x sequences from $\mathscr{T}_x(\delta)$, codebin $\mathscr{B}_2$ is formed by randomly choosing N_x more sequences from $\mathscr{T}_x(\delta)$, and so on. Codebins in the Y encoder are formed in the same way.

Let $m(\mathbf{x})$ be the smallest index of a codebin in the X encoder that contains the sourceword $\mathbf{x}$, unless sourceword $\mathbf{x}$ is in no codebin, in which case $m(\mathbf{x})$ is equal to the default index $M_x - 1$. Let $m'(\mathbf{y})$ be the smallest index of a codebin in the Y encoder that contains the sourceword $\mathbf{y}$, unless sourceword $\mathbf{y}$ is in no codebin, in which case $m'(\mathbf{y})$ is equal to the default index $M_y - 1$.

Suppose that the product set $\mathcal{B}_m \times \mathcal{B}'_{m'}$ defined by

$$\mathcal{B}_m \times \mathcal{B}'_{m'} = \{(\mathbf{x}, \mathbf{y}) : \mathbf{x} \in \mathcal{B}_m, \mathbf{y} \in \mathcal{B}'_{m'}\}$$

has only one entry that is also an element of the pairwise δ-typical set $\mathcal{T}_{xy}(\delta)$. Then the m, m' entry of the decoding table will be the single element of the set $\mathcal{T}_{xy}(\delta) \cap (\mathcal{B}_m \times \mathcal{B}'_{m'})$. We shall show that with high probability the m, m' entry of the decoding table is that pair $(\mathbf{x}, \mathbf{y})$ produced by the pair of sources.

A decoding failure will occur if the sourcewords $\mathbf{x}$ and $\mathbf{y}$ are not jointly typical and each in a codebin, or if there is another pair of jointly typical sourcewords $(\mathbf{x}', \mathbf{y}')$ in the same pair of codebins as the pair $(\mathbf{x}, \mathbf{y})$. The union bound on the probability of decoding failure then allows us to write:

$$p_e \leq Pr\big[(\mathbf{x}, \mathbf{y}) \notin \mathcal{T}_{xy}(\delta) \cap (\mathcal{B}_{m(\mathbf{x})} \times \mathcal{B}'_{m'(\mathbf{y})})\big]$$
$$+ Pr\big[(\mathbf{x}', \mathbf{y}') \in \mathcal{T}_{xy}(\delta) \cap (\mathcal{B}_{m(\mathbf{x})} \times \mathcal{B}'_{m'(\mathbf{y})}) : \text{for some } (\mathbf{x}', \mathbf{y}') \neq (\mathbf{x}, \mathbf{y})\big]$$

The complement of the first term on the right says that the pair of sourcewords to be encoded is almost always weakly typical and that both sourcewords can be successfully encoded. Then the only thing that can go wrong is that the decoder finds an ambiguity. The complement of the second term on the right says that an alternative weakly typical pair will almost never be found in the received pair of codebins, so there is almost never an ambiguity.

We abbreviate the inequality for p_e by

$$p_e \leq p_{e1} + p_{e2}$$

The expected probability of error over the random ensemble of codes satisfies

$$E[p_e] \leq E[p_{e1}] + E[p_{e2}]$$

That the pair of sourcewords $(\mathbf{x}, \mathbf{y})$ is jointly typical with high probability is an elementary property of the set of weakly typical sequences, which follows from Theorem 5.5.2. To prove that sourceword $\mathbf{x}$ can be encoded, it suffices to prove that $Pr[m(\mathbf{x}) \neq M_x - 1] \to 1$ as $n \to \infty$. We may assume that $\mathbf{x}$ is a typical sequence because this is true with probability close to 1. We will prove the complementary statement, that $Pr[m(\mathbf{x}) = M_x - 1 | \mathbf{x} \in \mathcal{T}_x(\delta)] \to 0$ as $n \to \infty$. But $m(\mathbf{x}) = M_x - 1$ only if $\mathbf{x}$ does not appear in any codebin. There are a total of

$$N = N_x M_x$$
$$= 2^{n[H(X) + 2\delta]}$$

randomly selected sourcewords in the set of all codebins in the X encoder, and every such sourceword has the same probability of equaling $\mathbf{x}$.

Consequently,

$$Pr[m(\mathbf{x}) = M_x - 1 | \mathbf{x} \in \mathcal{T}_x(\delta)] = Pr[\mathbf{x} \neq \mathbf{c}_1 | \mathbf{x} \in \mathcal{T}_x(\delta)]^N$$
$$= [1 - |\mathcal{T}_x(\delta)|^{-1}]^N$$

where $\mathbf{c}_1$ is the first sourceword in the first codebin. Now use the fact that $|\mathcal{T}_x(\delta)| \leq 2^{n[H(X)+\delta]}$ and the inequality $\log x \leq x - 1$ to write

$$\log Pr[m(\mathbf{x}) = M_x - 1 | \mathbf{x} \in \mathcal{T}_x(\delta)] \leq N \log (1 - 2^{-n[H(X)+\delta]})$$
$$\leq -N2^{-n[H(X)+\delta]}$$
$$= -2^{n[H(X)+2\delta]}2^{-n[H(X)+\delta]}$$
$$= -2^{n\delta}$$

which goes to negative infinity as n goes to infinity. Therefore the probability that sourceword $\mathbf{x}$ cannot be encoded goes to zero as n goes to infinity. The same is seen to be true also for sourceword $\mathbf{y}$ simply by interchanging the roles of X and Y. Therefore we see that

$$E[p_{e1}] \leq \varepsilon/2$$

for sufficiently large n.

Finally, we bound $E[p_{e2}]$ as follows: In the product set $\mathcal{B}_m \times \mathcal{B}'_{m'}$, there are $N_x N_y - 1$ wrong pairs $(\mathbf{x}', \mathbf{y}')$ that are not the correct pair $(\mathbf{x}, \mathbf{y})$ and so must not be jointly typical. The probability p_{e2} cannot be larger than when all the events are disjoint. In particular,

$$E[p_{e2}] \leq (N_x N_y - 1)Pr[(\mathbf{x}', \mathbf{y}') \in \mathcal{T}_{xy}(\delta)]$$

where $\mathbf{x}'$ is randomly chosen from $\mathcal{T}_x(\delta)$ and $\mathbf{y}'$ is randomly chosen from $\mathcal{T}_y(\delta)$ independently of $\mathbf{x}'$. Because

$$|\mathcal{T}_{xy}(\delta)| \leq 2^{n[H(X,Y)+\delta]}$$
$$|\mathcal{T}_x(\delta)| \geq (1 - \delta)2^{n[H(X)-\delta]}$$
$$|\mathcal{T}_y(\delta)| \geq (1 - \delta)2^{n[H(Y)-\delta]}$$

we have

$$E[p_{e2}] \leq N_x N_y 2^{n[H(X,Y)+\delta]}2^{-n[H(X)-\delta-(1/n)\log(1-\delta)]}2^{-n[H(Y)-\delta-(1/n)\log(1-\delta)]}$$
$$\leq 2^{-n[R_x + R_y - H(X,Y) - 7\delta]}/(1 - \delta)^2$$

For any rate pair satisfying

$$R_x + R_y > H(X, Y)$$

δ can be chosen small enough to make $R_x + R_y - H(X, Y) - 7\delta$ positive. Consequently, $E[p_{e2}] \rightarrow 0$ as $n \rightarrow \infty$.

It now follows that for sufficiently large n

$$E[p_e] \leq \varepsilon$$

There must be at least one code for which $p_e \leq \varepsilon$, so the theorem is proved. $\square$

9.6 DATA COMPACTION WITH SIDE INFORMATION

The problem of data compaction with side information, illustrated in Fig. 9.18, seems to resemble the problem studied in the previous section and illustrated in Fig. 9.16. However, the two problems are very different. Now the decoder only wishes to estimate the output of the X source. Data from the Y source is encoded as side information in a way that aids the decoder to recover X. There is no need for the Y encoder to preserve information about Y itself. The solution to this problem is quite different from the solution to the problem in the previous section. This time the side information from the Y source will be compressed to a rate below its entropy in such a way that the data from the X source can be better compacted.

It is possible to propose a simple model of how the data compaction behaves on the level of a single source symbol. It is very satisfying that the model, shown in Fig. 9.19, provides a valid picture of the data compaction. Because Y is dependent on X, the input of the Y encoder can be thought of as the output of a dummy channel with X as the input. The output of the random Y encoder is described in terms of a somewhat mysterious auxiliary random variable Z. This is a dummy random variable that represents the single-letter output of the Y encoder.

At the level of a single output, the encoder appears to be a probabilistic device, even though it is actually a deterministic operation on the block level. Each symbol from the Y alphabet $\{a'_j\}$ appears to be encoded into a letter of the discrete alphabet corresponding to Z by means of a probability transition matrix $Q_{k|j}$. The size of the Z alphabet and of the transition matrix is chosen to minimize the code rate. The decoder works with Z, which depends indirectly on X, and with the compacted X data stream, which depends directly on X. Based on its two inputs, the decoder must recover $\hat{X}$, the decompacted reproduction of X.

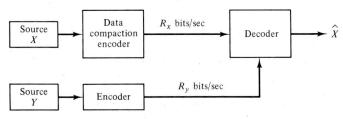

Figure 9.18   Data compaction with side information.

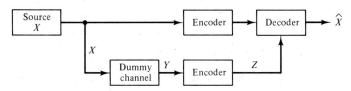

Figure 9.19   Single-letter view of data compaction with side information.

The achievable-rate region is defined as the convex hull of the set of all R_x and R_y for which codes exist from which the decoder can reproduce long blocks of outputs of source X with arbitrarily small probability of decoding failure. The achievable-rate region will be described with the aid of the single-letter description shown in Fig. 9.19.

□ **Theorem 9.6.1 (Converse theorem)** If the decoder has side information from source Y encoded at rate R_y, then every data compaction code of arbitrarily small probability of decoding error for the finite alphabet memoryless source X has rate R_x satisfying

$$R_x \geq \min H(X|Z)$$

where the minimum is over the set of random variables Z conditionally independent of X given Y, and satisfying

$$R_y \geq I(Y, Z)$$

Proof The proof employs a conditional version of Fano's inequality to bound the probability of symbol error away from zero when the conditions of the theorem are not satisfied. Refer to Theorem 6.1.2. We can apply this theorem, noticing that input blocks of length n are encoded into codewords of blocklength n. Conditional on a side random variable $S = m'$, the average probability of symbol error in the reconstruction $\hat{X}$ satisfies

$$\langle p_{e|m'} \rangle \log (J - 1) + H_b(\langle p_{e|m'} \rangle) \geq \frac{1}{n} H(X^n|\hat{X}^n, S = m')$$

Now take the expectation with respect to S. Because the binary entropy is concave, the expectation can be moved inside the binary entropy function. We get

$$\langle p_e \rangle \log (J - 1) + H_b(\langle p_e \rangle) \geq \frac{1}{n} H(X^n|\hat{X}^n, S)$$

as a conditional form of the per-letter Fano inequality.

Now we are ready to bound the code rates. Denote the operation of the Y encoder by $S = e(Y^n)$ where S is a random variable denoting the codeword index. Then we have the following chain of information-theoretic inequalities:

$$nR_y \geq H(S)$$
$$\geq H(S) - H(S|Y^n)$$
$$= H(Y^n) - H(Y^n|S)$$
$$= \sum_{l=1}^{n} H(Y_l) - \sum_{l=1}^{n} H(Y_l|S, Y_1, \ldots, Y_{l-1})$$

Define the discrete random variable Z_l by

$$Z_l = (S, Y_1, \ldots, Y_{l-1})$$

and we can conclude that

$$nR_y \geq \sum_{l=1}^{n} I(Y_l; Z_l)$$

To develop an inequality on rate R_x, start with the inequality

$$nR_x \geq H(\hat{X}^n | S = m')$$

This is valid because, conditional on $S = m'$, $\hat{X}^n$ can only take on 2^{nR_x} different values. Therefore taking the expectation with respect to S leads to the following string of implications:

$$nR_x \geq H(\hat{X}^n | S)$$
$$= H(\hat{X}^n | S) - H(\hat{X}^n | X^n, S)$$
$$= I(X^n; \hat{X}^n | S)$$
$$= H(X^n | S) - H(X^n | \hat{X}^n, S)$$

The first term on the right can be bounded as follows:

$$H(X^n | S) = \sum_{l=1}^{n} H(X_l | S, X_1, \ldots, X_{l-1})$$

$$\geq \sum_{l=1}^{n} H(X_l | S, X_1, \ldots, X_{l-1}, Y_1, \ldots, Y_{l-1})$$

$$= \sum_{l=1}^{n} H(X_l | S, Y_1, \ldots, Y_{l-1})$$

The last equality is a subtle one, and may call for a side computation to be convincing. It says that because X_l is independent of $X_1, \ldots, X_{l-1}$, and S depends on $X_1, \ldots, X_{l-1}$ only through $Y_1, \ldots, Y_{l-1}$, the conditioning on $X_1, \ldots, X_{l-1}$ is now superfluous and can be dropped. Thus recalling that $Z_l = (S, Y_1, \ldots, Y_{l-1})$, we have the inequality

$$\sum_{l=1}^{n} H(X_l | Z_l) - nR_x \leq H(X^n | \hat{X}^n, S)$$

Applying the conditional form of Fano's inequality gives

$$\langle p_e \rangle \log (J - 1) + H_b(\langle p_e \rangle) \geq \frac{1}{n} \left[\sum_{l=1}^{n} H(X_l | Z_l) - nR_x \right]$$

For $\langle p_e \rangle$ to be arbitrarily small, the right side must not be positive. We can conclude that an achievable coding scheme must satisfy

$$R_x \geq n^{-1} \sum_{l=1}^{n} H(X_l | Z_l)$$

for some Z_l satisfying

$$R_y \geq n^{-1} \sum_{l=1}^{n} I(Y_l; Z_l)$$

We know little else about the Z_l except that Z_l is conditionally independent of X_l, given Y_l. This is because knowledge of the value assumed by $Z_l = (S, Y_1, \ldots, Y_{l-1})$ can affect the distribution of X_l only by way of what it says about the distribution of Y_l. Because we don't know Z_l, we choose it, consistent with known constraints, to make the bound on R_x the smallest. The minimum will be the same for every l, so we have completed the proof of the theorem. □

Now we turn to the development of the direct theorem. First we must define the code more specifically.

□ **Definition 9.6.2**   Let $M_x = 2^{nR_x}$ and $M_y = 2^{nR_y}$. A block code $\mathscr{C}$ of blocklength n and rates R_x, R_y for a pair of dependent sources consists of two component codes, $\mathscr{C}_x$ and $\mathscr{C}_y$. Code $\mathscr{C}_x$ consists of M_x codebins, each codebin containing N_x sourcewords of blocklength n from source X. Code $\mathscr{C}_y$ consists of M_y codewords of blocklength n in the alphabet of a random variable Z. □

The codebins for source X are denoted $\mathscr{B}_m$ for $m = 0, \ldots, M_x - 1$ and codewords for source Y are denoted $\mathbf{c}_{m'}$ for $m' = 0, \ldots, M_y - 1$. The first $M_x - 1$ codebins of $\mathscr{C}_x$ and the first $M_y - 1$ codewords of $\mathscr{C}_y$ are called *normal codebins* and *normal codewords*, respectively. The M_xth codebin of $\mathscr{C}_x$ and the M_yth codeword of $\mathscr{C}_y$ are called the *default codebin* and *default codeword*, respectively. To use the block code, each source encoder breaks the stream of source output symbols into sourcewords of blocklength n. (The X and Y encoders must be synchronized so they begin new source blocks at the same time.) Each sourceword of source X is represented by any codebin containing that sourceword. In turn, that codebin is designated by the nR_x-bit binary number that indexes that codebin. If the sourceword appears in no codebin, it is assigned to the default codebin of $\mathscr{C}_x$ and is represented by the largest index $M_x - 1$.

To encode the side information, the sourcewords of source Y are encoded into that codeword $\mathbf{c}_{m'}$ of $\mathscr{C}_y$ such that the sourceword $\mathbf{y}$ and codeword $\mathbf{c}_{m'}$ are jointly strongly typical. If there is no such codeword, the default codeword is used.

The decoder makes use of a decoding table consisting of an nR_x-by-nR_y array, which is used as follows: The decoder receives the indices of codebin $\mathscr{B}_m$ and of codeword $\mathbf{c}_{m'}$ and looks in the decoding table under that pair of indices to find the decoded sourceword $\mathbf{x}$. The decoding table is constructed as follows: Choose $\delta > 0$. For each codebin $\mathscr{B}_m$, and codeword $\mathbf{c}_{m'}$, choose a pair of sourcewords $\mathbf{x}$ and $\mathbf{y}$ such that the triplet $(\mathbf{x},\mathbf{y},\mathbf{c}_{m'})$ is jointly strongly δ-typical and $\mathbf{x}$ is in codebin $\mathscr{B}_m$. The sourceword $\mathbf{x}$ then composes the entry in the decoding table corresponding to that pair of indices. If there is no such jointly strongly typical triplet or if there is more than one, then any null symbol can compose that entry in the decoding table. Such a case will be counted as a decoding error.

The proof of the direct coding theorem will employ a random-coding argument. We will randomly construct the block code consisting of the codewords into which each block $\mathbf{y}$ from the Y source is encoded and codebins into which each block $\mathbf{x}$ from the X source is encoded. To prove the coding theorem we will make use of the fact that if $\mathbf{y}$ is encoded into a codeword with which it is jointly strongly typical, then usually that codeword is also jointly strongly typical with $\mathbf{x}$. We will prove that this is so as a consequence of the fact that there is a Markov relationship between X, Y, and Z. In general, three random variables X, Y, and Z form a Markov chain, denoted $X \to Y \to Z$, if Z is conditionally independent of X given Y. This can be written

$$p_{X,Y,Z}(x, y, z) = p_X(x)p_{Y|X}(y|x)p_{Z|Y}(z|y)$$

By the Bayes formula,

$$p_X(x)p_{Y|X}(y|x) = p_Y(y)p_{X|Y}(x|y)$$

so that whenever $X \to Y \to Z$ we also have

$$p_{X,Y,Z}(x, y, z) = p_Y(y)p_{X|Y}(x|y)p_{Z|Y}(z|y)$$
$$= p_Z(z)p_{Y|Z}(y|z)p_{X|Y}(x|y)$$

where the second equation follows from a second application of the Bayes formula. Therefore $Z \to Y \to X$ whenever $X \to Y \to Z$.

Given three discrete random variables X, Y, and Z, not necessarily forming a Markov chain, with joint probability distribution abbreviated as p_{ijk}, the set of jointly strongly δ-typical sequences is defined as

$$\mathscr{S}_{xyz}(\delta) = \left\{ (\mathbf{x},\mathbf{y},\mathbf{z}) : \left| \frac{1}{n} n_{ijk}(x,y,z) - p_{ijk} \right| < \frac{\delta}{IJK}; \right.$$

$$\left. i = 0, \ldots, I - 1, j = 0, \ldots, J - 1, k = 0, \ldots, K - 1 \right\}$$

Clearly, if $(\mathbf{x}, \mathbf{y}, \mathbf{z}) \in \mathscr{S}_{xyz}(\delta)$, then $(\mathbf{x}, \mathbf{y}) \in \mathscr{S}_{xy}(\delta)$ and $(\mathbf{y}, \mathbf{z}) \in \mathscr{S}_{yz}(\delta)$. However, the converse is not true. Joint δ-typicality of both $(\mathbf{x}, \mathbf{y})$ and $(\mathbf{y}, \mathbf{z})$ does not imply joint Δ-typicality of $(\mathbf{x}, \mathbf{z})$, even if Δ is chosen considerably larger than δ. For example, suppose X^n, Y^n, and Z^n are independent, equiprobable vector random variables with binary components. Any two of their realizations are a jointly typical pair if they agree in approximately half of their places. If the pair $(\mathbf{x},\mathbf{y})$ is jointly typical of (X^n, Y^n), and $\mathbf{z} = \mathbf{x}$, then $(\mathbf{y},\mathbf{z})$ is also a jointly typical pair. However, $(\mathbf{x},\mathbf{z})$ is definitely not a jointly typical pair because $\mathbf{x}$ and $\mathbf{z}$ agree in all places.

Lemma 9.6.4 says that such cases are rare; given $X \to Y \to Z$ and any realization $\mathbf{z}$ of Z^n, if Y^n assumes a value $\mathbf{y}$ jointly strongly typical with $\mathbf{z}$, then X^n will almost always assume a value $\mathbf{x}$ jointly strongly typical with $\mathbf{z}$.

$\square$ **Lemma 9.6.3** In the space of vectors of blocklength n, let

$$\mathscr{S}_{y|x}(\delta) = \{\mathbf{y} : (\mathbf{x}, \mathbf{y}) \in \mathscr{S}_{xy}(\delta)\}$$

where $\mathbf{x}$ is a fixed element of $\mathscr{S}_x(\delta)$. Then

$$|\mathscr{S}_{y|x}(\delta)| = e^{nH(Y|X) + o(n)}$$

Proof The proof is based on Stirling's approximation. Let $\mathbf{x} \in \mathscr{S}_x(\delta)$ be given. For any $\mathbf{y}$, let $n_{ij}(\mathbf{x}, \mathbf{y})$ be the joint composition of $\mathbf{x}$ and $\mathbf{y}$. Choose a joint composition array $\{N_{ij}\}$ such that $N_{ij} \sim nP_{ij}$ within an $o(n)$ term and $\sum_j N_{ij} = n_i(\mathbf{x})$. There are only algebraically many such joint compositions. The number of $\mathbf{y}$ such that $n_{ij}(\mathbf{x}, \mathbf{y}) = N_{ij}$ for all i and j is given by

$$|\{\mathbf{y} : n_{ij}(\mathbf{x}, \mathbf{y}) = N_{ij}\}| = \prod_i \frac{n_i(\mathbf{x})!}{\prod_j [N_{ij}!]}$$

Stirling's approximation to the factorial is $\log n! \approx n \log n$. Therefore

$$\log |\mathscr{S}_{y|x}(\delta)| = \log |\{\mathbf{y} : n_{ij}(\mathbf{x}, \mathbf{y}) = N_{ij}\}| + o(n)$$

$$= \sum_i \left\{ n_i(\mathbf{x})[\log n_i(\mathbf{x}) + o(n)] - \sum_j N_{ij}[\log N_{ij} + o(n)] \right\}$$

$$= \sum_i \left\{ n_i(\mathbf{x})[\log p_i + o'(n)] - \sum_j N_{ij}[\log P_{ij} + o'(n)] \right\}$$

$$+ \left\{ \sum_i [n_i(\mathbf{x}) - \sum_j N_{ij}] \right\} \log n + o(n)$$

The last term is zero because $\sum_j N_{ij} = n_i(\mathbf{x})$. Finally,

$$\frac{1}{n} \log |\mathscr{S}_{y|x}(\delta)| = \sum_i p_i \log p_i - \sum_{ij} P_{ij} \log P_{ij} + o(n)$$

$$= H(Y|X) + o(n)$$

which completes the proof of the lemma. $\square$

This lemma is the first time we have worked closely with strongly typical sequences. Up to now, weakly typical sequences satisfied our needs. For the remainder of this chapter, however, we will use strongly typical sequences. The next two lemmas provide some properties that will be needed. The derivations of such properties for strongly typical sequences are more combinatoric and more difficult than for weakly typical sequences.

☐ **Lemma 9.6.4** **(Markov typicality lemma)** Let $\delta > 0$ and $\varepsilon > 0$ be given. Suppose that $X_l \to Y_l \to Z_l$ are identically distributed Markov chains for $l = 1, \ldots, n$ such that the pair (X_l, Y_l) is independent of the pair $(X_{l'}, Y_{l'})$ if $l \neq l'$. Then, for each $\mathbf{z}$,

$$Pr[(X^n, \mathbf{z}) \in \mathscr{S}_{xz}(\delta) | (Y^n, \mathbf{z}) \in \mathscr{S}_{yz}(\delta)] \geq 1 - \varepsilon$$

provided n is sufficiently large.

Proof By the general definition of conditional probability, for any events $\mathscr{A}$ and $\mathscr{B}$, we have

$$Pr[\mathscr{A} | \mathscr{B}] = \frac{Pr[\mathscr{A} \cap \mathscr{B}]}{Pr[\mathscr{B}]}$$

Let $\mathscr{A}$ be the event that $(X^n; \mathbf{z})$ is a strongly δ-typical pair, and let $\mathscr{B}$ be the event that $(Y^n; \mathbf{z})$ is a strongly δ-typical pair. The elements of $\mathscr{S}_y(\delta)$ are approximately equiprobable. Therefore, using Lemma 9.6.3,

$$Pr[\mathscr{B}] = |\mathscr{S}_{y|z}(\delta)| e^{-nH(Y) + o(n)}$$
$$= e^{-nI(y;z) + o(n)}$$

Similarly, using Lemma 9.6.3 and the Markov property,

$$Pr[\mathscr{A} \cap \mathscr{B}] = |\mathscr{S}_{xy|z}| e^{-nH(X,Y) + o(n)}$$
$$= e^{-nI(X,Y;Z) + o(n)} = e^{-nI(Y;Z) + o(n)}$$

and the lemma follows.   ☐

☐ **Lemma 9.6.5** Given discrete random variables X and Y, let $M = 2^{nR}$ and let $\mathbf{y}_0, \ldots, \mathbf{y}_{M-1}$ be vectors of blocklength n chosen independently and equiprobably from the set of strongly δ-typical Y sequences. Then for small enough δ, the probability that X^n takes on a realization $\mathbf{x}$ that is jointly strongly δ-typical with at least one vector in the set $\{\mathbf{y}_0, \ldots, \mathbf{y}_{M-1}\}$ goes to 1 as n goes to infinity, provided $R > I(X; Y)$.

Proof It suffices to prove the theorem under the assumption that $\mathbf{x}$ is itself strongly δ-typical, because the contrary case has arbitrarily small probability of occurring. Let p_e be the probability that no such sequence is jointly strongly δ-typical with $\mathbf{x}$, given that $\mathbf{x}$ is strongly δ-typical. Because the $\mathbf{y}_m$ are chosen independently, we can write

$$p_e = Pr[(\mathbf{x}, \mathbf{y}_m) \notin \mathscr{S}_{xy}(\delta), 0 \leq m \leq M - 1 | \mathbf{x} \in \mathscr{S}_x(\delta)]$$
$$= \{1 - Pr[(\mathbf{x}, \mathbf{y}) \in \mathscr{S}_{xy}(\delta) | \mathbf{x} \in \mathscr{S}_x(\delta)]\}^M$$

To find $Pr[(\mathbf{x}, \mathbf{y}) \in \mathscr{S}_{xy}(\delta) | \mathbf{x} \in \mathscr{S}_x(\delta)]$, we need to find the ratio of the total number of $\mathbf{y}$ sequences that are jointly δ-typical with a given $\mathbf{x}$ to the total number of δ-typical **y** sequences. By Lemma 9.6.3, this is

$$Pr\left[(\mathbf{x},\mathbf{y})\in\mathscr{S}_{xy}(\delta)\,\middle|\,\mathbf{x}\in\mathscr{S}_x(\delta)\right] = \frac{\left|\mathscr{S}_{y|x}(\delta)\right|}{\left|\mathscr{S}_y(\delta)\right|}$$

$$\geq \frac{2^{nH(Y|X)+o'(n)}}{2^{nH(Y)+o''(n)}}$$

and

$$p_e \leq \left\{1 - 2^{-nI(X;Y)+o(n)}\right\}^M$$

Therefore

$$\log p_e \leq M \log \left\{1 - 2^{-nI(X;Y)+o(n)}\right\}$$

$$\leq \left\{-M2^{-nI(X;Y)+o(n)}\right\}$$

where we have used the inequality $\log x \leq x - 1$. Consequently,

$$\log p_e \leq -2^{n[R-I(X;Y)]-o(n)}$$

Because $R > I(X;Y)$, $\log p_e \to -\infty$ as $n \to \infty$. Hence $p_e \to 0$ and the proof is complete. $\square$

$\square$ **Theorem 9.6.6 (Direct theorem)** If the decoder can have side information from source Y encoded at rate R_y, then, if the blocklength is sufficiently large, there exists a block code for data compaction of arbitrarily small probability of block decoding error for the finite alphabet memoryless source X for every rate R_x satisfying

$$R_x \geq \min H(X|Z)$$

where the minimum is over the set of random variables Z satisfying both the Markov property $X \to Y \to Z$ and the inequality

$$R_y \geq I(Y;Z)$$

Proof The proof is based on a random-coding argument and on the Markov typicality lemma. Fix $\varepsilon > 0$ and $\delta > 0$. Let

$$\gamma_x = \delta\sum_j[-\log p_j]$$

where p_j denotes the probability that X takes the value a_j for $j = 0, \ldots, J - 1$. There are at most $2^{n[H(X)+\gamma_x]}$ strongly δ-typical **x** sequences.

To construct the code, first construct $2^{n[H(X|Z)+\varepsilon]}$ codebins; each codebin contains a fraction of the $2^{n[H(X)+o(n)]}$ strongly δ-typical X sequences assigned randomly. Specifically, the strongly δ-typical **x** sequences are shuffled and dealt into the codebins so that each codebin contains $2^{n[H(X)+o(n)]}/2^{n[H(X|Z+\varepsilon]}$ strongly δ-typical **x** sequences. Next choose the codewords for the side information as follows. Choose any discrete random variable Z jointly distributed with Y and satisfying the Markov condition $X \to Y \to Z$. Randomly choose a set of $2^{n[I(Y;Z)+\varepsilon]}$ codewords from the set $\mathcal{S}_z(\delta)$ of strongly δ-typical $\mathbf{z}$ blocks. We know by Lemma 9.6.5 that the probability that Y^n takes a value that is strongly jointly δ-typical with one of these codewords goes to 1 as n goes to infinity.

To encode, represent sourceword $\mathbf{x}$ by any codebin that contains it and represent sideword $\mathbf{y}$ by the codeword $\mathbf{c}$ of smallest index that is jointly typical with $\mathbf{y}$. The Markov typicality lemma asserts that with probability going to 1 as n goes to infinity, sourceword $\mathbf{x}$ will take on a value that is jointly strongly δ-typical with $\mathbf{c}$.

At encoded rates of $R_x = H(X|Z) + \varepsilon$ and $R_y = I(Y;Z) + \varepsilon$, we can specify to the decoder, with probability approaching 1 as n goes to infinity, both the codebin containing the realization $\mathbf{x}$ and a value of $\mathbf{z}$ that is jointly typical with it. Because the sourceword $\mathbf{x}$ is jointly δ-typical with the specified $\mathbf{z}$, the decoder will be able to uniquely recover $\mathbf{x}$ as long as no other sequence in the codebin is also jointly typical with $\mathbf{z}$. This will be so with probability very close to 1 as n goes to infinity if, in codebin $\mathcal{B}_x$, the number of codewords N_x is not too large—specifically (by Problem 9.11) if N_x is chosen so that

$$\lim_{n \to \infty} \frac{1}{n} \log N_x < I(X;Z)$$

with probability approaching 1, there will be no ambiguous sourceword in codebin $\mathcal{B}_x$. But

$$\frac{1}{n} \log N_x = H(X) - H(X|Z) + \gamma_x - \varepsilon$$

$$= I(X;Z) - \varepsilon + \delta \sum_j [-\log p_j]$$

so it suffices to choose δ small enough so that

$$\varepsilon > \delta \sum_j [-\log p_j]$$

and the proof is complete. $\square$

9.7 DATA COMPRESSION WITH SIDE INFORMATION

For the multiterminal source-coding problem that was shown in Fig. 9.17, we know that if $R_x < H(X|Y)$, the output of source X cannot be reconstructed with arbitrarily small probability of error. This is a consequence of the Slepian-Wolf converse theorem, as given in Theorem 9.5.1. Consequently, we must accept some errors in the decoder output. In this section we shall determine how small we can make the probability of decoding error.

Without any extra effort, we can treat a more general notion of distortion in the decoder output rather than simply treat the probability of decoding error. We will introduce a distortion matrix $\{\rho_{jk}\}$ as we did in Chapter 6, so this section is a generalization of that chapter. The element ρ_{jk} specifies the distortion when source symbol a_j is reproduced at the decoder by reproducing symbol b_k.

Figure 9.20 illustrates how the R_x, R_y plane is partitioned into four regions. In the region where both rates are large, the source coding is a two-terminal data compaction code. The Slepian-Wolf theorem defines this region. In the region where one rate is small, a data compression code is needed, albeit one that uses side information from the other source. Such codes are described by the theorems of this section. For the region where both rates are small, a data compression code is needed simultaneously on both axes, but the decoder can use the a priori knowledge of the dependence between the two sources to reduce the distortion in each reproduction. To determine the performance of simultaneous multiterminal source compression codes is a difficult problem that has not yet been solved.

In this section we shall study those regions of the R_x, R_y plane in which data compaction can be used for one source, say source Y, but data compression must be used for the other, say source X. We shall model the problem more simply, as seen in Fig. 9.21, by giving the decoder directly the

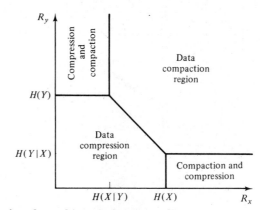

Figure 9.20   Regions for multiterminal source coding.

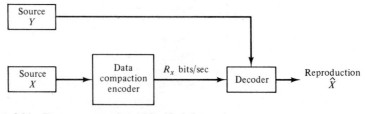

Figure 9.21   Data compression with side information.

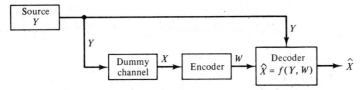

Figure 9.22 **Single-letter view of data compression with side information.**

output of source Y without compaction. The output of source Y then is thought of as side information available only to the decoder. We wish to determine the average distortion necessary to compress the X source output to R_x bits per source symbol when the decoder knows the output of source Y.

It is possible to propose a simple model of how the data compression behaves on the level of a single source symbol. In this model, shown in Fig. 9.22, the encoder output is described in terms of a dummy random variable W that represents the compressed data stream at the level of a single source symbol. The decoder works with Y and W, each of which depends on X. The decoder recovers $\hat{X}$, a reproduction of X as a function $\hat{X} = f(Y, W)$ of its two inputs Y and W.

At the level of a single source symbol, the encoder appears to be a probabilistic device, even though it is actually a deterministic device on the block level. Each source symbol is encoded into a letter of a discrete alphabet W by means of a transition matrix $\mathbf{Q}$. The size of W, the transition matrix $\mathbf{Q}$ and the function $f(Y, W)$, are chosen to minimize the code rate consistent with the allowable distortion. When there is no side information, this model reduces to that studied in Chapter 6 by equating W and $\hat{X}$.

We shall see that we can express the achievable performance of data compression codes based upon this single-letter picture. First we will define the abridged information content at distortion D with side information. Then we will prove the coding theorems.

□ **Definition 9.7.1** The source-distortion function with side information Y is given by the function[†]

$$B_{X|Y}(D) = \min_f \ \min_{\mathbf{Q} \in \mathcal{D}_D} \ [I(X; W) - I(Y; W)]$$

where $\mathbf{Q}$ is a probability transition matrix from X to W constrained to lie in the set

$$\mathcal{D}_D = \left\{ \mathbf{Q} : \sum_j \sum_k p_j T_{k|j} \rho_{jk} \leq D \right\}$$

and $T_{k|j}$ is the probability transition matrix induced on random variable $\hat{X}$ by the mapping $\hat{X} = f(Y, W)$, and $f(Y, W)$ is any mapping from Y and W to $\hat{X}$. □

[†]The same notation $B_{X|Y}(D)$ is also used for a different problem in which the side information Y is known to *both* the encoder and the decoder.

We shall see that $B_{X|Y}(D)$ denotes the least value of R_x for which a code exists that achieves an average distortion not exceeding D when the decoder knows the corresponding output of source Y. Clearly the code construction can choose to ignore source Y, so that

$$B_{X|Y}(D) \le B(D)$$

However, we expect the performance to be improved if the X decoder uses its knowledge of source Y. The problem, however, runs deeper than this. Not only does the decoder use its knowledge of source Y, but the X encoder anticipates that the X decoder will know the output of source Y. The code is designed anticipating that the decoder will have this side information.

□ **Theorem 9.7.2 (Converse theorem)** If the decoder has side information Y, every data compression block code of average per-letter distortion D for the finite-alphabet, memoryless source X has rate R satisfying

$$R \ge B_{X|Y}(D)$$

Proof Denote the operation of the X encoder by $S = e(X^n)$ where S is a random variable denoting the codeword index. Then we have the following chain of information-theoretic inequalities:

$$nR_x \ge H(S)$$

$$\ge H(S|Y^n) = H(S|Y^n) - H(S|X^n, Y^n)$$

$$= I(X^n; S|Y^n)$$

$$= H(X^n|Y^n) - H(X^n|S, Y^n)$$

$$= \sum_{l=1}^{n} H(X_l|Y_l) - \sum_{l=1}^{n} H(X_l|S, Y^n, X_1, \ldots, X_{l-1})$$

Drop $X_1, \ldots, X_{l-1}$ from the conditioning without violating the inequality. Then rewrite the remaining conditioning in the second sum on the right as $(S, Y^n) = (Y_l, W_l)$ where W_l is defined as the discrete random variable $(S, Y_1, \ldots, Y_{l-1}, Y_{l+1}, \ldots, Y_n)$. This gives the inequality

$$nR_x \ge \sum_{l=1}^{n} H(X_l|Y_l) - \sum_{l=1}^{n} H(X_l|W_l, Y_l)$$

$$= \sum_{l=1}^{n} I(X_l; W_l|Y_l)$$

Now S is independent of Y_l given X_l, so we have the Markov condition $Y_l \to X_l \to W_l$. Therefore

$$I(X_l; W_l|Y_l) = I(X_l; W_l) - I(Y_l; W_l)$$

and

$$R_x \geq \frac{1}{n} \sum_{l=1}^{n} B_{X|Y}(D_l)$$

where

$$D_l = E[d(X_l; \hat{X}_l)]$$

By the convexity[†] of $B_{X|Y}(D)$, this becomes

$$R_x \geq B_{X|Y}\left(\frac{1}{n} \sum_{l=1}^{n} D_l\right)$$

Because

$$D = \frac{1}{n} \sum_{l=1}^{n} D_l$$

the proof is complete. $\square$

$\square$ **Theorem 9.7.3 (Direct theorem)** If the decoder can have unrestricted side information from source Y, then, if the blocklength is sufficiently large, there exists a data compression code with distortion D and rate arbitrarily close to $B_{X|Y}(D)$.

Proof The proof is based on the Markov typicality lemma. Choose any random variable W dependent on X such that the conditional probability distribution $\mathbf{Q}$ lies in $\mathcal{Q}_D$. Form a code consisting of $2^{n[I(X;W)+\varepsilon]}$ codewords that are randomly chosen sequences of blocklength n generated by W^n. Arrange the $2^{n[I(X;W)+\varepsilon]}$ codewords into codebins with $2^{n[I(Y;W)-\varepsilon]}$ codewords to a codebin. There are $2^{n[I(X;W)-I(Y;W)]}$ codebins. With probability approaching 1 as n goes to infinity, the encoder can map X^n into a codeword $\mathbf{w}$ that is jointly typical with it, and then specify the codebin to which $\mathbf{w}$ belongs. The decoder, which already knows the realization $\mathbf{y}$ of Y^n, can be given the index of the codebin that contains $\mathbf{w}$ at any rate R_x satisfying

$$R_x \geq I(X; W) - I(Y; W)$$

From that codebin the decoder recovers that vector $\mathbf{w}$ that is jointly typical with $\mathbf{y}$. It will be unique with probability approaching 1.

We now have an encoding procedure that satisfies the rate constraint. We only need to verify that the decoder can form the reproduction $\hat{X}$ such that the distortion constraint is satisfied.

Having $\mathbf{w}$, the decoder forms $\hat{\mathbf{x}}$ symbol by symbol using the rule

$$\hat{x}_l = f(y_l, w_l)$$

[†]We are leaving a gap here because we have not proved the convexity of $B_{X|Y}(D)$. It is a lengthy proof. To be mathematically precise we should replace $B_{X|Y}(D)$ with its lower convex envelope in the statement of the theorem. Then there would be no gap in the proof.

By assumption of the theorem, the function $f(Y, W)$ ensures that

$$E[d(X, \hat{X})] \leq D$$

because we initially selected W as a conditional probability distribution in $\mathcal{Q}_D$. Now write

$$d(\mathbf{x}, \hat{\mathbf{x}}) = \frac{1}{n} \sum_{l=1}^{n} d(x_l, \hat{x}_l)$$

$$= \frac{1}{n} \sum_{ijk} n_{ijk}(Y^n, X^n, \mathbf{w}) d(j, f(i, k))$$

Now it follows from the Markov typicality lemma and its proof that the triplet $(Y^n, X^n, \mathbf{w})$ is strongly δ-typical with probability approaching 1 as n goes to infinity. Therefore, with probability approaching 1 as n goes to infinity, we have the inequality:

$$d(\mathbf{x}, \hat{\mathbf{x}}) \leq \frac{1}{n} \sum_{ijk} (np_{ijk} + n\delta |YZ|^{-1}) d(j, f(i, k))$$

Now sum over i, j, and k:

$$d(\mathbf{x}, \hat{\mathbf{x}}) \leq E\left[d(X, \hat{X}(Y, W))\right] + \delta |Y| d_{\max}]$$

$$\leq D + \delta'$$

for some small δ' that can be sent to zero. Hence the rate $I(X; W) - I(Y; W)$ is an achievable rate for all W compatible with $\mathcal{Q}_D$. $\square$

9.8 DATA COMPRESSION FOR DIVERSITY SYSTEMS

A *diversity system* for communication sends several copies of the same message to a user through several different channels, so that even if all but one channel is broken, the message will still arrive at the receiver. In the simplest case there are two diversity channels. If neither channel is broken, then the user receives the same message twice. The duplicate copy of the message has no value.

A *degraded diversity system* is more subtle and requires only half the channel capacity. It sends half the message through each of two channels, as shown in Fig. 9.23, but it does this in such a way that either half suffices to reconstruct a degraded copy of the message. A high-fidelity reproduction is obtained if both channels are intact; a low-fidelity reproduction is obtained if only one channel is intact. Each of the two half-messages must preserve the main content of the message but can suppress some minor details; yet the two half-messages together contain everything. A possible application is to voice telephony. A digitized voice signal could be divided in half and sent over two routes. If either route is blocked or disconnected, a reduced-fidelity reproduction is still available to the receiver.

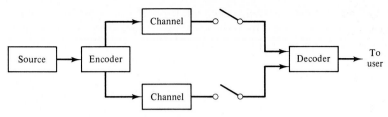

Figure 9.23 A degraded diversity system.

We shall prove that codes exist for degraded diversity systems, though we do not yet know how to construct them. Only the most rudimentary form of this problem has been studied. The simplest model of a degraded diversity system consists of a binary symmetric source and two channels, each with capacity one-half of the source entropy. The theory shows that the data can be encoded into codewords of rate 1/2 so that the decoder can reconstruct the sourceword from either half-rate codeword with a bit error rate of 20.7%, and can reconstruct the sourceword from both half-rate codewords with arbitrarily small bit error rate.

It is interesting to contrast this with the source-distortion function $B(D)$ for the binary source. When $B(D) = 0.5$, the distortion is 0.11; only 11% of the bits need to be received in error for a rate 1/2 code. What is different about the new problem is that it must be possible to eliminate essentially all errors by supplementing the rate 1/2 code with a second rate 1/2 code of the same kind. This is a more restrictive requirement on the design of the code, and that is why the distortion must increase to 20.7%.

Figure 9.24 shows an equivalent form of the degraded diversity system that may be easier to visualize. In the representation, the decoder is shown in

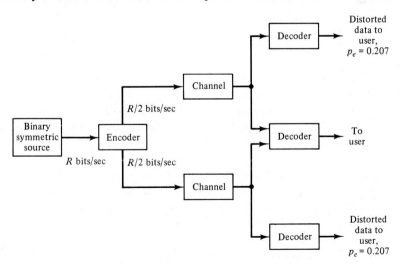

Figure 9.24 A representation of a binary degraded diversity system.

the diagram as three decoders, although these are really just three operating modes of a single decoder. In the simplest case, the central decoder is required to reproduce the stream of source symbols. Without any extra effort, we can study a more general case in which the central decoder is required only to reproduce the source data within average distortion D under distortion matrix $\{\rho_{jk}\}$. The original problem is included simply by using the probability-of-error distortion matrix and setting D to zero.

We formulate the general problem as follows: There are four alphabets— the source alphabet $\{a_j\}$ and three reproducing alphabets $\{b_k\}$, $\{b'_{k'}\}$, and $\{b''_{k''}\}$, possibly of different sizes. A stream of symbols from the source alphabet enters the encoder, and two bit streams leave the encoder at rates R_1 bits per input symbol and R_2 bits per input symbol. Both bit streams enter the central decoder.

Only one bit stream enters each side decoder. Side decoder 1 is required to describe the source data using alphabet $\{b'_{k'}\}$ within average distortion D_1 under distortion matrix $\{\rho'_{jk'}\}$. Side decoder 2 is required to describe the source data using alphabet $\{b''_{k''}\}$ within average distortion D_2 under distortion matrix $\{\rho''_{jk''}\}$. The central decoder is required to describe the source data using alphabet $\{b_k\}$ within average distortion D_0 under distortion matrix $\{\rho_{jk}\}$.

For each value of the distortion vector (D_0, D_1, D_2), there is an achievable-rate region defined as the set of rate pairs (R_1, R_2) for which there exist codes of distortion at most (D_0, D_1, D_2). The achievable-rate region is not known except for simple cases such as that discussed in conjunction with Fig. 9.24. In this section we shall develop only an inner bound on the achievable-rate region; the actual region may be larger.

A crude outer bound on the achievable-rate region is easy to state. Specifically, (R_1, R_2) is not in the achievable-rate region unless

$$R_1 + R_2 \geq B(D_0)$$

$$R_1 \geq B(D_1)$$

$$R_2 \geq B(D_2)$$

However, we should not expect that all rate pairs satisfying these inequalities are in the achievable-rate region. This is because part of the information in the two codewords must be dependent so that the needs of the side decoders can be satisfied. The redundant portion of the information will be useless to the central decoder. In addition, the central decoder may need some detailed information that neither side decoder needs. The way that we will prove the inner bound is by starting with codewords that satisfy the needs of the side decoders and appending to these codewords additional information that will satisfy the needs of the central decoder. However, we do not know that this two-step method for forming codes is the most efficient method, since we do not know a corresponding outer bound.

The inner bound on the achievable-rate region will be developed by using

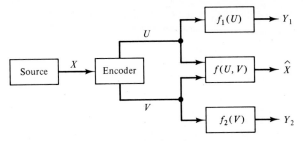

Figure 9.25   Single-letter view of a degraded diversity system.

a single-letter view of the data compression, even though the encoder and decoder work on blocks. The random variable X is mapped into random variables Y, Y_1, and Y_2 by the encoder and decoders, as is shown in Fig. 9.25. Source symbol a_j is transformed into the three reproducing symbols $(b_k, b'_{k'}, b''_{k''})$ with probability $Q(b_k, b'_{k'}, b''_{k''}|a_j)$, abbreviated $Q_{kk'k''|j}$.

□ **Theorem 9.8.1**   Let **p** be a discrete source. Given a distortion vector (D_0, D_1, D_2), the achievable-rate region for a degraded diversity system contains the convex hull of the set of all (R_1, R_2) such that

$$R_1 \geq I(X; Y_1)$$
$$R_2 \geq I(X; Y_2)$$
$$R_1 + R_2 \geq I(X; (Y, Y_1, Y_2)) + I(Y_1, Y_2)$$

for some conditional probability distribution $Q_{kk'k''|j}$ such that

$$D_0 \geq E[d(X, Y)]$$
$$D_1 \geq E[d(X, Y_1)]$$
$$D_2 \geq E[d(X, Y_2)]$$

Proof   The proof involves a random-coding argument. Select numbers $\tilde{R}_1, \delta R_1, \tilde{R}_2$, and δR_2, such that $R_1 = \tilde{R}_1 + \delta R_1$ and $R_2 = \tilde{R}_2 + \delta R_2$. First we will randomly choose a set of reproducing words for each side decoder, with rates $\tilde{R}_1$ and $\tilde{R}_2$, respectively; then we will randomly choose some conditional information for the central decoder with rates δR_1 and δR_2, respectively. This establishes a set of rate pairs (R_1, R_2) in the achievable-rate region. The achievable-rate region is convex because by timesharing, the line joining any two points in the achievable-rate region is also in the achievable-rate region. Therefore it is permissible to include the convex hull in the statement of the theorem.

The proof is in two steps. In step 1 we give a procedure for designing the code of rate (R_1, R_2), the encoding procedure, and the decoding procedure. In step 2 we show that the probability of decoding failure can be made arbitrarily small by making the blocklength large enough.

Step 1: Given the joint probability distribution

$$P_{jkk'k''} = p_j Q_{kk'k''|j}$$

let

$$Q'_{k'|j} = \sum_{kk''} Q_{kk'k''|j}$$

$$Q''_{k''|j} = \sum_{kk'} Q_{kk'k''|j}$$

and

$$Q_{k|j} = \sum_{k'k''} Q_{kk'k''|j}$$

We know from Theorem 6.5.1 and its proof that we can choose a set of reproducing codewords c'_r of rate R_1 and blocklength n that can encode sourceword X^n with average distortion satisfying

$$\sum_{jk} p_j Q'_{k|j} \rho'_{jk'} \le D_1$$

for all $\mathbf{Q}'$ satisfying

$$\tilde{R}_1 \ge I(\mathbf{p}; \mathbf{Q}')$$

Randomly choose such a set of reproducing codewords. The random selection is based on the product probability distribution on vectors generated by the per-letter probability distribution

$$q'_{k'} = \sum_j p_j Q'_{k'|j}$$

However, instead of using $q'(\mathbf{y})$ to randomly select $\mathbf{y}$ as a codeword, we will choose $\mathbf{y}$ equiprobably from the set of all strongly δ-typical $\mathbf{y}$ sequences. The Shannon-McMillan theorem says that this is essentially the same thing.

Similarly, from the set of strongly δ-typical sequences generated by $q''_{k''} = \sum_j p_j Q''_{k''|j}$, randomly choose a set of reproducing codewords c''_s of rate $\tilde{R}_2$ and blocklength n that can encode the sourcewords to within distortion at most D_2.

The next step is to supplement these two codes with additional information needed by the central decoder. The rates will be increased by δR_1 and δR_2, respectively. For every pair (c'_r, c''_s), of codewords drawn above, choose a set of $2^{n(\delta R_1 + \delta R_2)}$ conditional codewords $c_{m|r,s}$ independently and uniformly from the set of strongly conditionally δ-typical sequences $\mathcal{S}_{z|c'_r c''_s}(\delta)$, provided the set is nonempty. If c'_r and c''_s are not themselves jointly δ-typical, the set will be empty. In such cases, any default policy can be followed; we will assume that a decoding error ensues.

The encoding is as follows. Given the sourceword $\mathbf{x}$, find a jointly typical quadruple $(\mathbf{x}, \mathbf{c}'_r, \mathbf{c}''_s, \mathbf{c}_{m|r,s})$, provided such exists. Otherwise, follow any default policy. Rewrite the index m as a pair of indices $m = (m', m'')$, where $m' = 0, \ldots, 2^{n\delta R_1} - 1$ and $m'' = 0, \ldots, 2^{n\delta R_2} - 1$ using the one-to-one map

$$m = m' + m'' 2^{n\delta R_1}$$

Send the pair (r, m') to side decoder 1. This requires $n\tilde{R}_1 + n\delta R_1$ bits. Send the pair (s, m'') to side decoder 2. This requires $n\tilde{R}_2 + n\delta R_2$ bits.

Side decoder 1, given (s, m'), simply announces $\mathbf{c}'_s$ as its reproduction of $\mathbf{x}$. Side decoder 2, given (r, m''), simply announces $\mathbf{c}''_r$ as its reproduction of $\mathbf{x}$. The central decoder, given (s, r, m), simply announces $\mathbf{c}_{m|r,s}$ as its reproduction of $\mathbf{x}$.

Step 2: First notice that the average distortion meets the requirements at the three decoders because of the way we have specified the probability distributions that were used to randomly choose codewords. If the probability of decoding failure is small, then the average distortion increases insignificantly because of decoding failure. We need only to prove that the probability of decoding failure can be made arbitrarily small under the conditions that δR_1 and δR_2 are nonnegative and that

$$\tilde{R}_1 > I(X; Y_1)$$
$$\tilde{R}_2 > I(X; Y_2)$$
$$\tilde{R}_1 + \tilde{R}_2 > I(X; Y_1, Y_2) + I(Y_1; Y_2)$$
$$\delta R_1 + \delta R_2 > I(X; Y | Y_1, Y_2)$$

The theorem follows by adding these inequalities to get

$$R_1 \geq \tilde{R}_1 > I(X; Y_1)$$
$$R_2 \geq \tilde{R}_2 > I(X; Y_2)$$
$$R_1 + R_2 = \tilde{R}_1 + \tilde{R}_2 + \delta R_1 + \delta R_2$$
$$> I(X; Y_1, Y_2) + I(X; Y | Y_1, Y_2) + I(Y_1; Y_2)$$
$$= I(X; (Y, Y_1, Y_2)) + I(Y_1; Y_2)$$

A decoding failure does not occur unless at least one of the following five events occurs:

$$\mathcal{E}_0 = \{\mathbf{x} \text{ is not typical}\}$$
$$\mathcal{E}_1 = \{(\mathbf{x}, \mathbf{c}'_r) \text{ is not jointly typical for any } r\}$$
$$\mathcal{E}_2 = \{(\mathbf{x}, \mathbf{c}''_s) \text{ is not jointly typical for any } s\}$$
$$\mathcal{E}_3 = \{(\mathbf{x}, \mathbf{c}'_r, \mathbf{c}''_s) \text{ is not jointly typical for any } r \text{ and } s\}$$

$\mathcal{E}_4 = \{(\mathbf{x}, \mathbf{c}'_r, \mathbf{c}''_s, \mathbf{c}_{m|r,s})$ is not jointly typical for any r and

s for which $(\mathbf{x}, \mathbf{c}'_r, \mathbf{c}''_s)$ is jointly typical$\}$

Notice that event $\mathcal{E}_4$ is conditioned in such a way that it excludes examples of cases already included in other events.

Using the union bound, we can write

$$p_e \le Pr\left[\bigcup_{i=0}^{4} \mathcal{E}_i\right]$$

$$\le Pr[\mathcal{E}_0] + \sum_{i=1}^{4} Pr[\mathcal{E}_i \cap \mathcal{E}_0^c]$$

Clearly, $Pr[\mathcal{E}_0] \to 0$ as $n \to \infty$. Further, we already know from the study of data compression codes that

$$\tilde{R}_1 > I(X; Y_1)$$

implies that $Pr[\mathcal{E}_1 \cap \mathcal{E}_0^c] \to 0$ as blocklength increases; that

$$\tilde{R}_2 > I(X; Y_2)$$

implies that $Pr[\mathcal{E}_2 \cap \mathcal{E}_0^c] \to 0$ as blocklength increases; and that

$$\delta R > I(X; Y | Y_1, Y_2)$$

implies that $Pr[\mathcal{E}_4 \cap \mathcal{E}_0^c] \to 0$ as blocklength increases.

It only remains to be shown that $Pr[\mathcal{E}_3 \cap \mathcal{E}_0^c] \to 0$ with blocklength. Specifically, we wish to show that there are enough individually typical codewords $\mathbf{c}'_r$ and $\mathbf{c}''_s$ so that we can find at least one jointly strongly δ-typical triple $(\mathbf{x}, \mathbf{c}'_r, \mathbf{c}''_s)$. Let

$$\phi(\mathbf{x}, \mathbf{c}'_r, \mathbf{c}''_s) = \begin{cases} 1 & \text{if } (\mathbf{x}, \mathbf{c}'_r, \mathbf{c}''_s) \in \mathcal{S}_{xy_1y_2}(\delta) \\ 0 & \text{otherwise} \end{cases}$$

The number of pairs of codewords with which $\mathbf{x}$ is jointly strongly δ-typical is given by

$$\psi(\mathbf{x}) = \sum_{r,s} \phi(\mathbf{x}, \mathbf{c}'_r, \mathbf{c}''_s)$$

There is a decoding failure when $\psi(\mathbf{x}) = 0$. To bound $Pr[\mathcal{E}_3 \cap \mathcal{E}_0^c]$, we will bound $Pr[\psi(\mathbf{x}) = 0]$. Specifically, notice that

$$Pr[\psi(\mathbf{x}) = 0] \le Pr[\{|\psi(\mathbf{x}) - E[\psi(\mathbf{x})]| \ge \alpha E[\psi(\mathbf{x})]\}]$$

$$\le \frac{\text{var}\,[\psi(\mathbf{x})]}{\alpha^2 (E[\psi(\mathbf{x})])^2}$$

where the second inequality is Chebychev's inequality.

To compute the denominator, first compute $E[\psi(\mathbf{x})]$ with the sourceword $\mathbf{x}$ fixed and the expectation taken with respect to the random coding. Then

$$E[\psi(\mathbf{x})] = \sum_r \sum_s Pr[(\mathbf{x}, \mathbf{c}'_r, \mathbf{c}''_s) \in \mathcal{S}_{xy_1y_2}(\delta)]$$

To within $o(n)$ terms in the exponents, we can write for fixed $\mathbf{x}$:

$$Pr[(\mathbf{x}, \mathbf{c}'_r, \mathbf{c}''_s)] = \frac{e^{nH(Y_1, Y_2|X)}}{e^{nH(Y_1)}e^{nH(Y_2)}}$$

because there are about $e^{nH(Y_1)}e^{nH(Y_2)}$ pairs $(\mathbf{c}'_r, \mathbf{c}''_s)$ of which about $e^{nH(Y_1, Y_2|X)}$ are jointly typical with $\mathbf{x}$. This estimate, within terms of order $o(n)$ in the exponents, is the same for every $\mathbf{x}$. Therefore

$$E[\psi(\mathbf{x})] = \sum_r \sum_s e^{-n[H(Y_1) + H(Y_2) - H(Y_1, Y_2|X)] + o(n)}$$

$$= e^{n[\tilde{R}_1 + \tilde{R}_2 - H(Y_1) - H(Y_2) + H(Y_1, Y_2|X)] + o(n)}$$

To bound var $[\psi(\mathbf{x})]$, fix the sourceword $\mathbf{x}$ and write

$$\text{var } [\psi(\mathbf{x})] = \text{var} \left[\sum_r \sum_s \phi(\mathbf{x}, \mathbf{c}'_r, \mathbf{c}''_s) \right]$$

$$= \sum_r \sum_s \text{var } [\phi(\mathbf{x}, \mathbf{c}'_r, \mathbf{c}''_s)]$$

because the codewords are independently selected, and the variance of the sum of independent random variables equals the sum of their variances. Finally, because $\phi(\mathbf{x}, \mathbf{c}'_r, \mathbf{c}''_s)$ takes on only the values 0 and 1, we have the bound:

$$\text{var } [\phi(\mathbf{x}, \mathbf{c}'_r, \mathbf{c}''_s)] \leq Pr[(\mathbf{x}, \mathbf{c}'_r, \mathbf{c}''_s) \in \mathcal{S}_{xy_1y_2}(\delta)]$$

$$= \frac{e^{nH(Y_1, Y_2|X) + o(n)}}{e^{nH(Y_1)}e^{nH(Y_2)}}$$

Consequently

$$\text{var } [\psi(\mathbf{x})] \leq e^{n[\tilde{R}_1 + \tilde{R}_2 - H(Y_1) - H(Y_2) + H(Y_1, Y_2|X)] + o'(n)}$$

We now have the bound

$$Pr[\mathcal{E}_3 \cap \mathcal{E}_0^c] = Pr[\psi(\mathbf{x}) = 0]$$

$$\leq \alpha^{-2} e^{-n[\tilde{R}_1 + \tilde{R}_2 - H(Y_1) - H(Y_2) + H(Y_1, Y_2|X)] + o(n)}$$

which goes to zero as $n \to \infty$ if

$$\tilde{R}_1 + \tilde{R}_2 > H(Y_1) + H(Y_2) + H(Y_1, Y_2|X)$$

$$= I(X; Y_1, Y_2) + I(Y_1; Y_2)$$

This completes the proof of the theorem.   □

PROBLEMS

9.1. (Binary adder channel) A two-way channel has a binary input alphabet and a binary output alphabet at each terminal. The outputs at the two terminals are the same and are equal to the modulo-2 sum of the two inputs. Find the capacity region.

9.2. (Push-to-talk channel) A two-way channel has a ternary input alphabet and a binary output alphabet at each terminal. The transition matrix $Q_{kk'|jj'}$ is given by

jj' \ kk'	00	01	10	11
00	1/4	1/4	1/4	1/4
01	1/2	1/2	0	0
02	0	0	1/2	1/2
10	1/2	0	1/2	0
11	1/4	1/4	1/4	1/4
12	1/4	1/4	1/4	1/4
20	0	1/2	0	1/2
21	1/4	1/4	1/4	1/4
22	1/4	1/4	1/4	1/4

a. Show that data can be sent at rate 1 in either direction, and, by apportioning time appropriately, data can be sent at the rate pair $(\lambda, 1 - \lambda)$.

b. Show further that the capacity region is a triangular region and therefore that one cannot improve on the "push-to-talk" strategy.

c. Finally, show that there is no probability distribution on the inputs that achieves the point $(\frac{1}{2}, \frac{1}{2})$. This shows that it is necessary to include the convex hull in the definition of the capacity region.

9.3. (Binary multiplier channel) A two-way channel has a binary input alphabet and a binary output alphabet at each terminal. The outputs at the two terminals are the same and are equal to the product of the two inputs. Find upper and lower bounds on the capacity region.

9.4. The Hagelbarger code for the two-way binary multiplying channel is a fixed-to-variable-length tree code having average rate greater than 1/2 simultaneously in both directions. Each encoder is a two-state machine. An encoder is in state S_0 if it last received a 0 and was not in state S_0 at the previous clock time. It is in state S_1 if it last received a 1 or if it was in state S_0 previously. If in state S_1, the encoder accepts the next information bit and transmits this bit unchanged as the next code bit. If in state S_0, the encoder accepts no information bit but transmits the complement of the previous code bit.

a. Find the average rate in each direction of this code.

b. Describe the decoder.

c. By showing that the average number of code bits per data bit decreases faster than $H(\mathbf{p})$, show that the average rate can be increased if the input to the encoder is precoded such that a 1 data bit occurs with probability 0.63.

9.5. The *interference channel* is a channel with two inputs, X_1 and X_2, and two outputs, Y_1 and Y_2. It is used by two transmitters to send two independent messages to two destinations, so the channel can be thought of as two point-to-point channels. However, the channels are not independent, but rather are described by the joint transition matrix $Q(b_k, b'_{k'}|a_j, a'_{j'})$, abbreviated $Q_{kk'|jj'}$.

a. Express the points in the capacity region for which one or the other rate is zero.

b. What are these points if $Q_{kk'|jj'}$ can be factored as $Q'_{k|j}Q''_{k'|j'}$? What is the capacity region in this case?

c. Show that if $R_1 \leq I(X_1; Y_1)$, $R_2 \leq I(X_2; Y_2)$, and $R_1 + R_2 \leq I(X_1, X_2; Y_1, Y_2)$, then (R_1, R_2) is in the capacity region, provided X_1 and X_2 are independent, and Y_1 and Y_2 depend on X_1 and X_2 by means of the channel **Q**.

9.6. The problem of data compression with side information is much simpler if both the encoder and the decoder see the side information X. Show that the appropriate definition now is

$$B_{Y|X}(D) = \min I(Y; \hat{Y}|X)$$

where the minimum is over all $\hat{Y}$ satisfying $E[d(Y; \hat{Y})] \leq D$.

9.7. A broadcast channel consists of two binary symmetric channels, one with crossover probability ρ and one with crossover probability 2ρ.

a. Show this is a degraded broadcast channel.

b. Find the achievable-rate region.

9.8. Find an outer bound for the restricted two-way channel that corresponds to the inner bound. Conclude that the capacity region for the restricted two-way channel is known.

9.9. **a.** The gaussian multiaccess channel is a multiaccess channel with a continuous input alphabet and for which the noise is additive gaussian noise. The output is given by $Y = X_1 + X_2 + Z$. Find the achievable-rate region for the gaussian multiaccess channel.

b. The gaussian broadcast channel is a broadcast channel with continuous input alphabet and for which the noise is additive gaussian noise. Show that every gaussian broadcast channel is a degraded broadcast channel. Find the capacity region for the gaussian broadcast channel.

9.10. A multiaccess channel has two binary inputs and a ternary output with symbols $\{0, 1, e\}$. The channel output is always 0 if both inputs are 0, is always 1 if both inputs are 1, and is symbol e if the two inputs differ. Find the capacity region of this deterministic multiaccess channel.

9.11. Prove the converse to Lemma 9.6.5, that if $R < I(X; Y)$, the probability of a jointly strongly δ-typical sequence goes to 0 as n goes to infinity.

9.12. A continuous-time gaussian multiaccess channel with M users, each of power S, has output

$$Y = \sum_{i=1}^{M} X_i + Z$$

where Z is bandlimited white noise of variance N and the inputs X_i are all constrained to lie in a common band of W hertz.

a. Show that the capacity region is completely specified by the equation

$$\sum_{i=1}^{M} R_i \leq W \log\left(1 + M\frac{S}{N}\right)$$

b. Let $S = E_b R$, $N = N_o W$, and $r = MR/W$. Show that

$$\frac{E_b}{N_o} > \frac{2^r - 1}{r}$$

How does this compare with the point-to-point continuous-time gaussian channel? What can be concluded about the efficiency of using energy in the multiaccess channel?

9.13. A binary diversity communication system with no "excess rate" has rates $R_1 = R_2 = 1/2$ code bits per source bit and zero distortion at the central decoder. Prove that the distortion at each of the side decoders need not exceed any value greater than $(\sqrt{2} - 1)/2$.

NOTES

Multiterminal information theory has been under study for some time, but the problems are very difficult and progress has been slow. The problem treated earliest was the capacity of the feedback channel, which was studied by Shannon (1956) and Dobrushin (1958). The first true multiterminal channel to be studied was the two-way channel studied by Shannon (1961). Ahlswede (1973) and Liao (1972) gave the capacity region of the multiaccess channel. The capacity region of the broadcast channel was studied by Cover (1972). The direct theorem for the degraded broadcast channel was proved by Bergmans (1973), and the converse was proved by Gallager (1974). The general case of the broadcast channel has never been solved; only an inner bound of Marton (1979) is known. Survey articles on multiterminal channel coding have been prepared by van der Meulen (1977) and by El Gamal and Cover (1980). Our proofs follow the unifying methods of El Gamal and Cover, which are based on typical sequences.

The study of multiterminal source coding began with the work of Slepian and Wolf (1973). They gave the achievable-rate region for the problem of compaction of dependent data at remote sites. The problem of data compaction with side information, despite its apparent similarity to the compaction of dependent data, requires a much different solution. It was solved by Ahlswede and Körner (1975) and by Wyner (1975). The problem of data compression with side information was solved by Wyner and Ziv (1976). The Markov lemma is taken from Berger's 1977 unifying survey paper. Data compression for diversity systems was treated by Cover and El Gamal (1982), who gave a region of achievable rates and distortions, and by Berger and Zhang (1983), who established tightness in a special case.

CHAPTER 10

Performance Bounds for Data Transmission

There are now many good block codes in use for data transmission. However, there is room for improvement; we still do not know how to find the best codes for a given channel—perhaps we shall never know. We can only know the best code of blocklength n if we can describe it, say by a rule for generating the codewords. We can only know a rule if we can write it down, say in the form of a computer program. If the number of bits needed by the most concise description of every good code of blocklength n and rate R is exponential in n, then we may say that the best codes of large blocklength are unknowable. Even if we could find the best codes as judged by the probability of decoding error, we might not like them because of the great complexity of the encoder and the decoder. However, we would still want to know something about the best such codes.

In this chapter we shall try to find upper and lower exponential bounds on the performance of the best, or nearly best, block codes for data transmission, without finding the codes themselves and without regard for their complexity. The new exponential bounds supplement the random-coding bound, which was derived in Chapter 5. We shall work quite hard for the little we get, and there will be nothing of direct practical use. All that we can promise for reading this difficult chapter is some sharper insight into the nature of data transmission codes.

10.1 THE CHANNEL RELIABILITY FUNCTION AT HIGH RATES

The random-coding bound, proved in Section 5.7, involves a function $E_r(R)$. In this section we shall study the properties of $E_r(R)$. We shall begin anew, defining a function $E(R)$ in terms of the discrimination. This definition looks much different from the function $E_r(R)$, but we shall prove that it is the same function for $R \geq R_{crit}$. In the next section we shall prove further that $E(R)$ is the channel reliability function $E^*(R)$ for $R \geq R_{crit}$.

☐ **Definition 10.1.1**   The channel reliability exponent $E(R)$ for the channel **Q** is given by

$$E(R) = \max_{\mathbf{p}} \ \min_{\hat{\mathbf{Q}} \in \mathcal{Q}_R(\mathbf{p})} \ L(\hat{\mathbf{Q}}; \mathbf{Q} | \mathbf{p})$$

where the minimum is over the set of $\hat{\mathbf{Q}}$ given by

$$\mathcal{Q}_R(\mathbf{p}) = \{\hat{\mathbf{Q}} : I(\mathbf{p}; \hat{\mathbf{Q}}) \leq R\} \qquad\qquad ☐$$

The reliability exponent $E(R)$ uses the discrimination as a distance between the true channel **Q** and each dummy channel $\hat{\mathbf{Q}}$.

Denote the inner minimum of the definition $E(\mathbf{p}, R)$. It is the minimum discrimination with **p** fixed between the true channel and all conceivable hypothetical channels with mutual information at most R. This means that in turn $E(R)$ is the minimum discrimination between the true channel and those hypothetical channels with mutual information at most R, provided **p** is chosen to maximize this minimum.

The channel exponent $E(R)$ should be compared with the error exponent $e(r)$ for the hypothesis-testing problem as given in Definition 4.6.1. The two have many analogous properties, though these properties are more difficult to prove for $E(R)$.

☐ **Theorem 10.1.2** $E(R)$ is positive for $R < C$ and zero for $R \geq C$, where C is the channel capacity.

Proof $E(R) = 0$ if and only if $\hat{\mathbf{Q}} = \mathbf{Q}$, which occurs if and only if $\mathbf{Q}$ is an element of $\mathcal{Q}_R(\mathbf{p})$ for every $\mathbf{p}$. Hence $E(R) = 0$ if and only if

$$\sum_j \sum_k p_j Q_{k|j} \log \frac{Q_{k|j}}{\sum\limits_j p_j Q_{k|j}} \leq R$$

for every value of $\mathbf{p}$. This is true if and only if $R \geq C$. $\square$

□ **Theorem 10.1.3** $E(R)$ is a decreasing, convex, and hence continuous function defined for $R \geq 0$. It is strictly decreasing in the interval $0 \leq R \leq C$, and in this interval the solution satisfies the constraint with equality.

Proof   Let $E(\mathbf{p}, R)$ denote the inner minimum. Suppose that $R > R'$; then $\mathcal{Q}_R(\mathbf{p}) \supset \mathcal{Q}_{R'}(\mathbf{p})$. Hence $E(\mathbf{p}, R) \leq E(\mathbf{p}, R')$, and the constraint is satisfied with equality in the region where $E(\mathbf{p}, R)$ is strictly decreasing. For each $\mathbf{p}$, convexity follows because $E(\mathbf{p}, R)$ is the minimum of a convex function subject to a convex constraint. Finally $E(R)$ is convex because it is the pointwise maximum of a set of convex functions. $\square$

Let $\mathbf{p}^*$ and $\mathbf{Q}^*$ achieve $E(R)$ at the point R and let $q_k^* = \sum_j p_j^* Q_{k|j}^*$. The following theorem says that the variable $\sum_j p_j \hat{Q}_{k|j}$ can be replaced by the constant q_k^* inside the logarithm of the constraint equation in the expression for $E(R)$. This is a significant reformulation because now $E(R)$ is analogous to the error exponent $e(r)$ of Chapter 4. This association of $E(R)$ with the error exponent $e(r)$ will be used later to analyze the performance of data transmission codes by using the ideas of hypothesis testing.

□ **Theorem 10.1.4**   Suppose that $\mathbf{p}^*$ and $\mathbf{Q}^*$ achieve $E(R)$, and $q_k^* = \sum_j p_j^* Q_{k|j}^*$. Then

$$E(R) = \max_{\mathbf{p}} \min_{\hat{\mathbf{Q}} \in \mathcal{Q}_R'(\mathbf{p})} \sum_j p_j \sum_k \hat{Q}_{k|j} \log \frac{\hat{Q}_{k|j}}{Q_{k|j}}$$

where

$$\mathcal{Q}_R'(\mathbf{p}) = \left\{ \hat{\mathbf{Q}} : \sum_j p_j \sum_k \hat{Q}_{k|j} \log \frac{\hat{Q}_{k|j}}{q_k^*} \leq R \right\}$$

Proof   Let $\mathbf{p}$ be fixed. Define $E(R, \mathbf{p})$ as

$$E(R, \mathbf{p}) = \min_{\hat{\mathbf{Q}} \in \mathcal{Q}_R(\mathbf{p})} \sum_j p_j \sum_k \hat{Q}_{k|j} \log \frac{\hat{Q}_{k|j}}{Q_{k|j}}$$

where

$$\mathcal{Q}_R(\mathbf{p}) = \left\{ \hat{\mathbf{Q}} : \sum_j p_j \sum_k \hat{Q}_{k|j} \log \frac{\hat{Q}_{k|j}}{\sum\limits_j p_j \hat{Q}_{k|j}} \leq R \right\}$$

Define $E'(R, \mathbf{p}, \mathbf{q})$ as

$$E'(R, \mathbf{p}, \mathbf{q}) = \min_{\hat{Q} \in \mathcal{Q}'_R(\mathbf{p}, \mathbf{q})} \sum_j p_j \sum_k \hat{Q}_{k|j} \log \frac{\hat{Q}_{k|j}}{Q_{k|j}}$$

where

$$\mathcal{Q}'_R(\mathbf{p}, \mathbf{q}) = \left\{ \hat{Q} : \sum_j p_j \sum_k \hat{Q}_{k|j} \log \frac{\hat{Q}_{k|j}}{q_k} \le R \right\}$$

and $\mathbf{q}$ is any probability distribution on the output alphabet.
Because, by Theorem 5.2.6,

$$I(\mathbf{p}; \hat{Q}) \le \sum_j \sum_k p_j \hat{Q}_{k|j} \log \frac{\hat{Q}_{k|j}}{q_k}$$

we have that

$$\mathcal{Q}_R(\mathbf{p}) \supset \mathcal{Q}'_R(\mathbf{p}, \mathbf{q})$$

Consequently,

$$E(R, \mathbf{p}) \le E'(R, \mathbf{p}, \mathbf{q})$$

This inequality holds for any $\mathbf{q}$.

On the other hand, because it is defined as a minimum,

$$E'(R, \mathbf{p}, \mathbf{q}) \le \sum_j p_j \sum_k \hat{Q}_{k|j} \log \frac{\hat{Q}_{k|j}}{Q_{k|j}}$$

for every $\hat{Q}$ in the set $\mathcal{Q}'_R(\mathbf{p}, \mathbf{q})$. Now choose $q_k^* = \sum_j p_j^* Q_{k|j}^*$, recalling that $\mathbf{p}^*$ and $\mathbf{Q}^*$ achieve $E(R)$. Then

$$E'(R, \mathbf{p}^*, \mathbf{q}^*) \le \sum_j p_j^* \sum_k Q_{k|j}^* \log \frac{Q_{k|j}^*}{Q_{k|j}} = E(R, \mathbf{p}^*)$$

Thus we have shown that

$$E(R, \mathbf{p}^*) \le E'(R, \mathbf{p}^*, \mathbf{q}^*) \le E(R, \mathbf{p}^*)$$

Because $E(R, \mathbf{p}^*) = E(R)$, the proof of the theorem is complete. $\square$

The purpose of Theorem 10.1.4 is to show the channel exponent $E(R)$ in the form of an error exponent for a hypothesis-testing problem for a specific alternative probability distribution $\mathbf{q}^*$. This distribution has the form of an average probability distribution on the channel output alphabet. In Section 10.2 we will use this theorem to obtain a lower bound on p_e by posing the channel decoding problem as a binary hypothesis-testing problem.

Our next task is to show that $E(R) = E_r(R)$ for $R > R_{crit}$. Equality holds only for the optimum $\mathbf{p}$; more generally it is only true that $E_r(R, \mathbf{p}) \le E(R, \mathbf{p})$. This theorem is the key link that establishes equality between the random-coding lower bound on $E^*(R)$ and the partitioning upper bound on $E^*(R)$.

The fact that it is difficult to prove may be somehow related to the fact that it is intuitively surprising that the two bounds are asymptotically equal.[†]

☐ **Theorem 10.1.5** The channel exponent can be written

$$E(R) = \max_{\mathbf{p}} \max_{s \geq 0} \left[-sR - \log \sum_k \left(\sum_j p_j Q_{k|j}^{1/(1+s)} \right)^{1+s} \right]$$

Proof Step 1: Referring to the definition of $E(R)$, let

$$E(R, \mathbf{p}) = \min_{\mathbf{q}} \min_{\hat{\mathbf{Q}} \in \mathscr{Q}'_R(\mathbf{p}, \mathbf{q})} \sum_j p_j \sum_k \hat{Q}_{k|j} \log \frac{\hat{Q}_{k|j}}{Q_{k|j}}$$

where

$$\mathscr{Q}'_R(\mathbf{p}, \mathbf{q}) = \left\{ \hat{\mathbf{Q}} : \sum_j p_j \sum_k \hat{Q}_{k|j} \log \frac{\hat{Q}_{k|j}}{q_k} \leq R \right\}$$

This is an equivalent representation of $E(R, \mathbf{p})$ because, as we have seen, $\mathscr{Q}_R(\mathbf{p}) \supset \mathscr{Q}'_R(\mathbf{p}, \mathbf{q})$; so for each $\mathbf{q}$, the minimum on $\hat{\mathbf{Q}}$ is larger than or equal to $E(R, \mathbf{p})$ and is equal to it when $\mathbf{q} = \mathbf{q}^*$, as shown in the previous theorem. Hence by Theorem 4.6.3, we find the minimum over $\hat{\mathbf{Q}}$ is

$$E(R, \mathbf{p}) = \min_{\mathbf{q}} \left[-sR_s - (1 + s) \sum_j p_j \log \left(\sum_k Q_{k|j}^{1/(1+s)} q_k^{s/(1+s)} \right) \right]$$

where R_s is given, as in Theorem 4.6.3, in terms of the tilted distribution $\mathbf{Q}^*$ that achieves the minimum over $\hat{\mathbf{Q}}$, and s is nonnegative.

Step 2: Next we proceed, as in Theorem 4.6.4, to replace the final equation in step 1 with an equation involving a maximum over s. Starting with the definition of $E(R, \mathbf{p})$ at the start of step 1, write

$$E(R, \mathbf{p}) \geq \min_{\mathbf{q}} \min_{\hat{\mathbf{Q}} \in \mathscr{Q}'_R(\mathbf{p}, \mathbf{q})} \left[\sum_{jk} p_j \hat{Q}_{k|j} \log \frac{\hat{Q}_{k|j}}{Q_{k|j}} + s \left(\sum_{jk} p_j \hat{Q}_{k|j} \log \frac{\hat{Q}_{k|j}}{q_k} - R \right) \right]$$

for any $s \geq 0$. The inequality holds because the term multiplying s is negative for $\hat{\mathbf{Q}}$ in $\mathscr{Q}'_R(\mathbf{p}, \mathbf{q})$. The inequality is still valid if the domain of the minimum on $\hat{\mathbf{Q}}$ is enlarged to include all probability transition matrices of the right dimension. Now pick s to maximize the right side. Then

$$E(R, \mathbf{p}) \geq \max_{s \geq 0} \min_{\mathbf{q}} \min_{\hat{\mathbf{Q}}} \left[\sum_{jk} p_j \hat{Q}_{k|j} \log \frac{\hat{Q}_{k|j}}{Q_{k|j}} + s \left(\sum_{jk} p_j \hat{Q}_{k|j} \log \frac{\hat{Q}_{k|j}}{q_k} - R \right) \right]$$

The right side is minimized over $\hat{\mathbf{Q}}$ by the tilted distribution

$$Q_{k|j}^* = \frac{Q_{k|j}^{1/(1+s)} q_k^{s/(1+s)}}{\sum_k Q_{k|j}^{1/(1+s)} q_k^{s/(1+s)}}$$

[†]It is possible to avoid the need for this proof if the development of the random-coding bound is replaced by an argument involving typical sequences. This is an elegant combinatoric argument, but we prefer to retain the earlier approach to the random-coding bound.

which gives

$$E(R,\mathbf{p}) \geq \max_{s \geq 0} \min_{\mathbf{q}} \left[-sR - (1+s) \sum_j p_j \log \sum_k Q_{k|j}^{1/(1+s)} q_k^{s/(1+s)} \right]$$

Now compare this to the equation at the end of step 1. This shows that there is a value of s for which the inequality above is satisfied with equality whenever the rate R is associated with a Lagrange multipier s; that is, whenever $E(R,\mathbf{p})$ is nonzero. Thus we can conclude that

$$E(R,\mathbf{p}) = \max_{s \geq 0} \min_{\mathbf{q}} \left[-sR - (1+s) \sum_j p_j \log \sum_k Q_{k|j}^{1/(1+s)} q_k^{s/(1+s)} \right]$$

To complete this proof, we must evaluate the minimum over $\mathbf{q}$. This is done in the next two steps by deriving upper and lower bounds on $E(R,\mathbf{p})$ that are equal for the maximizing $\mathbf{p}$.

Step 3: The logarithm is concave, so we can use Jensen's inequality to write

$$E(R,\mathbf{p}) \geq \max_{s \geq 0} \min_{\mathbf{q}} \left[-sR - (1+s) \log \sum_j p_j \sum_k Q_{k|j}^{1/(1+s)} q_k^{s/(1+s)} \right]$$

The form of the right side has the advantage that we can evaluate the minimum over $\mathbf{q}$. To minimize over $\mathbf{q}$ we will maximize the argument of the logarithm over $\mathbf{q}$. Note that for each s, $q_k^{s/(1+s)}$ is a concave function, so any maximum is the global maximum. It suffices to maximize the augmented function:

$$\sum_k q_k^{s/(1+s)} \sum_j p_j Q_{k|j}^{1/(1+s)} + \lambda \left(\sum_k q_k - 1 \right)$$

where λ is a Lagrange multiplier. Differentiation gives

$$\frac{s}{1+s} q_k^{s/(1+s)-1} \sum_j p_j Q_{k|j}^{1/(1+s)} + \lambda = 0$$

which yields

$$q_k = \frac{\left(\sum_j p_j Q_{k|j}^{1/(1+s)} \right)^{1+s}}{\sum_k \left(\sum_j p_j Q_{k|j}^{1/(1+s)} \right)^{1+s}}$$

Substitution into the expression for $E(R,\mathbf{p})$ gives

$$E(R,\mathbf{p}) \geq \max_{s \geq 0} \left[-sR - \log \sum_k \left(\sum_j p_j Q_{k|j}^{1/(1+s)} \right)^{1+s} \right]$$

Therefore

$$E(R) \geq \max_{s \geq 0} \max_{\mathbf{q}} \left[-sR - \log \sum_k \left(\sum_j p_j Q_{k|j}^{1/(1+s)} \right)^{1+s} \right]$$

Step 4: Now we prove the inequality in the opposite direction. Start with the representation at the end of step 2:

$$E(R, \mathbf{p}) \le \max_{s \ge 0} \left[-sR - (1 + s) \sum_j p_j \log \sum_k Q_{k|j}^{1/(1+s)} q_k^{s/(1+s)} \right]$$

for any vector $\mathbf{q}$. This holds even if a different $\mathbf{q}$ is chosen for each value of s. Choose

$$q_k = \frac{\left(\sum_j p_j^* Q_{k|j}^{1/(1+s)} \right)^{1+s}}{\sum_k \left(\sum_j p_j^* Q_{k|j}^{1/(1+s)} \right)^{1+s}}$$

where $\mathbf{p}^*$ will be chosen later. Substitution into the expression for $E(R, \mathbf{p})$ gives

$$E(R, \mathbf{p}) \le \max_{s \ge 0} \left\{ -sR - (1 + s) \sum_j p_j \log \left[\sum_k Q_{k|j}^{1/(1+s)} \left(\sum_j p_j^* Q_{k|j}^{1/(1+s)} \right)^s \right] \right.$$
$$\left. + s \log \sum_k \left(\sum_j p_j^* Q_{k|j}^{1/(1+s)} \right)^{1+s} \right\}$$

We would be finished if we could push the sum on p_j inside the logarithm in the second term on the right and equate $\mathbf{p}$ to $\mathbf{p}^*$. Unfortunately, the inequality goes in the wrong direction to use Jensen's inequality. However, if we limit ourselves to those $\mathbf{p}^*$ for which the argument of the logarithm is the same for all j, we could move p_j inside the logarithm. It so happens that the maximizing $\mathbf{p}$ has this property.

It is easier to work backwards. Consider

$$E'(R) = \max_{s \ge 0} \max_{\mathbf{p}} \left[-sR - \log \sum_k \left(\sum_j p_j Q_{k|j}^{1/(1+s)} \right)^{1+s} \right]$$

The goal of our proof is to show that $E'(R) = E(R)$. A necessary condition, though perhaps not a sufficient one, for $\mathbf{p}$ to achieve the maximum defining $E'(R)$ is that the derivative with respect to p_j satisfies

$$\frac{\partial}{\partial p_j} \left[\sum_k \left(\sum_j p_j Q_{k|j}^{1/(1+s)} \right)^{1+s} - \lambda \sum_j p_j \right] \ge 0$$

with equality, unless $p_j = 0$. By differentiating and evaluating λ, we obtain

$$\sum_k Q_{k|j}^{1/(1+s)} \left(\sum_j p_j^* Q_{k|j}^{1/(1+s)} \right)^s \ge \sum_k \left(\sum_j p_j^* Q_{k|j}^{1/(1+s)} \right)^{1+s}$$

if $\mathbf{p}^*$ achieves $E'(R)$, with equality for all j such that $p_j^* = 0$. In the bound on $E(R,\mathbf{p})$, we choose the value of $\mathbf{p}^*$ achieving $E'(R)$. Then

$$E(R) \leq \max_{s \geq 0} \max_{\mathbf{p}} \left\{ -sR - (1 + s) \sum_j p_j \log \left[\sum_k Q_{k|j}^{1/(1+s)} \left(\sum_j p_j^* Q_{k|j}^{1/(1+s)} \right)^s \right] \right.$$
$$\left. + s \log \sum_k \left(\sum_j p_j^* Q_{k|j}^{1/(1+s)} \right)^{1+s} \right\}$$

Because of the Kuhn-Tucker inequality that $\mathbf{p}^*$ satisfies, the maximum must occur for a $\mathbf{p}$ that has component $p_j = 0$ whenever $p_j^* = 0$, and is otherwise arbitrary. But $\mathbf{p}^*$ itself has this property. We choose $\mathbf{p} = \mathbf{p}^*$ and pass the sum on p_j inside the logarithm, which is permissible because the argument of the logarithm is constant whenever p_j is nonzero. Therefore we have obtained

$$E(R) \leq \max_{s \geq 0} \left[-sR - \log \sum_k \left(\sum_j p_j^* Q_{k|j}^{1/(1+s)} \right)^{1+s} \right]$$

The right side, by the definition of $\mathbf{p}^*$, is $E'(R)$. Therefore

$$E(R) \leq \max_{s \geq 0} \max_{\mathbf{p}} \left[-sR - \log \sum_k \left(\sum_j p_j Q_{k|j}^{1/(1+s)} \right)^{1+s} \right]$$

and the theorem is proved.   □

□ **Corollary 10.1.6** Let R_{crit} be the value of R parameterized by $s = 1$ in the $E(R)$ function. Then the random-coding exponent can be written

$$E_r(R) = E(R) \qquad \text{for } R \geq R_{\mathrm{crit}}$$
$$E_r(R) = E(R_{\mathrm{crit}}) - R + R_{\mathrm{crit}} \quad \text{for } R \leq R_{\mathrm{crit}}$$ □

□ **Corollary 10.1.7** The parameter s satisfies

$$\frac{dE(R)}{dR} = -s$$

wherever $E(R)$ has a derivative.

Proof From Theorem 10.1.5, for any $s \geq 0$,

$$E(R) \geq -sR + \max_{\mathbf{p}} \left[-\log \sum_k \left(\sum_j p_j Q_{k|j}^{1/(1+s)} \right)^{1+s} \right]$$

For fixed s, the right side describes a straight line that touches the convex function $E(R)$ at one point and otherwise lies beneath it. The corollary follows.   □

10.2 LOWER BOUNDS BY PARTITIONING

The probability of decoding error of data transmission codes for a channel $\mathbf{Q}$ has been upper-bounded using a function $E(R)$. The upper bound is quite similar to the upper bound on the probability of error using the error-exponent function $e(r)$ in the hypothesis-testing problem of Chapter 4. In this section, we turn to a lower bound for the probability of decoding error. We shall prove that for any code of rate R and blocklength n,

$$p_e \geq e^{-nE(R) + o(n)}$$

for $0 \leq R \leq C$, whereas we have already proved that for the best code,

$$p_e \leq e^{-nE(R)}$$

for $R_{crit} \leq R \leq C$. The combination of these two statements shows that

$$E^*(R) = E(R)$$

for $R_{crit} \leq R \leq C$.

Suppose that $\{\mathcal{U}_m : m = 0, \ldots, M - 1\}$ is any partition of the set of received words into M decoding regions. There are K^n received words, so that there must be at least one decoding region with not more than K^n/M received words in it. For a stronger statement of this kind, suppose that $\hat{\mathbf{q}}$ is any probability distribution on this same set. Then for some $\mathcal{U}_m$

$$\sum_{\mathbf{y} \in \mathcal{U}_m} \hat{q}(\mathbf{y}) \leq \frac{1}{M}$$

which is a simple consequence of the equality

$$\sum_{m=0}^{M-1} \sum_{\mathbf{y} \in \mathcal{U}_m} \hat{q}(\mathbf{y}) = \sum_{\mathbf{y}} \hat{q}(\mathbf{y}) = 1$$

We will work with such a region and bound the probability of error for the codeword associated with that decoding region. Then we will argue that this bound can be converted to a bound on the probability of error of the average codeword.

The lower bound to be derived in this section relies heavily on the lower bound on the probability of error for binary hypothesis testing, as derived in Chapter 4. Although the channel-decoding problem is a problem of testing among M hypotheses, we shall find that, with a little effort, we can approximate this problem by finding a binary hypothesis-testing problem in the original problem. Pick an m and consider the binary hypothesis-testing problem:

$$H_0 : \mathbf{c}_m = \text{codeword transmitted}$$

$$H_1 : \mathbf{c}_m \neq \text{codeword transmitted}$$

If we choose the right m, we will find that a lower bound on this problem can be used as a starting point to derive a bound on the original problem.

The code consists of a fixed set of M codewords, each used with probability $1/M$. The decoder consists of a partition of the space of output words into M decode regions $\{\mathcal{U}_m : m = 0, \ldots, M - 1\}$. Reception of an output in $\mathcal{U}_m$ will cause the decoder to choose the mth codeword. Therefore a lower bound must underestimate the probability of error under the assumption that the codewords and the decode regions have been selected optimally.

The performance of the code can be characterized by either the maximum probability of error over the set of codewords or the average probability of error over the set of codewords. We shall start with a bound on the maximum probability of error; later we convert it into a bound on the average probability of error.

The theorem giving a lower bound on $p_e(n, R)$ is then as follows.

□ **Theorem 10.2.1   (Partitioning bound)** The average probability of error of a block code having $M = e^{nR}$ codewords satisfies

$$p_e \geq e^{-nE(R) - o(n)}$$

Proof The proof is in two steps, first developing a bound on the probability of error of the codeword with the largest probability of error, then turning that bound into a bound on the average probability of decoding error.

For any R^*, let $\mathbf{q}^*$ be the probability distribution on the channel output that achieves $E(R^*)$, and let $q^*(\mathbf{y})$ be the associated product probability distribution on the output sequence $\mathbf{y}$. Select m so that

$$\sum_{\mathbf{y} \in \mathcal{U}_m} q^*(\mathbf{y}) \leq \frac{1}{M}$$

We have already seen that there must be such an m.

Step 1: We are now ready to apply the theory of Chapter 4 here by viewing this as a hypothesis-testing problem. The hypotheses are now characterized by $Q(\mathbf{y}|\mathbf{c}_m)$ and $q^*(\mathbf{y})$, which replace $Q_0(\mathbf{y}|\mathbf{x})$ and $Q_1(\mathbf{y}|\mathbf{x})$, respectively. The probability of error $p_{e|m}$ replaces α and $1/M$ replaces β. Because the dummy alternative hypothesis characterized by $q^*(\mathbf{y})$ has probability of resulting in $\mathcal{U}_m$ of less than $1/M$, we can lower-bound $p_{e|m}$ using Theorem 4.5.3. Consider the pair of sets $\{\mathcal{U}_m, \mathcal{U}_m^c\}$ and let

$$p_{e|m} = \sum_{\mathbf{y} \in \mathcal{U}_m^c} Q(\mathbf{y}|\mathbf{c}_m)$$

By Theorem 4.5.3 we have the lower bound on $p_{e|m}$:

$$p_{e|m} = \sum_{\mathbf{y} \in \mathcal{U}_m^c} Q(\mathbf{y}|\mathbf{c}_m)$$

$$\geq e^{-nL(Q^*; Q|\mathbf{p}) - o''(n)}$$

and also the lower bound on $1/M$:

$$\frac{1}{M} \geq \sum_{\mathbf{y} \in \mathcal{U}_m} q^*(\mathbf{y}) \geq e^{-nL(Q^*; q^*|\mathbf{p}) - o'(n)}$$

Referring to Theorem 10.1.4, these become

$$p_{e|m} \geq e^{-nE(R^*) - o''(n)}$$

and

$$R \leq R^* + o'(n)$$

Because $E(R)$ is a decreasing function, the bound on $p_{e|m}$ can be written as

$$p_{e|m} \geq e^{-nE(R - o'(n)) - o''(n)}$$

Step 2: Of the M codewords, remove those $M/2$ codewords whose probability of error is largest. This results in a code having $M/2 = e^{nR - \log 2}$ codewords that must satisfy step 1. Let $\mathscr{C}'$ denote the set of codewords in the purged code. Let $(p'_e)_{max}$ denote the maximum error of any codeword in this purged code. Then by step 1,

$$(p'_e)_{max} \geq e^{-nE(R - (\log 2/n) - o'(n)) - o''(n)}$$

The average error of the original code is bounded as follows:

$$p_e = \frac{1}{M} \sum_m p_{e|m} \geq \frac{1}{M} \sum_{m \notin \mathscr{C}'} p_{e|m}$$

$$\geq \frac{1}{M} \sum_{m \notin \mathscr{C}'} (p'_e)_{max} = \frac{1}{2} (p'_e)_{max}$$

$$\geq \frac{1}{2} e^{-nE(R - (\log 2/n) - o'(n)) - o''(n)}$$

$$= e^{-nE(R) - o(n)}$$

which completes the proof of the theorem.   □

10.3 UPPER BOUNDS BY EXPURGATION

The random-coding lower bound and the partitioning upper bound tell us that the probability of decoding error satisfies

$$e^{-nE(R) + o(n)} \leq p_e(n, R) \leq e^{-nE_r(R)}$$

Hence for each fixed R, $p_e(n, R)$ is asymptotically exponential in n, and we have

$$E(R) \geq \lim_{n \to \infty} \frac{1}{n} \log p_e(n, R)^{-1} \geq E_r(R)$$

For rates larger than R_{crit}, the outer terms are equal, so the limit does exist, and $E^*(R) = E(R) = E_r(R)$. For rates larger than R_{crit}, we have found $E^*(R)$.

For rates smaller than R_{crit}, the end terms are not equal; there is a gap. It is not even known if $E^*(R)$ then exists, but if it does, it satisfies

$$E(R) \geq E^*(R) \geq E_r(R)$$

The function $E^*(R)$ lies in the gap between $E(R)$ and $E_r(R)$. We will partially close the gap by proving another lower bound and another upper bound. The bounds will tell us that the probability of decoding error satisfies

$$e^{-nE_U(R)+o'(n)} \leq p_e(n, R) \leq e^{-nE_L(R)+o''(n)}$$

for two functions $E_U(R)$ and $E_L(R)$. Then $E^*(R)$ satisfies

$$E_U(R) \geq E^*(R) \geq E_L(R)$$

When $R = 0$, the outer terms are equal. Hence $E^*(0) = E_L(0)$. At other values of R, the outer terms are not equal, and $E^*(R)$ is unknown.

In this section we derive the expurgated bound, an upper bound on $p_e(n, R)$ and a lower bound on $E^*(R)$.

The expurgated bound is proved by a different version of the random-coding argument. This time the argument is reformulated in such a way that many of the bad codes can be improved before the average probability of error is computed. This has the effect of reducing the average probability of error over the ensemble, and hence of strengthening the bound. Each code in the ensemble of codes has M codewords. The ensemble will be created by starting with a different ensemble whose codes are larger; each of the larger codes has $2M$ codewords. After a code is chosen at random from the ensemble, bad codewords are purged from it. Accordingly, from the $2M$ codewords, a good subcode is chosen having only M codewords. We shall bound the ensemble average of the probability of decoding error for codes that can be obtained in this way.

Let $\mathcal{C}^+$ denote a code with $2M$ codewords of blocklength n, and let $\{\mathcal{C}^+\}$ denote the ensemble of all possible codes that each have $2M$ codewords of blocklength n. Given a code $\mathcal{C}^+$ together with a maximum-likelihood decoder for that code, let $p_{e|m}$ be the probability of decoding error when using that code and transmitting its mth codeword.

☐ **Lemma 10.3.1**   Let $\rho > 0$ be given. Let $\mathbf{c}_m$ denote the mth codeword of a code $\mathcal{C}^+$, and let $p_{e|m}$ be the probability of decoding error of codeword $\mathbf{c}_m$. There is at least one code in the ensemble $\{\mathcal{C}^+\}$ for which at least M of the codewords $\mathbf{c}_m$ satisfy

$$p_{e|m} \leq 2^{1/\rho}[E[p_{e|m}^{\rho}]]^{1/\rho}$$

where E denotes the ensemble average.

Proof   For each m, let $\phi_m(\mathcal{C}^+)$ be a function defined on the ensemble $\{\mathcal{C}^+\}$ as follows: Let $\phi_m(\mathcal{C}^+) = 1$ for codes in which, for the mth codeword, the inequality of the theorem holds. Let $\phi_m(\mathcal{C}^+) = 0$ otherwise. Now choose $\mathcal{C}^+$ randomly from the ensemble. By Chebychev's inequality, for a randomly chosen code,

$$Pr[p_{e|m}^{\rho} \geq 2E[p_{e|m}^{\rho}]] \leq \frac{1}{2}$$

or

$$Pr\left[p_{e|m} < \left[2E\left[p_{e|m}^{\rho}\right]\right]^{1/\rho}\right] \geq \frac{1}{2}$$

From which we see that, for each m, $E[\phi_m(\mathscr{C}^+)] \geq 1/2$.

The number of codewords in code $\mathscr{C}^+$ that satisfy the inequality of the lemma is

$$\sum_{m=0}^{2M-1} \phi_m(\mathscr{C}^+)$$

Hence the ensemble average of the number of codewords that satisfy the inequality is

$$E\left[\sum_{m=0}^{2M-1} \phi_m(\mathscr{C}^+)\right] \geq \frac{2M}{2} = M$$

On average, a code has at least M codewords satisfying the bound, so there must be at least one code that has at least M codewords satisfying the inequality. □

If the M codewords satisfying Lemma 10.3.1 are chosen from a code $\mathscr{C}^+$, a new code $\mathscr{C}$ having M codewords is obtained. The maximum-likelihood decision regions for the original code $\mathscr{C}^+$ will be contained within the maximum-likelihood decision regions for $\mathscr{C}$. Hence the probability of error of $\mathscr{C}$ is at least as small as $2^{1/\rho}[E[p_{e|m}^{\rho}]]^{1/\rho}$.

We now have obtained a starting point from which to find an upper bound on $E[p_{e|m}^{\rho}]$.

□ **Theorem 10.3.2**   For the memoryless channel **Q**, there exist codes of rate R and blocklength n for which every codeword has probability of error $p_{e|m}$ satisfying

$$p_{e|m} \leq e^{-nE_{ex}(R + n^{-1}\log 4)}$$

where

$$E_{ex}(R) = \max_{s \geq 1} \max_{q} \left\{ -sR - s\log\left[\sum_{ij} p_i p_j \left(\sum_k \sqrt{Q_{k|i} Q_{k|j}} \right)^{1/s} \right] \right\}$$

Proof   Step 1: As in the proof of the random-coding bound, we can say that if $\mathbf{y} \in \mathscr{U}_m^c$, then for at least one $m' \neq m$,

$$1 \leq \left[\frac{Q(\mathbf{y}|\mathbf{c}_{m'})}{Q(\mathbf{y}|\mathbf{c}_m)} \right]^{1/2}$$

Therefore

$$1 \leq \sum_{m' \neq m} \left[\frac{Q(\mathbf{y}|\mathbf{c}_{m'})}{Q(\mathbf{y}|\mathbf{c}_m)} \right]^{1/2}$$

So for the mth codeword of code $\mathscr{C}$ we have

$$p_{e|m}(\mathscr{C}) = \sum_{\mathbf{y} \in \mathscr{U}_m^c} Q(\mathbf{y}|\mathbf{c}_m)$$

$$\leq \sum_{\mathbf{y} \in \mathscr{U}_m^c} \sum_{m' \neq m} Q(\mathbf{y}|\mathbf{c}_m) \left[\frac{Q(\mathbf{y}|\mathbf{c}_{m'})}{Q(\mathbf{y}|\mathbf{c}_m)} \right]^{1/2}$$

$$\leq \sum_{m' \neq m} \sum_{\mathbf{y}} [Q(\mathbf{y}|\mathbf{c}_m)Q(\mathbf{y}|\mathbf{c}_{m'})]^{1/2}$$

Now use Jensen's inequality. Because x^ρ is a concave function of x for $0 \leq \rho \leq 1$, Jensen's inequality says that for a vector $\mathbf{a}$ with all components nonnegative and for all ρ satisfying $0 < \rho \leq 1$,

$$\left(\sum_i a_i \right)^\rho \leq \left(\sum_i a_i^\rho \right)$$

Therefore

$$[p_{e|m}(\mathscr{C})]^\rho \leq \sum_{m' \neq m} \left\{ \sum_{\mathbf{y}} [Q(\mathbf{y}|\mathbf{c}_m)Q(\mathbf{y}|\mathbf{c}_{m'})]^{1/2} \right\}^\rho$$

Next consider all codes of blocklength n and with $2M$ codewords. We randomly choose a code from this ensemble. The code is chosen by taking $\mathbf{x}$ as a codeword with probability $p(\mathbf{x})$. The average of the previous inequality over all codes is

$$E[p_{e|m}^\rho] \leq \sum_{m' \neq m} E\left[\sum_{\mathbf{y}} [Q(\mathbf{y}|\mathbf{c}_m)Q(\mathbf{y}|\mathbf{c}_{m'})]^{1/2} \right]^\rho$$

Because all of the codewords are chosen randomly in the same way, the expectation is the same for every m'; the outer summation sums $2M - 1$ identical terms:

$$E[p_{e|m}^\rho] \leq 2M E\left[\sum_{\mathbf{y}} [Q(\mathbf{y}|\mathbf{x})Q(\mathbf{y}|\mathbf{x}')]^{1/2} \right]^\rho$$

where $\mathbf{c}_m$ and $\mathbf{c}_{m'}$ are now replaced by $\mathbf{x}$ and $\mathbf{x}'$, and $2M - 1$ has been replaced by $2M$ without violating the inequality.

Step 2: By Lemma 10.3.1 there is a code $\mathscr{C}$ with M codewords such that

$$p_{e|m} \leq 2^{1/\rho} \left[2M E\left[\sum_{\mathbf{y}} [Q(\mathbf{y}|\mathbf{x})Q(\mathbf{y}|\mathbf{x}')]^{1/2} \right]^\rho \right]^{1/\rho}$$

for $m = 1, \ldots, M$.

Step 3: For the probability of choosing $\mathbf{x}$ as a codeword, take $p(\mathbf{x})$ as a product distribution and use the fact that $Q(\mathbf{y}|\mathbf{x})$ is a product distribution to rearrange the expectation:

$$E\left[\sum_{\mathbf{y}}[Q(\mathbf{y}|\mathbf{x})Q(\mathbf{y}|\mathbf{x}')]^{1/2}\right]^{\rho} = E\left[\prod_{l=1}^{n}\sum Q(y_l|x_l)Q(y_l|x_l')\right]^{1/2}\right]^{\rho}$$

$$= \left[\sum_{ij}p_ip_j\left(\sum_{k}\sqrt{Q_{k|i}Q_{k|j}}\right)^{\rho}\right]^{n}$$

where we have used the identity

$$\prod_{l=1}^{n}\left(\sum_{j_l}A_{j_l}\right) = \sum_{j_1}\sum_{j_2}\cdots\sum_{j_n}\left(\prod_{l=1}^{n}A_{j_l}\right)$$

Next replace $1/\rho$ with s. Because $0 \le \rho \le 1$, s must satisfy $1 \le s \le \infty$. We now have the bound

$$p_{e|m} \le [4M]^s\left[\sum_{ij}p_ip_j\left(\sum_{k}\sqrt{Q_{k|i}Q_{k|j}}\right)^{1/s}\right]^{sn}$$

Because $M = e^{nR}$, the theorem follows. □

10.4 THE CHANNEL RELIABILITY FUNCTION AT LOW RATES

The expurgated bound, proved in Section 10.3, involves a function $E_{\text{ex}}(R)$. In this section we shall begin anew, defining a function $E_L(R)$ in terms of the Bhattacharyya distance. This definition looks much different from the expurgated error exponent $E_{\text{ex}}(R)$, but we shall prove that it is the same function for small values of the rate.

The reason for defining the function $E_L(R)$ is that it will turn out to be a lower bound on the packing of Bhattacharyya spheres. Relating $E_L(R)$ to $E_x(R)$ exposes the relationship between the expurgated bound and Bhattacharyya distance. In this way, we can see that the expurgated bound is related to the minimum pairwise Bhattacharyya distance of a code. However, we cannot prove an upper bound to $E^*(R)$ using $E_L(R)$, so the payoff is limited.

□ **Definition 10.4.1**   The low-rate reliability function for the channel **Q** is given by

$$E_L(R) = \max_{\mathbf{p}} \min_{\hat{\mathbf{P}}\in\mathscr{P}_R(\mathbf{p})}\left[-\sum_{ij}\hat{P}_{ij}\log\sum_{k}Q_{k|i}^{1/2}Q_{k|j}^{1/2}\right]$$

where

$$\mathscr{P}_R(\mathbf{p}) = \left\{\hat{\mathbf{P}}\colon \sum_{ij}\hat{P}_{ij}\log\frac{\hat{P}_{ij}}{p_ip_j} \le R; \sum_{i}\hat{P}_{ij} = p_j; \sum_{j}\hat{P}_{ij} = p_i\right\}$$ □

The definition of $E_L(R)$ is similar to that of $E(R)$. Comparing this definition with that of $E(R)$ as given by Definition 10.1.1 shows that $E_L(R)$ uses the Bhattacharyya distance between pairs of codewords, whereas $E(R)$ uses the discrimination as a distance between the true channel and a dummy channel.

The definition of $E_L(R)$ also is closely related to the inverse form of the source-distortion function $D(B)$, studied in Chapter 6, which measures the distortion a data compression code must have when compressing to an information rate B. In that analogy, the Bhattacharyya distance plays the role of a distortion measure.

The joint probability distribution $\hat{P}_{ij}$ can be thought of as the probability that a pair of codewords has an i in a given position of the first codeword and a j in the same position of the second codeword. Therefore we expect $\hat{P}_{ij}$ to be symmetric, and so we impose explicitly the symmetry condition that $\hat{P}_{ij}$ satisfies $p_i = \sum_j \hat{P}_{ij}$ and $p_j = \sum_i \hat{P}_{ij}$.

□ **Theorem 10.4.2** The function $E_L(R)$ is a convex and hence continuous function, positive and strictly decreasing in the interval $0 < R < \log J$ and equal to zero for R larger than $\log J$.

Proof Let $E_L(\mathbf{p}, R)$ denote the inner minimum. Suppose $R > R'$; then $\mathscr{P}_R \supset \mathscr{P}_{R'}$. Hence $E_L(\mathbf{p}, R) \le E_L(\mathbf{p}, R')$, and the constraint is satisfied with equality in the region where $E(\mathbf{p}, R)$ is strictly decreasing. For each $\mathbf{p}$, convexity follows because $E(\mathbf{p}, R)$ is the minimum of a convex function subject to a convex constraint. Finally, $E_L(R)$ is convex because it is the pointwise maximum of a set of convex functions.

When $R = \log J$, we are free to choose for $\hat{\mathbf{P}}$ a diagonal matrix such that $\hat{P}_{ij} = p_i$ when $i = j$ and otherwise $\hat{P}_{ij} = 0$; the constraint is then satisfied for every $\mathbf{p}$. Hence $E_L(R) = 0$. For $R < \log J$, there are some $\mathbf{p}$ for which this choice of $\hat{\mathbf{P}}$ will not satisfy the constraint. Hence $E_L(R) > 0$, and the proof is complete. □

The following theorem is a companion to Theorem 10.1.5 in that it represents $E_L(R)$ in a way that parallels the representation of $E(R)$ in that theorem. By comparing Theorem 10.4.3 with Theorem 10.3.2, we can see that $E_L(R) = E_{ex}(R)$ whenever the supremum occurs for $s \ge 1$. In fact, the parameter s is the negative of the slope of $E_L(R)$, so the equality holds whenever the negative slope is equal to at least 1.

□ **Theorem 10.4.3** The low-rate reliability function can be written

$$E_L(R) = \sup_{s \ge 0} \max_{\mathbf{p}} \left\{ -sR - s \log \left[\sum_{ij} p_i p_j \left(\sum_k Q_{k|i}^{1/2} Q_{k|j}^{1/2} \right)^{1/s} \right] \right\}$$

Proof The proof is broken into three steps using the notation

$$d_{ij} = -\log \sum_k Q_{k|i}^{1/2} Q_{k|j}^{1/2}$$

throughout.

Step 1: Referring to the definition of $E_L(R)$, let

$$E_L(R, \mathbf{p}) = \min_{\mathbf{P} \in \mathscr{P}'_R(\mathbf{p})} \sum_{ij} \hat{P}_{ij} d_{ij}$$

where

$$\mathscr{P}'_R \mathbf{p} = \left\{ \hat{\mathbf{P}} : \sum_{ij} \hat{P}_{ij} \log \frac{\hat{P}_{ij}}{p_i p_j} \leq R; \sum_i \hat{P}_{ij} = p_j; \sum_j \hat{P}_{ij} = p_i \right\}$$

For any $s \geq 0$, this implies that

$$E_L(R, \mathbf{p}) \geq \min_{\hat{\mathbf{P}} \in \mathscr{P}'_R(\mathbf{p})} \left[\sum_{ij} \hat{P}_{ij} d_{ij} + s \left(\sum_{ij} \hat{P}_{ij} \log \frac{\hat{P}_{ij}}{p_i p_j} - R \right) \right]$$

because the term multiplying s is negative for $\hat{\mathbf{P}}$ in $\mathscr{P}'_R(\mathbf{p})$. The inequality is not violated if the minimum is allowed to range over all $\hat{\mathbf{P}}$ with the required marginals. Then, picking s to make the right side as large as possible, we have

$$E_L(R, \mathbf{p}) \geq \sup_{s \geq 0} \min_{\hat{\mathbf{P}}} \left[\sum_{ij} \hat{P}_{ij} d_{ij} + s \left(\sum_{ij} \hat{P}_{ij} \log \frac{\hat{P}_{ij}}{p_i p_j} - R \right) \right]$$

Next we will show that the maximizing nonnegative s makes the inequality into an equality. Because $E_L(R, \mathbf{p})$ is convex and decreasing, there is a line of negative slope tangent to $E_L(R, \mathbf{p})$ at the value R and never larger than $E_L(R, \mathbf{p})$ for any other value of R. Let $-s$ be the slope of this line. For any R', this implies that

$$E_L(R', \mathbf{p}) \geq E_L(R, \mathbf{p}) - s(R' - R)$$

or

$$E_L(R, \mathbf{p}) + sR \leq E_L(R', \mathbf{p}) + sR'$$

for any R'. Given any $\hat{\mathbf{P}}$, let $P_{j|i} = \hat{P}_{ij}/p_i$ and $R' = I(\mathbf{p}; \mathbf{P})$. By Definition 10.4.1, this implies that

$$E_L(R', \mathbf{p}) + sR' \leq \sum_{ij} \hat{P}_{ij} d_{ij} + sI(\mathbf{p}; \mathbf{P})$$

Consequently, for any $\hat{\mathbf{P}}$,

$$E_L(R, \mathbf{p}) + sR \leq \sum_{ij} \hat{P}_{ij} d_{ij} + sI(\mathbf{p}; \mathbf{P})$$

so that

$$E_L(R, \mathbf{p}) \leq \min_{\hat{\mathbf{P}}} \left\{ \sum_{ij} \hat{P}_{ij} d_{ij} + s[I(\mathbf{p}; \mathbf{P}) - R] \right\}$$

Combining this with the earlier inequality in the opposite direction gives

$$E_L(R,\mathbf{p}) = \sup_{s \geq 0} \min_{\hat{\mathbf{P}}} \left[\sum_{ij} \hat{P}_{ij} d_{ij} + s \left(\sum_{ij} \hat{P}_{ij} \log \frac{\hat{P}_{ij}}{p_i p_j} - R \right) \right]$$

where now the minimum is over all $\hat{\mathbf{P}}$ satisfying $\sum_i \hat{P}_{ij} = p_j$ and $\sum_j \hat{P}_{ij} = p_i$.

Step 2: Introduce Lagrange multipliers α_i to constrain $\sum_j \hat{P}_{ij} = p_i$ and β_j to constrain $\sum_i \hat{P}_{ij} = p_j$. We can then carry out the minimization over $\hat{\mathbf{P}}$ explicitly by differentiation. The minimum occurs at

$$\hat{P}_{ij} = \frac{(e^{-(1/s)\alpha_i} p_i)(e^{-(1/s)\beta_j} p_j) e^{-(1/s)d_{ij}}}{\sum_{ij} (e^{-(1/s)\alpha_i} p_i)(e^{-(1/s)\beta_j} p_j) e^{-(1/s)d_{ij}}}$$

and by symmetry, $\alpha_i = \beta_j$. Define

$$q_i = \gamma e^{-(1/s)\alpha_i} p_i$$

where γ is a normalizing constant. Then

$$\hat{P}_{ij} = \frac{q_i q_j e^{-(1/s)d_{ij}}}{\sum_{ij} q_i q_j e^{-(1/s)d_{ij}}}$$

and

$$E_L(R,\mathbf{p}) = \sup_{s \geq 0} \left[-sR - s \log \left(\sum_{ij} q_i q_j e^{-(1/s)d_{ij}} \right) - s2L(\mathbf{p};\mathbf{q}) \right]$$

where we have made the substitution

$$L(\mathbf{p};\mathbf{q}) = \frac{1}{2} \sum_{ij} P_{ij} \log \frac{p_i p_j}{q_i q_j}$$

But the discrimination is nonnegative, so that

$$E_L(R,\mathbf{p}) \leq \sup_{s \geq 0} \left[-sR - s \log \sum_{ij} q_i q_j e^{-(1/s)d_{ij}} \right]$$

Because we do not know $\mathbf{q}$, we can choose the maximizing $\mathbf{q}$ in the inequality:

$$E_L(R,\mathbf{p}) \leq \sup_{s \geq 0} \max_{\mathbf{q}} \left[-sR - s \log \sum_{ij} q_i q_j e^{-(1/s)d_{ij}} \right]$$

This holds for every $\mathbf{p}$, so we have proved that

$$E_L(R) \leq \sup_{s \geq 0} \max_{\mathbf{p}} \left[-sR - s \log \sum_{ij} p_i p_j e^{-(1/s)d_{ij}} \right]$$

Step 3: To show the inequality in the other direction, we ignore the constraints associated with the equation at the end of step 1. Introduce a

Lagrange multiplier and differentiate to obtain

$$\hat{P}_{ij} = \frac{p_i p_j e^{-(1/s)d_{ij}}}{\sum_{ij} p_i p_j e^{-(1/s)d_{ij}}}$$

Because the constraints were ignored this leads to an inequality:

$$E_L(R, \mathbf{p}) \geq \sup_{s \geq 0} \left[-sR - s\log \sum_{ij} p_i p_j e^{-(1/s)d_{ij}} \right]$$

and

$$E_L(R) \geq \max_{\mathbf{p}} \sup_{s \geq 0} \left[-sR - s\log \sum_{ij} p_i p_j e^{-(1/s)d_{ij}} \right]$$

This completes the proof of the theorem. □

10.5 PACKING OF BHATTACHARYYA SPHERES

The expurgated bound can be expressed in terms of the Bhattacharyya distance even though the derivation does not involve the Bhattacharyya distance. What does this tell us? It suggests that the Bhattacharyya distance between codewords plays a role in the performance of low-rate codes. We will return to this suggestion in Section 10.6. For now we will study the minimum pairwise Bhattacharyya distance between codewords without considering the relationship to probability of error. Everything we will prove about minimum Bhattacharyya distance is also true for minimum Hamming distance. Simply choose an equidistant channel on a J-ary input alphabet so that Hamming distance on this alphabet is a fixed multiple of Bhattacharyya distance. In proving the bounds, we will deal only with the case of constant-composition codes. This is not much of a restriction because any code must have a constant-composition subcode of nearly the same rate.

We wish to determine the largest value of the minimum Bhattacharrya distance over all codes of rate R, composition $n\mathbf{p}$, and blocklength n. The largest such value is a measure of how efficiently we can pack Bhattacharyya spheres, because it tells us how large the spheres may be if we have 2^{nR} of them that do not intersect. This is too hard a problem to solve, so we settle for an asymptotic analysis. Define

$$d^*(R, \mathbf{p}, n) = \max_{\mathscr{C}} d^*(\mathscr{C})$$

where $d^*(\mathscr{C})$ is the minimum Bhattacharyya distance of code $\mathscr{C}$ and the maximum is taken over all codes of rate R, composition $n\mathbf{p}$, and blocklength n. Next define

$$d^*(R, \mathbf{p}) = \lim_{n \to \infty} \frac{1}{n} d^*(R, \mathbf{p}, n)$$

The function $d^*(R, \mathbf{p})$ need not exist because the limit need not exist. If it does exist, however, then for large n, codes of blocklength n and composition $n\mathbf{p}$ exist having minimum Bhattacharyya distance about $nd^*(R, \mathbf{p})$. Finally, define

$$d^*(R) = \max_{\mathbf{p}} d^*(R, \mathbf{p})$$

The functions $d^*(R, \mathbf{p})$ and $d^*(R)$ are not known. We will bound them below by a lower bound known as the *Gilbert bound* and above by an upper bound known as the *Elias bound*. These bounds are shown in Fig. 10.1. Similar results can be proved for more general channels, but we will restrict our treatment of the Elias bound to equidistant channels. The Gilbert bound, on the other hand, will be proved for a general channel.

To develop the Gilbert bound, we begin by counting the number of codewords in a sphere of radius d about each point in the space, not necessarily a codeword, and then averaging. Let V be the number of points in a Bhattacharyya sphere of radius d about any point. Given a code $\mathscr{C}$ with M codewords, let $\bar{T}_s$ denote the average number of codewords in a sphere of radius d about an arbitrary point in a space of N points. It is

$$\bar{T}_s = \frac{MV}{N}$$

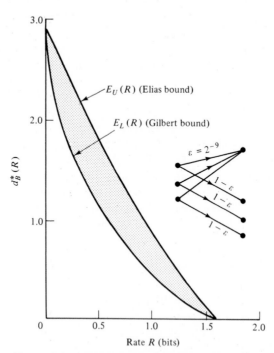

Figure 10.1 **Bounds on minimum Bhattacharyya distance for a ternary erasure channel.**

This can be seen as follows: Consider a sphere of radius d about each point in the space. Count the number of codewords in each such sphere and then sum over all spheres. How many times is a particular codeword counted? A codeword has V points within distance d, so it lies in V such spheres and is counted V times. Therefore the sum over all spheres of the number of codewords in each sphere must equal MV, and so the average number of codewords per sphere is MV/N.

☐ **Theorem 10.5.1   (Gilbert bound)** Let $\varepsilon > 0$ be given. Given the channel **Q**, for sufficiently large n, there exists a code $\mathscr{C}$ of blocklength n such that the Bhattacharyya distance satisfies

$$d(\mathbf{c}_m, \mathbf{c}_{m'}) \geq n[E_L(R) - \varepsilon]$$

for all pairs of codewords $\mathbf{c}_m$, $\mathbf{c}_{m'}$ with $m \neq m'$.

Proof   We will actually prove a stronger result, that there exist *constant-composition codes* satisfying the conditions of the theorem. Consider the set of all n-tuples with constant composition such that symbol a_j occurs n_j times, and let $p_j = n_j/n$. There are

$$N = \frac{n!}{\prod_j n_j!}$$

words in the set. Of these, we wish to select a subset of M codewords.

Step 1: Consider the set of Bhattacharyya spheres of radius d defined as the set of points within Bhattacharyya distance d from a given point, and let V be the number of points in such a sphere. We have seen that

$$\bar{T}_s = \frac{MV}{N}$$

We may assume in this equation that $\bar{T}_s \geq 1$. Otherwise we would enlarge the code by choosing any point that has no codeword within distance d and declaring it to be a codeword. Hence

$$\frac{MV}{N} \geq 1$$

Take the logarithm and divide by n to obtain

$$R \geq \frac{1}{n} \log \frac{N}{V}$$

To complete the bound, we need to bound V.

Step 2: Consider a sphere of radius d in the space of n-tuples of composition $\{n_j\}$. Suppose the n-tuple at the sphere center and a second n-tuple have joint composition $\{n_{ij}\}$. The second n-tuple lies in the sphere of radius d about the first if

$$-\sum_{ij} \hat{n}_{ij} \log \sum_k Q_{k|i}^{1/2} Q_{k|j}^{1/2} \leq d$$

There are

$$\prod_i \frac{n_i!}{\prod_j n_{ij}!}$$

such words in the sphere, and there are certainly not more than n^{J^2} possible joint compositions. Therefore we can bound V as

$$V \leq n^{J^2} A_s(d)$$

where

$$A_s(d) = \max_{\{\hat{n}_{ij}\} \in \mathcal{N}_r} \prod_i \frac{n_i!}{\prod_j \hat{n}_{ij}!}$$

and

$$\mathcal{N}_r = \left\{ \{\hat{n}_{ij}\} : -\sum_{ij} \hat{n}_{ij} \log \sum_k Q_{k|i}^{1/2} Q_{k|j}^{1/2} \leq d, \sum_i \hat{n}_{ij} = n_j, \sum_j \hat{n}_{ij} = n_i \right\}$$

Step 3: Combine the results of steps 1 and 2 and use Stirling's approximation for N in the definition of $A_s(d)$. Then

$$nR \geq -\sum_j n_j \log \frac{n_j}{n} - J^2 \log n - \log A_s(d) - o(n)$$

and

$$\log A_s(d) \leq \max_{\mathcal{N}_r} \left[-\sum_{ij} \hat{n}_{ij} \log \frac{\hat{n}_{ij}}{n_i} \right] + o(n)$$

Therefore

$$nR \geq \min_{\mathcal{N}_r} \left[\sum_{ij} \hat{n}_{ij} \log \frac{\hat{n}_{ij} n}{n_i n_j} \right] - J^2 \log n - o(n)$$

Finally, expressing $\hat{n}_{ij}$ in terms of $\hat{P}_{ij}$, we have

$$R \geq \min_{\hat{\mathbf{P}} \in \mathscr{P}_R(\mathbf{p})} \left[\sum_{ij} \hat{P}_{ij} \log \frac{\hat{P}_{ij}}{p_i p_j} \right] - \frac{1}{n} J^2 \log n - o(n)$$

where

$$\mathscr{P}_R(\mathbf{p}) = \left\{ \hat{\mathbf{P}} : -\sum_i \hat{P}_{ij} \log \sum_k Q_{k|i}^{1/2} Q_{k|j}^{1/2} \leq \frac{d}{n}, \sum_i \hat{P}_{ij} = p_j, \sum_j \hat{P}_{ij} = p_i \right\}$$

This bound is closely related to $E_L(R)$. In fact, because $E_L(R)$ is monotonically decreasing, it is just the inverse $R(E_L)$. We can interchange the object function of the minimization and the constraint, thereby obtaining the statement of the theorem. □

Now we turn to the development of the Elias bound. The development will be completed only for the case of equidistant channels. The Elias bound will be derived for constant-composition codes so that we can express the bound in a form that parallels the Gilbert bound. By noting that every code has a constant-composition subcode of very nearly the same rate, we see that the Elias bound also applies to codes other than constant-composition codes.

As in proving the Gilbert bound, we use the Bhattacharyya distance to visualize "spheres" in the space of all constant-composition n-tuples over the input alphabet. Now, however, we are proving an upper bound, so we only count codewords on the surface of one of these spheres. Codewords in the interior are not counted.

Fix the composition $\{n_i\}$. There are $N = n!/\prod_i n_i!$ words with this composition. Pick a joint composition n_{ij} such that $\sum_i n_{ij} = n_j$ and $\sum_j n_{ij} = n_i$, and any word $\mathbf{x}$ of composition $\{n_i\}$. The word $\mathbf{x}$ has a total of

$$A_s = \prod_i \frac{n_i!}{\prod_j n_{ij}!}$$

words with which it shares a joint composition n_{ij}. The set will be called a *spherical surface* about $\mathbf{x}$, and A_s will be called the *surface area* of the spherical surface. Every $\mathbf{x}$ has such a spherical surface about it. A constant-composition code will have some of its codewords lying on some of these spherical surfaces. Our bound is derived by showing that, if we choose M big enough, on the average there must be several codewords on a spherical surface, and so their distance is upper-bounded by the size of the spherical surface.

Given a constant-composition code $\mathscr{C}$ with M codewords, on the average the number of codewords $\bar{T}$ on a spherical surface defined by joint composition n_{ij} is found as follows: Consider a spherical surface for every word $\mathbf{x}$. There are N of them, which we index by r in any fixed order. Because each of the M codewords shares joint composition n_{ij} with A_s words, it is on A_s spherical surfaces. Let T_r be the number of codewords on the rth spherical surface. Then

$$\sum_r T_r = M A_s$$

because in carrying out the sum, each codeword must get counted A_s times. But there are N such spheres, so we have proved that $\bar{T}$, the average number of codewords on a spherical surface, satisfies

$$\bar{T} = M \frac{A_s}{N}$$

Later we will choose M so as to ensure that $\bar{T}$ is sufficiently large. For the moment, we will choose any one of these spherical surfaces denoted by $\mathscr{S}$ and study the distance structure of those codewords that lie in $\mathscr{S}$. Of the M codewords, let T denote the number that appear in the spherical surface under study. We will calculate the average distance between pairs of codewords on this spherical surface. The average Bhattacharyya distance is given by

$$d_{av} = \frac{1}{T(T-1)} d_{tot}$$

where d_{tot} is the total distance obtained as the sum of the distances between all unordered pairs of codewords in $\mathscr{S}$ not necessarily distinct. Then

$$d_{av} = \frac{1}{T(T-1)} \sum_{mm'} d(\mathbf{c}_m, \mathbf{c}_{m'})$$

where the sum on m and m' ranges only over those codewords that are in $\mathscr{S}$. Let $n_{ij}^{mm'}$ be the joint composition of codewords $\mathbf{c}_m$ and $\mathbf{c}_{m'}$. Then

$$d_{av} = \frac{1}{T(T-1)} \sum_{mm'} \left[-\sum_{ij} n_{ij}^{mm'} \log \sum_k Q_{k|i}^{1/2} Q_{k|j}^{1/2} \right]$$

We now can simplify the sum on m and m'. Define the variable $n_{ij|l}^{mm'}$ to be equal to 1 if $\mathbf{c}_m$ has an i in the lth place and $\mathbf{c}_{m'}$ has a j in the lth place, and otherwise to be equal to 0. Let $T_{i|l}$ be the number of codewords in $\mathscr{S}$ that have an i in the lth place. Then

$$d_{av} = \frac{1}{T(T-1)} \sum_l \left[-\sum_{mm'} \sum_{ij} n_{ij|l}^{mm'} \log \sum_k Q_{k|i}^{1/2} Q_{k|j}^{1/2} \right]$$

$$= \frac{T}{T-1} \sum_l \left[-\sum_{ij} \frac{T_{i|l} T_{j|l}}{T^2} \log \sum_k Q_{k|i}^{1/2} Q_{k|j}^{1/2} \right]$$

Next define

$$\lambda_{i|l} = \frac{T_{i|l}}{T}$$

as the fraction of codewords in $\mathscr{S}$ with an i in the lth component. We then have

$$d_{av} = \frac{T}{T-1} \sum_l \left[-\sum_{ij} \lambda_{i|l} \lambda_{j|l} \log \sum_k Q_{k|i}^{1/2} Q_{k|j}^{1/2} \right]$$

We cannot evaluate this expression because we do not know λ. To obtain a bound on d_{av}, we determine the largest value that the right side can have consistent with known constraints on λ. The first constraint on λ is

$$\sum_i \lambda_{i|l} = 1$$

To derive the second constraint, define the variable $\gamma_{j|l}$ as equal to 1 if the center of the spherical surface $\mathscr{S}$ has a j in the lth component, and as equal to 0 otherwise. Then λ must satisfy

$$\sum_l \lambda_{i|l} \gamma_{j|l} = n_{ij}$$

Of those λ satisfying the two constraints, we now take the worst case by choosing the one that makes d_{av} the largest to get a bound in terms of known quantities. Thus

$$d_{av} \le \frac{T}{T-1} \max_\lambda \sum_l \left[-\sum_{ij} \lambda_{i|l} \lambda_{j|l} \log \sum_k Q_{k|i}^{1/2} Q_{k|j}^{1/2} \right]$$

where the maximum is over all λ satisfying the constraints.

We are now ready to develop the Elias bound by evaluating the maximum. We will carry out this maximization in a way that avoids the need to prove that the argument is a concave function. We will postulate a maximizing value for $\lambda_{i|l}$ and then prove that it does indeed give a maximum.

□ **Theorem 10.5.2** Suppose that a constant composition code is given for an equidistant channel $\mathbf{Q}$. The average distance between the T codewords in a spherical collection defined by joint composition n_{ij} satisfies

$$d_{av} \le \frac{T}{T-1} \left[-\sum_{ij} \sum_k \frac{n_{ik} n_{jk}}{n_k} \log \sum_k Q_{k|i}^{1/2} Q_{k|j}^{1/2} \right]$$

Proof Let

$$\lambda_{i|l}^* = \sum_k \frac{n_{ik}}{n_k} \gamma_{k|l}$$

We will see that this achieves the maximum. Notice that

$$\sum_l \lambda_{i|l}^* \lambda_{j|l} = \sum_k \frac{n_{ik}}{n_k} \sum_l \lambda_{j|l} \gamma_{k|l} = \sum_k \frac{n_{ik} n_{jk}}{n_k}$$

for all λ satisfying the constraints, including $\lambda = \lambda^*$. Hence

$$\sum_l (\lambda_{i|l} \lambda_{j|l} - \lambda_{i|l}^* \lambda_{j|l}^*) = \sum_l (\lambda_{i|l} - \lambda_{i|l}^*)(\lambda_{j|l} - \lambda_{j|l}^*)$$

If we define $c_{i|l} = \lambda_{i|l} - \lambda_{i|l}^*$, then

$$\sum_l \left[\sum_{ij} \lambda_{i|l} \lambda_{j|l} d_{ij} \right] - \sum_l \left[\sum_{ij} \lambda_{i|l}^* \lambda_{j|l}^* d_{ij} \right] = \sum_{ij} \sum_l c_{i|l} c_{j|l} d_{ij}$$

where

$$d_{ij} = -\log \sum_k Q_{k|i}^{1/2} Q_{k|j}^{1/2}$$

To complete the proof, we must prove that the right side is nonpositive, using the observation that $\sum_i c_{i|l} = 0$ for all l.

Up to this point, we have not made use of the condition that the channel is an equidistant channel. Now we do. Because $d_{ij} = 0$ when $i = j$, and otherwise is equal to a positive constant A, we have

$$\sum_{ij} c_{i|l} c_{j|l} d_{ij} = \sum_{ij} c_{i|l} c_{j|l} A - \sum_i c_{i|l}^2 A$$

$$= A\left(\sum_i c_{i|l}\right)\left(\sum_j c_{j|l}\right) - A \sum_i c_{i|l}^2$$

$$\leq 0$$

Consequently, for equidistant channels,

$$\sum_l \sum_{ij} \lambda_{i|l} \lambda_{j|l} d_{ij} \leq \sum_l \sum_{ij} \lambda_{i|l}^* \lambda_{j|l}^* d_{ij}$$

We have already seen that

$$\sum_l \lambda_{i|l}^* \lambda_{j|l}^* = \sum_k \frac{n_{ik} n_{jk}}{n_k}$$

so the theorem is proved. □

We want to contrast this theorem with the Gilbert bound, so we define another reliability exponent as follows.

□ **Definition 10.5.3** The upper reliability exponent $E_U(R)$ of the channel $\mathbf{Q}$ is given by

$$E_U(R) = \max_{\mathbf{p}} \min_{\hat{\mathbf{P}} \in \mathscr{P}_R(\mathbf{p})} \left[-\sum_{ij} \sum_k \hat{P}_{ik} \frac{\hat{P}_{jk}}{P_k} \log \sum_k Q_{k|i}^{1/2} Q_{k|j}^{1/2} \right]$$

where

$$\mathscr{P}_R(\mathbf{p}) = \left\{ \hat{\mathbf{P}} : \sum_{ij} \hat{P}_{ij} \log \frac{\hat{P}_{ij}}{p_i p_j} \leq R; \sum_i \hat{P}_{ij} = p_j; \sum_j \hat{P}_{ij} = p_i \right\} \qquad □$$

The definition of $E_U(R)$ is similar to that of $E_L(R)$. Here $\hat{\mathbf{P}}$ appears quadratically in the object function rather than linearly. Otherwise the definitions are the same. In the limit as $R \to 0$, $E_U(R) = E_L(R)$. This follows because the mutual information in the constraint can equal zero only if $\hat{P}_{ij} = p_i p_j$.

□ **Theorem 10.5.4 (Elias bound)** Every constant composition code for the equidistant channel $\mathbf{Q}$ has a pair of codewords whose Bhattacharyya distance satisfies

$$d(\mathbf{c}_m, \mathbf{c}_{m'}) \leq E_U(R)$$

Proof Choose $\varepsilon > 0$. Suppose the code has composition $n\mathbf{p}^*$ achieving $E_U(R - \varepsilon)$. (Otherwise the proof holds for the weaker bound $E_U(R, \mathbf{p})$.) Let

$\mathbf{P}^*$ achieve $\dot{E}_U(R - \varepsilon)$. Use $n_{ij} = nP_{ij}^*$ to define a spherical collection about each word. Recall that $\bar{T} = MA_s/N$ and use Stirling's approximation to bound the average number of codewords in a spherical collection:

$$\bar{T} = Me^{-H(\mathbf{y}) + o(n)}e^{H(\mathbf{x}|\mathbf{y}) + o(n)}$$

$$= Me^{-nI(\mathbf{p};\mathbf{P}^*) + o(n)} \geq e^{n[\varepsilon - \varepsilon(n)]}$$

because $R \geq I(\mathbf{p};\mathbf{P}^*) + \varepsilon$ by definition of $E_U(R - \varepsilon)$. Some spherical collection $\mathscr{S}$ has a number of codewords T that is at least as large as the average number of codewords in a spherical collection. Hence the average number of codewords $\bar{T}$ grows exponentially in n, and $T/(T - 1) \to 1$. Combining this with Theorem 10.5.2 and noting that the minimum distance between codewords in $\mathscr{C}$ is not larger than the average distance between codewords in $\mathscr{S}$ leads to

$$d(\mathbf{c}_m, \mathbf{c}_{m'}) \leq E_U(R - \varepsilon)$$

The proof is complete because ε is arbitrary and $E_U(R)$ is continuous. $\square$

10.6 LOWER BOUNDS BY SPHERE PACKING

If we know the minimum Bhattacharyya distance of a code for a channel $\mathbf{Q}$, then we can make some estimates of the probability of decoding error when the code is used on channel $\mathbf{Q}$. This we do by studying the probability of confusing two codewords that differ by the minimum distance. Hence, if we know the largest possible minimum Bhattacharyya distance of any code of rate R and blocklength n, then we can give some bounds on the probability of decoding error of the best code of rate R and blocklength n. We can hope to find such a bound without actually finding the best code.

We do not know the maximum of the minimum Bhattacharyya distance over all codes of rate R and blocklength n, but in Section 10.5, we found the Elias upper bound on it. The Elias upper bound can be used to obtain an upper bound on $E^*(R)$, which we derive in this section.

Suppose that codewords $\mathbf{c}_m$ and $\mathbf{c}_{m'}$ have joint composition n_{ij}. We wish to lower-bound the probability of confusing these two codewords. The analysis will go through more cleanly if we treat only the case in which the two codewords have the same composition. This limitation will turn out to be of no significance because it can be removed later.

Let $p_{e|m}$ denote the probability of error given that codeword $\mathbf{c}_m$ was transmitted. Let

$$p_{e|m,m'} = \frac{1}{2}p_{e|m} + \frac{1}{2}p_{e|m'}$$

We will lower-bound $p_{e|m,m'}$. We imagine that whenever either codeword $\mathbf{c}_m$ or $\mathbf{c}_{m'}$ is transmitted, the decoder is given the side information that one of these two codewords was transmitted. We shall lower-bound $p_{e|m,m'}$ by pretending that the decoder has this artificial information; the true error probability can only be larger. The lower-bounding technique will be a familiar one; we have already used it for the problem of hypothesis testing.

The channel block output takes vector value $\mathbf{y}$ with probability $Q(\mathbf{y}|\mathbf{c}_m)$, abbreviated $Q_m(\mathbf{y})$, if codeword $\mathbf{c}_m$ is transmitted, and with probability $Q(\mathbf{y}|\mathbf{c}_{m'})$, abbreviated $Q_{m'}(\mathbf{y})$, if codeword $\mathbf{c}_{m'}$ is transmitted. Define the tilted distribution

$$Q^*(\mathbf{y}) = \frac{Q(\mathbf{y}|\mathbf{c}_m)^{1/2}Q(\mathbf{y}|\mathbf{c}_{m'})^{1/2}}{\sum_{\mathbf{y}} Q(\mathbf{y}|\mathbf{c}_m)^{1/2}Q(\mathbf{y}|\mathbf{c}_{m'})^{1/2}}$$

Let the discrimination on the blocks be denoted by

$$L^{(n)}(\mathbf{Q}^*;\mathbf{Q}_m) = \frac{1}{2}\sum_{\mathbf{y}} Q^*(\mathbf{y})\log\frac{Q(\mathbf{y}|\mathbf{c}_{m'})}{Q(\mathbf{y}|\mathbf{c}_m)} - \log\sum_{\mathbf{y}} Q(\mathbf{y}|\mathbf{c}_m)^{1/2}Q(\mathbf{y}|\mathbf{c}_{m'})^{1/2}$$

The first term on the right is equal to zero because $\mathbf{c}_m$ and $\mathbf{c}_{m'}$ have the same composition, and $Q^*(\mathbf{y})$ is symmetric in $\mathbf{c}_m$ and $\mathbf{c}_{m'}$. Thus

$$L^{(n)}(\mathbf{Q}^*;\mathbf{Q}_m) = nL(\mathbf{Q}^*;\mathbf{Q}_m|\mathbf{p})$$

$$= -\log\sum_{\mathbf{y}} Q(\mathbf{y}|\mathbf{c}_m)^{1/2}Q(\mathbf{y}|\mathbf{c}_{m'})^{1/2}$$

which is the Bhattacharyya distance. The same argument applies to $L^{(n)}(\mathbf{Q}^*;\mathbf{Q}_{m'})$, so

$$nL(\mathbf{Q}^*;\mathbf{Q}_m|\mathbf{p}) = nL(\mathbf{Q}^*;\mathbf{Q}_{m'}|\mathbf{p}) = d(\mathbf{c}_m,\mathbf{c}_{m'})$$

We are now ready to lower-bound the error probability for two codewords in a constant-composition code.

☐ **Theorem 10.6.1** Suppose that $\mathscr{C}$ is an arbitrary block code with $M = e^{nR}$ codewords of blocklength n, used on an indivisible channel $\mathbf{Q}$. Then

$$p_e \geq e^{-nd^*((R-o(n))+o'(n)}$$

where both $o(n)$ and $o'(n) \to 0$ as $n \to \infty$.

Proof The proof is in three steps, first developing a bound for a constant-composition code on the probability of error of the codeword with the largest probability of error, then turning that bound into a bound on the average probability of error, and finally removing the need for a constant composition.

Step 1: We will apply the theory of Chapter 4 here by viewing this as a hypothesis-testing problem. The hypotheses are now characterized by $Q(\mathbf{y}|\mathbf{c}_m)$ and $Q(\mathbf{y}|\mathbf{c}_{m'})$, which replace $Q_0(\mathbf{y}|\mathbf{x})$ and $Q_1(\mathbf{y}|\mathbf{x})$, respectively. The probability of error $p_{e|m}$ replaces α, and $p_{e|m'}$ replaces β. We can lower-bound $p_{e|m}$ using Theorem 4.5.3. Consider the pair of sets

$\{\mathcal{U}_m, \mathcal{U}_m^c\}$. By Theorem 4.5.3 we have the lower bound on $p_{e|m}$:

$$p_{e|m} = \sum_{\mathbf{y} \in \mathcal{U}_m^c} Q(\mathbf{y}|\mathbf{c}_m)$$

$$\geq e^{-nL(Q^*; Q_m|\mathbf{p}) - o(n)} = e^{-nd(\mathbf{c}_m, \mathbf{c}_{m'}) - o(n)}$$

and also the lower bound on $p_{e|m'}$:

$$p_{e|m'} = \sum_{\mathbf{y} \in \mathcal{U}_m} \mathbf{Q}(\mathbf{y}|\mathbf{c}_{m'})$$

$$\geq e^{-nL(Q^*; Q_{m'}|\mathbf{p}) - o'(n)}$$

$$= e^{-nd(\mathbf{c}_m, \mathbf{c}_{m'}) - o(n)}$$

By the definition of the asymptotic minimum Bhattacharyya distance $nd^*(R, \mathbf{p})$, some pair of codewords has Bhattacharyya distance that satisfies

$$d(\mathbf{c}_m, \mathbf{c}_{m'}) \leq nd^*(R, \mathbf{p}) + o(n)$$

Therefore, there are two codewords $\mathbf{c}_m$ and $\mathbf{c}_{m'}$ such that

$$p_{e|m,m'} \geq e^{-nd^*(R, \mathbf{p}) - o(n)}$$

We shall extend this bound in two stages—first to the average probability of error of constant-composition block codes, then to the average probability of error of block codes that need not have constant composition.

Step 2: Given a code $\mathscr{C}$, remove $M/2$ codewords whose probability of error is largest. This results in a smaller code, denoted $\mathscr{C}'$, having $M/2 = e^{nR - \log 2}$ codewords of composition $n\mathbf{p}$, which must satisfy step 1. If n is sufficiently large, there are two codewords $\mathbf{c}_m$ and $\mathbf{c}_{m'}$ in the new code whose two-codeword probability of error satisfies

$$p_{e|m,m'} \geq e^{-nd^*(R - (1/n)\log 2, \mathbf{p}) + o(n)}$$

When the full code is used, the average probability of error of these two codewords is at least this large. Let $(p_e)_{\max}^p$ denote the maximum error of the purged code $\mathscr{C}'$. The average error of the original code is bounded as follows:

$$\frac{1}{M} \sum_m p_{e|m} \geq \frac{1}{M} \sum_{\mathbf{c}_m \notin \mathscr{C}'} p_{e|m}$$

$$\geq \frac{1}{M} \sum_{\mathbf{c}_m \notin \mathscr{C}'} (p_e)_{\max}^p \geq \frac{1}{M} \sum_{\mathbf{c}_m \notin \mathscr{C}'} p_{e|m,m'}$$

$$= \frac{1}{2} p_{e|m,m'}$$

Therefore

$$p_e \geq e^{-n[d^*(R - (1/n)\log 2,\mathbf{p}) + (1/n)\log 2] + o(n)}$$

We have obtained a lower bound that depends on the code composition $\mathbf{p}$. This composition we are free to select. We select the $\mathbf{p}$ that maximizes $d^*(R - n^{-1}\log 2, \mathbf{p})$ so as to bound p_e for any choice of composition $n\mathbf{p}$, and redefine $o(n)$ to obtain

$$p_e \geq e^{-nd^*(R - (1/n)\log 2) + o(n)}$$

Finally, we must remove the assumption of a constant-composition code.

Step 3: There are less than $(n + 1)^J$ different compositions in the code. Let M' be the number of codewords having the most frequently occurring composition; then

$$M \leq (n + 1)^J M'$$

Selecting all codewords with the most frequently occurring composition gives a smaller constant-composition code $\mathscr{C}'$ of rate

$$R' \geq R - \frac{1}{n} J \log (n + 1)$$

and, for this reduced code,

$$p_e(\mathscr{C}') \geq e^{-nd^*(R' - o(n)) + o'(n)}$$

The original code surely has a larger probability of error; thus

$$p_e \geq e^{-nd^*(R' - o(n)) + o'(n)}$$

$$\geq e^{-nd^*(R - (1/n)J \log (n + 1) - o(n)) + o'(n)}$$

Finally, redefine $o(n)$ to complete the proof.   □

Theorem 10.6.1 underbounds the probability of decoding error in terms of the Bhattacharyya distance rate function $d^*(R)$. This can be translated into a bound on $E^*(R)$ because we have the Elias bound as an upper bound on $d^*(R)$.

□   **Theorem 10.6.2   (Sphere-packing bound)** Let $\mathbf{Q}$ be an equidistant channel. Then

$$E^*(R) \leq E_U(R)$$

Proof   By Theorem 10.6.1,

$$E^*(R) \leq d^*(R)$$

and by Theorem 10.5.4,

$$d^*(R) \leq E_U(R)$$

□

10.7 THE STRAIGHT-LINE BOUND

If the conjecture that the function $E^*(R)$ is convex were true, then any straight line between two points on two upper bounds would be an upper bound also. However, convexity of $E^*(R)$ has never been proved. In this section we shall prove the weaker statement that any straight line between $E_U(R)$ and any point on the partitioning bound is an upper bound on $E^*(R)$.

The development will be baséd on the notion of a list decoder. A *list decoder* forms a list of L candidate codewords rather than a single codeword. The list decoder will make an error if the correct codeword is not on the list of L codewords. A subsequent final decoder can select the correct codeword from the list of L codewords. If we view a decoder as containing a list decoder, we will be able to bound the probability of error based on a combination of two kinds of terms.

A codeword $\mathbf{c}$ of blocklength n will be treated as the concatenation of a prefix of length n_1 and a suffix of length n_2 where $n = n_1 + n_2$. Likewise, a received word $\mathbf{y}$ will consist of a prefix of length n_1 and a suffix of length n_2. To prove the next theorem, different arguments will be applied to the prefix and the suffix.

□ **Theorem 10.7.1**   For discrete memoryless channel $\mathbf{Q}$, let

$$p_{e,\max}(n, M) = \min_{\mathscr{C}} \max_{m} p_{e|m}$$

where the minimum is over all codes of blocklength n and size M. The average error probability $p_e(n,M)$ for a code of M codewords of blocklength n is bounded by

$$p_e(n, M) \geq p_e(n_1, M, L)p_{e,\max}(n_2, L + 1)$$

where $n = n_1 + n_2$ and $p_e(n, M, L)$ is the probability of error of a list decoder of size L for a code of M codewords and blocklength n.

Proof   Consider each codeword as broken into a prefix of length n_1 and a suffix of length n_2. Likewise, consider received words as broken into a prefix of length n_1 and a suffix of length n_2. Thus

$$\mathbf{c} = (c_1, c_2)$$

$$\mathbf{y} = (y_1, y_2)$$

For a discrete memoryless channel,

$$Q(\mathbf{y}|\mathbf{c}) = Q(y_1|c_1)Q(y_2|c_2)$$

The error probability for the code is

$$p_e = \sum_{m=0}^{M-1} \frac{1}{M} \sum_{y \in \mathscr{U}_m^c} Q(\mathbf{y}|c_m)$$

where $\mathcal{U}_m$ for $m = 0, \ldots, M - 1$ is the set of $\mathbf{y}$ that decode into codeword $\mathbf{c}_m$. Rewrite this as

$$p_e = \frac{1}{M} \sum_{m=0}^{M-1} \sum_{y_1} Q(y_1|c_{m1}) \sum_{y_2 \in \mathcal{U}_{m2}^c(y_1)} Q(y_2|c_{m2})$$

where for each y_1 and $m = 0, \ldots, M - 1$, $\mathcal{U}_{m2}(y_1)$ is the set of suffixes y_2 such that a maximum-likelihood decoder will decode $y_1 y_2$ into codeword $\mathbf{c}_m$.

Fix any prefix y_1. We can regard the set of M codeword suffixes as a code and the set of regions $\mathcal{U}_{m2}(y_1)$ for $m = 0, \ldots, M - 1$ as a set of decoding regions for this code. (Possibly $\mathcal{U}_{m2}(y_1)$ is empty for some values of m. This only means that the decoder or code is a poor one; it is still valid.) In this way we have a collection of decoders, one decoder for every received prefix y_1. Each decoder is associated with a probability of decoding error for each m given by

$$p_{e|m}(y_1) = \sum_{y_2 \in \mathcal{U}_{m2}^c(y_1)} Q(y_2|c_{m2})$$

For each prefix y_1, rank the codewords in order of their error probability. Let $m_1(y_1)$ be that m for which $p_{e|m}(y_1)$ is smallest; let $m_2(y_1)$ be that m for which $p_{e|m}(y_1)$ is the next smallest; and so on. We now have the lower bound

$$p_{e|m}(y_1) \geq \begin{cases} 0 & m = m_1(y_1), \ldots, m_L(y_1) \\ p_{e,\max}(n_2, L + 1) & m = m_{L+1}(y_1), \ldots, m(y_1) \end{cases}$$

because otherwise the definition

$$p_{e,\max}(n_2, L + 1) = \min_{\mathcal{C}} \max_{m} p_{e|m}$$

would be violated.

Now return to the expression for p_e:

$$p_e = \frac{1}{M} \sum_{m=0}^{M-1} \sum_{y_1} Q(y_1|c_{m1}) p_{e|m}(y_1)$$

$$\geq \frac{1}{M} \sum_{y_1} \sum_{\substack{m_l(y_1) \\ l > L}} Q(y_1|c_{m1}) p_{e,\max}(n_2, L + 1)$$

Finally, consider the set of prefixes $\{\mathbf{c}_{m1}\}$ as a set of M codewords of blocklength n_1, and consider $m_l(y_1)$ for $l = 1, \ldots, L$ as a list-decoding rule for this set of codewords. This implies that

$$\frac{1}{M} \sum_{y_1} \sum_{\substack{m_l(y_1) \\ l > L}} Q(y_1|c_{m1}) \geq p_e(n_1, M, L)$$

Combining this with the previous inequality completes the proof.   □

We would now like to use the partitioning bound to upper-bound $p_e(n_1, M, L)$. Before we can do so, we must prove a form of the partitioning bound suitable for list decoding. This bound is derived by mimicking the proof of Theorem 10.2.1. The point of departure is that the decoding regions are enlarged to

$$\mathscr{U}_m = \{\mathbf{y} : Q(\mathbf{y}|\mathbf{c}_m) > Q(\mathbf{y}|\mathbf{c}_k) \text{ for all but } L \text{ values of } k\}$$

Any subrule can be chosen to break ties with no change in the argument. Consequently, every $\mathbf{y}$ will appear in exactly L of the decoding regions $\mathscr{U}_m$. The calculation for the probability of error is

$$p_e = \sum_{m=0}^{M-1} \frac{1}{M} \sum_{\mathbf{y} \notin \mathscr{U}_m} Q(\mathbf{y}|\mathbf{c}_m)$$

☐ **Theorem 10.7.2**   The average probability of error of a list decoder of size L for a block code having $M = e^{nR}$ codewords satisfies

$$p_e \geq e^{-nE(R - (1/n)\log L - o(n)) + o'(n)}$$

Proof   The proof is nearly the same as the proof of the steps leading up to Theorem 10.2.1. The only change is that for any probability distribution $\hat{\mathbf{q}}$ on the set of received words, we have

$$\sum_{m=0}^{M-1} \sum_{y \in \mathscr{U}_m} \hat{q}(y) = L$$

Then for some $\mathscr{U}_m$,

$$\sum_{y \in \mathscr{U}_m} \hat{q}(y) \leq \frac{L}{M}$$

which is just L times larger than for the decoder treated in Theorem 10.2.1. If M in that analysis is replaced by M/L, the rest of that analysis can be borrowed without change, which completes the proof here.   ☐

The following theorem says that if $E_{sl}(R)$ is the straight line that satisfies $E_{sl}(0) = E_U(0)$ and is tangent to $E(R)$, then

$$E^*(R) \leq E_{sl}(R)$$

More generally, any line between a point on $E_U(R)$ and a point on $E(R)$ is an upper bound on $E^*(R)$.

☐ **Theorem 10.7.3**   (**Straight-line bound**) For any indivisible channel,

$$E^*(\lambda R' + (1 - \lambda)R'') \leq \lambda E(R') + (1 - \lambda)E_U(R'')$$

for all $\lambda \in (0, 1)$.

Proof   By Theorem 10.7.1,

$$p_e(n, M) \geq p_e(n_1, M, L)p_{e,\max}(n_2, L + 1)$$

where $n_1 + n_2 = n$ and L is an arbitrary integer. The proof will use Theorem 10.7.2 and $E(R)$ to bound the first term on the right and will use Theorem 10.6.2 (which also applies to maximum probability of error) and $E_U(R)$ to bound the second term on the right. This allows us to write

$$p_e(n_1 + n_2, M) \geq e^{-n_1 E(n_1^{-1} \log (M/L)) + o'(n_1)} e^{-n_2 E(n_2^{-1} \log L) + o''(n_2)}$$

Let

$$\lambda = \frac{n_1}{n_1 + n_2} \qquad 1 - \lambda = \frac{n_2}{n_1 + n_2}$$

Then we have

$$R = \frac{1}{n} \log M$$

$$= \lambda \frac{\log (M/L)}{n_1} + (1 - \lambda) \frac{\log L}{n_2}$$

$$= \lambda R' + (1 - \lambda)R''$$

where the last line defines R' and R''. Finally,

$$p_e(n, M) \geq e^{-n[\lambda E(R') + (1 - \lambda)E_U(R'')] + o(n)}$$

to complete the proof of the theorem. $\square$

10.8 ZERO-ERROR CAPACITY

Given a channel with probability transition matrix $\mathbf{Q}$, suppose that two input symbols a_i and a_j are at infinite Bhattacharyya distance. Then $\sum_k Q_{k|i}^{1/2} Q_{k|j}^{1/2} = 0$. This can be so only if there is no channel output symbol b_k that can be produced by both input symbol a_i and input symbol a_j. More briefly, we can say that no k can be reached from both i and j. Every output k either cannot be reached from i or cannot be reached from j.

The same expression can be applied to codewords of blocklength n. If

$$\sum_y Q(\mathbf{y}|\mathbf{c}_m)^{1/2} Q(\mathbf{y}|\mathbf{c}_{m'})^{1/2} = 0$$

then it is not possible for output word $\mathbf{y}$ to be a consequence of both input $\mathbf{c}_m$ and input $\mathbf{c}_{m'}$.

$\square$ **Definition 10.8.1** For each n, let $\mathscr{C}(n)$ be a largest code of blocklength n such that, for all $\mathbf{c}_m$ and $\mathbf{c}_{m'}$ in $\mathscr{C}(n)$,

$$\sum_y Q(\mathbf{y}|\mathbf{c}_m)^{1/2} Q(\mathbf{y}|\mathbf{c}_{m'})^{1/2} = 0$$

provided $m \neq m'$, and let M_n be the size of $\mathscr{C}(n)$. The *zero-error capacity* is defined as

$$C_0 = \sup_n \frac{1}{n} \log M_n \qquad \square$$

The zero-error capacity is the largest rate of any block code that can transmit data through a channel such that the probability of decoding error is zero. Because the definition involves a supremum over blocklength, it is a nonconstructive definition. To numerically evaluate the zero-error capacity can be an extremely difficult task for many channels.

□ **Theorem 10.8.2**   Either $C_0 = 0$ or $C_0 \geq 1$.

Proof   If $C_0 \neq 0$, then for some i and j

$$\sum_k Q_{k|i}^{1/2} Q_{k|j}^{1/2} = 0$$

Use only two codewords of blocklength 1 given by $c_1 = a_i$ and $c_2 = a_j$. These two codewords are never confused by the decoder, so the probability of decoding error is zero. Using these two codewords, it is possible to communicate at a rate of 1 bit per channel symbol.   □

Define the J^n-by-J^n matrix:

$$\phi(\mathbf{x}, \mathbf{x}') = \begin{cases} 1 & \text{if } \sum_y Q(\mathbf{y}|\mathbf{x})^{1/2} Q(\mathbf{y}|\mathbf{x}')^{1/2} \neq 0 \\ 0 & \text{if } \sum_y Q(\mathbf{y}|\mathbf{x})^{1/2} Q(\mathbf{y}|\mathbf{x}')^{1/2} = 0 \end{cases}$$

The words $\mathbf{x}$ and $\mathbf{x}'$ can be codewords in the same zero-error code only if $\phi(\mathbf{x}, \mathbf{x}') = 0$. One way to design such a code is to repeatedly discard candidate words $\mathbf{x}$ by striking any row and the corresponding column from $\phi(\mathbf{x}, \mathbf{x}')$ until the matrix is reduced to a diagonal matrix.

□ **Theorem 10.8.3**   The zero-error capacity can be written

$$C_0 = \sup_n \max_{\mathbf{p}} \left[-\frac{1}{n} \log \sum_{\mathbf{x}} \sum_{\mathbf{x}'} p(\mathbf{x}) p(\mathbf{x}') \phi(\mathbf{x}, \mathbf{x}') \right]$$

Proof   Clearly there is no need to consider any but equiprobable $p(\mathbf{x})$ because every $\mathbf{x}$ that is a codeword should be used with equal probability. Either $\mathbf{x}$ is not used at all or it is used with the same frequency as the other codewords. There are M_n codewords in $\mathscr{C}(n)$. Take

$$p(\mathbf{x}) = \begin{cases} \dfrac{1}{M_n} & \mathbf{x} \in \mathscr{C}(n) \\ 0 & \mathbf{x} \notin \mathscr{C}(n) \end{cases}$$

Then

$$\sum_{xx'} p(\mathbf{x})p(\mathbf{x'})\phi(\mathbf{x}, \mathbf{x'}) = \sum_{m,m'} \frac{1}{M_n^2} \phi(\mathbf{c}_m, \mathbf{c}_{m'})$$

If we examine the structure of the M_n-by-M_n matrix $\phi(\mathbf{c}_m, \mathbf{c}_{m'})$ that is obtained by restricting $\phi(\mathbf{x}, \mathbf{x'})$ to codewords, we see that all diagonal elements are equal to 1 (as is also the case for $\phi(\mathbf{x}, \mathbf{x'})$). Further, every off-diagonal term must equal zero or else that pair of codewords would not be at infinite Bhattacharyya distance. Consequently,

$$\sum_{m,m'} \frac{1}{M_n^2} \phi(\mathbf{c}_m, \mathbf{c}_{m'}) = \frac{1}{M_n}$$

and

$$C_0 = \sup_n \frac{1}{n} \log M_n$$

which completes the proof of the theorem.   □

The following theorem develops the relationship between zero-error capacity and the expurgated bound, showing that the expurgated bound is infinite whenever the rate R is less than the zero-error capacity.

□   **Theorem 10.8.4**   For any discrete, memoryless channel, $E_x(R) < \infty$ if and only if

$$R > \max_{\mathbf{p}} \left[-\log \sum_{ij} p_i p_j \phi_{ij} \right]$$

Proof   In the limit as $s \to \infty$, the $\hat{\mathbf{P}}$ achieving $E_x(R, \mathbf{p})$ as given by Theorem 10.8.3 goes to

$$P_{ij}^* = \frac{p_i p_j \phi_{ij}}{\displaystyle\sum_{ij} p_i p_j \phi_{ij}}$$

The rate R goes to

$$R = \sum_{ij} P_{ij}^* \log \frac{P_{ij}^*}{p_i p_j}$$

$$= -\log \sum_{ij} p_i p_j \phi_{ij}$$

Evaluating $E_x(R, \mathbf{p})$ shows that it is finite because $P_{ij} = 0$ if $\phi_{ij} = 0$. For each $\mathbf{p}$, a value of R is so obtained below which $E_x(R, \mathbf{p})$ is infinite. Hence $E_x(R)$ is infinite below the largest of these values of R. This completes the proof.   □

PROBLEMS

10.1. Calculate $E(R)$ for the binary erasure channel and for the ternary symmetric channel.

10.2. **a.** Use the "triangle" $\{\frac{1}{2},\frac{1}{2}\}$, $\{\varepsilon,(1-\varepsilon)\}$, $\{(1-\varepsilon),\varepsilon\}$ to show that the Bhattacharyya distance does not satisfy the triangle inequality.

b. Prove that for an equidistant channel the Bhattacharyya distance does satisfy the triangle inequality. For such a channel, the Bhattacharyya distance is a metric.

10.3. Modify the derivation of the expurgated bound to use the distance

$$d'(\mathbf{x}_i, \mathbf{x}_j) = \max_{\alpha \in [0,1]}\left[-\log\sum_{\mathbf{y}} Q(\mathbf{y}|\mathbf{x}_i)^{\alpha} Q(\mathbf{y}|\mathbf{x}_j)^{1-\alpha}\right]$$

Show that even though for some pairs of codewords

$$d'(\mathbf{x}_i, \mathbf{x}_j) > d(\mathbf{x}_i, \mathbf{x}_j)$$

with strict inequality, the resulting bound is not an improvement on the expurgated bound for any channel.

10.4. **a.** Prove that $dE(R)/dR = -s$ directly by computing the derivative.

b. Prove that $dE_L(R)/dR = -s$ directly by computing the derivative.

10.5. Find the expurgated exponent for the channel with probability transition matrix

$$\mathbf{Q} = \begin{bmatrix} \frac{1}{2} & \frac{1}{2} & 0 \\ 0 & 1 & 0 \\ 0 & \frac{1}{2} & \frac{1}{2} \end{bmatrix}$$

What does the expurgated bound suggest about the relative frequency with which channel input letters should be used for very low rate codes?

10.6. (Sum channels) Suppose that we have N independent discrete memoryless channels which need not have the same input and output alphabets nor the same probability transition matrices. At each time, a symbol can be sent over only one of these channels. We can view this system as a larger channel, called a *sum channel*, by attaching a channel index to each symbol, then pooling the input symbols as well as the output symbols.

a. Prove that the capacity of the sum channel is related to the capacities of the individual channels by

$$e^C = \sum_{i=1}^{N} e^{C_i}$$

b. Show that the zero-error capacity of the sum channel satisfies

$$C_0 \geq \log N$$

c. Find $E(R)$ for the sum of two binary symmetric channels.

10.7. (Degraded channels) A channel $\mathbf{Q}'$ is called a *degraded* version of channel $\mathbf{Q}$ if they are related by

$$Q'_{k|j} = \sum_{i} W_{k|i} Q_{i|j}$$

for some probability transition matrix $\mathbf{W}$. A degraded channel $\mathbf{Q}'$ can be visualized as the cascade of the channel $\mathbf{Q}$ and a channel $\mathbf{W}$. Prove that a code with error probability p_e for channel $\mathbf{Q}'$ can be used on channel $\mathbf{Q}$ with error probability not larger than p_e.

10.8. Prove that the expression

$$-\log \sum_j p_j Q_{k|j} \left(\frac{P_{j|k}}{p_j}\right)^{-\rho}$$

for ρ positive, is maximized by

$$P_{j|k} = \frac{p_j Q_{k|j}^{1/(1+\rho)}}{\sum_j p_j Q_{k|j}^{1/(1+\rho)}}$$

Use this fact to construct an algorithm for computing $E(R)$ that is analogous to the algorithm for computing channel capacity given in Fig. 5.7.

10.9. Given the channel

$$\mathbf{Q} = \begin{bmatrix} 1/4 & 5/8 & 1/8 & 0 \\ 0 & 1/2 & 1/2 & 0 \\ 0 & 1/8 & 5/8 & 1/4 \end{bmatrix}$$

show that the expurgated bound is achieved by the probability distribution $(1/2, 0, 1/2)$.

10.10. Prove that the equiprobable distribution achieves the expurgated bound for an equidistant channel. Express $E_L(R)$ and R parametrically.

10.11. The random-coding bound is a statement about the average probability of error of a code. It can be changed to a statement about the maximum probability of error over all codewords. By starting with a code with $2M$ codewords and purging M of them, show that one can obtain a code such that

$$p_{e|m} \le 4e^{-nE_r(R)}$$

for all m.

10.12. The channel

$$\mathbf{Q} = \begin{bmatrix} 1/2 & 1/2 & 0 & 0 & 0 \\ 0 & 1/2 & 1/2 & 0 & 0 \\ 0 & 0 & 1/2 & 1/2 & 0 \\ 0 & 0 & 0 & 1/2 & 1/2 \\ 1/2 & 0 & 0 & 0 & 1/2 \end{bmatrix}$$

has a nonzero zero-error capacity.

a. What is the largest zero-error code that can be obtained with blocklength equal to 1?

b. What is the largest zero-error code that can be obtained with blocklength equal to 2? (It is known, but difficult to prove, that one cannot increase the rate by using a blocklength larger than 2.)

10.13. Evaluate $E_x(R)$ at zero rate. Specifically, show that

$$E_x(0) = \max_{\mathbf{p}} \left[-\sum_i \sum_j p_i p_j \log \sum_k Q_{k|i}^{1/2} Q_{k|j}^{1/2} \right]$$

10.14. A list decoder of list size L, instead of decoding a single codeword, constructs a list of the L most likely codewords. The probability of error for codeword m is the probability that $\mathbf{c}_m$ is not on the list:

$$p_{e|m} = \sum_{\mathbf{y} \in \mathscr{U}_m^c} Q(\mathbf{y}|\mathbf{c}_m)$$

where

$$\mathscr{U}_m^c = \{\mathbf{y} : Q(\mathbf{y}|\mathbf{c}_m) > Q(\mathbf{y}|\mathbf{c}_k) \text{ for all but } L-1 \text{ values of } k\}$$

Derive the random-coding bound for list decoding. Specifically show that

$$p_e \le e^{-nE_{Lr}(R)}$$

where

$$E_{Lr}(R) = \max_{0 \le s \le L} \max_{\mathbf{p}} \left[-sR - \log \sum_{k=0}^{K-1} \left(\sum_{j=0}^{J-1} p_j Q_{k|j}^{1/(1+s)} \right)^{1+s} \right]$$

NOTES

The determination of the exponential dependence of probability of error on blocklength and rate of a data transmission code has been an open problem for some time. Fano (1961) introduced a random-coding upper bound on the error behavior in which probability of error exhibited an exponential decay in blocklength. Later Gallager (1965) reduced considerably the mechanics of developing the random-coding bound. Forney (1968) reached the same bound by using the Neyman-Pearson theorem for a somewhat different formulation of the problem. Csiszár, Körner, and Marton (1977) gave a universal form of the random-coding bound by selecting codes randomly in a much different way. This method is published in Csiszár and Körner (1981). Fano (1961) also introduced another function, which for historical reasons is called the *sphere-packing exponent*, that has been used by Shannon, Gallager, and Berlekamp (1967) in a rigorous proof of a lower bound to error behavior. The form of the upper bound and the proof given here come from Haroutunian (1968) and Blahut (1974).

For the special case of binary codes, extensive study has been devoted not only to bounds on the probability of decoding error but also to bounds on the minimum Hamming distance. The asymptotically best lower bound on the minimum Hamming distance comes from Gilbert (1952) and its generalization to Bhattacharyya distance is by Blahut (1977). For many years, the asymptotically best upper bound on the minimum Hamming distance was the bound first given in unpublished work by Elias. The Elias bound has been improved by McEliece, Rodemich, Rumsey, and Welch (1974) and by Levenshtein (1975) and Sidelnikov (1975). The best upper and lower bounds still are asymptotically different, so the actual asymptotic behavior of the best obtainable minimum Hamming distance also remains an open question.

Gallager partly closed the gap between the random-coding bound and the partitioning bound from above by introducing a technique to purge poor codewords from a random code. This bound, called the *expurgated bound*, is an improvement over the random-coding bound at low rates. Jelinek (1968) studied the properties of the expurgated exponent. Omura (1973, 1974) simplified the proof of the expurgated bound and developed its relationship to the Gilbert bound. Berlekamp (1964) found a lower bound for very low (asymptotically zero) rate codes. Shannon, Gallager, and Berlekamp further closed the gap between known bounds from below by combining the zero-rate bound with the partitioning bound. This procedure resulted in a new lower bound, the *straight-line bound*, which is an asymptotic improvement over the partitioning bound at low rates. The straight-line bound is asymptotically different from the expurgated bound, so the actual performance of optimum low-rate block codes has remained an open question. By generalizing the Elias bound to Bhattacharyya distance, Blahut (1977) gave a bound for all rates that agrees with the low-rate bound at $R = 0$. Algorithms for computing channel exponents have been discovered by Arimoto (1976) and Lesh (1976).

To zero-error capacity was introduced by Shannon (1956). Lovász (1979) was the first to evaluate the zero-error capacity for a nontrivial case.

APPENDIX A

Minimization of Convex Functions

Many of the functions that arise in information theory are convex. Convex functions have many important properties,[†] including those described below. They are convenient to minimize because any local minimum is also a global minimum. They also have many useful inequality properties.

    □ **Definition A.1**   A subset $\mathscr{S}$ of a real vector space is called *convex* if for all λ in the interval $[0, 1]$ whenever $\mathbf{r}_1$ and $\mathbf{r}_2$ are in $\mathscr{S}$, then $\lambda\mathbf{r}_1 + (1 - \lambda)\mathbf{r}_2$ is also in $\mathscr{S}$. □

Another way to say this is that the line segment joining any two points in a convex set is entirely in the convex set. Figure A.1 shows a subset of $\mathbf{R}^2$ that is convex, and one that is not convex.

[†]Roberts, A. W., and D. E. Varberg, *Convex Functions*, Academic Press, New York, 1973.

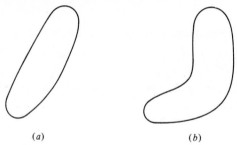

(a)   (b)

Figure A.1   Set convexity.

□   **Definition A.2**   A real function $f(\mathbf{r})$ on a convex set $\mathscr{S}$ is called a *convex function* if, for all λ in the interval $[0, 1]$ and for all $\mathbf{r}_1$ and $\mathbf{r}_2$ in $\mathscr{S}$,

$$f(\lambda \mathbf{r}_1 + (1 - \lambda)\mathbf{r}_2) \leq \lambda f(\mathbf{r}_1) + (1 - \lambda)f(\mathbf{r}_2)$$

If the inequality holds with strict inequality, the function is called a *strictly convex function*.   □

Geometrically, the definition says that if we draw the straight line between the points $(\mathbf{r}_1, f(\mathbf{r}_1))$ and $(\mathbf{r}_2, f(\mathbf{r}_2))$, then the straight line always lies above the function $-f(\mathbf{r})$. Figure A.2 illustrates this for a real convex function of one variable and a real convex function of two variables.

A real function $f(\mathbf{r})$ on a convex set is called a *concave function* if the function $-f(\mathbf{r})$ is a convex function.

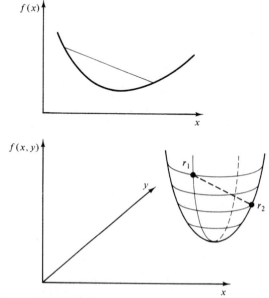

Figure A.2   Convex functions.

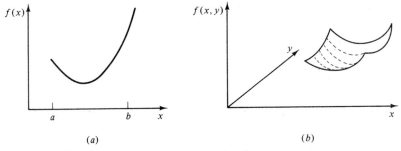

Figure A.3   Illustrating a property of convex functions.

The simplest convex functions are those defined on a one-dimensional space. Figure A.3 shows a convex function on a one-dimensional space and also a convex function on a two-dimensional space. We will develop in some detail the properties of real convex functions defined on the real line and on some open interval (a, b) of the real line.

☐ **Theorem A.3** Suppose $f(x)$ has a second derivative $f''(x)$ on the open interval (a, b). Then $f(x)$ is a convex function on (a, b) if and only if

$$f''(x) \geq 0$$

for all x in the interval (a, b), and is a strictly convex function only if the inequality holds with strict inequality.

Proof First suppose that $f(x)$ is convex and that f'' exists. By definition

$$f''(x) = \lim_{\Delta \to 0} \frac{f(x + \Delta) - 2f(x) + f(x - \Delta)}{\Delta^2}$$

By Definition A.2, with $\lambda = 1/2$,

$$f(x) \leq \frac{1}{2} f(x + \Delta) + \frac{1}{2} f(x - \Delta)$$

which implies that $f''(x) \geq 0$.

Now suppose that $f''(x) \geq 0$. By the Taylor formula with remainder of elementary calculus,

$$f(t) = f(x) + f'(x)(t - x) + \frac{1}{2} f''(\gamma)(t - x)^2$$

for some γ lying between t and x. Let $x = \lambda x_1 + (1 - \lambda)x_2$. In turn, let $t = x_1$ and multiply $f(t)$ by λ; then let $t = x_2$ and multiply $f(t)$ by $(1 - \lambda)$.

Adding these two equations gives

$$\lambda f(x_1) + (1 - \lambda)f(x_2) = f(\lambda x_1 + (1 - \lambda)x_2)$$

$$+ \frac{1}{2}\lambda f''(\gamma_1)(x_1 - x)^2$$

$$+ \frac{1}{2}(1 - \lambda)f''(\gamma_2)(x_2 - x)^2$$

$$\geq f(\lambda x_1 + (1 - \lambda)x_2)$$

with strict inequality if $f''(x)$ is strictly positive. $\quad\square$

$\square$ **Theorem A.4 (Jensen's inequality)** Suppose $f(x)$ is a convex function and $\{x_j\}$ is any finite set of positive numbers in the domain of f; let **p** be a probability distribution on $\{x_j\}$. Then

$$\sum_{j=1}^{n} p_j f(x_j) \geq f\left(\sum_{j=1}^{n} p_j x_j\right)$$

Proof   The theorem is true for $n = 2$ because this is then the definition of a convex function. Suppose the theorem is true for $n = r - 1$. Then write $p_j' = p_j/(1 - p_1)$ and

$$\sum_{j=1}^{n} p_j f(x_j) = p_1 f(x_1) + (1 - p_1) \sum_{j=2}^{n} p_j' f(x_j)$$

$$\geq p_1 f(x_1) + (1 - p_1)f\left(\sum_{j=2}^{n} p_j' x_j\right)$$

$$\geq f\left(p_1 x_1 + (1 - p_1) \sum_{j=2}^{n} p_j' x_j\right)$$

$$= f\left(\sum_{j=1}^{n} p_j x_j\right)$$

where the first inequality follows from the induction hypothesis and the second follows from the definition of convexity. $\quad\square$

Elementary calculus shows how to find local minima of differentiable functions by setting the derivative equal to zero. There are two directions in which we need to strengthen this procedure; minimization over the region of nonnegative arguments, and minimization in the presence of an equality constraint. When the minimum of a convex function over the region of nonnegative arguments is to be computed and that minimum lies on the boundary, the derivative need not be equal to zero. However, if the minimum lies on the boundary, then the function must not decrease as one moves away from the boundary in the positive direction. This is the gist of the following theorem.

□   **Theorem A.5**   Let $g(x)$ be a convex differentiable function defined on some vector space, and let $G = \min_{x \geq 0} g(x)$ where $x \geq 0$ means that all components of $\mathbf{x}$ are nonnegative. Then $\mathbf{x}^*$ achieves this minimum if and only if

$$\frac{\partial g}{\partial x_i}\bigg|_{\mathbf{x}=\mathbf{x}^*} \geq 0$$

with equality if component x_i^* is nonzero.

Proof   By elementary calculus, the minimum occurs where

$$\frac{\partial g}{\partial x_i}\bigg|_{\mathbf{x}=\mathbf{x}^*} = 0$$

for all i such that $x_i^* \neq 0$. However, it is also clear that the minimum occurs on the boundary if and only if displacement from the boundary to the interior increases $g(\mathbf{x})$.   □

Minimization in the presence of an equality constraint is a standard problem of calculus. The procedure of Lagrange multipliers[†] is usually the most convenient method of dealing with the constraints.

To minimize the convex function $g(\mathbf{x})$ subject to the constraint

$$f(\mathbf{x}) = F$$

where, in our applications, $f(\mathbf{x})$ is also a convex function and F is a constant, simply introduce the *Lagrange multiplier s* and write the augmented object function

$$g'(\mathbf{x}) = g(\mathbf{x}) + s(f(\mathbf{x}) - F)$$

The parameter s is an initially unspecified real number. If the constraint equation is satisfied, then the Lagrange multiplier s multiplies zero and $g'(\mathbf{x}) = g(\mathbf{x})$.

The procedure of Lagrange multipliers is to set the derivative of $g'(\mathbf{x})$ equal to zero:

$$\frac{\partial g'}{\partial x_i}\bigg|_{\mathbf{x}=\mathbf{x}^*} = 0$$

In general, $\mathbf{x}^*$ that solves this equation will be a function of s. Then s is chosen so that the constraint is satisfied.

The procedure of Lagrange multipliers can be incorporated into Theorem A.5 as follows:

□   **Theorem A.6   (Kuhn-Tucker theorem)**   Let $g(x)$ be a convex differentiable function on some vector space, and let

$$\mathscr{V}_F = \{\mathbf{x} \mid \mathbf{x} \geq 0, f(\mathbf{x}) = F\}$$

[†]Kaplan, W., *Advanced Calculus*, Addison-Wesley, Reading, Mass., 1952.

where $f(\mathbf{x})$ is a convex differentiable function and F is a constant. Then $\mathbf{x}^*$ minimizes $g(\mathbf{x})$ over $\mathcal{V}_F$ if and only if there exists $s \leq 0$ so that $f(\mathbf{x}^*) = F$ and

$$\frac{\partial}{\partial x_i}(g(\mathbf{x}) - sf(\mathbf{x}))\big|_{\mathbf{x}=\mathbf{x}^*} \geq 0$$

with equality if component x_i is nonzero.

Proof Introduce s as a Lagrange multiplier in Theorem A.5. $\square$

APPENDIX B

Karhunen-Loeve Expansions

An arbitrary real function on the interval $[-T/2, T/2]$ can usually be described compactly by the coefficients of a series expansion, although the expansion may be incorrect at a countable number of points. Such an expansion closely parallels the behavior of a block code for data compaction. We can think of such an expansion as a kind of data compaction code for functions on an interval.

The best-known expansion for an arbitrary function in an interval is the Fourier series expansion, in which case the signal is written

$$v(t) = \sum_{i=-\infty}^{\infty} v_i e^{j2\pi it/T} \qquad -T/2 \leq t \leq T/2$$

where the v_i are known as the Fourier coefficients and are given by

$$v_i = \frac{1}{T} \int_{-T/2}^{T/2} v(t)e^{-j2\pi it/T} dt \qquad i = 0, \pm 1, \pm 2, \ldots$$

This expansion can also be used for random processes. If the random process is a gaussian process, then each of the Fourier coefficients is a gaussian random variable. Each realization of the countably infinite set of Fourier coefficients leads to a realization of the random process. Every random process leads to a Fourier expansion, with the representation understood to be valid in a mean-square sense.

The Fourier coefficients representing a random process do not form an independent set of random variables. In general,

$$E[v_i v_j] \neq 0$$

and the infinite-dimensional covariance matrix will have nonzero entries in off-diagonal locations. For this reason, the Fourier expansion can be inconvenient to deal with.

The Karhunen-Loeve expansion is another kind of series expansion. Rather than using complex exponentials as in the Fourier expansion, the expansion functions are selected so as to make the correlation between the expansion coefficients equal to zero. Whereas the Fourier expansion has simple expansion functions and a complicated covariance matrix, the Karhunen-Loeve expansion has complicated expansion functions and a simple covariance matrix.

Let the real signal $v(t)$ be expressed as

$$v(t) = \sum_k v_k \psi_k(t)$$

where the real functions $\psi_k(t)$ are an orthonormal set of functions on the interval $[-T/2, T/2]$:

$$\int_{-T/2}^{T/2} \psi_k(t)\psi_{k'}(t) \, dt = \delta_{kk'} = \begin{cases} 1 & \text{if } k = k' \\ 0 & \text{if } k \neq k' \end{cases}$$

for all values of k and k'. The expansion coefficients v_k are calculated from

$$v_k = \int_{-T/2}^{T/2} \psi_k(t)v(t) \, dt$$

We wish to choose the $\psi_k(t)$ so that the expansion coefficients are uncorrelated:

$$E[v_k v_{k'}] = 0 \qquad k \neq k'$$

The following theorem tells us how to do this.

☐   **Theorem B.1   (Karhunen-Loeve theorem)** Let $\psi_k(t)$ and λ_k for $k = 1, \ldots$ be the eigenfunctions and the eigenvalues,[†] respectively, of the

[†]The terms "eigenfunction" and "eigenvalue" have the same meaning as in the study of matrix equations. That is, they satisfy

$$\int_{-T/2}^{T/2} \phi(t-s)\psi_k(s)ds = \lambda_k\psi_k(t) \qquad -T/2 \leq t \leq T/2$$

For each there will be a countable infinity of eigenfunctions, each one paired with an eigenvalue. Fortunately, the eigenfunctions and eigenvalues play only a passing role in developing the theory. We rarely need to know them explicitly.

integral equation

$$\int_{-T/2}^{T/2} \phi(t - s)\psi(s)\, ds = \lambda\psi(t) \qquad -T/2 \le t \le T/2$$

where $\phi(\tau) = E[v(t)v(t + \tau)]$ is the correlation function of a covariance stationary random process. The expansion coefficients

$$v_k = \int_{-T/2}^{T/2} \psi_k(t)v(t)\, dt$$

for $k = 1, 2, \ldots$ are uncorrelated random variables of variance λ_k. If $v(t)$ is gaussian, then the v_k are independent gaussian random variables.

Proof The normalized eigenfunctions of an integral equation with symmetric kernel are always orthonormal. Therefore

$$E[v_k v_{k'}] = E\left[\int_{-T/2}^{T/2} \psi_k(t_1)v(t_1)\, dt_1 \int_{-T/2}^{T/2} \psi_{k'}(t_2)v(t_2)\, dt_2\right]$$

$$= \int_{-T/2}^{T/2} \psi_k(t_1) \int_{-T/2}^{T/2} \phi(t_1 - t_2)\psi_{k'}(t_2)\, dt_2\, dt_1$$

$$= \int_{-T/2}^{T/2} \lambda_{k'}\psi_k(t)\psi_{k'}(t)\, dt$$

$$= \lambda_k \delta_{kk'}$$

Hence the random variables $\{v_k\}$ are uncorrelated and have variance λ_k for $k = 1, \ldots$.

The last line of the theorem is immediately apparent because, if two random variables are both gaussian and uncorrelated, then they are independent. $\square$

A set of Karhunen-Loeve functions can be used to expand any sufficiently nice function. Several functions, either random or deterministic, can be expanded in terms of the same set of Karhunen-Loeve functions. We then have the following analog to Parseval's formula.

$\square$ **Theorem B.2** Suppose s_k and r_k are the Karhunen-Loeve expansion coefficients of two functions $s(t)$ and $r(t)$, possibly complex. Then

$$\int_{-T/2}^{T/2} s^*(t)r(t)\, dt = \sum_k s_k^* r_k$$

Proof

$$\int_{-T/2}^{T/2} s^*(t)r(t)\,dt = \int_{-T/2}^{T/2} \sum_k s_k^* \psi_k(t) \sum_{k'} r_{k'} \psi_{k'}(t)\,dt$$

$$= \sum_k \sum_{k'} s_k^* r_{k'} \int_{-T/2}^{T/2} \psi_k(t)\psi_{k'}(t)\,dt$$

$$= \sum_k \sum_{k'} s_k^* r_{k'} \delta_{kk'}$$

$$= \sum_k s_k^* r_k \qquad\qquad \square$$

Any two distinct functions in a set of Karhunen-Loeve functions are orthonormal. The following theorem gives a property that is analogous to the orthogonality property, but it involves a sum on k rather than an integration on t.

□   **Theorem B.3**   The Karhunen-Loeve eigenfunctions satisfy

$$\sum_k \psi_k(t_1)\psi_k(t_2) = \delta(t_1 - t_2)$$

where the delta function is understood in the sense of a distribution satisfying the property

$$\int_{-T/2}^{T/2} f(t_1)\delta(t_1 - t_2)\,dt_1 = f(t_2)$$

Proof

$$\int_{-T/2}^{T/2} f(t_1)\sum_k \psi_k(t_1)\psi_k(t_2)\,dt_1 = \sum_k \psi_k(t_2) f_k$$

$$= f(t_2)$$

□   **Theorem B.4   (Mercer's theorem)**   The Karhunen-Loeve eigenfunctions satisfy

$$\phi(t_1 - t_2) = \sum_k \lambda_k \psi_k(t_1)\psi_k(t_2)$$

Proof   From the defining integral equation,

$$\lambda_k \psi_k(t_1) = \int_{-T/2}^{T/2} \phi(t_1 - t_2')\psi_k(t_2')\,dt_2'$$

Multiply by $\psi_k(t_2)$ and sum on k:

$$\sum_k \lambda_k \psi_k(t_1)\psi_k(t_2) = \int_{-T/2}^{T/2} \phi(t_1 - t_2') \sum_k \psi_k(t_2')\psi_k(t_2)\, dt_2'$$

$$= \int_{-T/2}^{T/2} \phi(t_1 - t_2')\delta(t_2' - t_2)\, dt_2'$$

$$= \phi(t_1 - t_2)$$

which proves the theorem.   □

The final theorem of this appendix is concerned with the solution of integral equations in terms of a Karhunen-Loeve expansion.

□   **Theorem B.5**   Suppose that λ_k is the eigenvalue of the Karhunen-Loeve integral equation, with the positive-definite function $\phi(\tau)$ as kernel, and v_k and w_k are the Karhunen-Loeve expansion coefficients of $v(t)$ and $w(t)$, respectively. Then

$$v(t) = \int_{-T/2}^{T/2} \phi(t - \tau)w(\tau)\, d\tau$$

if and only if

$$w_k = \frac{v_k}{\lambda_k}$$

Proof

$$v(t) = \sum_k v_k \psi_k(t)$$

$$w(t) = \sum_k w_k \psi_k(t)$$

Therefore

$$\sum_k v_k \psi_k(t) = \int_{-T/2}^{T/2} \phi(t - \tau) \sum_k w_k \psi_k(\tau)\, d\tau$$

$$= \sum_k w_k \lambda_k \psi_k(t)$$

The theorem follows from the uniqueness of the expansion.   □

APPENDIX C

The Toeplitz Distribution Theorems

A stationary discrete-time stochastic process is characterized in part by its covariance matrix. If the process is also gaussian, then it is completely specified by its mean and covariance matrix. The covariance matrix is an example of a kind of matrix known as a *Toeplitz matrix*, which we study in this appendix.

    ☐ **Definition C.1** A *Toeplitz matrix* is one whose *ij* element depends only on the difference between *i* and *j*. That is,

$$\phi_{ij} = \phi_{i-j} \qquad\qquad\qquad\qquad ☐$$

    A Toeplitz matrix may be of finite or of infinite dimension. If X_i is a discrete-time stationary random process, then $E[X_i X_j]$ is a Toeplitz matrix. Toeplitz matrices have valuable asymptotic properties. Intuitively, the eigenvalues of Toeplitz matrices become densely distributed on the real line as

436

the dimension of the matrix becomes large. We will state these well-known[†] properties in this appendix, but the proofs will be omitted.

The Toeplitz distribution theorems deal with the limiting density of the distribution of eigenvalues as the matrix size goes to infinity. These theorems are useful in the study of random processes with memory. Such processes are studied by analyzing a segment of the process of finite time duration and then taking limits. The transition from the finite-time segment to the limiting case is based on the Toeplitz distribution theorems. The theorems give a rigorous justification for a solution expressed in terms of the power spectral density of the process.

Suppose that $\mathbf{\Phi}_\infty$ is an infinite Toeplitz matrix, with entry ϕ_k on the kth diagonal. The spectrum of the matrix is defined in terms of any row by

$$\Phi(f) = \sum_{k=-\infty}^{\infty} \phi_k e^{-j2\pi f k}$$

For each n, consider the finite-dimensional n-by-n Toeplitz matrix centered about the main diagonal of $\mathbf{\Phi}_\infty$. Each of these n-by-n matrices has a set of eigenvalues. The Toeplitz distribution theorem describes the behavior of these eigenvalues in the limit as $n \to \infty$.

☐ **Theorem C.2 (Toeplitz distribution theorem for discrete processes)** Let $\mathbf{\Phi}_\infty$ be an infinite Toeplitz matrix, with entry ϕ_k on the kth diagonal such that the spectrum $\Phi(f)$ is bounded. Let $\lambda_k^{(n)}$ denote the eigenvalues of the nth-order matrix $\mathbf{\Phi}_n$ centered about the main diagonal of $\mathbf{\Phi}_\infty$. If $G(x)$ is any continuous function, then

$$\lim_{n \to \infty} n^{-1} \sum_{k=1}^{n} G(\lambda_k^{(n)}) = \int_{-1/2}^{1/2} G[\Phi(f)]\, df$$

Proof The proof is not given here. ☐

A similar theorem is useful to analyze continuous-time gaussian processes. The procedure is more elaborate because a Karhunen-Loeve expansion must be used to represent the process by a sequence of samples. Consider a finite-time segment of the gaussian process and expand in a Karhunen-Loeve expansion:

$$v(t) = \sum_{k=1}^{\infty} v_k \psi_k(t) \qquad -T/2 \le t \le T/2$$

[†]Kac, M., W. L. Murdock, and G. Szegö. On the Eigenvalues of Certain Hermitian Forms, *J. Rat. Mech. Anal.* 2 (1953): 767–800.
Gray, R. M., On the Asymptotic Eigenvalue Distribution of Toeplitz Matrices, *IEEE Trans. Inform. Theory* IT-18 (1972): 725–730.
Grenander, U., and G. Szegö, *Toeplitz Forms and Their Applications*, Univ. California Press, Berkeley, Calif., 1958.

The $\psi_k(t)$ are the orthonormal eigenfunctions of the integral equation

$$\int_{-T/2}^{T/2} \phi(t - s)\psi(s)\, ds = \lambda\psi(t) \qquad -T/2 \le t \le T/2$$

The expansion coefficients v_k for $k = 1, 2, \ldots$ are uncorrelated random variables with variance λ_k where λ_k is the eigenvalue of the above integral equation corresponding to the eigenfunction $\psi_k(t)$.

□ **Theorem C.3 (Toeplitz distribution theorem for continuous processes)** Consider a zero-mean stationary random process with autocorrelation function $\phi(\tau)$, power spectral density $\Phi(f)$, and finite second moment

$$\sigma^2 = \phi(0) = \int_{-\infty}^{\infty} \Phi(f)\, df < \infty$$

Denote the eigenvalues of the Karhunen-Loeve integral equation by $\lambda_k(T)$ for $k = 1, 2, \ldots$. Let $G(\cdot)$ be any continuous function satisfying $G(\lambda) \le K\lambda$ for $\lambda \in [0, \max \Phi(f)]$ for any finite constant K. Then

$$\lim_{T \to \infty} T^{-1} \sum_{k=1}^{\infty} G[\lambda_k(T)] = \int_{-\infty}^{\infty} G[\Phi(f)]\, df$$

Proof The proof is not given here. □

References

GENERAL

1. Abramson, N. M., *Information Theory and Coding*, McGraw-Hill, New York, 1963.
2. Ash, R. B., *Information Theory*, Interscience, New York, 1965.
3. Berger, T., *Rate Distortion Theory: A Mathematical Basis for Data Compression*, Prentice-Hall, Englewood Cliffs, N.J., 1971.
4. Brillouin, L., *Science and Information Theory*, 2nd ed., Academic Press, New York, 1962.
5. Csiszár, I., and J. Körner, *Information Theory*, Akademiai Kiado, Budapest, and Academic Press, New York, 1981.
6. Fano, R. M., *Transmission of Information: A Statistical Theory of Communication*, Wiley, New York, 1961.
7. Feinstein, A., *Foundations of Information Theory*, McGraw-Hill, New York, 1958.
8. Gallager, R. G., *Information Theory and Reliable Communication*, Wiley, New York, 1968.
9. Goldman, S., *Information Theory*, Prentice-Hall, Englewood Cliffs, N.J., 1953.
10. Guiasu, S., *Information Theory with Applications*, McGraw-Hill, New York, 1976.
11. Jelinek, F., *Probabilistic Information Theory*, McGraw-Hill, New York, 1968.

12. Khinchin, A. Ya., *Mathematical Foundations of Information Theory*, Dover, New York, 1957.
13. Kotel'nikov, V. A., *The Theory of Optimum Noise Immunity*, McGraw-Hill, New York, 1959.
14. Kullback, S., *Information Theory and Statistics*, Wiley, New York, 1959, and Dover, New York, 1968.
15. McEliece, R. J., *The Theory of Information and Coding*, Addison-Wesley, Reading, Mass., 1977.
16. Pinsker, M. S., *Information and Information Stability of Random Variables and Processes*, trans. by A. Feinstein, Holden Day, San Francisco, 1964.
17. Reza, F. M., *An Introduction to Information Theory*, McGraw-Hill, New York, 1961.
18. Shannon, C. E., and W. W. Weaver, *The Mathematical Theory of Communication*, Univ. Ill. Press, Urbana, 1949.
19. Viterbi, A. J., and J. K. Omura, *Principles of Digital Communication and Coding*, McGraw-Hill, New York, 1979.
20. Wolfowitz, J., *Coding Theorems of Information Theory*, 3rd ed., Springer-Verlag, Berlin, and Prentice-Hall, Englewood Cliffs, N.J., 1978.
21. Woodward, P. M., *Probability and Information Theory with Applications to Radar*, McGraw-Hill, New York, 1953.
22. Wozencraft, J. M., and I. M. Jacobs, *Principles of Communication Engineering*, Wiley, New York, 1965.

CHAPTER 1

1. Nyquist, H., Certain Factors Affecting Telegraph Speed, *Bell Sys. Tech. J.* 3 (1924): 324.
2. Hartley, R. V. L., Transmission of Information, *Bell Sys. Tech. J.* 7 (1928): 535.
3. Fisher, R. A., Theory of Statistical Estimation, *Proc. Cambridge Phil. Soc.* 22 (1925): 700–725.
4. Shannon, C. E., A Mathematical Theory of Communication, *Bell Sys. Tech. J.* 27 (1948): 379–423, 623–656.
5. Shannon, C. E., and W. Weaver, *The Mathematical Theory of Communication*, Univ. Ill. Press, Urbana, 1949.
6. Wiener, N., *Extrapolation, Interpolation, and Smoothing of Stationary Time Series*, MIT Press, Cambridge, Mass., and Wiley, New York, 1949.
7. Wiener, N., *Cybernetics*, MIT Press, Cambridge, Mass., and Wiley, New York, 1948.
8. Kotel'nikov, V. A., The Theory of Optimum Noise Immunity, Ph.D. dissertation, Molotov Energy Institute, Moscow, 1947, transl. by R. A. Silverman, McGraw-Hill, New York, 1959.
9. Feinstein, A., A New Basic Theorem of Information Theory, *IRE Trans. Inform. Theory* IT-4 (1954): 2–22.
10. Fano, R. M., *Transmission of Information*, MIT Press, Cambridge, Mass., 1961.
11. Gallager, R. G., A Simple Derivation of the Coding Theorem and Some Applications, *IEEE Trans. Inform. Theory* IT-11 (1965): 3–18.

12. Fano, R. M., Class Notes for Transmission of Information, Course 6.574, MIT, Cambridge, Mass., 1952.

13. Wolfowitz, J., The Coding of Messages Subject to Chance Errors, *Ill. J. Math.* 1 (1957): 4.

14. Shannon, C. E., Coding Theorems for A Discrete Source with a Fidelity Criterion, *IRE Nat. Conv. Rec.* (1959): 142–163.

15. Shannon, C. E., Channels with Side Information at the Transmitter, *IBM J. Res. Develop.* 2 (1958): 289–293.

16. Shannon, C. E., Two-Way Communication Channels, *Proc. 4th Berkeley Symp. Math. Stat. Prob.* 1 (1961): 611–644.

17. Cover, T. M., Broadcast Channels, *IEEE Trans. Inform. Theory* IT-18 (1972): 2–14.

18. Slepian, D., and J. K. Wolf, Noiseless Coding of Correlated Information Sources, *IEEE Trans. Inform. Theory* IT-19 (1973): 471–480.

19. Kullback, S., *Information Theory and Statistics*, Wiley, New York, 1959, and Dover, New York, 1968.

20. Cramer, H., *Mathematical Methods of Statistics*, Princeton Univ. Press, Princeton, N.J., 1946.

21. Rao, C. R., Information and Accuracy Attainable in the Estimation of Statistical Parameters, *Bull. Calcutta Math. Soc.* 37 (1945): 81–91.

22. Neyman, J., and E. S. Pearson, On the Problem of the Most Efficient Tests of Statistical Hypotheses, *Phil. Trans. Roy. Soc. London*, Series A, 231 (1933): 289–337.

23. North, D. O., *An Analysis of the Factors Which Determine Signal/Noise Discrimination in Pulsed-Carrier Systems*, RCA Tech. Rpt. PTR-6C, 1943.

24. Wald, A., *Sequential Analysis*, Wiley, New York, 1947.

25. Elias, P., Error-Free Coding, *IRE Trans. Inform. Theory* IT-4 (1954): 29–37.

CHAPTER 2

1. Shannon, C. E., A Mathematical Theory of Communication, *Bell Sys. Tech. J.* 27 (1948): 379–423, 623–656.

2. Freiman, C. V., and A. D. Wyner, Optimum Block Codes for Noiseless Input Restricted Channels, *Inform. Contr.* 7 (1964): 398–415.

3. Franaszek, P. A., On Synchronous Variable Length Coding for Discrete Noiseless Channels, *Inform. Contr.* 15 (1969): 155–164.

4. Tang, D. L., and L. R. Bahl, Block Codes for a Class of Constrained Noiseless Channels, *Inform. Contr.* 17 (1970): 436–461.

5. Blake, I. F., The Enumeration of Certain Run Length Sequences, *Inform. Contr.* 55 (1982): 222–237.

6. Zehavi, E., and J. K. Wolf, On Run-Length Codes, *IEEE Trans. Inform. Theory* (in press).

7. Kraft, L. G., A Device for Quantizing, Grouping, and Coding Amplitude Modulated Pulses, M.S. thesis, EE Dept., MIT, Cambridge, Mass., 1949.

8. Forney, G. D., Jr., Review of Random Tree Codes, NASA Contract NAS2-3637 Final Report, Appendix A, 1967.

CHAPTER 3

1. C. E. Shannon, A Mathematical Theory of Communication, *Bell Sys. Tech. J.* 27 (1948): 379–423, 623–656.
2. McMillan, B., Two Inequalities Implied by Unique Decipherability, *IRE Trans. Inform. Theory* IT-2 (1956): 115–116.
3. Karush, J., A Simple Proof of an Inequality of McMillan, *IRE Trans. Inform. Theory* IT-7 (1961): 118.
4. McMillan, B., The Basic Theorems of Information Theory, *Ann. Math. Stat.* 24 (1953): 196–219.
5. Breiman, L., The Individual Ergodic Theorem of Information Theory, *Ann. Math. Stat.* 28 (with correction in 31: 809–810) (1957): 809–811.
6. Kolmogorov, A. N., A New Invariant for Transitive Dynamical Systems (in Russian), *Dokl. An. SSR.* 119 (1958): 861–864.
7. Ornstein, D. S., Bernoulli Shifts with the Same Entropy Are Isomorphic, *Advances in Math.* 4 (1970): 337–352.
8. Sinai, J. G., On the Notion of Entropy of a Dynamical System (in Russian), *Dokl. Akad. Nauk. SSSR.* 124 (1959): 708–711.
9. Huffman, D. A., A Method for the Construction of Minimum Redundancy Codes, *Proc. IRE* 40 (1952): 1098–1101.
10. Jelinek, F., Buffer Overflow in Variable Length Coding of Fixed Rate Sources, *IEEE Trans. Inform. Theory* IT-14 (1968): 490–501.
11. Pasco, R., Source Coding Algorithms for Fast Data Compression, Ph.D. dissertation, EE Dept., Stanford Univ., Stanford, Calif., 1976.
12. Jones, C. B., An Efficient Coding System for Long Source Sequences, *IEEE Trans. Inform. Theory* IT-27 (1981): 280–291.
13. Rissanen, J. J., Generalized Kraft Inequality and Arithmetic Coding, *IBM J. Res. Develop.* 20 (1976): 198–203.
14. Jelinek, F., *Probabilistic Information Theory*, McGraw-Hill, New York, 1968.
15. Csiszár, I., and G. Longo, *On the Error Exponent for Source Coding and for Testing Simple Statistical Hypotheses*, Hungarian Academy of Sciences, Budapest, 1971.
16. Davisson, L. D., G. Longo, and A. Sgarro, The Error Exponent for the Noiseless Encoding of Finite Ergodic Markov Sources, *IEEE Trans. Inform. Theory* IT-27 (1981): 431–438.
17. Fitingoff, B. M., Coding in the Case of Unknown and Changing Message Statistics (in Russian), *Problemy Peredaci Informatsii* 2 (1966): 3–11.
18. Davisson, L. D., Universal Noiseless Coding, *IEEE Trans. Inform. Theory* IT-19 (1973): 783–795.
19. Davisson, L. D., R. J. McEliece, M. B. Pursley, and M. S. Wallace, Efficient Universal Noiseless Source Codes, *IEEE Trans. Inform. Theory* IT-27 (1981): 269–279.

CHAPTER 4

1. Neyman, J., and E. S. Pearson, On the Problem of the Most Efficient Tests of Statistical Hypotheses, *Phil. Trans. Roy. Soc. London*, Series A, 231 (1933): 289–337.
2. Kullback, S., and R. A. Leibler, On Information and Sufficiency, *Ann. Math. Stat.* 22 (1951): 79–86.

3. Kullback, S., *Information Theory and Statistics*, Wiley, New York, 1959, and Dover, New York, 1968.
4. Sanov, I. N., On the Probability of Large Deviations of Random Variables, *Mat. Sbornik* 42 (1957): 11–44.
5. Hoeffding, W., Asymptotically Optimal Tests for Multinominal Distributions, *Ann. Math. Stat.* 36 (1965): 369–400.
6. Csiszár, I., Sanov Property, Generalized I-Projection, and a Conditional Limit Theorem, *Ann. Probab.* 12 (1984): 768–793.
7. Csiszár, I., and Longo, G., On the Error Exponent for Source Coding and for Testing Simple Statistical Hypotheses, Hungarian Academy of Sciences, Budapest, 1971.
8. Blahut, R. E., An Hypothesis Testing Approach to Information Theory, Ph.D. dissertation, Cornell Univ., Ithaca, N.Y., August 1972.
9. Chernoff, H., A Measure of Asymptotic Efficiency for Tests of a Hypothesis Based on a Sum of Observations, *Ann. Math. Stat.* 23 (1952): 493–507.
10. North, D. O., *An Analysis of the Factors Which Determine Signal/Noise Discrimination in Pulsed-Carrier Systems*, RCA Tech. Rpt. PTR-6C, 1943.
11. Turin, G. L., An Introduction to Matched Filters, *IRE Trans. Inform. Theory* IT-6 (1960): 311–329.

CHAPTER 5

1. Shannon, C. E., A Mathematical Theory of Communication, *Bell Sys. Tech. J.* 27 (1948): 379–423, 623–656.
2. Dobrushin, R. L., General Formulation of Shannon's Main Theorem in Information Theory, *Usp. Math. Nauk* 14 (1959): 3–104., transl. in *Am. Math. Soc. Trans.*: 33, 323–438.
3. Fano, R. M., Class Notes for Transmission of Information, Course 6.574, MIT, Cambridge, Mass., 1952.
4. Wolfowitz, J., The Coding of Messages Subject to Chance Errors, *Ill. J. Math.* 1 (1957): 591–606.
5. Arimoto, S., On the Converse to the Coding Theorem for Discrete Memoryless Channels, *IEEE Trans. Inform. Theory* IT-19 (1973): 357–359.
6. Wolfowitz, J., *Coding Theorems of Information Theory*, Springer, Berlin, 1961.
7. Csiszár, I., and J. Körner, *Information Theory*, Akademiai Kiado, Budapest, and Academic Press, New York, 1981.
8. Gallager, R. G., A Simple Derivation of the Coding Theorem and Some Applications, *IEEE Trans. Inform. Theory* IT-11 (1965): 3–18.
9. Arimoto, S., An Algorithm for Computing the Capacity of an Arbitrary Discrete Memoryless Channel, *IEEE Trans. Inform. Theory* IT-18 (1972): 14–20.
10. Blahut, R. E., Computation of Channel Capacity and Rate Distortion Functions, *IEEE Trans. Inform. Theory* IT-18 (1972): 460–473.
11. Bhattacharyya, A., On a Measure of Divergence between Two Statistical Populations Defined by Their Probability Distributions, *Bull. Calcutta Math. Soc.* 35 (1943): 99–110.
12. Yudkin, H. L., Channel State Testing in Information Decoding, Ph.D. dissertation, EE Dept., MIT, Cambridge, Mass., 1964.

13. Viterbi, A. J., Error Bounds for Convolutional Codes and an Asymptotically Optimum Decoding Algorithm, *IEEE Trans. Inform. Theory* IT-13 (1967): 260–269.
14. Forney, G. D., Jr., Convolutional Codes II: Maximum-Likelihood Decoding and Convolutional Codes III: Sequential Decoding, *Inform. Contr.* 25 (1974): 222–297.
15. Arikan, E., Sequential Decoding for Multiple Access Channels, Ph.D. dissertation, EE Dept., MIT, Cambridge, Mass., 1985.

CHAPTER 6

1. Shannon, C. E., Coding Theorems for a Discrete Source with a Fidelity Criterion, *IRE Nat. Conv. Rec.*, Part 4 (1959): 142–163.
2. Berger, T., *Rate Distortion Theory: A Mathematical Basis for Data Compression*, Prentice-Hall, Englewood Cliffs, N.J., 1971.
3. Omura, J., A Coding Theorem for Discrete Time Sources, *IEEE Trans. Inform. Theory* IT-19 (1973): 490–498.
4. Gray, R. M., Sliding Block Source Coding, *IEEE Trans. Inform. Theory* IT-21 (1975): 357–368.
5. Blahut, R. E., Computation of Channel Capacity and Rate Distortion Functions, *IEEE Trans. Inform. Theory* IT-18 (1972): 460–473.
6. Marton, K., Error Exponent for Source Coding with a Fidelity Criterion, *IEEE Trans. Inform. Theory* IT-20 (1974): 197–199.
7. Blahut, R. E., Information Bounds of the Fano-Kullback Type, *IEEE Trans. Inform. Theory* IT-22 (1976): 410–421.
8. Blahut, R. E., Hypothesis Testing and Information Theory, *IEEE Trans. Inform. Theory* IT-20 (1974): 405–417.
9. Sakrison, D. J., The Rate Distortion Function for a Class of Sources, *Inform. Contr.* 15 (1969): 165–195.
10. Ziv, J., Coding of Sources with Unknown Statistics—Part II: Distortion Relative to a Fidelity Criterion, *IEEE Trans. Inform. Theory* IT-18 (1972): 389–394.
11. Pursley, M. B., and L. D. Davisson, Variable Rate Coding for Nonergodic Sources and Classes of Ergodic Sources Subject to a Fidelity Constraint, *IEEE Trans. Inform. Theory* IT-22 (1976): 324–337.
12. Singh, S., and N. S. Kambo, Source Code Error Bound in the Excess Rate Region, *IEEE Trans. Inform. Theory* IT-23 (1977): 65–70.
13. Fano, R. M., Class Notes for Transmission of Information, Course 6.574, MIT, Cambridge, Mass., 1952.
14. Wolfowitz, J., The Coding of Messages Subject to Chance Errors, *Ill. J. Math.* 1 (1957): 591–606.
15. Arimoto, S., On the Converse to the Coding Theorem for Discrete Memoryless Channels, *IEEE Trans. Inform. Theory* IT-19 (1973): 357–359.
16. Dueck, G., and J. Körner, Reliability Function of a Discrete Memoryless Channel at Rates above Capacity, *IEEE Trans. Inform. Theory* IT-25 (1979): 82–85.

CHAPTER 7

1. Shannon, C. E., A Mathematical Theory of Communication, *Bell Sys. Tech. J.* 27 (1948): 379–423, 623–656.

2. Ebert, P. M., Error Bounds for Parallel Communication Channels, MIT Research Lab of Electronics, Tech. Rpt. 448, 1966.

3. Holsinger, J. L., Digital Communication over Fixed Time-Continuous Channels with Memory, with Special Application to Telephone Channels, MIT Research Lab of Electronics, Tech. Rpt. 430, 1964.

4. Blachman, N. M., A Comparison of the Informational Capacities of Amplitude- and Phase-Modulation Communication Systems, *Proc. IRE* 41 (1953): 748–759.

5. Stam, A. J., Some Inequalities Satisfied by the Quantities of Information of Fisher and Shannon, *Inform. Contr.* 2 (1959): 101–112.

6. Stam, A. J., Some Mathematical Properties of Quantities of Information, Ph.D. dissertation, Technische Hogeschool te Delft, Uitgeverij Excelsior, The Hague, 1959.

7. Blachman, N. M., The Convolution Inequality for Entropy Powers, *IEEE Trans. Inform. Theory* IT-11 (1965): 267–271.

8. Barron, A. R., Monotonic Central Limit Theorem for Densities, Stanford Univ. Dept. of Statistics Tech. Rpt. 50, 1984.

9. Brown, L. D., A Proof of the Central Limit Theorem Motivated by the Cramer-Rao Inequality, *Statistics and Probability: Essays in Honor of C. R. Rao*, ed. by Kallianpur, Krishnaiah, and Ghosh, North-Holland, Amsterdam, 1982.

10. Barron, A. R., Entropy and the Central Limit Theorem, *Ann. Probab.* 14 (1986): 336–342.

11. Csiszár, I., Information-Type Measures of Difference of Probability Distributions and Indirect Observations, *Studia Sci. Math. Hungary* 2 (1967): 299–318.

CHAPTER 8

1. Cramer, H., *Mathematical Methods of Statistics*, Princeton Univ. Press, Princeton, N.J., 1946.

2. Rao, C. R., Information and Accuracy Attainable in the Estimation of Statistical Parameters, *Bull. Calcutta Math. Soc.* 37 (1945): 81–91.

3. Fisher, R. A., Theory of Statistical Estimation, *Proc. Cambridge Phil. Soc.* 22 (1925): 700–725.

4. Slepian, D., Estimation of Signal Parameters in the Presence of Noise, *IRE Trans. Inform Theory* IT-3 (1954): 68–69.

5. Mallinckrodt, A. J., and T. E. Sollenberger, Optimum-Pulse-Time Determination, *IRE Trans. Inform. Theory* IT-3 (1954): 151–159.

6. Ziv, J., and M. Zakai, Some Lower Bounds on Signal Parameter Estimation, *IEEE Trans. Inform. Theory* IT-15, No. 2 (1969): 386–391.

7. Seidman, L. P., Performance Limitations and Error Calculations for Parameter Estimation, *Proc. IEEE* 58, No. 5 (1970): 644–652.

8. Kalman, R. E., A New Approach to Linear Filtering and Prediction Problems, *Trans. ASME J. Basic Eng.* 82D (1960): 34–45.

9. Kalman, R. E., and R. S. Bucy, New Results in Linear Filtering and Prediction Theory, *Trans. Am. Soc. Mech. Eng., Series D, J. Basic Eng.*, 83 (1961): 95–108.

10. Jaynes, E. T., Information Theory and Statistical Mechanics I, *Phys. Rev.* 106 (1957): 620–630.

11. Kullback, S., *Information Theory and Statistics*, Wiley, New York, 1959, and Dover, New York, 1969.

12. Shore, J. E., and R. W. Johnson, Axiomatic Derivation of the Principle of Maximum Entropy and the Principle of Minimum Cross-Entropy, *IEEE Trans. Inform. Theory* IT-26 (1980): 26–37.
13. Van Campenhout, J. M., and T. M. Cover, Maximum Entropy and Conditional Probability, *IEEE Trans. Inform. Theory* IT-27 (1981): 483–489.
14. Csiszár, I., Sanov Property, Generalized I-Projection, and a Conditional Limit Theorem, *Ann. Prob.* 12 (1984): 768–793.
15. Burg. J. P., Maximum Entropy Spectral Analysis, Ph.D. dissertation, Dept. of Geophysics, Stanford Univ., Stanford, Calif., 1975.
16. Choi, B. S., and T. M. Cover, An Information-Theoretic Proof of Burg's Maximum Entropy Spectrum, *Proc. IEEE* 72 (1984): 1094–1095.

CHAPTER 9

1. Shannon, C. E., The Zero-Error Capacity of a Noisy Channel, *IRE Trans. Inform. Theory* IT-2 (1956): 8–19.
2. Dobrushin, R. L., Information Transmission in a Channel with Feedback, *Theory Prob. Appl.* 34 (1958): 367–383.
3. Shannon, C. E., Two-Way Communication Channels, *Proc. 4th Berkeley Symp. Math. Stat. Prob.* 1 (1961): 611–644.
4. Ahlswede, R., Multi-Way Communication Channels, *Proc. 2nd Int. Symp. Inform. Theory*, Tsahkadsor, Armenian S.S.R., Hungarian Academy of Sciences, Budapest, 1973, 23–52.
5. Liao, H., Multiple Access Channels, Ph.D. dissertation, EE Dept., Univ. Hawaii, Honolulu, 1972.
6. Cover, T. M., Broadcast Channels, *IEEE Trans. Inform. Theory* IT-18 (1972): 2–14.
7. Bergmans, P. P., Random Coding Theorems for Broadcast Channels with Degraded Components, *IEEE Trans. Inform. Theory* IT-19 (1973): 197–207.
8. Gallager, R. G., Capacity and Coding for Degraded Broadcast Channels, *Problemy Peredaci Informatsii* 10 (1974): 3–14.
9. Marton, K., A Coding Theorem for the Discrete Memoryless Broadcast Channel, *IEEE Trans. Inform. Theory* IT-25 (1979): 306–311.
10. van der Meulen, E. C., A Survey of Multi-Way Channels in Information Theory: 1961–1976, *IEEE Trans. Inform. Theory* IT-23 (1977): 1–37.
11. El Gamal, A., and T. M. Cover, Multiple User Information Theory, *Proc. IEEE* 68 (1980): 1466–1483.
12. Slepian, D., and J. K. Wolf, A Coding Theorem for Multiple Accesss Channels with Correlated Sources, *Bell Sys. Tech. J.* 52 (1973): 1037–1076.
13. Slepian, D., and J. K. Wolf, Noiseless Coding of Correlated Information Sources, *IEEE Trans. Inform. Theory* IT-19 (1973): 471–480.
14. Ahlswede, R., and J. Körner, Source Coding with Side Information and a Converse for the Degraded Broadcast Channel, *IEEE Trans. Inform. Theory* IT-21 (1975): 629–637.
15. Wyner, A., On Source Coding with Side Information at the Decoder, *IEEE Trans. Inform. Theory* IT-21 (1975): 294–300.
16. Wyner, A., and J. Ziv., The Rate-Distortion Function for Source Coding with Side Information at the Decoder, *IEEE Trans. Inform. Theory* IT-22 (1976): 1–10.

17. Berger, T., Multiterminal Source Coding, in *The Information Theory Approach to Communications*, ed. by G. Longo, Springer-Verlag, New York, 1977.
18. Cover, T. M., and A. El Gamal, Achievable Rates for Multiple Descriptions, *IEEE Trans. Inform. Theory* IT-28 (1982): 851–857.
19. Berger, T., and Z. Zhang, Minimum Breakdown Degradation in Binary Source Encoding, *IEEE Trans. Inform. Theory* IT-29 (1983): 807–814.

CHAPTER 10

1. Fano, R. M., *Transmission of Information*, MIT Press, Cambridge, Mass., 1961.
2. Gallager, R. G., A Simple Derivation of the Coding Theorem and Some Applications, *IEEE Trans. Inform. Theory* IT-11 (1965): 3–18
3. Forney, G. D., Exponential Error Bounds for Erasure, List, and Decision Feedback Schemes, *IEEE Trans. Inform. Theory* IT-11 (1968): 549–557.
4. Csiszár, I., J. Körner, and K. Marton, A New Look at the Error Exponent of a Discrete Memoryless Channel, *Abstracts—1977 IEEE Internat. Symp. Inform. Theory*, Ithaca, N.Y., 1977.
5. Csiszár, I., and J. Körner, *Information Theory*, Akademiai Kiado, Budapest, and Academic Press, New York, 1981.
6. Shannon, C. E., R. G. Gallager, and E. Berlekamp, Lower Bounds to Error Probability for Coding on Discrete Memoryless Channels, Part 1, *Inform. Contr.* 10 (1967): Part 1, 65–103; Part 2, 522–552.
7. Haroutunian, E. A., Estimates of the Error Exponent for the Semi-Continuous Memoryless Channel (in Russian), *Problemy Peredaci Informatsii* 13 (1968) 37–48.
8. Blahut, R. E., Hypothesis Testing and Information Theory, *IEEE Trans. Inform. Theory* IT-20 (1974): 405–417.
9. Gilbert, E. N., A Comparison of Signalling Alphabets, *Bell Sys. Tech. J.* 31 (1952): 504–522.
10. Blahut, R. E., Composition Bounds for Channel Block Codes, *IEEE Trans. Inform. Theory* IT-23 (1977): 656–674.
11. McEliece, R. J., E. R. Rodemich, H. Rumsey, Jr., and L. R. Welch, New Upper Bounds on the Rate of a Code via the Delsarte-MacWilliams Inequalities, *IEEE Trans. Inform. Theory* IT-20 (1974): 356–365.
12. Levenshtein, V. I., On the Minimal Redundancy of Binary Error-Correcting Codes, *Problemy Peredaci Informatsii* 10 (1974): 26–42; English trans., *Inform. Contr.* 28 (1975).
13. Sidelnikov, V. M., Upper Bounds on the Cardinality of a Binary Code with a Given Minimum Distance, *Problemy Peredaci Informatsii* 10 (1974): 43–51; English transl., *Inform. Contr.* 28 (1975).
14. Jelinek, F., Evaluation of Expurgated Bound Exponents, *IEEE Trans. Inform. Theory* IT-14 (1968): 501–505.
15. Omura, J. K., On General Gilbert Bounds, *IEEE Trans. Inform. Theory* IT-19 (1973): 661–666.
16. Omura, J. K., Expurgated Bounds, Bhattacharyya Distance and Rate Distortion Functions, *Inform. Contr.* 24 (1974): 358–383.
17. Berlekamp, E. R., Block Coding with Noiseless Feedback, Ph.D. dissertation, EE Dept., MIT, Cambridge, Mass., 1964.

18. Arimoto, S., Computation of Random Coding Exponent Functions, *IEEE Trans. Inform. Theory* IT-22 (1976): 665–671.
19. Lesh, J. R., Computational Algorithms for Coding Bound Exponents, Ph.D. dissertation, Univ. California, Los Angeles, 1976.
20. Sloane, N. J. A., The Packing of Spheres, *Scientific American* 250 (January 1984): 116–125.
21. Shannon, C. E., The Zero Error Capacity of a Noisy Channel, *IRE Trans. Inform. Theory* IT-2 (1956): 8–19.
22. Lovász, L., On the Shannon Capacity of a Graph, *IEEE Trans. Inform. Theory*, IT-25 (1979): 1–7.

Index